# Discipline and Discharge in Arbitration

## Other BNA Books Authored by the
## ABA Section of Labor & Employment Law

*Covenants Not to Compete: A State-by-State Survey*

*The Developing Labor Law*

*Employee Benefits Law*

*Employment Discrimination Law*

*Employee Duty of Loyalty: A State-by-State Survey*

*Equal Employment Law Update*

*Elkouri and Elkouri: How Arbitration Works*

*International Labor and Employment Laws*

*Labor Arbitration: A Practical Guide for Advocates*

*Labor Arbitration: Cases and Materials for Advocates*

*Labor Arbitrator Development: A Handbook*

*Occupational Safety and Health Law*

*The Railway Labor Act*

*Trade Secrets: A State-by-State Survey*

# Discipline and Discharge in Arbitration

### *Editor-in-Chief*

**Norman Brand**
Arbitrator, Mediator, and Attorney
*San Francisco, CA*

### *Associate Editors*

**Patricia Thomas Bittel**
Arbitrator and Mediator
*Cleveland, OH*

**Charles W. Kohler**
Arbitrator and Attorney
*Columbus, OH*

**Jacquelin F. Drucker**
Arbitrator
*New York, NY*

**Thomas Y. Mandler**
Schwartz & Freeman
*Chicago, IL*

**Julius Mel Reich**
Reich, Adell, Crost & Cvitan
*Los Angeles, CA*

### *Assistant Editor*

**Henry G. Stewart**
Palmer & Dodge
*Boston, MA*

Committee on ADR in Labor and Employment Law
Section of Labor and Employment Law
American Bar Association

The Bureau of National Affairs, Inc., Washington, D.C.

Copyright © 1998
The American Bar Association
Chicago, IL

**Library of Congress Cataloging-in-Publication Data**

Discipline and discharge in arbitration / editor in chief, Norman
  Brand ; associate editors, Patricia Thomas Bittel . . . [et al.] ;
  assistant editor, Henry G. Stewart.
      p.   cm.
    ISBN 1-57018-060-1
    1. Arbitration, Industrial—United States.   2. Labor disputes—
  United States.   I. Brand, Norman.   II. Bittel, Patricia Thomas.
  KF3424.D57   1998
  344.7301′89143—dc21

                                                              98-42447
                                                              CIP

Published by BNA Books
1250 23rd St., NW, Washington, DC

International Standard Book Number: 1-57018-060-1

JERRY M. CUTLER
Attorney
Wilmington, DE

PHYLLIS E. FLORMAN
Arbitrator and Mediator
Louisville, KY

JOSEPH F. GENTILE
Arbitrator and Attorney
Los Angeles, CA

DAVID L. GREGORY
Professor of Law and
   Arbitrator
St. John's University
Jamaica, NY

JERALD A. HOCHSZTEIN
Newburger & Vossmeyer
St. Louis, MO

EDWIN S. HOPSON
Wyatt, Tarrant & Combs
Louisville, KY

SUSAN L. HUGHES
Attorney
Michigan Education Association
Kalamazoo, MI

ROBERT KINGSLEY HULL
Arbitrator
Penn Yan, NY

ANITA CHRISTINE KNOWLTON
Chvany, Silbert & Knowlton
Berkeley, CA

KENNETH A. PEREA
Arbitrator and Attorney
Del Mar, CA

HERBERT L. SEGAL
Segal, Isenberg, Sales, Stewart
   & Cutler
Louisville, KY

RICHARD K. ZUCKERMAN
Rains & Pogrebin, PC
Mineola, NY

## CONTRIBUTING EDITORS

PATRICK L. ABRAMOVICH

SALLY ADAMS
Palmer & Dodge
Boston, MA

JOSEPH J. ALLOTTA
Allotta and Farley
Toledo, OH

CATHERINE ANDREWS
Union Pacific Railroad
Omaha, NE

MARGARET A. ANGELUCCI
Asher, Gittler, Greenfield,
   Cohen & D'Alba
Chicago, IL

LOUIS ARONIN
Arbitrator and Attorney
Baltimore, MD

DON BANTA
Banta, Cox & Hennessy
Chicago, IL

SHARON BERLIN
Rains & Pogrebin, PC
Mineola, NY

STEVEN BIERIG
Katten, Muchin & Zavis
Chicago, IL

RICHARD L. BITTNER
Attorney
Fort Collins, CO

ELLEN O. BOARDMAN
O'Donoghue & O'Donoghue
Washington, DC

BRIAN BOCK
Atkinson & Andelson
Riverside, CA

JAY E. BOVILSKY
Cummings & Lockwood
Hartford, CT

LINDA BUNGE
Varnum, Riddering, Schmidt &
    Howlett LLP
Grand Rapids, MI

LAWRENCE J. CASAZZA
Veder, Price, Kaufman &
    Kammholz
Chicago, IL

JAMES P. CLARK
Rains & Pogrebin, PC
Mineola, NY

DAVID A. COHEN
Carpenter, Bennett &
    Morrissey
Newark, NJ

FRED CORY
Attorney
Washington, DC

HENRY R. COX
Blackwell, Sanders, Matheny,
    Weary & Lom
Kansas City, MO

MARTIN J. CRANE
Sherman, Dunn, Cohen, Leifer
    & Yellig, PC
Washington, DC

BENJAMIN N. DAVIS
Washington, DC

JOSEPH D'ARRIGO
Attorney
York Harbor, ME

BENJAMIN DAVIS
Attorney
Washington, DC

NEAL M. DAVIS
Schuchat, Cook & Werner
St. Louis, MO

ANNE L. DRAZNIN
Arbitrator and Attorney
Chicago, IL

WILLIAM M. EARNEST
Elarbee, Thompson & Trapnell,
    LLP
Atlanta, GA

KATHLEEN JOHNSON EHLERS
Attorney
New York, NY

JOHN ENTENMAN
Dykema Gossett
Detroit, MI

GARY R. FISCHER
Dreher, Simpson and Jensen,
    PC
Des Moines, IA

B. FRANK FLAHERTY
Attorney
Garden City, NY

SUSAN GROMIS FLYNN
Marcus & Shapiro
Pittsburgh, PA

JOSH M. FRIEDMAN
Bates, Meckler, Bulger & Tilson
Chicago, IL

JAMES V. GARVEY
Vedder, Price, Kaufman &
    Kammholz
Chicago, IL

JOSEPH P. GIROLAMO
Joseph P. Girolamo Law Offices
Detroit, MI

JEROLD E. GLASSMAN
Grotta, Glassman & Hoffman
Roseland, NJ

MARGERY GOOTNICK
Attorney
Rochester, NY

MICHAEL GORDON
Attorney
Kansas City, MO

LYLE J. GUILBEAU
Tredegar Industries, Inc.
Richmond, VA

MELVA HARMON
Levy, Harmon & Burnett
Little Rock, AK

LYNNE L. HICKS
MacDonald & Hicks PC
Denver, CO

ONDREA DAE HIDLEY
GTE California, Inc.
Thousand Oaks, CA

SCOTT HINCKLEY
Attorney
Omaha, NE

FREDRIC HOROWITZ
Arbitrator and Attorney
Santa Monica, CA

CHARLES F. IPAVEC
Attorney
Cleveland, OH

JOHN KAGEL
Arbitrator and Attorney
Redwood City, CA

GAIL KALINICH
Ross & Hardies
Chicago, IL

IRA KATZ
UNITE
New York, NY

HERBERT G. KEENE, JR.
Stradley, Romon, Stevens &
    Young
Philadelphia, PA

WESLEY KENNEDY
Allison, Slutsky & Kennedy
Chicago, IL

LLOYD C. LOOMIS
ARCO
Los Angeles, CA

FRANK T. MAMAT
Clark Hill, PLC
Detroit, MI

KELLY S. MAY

FRANK MARTORANA
O'Donoghue & O'Donoghue
Washington, DC

KEVIN M. McCARTHY
Miller, Canfield, Paddock and
   Stone, PLC
Kalamazoo, MI

JOHN P. McGURY
Attorney
Chicago, IL

THOMAS METZGER
Emens, Kegler, Brown, Hill &
   Ritter
Columbus, OH

JOHN J. MICHELS, JR.
McGuire, Woods, Battle &
   Boothe
McLean, VA

DAVID R. MILLER
Merck-Medco Managed Care,
   LLC
Montvale, NJ

LUELLA E. NELSON
Attorney
Portland, OR

LAWRENCE M. OBERDAWK

CLIFFORD R. OVIATT, JR.
McGuire, Woods, Battle &
   Boothe
Washington, DC

MARY S. PETERSEN
Reed McClure
Seattle, WA

PETER C. PHILLIPS
Morris, Rogers & Phillips
Andover, MA

CHARLES REHMUS
Attorney
Poway, CA

MICHAEL T. REYNVAAN
Perkins Cole
Seattle, WA

DONALD A. ROMANO
Carpenter, Bennett & Morrisey
Newark, NJ

GEORGE T. ROUMELL, JR.
Riley and Roumell
Detroit, MI

STEPHEN RUBIN
Oak Park, IL

MITCHELL H. RUBINSTEIN
New York State United
   Teachers
New York, NY

ARTHUR D. RUTKOWSKI
Bowers, Harrison, Kent &
   Miller
Evansville, IN

LAURA J. SCHANK
Toledo, OH

JON SCHAUER
Seyfarth, Shaw, Fairweather &
   Geraldson
Chicago, IL

DAVID SCHOOLCRAFT
Reed McClure
Seattle, WA

FRANCIS R. A. SHEED
Osborne Law Offices
Washington, DC

LORI M. SMITH
UNITE
New York, NY

# Foreword

Since 1945 the ABA Section of Labor and Employment Law has had as its stated purposes (1) to study and report upon continuing developments in the law affecting labor relations, (2) to assist the professional growth and development of practitioners in the field of employment and labor relations law, and (3) to promote justice, human welfare, industrial peace, and the recognition of the supremacy of law in labor-management relations.

Through the publication of books such as *Discipline and Discharge in Arbitration,* and through annual and committee meeting programs designed to provide a forum for the exchange of ideas, the Section has pursued these stated goals. Gradually, the Section has built a library of comprehensive legal works intended for the use of the Section membership as well as the bar generally.

The Section of Labor and Employment Law is pleased to provide this treatise on discipline and discharge in arbitration as part of its library of books published by BNA Books, a Division of The Bureau of National Affairs, Inc. The combined efforts of many individual authors recruited by the Committee on ADR in Labor and Employment Law of the Section are reflected in this work.

The Section wishes to express its appreciation to the subcommittee, and in particular to the editor-in-chief, Norman Brand; to the associate editors, Patricia Thomas Bittel, Jacquelin F. Drucker, Charles W. Kohler, Thomas Y. Mandler, and Julius Mel Reich; to the Assistant Editor, Henry G. Stewart; and to the chapter editors and contributors. This group has tried to accomplish two primary objectives: (1) to be equally balanced and nonpartisan in their viewpoints, and (2) to ensure the book is of significant value to the practitioner, student, and sophisticated nonlawyer.

The views expressed herein do not necessarily represent the views of the American Bar Association, or its Section of Labor and Employment Law, or any other organization, but are simply the collective, but not necessarily the individual, views of the authors.

STEPHEN E. TALLENT
*Chair*

MAX ZIMNY
*Chair-Elect*

Section of Labor
and Employment Law
American Bar Association

*September 1998*

# Preface

This is not a book you are likely to read through at one sitting. For one thing, it has no plot, too many characters, and an overwhelming variety of individual stories. For another, you are most likely to use it when you have a particular problem for which you need to consult a specific part of the book. Each story—the facts of a particular case—is likely to be most interesting to you as the advocate or arbitrator in a specific labor or employment arbitration. You can look at the case to learn how an arbitrator applied the general theory of just cause to the specific facts and decided whether to uphold the discipline. Then you can use that information to help you decide how best to present or decide a case. The first time you need to consult this book for a specific case—or better still—before then, you should read the first chapter. It will provide you with a useful general framework for analyzing cases. Every time you consult this book about a specific issue, that analytical framework will help you get the most out of your research.

Just cause is the underlying equitable principle by which arbitrators determine whether the discipline or discharge of an employee should be upheld. And while only one chapter is entitled just cause, that is what this entire book is about. Each case in this book is part of the underlying material upon which the theory of just cause has been built. Each one demonstrates what just cause means when applied to specific facts. Most of the chapter are organized around general areas of behavioral problems that lead to discipline and the specific sub-theories of just cause that have developed within those general areas. Some chapters explore the relationship between just cause and the law, or the courts. Finally, Chapter 1 provides advocates with an approach to using this book effectively and a helpful general framework for analyzing cases.

As the list of editors and contributors shows, many people worked on this book. What the list does not show is the pervasive impact of

Sara Adler, former neutral chair of the Committee on ADR in Labor and Employment Law, whose determination brought this book from an inchoate idea to reality.

NORMAN BRAND

*San Francisco, CA*
*August 1998*

# Detailed Table of Contents

# Chapter 1

# Arbitration Advocacy

## I. Introduction

The chapters that follow describe the theories employed by arbitrators in a wide variety of discipline cases. In some areas of discipline, arbitrator's views are almost uniform about the appropriate theory; in other areas there are recognized minority views, and in some instances there are aberrant decisions that practitioners need to know to avoid being surprised by an unusual theory. But there is a difference between knowing a disciplinary theory and using it effectively to argue a specific case. This chapter is about the latter; the rest of this book is about the former. The tools in this chapter will help an advocate prepare and present a case, choose an arbitrator, and effectively advance his or her position.

Consider what advocates do in a typical case.

Good advocates investigate their case, choose a theory of discipline that they posit is appropriate, review what arbitrators consider the essential factual elements of that theory, and then match the facts of their case against the essential factual elements of the theory. This interplay of facts and theory presents a quandary—the theory cannot be chosen until the facts have been reviewed, but the facts cannot be effectively developed until the theory has been chosen. Good advocates do not feel paralyzed by the appearance of contradiction. They have a sense of the likely best theory and begin to slot the facts into the theory. Then, as discussed in "Analyzing the Case" below, they engage in "feedback loops" as they organize facts according to the theory they have chosen. When they realize they do not have all the facts, they go back to investigate and get the facts they need. And when the facts do not fit the theory properly, they examine alternative theories of discipline or review whether it will be possible to prove or disprove just cause after all, given the missing facts. Only when

1

they have matched the facts of their case against the essential elements required by arbitrators under a specific theory of discipline can they make a reasoned judgment to investigate further, modify discipline, settle a grievance, or go to arbitration.

Good advocates also recognize that the same facts may strike a different chord when viewed through the lenses of different disciplinary theories. Thus, they look not only for an appropriate theory but for the disciplinary theory that will help their client win. They know they cannot change the facts, but the facts they emphasize and the disciplinary theory they use can make the difference between winning and losing. Good advocates evaluate the strength of each element of the theory of discipline they are espousing or challenging. They recognize that there is a difference between what they "know" to be true and what they can prove.

Good advocates choose their arbitrators carefully. They know that the background and decisional predilections of the arbitrator can make a difference in the outcome of the case. Good advocates know that both the mechanics of how they present the case and the way they argue the case can be crucial to winning. All four of these activities—developing facts and theory, evaluating the case, choosing an arbitrator, and presenting and arguing a case—are discussed in greater detail below.

This chapter is not the definitive text on effective arbitration advocacy. Books have been written on arbitration advocacy (some of which are listed at the end of this chapter), and a chapter is simply too little space to cover all the complexities of case presentation. This chapter only provides an introductory discussion of some techniques to help the advocate analyze, evaluate, and integrate the facts of a specific case in the context of disciplinary theories presented in the rest of the book.

## II. Preliminary Research and Investigation

Many lawyers and advocates have had the unpleasant experience of learning at the arbitration just how inadequate the investigation of their case was. Some make a fabulous comeback, acting as if they always knew that immediately after the event their client wrote an account that contradicts his current story. But why let it happen? While investigating a case is beyond the scope of this chapter, it is very important. The advocate must know all the facts and have all the documents essential to prove (and disprove) the case's essential elements. The disciplinary theories discussed in the rest of this book establish the essential elements that determine what proofs must be adduced to prevail. The case matrix—which is discussed below—will help the advocate discover when more facts or different proofs are needed. If investigation shows the proofs exist, the case will be stronger. If not, settlement may be preferable to arbitration.

## A. *Analyzing the Case*

In this discussion, analysis and evaluation are treated as different processes. Analysis precedes evaluation of a case. Analyzing a case means examining the elements arbitrators have found essential to determining whether there is just cause to discipline an employee for some specific behavior. While just cause always provides the context, specific disciplinary theories have been developed for particular behavior. For instance, in theft cases arbitrators require employers to prove four specific elements (see Chapter 7) and the advocate would have to know whether each of these essential elements was present. The absence of a single element may be fatal to the case. On the other hand, decisions may show how an advocate can prevail without proving that one essential element. In either case, of course, analysis only shows whether the elements necessary to a particular theory of discipline are present, not how persuasive the proofs will be; determining persuasiveness involves evaluation.

## B. *Evaluating the Case*

Evaluation is a separate process. It goes beyond analysis and looks at the sources of proof to determine their probative value and likely persuasive impact. These latter determinations indicate the strength of the case and are critical to deciding whether to pursue or settle the case. In evaluating a case, it is helpful to learn how persuasive arbitrators found specific types of evidence that were adduced to prove the essential elements of a specific case.

## III. Analyzing and Evaluating the Case Using the Case Matrix

A case matrix can facilitate both analysis and evaluation by organizing the information.

## A. *Analyzing the Case Using the Case Matrix*

A supervisor found Smedlap sleeping on a bed of bubble wrap in the tool shed. Or Jones failed to come to work for the fifth day in a row without calling in. Usually the basic investigation into an incident will have been done by supervisors, perhaps with the help of human resources or labor relations staff. They will have gathered data about the employee behavior at issue by talking with supervisors and other employees, perhaps even taking written statements. They will have investigated any reason given by the employee for the alleged behavior. (Sometimes the only reason is a denial that the behavior occurred.)

They will have looked at the employee's personnel record in order to determine if he was previously warned or disciplined for this or other behavior. In some instances, a specific rule may have been violated, and this will be noted. All of this information needs to be analyzed in light of the relevant just cause theory of discipline.

There is a standard sequence and process to be followed by both management and union advocates in analyzing these cases. First, all the elements of the theory of discipline applicable to this type of offense must be listed. For instance, if Jones failed to come to work or call in for the fifth day in a row, the applicable theories are found in Chapter 3's discussion of absenteeism and in the just cause criteria contained in Chapter 2.[1] According to Chapter 2, the rule breached must be clear and consistent with the collective bargaining agreement (2.IV.A.2.), communicated to the employee (2.IV.A.), and consistently enforced with like penalties (2.IV.B.). In addition, there are specific mitigating and aggravating circumstances that may apply in absence cases (3.I.C.) as well as specific considerations when there is absence without leave (3.I.D.). These are all essential elements of a potential disciplinary case against Jones. Obviously, for the union advocate the essential elements are the negatives of these. In addition there are affirmative defenses. For instance, a sudden overwhelming illness, or a lack of ability to call in or direct someone to do so could be defenses to the charge. A brief review of the facts will establish the applicability of specific mitigating or aggravating factors listed in Chapter 3 and alert both sides to potential arguments for which the facts are incomplete.

As noted above, the case matrix is a device for organizing this mass of information and for moving from analysis to evaluation. Typical case matrices for the employer and union look like this:

## Case Matrix
## Employer
### Obligation: Just Cause

| ANALYSIS | EVALUATION | | | |
|---|---|---|---|---|
| Essential Elements | Necessary Facts | Sources of Proof | Probative Value | Persuasive Impact |
| 1. Clear Standard | | | | |
| 2. Notice/ Knowledge | | | | |
| 3. Breach | | | | |

---

[1] As Chapter 2 explains, just cause is a pervasive theory, applicable to all disciplinary cases. It is often shaped in its particulars by the specific theory of discipline applicable to the particular behavior.

| | | | | |
|---|---|---|---|---|
| 4. Appropriate Consequences | | | | |
| 5. Affirmative Defenses | | | | |
| a. Mitigation | | | | |
| b. Special Rules | | | | |
| c. Past Practice | | | | |

## Case Matrix
## Union
## Obligation: Just Cause

| ANALYSIS | EVALUATION | | | |
|---|---|---|---|---|
| Essential Elements | Necessary Facts | Sources of Proof | Probative Value | Persuasive Impact |
| 1. Unclear Standard | | | | |
| 2. No Notice/ Knowledge | | | | |
| 3. No Breach | | | | |
| 4. Inappropriate Consequences | | | | |
| 5. Affirmative Defenses | | | | |
| a. Mitigation | | | | |
| b. Special Rules | | | | |
| c. Past Practice | | | | |

This simple organizing tool allows the advocate to examine sys-tematically all the essential components of the case.

The first column is titled "essential elements." These are the requirements of just cause in this specific case. For instance, in the Jones case an essential element (element number 2 in the matrix) is whether there is a clear rule requiring an employee to call in if she is going to be out sick.

The next column is "necessary facts." These are the specific facts of Jones' case that must be shown in order to satisfy each essential element of that disciplinary theory. The necessary fact is the com-pany's written rule that literally says an employee must call in if she

is going to be absent. Or it may be the written rule that says an employee is deemed to have abandoned his job if he does not show up, or call in, for five days.

The third column, and the third step in the analysis, involves determining the "source of proof" for each necessary fact. This is the documentary, testimonial, or circumstantial evidence that shows the existence of the necessary fact. For instance, a company handbook may contain the rule requiring calling in for absence. This handbook would be the source of proof (documentary) for the necessary fact in column 2 (a writing that says "employees must call in before or within two hours of any absence") which proves the existence of an essential element in column 1 ("clear standard") of the disciplinary theory.

Suppose, however, that after examining the material produced by the investigation no document containing a rule about calling in or job abandonment can be found. There is no source of proof for a necessary fact. Without that source of proof an essential element cannot be proved, and the employer will be unable to prove there was just cause for the discipline. The advocate must consider whether the investigation was incomplete and the analysis must be suspended to investigate if there is a source of proof for the rule. This results in a feedback loop. Either an appropriate source of proof will be found, in which case analysis can continue, or no source of proof will be found. If no written rule can be found in the collective bargaining agreement, company handbook, or work rules, then it is clear that a documentary source of proof for an essential element of a failure to call in or job abandonment case is missing. There may be an alternative source of proof, such as the testimony of the human resources manager that all new employees receive orientation lectures about calling in. There may be an alternative disciplinary theory, or the case may have to be compromised or settled if discipline has already been taken. If the rule is in a handbook or set of work rules, that document will be the source of proof for the necessary fact that there is a rule.

The second essential element in column 1 is that the rule must be communicated to the employee. The necessary fact in column 2 is that the rule was actually communicated. The source of proof could be the collective bargaining agreement (which employees are responsible for knowing), a signed receipt for a company handbook, or a copy of the work rules signed by the grievant. Alternatively, the rules may have been posted on a bulletin board, which would require testimony to establish that they were actually posted during a certain time.

To complete the analysis, the advocate should review the applicable mitigating and aggravating circumstances described in Chapter 3, as well as the special rules for absences without leave (if that was the theory used), further using the case matrix. The essential elements, necessary facts, and sources of proof should be listed on the case matrix. In filling in the matrix, every time a fact or source of proof is missing it creates a new feedback loop, requiring further investigation. In some instances, the investigation will show no source

of proof for a necessary fact. In those cases, the advocate can examine alternative theories of discipline or decide that even if there was inappropriate behavior it will not be possible to show there was just cause for discipline.

Two other areas for investigation and analysis highlight the differences between the employer and union case matrices: past practice and the appropriateness of the penalty. The employee behavior for which management is imposing discipline may have long been tolerated. A rule that is clear in its apparent requirements may have been long ignored with the implicit consent of management, or applied in a way that is not obvious from the statement of the rule. There may be contractual requirements for expunging disciplinary records, or long-standing practices that limit the period during which prior discipline will be considered in determining the current penalty. It is critical that the union advocate look into these areas. A careful investigation may show that the "real rule" was not broken. Investigating past practice and prior penalties is often fruitful for the union, helping it to identify affirmative defenses. Management advocates should also investigate these areas to avoid being surprised at the hearing.

For the union advocate, past practice and unenforced rules may be the only defenses when inappropriate behavior can easily be proved. In asserting these defenses, however, it is vitally important to use the case matrix to determine the probative value and persuasive impact of the sources of proof. It may be that everybody in the workplace believes the rule has never been enforced this way. But if the witnesses cannot testify to anything more probative than rumor, their testimony is unlikely to be persuasive. This creates a feedback loop for the union, causing it to seek more persuasive evidence (perhaps from the employer's records) of how the rule was actually enforced.

The appropriateness of the penalty is almost always at issue.[2] Sometimes the argument is that the penalty is highly disproportionate to the seriousness of the acts alleged; sometimes the argument is that the penalty is impermissibly different from the penalty ordinarily meted out in like circumstances. In both cases, the management advocate argues consistency, while the union advocate argues inconsistency. In both cases, a careful investigation is necessary to determine what happened in previous cases. Again, it is vital to use the case matrix to determine the likely persuasive impact of the available sources of proof. Using the case matrix to determine persuasive impact is explored below.

## B. Evaluating the Case Using the Case Matrix

After identifying the essential elements, necessary proofs, and sources of proof for the case, the advocate needs to evaluate and assess

---

[2]Some collective bargaining agreements do not give the arbitrator any ability to change the penalty imposed if the employer proves the behavior.

the probative value of each source of proof and determine its likely persuasive impact. Probative value is a measure of the directness with which the proof establishes an essential element. There are three types of probative value: direct, indirect, and circumstantial. For example, to show that a rule requires calling in for any absence, a collective bargaining agreement containing the rule would be direct proof of the rule's existence. If no written rule is available, a supervisor may testify that he understood there was such a rule and he told the grievant he had to call in. This would be indirect evidence of the existence of the rule because it is not the rule itself, but an assertion that the rule exists. It is however, direct evidence that the grievant was told about the rule. If such supervisorial testimony is not available, an advocate may use circumstantial evidence of the rule, such as a "call-in" log maintained by the personnel department, on which calls about absences are recorded each day. This "call-in" log is not the rule itself, but tends to establish the existence of the rule through inference. That is, it is unlikely that this log would exist if there were not a known rule requiring employees to call in. In general, direct proof has more impact than indirect proof or circumstantial evidence. But that is not always the case.

In many disciplinary cases circumstantial evidence can be more compelling than eyewitness testimony. Eyewitnesses can tell conflicting stories because they confused what they saw with what they believe happened. Or they can have motives that lead them to forget parts of what they saw. Or they may simply intend to deceive and be effective liars. While circumstantial evidence does not have the immediacy of someone saying, "I saw the fight," it is usually more difficult to fabricate. And sometimes it has greater persuasive impact than direct testimonial evidence. For example, in fighting cases the employees involved in the altercation often assert that they were merely fooling around, not fighting. Eyewitness testimony about the "seriousness" of the fight is subject to being undercut on cross-examination. A supervisor who did not see the fight, but saw one of the employees with a bloody nose immediately afterwards, may provide good circumstantial evidence that the altercation was not mere horseplay.

Persuasive impact involves the credibility of the evidence and the credence that arbitrator is likely to give to the advocate's proof. The credibility of a witness's testimony depends on such things as the internal consistency of the story she tells, the consistency of her story over time, the consistency of her story with other facts established in the case, the consistency of her story with the way common sense suggests things happen in the real world, her reputation for honesty, her interest in the outcome of the case, and her demeanor. The credence an arbitrator gives to a particular witness's testimony depends on the witness's credibility. The credence an arbitrator gives other proofs depends on such things as whether they are originals, whether they have internal indicia of reliability or unreliability, and whether they meet the consistency tests listed above. For instance, where a handbook contains the rule, it is often necessary to show that this handbook was the one in force at the time rather than a more recent update. Indeed, many documents bear either creation or revision dates that are not, on their face, consistent with what they are introduced to prove. A witness must explain that this later handbook contains exactly the same rule as the previous handbook. The probative value of the handbook is slightly diminished if it is a later version and the arbitrator has only testimony to show that the earlier handbook contained the same rule. In effect, the arbitrator is relying on the testimony, not the document.

## IV. Utilizing the Case Matrix: A Hypothetical Case

A hypothetical "typical" just cause discipline case shows the case matrices that would be constructed by the employer and the union in preparing this case for arbitration.

### A. *Facts of the Hypothetical Case*

Rocky Farms is a processor of fresh chickens and chicken parts located in Modesto, California. Ed is a driver for the company, responsible for moving truckloads of freshly processed chickens from the line to the distribution facility. At the loading dock, production employees move the product in large containers onto the trailer. Ed is small man, and he always wears cowboy boots, a cowboy shirt, and a Stetson hat. One of the loaders who works the graveyard shift with Ed, a large man named Carl began calling Ed "Tex" about six months ago. Ed told Carl he did not like being called Tex, but Carl persisted. Ed told his supervisor that he would like to be called by his name, but his supervisor said that Carl was just kidding around and that Ed should not be so thin-skinned.

Very early Tuesday morning Ed hooked up his tractor to a trailer that had just been loaded and climbed onto the loading dock to check that the doors were properly closed. Carl greeted him by saying: "Hey, Tex, lemme try on that cowboy hat of yours, I'm thinking of getting one myself." Ed said: "Don't call me Tex." Carl responded by shouting to the supervisor, Jim: "Hey, Jim, don't you think Tex should let me try on his cowboy hat?" Jim did not respond.

As Ed was checking the trailer doors Carl grabbed Ed's hat and ran off a few steps with the hat on shouting to co-workers: "Hey, I'm Tex, the baddest cowboy in town." As Ed attempted to grab his hat back, Carl moved to put his hand on Ed's chest and push him off. Ed, who is a judo expert, grabbed Carl's hand and put it into a painful wrist lock while demanding his hat back. Carl gave him the hat back, and Ed let him go. Then Carl swung at Ed, who parried the blow and swept Carl to the ground. Carl tried to get up to hit Ed, but Ed swept an arm or a leg out from under Carl each time he tried to rise. Jim called Security and came running over. He told Ed to move away, Carl to get up, and both that they were suspended pending termination. Security escorted both of them off the plant grounds.

Rocky Farms has a standard discipline and grievance arbitration clause which permits it to discipline and discharge employees only for just cause. Just cause is not defined in the collective bargaining agreement. Rocky Farms has a set of House Rules, for which each employee signs when he is hired and which is posted on each bulletin board at the plant and distribution facility. House Rule 6 reads: "Fighting on company premises will not be tolerated and may be cause for immediate termination." Human Resources subsequently reviewed the facts, the personnel records, and company policy. After the review both Carl and Ed were sent registered letters, stating that they were terminated for violating Rule 6. Ed grieved the termination. Fights at the plant are rare. The only other fight was about eight years ago, and it resulted in one employee being fired. The employee who was fired had accused the other employee of dating his girlfriend and had begun punching him. The other employee fought back until co-workers pulled the two apart.

## B. Analyzing and Evaluating the Hypothetical Case

In this hypothetical situation, the employer and union case matrices diverge on only a few points. Both contain the essential elements of a just cause discharge as they relate to this specific case of fighting. One way of analyzing the case is as a rule violation. The essential elements of the rule violation are the existence of a clear rule that is not inconsistent with the collective bargaining agreement, its communication to the employee, breach of the rule, and its consistent enforcement with an appropriate penalty. As Chapter 8 indicates, there are specific rules governing provocation and self-defense in fighting cases. The essential elements of due process are timely action by the employer, a fair investigation, and a precise statement of the charges. Since these facts demonstrate immediate action by the employer based on a single event witnessed by the supervisor and reviewed by Human Resources, and a termination letter that lists a specific rule as the reason for discharge, it is unlikely that there are any due process issues. The principles of progressive discipline are not likely to be successfully invoked in this case either, since striking another employee is generally seen as grounds for discharge, even in the absence of progressive discipline. Consequently, the case matrix need be constructed only for the rule violation and specific principles for fighting cases.

The first essential element is the existence of a clear rule that is not inconsistent with the collective bargaining agreement. The necessary fact is Rule 6. The source of proof is a copy of the House Rules that are posted on the bulletin board. The probative value is direct, and the persuasive impact is likely to be conclusive. The facts suggest nothing that make a rule against fighting on the premises inconsistent with the collective bargaining agreement.

The second essential element is that the rule be communicated. The necessary fact is that Ed knew or could be presumed to have known about the rule. There are three potential sources of proof. Since employees are asked to sign for the House Rules when they are given a copy, there should be a document that Ed signed. Such a document constitutes direct proof of Ed's receipt and is likely to be conclusive. A second source of proof, if that document is not found, is testimony from the person who is responsible for giving the rules to new employees. The probative value is either direct or circumstantial. If the testimony is, "I gave him a copy of the rules," it would be direct. Its persuasive value depends on how long ago Ed was hired and any apparent bias of the witness. Since it is unlikely someone could remember a trivial act done many years ago, the persuasive impact is limited, depending on the credibility of the witness and her motive, if any, to lie to support the company position. If there were strong motivation to lie (for instance, if the person testifying made the decision to terminate on behalf of Human Resources) circumstantial evidence would be more persuasive.

The evidence is circumstantial if the testimony is, "I can't say I specifically remember giving this to him, but I always give the rules to every new employee as part of the orientation." If the person doing the orientation used a checklist with the House Rules as one item on it, that increases the persuasive impact of his testimony. It also provides a neutral document to buttress the witness's credibility. In either case, the persuasive impact is likely to be substantial. If Ed remembers getting the rules, there is no issue. If he testifies that he simply does not remember whether he was given the rules, it is likely that the employer evidence will have greater persuasive value.

Breach of the rule is unlikely to be at issue in this case. The necessary fact is a fight. The source of proof is the supervisor who was present and saw Ed and Carl fighting. His testimony is direct evidence of the necessary fact and is likely to be conclusive. It may be buttressed by Carl's testimony. Or Ed may agree that there was a fight and there could be a stipulation about it. It is unlikely that Ed will deny a fight occurred, although he is likely to characterize his role in it as self-defense.

The company is likely to argue that the essential element of a consistent and appropriate penalty is proved by the necessary fact that it terminated both employees in the fight. The source of proof is the termination letters to Carl and Ed. They are competent documentary evidence and are conclusive proof that both participants in the fight were terminated. In creating the case matrix, however, the employer will be faced with the affirmative defense of the instance eight years ago in which an employee was not fired because he was defending himself. The employer should examine all available evidence on the earlier fight to distinguish it from this one. The company may call the distinguishing feature an "extraordinary circumstance" and argue that it has consistently terminated employees for fighting, except when there was an extraordinary circumstance.

The union should look to the essential elements of self-defense. Chapter 8 indicates that the person claiming self-defense must be a nonaggressor and engaged solely in defending himself. The necessary fact to show Ed was the nonaggressor is the initial aggressive act by Carl. There are three possibilities: grabbing the hat (a technical battery), attempting to shove Ed off, and Carl's swing at Ed. Both Ed and the supervisor should be able to testify to all acts. The supervisor's testimony, however, is likely to be colored by his failure to take any action when Carl called his attention to the fact he was about to give Ed a hard time. So the supervisor may undercut the aggressive nature of the acts or claim to have been unable to see Carl's swing. In addition, if he supports the management decision to terminate Ed, he is likely to underplay the significance of Carl's attempt to hold off Ed and characterize it as not being an aggressive act. Ed, on the other hand, is likely to testify that Carl acted aggressively in taking his hat and continued to act aggressively by attempting to push him away.

Ed's testimony, which provides direct proof of the aggression by Carl, creates a feedback loop for the union. Since the supervisor and Carl both have a motive to characterize Carl's acts as nonaggressive, the union should look for other possible witnesses. If there are none, it may want to seek out people the supervisor, Carl, or Ed spoke to immediately after the incident, who may be able to corroborate Ed's version. In addition, the union should want to examine any written document the supervisor created after the incident to see if it supports or undercuts his likely testimony.

The second essential element in the union's case is that Ed acted solely in self-defense. The necessary facts are that he used a wrist lock only after Carl attempted to shove him, that he parried Carl's swing, and that all the blows against Carl were defensive. Ed is the primary source of proof for the timing of the wrist lock. His testimony is direct evidence, but its persuasive impact is limited by his self-interest. The supervisor may also testify to the wrist lock, but he may be inclined to fudge the timing to create confusion about whether Carl attempted a shove. While his testimony is direct evidence, he may understate or claim confusion about what he saw to buttress the employer's position. Similarly, Ed can provide direct evidence of the parry and "sweeps" he used to keep Carl from getting up. His testimony is direct evidence but is limited in its persuasive value by his self-interest. The supervisor can again provide direct testimony of what he saw. If he testifies honestly, he will have to concede the attempted blow by Carl, which undercuts any later attempt to characterize the parry and sweeps as aggressive. If the union is unable to find an additional witness, it might call a judo expert to testify to—and perhaps demonstrate—the essentially defensive nature of the actions the supervisor and Ed describe.

The employer and union case matrices look like this:

## Obligation: <u>Just Cause/Self-Defense (Employer)</u>

| ANALYSIS | EVALUATION | | | |
|---|---|---|---|---|
| Essential Elements | Necessary Facts | Sources of Proof | Probative Value | Persuasive Impact |
| 1. Clear Standard | Rule 6 | House Rules | Direct | Conclusive |
| 2. Communicated | Ed Knew or Could Be Presumed to Know Rule | Signed House Rules | Direct | Conclusive |
| | | HR Testimony: "I gave it." | Direct | Possibly Limited |
| | | HR "I always give it." | Circum-stantial | Sub-stantial |
| 3. Breach | Fight | Supervisor | Direct | Conclusive |
| 4. Consistent and Appro-priate Penalty | Carl Ter-mination Letter | Letter | Direct | Relevant? Conclusive |

## Obligation: <u>Self-Defense (Union)</u>

| ANALYSIS | EVALUATION | | | |
|---|---|---|---|---|
| Essential Elements | Necessary Facts | Sources of Proof | Probative Value | Persuasive Impact |
| 1. Nonaggressor | Hat Grabbed | Supervisor | Direct | May Undercut |
| | | Ed | Direct | Interested |
| | | Other Witness? | Direct | Unknown |
| | Attempted Shove | Ed | Direct | Interested |
| | | Supervisor | Direct | May Undercut |
| | | Other? | Indirect | Unknown |
| | Carl's Swing | Ed | Direct | Persuasive/ Interested |
| | | Supervisor | Direct | Interested |
| 2. Only Self-Defense | Defensive Acts: Wrist Lock, Sweep | Ed | Direct | Persuasive/ Interested |
| | | Supervisor | Direct | Persuasive |
| | | Judo Expert | Indirect | Persuasive |

In examining the case matrices both advocates become aware of the weaknesses and strengths in their cases.

## V. Choosing an Arbitrator

In the hypothetical fighting situation analyzed in the previous section, the advocates may be concerned about which arbitrator will hear the case. The employer will want someone to whom a fight is a fight and there is no exception for self-defense. The union will want an arbitrator who subscribes to the self-defense theory. Choosing an arbitrator is a significant concern for both sides.

In using this book to prepare for a specific case, the advocate may be struck by arbitrators arriving at different results in similar cases. There are a variety of reasons for this seeming inconsistency. In some areas there is a well-accepted theory and variations in result exist only because of unique factual elements. In other areas there are majority and minority views about the essential elements of a disciplinary theory. In those cases a genuine theoretical split exists among arbitrators, and the view an arbitrator takes is often outcome-determinative.

In some areas, however, there is no overriding intellectual principle that can unify all the decisions. In trying to reconcile the theories in these confusing areas—to understand how a potential arbitrator may rule—three things must be remembered. First, there are an enormous number of factual situations and advocates. Sometimes a unique set of facts, combined with good advocacy, leads an arbitrator to write a decision that does not appear to follow the disciplinary theory enunciated. Because the arbitrator is convinced that a particular result is correct, her explanation of how the disciplinary theory leads to this result may be strained. These decisions, if read carefully, can suggest how good advocacy may affect a case.

Second, only a portion of all awards are submitted for publication. The Code of Professional Responsibility for Labor Management Arbitrators requires arbitrators to seek permission to publish an award only after it has been issued. Some arbitrators regularly ask for permission to publish their awards; others have no interest in publication. Often, when asked, a party will not want an award published in a case it lost. Of those cases submitted for publication each year, fewer than 3 percent are published. Consequently, published awards represent a minuscule and possibly unrepresentative fraction of all awards issued in a given year.

Third, there is little interest in publishing one more award that simply follows a well-accepted disciplinary theory. If a new technology is emerging (such as genetic testing), an award applying traditional principles to this new area will have a good chance of being published. If a case has a unique factual twist with inherent interest, or relates to an interesting new workplace tool (such as computers in the 1970s), the decision may catch the attention of publishers. Aberrant decisions have their own inherent fascination. An award that statisticians might call an outlier because it does not fit within the body of accepted principles may be published just because it is aberrant. It may help to define what is beyond the pale, but advocates must remember it is not likely to convince other arbitrators. The aberrant award simply confirms the range of the possible in arbitration.

These variations in the way arbitrators view disciplinary theories make this book a valuable—although certainly not exclusive—resource for choosing an arbitrator. As a preliminary matter, this book shows the range of arbitral views, and advocates can see where their case fits into that range. If they fit easily into a well-accepted disciplinary theory, it will be relatively easy to choose an arbitrator, since any mainstream arbitrator is likely to use the well-accepted theory. On the other hand, it may become apparent that whether the arbitrator follows the majority or minority view will be outcome-determinative in a case. Although it may be possible to choose an arbitrator cited in this book for a particular minority theory, it is not likely. If the theory used by the arbitrator is outcome-determinative, it is likely that both sides will be researching arbitrators and will reach an impasse in choosing an arbitrator because each side wants someone who uses the disciplinary theory that will win the case.[3]

Choosing an arbitrator involves inferring the arbitrator's predilections, views, and decisional style from a written award. Predilections are based on the arbitrator's experience and background and may be inferable from a biographical sketch as well as awards.[4] For example, an advocate may believe an arbitrator who is a professor without real-world experience might be more likely to buy an abstruse theory than an experienced arbitrator "from the trenches." Or an advocate may believe an inexperienced arbitrator might provide a decision that is outside the normal range of arbitral opinion. Views of disciplinary theories may be expressed in written awards, published articles, or books. Decisional style—whether the arbitrator is a splitter, a "visceral" decider, or a decision avoider—is often most clearly expressed in written awards. These same characteristics—predilections, views, and decisional style—are also important in cases where the arbitrator's view of a disciplinary theory is not outcome-determinative.

---

[3]Since so few decisions are published, one party may be advantaged because it has available to it unpublished decisions in its industry. This underscores the importance of consulting with colleagues when choosing an arbitrator.

[4]The worst source of information on predilections are the statistics provided by certain management services that purport to list how many times the arbitrator has decided for or against management or split the decision. There are so many confounding factors that these statistics can be extremely misleading.

There are two major sources for learning about arbitrators: their written awards and the experience of other advocates. Of course, an agreed-upon arbitrator must also be available.

## A. *Reading the Award*

Learning about arbitrators by reading their awards is not a science, but there are techniques that can help the advocate to infer arbitral characteristics and to decide if this is the right arbitrator for a particular case. There are five aspects of an award to consider: directness, economy, sensitivity, remedy, and the intellectual predilections of the arbitrator.

*1. Directness.* An award should be direct. The facts and disciplinary theory should be clearly stated and the relevant arguments of the parties directly addressed. The arguments about disciplinary theory that the arbitrator accepts should focus the award so that it contains only the relevant facts. Where the arbitrator has made credibility determinations they should be clear, and the reason for them should be stated. The award must expose the mental processes the arbitrator went through in deciding the case. An award that recites all the testimony and all the arguments in excruciating detail, and then states the outcome without any rationale, is suspect. If it is impossible to extract from the decision the arbitrator's reason for deciding the case as he did, the advocate can suspect the clarity of the arbitrator's thinking. Similarly, an arbitrator who recites the facts and theories, mentions "considerations," and then goes on to reach a conclusion without providing the link among them has not provided a direct award. If there is no statement of the reason for a decision, it should create suspicion about whether the arbitrator engaged in rigorous analysis. The arbitrator who fails to share the mental process by which he or she reached a decision may have reached a visceral, rather than a reasoned decision. The "guts" decider listens to all the testimony, develops a feeling for who should prevail, and then writes an award embodying the decision as to who prevails, but little more. Where the award contains no explicit credibility determinations—and they are crucial to the outcome—the arbitrator may be a "decision avoider," someone who does not want to offend by deciding that testimony is not credible.

*2. Economy.* The facts and arguments should be stated concisely. A long recitation that combines relevant and irrelevant facts may indicate an inability to distinguish between the two. A synopsis of each witness's testimony simply shows that the arbitrator was awake or read the transcript, not that he understood the significance of the testimony. If the arguments of the parties are quoted at great length, it may indicate that the arbitrator failed to assimilate those arguments. On the other hand, a succinct paraphrase shows the arbitrator understood the arguments.

An economical decision is one in which the arbitrator supports her conclusion simply, using no surplus words. Arbitral statements that are unnecessary to support the conclusion are potentially mischievous. General statements tend to take on a life of their own and may lead from this grievance to a new one embodying a disciplinary theory the arbitrator seemed implicitly to endorse. In addition, a multiplicity of reasons for arriving at a single conclusion may leave the advocate guessing as to precisely why the arbitrator decided as she did. What should the employer have done differently to have the discipline upheld? How could the employee have behaved differently to avoid discipline? If the answers are not clear from the award, it has limited value for guiding the parties in their future behavior or as a predictor of future decisions.

3. *Sensitivity.*   The third aspect of an award is the arbitrator's sensitivity to the continuing relationship of the parties. Sometimes it is necessary to call a liar precisely that. At other times it may be more polite to speak of a lack of credibility. Most good arbitrators know when to do which, but the "decision avoider" is constrained by a desire never to offend anyone by a clear decision. The consequence may be that one side or the other is encouraged to lie because there seems to be no consequences—in outcome or personal status—in being untruthful.

If the arbitrator uses emotionally toned language, that may be a clue about the arbitrator's ability to remain neutral. In some cases it is a reflection of a hearing that was acrimonious and out of control. In other instances it is an indication that the arbitrator was not successful in separating his feelings from the issue in the case. It is possible to describe bad actions without impugning the actors. If the arbitrator does not do so it may be an indication of a visceral decision.

4. *Remedy.*   The fourth aspect of reading an award is how the arbitrator deals with remedies. For most parties the remedy is the key part of the award. Arbitrators vary in the amount of attention they give to the remedy. In some instances the reason for the remedy is fully explored in the opinion, so that it is inevitable that the award will sustain the grievance. Some arbitrators seem satisfied to have decided the issue and give almost no explanation for the remedy, characterizing a reduced penalty (for example) as "appropriate." Some arbitrators simply announce a remedy and leave it to the reader to determine how they got from the conclusion to the remedy. The classic "splitter" may regularly reduce the penalty for no identifiable reason or put an employee back to work with no back pay, despite a long period of time between the termination and the award. Whether this is a desirable or undesirable trait depends on which side an advocate represents. The specificity with which the arbitrator describes the

remedy is important to the parties' ability to execute it without dispute. In some instances, the arbitrator may leave the parties to work out a remedy and retain jurisdiction.

Arbitrators disagree about the propriety of retaining jurisdiction over the creation or execution of the remedy. A classic "decision avoider" may simply leave the remedy to be worked out by the parties while retaining jurisdiction if they do not agree. The disagreement over retained jurisdiction comes from the general principle of *functus officio*: once an arbitrator has issued the award he or she has no further powers, unless some are given by statute or contract. While arbitration statutes generally provide for "correction" of an award, there are no provisions for retaining jurisdiction: it is an arbitral invention. Many question whether an arbitrator can simply announce in the award that he has retained jurisdiction. The arbitrator who believes that his jurisdiction is decided by the parties is likely to ask them if they wish to stipulate that he can retain jurisdiction over the remedy. This stipulation will then appear in the award.

5. *Intellectual Predilections.*   Certain intellectual predilections are easily ascertained from reading a few of the arbitrator's awards. The most common misperception about arbitrators is that they are all "splitters." While the general proposition is not true, there are some arbitrators who always endeavor to give something to each side. Their awards make it clear that these arbitrators can never decide cleanly, always feeling obliged to find a middle way. This is a very important consideration when choosing an arbitrator, since it may be advantageous to one side to have a split decision.

Arbitrators differ significantly in their views of discharge cases. Some arbitrators view discharge as the industrial equivalent of capital punishment. These arbitrators may reveal this explicitly or implicitly in their awards. If an arbitrator requires strict adherence to rules of evidence and proof of facts "beyond a reasonable doubt," that is implicit proof that the arbitrator sees termination as industrial capital punishment. Similarly, if the arbitrator requires extensive progressive discipline, it may be evidence of a bias toward seeing termination as industrial capital punishment. In both instances it is important to distinguish between the arbitrator who is simply being cautious because a lot is at stake and the arbitrator with a predilection against termination. It requires reading many of the arbitrator's awards to see if there is a predilection against termination. Where the arbitrator almost always finds unacceptable evidence, a failure of proof, or insufficient progressive discipline, it is likely that the arbitrator has a bias against termination. The arbitrator may be so uncomfortable with upholding a termination that he or she will only do it in the most egregious circumstances.

Arbitrators also differ over the weight to be given management decisions. Most view the arbitration as a de novo proceeding in which the employer must establish just cause for taking disciplinary action and for the specific discipline imposed. They ignore what the employer has done before imposing discipline—unless the behavior violates contractual obligations or offends just cause—and look only to what is proved at the hearing. The employer's good faith belief about what the employee did and whether it had a good faith belief the discipline was appropriate are irrelevant to the arbitrator's decision. Other arbitrators see their function as reviewing the discipline and penalty as actions already taken and simply imposing some test of reasonability on the employer's decision. Finally, some arbitrators make it clear in their award that they view themselves as chancellors in equity whose task is to right wrongs. Again, there are no right or wrong styles. The effective advocate recognizes the differences and chooses what each case needs for a better chance of winning.

Some additional intellectual predilections may appear in the award itself or be inferable from the arbitrator's biographical sketch. Consider this example: Suppose it is 1980 and an employee was terminated for being at a party where marijuana was smoked. The union would probably want an arbitrator who was in college in the late 1960s. It would be reasonable to expect that she would have been exposed to marijuana smoking and might not think that being in a place where it was smoked was evidence of moral turpitude. The company might want an arbitrator who went to college in the 1950s, who might believe marijuana smokers are evildoers who corrupt everyone they come in contact with. Neither is necessarily true, but it is reasonable to believe that these two arbitrators have very different relevant experiences which may lead to different intellectual predilections. These predilections may also show up clearly in the language of awards. An arbitrator may use emotionally toned language in the award such as "evils (as opposed to "effects") of pot smoking, "illicit (as opposed to "illegal") activities," or "den" (as opposed to "roomful") of pot smokers.

In some respects the information gleaned from reading arbitral awards is neutral. For an advocate, the abstract question of which arbitral school of thought is correct is secondary to the pragmatic question of whether this arbitrator is right for this specific case. By using the case matrix to analyze and evaluate a case, an advocate should know what disciplinary theory will provide the greatest chance of success. After reading arbitration awards, an advocate should know something about the theories accepted by potential arbitrators and their decisional style.

## B. Consulting With Colleagues

In choosing an arbitrator an advocate should consult with colleagues. A colleague who has used the arbitrator is an invaluable resource. While the award of an experienced arbitrator will almost always reflect a view of the facts that is consistent with the decision, it will rarely reveal anything about the way the hearing was conducted. Nor will it tell you anything about the arbitrator's ability to grasp concepts and apply them sensibly. For all this information it is best to confer with a colleague who has used the arbitrator. In addition, it is important to know the right questions to ask a colleague.

The first question to ask a colleague is whether he or she has won or lost cases with a particular arbitrator. It is amazing how intelligent, evenhanded, and capable the arbitrator looks to the advocate who won the case. Yet that same arbitrator may look like an ignorant, biased bumbler to the loser. The second question to ask is how many times the colleague has used the arbitrator. Obviously, the more experience she has with the arbitrator the more rooted the evaluation. After that, there are two general areas to question your colleague about: the conduct of the hearing and the arbitrator's post-hearing conduct.

Whether the arbitrator controls the hearing, and what he or she permits advocates to do, are important considerations in choosing an arbitrator. Some arbitrators take the view that the case belongs to the parties but the hearing belongs to the arbitrator. They will never suggest what evidence should be presented, but they tightly control how evidence is presented. Ask the colleague if the arbitrator runs a tight hearing, one in which he or she controls the conduct of the advocates, rather than reacting to it. Does the arbitrator permit yelling, screaming, and advanced histrionics? Or does she insist that the hearing be conducted civilly? Does the arbitrator make evidentiary rulings that make for an orderly record? Some arbitrators are in the habit of taking any proffered evidence "for what it is worth," and advocates may not know what the arbitrator thinks it is worth, what it says about the arbitrator's view of the issues in the case, and how much time should be spent refuting that evidence. On the other hand, an arbitrator who refuses to admit that odd bit of evidence avoids uncertainty as to "what it is worth" and ensures a useful record.

Other arbitrators rule on evidentiary matters, excluding evidence that has too little probative value to assist in determining any material issue. Some of this behavior will be determined by the arbitrator's training: a lawyer is more likely to make evidentiary rulings than an industrial relations expert. Not all lawyer arbitrators, however, keep tight control over a hearing by making evidentiary rulings, and this is something other advocates will know.

At times an arbitrator will admit a piece of evidence about which there is protracted wrangling and advise the parties of the probative value he or she attaches to that piece of evidence. If the arbitrator says that the weight of the evidence is, in the words of the metaphysical poet John Donne, "like gold to aery thinness beat," even the most nonliterary advocate will recognize that this evidence should not be relied upon by its proponent and need not be rebutted by its opponent. In considering a specific arbitrator for a specific case, an advocate's evaluation of the probative value of the available evidence will determine whether it is preferable to choose an arbitrator who lets everything in or one who makes evidentiary rulings.

A critical area of arbitral behavior at the hearing is the degree to which the arbitrator intrudes inappropriately into the case. There is nothing more frustrating to an advocate than to have an arbitrator force him to conduct the case the way the arbitrator would have presented it, rather than as the advocate wishes to present it. There are two extremes of arbitral behavior, each posing its own dangers. At one extreme is the arbitrator who, during the entire hearing, sits unmoving as evidence comes in. It is difficult to know if the arbitrator understands the testimony, the documents, or the points the advocate is making. At the other extreme is the arbitrator who takes such complete control of the case that neither side gets to present its evidence the way it had planned. This arbitrator may have decided his theory of the case during the first few minutes and then directs the presentation to conform with that theory. An arbitrator who behaves this way presents the greatest danger to a well-prepared advocate trying to present the case using the theory most favorable to his client.

Finally, some arbitrators conduct a hearing by trying to avoid holding it. There are arbitrators who have a reputation for trying to mediate all the disputes that come before them. Some are very successful at settling cases. If the case matrix shows an advocate has a weak case, that side may want to choose an arbitrator who will push to mediate. If you have a strong case, and a need to have it serve as an example to promote or prevent certain behavior, you should choose a different arbitrator.

It is critical to learn from colleagues whether an arbitrator is educable. Does the arbitrator asks intelligent questions during the hearing to clarify matters that puzzle him or her? The most dangerous arbitrator is one who is not following an advocate's case and is afraid to ask questions that will expose his or her ignorance. This is unusual behavior, since most experienced arbitrators are sufficiently self-assured that they are not afraid to ask questions.

Closely related to asking questions is the willingness of an arbitrator to grapple with difficult theories, scientific concepts, or highly complex factual situations. Some arbitrators are not comfortable with a high degree of complexity or uncertainty. Their tendency is to oversimplify, rather than struggle to understand the complexity. If an arbitrator is unwilling to expose his or her lack of understanding at a time when it can be remedied, or is unwilling to struggle with complexity, she may be unsuitable for a particular case. The best way to learn this is from a colleague who has used the arbitrator.

The second major area for questioning colleagues is the arbitrator's posthearing conduct. Three questions should be asked about the decision, the answers to which will not be apparent on the face of the award. First, was the decision timely—i.e., was it mailed within the period provided by the contract or administering agency? Second, did the arbitrator's statement of the facts fairly reflect the evidence introduced at the hearing? In asking this, of course, the arbitrator's stated judgments about credibility and relevance should be considered. The key is not whether the arbitrator believed a particular witness or document, but whether the arbitrator simply ignored evidence that was inconsistent with her view of the case. Third, ask whether the award completely resolved the controversy and was sensitive to the continuing relationship of the parties. To an outsider reading an award a particular remedy may seem perfectly appropriate. The parties, however, may be aware of difficulties that were explained to the arbitrator but inadequately handled in the remedy. Even more important is the way in which the arbitrator reached a certain conclusion may help or hinder the continuing relationship. Only someone who is keenly aware of the relationship can assess whether the arbitrator helped or unnecessarily hindered the ongoing relationship.

There are two other questions to ask a colleague. First, would the colleague use this arbitrator again? (If not, why not? If so, for what kind of case?) Some cases can be competently handled by a relatively inexperienced arbitrator, while others require only the most seasoned arbitrator. Second, does this arbitrator make tough decisions? There are some cases in which one party clearly wins or loses; no compromise is possible. It is likely that the loser will be unhappy with the arbitrator. Can this arbitrator take the heat? If not, an advocate may consider using an arbitrator from outside the area, who will be unaffected by alienating one side in this dispute.

## C. Arbitrator Availability

One final consideration is arbitrator availability. There are two important factors to consider when looking at arbitrator availability. First, is this a case in which a quick decision is the most important factor? Second, is this a complex case that requires an arbitrator with a technical grounding in the industry or many years of experience?

In many disciplinary cases it is more important to resolve the matter quickly than absolutely correctly. For instance, where the employer has a progressive discipline program for time and attendance it is important to get a quick decision to know whether an employee has broken the rules and moved from one step to the next. While parties always want the decision to be correct, for progressive discipline to succeed the arbitration needs to occur quickly before further infractions occur or existing infractions become stale. Other discipline cases that involve a penalty less than discharge also need to be quickly decided for progressive discipline to effectively correct employee behavior. Ordinarily, in nondischarge cases the consequences of an incorrect decision (from the losing side's perspective) are not devastating to a program or the employee's career. Similarly, discharge cases where the back-pay liability may be more significant than the reason for discharge require speedy, rather than perfect, decisions. This may suggest using an arbitrator who is newer, more available, and willing to get a decision out in a short time.

In other discharge cases, where the behavior was notorious or there is new ground to be broken, a correct decision is more important than a speedy one. For instance, if an employee had been fired in 1986 for refusing to take a drug test it would have been quite important to have an experienced arbitrator capable of understanding constitutional and technical issues. The precedential value of the decision would have been as important to the parties as the actual discharge decision.

## VI. Preparing for Arbitration

There are many books about case preparation, some of which are noted at the end of this chapter. They cover the specifics of matters such as witness and document preparation. Those technical areas are not covered in this section. Instead, this section focuses on working with the opposing advocate and the arbitrator—before the hearing—to help ensure a smooth hearing.

By the time an arbitrator has been chosen, the parties should have a good enough idea of their cases to determine whether more than one day will be needed for hearing. If the parties share their preliminary estimate of how many witnesses they will present, they can predict—reasonably well—the number of days required for the hearing. While most disciplinary cases are completed in a single day, if it appears that more than one day will be needed, a multiday hearing should be scheduled. There are three advantages to scheduling multiday hearings. First, the arbitrator's availability is ensured. Otherwise, if the parties wait until the end of the first day of hearing to schedule a second date, it is likely that the arbitrator will have to offer a date a month or more away because he or she does not have earlier available dates. Second, it ensures the client will only pay once for preparing the case. If a second date is weeks after the first, the advocate must spend significant time repreparing himself as well as witnesses who were not called. Third, it eliminates the possible necessity of truncating the case in order to finish and avoid delays. The disadvantage of scheduling a multiday hearing is that if the hearing concludes on the first day, the parties may wind up paying the arbitrator a late cancellation fee. The cost of this fee should be weighed against the costs of continuing a hearing when deciding whether to schedule multiple days.

After scheduling the case, it is often useful to have a prehearing conference if there are potential differences between the parties that can take up hearing time. For instance, where a witness is no longer in the area it may make sense to one side to have telephone testimony. If the other side disagrees, the arbitrator can resolve it before the hearing. The arbitrator can also resolve disagreements about production of records, hearing location, and issues of confidentiality or privilege. The arbitrator can issue subpoenas for witnesses and documents to be produced at the hearing. In a very complex case it may be useful to have the arbitrator set forth a timetable for the parties to reach a stipulation of uncontested facts, to mark and agree to documents, and to stipulate the issue.

Some arbitrators insist upon a court reporter, while others leave that decision to the parties. In a simple disciplinary case it is hard to justify the expense of a transcript. On the other hand, if there is a multiday hearing spread out over several months, or some technically difficult matter, or lots of conflicting testimony, a transcript may be justified. In choosing an arbitrator for a specific case it is important to ascertain whether her transcript requirements match the needs of the case.

# VII. Presenting the Case

The mechanics of case presentation, such as direct and cross-examination, have been covered in many books, and are not covered in this section. Rather, this section addresses only the arbitrator's needs in an advocate's presentation. That is, having analyzed and evaluated the case on the case matrix, what can the advocate do to ensure that the arbitrator has the best chance of understanding the case? Approached from that perspective, there are four important areas: the rolling hypothesis, opening statements, witness sequestration, and aids to comprehension.

## A. *Rolling Hypothesis*

Decision making in arbitration begins the moment the arbitrator looks at the first piece of paper, conducts a conference call, or hears the first words of the case. The arbitrator strives, from the first moment, to understand the nature of the dispute, its factual basis and theoretical underpinning. In most cases, the parties have been actively engaged in investigating the underlying facts, analyzing and evaluating the case, and preparing their theories and proofs well before they first speak with the arbitrator. The arbitrator ordinarily comes to the first encounter with no information about the case. The arbitrator's job is to quickly make some sense of the mass of materials presented, so that she can make rulings on motions and evidence. In order to bring some mental order to the facts as they are presented, arbitrators employ a "rolling hypothesis." This is a tentative theory, or set of theories, about what the case entails, which the arbitrator uses for categorizing and remembering evidence as it is presented.

The rolling hypothesis is a tentative series of pigeonholes into which the arbitrator can fit facts so she can see the relationships among them and how they support (or defeat) the disciplinary theory involved in the case. For instance, at the beginning of an absenteeism case the employer might present bargaining history evidence to show that the attendance rules, although not incorporated into the collective bargaining agreement, were presented to the union. While bargaining history is not normally a part of a disciplinary case, the arbitrator would have a rolling hypothesis that this is part of the employer's attempt to show the rules do not contravene the collective bargaining agreement, were properly promulgated, and known to the employee. Thus, the arbitrator would know where this evidence fits and have an expectation that certain other evidence would be forthcoming.

### B. Opening Statements

A rolling hypothesis is both a mental organizing device and a device for setting arbitral expectations of what is to come. It is important to the advocate because it shapes how the arbitrator sees the evidence as it comes in. The first chance an advocate has to shape the arbitrator's rolling hypothesis is the opening statement. The opening statement is a brief outline of the theories of the case and what the advocate believes the evidence will show. In many instances the advocate includes the strongest facts that will be adduced as a way of indicating to the arbitrator the strength of the case.

While many advocates forego an opening statement, or reserve it until the beginning of their case, both strategies waste an important opportunity. The sooner an advocate can tell an arbitrator his theory of the case, the better. The reason is simple. The rolling hypothesis is always tentative, but the more evidence that is provided by one side to support a specific rolling hypothesis, the less tentative it becomes. If the employer fails to make an opening statement it misses the opportunity to initially shape the rolling hypothesis to conform to its theory of the case. Since the arbitrator is obliged to create a rolling hypothesis based solely on the evidence, it is likely to be extremely tentative. If the union fails to make an opening statement immediately after the employer, it wastes the opportunity to undercut the employer's theory of the case with its own and to ensure the rolling hypothesis contains both theories as alternative means of organizing the evidence as it comes in. The best strategy is for both sides to provide an opening statement in all cases in which the employer has set forth a clear reason for the discipline. In those rare cases when the employer fails to allege specific reasons for the discipline in the grievance procedure and the opening statement, the union would be wise to decline to make an opening statement since it may be an exercise in futility. The union may simply want to make a motion to dismiss at the end of the employer's case-in-chief.

## C. Witness Sequestration

Sequestering witnesses—excluding from the hearing room all potential witnesses who are not actually testifying—is important when credibility questions are anticipated. It serves two purposes. First, it ensures that witnesses will not learn information from each others testimony, so as to vary their own testimony to match or dispute that which preceded it. Second, arbitrators deciding credibility issues use consistency to evaluate testimony. They consider the internal consistency of the story, its consistency over time, the consistency of each story with other facts established in the case, the consistency of each story with what common sense suggests is how things happen in the real world, and the witness's reputation for honesty, interest in the outcome of the case, and demeanor. As to all these tests, the arbitrator has much more to work with when each witness's testimony is unaffected by someone else's words.

A motion to sequester witnesses should be made before the opening statements. It will defeat the purpose of sequestration if witnesses hear detailed statements of what each side intends to prove and how they intend to prove it. Where credibility will be the major determinant of the outcome of the hearing it is important to treat the hearing as a laboratory in which the samples must be kept uncontaminated.

## D. Aids to Comprehension

Most advocates are well aware that arbitrators sell curable ignorance. Arbitrators come into a case ignorant of the facts and not knowing which disciplinary theories they will be asked to apply. By the end of the hearing they need to have all the evidence necessary for making a decision. Two useful devices, used by sophisticated advocates to help educate arbitrators, are the glossary and the chronology. A glossary is often necessary, even if the arbitrator is familiar with the industry, because there are many different acronyms, initialisms, and jargon terms that people in the industry use. Witnesses will use these terms frequently: it is how they normally talk. But the arbitrator may be struggling to remember the acronym that was explained an hour ago. An arbitrator who is provided with a glossary at the beginning of the hearing will be able to refer to it any time he hears a word or phrase that is only barely familiar. Similarly, when there is a complex chain of events, a timeline showing all the major events, or a chronology presented in some other graphic format, will be an invaluable resource for the arbitrator. Frequently the parties will be able to prepare a joint chronology, simply highlighting areas in which they have a difference. If they present this to the arbitrator at the beginning of the hearing, it can be incorporated into the arbitrator's rolling hypothesis.

## VIII.  Conclusion

This chapter provides some tools for effectively using the rest of the book. While it is important to know the theories of discipline contained in the following chapters, it is equally important to know how to use them to prepare and win your cases. This book will be most useful if the advocate analyzes and evaluates cases using the case matrix and theories of discipline. It will also help the advocate choose the theory that works best for her case, and the arbitrator who is most suited to the case.

## Books on Advocacy in Arbitration

How to Prepare and Present a Labor Arbitration Case by Charles S. Loughhran (BNA Books, 1996)

Labor Arbitration: A Practical Guide for Advocates edited by Max Zimny, William F. Dolson, and Christopher A. Barreca (BNA Books, 1990)

Labor Arbitration: Cases and Materials for Advocates by William F. Dolson, Christopher A. Barreca, and Max Zimny (BNA Books, 1997)

Labor Arbitration: The Strategy of Persuasion by Norman Brand (Practising Law Institute, 1987) An earlier version of the case matrix appears in this book. The editor-in-chief appreciates the Practising Law Institute's permission to adapt and reprint this material.

Winning Arbitration Advocacy by Marvin F. Hill, Jr., Anthony V. Sinicropi, and Amy L. Evenson (BNA Books, 1997)

# Chapter 2

# Just Cause

The central concept permeating discipline and discharge arbitrations is "just cause." Most collective bargaining agreements explicitly prohibit the employer from disciplining or discharging employees without just cause. Even in the absence of specific contract language, just cause is the touchstone by which arbitrators judge employer actions. If the arbitrator concludes that the employer lacked just cause to discipline or discharge an employee, the action will be overturned. If there was just cause, the action will be upheld.

Just cause is not an easily defined concept. In one respect, just cause can be shorthand for what an arbitrator thinks is fair. If, after considering the facts, the arbitrator concludes that the employer failed to treat the employee fairly, she will find there was no just cause for the discipline. Or she will find there was just cause if the employer treated the employee fairly. Since individual notions of fairness vary and the specific facts that lead to discipline are often unique, it can be difficult to extract the principle that led this arbitrator to her conclusion. Over many arbitrators and many cases, however, some principles of just cause emerge.

Two principles that are central to just cause are employed by all arbitrators: due process and progressive discipline. Due process, as it is used in determining just cause, has its origins in both constitutional and criminal law. Arbitrators have made analogies to both types of law in creating a hybrid called "industrial due process."[1] Industrial due process encompasses the employer's procedural responsibilities in disciplining employees. In general, arbitrators apply

---

[1] See Tucson Unified Sch. Dist., 89-1 ARB ¶8236 (White, 1989); United Tel. Co. of Fla., 61 LA 443 (Taylor, 1973).

principles of industrial due process when determining whether an employer had just cause for discipline.

Progressive discipline has its origins in both collective bargaining and shared notions of fairness. Some collective bargaining agreements specify the steps an employer must take before disciplining or discharging an employee. Even in the absence of bargained-for steps, however, arbitrators have generally asserted that an employee must be given some warning that his behavior is unacceptable and some opportunity to conform his behavior to the employer's legitimate expectations. In the most egregious circumstances—such as stealing or destroying company property—societal norms can substitute for warnings and employees can be fired for a first offense. Ordinarily, however, notice and an opportunity to improve, together with the imposition of increasingly severe disciplinary penalties, are at the heart of progressive discipline as that principle is applied by arbitrators.

It should be clear by now that arbitrators did not sit down together in the dim past and agree upon the principles of just cause. Rather, arbitrators build upon what other arbitrators said in their opinions, developing principles of just cause by accretion. Over time, as societal notions of fairness changed, the outer contours of just cause changed while the basic principles became more solidified. The discussion of just cause is organized into four sections: (1) a survey of attempts to describe the underlying principles of just cause; (2) a discussion of industrial due process, including remedies arbitrators have awarded for failures of due process; (3) a discussion of progressive discipline; and (4) a discussion of arbitral concepts of "fairness." Taken together, these sections should help explain the myriad opinions discussed in subsequent chapters.

## I. Theories of Just Cause

The concept of just cause draws its origin from the Statute of Laborers enacted in 1562.[2] This statute prohibited employers from discharging employees without a "reasonable cause."[3] While most American jurisdictions initially followed this rule, it was replaced by the employment at-will doctrine in 1877.[4]

Just cause resurfaced in the 1930s when unions, concerned about their members' job security, began including just cause provisions

---

[2]Delmendo, "Determining Just Cause: An Equitable Solution for the Workplace," 66 Wash. L. Rev. 831, 832 (1991).

[3]Id., citing Blackstone, Commentaries 425 (1847) (discussing 5 Eliz. 1., Ch. 4, The Statute of Laborers).

[4]Id., citing Feinman, "The Development of the Employment at Will Rule," 20 Am. J. Legal Hist. 118, 124 (1976).

in their collective bargaining agreements.[5] Early arbitration cases provided little guidance as to the meaning of just cause. Just cause was (and frequently still is) what a reasonable arbitrator thought it was. This 1947 statement is typical:[6]

> It is ordinarily the function of an Arbitrator in interpreting a contract provision which requires "sufficient cause" as a condition precedent to discharge not only to determine whether the employee involved is guilty of wrongdoing * * * but also to safeguard the interests of the discharged employee by making reasonably sure that the causes for discharge were just and equitable and such as would appeal to reasonable and fair-minded persons as warranting discharge. To be sure, no standards exist to aid an Arbitrator in finding a conclusive answer to such a question and, therefore, perhaps the best he can do is to decide what a reasonable man, mindful of the habits and customs of industrial life and of the standards of justice and fair dealing prevalent in the community, ought to have done under similar circumstances and in that light to decide whether the conduct of the discharged employee was defensible and the disciplinary penalty just.[7]

## A. *The Seven Tests*

In 1964, Arbitrator Carroll Daugherty tried to crystalize the existing "common law" definition of just cause into seven independent questions. If the answer to any of them was "no," in Daugherty's view, just cause did not exist for discipline.[8] Although there has been much subsequent criticism of the "seven tests" as mechanistic, they provide a good preliminary tool for our discussion of just cause. The questions are:

(1) Did the employer give to the employee forewarning or foreknowledge of the possible or probable disciplinary consequences of the employee's conduct? According to Daugherty, this forewarning could be communicated either orally or in writing, but there had to be actual communication of the rules and penalties to the employee. He noted the employer has the right to unilaterally promulgate reasonable rules and give reasonable orders unless it is limited by the collective bargaining agreement. He recognized that in some circumstances this communication was not necessary because certain offenses are so serious that an employee could be expected to know his conduct is improper and heavily punishable.[9]

---

[5]Id.

[6]"[T]his definition by Platt may be as good as anything that has been offered in the intervening years." Dunsford, "Arbitral Discretion: The Tests of Just Cause," Proceedings of the 42nd Annual Meeting of NAA, 23, 25 (BNA Books, 1990). See also Koven, Smith & Farwell, Just Cause: The Seven Tests, 2d ed., 3, 21–23 (BNA Books, 1992), where Platt's and similar formulae are collected.

[7]Riley Stoker Corp., 7 LA 764, 767 (Platt, 1947).

[8]Grief Bros. Cooperage Corp., 42 LA 555, 557–59 (Daugherty, 1964).

[9]Theft of the employer's money is often cited as an example of conduct that requires no explicit communication to employees.

(2) Was the employer's rule or managerial order reasonably related to the orderly, efficient, and safe operation of the company's business? Daugherty acknowledged that an employee should generally obey an order, even if it is unreasonable, then file a grievance. There is an exception where obeying the order would seriously and immediately jeopardize the employee's personal safety or integrity.

(3) Did the employer, before administering discipline to an employee, make an effort to discover whether the employee violated or disobeyed a rule or order of management? Daugherty felt an employee has the right to know, with reasonable precision, the offense he is being charged with and must be given an opportunity to defend his behavior. He noted the investigation should be made prior to a disciplinary decision, and observed this is not met by reliance on the grievance procedure. Where management must react immediately to the employee's behavior, suspension pending investigation is generally recognized as acceptable, so long as the employee is reinstated with full pay for time lost if found innocent.

(4) Was the employer's investigation conducted fairly and objectively? According to Daugherty, the management official may be both "prosecutor" and "judge," but may not also be a witness against the employee.

(5) At the investigation did the "judge" obtain substantial evidence or proof that the employee was guilty as charged? Daugherty disdained imposing any particular burden of proof, stating instead that the evidence must be truly substantial and not flimsy.

(6) Has the employer applied its rules, orders, and penalties evenhandedly and without discrimination to all employees? Discriminatory enforcement is the antithesis of just cause. An employee cannot be singled out for discipline based on a rule that is not enforced against any other employees. Daugherty said prior lax enforcement can be cured by advising all employees of the intent to enforce all rules as written.

(7) Was the degree of discipline administered by the employer reasonably related to (a) the seriousness of the employee's proven offense and (b) the record of the employee's service? Daugherty explained this criterion as follows: "A trivial proven offense does not merit harsh discipline unless the employee has properly been found guilty of the same or other offenses a number of times in the past."[10] He pointed out however, that previous offenses may never be used to determine guilt or innocence of the current charge. Rather, the only proper use of an employee's record is in evaluating the severity of discipline for a proven offense.

Daugherty's adherents see the tests as a major advance in arbitral thought.[11] The tests have been touted as "the most specifically articulated analysis of the just cause standard as well as an extremely

---

[10]Grief Bros. Cooperage Corp., 42 LA at 558.
[11]Koven, Smith & Farwell, Just Cause: The Seven Tests, 2d ed., 5, 23 (BNA Books, 1992).

practical approach" and described as an "incisive codification" that "sets the standard for exploring the relationship between disciplinary due process and just cause."[12] The seven tests are included in training manuals for arbitrators and advocates[13] and are the subject of a book by another arbitrator.[14]

Enthusiasm about the seven tests is, however, far from universal. Those tests pertaining to issues of prearbitration due process have been particularly controversial. Many arbitrators believe that the tests relating to the propriety of the investigation do not embody essential elements of industrial due process. Moreover, since the tests purport to be objective and lead to "yes" or "no" answers, they are susceptible to rigid or formulaic application. Daugherty applied the tests flexibly. He explained: "The answers to the questions in any particular case are to be found in the evidence presented to the arbitrator at the hearing thereon. Frequently, of course, the facts are such that the guide lines cannot be applied with slide-rule precision."[15]

One critic suggests that the tests could cause an arbitrator to focus on issues that the parties may not want resolved.[16] Admittedly, Daugherty suggests the arbitrator take the initiative in examining each issue out of concern for fair treatment of the disciplined grievant. Daugherty's view that the arbitrator should take the initiative is not universally accepted; many arbitrators believe their proper role is to refrain from introducing issues not addressed by the parties.

## B. A "Systematic" Theory

The next step in the evolution of "just cause" was taken by Arbitrators Abrams and Nolan, whose article on just cause set out to develop

> a systematic theory of just cause in employee discipline cases by exploring the fundamental understanding of the employment relationship and the effect of the collective bargaining agreement on the fundamental understanding. It [the article] presents a model of just cause, identifying the components of the employee's obligation to provide satisfactory work, management's objectives for imposing discipline and the union's objective of achieving fairness in discipline administration. By illustrating the application of the theory, the article demonstrates the value of a

---

[12]McPherson, "The Evolving Concept of Just Cause: Carroll R. Daugherty and the Requirement of Disciplinary Due Process," 38 Lab. L.J. 387 (July, 1987).

[13]The tests are included in American Arbitration Association training manuals for advocates and arbitrators. Enterprise Wire Co., 46 LA 359 (1966), a Daugherty decision implementing the tests, is featured in Barreca, Miller & Zimny, Labor Arbitrator Development: A Handbook, 313, 408 (BNA Books, 1983).

[14]See note 11.

[15]Grief Bros., 42 LA 555, 557 (Daugherty, 1964).

[16]Dunsford, "Arbitral Discretion: The Tests of Just Cause," Proceedings of the 42nd Annual Meeting of NAA, 23, 35–37 (BNA Books, 1990).

principled approach to just cause—employers and employees can better shape their day-to-day conduct, and arbitrators can more consistently honor the expectations of the parties.[17]

The arbitrators explain that just cause for discipline can exist only when an employee fails to meet a fundamental obligation that exists in the employment relationship. They identify employee obligations, legitimate management interests, and employee protections applicable to the disciplinary setting.

Under this theory of just cause, the employee's general obligation is to provide satisfactory work, consisting of four components: regular attendance, obedience to reasonable work rules, reasonable quality and quantity of work, and avoidance of conduct that would interfere with the employer's ability to carry on the business effectively.[18] For just cause to exist, discipline must further one or more of management's three legitimate interests: rehabilitation of a potentially satisfactory employee, deterrence of similar conduct, and protection of the employer's ability to operate the business successfully.[19]

This concept of just cause includes certain employee protections that reflect the union's interest in guaranteeing "fairness" in disciplinary situations. For example, the employee is entitled to industrial due process. This includes actual or constructive notice of the expected standards of conduct and the penalties for failure to meet them. The disciplinary decision must be based on facts acquired through an investigation, which provides the employee an opportunity to state his case, with union assistance if he desires it.[20]

Fundamental employee protections include progressive discipline. Discipline is to be imposed in gradually increasing degrees, except in cases involving the most extreme breaches of the fundamental understanding. In particular, discharge may be imposed only when less severe penalties will not protect legitimate management interests. This is the case when the employee's past record indicates the unsatisfactory conduct will continue. Discharge may also be necessary to protect the system of work rules. Where continued employment would inevitably interfere with the successful operation of the business, discharge will be upheld.[21]

Another fundamental employee protection is entitlement to industrial equal protection, which prohibits differing penalties for comparable offenses: "Like cases should be treated alike, but different

---

[17]Abrams & Nolan, "Toward a Theory of 'Just Cause' in Employee Discipline Cases," 1985 Duke L.J. 594 (1985).

[18]Id. at 597.

[19]Id. at 603.

[20]Id. at 607.

[21]Id. at 607–08.

cases should be treated differently."[22] Distinctive facts in the employee's record or pertaining to the event must be given appropriate weight.[23]

Reducing the concept of just cause to the universal obligations and interests of the parties provides a less structured alternative to Daugherty's seven tests. But no single formulation of the just cause concept has received exclusive acceptance. Just cause continues to be a flexible concept that takes specific shape only in the context of the facts it addresses.

## II. Due Process as an Element of Just Cause

Due process is an integral part of just cause, requiring employers to treat employees fairly during the disciplinary process.[24] As one arbitrator put it: "[T]he essence of 'just cause' is that the Employer, in carrying out its inherent or express right to discipline employees, must do so in a manner that is not unreasonable, arbitrary, capricious or discriminatory."[25] Unfair treatment of an employee during the disciplinary process undermines the process and may lead an arbitrator to reverse the penalty.[26] One arbitrator noted that the due process requirement benefits the employer as well as the employee. The employer who provides procedural protection is much less likely to be confronted later with an order of reinstatement and back pay.[27]

Most cases treat due process principles as so well settled that no explanation is necessary.[28] The requirements associated with industrial due process were not the product of collective bargaining. Rather, these principles were first expressed by arbitrators.[29] The term "due process" is borrowed from constitutional law, but all the complexities

---

[22]Id. at 609.

[23]Id. at 611–12.

[24]Meyer Prods., Inc., 91 LA 690 (Dworkin, 1988); DeVry Inst. of Tech., 87 LA 1149 (Berman, 1986); United Tel. Co. of Fla., 61 LA 443 (Murphy, 1973).

[25]Indiana Convention Ctr. & Hoosier Dome, 98 LA 713, 719 (Wolff, 1992).

[26]SK Hand Tool Corp., 98 LA 643 (Hodgson, 1992); Chromalloy Am. Corp., Chromalloy Div., 93 LA 828 (Wolff, 1989); Flinkote Co., 59 LA 329 (Kelliher, 1972).

[27]Gilman Paper Co., 61 LA 416 (Murphy, 1973).

[28]Industrial Due Process and Just Cause for Discipline: A Comparative Analysis of the Arbitral and Judicial Decisional Processes," UCLA L. Rev. 603 (1958–59); Getman, "What Price Employment? Arbitration, The Constitution and Personal Freedom," Proceedings of the 29th Annual Meeting, National Academy of Arbitrators, 62–63 (BNA Books, 1976); McPherson, "The Evolving Concept of Just Cause: Carroll R. Daugherty & the Requirement of Disciplinary Due Process," 38 Lab. L.J. 387, 394 (1987).

[29]Arkansas Power & Light Co., 92 LA 144 (Weisbrod, 1989) (denial of union representation); King Co., 89 LA 681 (Bard, 1987) (denial of Miranda rights); Gilman Paper Co., 61 LA 416 (Murphy, 1973) (failure to make fair investigation and to allow the employee explanation or defense); Spartan Printing Co., 50 LA 1263 (Bernstein, 1968) (failure to ascertain whether other exculpatory evidence is available); Pittsburgh Steel Co., 47 LA 923 (McDermott, 1966) (failure to allow the union or the grievant an opportunity to question the foreman).

and formality required in criminal and judicial proceedings have not been adopted in labor arbitration.[30] Industrial due process is not treated as a strict set of rules, because it balances, or accommodates, individual employees' rights and the interests of the employer.[31]

Negotiated due process protections complement or add to implicit due process standards.[32] When a contract contains express due process requirements, conflicting employer policies will not support disciplinary action. For example, an arbitrator overturned a company decision to suspend drivers for speeding pursuant to its professional drivers policy, because the policy was not displayed in compliance with a contractual requirement for posting rules.[33]

Public sector employees enjoy specific due process rights derived from federal or state constitutions. The United States Constitution's Fifth Amendment, applicable to the United States, and the Fourteenth Amendment, applicable to the states and local or municipal governments, guarantee that no person shall be deprived of life, liberty, or property without due process of law. When alleged procedural due process violations involve constitutional claims, the Supreme Court has recognized that public employees have a property or liberty interest in continued employment.[34] State law may also provide a protected interest in public employment.

Once a protected interest is identified, questions about whether the government deprived the employee of that interest without due process and what process was due the employee must be resolved.[35] Public sector employees have specific rights, including the right to oral or written notice of the charges against them, an explanation of the employer's evidence, and an opportunity to present relevant information in a pretermination hearing before being deprived of a

---

[30]Flintkote Co., Pipe Prods. Group, 59 LA 329 (Kelliher, 1972); Stockman, "Discussion— Due Process of Arbitration, The Arbitrator and the Parties," Proceedings of the 11th Annual Meeting, National Academy of Arbitrators, 39–40 (BNA Books, 1955); Fleming, "Some Problems of Due Process and Fair Procedure in Labor Arbitration," 13 Stan. L. Rev. 235 (1961); Carlson & Phillips, "Due Process Considerations in Grievance Arbitration Proceedings," 2 Hastings Const. L.Q. 519, 538–41 (1975); Fairweather, "Due Process Considerations," Practice and Procedure in Labor Arbitration, 3d ed., 267–70, Schoonhoven, ed., (BNA Books, 1991).

[31]Wirtz, "Due Process of Arbitration," Proceedings of the 11th Annual Meeting, National Academy of Arbitrators, 1, 2 (BNA Books, 1958).

[32]General Dynamics Convair Div., 95 LA 500 (Jones, 1990). See generally McPherson, "The Evolving Concept of Just Cause: Carroll R. Daugherty and the Requirement of Disciplinary Due Process," 38 Lab. L.J. 387, 393 (1987).

[33]Foster Food Prods., 98 LA 854 (D'Spain, 1992).

[34]Arnett v. Kennedy, 94 S.Ct. 1633 (1976). See also Stephen v. Department of the Air Force, 47 MSPB 671 (1991) (federal employees have constitutionally protected property interest in their employment and a constitutional right to due process under Cleveland Bd. of Educ. v. Loudermill, 105 S.Ct. 1487, 1491 (1985), in actions covered by 5 USC §§ 7511–13).

[35]Zinermon v. Burch, 110 S.Ct. 975, 984 (1990); Narumanchi v. Board of Trustees of Conn. State Univ., 850 F.2d 70, 72 (2d Cir. 1988); Cleveland Bd. of Educ. v. Loudermill, 105 S.Ct. 1487, 1491 (1985); Board of Regents v. Roth, 92 S.Ct. 2701 (1972).

job.[36] The hearing serves as an initial check against mistaken decisions and allows a determination of whether reasonable grounds exist to believe that the charges made against the employee are true and support the proposed action.[37] While these rights were created by law, and not collective bargaining, a contract embodying due process protections can satisfy constitutional requirements.[38]

## A. *Elements of Due Process*

For private sector employees, arbitrators have suggested at least five requirements that are part of industrial due process: (1) timely action by the employer; (2) a fair investigation; (3) a precise statement of the charges; (4) a chance for the employee to explain before the imposition of discipline;[39] and (5) no double jeopardy; that is, employees may not be punished twice for the same offense. Not all arbitrators agree that each of these tests must be met as a prerequisite to finding just cause, particularly when there is no showing of prejudice to the grievant.[40] Finally, the right of an employee to have a union representative present at an investigative interview (called a *Weingarten* right)[41] was created by the National Labor Relations Board (Board or NLRB), but is often enforced by arbitrators.

*1. Timely Employer Action.* Employers must impose discipline within a reasonable time after learning of misconduct.[42] When a dispute is investigated and action taken quickly, the positions of the

---

[36]Loudermill, 105 S.Ct. at 1495; Linton v. Frederick County Bd. of Comm'rs, 964 F.2d 1436, 1438–39 (4th Cir. 1992).

[37]Loudermill, 105 S.Ct. at 1495; Post v. Harper, 980 F.2d 491, 494 (8th Cir., 1992).

[38]Murphy, "Due Process and Fair Representation in Grievance Handling in the Public Sector," Proceedings of the 30th Annual Meeting, National Academy of Arbitrators, 121, 127 (BNA Books, 1977). See Armstrong v. Meyers, 964 F.2d 948, 950 (9th Cir., 1992); Narumanchi v. Board of Trustees of Conn. State Univ., 850 F.2d 70, 72 (2d Cir., 1988); Jackson v. Temple Univ., 721 F.2d 931, 933 (3d Cir., 1983); Lewis v. Hillsborough Transit Auth., 726 F.2d 664, 667 (11th Cir., 1983) (per curiam), cert. denied, 105 S.Ct. 95 (1984).

[39]Union Street Bus Co., 102 LA 976, 979 (Sweeney, 1994); Olin Corp., 86 LA 1096 (Seidman, 1986); Misco, Inc., 89 LA 137 (Fox, 1983); Moore's Seafood Prods., Inc., 50 LA 83 (Daugherty, 1968); Enterprise Wire Co., 46 LA 359, 363–64 (Daugherty, 1966); Grief Bros. Cooperage Corp., 42 LA 555 (Daugherty, 1964). See generally Getman, "Labor Arbitration and Dispute Resolution," 88 Yale L.J. 916, 921 (1979); Edwards, "Due Process Considerations in Labor Arbitration," 25 Arb. J. 141 (1970); Hogler, "Industrial Due Process and Judicial Review of Arbitration Awards," 31 Lab. L.J. 570 (1980).

[40]Lamar Constr. Co., 98 LA 500 (Kanner, 1992); United Tel. Co. of Fla., 61 LA 443 (Murphy, 1983); Steiger Tractor, Inc., 80 LA 219 (Flagler, 1982). See also Dunsford, "Arbitral Discretion: The Tests of Just Cause," Proceedings of the 42nd Annual Meeting, National Academy of Arbitrators, 23 (BNA Books, 1989).

[41]This is more fully discussed in Chapter 13.

[42]Caldor, Inc. 97 LA 1057 (Johnson, 1991); Furr's Supermarkets, 95 LA 1021 (Rezler, 1990); Bethlehem Steel Corp., 56 LA 705 (Porter, 1971); Railway Employees' Dep't, 52 LA 157 (Sembower, 1968); Clark Grave Vault Co., 37 LA 860 (McCoy, 1961).

parties are less likely to harden,[43] thereby increasing the possibility that the matter can be resolved without the need for arbitration. An unreasonable delay subjects employees to suspense or uncertainty. It also deprives the union and the employee of an early opportunity to investigate, gather evidence, and prepare a defense.[44] The passage of time may disadvantage the grievant if witnesses lose their recollections or become unavailable.[45]

Delay in notifying the employee of pending charges may be grounds for setting aside discipline if the employee's ability to find competent witnesses has actually been impaired.[46] A 54-day delay in acting on information about drug use, where the work rules required the employer to act promptly in imposing discipline, was grounds for finding no just cause to discharge an employee.[47] In another case, the employer delayed in discharging an employee for nine months after learning that the employee falsely stated on his job application that he had no criminal convictions. This delay caused the arbitrator to reduce the discharge to a suspension.[48]

If the labor agreement contains time limits for imposing discipline, the failure to comply with them can result in the reinstatement of an employee with full back pay.[49] In one case the arbitrator reduced a discharge to a suspension and gave the employee seven days of back pay where the contract required the company to act in 5 days and it took 12 days to impose discipline.[50]

If the employer provides an acceptable reason for a delay, however, arbitrators may excuse tardy imposition of discipline.[51] Arbitrators allow more time between the act and the administration of discipline where there is an extensive investigation to establish that the employee in fact committed an offense.[52] An arbitrator excused a 5-month delay in imposing discipline where the grievant was aware that he was under a continuing investigation as a possible participant in vandalizing company property.[53] Also, an employer that waited more than 6 months after undercover police officers told it of the employee's sale of illegal drugs did not waive its right to discipline

[43]City of Flint, Mich., 69 LA 574 (Bowles, 1977).

[44]Id.

[45]Piedmont Natural Gas Co., 59 LA 661 (Whyte, 1972); National Carbide Co., 27 LA 128 (Warns, 1956).

[46]National Carbide Co., 27 LA 128 (Warns, 1956).

[47]Vendo Co., 97 LA 271 (D'Spain, 1991).

[48]Veterans Admin. Med. Ctr., Houston, Tex., 91 LA 588 (Howell, 1988).

[49]United Tel.—Southeast, 101 LA 316 (Nolan, 1993). See also Inland Tool & Mfg., Inc., 65 LA 1203 (Lipson, 1975).

[50]Tropicana Prods., 96 LA 212, 213 (Abrams, 1990).

[51]Town of Windsor Locks, 98 LA 1015 (Halperin, 1991).

[52]Jefferson Smurfit Corp. Container Div., 94 LA 868 (Wyman, 1990).

[53]Peoples Natural Gas Co., 97 LA 55 (Jones, 1991).

the employee where the employer had agreed to cooperate with the police in an undercover investigation and was required to wait until the investigation was completed before acting.[54] The arbitrator found the failure to act promptly in that case was not from a lack of concern over a violation of its rule against possession of illegal drugs on company property, but was attributable to its agreement to cooperate with the police in the undercover drug investigation.[55] Another arbitrator excused a 1-year delay in discharging employees for stealing groceries where the contract did not establish a statute of limitations in theft cases and where the company did not have actual notice of the thefts until it received information from another employee.[56] In a different case, a 2-month delay in imposing discharge was found to be reasonable when the employer delayed action until two other grievances impacting the degree of punishment to be imposed were resolved.[57]

*2. Fair Investigation.* Many arbitrators maintain that an employer should conduct "a careful and unbiased investigation of the charge" that leads to "the conclusion that sufficiently sound reasons exist to discipline the employee before taking disciplinary action."[58] When an investigation is found to be less than thorough, some arbitrators have concluded that the just cause standard has not been met.[59] Where the employer failed to investigate the reasons behind the grievant's attendance problems, and took no corrective steps, this failure to investigate defeated just cause.[60] Likewise, an arbitrator overturned the discharge of a bus driver where the investigation failed

---

[54]Zenith Elects. Corp., Rauland Div., 90 LA 881 (Patterson, 1987).

[55]Id. at 885. See also Jefferson Smurfit Corp. Container Div., 94 LA 868 (Wyman, 1990); Union-Tribune Publishing Co., 93 LA 617 (McBrearty, 1989).

[56]Kroger Co., 79 LA 468 (Beckman, 1982).

[57]Id.

[58]Grace Indus., Inc., 102 LA 119, 123 (Knott, 1993); St. Clair County, 80 LA 516 (Roumell, 1983); ITT Continental Baking Co., 79 LA 166 (Modjeska, 1982); Ryder Truck Rental, Inc., 78 LA 542 (Allen, 1982); City of Portland, Bureau of Police, 77 LA 820 (Axon, 1981); Amoco Chems. Corp., 70 LA 504 (Helburn, 1978); Missouri Research Labs., 55 LA 197 (Erbs, 1970); Spartan Printing Co., 50 LA 1263 (Bernstein, 1968). See also Cissell Mfg. Co., 95 LA 937 (Kindig, 1990); National R.R. Passenger Corp., 95 LA 617 (Simons, 1990); Alpha Beta Co., 91 LA 1225 (Wilmoth, 1988); Bard Mfg. Co., 91 LA 193 (Cornelius, 1988); Great Midwest Mining Corp., 82 LA 52 (Mikrut, 1984).

[59]Goodyear Tire & Rubber Co., 98 LA 941 (Nicholas, 1992) (inadequate investigation constituted denial of due process); Alpha Beta Co., 91 LA 1225 (Wilmoth, 1988) (discharge of employee based upon missed shift and arrest, without effort to communicate with or interview employee); Grief Bros. Cooperage Corp., 42 LA 555 (Daugherty, 1964) (no just cause where employee discharged without investigation to determine whether damage was accidental or purposeful). But see Stroehmann Bakeries v. Teamsters Local 776, 969 F.2d 1436, 140 LRRM 2625 (3d Cir.), cert. denied, 113 S.Ct, 660, 141 LRRM 2984 (1992) (Third Circuit affirmed vacation of arbitration award finding just cause did not exist to discharge driver for alleged sexual assault on customer's clerk, where company's investigation wholly inadequate; court found violation of public policy due to failure to address merits of claim).

[60]American Smelting & Ref. Co., 31 LA 350 (Seligson, 1958).

to go beyond a telephone conversation with a complaining passenger.[61] Arbitrators differ, however, on whether an employer's failure to conduct a complete and fair investigation is a denial of due process that in and of itself warrants reversal of a disciplinary action.[62]

Arbitrators frequently look beneath the surface of an investigation to determine whether the employer made its decision at an earlier stage and then just "went through the motions" of conducting investigatory interviews and fact finding. Arbitrators often limit a company to evidence in its possession when the disciplinary decision was made if it fails to investigate before taking action and attempts to build a case after a grievance is filed.[63] As one arbitrator said:

> There is an inherent unfairness in discharging employees first, then determining whether they deserve it. The action, once taken, loads the scales with a desire to justify, and short of arbitration, the burden is put on the employee and the Union to persuade the Company that the employee is entitled to his job back.[64]

To ensure that disciplinary decisions are not made before investigations are completed, employers frequently suspend an individual "pending an investigation."[65] This mechanism is used most frequently in cases of serious misconduct that, if proven, would result in the employee's discharge.

The period of time an employer may keep an employee off the schedule while conducting an investigation is sometimes controlled by the collective bargaining agreement.[66] Whether restricted by contract or not, an employer may commit a due process violation if it does not conduct a timely investigation.[67]

Where there is a suspicion that an employee is impaired by alcohol or drugs, an employer has the right to make an inquiry and conduct

---

[61]Niagara Frontier Transit Sys., Inc., 32 LA 901 (Thompson, 1959).

[62]See Dunsford, "Arbitral Discretion: The Tests of Just Cause: Part I," Proceedings of the 42nd Annual Meeting, National Academy of Arbitrators, 23, 31 (BNA Books, 1990).

[63]Gulf States Paper Corp., 97 LA 60 (Welch, 1991); Wells Aluminum Corp., 86 LA 987 (Wies, 1986); Associated Grocers of Colo., Inc., 82 LA 414 (Smith, 1984). See also Chapter 14 on after-acquired evidence.

[64]Aerosol Techniques, Inc., 48 LA 1278, 1279–80 (Summers, 1967). But see Trailways Southeastern Lines, Inc., 81 LA 365 (Gibson, 1983) (arbitration record may be reopened for new evidence when special circumstances exist). See also Volz & Goggin, eds., Elkouri & Elkouri, How Arbitration Works, 5th ed., 414–19 (BNA Books, 1997).

[65]Beatrice/Hunt-Wesson, Inc., 89 LA 710, 715 (Bickner, 1987) (company's past practice of not interviewing grievant until first grievance meeting after "suspension pending investigation," and union's prior acquiescence thereto, found sufficient under due process analysis). But see Cyprus Bagdad Copper Corp., 99 LA 841 (White, 1992) (where company suspends pending "further investigation," failure to conduct further investigation violates due process).

[66]See The Effect of Due Process Violations in this chapter for a discussion of "justice and dignity" clauses. Some contracts provide for expedited arbitration to minimize time spent off schedule.

[67]Social Sec. Admin., Office of Hearing & Appeals, 81 LA 1051 (Muessig, 1983); Koven, Smith & Farwell, "Just Cause: The Seven Tests," 2d ed., 177–79 (BNA Books, 1992).

a search to assure the safety of other employees and employer property.[68] The search may include a drug detection dog[69] or an undercover agent hired by the employer to detect drug use and possession by employees.[70]

When a third party makes a finding regarding an employee's conduct, whether that third party is a judicial officer, an insurance carrier, or other person, the employer must still conduct an impartial, thorough investigation and make its own disciplinary determination based on the evidence obtained from its probe.[71] When a magistrate found in an administrative hearing that the grievant was "not responsible" for an incident, the employer was still able to discipline the employee after conducting its own independent investigation.[72] The results of criminal proceedings are not necessarily binding in an arbitration.[73] When an insurance company refuses liability coverage to an employee under a company policy, the employer must conduct its own investigation and take reasonable measures to protect the job of its employee.[74]

The breadth of the investigation required is a fact-specific determination. In one case, where the testimony of an eye witness was very credible and the testimony of the employee lacked credibility, the employer's failure to interview the supervisor regarding the employee's good employment record was of no import.[75] In seeking to comply with its duty to conduct a thorough investigation, the employer must be mindful of statutory and common law privileges because, although their applicability to arbitration proceedings is unsettled, many arbitrators respect such privileges.[76] In one commentary, the authors observed that some arbitrators treat communications between the grievant and the union as privileged communications.[77]

---

[68]Kansas City Cold Storage Corp., 94 LA 783 (Madden, 1990); Shell Oil Co., Deer Park Mfg. Complex, 84 LA 562 (Milentz, 1985); Kraft, Inc., 82 LA 360 (Denson, 1984); Prestige Stamping Co., 74 LA 163 (Keefe, 1980); Aldens, Inc., 73 LA 396 (Martin, 1979). See Chapter 6 for a thorough discussion of substance abuse issues.

[69]Georgia Power Co., 93 LA 846 (Holley, 1989); Locomotive Eng'rs v. Burlington N. RR., 117 LRRM 2739 (D. Mont. 1984); U.S. Air Force Logistics Command, 78 LA 1092 (Feldman, 1982).

[70]For a thorough discussion of the factors considered in determining the appropriate penalty for drug-related offenses, see Union-Tribune Publ'g Co., 93 LA 617 (McBrearty, 1989). See also Chapter 6.

[71]Cissell Mfg. Co., 95 LA 937 (Kindig, 1990); Bard Mfg. Co., 91 LA 193 (Cornelius, 1988).

[72]Union St. Bus Co., 102 LA 976 (Sweeney, 1994).

[73]AT&T, 102 LA 931 (Kanner, 1994); King Co., 89 LA 681 (Bard, 1987). See also ITT Continental Baking Co., 798 LA 166 (Modjeska, 1982) (agency review of grievant's claim inadmissible in arbitration because irrelevant).

[74]Boulder Yellow Cab, Yellow Cab Coop. Ass'n, 102 LA 848 (Watkins, 1993).

[75]Kellogg Co., 93 LA 884 (Clarke, 1989).

[76]Loomis Armored Inc., 94 LA 1097 (Gentile, 1990) (citing Gosline, "Witnesses," in Labor and Employment Arbitration, § 4.10 (Matthew Bender, 1988)).

[77]Grenig & Estes, Labor Arbitration Advocacy, § 7.51 (Butterworth, 1989). See also Hill & Sinicropi, Evidence in Arbitration, 2d ed., 164 (BNA Books, 1987).

The company may use outside experts during the course of its investigation. Experts relied upon by an employer may include medical experts where an employee's capacity to perform a position is at issue,[78] or other experts such as handwriting analysts in fraud or forgery cases.[79] Employers are not required to use every investigative technique available. Where there was no proof that the employer had the necessary equipment, the employer's failure to test physical evidence for fingerprints did not destroy its just cause for imposing discipline.[80] Employer use of polygraph tests in investigations is regulated by law.[81] Arbitrators generally do not admit the results of a polygraph test because of its unreliability and "its attempted usurping of the fact finding and decision making function of the arbitrator."[82]

A corollary to the employer's duty to investigate is the employee's duty to cooperate with the investigation. Arbitrators frequently sustain discipline for insubordination when the employee refuses to cooperate with the investigation.[83] Most arbitrators hold, however, that an employee who is suspected of violating an employer's policy or rule may refuse to answer questions when a related criminal proceeding is ongoing, on the grounds that a mandatory response would violate the Fifth Amendment right against self-incrimination.[84]

When an employee has a duty to answer questions, the arbitrator may not sustain discipline for refusing unless the employee is warned of the consequences of not answering the questions.[85] Not all arbitrators, however, will uphold discipline imposed on an employee who refuses to answer an employer's investigatory questions truthfully.[86] This is especially so if the conduct at issue is not work related and is the subject of criminal prosecution.[87]

The remedy for an inadequate investigation is not necessarily reversal of discipline, especially where the penalty is something less than discharge.[88] As one arbitrator said:

---

[78]Stowe-Woodward Co., 78 LA 1038 (Thomson, 1982); Zellerbach Paper Co., 68 LA 69 (Stashower, 1977); Weber Mfg. Co., 63 LA 56 (Yeager, 1974).

[79]Southern Cal. Rapid Transit Dist., 96 LA 20 (Gentile, 1990); Seaview Indus., Inc., 39 LA 125 (Duncan, 1962).

[80]Abbott-Northwestern Hosp., Inc., 94 LA 621 (Berquist, 1990).

[81]See Chapter 13.

[82]Abbott-Northwestern Hosp. Inc., 94 LA 621, at 627 (Berquist, 1990) (citing Hill & Sinicropi, Evidence in Arbitration, 2d. ed. (BNA Books, 1987)).

[83]Sauget Sanitary Dev. & Research Ass'n, 98 LA 1082 (Cipolla, 1992); Square D Co., 96 LA 541 (Allen, 1991); Shell Oil Co., Deer Park Mfg. Complex, 84 LA 562 (Milentz, 1985); Illinois Power Co., 84 LA 586 (Penfield, 1985); Koppers Co., Forest Prods. Div., 76 LA 175 (Amis, 1981); Prestige Stamping Co., 74 LA 163 (Keefe, 1980); Marhoefer Packing Co., 54 LA 649 (Sembower, 1970). See also St. Joe Minerals Corp., 76 LA 421 (Newmark, 1981) (refusal to obey order justifies discipline).

[84]AT&T, 102 LA 931 (Kanner, 1994); Illinois Power Co., 84 LA 586 (Penfield, 1985).

[85]Kansas City Cold Storage Corp., 94 LA 783 (Madden, 1990).

[86]Exact Weight Scale Co., 50 LA 8 (McCoy, 1967).

[87]King Co., 89 LA 681 (Bard, 1987).

[88]SK Hand Tool Corp., 98 LA 643 (Hodgson, 1992); Welco Mfg. Co., 80 LA 273 (Yarowsky, 1983).

Virtually every case that the Impartial Arbitrator is familiar with where an arbitrator set aside discipline due to a due process failure-to-interview defect, concerns the "capital punishment" penalty of discharge, and merely involves the concomitant reduction of the penalty to one of reinstatement without back pay, or reinstatement coupled with a short suspension.[89]

Where the union can show that a proper investigation might have changed the result, the discharge is more likely to be set aside.[90] In these cases, arbitrators reinstate the grievant, but without back pay. Where the evidence produced by a proper investigation would not have altered management's decision, arbitrators may generally conclude there was just cause for the discharge despite the lack of a thorough investigation.[91]

*3. Precise Statement of Charges.* Any reason the employer intends to rely on for a discharge must be either stated in writing or communicated to the employee, unless special grounds exist that excuse the failure to present the reasons for management's actions at the time discipline is imposed.[92] Surprise and lack of adequate notice about the basis for disciplinary action generally prejudices the union and the employee in investigating the charges and preparing a defense.[93] "[T]he discharge * * * must stand or fall upon the reason given at the time of discharge."[94] The employer may not give the reasons for the discharge and then alter or add to them at the arbitration hearing.[95]

The employer must provide employees facing discipline precise information about the charges they face. The employer does not have to disclose all information in its possession, only enough facts to show the reasons for taking disciplinary action.[96] The mere listing of rules without giving the particulars of the infraction is not sufficient notice.[97] An arbitrator found the notice to be insufficient for this reason when an employer mailed a letter to an employee stating that it was

---

[89]Snow Mountain Pine Co. & Tecton Laminates Corp., 94 LA 929, 936 (Levak, 1990).

[90]Wine Cellar, 81 LA 158 (Ray, 1983).

[91]Meyer Prods., Inc. 91 LA 690 (Dworkin, 1988); Grief Bros. Cooperage Corp., 42 LA 555 (Daugherty, 1964). Cf. Southwest Airlines, 80 LA 628 (King, 1983) (refused reinstatement but ordered back pay up to date when proper investigation established just cause).

[92]Singer Co., Link Simulation Sys. Div., 85 LA 152 (Yarowsky, 1985); Kidde Inc. Weber Aircraft Div., 86 LA 681 (Dunn, 1985); Mazza Cheese Co., 84 LA 947 (LaCugna, 1985); Great Midwest Mining Corp., 82 LA 52 (Mikrut, 1984); Southwest Airlines, 80 LA 628 (King, 1983); G. Heileman Brewing Co., 54 LA 1 (Solomon, 1969); Dow Chem. Co. Texas Div., 32 LA 71 (Larson, 1958).

[93]McKeown Transp. Co., 84 LA 600 (Armstrong, 1985); General Elec. Co., 74 LA 125 (Clark, 1979); Wagner Elec. Corp., 61 LA 363 (Ray, 1973); Bethlehem Steel Co., Sparrows Point Plant, 29 LA 635 (Seward, 1957).

[94]West Virginia Pulp & Paper Co., 10 LA 117 (Guthrie, 1947).

[95]City of St. Paul, 100 LA 105 (Berquist, 1992).

[96]Acme Boot Co., 52 LA 585 (Oppenheim, 1969); Eastern Air Lines, Inc., 41 LA 88 (Seidenberg, 1963).

[97]Champion Spark Plug Co., 93 LA 1277 (Dobry, 1989).

necessary to fire him because of posted rules and the Occupational Safety and Health Act.[98]

Notices that do not describe the type, scope, or nature of the alleged misconduct are also considered to be flawed for lack of specificity.[99] When employees were notified at night by telephone that they were being discharged for larceny against a customer under an unspecified and unidentified rule, the arbitrator found no cause for termination.[100] Similarly, an arbitrator overturned a termination for absenteeism and bad attitude on the basis of due process violations because no precise standards existed to measure excessive absenteeism and the written notice required by the contract was not issued.[101] The arbitrator explained:

> The notice procedure was included in the contract for a reason; and there is *good* reason for it. If the basis for suspension or discharge is known to the Union, the Union representatives may be able to take action resulting in an employee's correction of irresponsible behavior * * *. Unless the Union is notified, it does not have the knowledge provided by contract essential for performance of one of its functions as employee representative. * * * "Due process," like rain, is for the just and unjust alike.[102]

Specific notice must be given in sufficient time to allow the union and the employee to prepare for an arbitration. Subsequent clarification of charges may not be adequate notice. For example, a discharge for reporting unfit for work was overturned because the notice was inherently vague and overbroad. The employee was not told until the arbitration hearing that the company discharged him for being under the influence of alcohol. The arbitrator concluded that the employer failed to adequately inform the employee of the charges against him and the clarification of the charges in arbitration came too late to correct the error.[103]

Arbitrators frequently decline to uphold discipline based on a ground that the employer failed to rely on at the time of discharge.[104] In unusual cases where no prejudice results from an employer raising a new basis for discharge, however, the arbitrator may consider the new reason when it is presented at the hearing. In one case, the employer discovered a new basis for discharge, falsification of production records, after the employee had been terminated for other reasons. The arbitrator considered the charge because both the union

---

[98]Pillsbury Co., 67 LA 601 (Levy, 1976).

[99]National R.R. Passenger Corp., 95 LA 617 (Simons, 1990).

[100]United States Steel Corp., United States Steel Supply Div., 29 LA 272 (Babb, 1957).

[101]Calumet & Hecla, Inc., Calumet Div., 40 LA 660 (Howlett, 1963).

[102]Id. at 663.

[103]United States Steel Corp., Gary Works, 55 LA 677 (Wolff, 1970).

[104]White Pullman/Holt Corp., 98 LA 431 (Kanner, 1992); Pittsburgh Press Club, 89 LA 826 (Stoltenberg, 1987).

and the employee were advised of it before the initial grievance meeting and the employee was given an opportunity to present a defense.[105]

Where there is a contractual requirement to provide a termination notice to an employee, the failure to do so may not result in the arbitrator overturning the discharge. In one case the arbitrator did not consider the violation sufficient to sustain the grievance on due process grounds because the union received a copy of the termination letter and both the union and employee were adequately briefed on the reasons for discharge.[106]

Arbitrators are divided on whether lack of notice to a union, when required by the labor agreement, is sufficiently serious to void the discharge.[107] In one case the company violated a contract provision requiring "immediate" notification to the union of discharge decisions, when it waited 10 days before notifying the union. The arbitrator found that this delay deprived the union of the opportunity to gather evidence while it was fresh in witnesses' minds.[108] Furthermore, an arbitrator may find that the union waived its rights by not protesting its failure to receive notice.[109]

*4. Employee Right to Be Heard.*   A number of arbitrators maintain that an employee accused of violating an employer policy or rule has a right to be heard before the decision to impose discipline is made.[110] Some arbitrators also rule that an employee's right to be heard encompasses the right to confront his or her accuser.[111] In one case, the arbitrator reversed the discharge of an employee who had allegedly poured toxic solution on another employee because the company never interviewed the grievant before discharging him.[112] No valid reasons, such as personal jeopardy or necessity for secrecy,

---

[105]Wagner Elec. Corp., 61 LA 363 (Ray, 1973); Lyon, Inc., 24 LA 353 (Alexander, 1955). See McKennon v. Nashville Banner Publ'g Co., 115 S.Ct. 879 (1995) (the Court found that after-acquired evidence could not be used to deny all relief under the ADEA, but could be taken into account in determining the specific remedy).

[106]Hyatt Hotels Palo Alto, 85 LA 11 (Oestereich, 1985).

[107]Jefferson Smurfit Corp., Container Div., 99 LA 290 (Feldman, 1992) (one due process safeguard is notice of the reasons for discharge); Purina Mills, 98 LA 504 (Jacobs, 1992); Harry Davies Molding Co., 82 LA 1024 (Fish, 1984) (suspension overturned because steward not given notice); Thompson Bros. Boat Mfg. Co., 56 LA 973 (Shurke, 1971); In the Round Dinner Playhouse, Inc., 55 LA 118 (Kamin, 1970); Frito-Lay, Inc., 52 LA 1213 (Dykstra, 1969) (compliance excused where the employer made a good faith attempt to notify the union).

[108]Piedmont Natural Gas, 59 LA 661, 665 (Whyte, 1972).

[109]Joseph T. Ryerson & Son, Inc., 61 LA 977 (Zack, 1973).

[110]SK Hand Tool Corp., 98 LA 643 (Hodgson, 1992); McCartney's, Inc., 84 LA 799 (Nelson, 1985); Chromalloy Am. Corp., 93 LA 828, 835 (Woolf, 1989); Cleveland Bd. of Educ. v. Loudermill, 105 S.Ct. 1487, 118 LRRM 3041 (1985); Associated Grocers of Colo., Inc., 82 LA 414 (Smith, 1984); Great Midwest Mining Corp., 82 LA 52 (Mikrut, 1984); St. Clair County, 80 LA 516 (Roumell, 1983); United Tel. Co. of Fla., 61 LA 443 (Murphy, 1973). See also Ross Gear Tenn. Plant, 45 LA 959 (Sanders, 1965).

[111]Interstate Brands, 97 LA 675 (Ellmann, 1991); Marion Power Shovel Div., 82 LA 1014 (Kates, 1984); Pittsburgh Steel Co., Monnesen, Pa., Plant, 47 LA 923 (McDermott, 1966).

[112]Gilman Paper Co., 61 LA 416 (Murphy, 1973).

existed for failing to interview the grievant, and the company's decision to call him in only after the discharge letter was prepared was held to be unjustifiable.

> This procedure was a clear violation of a thoroughly settled principle of industrial due process that a decision to discharge must be based on a fair and thorough investigation of the facts, and that this includes an opportunity for the employee to make such statement or explanation as he can in his own behalf. The requirement that no one shall be found guilty and sentenced without a hearing and opportunity to defend is drawn from the law, but its basis is common fairness.[113]

When an employee is arrested and charged with a crime, the employer may suspend the employee pending investigation, but must then afford the individual an opportunity to respond to those charges.

> One of the basic tenets of our American system of justice requires that an accused person be permitted to respond to charges against him/her before any action is taken because of those charges. In the interest of justice and fair play, arbitrators, as a rule, have also found that the discharge of any employee based merely upon the arrest of that employee and without investigation is neither just nor fair.[114]

Other arbitrators disagree about the grievant's right to be heard. They hold—in the absence of prejudice—that an employer does not commit a due process violation by failing to give the grievant some chance to explain his side of the story.[115]

When an employer conducts an investigatory interview, arbitrators require the meeting to be held in a nonthreatening atmosphere and allow the employee to have a union representative present.[116] Information in the company's possession, documentary evidence or witness statements, is ordinarily described or shown to the grievant and the union. Production of requested relevant information has been required by arbitrators.[117] Where an employer refuses to produce documents requested by the union in the earlier stages of the grievance

---

[113]Id. at 420. See also Volt Energy Sys., Inc., 100 LA 212 (Sugerman, 1992) (grievance upheld where company's investigation was "totally one-sided" and violated due process); Kidde, Inc., Weber Aircraft Div., 86 LA 681 (Dunn, 1985). But see Phoenix Prods. Co., 82 LA 172 (Imes, 1983) (company's failure to interview grievant, while irregular, was not sufficiently improper to warrant reversal of suspension, where other evidence showed that grievant admitted guilt, there were other witnesses to incident, and grievant expected to be disciplined).

[114]Alpha Beta Co., 91 LA 1225, 1227–28 (Wilmoth, 1988). See also Bard Mfg. Co., 91 LA 193 (Cornelius, 1988); Kaiser Steel Corp., 78 LA 185 (Lennard, 1982).

[115]Safeway Stores, Inc., 93 LA 1147 (Wilkinson, 1989); A. Finkl & Sons Co., 90 LA 1027 (Wolff, 1988).

[116]NLRB v. J. Weingarten, 95 S.Ct. 959, 88 LRRM 2689 (1975). See discussion of *Weingarten* rights later in this chapter.

[117]Mobil Oil Corp., 63 LA 263 (Sinclitico, 1974) (company required to provide union with information about employees at other company plants operating under substantially identical labor contract, where information of sufficient relevance). See also NLRB v. Acme Indus. Co., 87 S.Ct. 565, 64 LRRM 2069, 2071 (1967) (finding that the NLRB's action in requiring an employer to provide information "was in aid of the arbitral process * * * [which] can function properly only if the grievance procedures leading to it can sift out unmeritorious claims").

process, arbitrators may preclude introduction of such evidence at the hearing.[118]

Failure to notify the grievant of the charges, or failure to conduct an interview prior to imposition of the discipline, may not warrant setting aside the penalty, especially where the grievant subsequently has the opportunity to present a defense during grievance proceedings.[119] In many cases, the discharge is sustained even though the grievant had no opportunity for a predischarge hearing, because there was no prejudice as a result of the employer's failure to produce a forum.[120] A predischarge hearing may not be required in obvious or heinous situations.[121]

On the other hand, in two cases where the employer made its decision to discharge the employee before allowing an opportunity to be heard and to confront the accuser, the arbitrator set aside the discharge despite the fact that the employer proved the employee had committed the infraction.[122] In one case, the grievant was returned to work as a new hire for a probationary period, at the end of which, if there were no further altercations, wages, seniority, and fringe benefits would be restored.[123]

*5. Double Jeopardy.* Disciplining an employee twice for the same act constitutes double jeopardy and is a due process basis for invalidating the discipline.[124] Where an employer issues discipline based upon information available to it, and then further investigation reveals facts justifying greater discipline, the employer may not—as a general rule—impose the greater discipline.[125] Where the employer's incomplete knowledge of the facts at the time discipline was imposed is not the employer's fault, however, it may not be double jeopardy to adjust the punishment based on the facts.[126]

---

[118]Avis Rent-A-Car Sys., Inc., 99 LA 277 (DeLoach, 1992).

[119]Dierbergs Mkts., Inc., 93 LA 1113 (Yarowsky, 1989); Beatrice/Hunt-Wesson, Inc., 89 LA 710 (Bickner, 1987). But see United Tel. Co. of Fla., 61 LA 443 (Murphy, 1973); Capitol Hill Hosp., 93 LA 947 (Jones, 1989). See also Carbonic Prods., 93 LA 189 (Gentile, 1989) (warning not required where misconduct at issue is spontaneous and unexpected).

[120]Snow Mountain Pine Co. & Tecton Laminates Corp., 94 LA 929 (Levak, 1990); Southern Bell Tel. & Tel. Co., 75 LA 409 (Seibel, 1980).

[121]Great Midwest Mining Corp., 82 LA 52 (Mikrut, 1984).

[122]SK Hand Tool Corp., 98 LA 643 (Hodgson, 1992); Capitol Hill Hosp., 93 LA 947 (Jones, 1989).

[123]SK Hand Tool Corp., 98 LA 643 (Hodgson, 1992).

[124]Double jeopardy does not attach where the delay is caused by the union's repeated requests to delay determination and imposition of discipline. See, e.g., Bethlehem Steel Corp., Burns Harbor Plant, 83 LA 833 (Sharnoff, 1984).

[125]Gulf States Paper Corp., 97 LA 60 (Welch, 1991) (where written warning imposed was based upon supervisor's mistaken determination that grievant had not run defective product, and later investigation showed grievant had done so, employer's subsequent imposition of suspension constituted double jeopardy).

[126]International Harvester Co., Louisville Works, 13 LA 610 (Wirtz, 1949).

Consideration of an employee's past employment record does not constitute double jeopardy.[127] But an employer may not base discipline on an employee's past record using a precipitating event as a pretext for its action. One arbitrator discussed the application of double jeopardy principles to arbitration in the following way:[128]

> Having assured grievant no discipline would result from their meeting on January 11, 1991, the Company is estopped to discipline grievant for those events. Having previously disciplined grievant for those events supporting Company warnings dated February 20, 1990, July 26, 1990 and October 12, 1990, to allow these same events to support discharge would constitute punishment twice for the same events.[129]

The employer may not reserve charges and revive them as a basis for discipline later.

> [I]t is a denial of procedural due process and just cause to hold a charge over an employee's head *indefinitely* and to revive it *whenever* corroborating or substantiating evidence might eventually surface.[130]

Double jeopardy concepts are relevant only when a disciplinary decision is final. For example, a supervisor's direction to "punch out and go home" until the company takes action the following day does not constitute the imposition of a suspension.[131] Similarly, it is not double jeopardy when a supervisor expresses an opinion about a potential disciplinary outcome but says that the investigation is still continuing or is subject to review by upper-level management.[132]

Prior or contemporaneous punishment or exoneration by another tribunal, followed by discipline from an employer, also does not constitute double jeopardy.[133] For example:

> Counsel for the Union suggested that the Grievant has somehow been improperly subjected to a form of double jeopardy by the Borough. However, the Borough did not cease to have an interest in regulating what sort of persons it employs just because the Grievant was punished by the criminal court. The Borough still had the duty to implement whatever disciplinary action is deemed to be in the best interest of its taxpayers.[134]

The fact that a civil or criminal fine or other criminal penalty was assessed for particular employee misconduct, or that an acquittal

---

[127]Troy Dep't of Pub. Works, 77 LA 153 (Lewis, 1981).

[128]McCorkle Mach. Shop, 97 LA 774 (Kilroy, 1991).

[129]Id. at 776. But see Southern Ind. Gas & Elec. Co., 100 LA 160 (Euker, 1992) (company's consideration of earlier infractions which led to earlier demotion not double jeopardy where arbitrators convinced that critical safety issues involved).

[130]DeVry Inst. of Tech., 87 LA 1149, 1157 (Berman, 1986).

[131]Ross Gear & Tool Co., 35 LA 293 (Schmidt, 1960).

[132]Montgomery Ward & Co., 84 LA 905 (Wilcox, 1985).

[133]Borough of Baldwin, 95 LA 851 (Duff, 1990).

[134]Id. at 854.

was obtained, does not preclude imposition of discipline or discharge.[135]

    *6. Weingarten Rights.*   A special aspect of due process, similar to the right of counsel enjoyed by individuals accused of crimes, is the employee's right to union representation. In *NLRB v. J. Weingarten, Inc.,*[136] the United States Supreme Court upheld the Board's decision that Section 7 of the National Labor Relations Act (Act) grants an employee the right "to refuse to submit without union representation to an interview which he reasonably fears may result in his discipline."[137]

    The right to union representation arises only in situations where the employee requests representation.[138] For instance, in one case, the employee participated in a closed-door meeting with his supervisor and manager where he was confronted by serious charges of sexual harassment. Although he may have felt intimidated, the grievant did not request the presence of a union representative. Therefore, the arbitrator found *Weingarten* rights did not apply.[139] The request for a union representative can be insincere or flippant and still must be honored so long as it is not made solely to delay the interview.[140] An employee can waive the right to representation by participating in a discussion with management, but the participation must be voluntary.[141]

---

[135]Department of the Air Force, Sacramento Air Logistics Ctr., McClellan Air Force Base, Cal., 74 LA 949 (Ward, 1980) (double jeopardy does not attach where misconduct by employee also amounts to criminal violation, resulting in conviction and suspended sentence; employer still free to take disciplinary action); Westinghouse Elec. Corp., 26 LA 837 (Simkin, 1956) (fact that strikers paid fines or served jail sentences for activity engaged in during strike does not preclude disciplinary action). But see City of Chillicothe, Ohio, 96 LA 657 (DiLeone, 1991) (where company discharged employee for drug-related misconduct, first arbitrator reinstated grievant with full back pay, and after criminal conviction, company discharged employee again; second arbitrator found that where second discharge based upon same facts as first discharge, double jeopardy precluded second discharge).

[136]NLRB v. J. Weingarten, 95 S.Ct. 959, 88 LRRM 2689 (1975).

[137]Id. at 963, 88 LRRM at 2691. See Heinz, U.S.A. Div. of H.J. Heinz Co., 95 LA 82 (Ellmann, 1990); Dow Chem. Co., U.S.A., 91 LA 1385 (Baroni, 1989); City of Sterling Heights, 80 LA 825 (Ellmann, 1983).

[138]NLRB v. J. Weingarten, Inc., 95 S.Ct. at 963, 88 LRRM at 2691. See also O.B. Williams Co., 87 LA 534 (Krebs, 1986) (employer did not violate "*Weingarten* rights" of two employees who were disciplined without union representation, when neither requested such representation); Bethlehem Steel Corp., 83 LA 833 (Sharnoff, 1984) (union failed to establish that employee was denied union representation either during or subsequent to his meeting with plant protection officer regarding discipline for his reckless driving on employer premises; employee was grievance committee man and should be knowledgeable concerning his rights under collective bargaining contract); Borough of Carlisle, PA., 82 LA 1 (Woy, 1984) (employer did not deprive the union of due process when union president was not represented by union during his meeting that led to suspension for alleged negligence and not tightening hose coupling that resulted in drip of water to electric motor that was encased in hosing; grievant was the union president and should have been aware of his right to union representation during an investigatory interview; not the responsibility of the employer to inform the grievant of his right).

[139]Tampa Elec. Co., 88 LA 781 (Vause, 1986).

[140]Consolidated Freightways Corp. of Del., 264 NLRB 541, 111 LRRM 1289 (1982).

[141]Penn-Dixie Steel Corp., 253 NLRB 91, 105 LRRM 1470 (1980).

Under *Weingarten*, an employee is required to request union representation. Arbitrators have sometimes broadened the employer's responsibility and placed a duty on the employer to either call in a union representative or inform the employee of the right to representation in situations where the employer should have known that the employee was unaware of these rights.[142] An arbitrator held that an employee who was an untutored immigrant, in a work force consisting largely of immigrants with limited command of English, was not chargeable with knowledge of his right to representation. The arbitrator found it immaterial that the presence and participation of a union representative might not have averted the discharge and that the employee returned to a second interview with the representative after the employee had been asked to sign a suspension paper.[143]

An employee may demand union representation as a condition of participation in an interview only "where the employee reasonably believes the investigation will result in disciplinary action."[144] The "exercise of the right may not interfere with legitimate employer prerogatives."[145] An employee is not entitled to union representation when asked to complete an accident report;[146] presented with a written warning;[147] presented with disciplinary charges;[148] asked to submit to random blood or urine testing;[149] asked to accept work assignments;[150] or requested to attend any other noninvestigatory meeting.[151]

---

[142]See Maurey Mfg. Co., 95 LA 148 (Goldstein, 1990) (finding an affirmative duty for the employer to provide union representation to a workforce of unskilled laborers that was not shown to be primarily made up of people with a command of the English language).

[143]Maui Pineapple Co., 86 LA 907 (Tsukiyama, 1986).

[144]NLRB v. J. Weingarten, Inc., 95 S.Ct. at 963–64. See Dow Chem. Co., 91 LA 1385 (Baroni, 1989); Lancaster City Sch., 81 LA 1024 (Abrams, 1983) (school board did not violate the representation procedure when it denied teacher's request for presence of union representative during conference that mother of student in teacher's class had sought with teacher and principal to discuss her concern about her daughter, when the principal was there only to ensure that the situation could be resolved amicably).

[145]NLRB v. J. Weingarten, Inc., 95 S.Ct. at 964, 88 LRRM at 2691.

[146]Twin Coast Newspapers, Inc., 89 LA 799, 799 (Brisco, 1987) ("[e]mployer did not violate Weingarten rights of employee if discharged for insubordination after he walked away when manager asked him to go to his office, where employee returned with union representative, but manager merely wanted him to complete accident report and did not intend to accompany him to office, no investigatory interview commenced on shop floor, and none was contemplated").

[147]Library of Congress, 80 LA 642 (Bernhardt, 1983).

[148]Baton Rouge Water Works Co., 246 NLRB 995, 103 LRRM 1056 (1979). See also Allied Aviation Serv. Co., New England Inc., 77 LA 45, 459 (Turkus, 1981) (exception to *Weingarten* found where the supervisor had already determined the discipline to be imposed, had already obtained witness statements, and had no further need to discuss the basis for discipline).

[149]Deaconess Med. Ctr., 88 LA 44 (Robinson, 1986) (nurse suspected of drug and alcohol abuse was not entitled to union representation at an interview at which she was neither asked questions nor was her job threatened, but only asked for written consent to be subjected to random blood and urine tests).

[150]Joseph F. Whelan, Co., 273 NLRB 340, 118 LRRM 1040 (1984) (*Weingarten* did not protect an employee who was discharged because he refused at the morning "shape," where work assignments were made, to meet with management unless he had union representation).

[151]Bridgeport Hosp., 265 NLRB 421 (1982) (employees who walked out of a noninvestigatory meeting after the request for union representation was refused could be disciplined for doing so).

The employee has a right to the presence of a union representative at an investigatory meeting, but has no inherent right to the presence of a specific union representative. Where the requested representative is available, the employer violates the Act by refusing to summon that representative.[152] The employer must permit an employee and his representative to consult privately on the employer's time in advance of the *Weingarten* interview, if the employee does not have an adequate opportunity to consult with the union representative outside of work.[153]

In *Coca-Cola Bottling Co. of Los Angeles,*[154] the Board upheld the employer's denial of an employee's request for a union representative who was not available for at least three days, reasoning that to decide the case otherwise would afford employees an undue advantage by allowing the employees to purposefully request the assistance of an unavailable union representative and postpone their interviews.[155]

The role of the union representative during an investigatory interview is to assist the employee. While the representative is permitted to clarify facts or suggest other employees who may have knowledge of them, the employer is free to insist that the employer is only interested at that time in hearing the employee's own account on the matter under investigation.[156] The employer is not required to bargain with any union representative attending the investigatory interview,[157] but may not impose a passive role on the union representative during the meeting.

If the collective bargaining agreement includes language similar to that used in the *Weingarten* case, arbitrators will enforce the employee's contractual right to have a union representative during an investigatory interview.[158] Some arbitrators have imposed greater protections than those afforded by *Weingarten* when the right to representation appears in the contract. For example, an arbitrator found that management had an obligation to offer union representation, instead of waiting for a request from the employee when there was a contractual right to representation. In another case the arbitrator found the employees had representation rights in circumstances other

---

[152]GHR Energy Corp., 294 NLRB 1011, (1989).

[153]United States Postal Serv., 288 NLRB 864 (1988).

[154]227 NLRB 1276 (1977).

[155]Pacific Gas & Elec. Co., 253 NLRB 1143 (1981) (where union representation is available at a given location, employer does violate employee's § 7 rights by denying a request for a specific union representative from a different location).

[156]NLRB v. Southwestern Bell Tel. Co., 730 F.2d 166, 116 LRRM 2211 (5th Cir., 1984); New Jersey Bell Tel. Co., 308 NLRB 277, 141 LRRM 1017 (1992) (union representative exceeded his "permissible role" and interfered with employer's ability to conduct the interview when he interrupted the questioning with objections to questions asked more than once and advised the employee not to answer questions he deemed repetitive). See also Herrom, "Ten Years After *Weingarten*: Are the Standards Really Clear?" 6 N. Ill. U.L.Rev. 81 (1986).

[157]NLRB v. J. Weingarten, 95 S.Ct. at 965, 88 LRRM at 2692.

[158]Defense Mapping Agency Aerospace Ctr., 88 LA 651 (Hilgert, 1986).

than disciplinary investigations.[159] In one case, the contract and management handbook made the presence of a union representative at disciplinary discussions mandatory if the employee requested one. The arbitrator held that the employee could not be subject to discipline for insubordination when the employee refused to discuss performance matters with a supervisor in the absence of a union representative.[160]

Arbitrators do not uniformly apply the *Weingarten* rule in the absence of specific contract language. Some arbitrators have held that it is the function of the Board to enforce *Weingarten* and not the function of the labor arbitrator.[161] Other arbitrators have held that even in the absence of explicit contractual language providing for the employee's right to union representation during an investigatory interview, an implied requirement of procedural due process includes rights granted under the *Weingarten* rule.[162]

Arbitrators have a number of views about the appropriate remedy for a *Weingarten* violation. Failure to allow union representation for the grievant may result in a remedy, but not affect the finding of cause for discipline.[163] Some arbitrators have held that an employer's failure to comply precisely with the procedural requirements of *Weingarten* will entirely nullify the discharge or disciplinary action taken and hence require the employee's reinstatement. One arbitrator nullified the employee's discharge for theft of company property even though the employer proved beyond a reasonable doubt that the employee misappropriated 35 feet of wire for a moonlighting job. The arbitrator overturned the discharge solely because the employer violated the employee's *Weingarten* rights.[164] Others have taken the position that an employer's failure to comply with the procedural requirements are of significance only where the employee can demonstrate prejudice. For example, an arbitrator held that the presence of a

---

[159]Department of the Air Force, Warner Robins Air Logistics Ctr., Robins Air Force Base, Ga., 75 LA 994 (Hart, 1980) (contract entitles grievants the right to union representation at informal counseling).

[160]Pacific Bell, 92 LA 127 (Oestreich, 1989).

[161]Defense Mapping Agency Aerospace Ctr., 88 LA 651 (Hilgert, 1986).

[162]Maui Pineapple Co., 86 LA 907 (Tsukiyama, 1986) ("*Weingarten* right" is an implied requirement of procedural "just cause" in management's disciplinary process). See also City of Edina, 90 LA 209 (Ver Ploeg, 1987) (*Weingarten* not binding on an arbitrator, but provides guidance in determining what a contract does and does not require, even where such a right is not explicitly provided in the agreement).

[163]Margolis, McTernan, Scope, Sacks & Epstein, 81 LA 740 (Richman, 1983) (discharge upheld but required employer to post notice regarding failure to have a union steward present at disciplinary meetings).

[164]Arkansas Power & Light Co., 92 LA 144 (Weisbrod, 1989). See also Bake Rite Rolls, 90 LA 1133 (DiLauro, 1988) (reversing suspension and discharge of theft because employer did not allow for union representative to be present at meeting with purported eyewitness); Hill & Sincropi, "External Law as a Remedy," Remedies in Arbitration, 2d ed., 91–92 (BNA Books, 1991); Fairweather, "Remedies," Practice and Procedure in Labor Arbitration, Schoonhover, 3d ed., 353 (BNA Books, 1991); Orkin & Schmoyer, "*Weingarten*: Rights, Remedies and the Arbitration Process," 40 Lab. L.J. 594 (1989).

steward would have drastically reduced the coercive impact of the setting and circumstances. Consequently, the arbitrator could not consider statements implicating the grievant as having probative value.[165]

Another view is that although adherence to the *Weingarten* rule is important and an employer who fails to comply will be penalized, the discipline is not necessarily rendered void.[166] Other remedies may be employed to address the violation. For example, where an employer refused to allow union representation to an employee facing possible discharge for assaulting a supervisor, the arbitrator sustained the discharge, finding the grievant was not prejudiced by the lack of representation and imposing on the employer the union's costs and fees for arbitration.[167]

## B. *The Effect of Due Process Violations*

Due process violations do not always warrant the reversal of the disciplinary action imposed by the employer.[168] Where there has been no prejudice to the grievant, the employer's action may be sustained. As one arbitrator said:

---

[165]Maurey Mfg. Co., 95 LA 148 (Goldstein, 1990). See Macmillan Bloedel Containers, 92 LA 592 (Nicholas, 1989) (employer required employees charged with violation of rule prohibiting use, possession, or being under influence of alcohol or drugs to be interviewed by private investigators without presence of supervisory personnel or union representatives which violated employees' contractual due process rights, but technical violation will be overlooked in view of time and resources invested by parties, together with employees' admissions and good proof offered by company); Gold Kist, Inc., 89 LA 66 (Byars, 1987) (discipline or discharge should be set aside only when employer's failure to comply with procedural requirements results in prejudice to grievant); Internal Revenue Serv., Jacksonville Dist., 78 LA 1016 (Render, 1982) (remedy for revenue representatives who were improperly denied union representation during an interview concerning the disappearance of certain monies collected from taxpayers was to strike statement of grievant from employer's case against her). See also Hill & Sinicropi, "External Law as a Remedy," Remedies in Arbitration, 2d ed., 91–92 (BNA Books, 1991); Fairweather's Practice and Procedure in Labor Arbitration, 3d ed., 307, Schoonover, ed. (BNA Books, 1991); Orkin & Schmoyer, "*Weingarten*, Rights, Remedies and the Arbitration Process," 40 Lab. L.J., 594 (1989).

[166]Heinz, U.S.A. Div. of H. J. Heinz Co., 95 LA 82 (Ellmann, 1990) (one of the factors the arbitrator considered in reducing a penalty from termination to a 4-month suspension is the fact that grievant was denied the right to representation in several disciplinary meetings). See Defense Mapping Agency Aerospace Ctr., 88 LA 651 (Hilgert, 1986) (remedy for improper refusal of employee's request for union representation is publication of essence of award to both bargaining unit employees and supervisors); Maui Pineapple Co., 86 LA 907 (Tsukiyama, 1986) (sustaining termination of grievant but awarding 1-month back pay as a penalty for denial of union representation at two disciplinary interviews); Margolis, McTernan, Scope, Sacks & Epstein, 81 LA 740 (Richman, 1983) (employer violated contract language by denying discharged employee's request that union representative be present during meeting with personnel officer and must post a notice to cease and desist in a conspicuous place on its premises for 60 days). See also Hill & Sinicropi, Remedies in Arbitration, 2d ed., 91–92 (BNA Books, 1981); Fairweather's Practice and Procedure in Labor Arbitration, 3d ed., 307, Schoonover, ed. (BNA Books, 1991); Orkin & Schmoyer, "*Weingarten*: Rights, Remedies and the Arbitration Process," 40 Lab. L.J. 594 (1989).

[167]Indiana Convention Ctr. & Hoosier Dome, 98 LA 713 (Wolff, 1992).

[168]Chapter 12 addresses due process violations in the context of arbitral reduction of penalties.

The essential question for an arbitrator is not whether disciplinary action was totally free from procedural error, but rather whether the process was fundamentally fair. [The arbitrator] must find in order to overturn the employer's action on procedural grounds, that there was at least a possibility, however remote, that the procedural error may have deprived the grievant of a fair consideration of his case.[169]

Due process violations may be addressed by the arbitrator when determining the appropriate remedy. As a result of the violation, the discipline may be modified but not entirely overturned. In serious due process violations, especially those involving violations of contractual due process obligations, reinstatement is often ordered. Where the arbitrator otherwise finds the discharge was for cause, the reinstatement often will be without back pay.[170] On occasion, however, the arbitrator will award back pay from the date of discharge until the arbitration hearing or award, but deny reinstatement.[171]

Where the employer complies with the spirit of the contract and the employee is not prejudiced by procedural violations, disciplinary action may be sustained by the arbitrator.[172] For example, an arbitrator upheld a discharge even though the employee was denied contractual due process when given an oral warning without an investigation or opportunity to be heard. The arbitrator reasoned that since the grievant was not prejudiced by the violation, no change would have been made to the penalty even if the employer had acted appropriately.[173] Discipline may be significantly reduced if important contractual rights of the employee have been compromised, even if the grievant committed the offense.[174] In some cases, where the employer did not comply with the procedural provisions of the contract, arbitrators have sustained the discipline because of clear evidence that the employee committed a serious offense.[175] Further, if the union fails to make timely objection to the procedural defect, waiver may be found.[176]

---

[169]Cameron Iron Works, 73 LA 878, 881–82 (Marlatt, 1979).

[170]Roadmaster Corp., 89 LA 126 (Doering, 1987); United Refrigerated Serv., Inc., 78 LA 243 (Youngblood, 1982).

[171]Shaefer's Ambulance Serv., 104 LA 481 (Calhoun, 1995); Chromalloy Div.–Okla., Div. of Chromalloy Am. Corp., 93 LA 828 (Woolf, 1989); Fairweather's Practice and Procedure in Labor Arbitration, 3d ed., 309, Schoonover, ed. (BNA Books, 1991).

[172]Monarch Sidney Co., 96 LA 477 (Millous, 1991); Intermountain Rural Elec. Ass'n, 86 LA 540 (Watkins, 1985); Shamrock Indus. Inc., 84 LA 1203 (Reynolds, 1985); American Ship Bldg. Co., 81 LA Capital Region, 75 LA 1158 (Lubic, 1980); Armstrong Rubber Co., 74 LA 362 (Williams, 1980).

[173]HBI Automotive Glass, 97 LA 121 (Richard, 1991).

[174]Ryder Truck Rental, Inc., 94 LA 7 (Bognanno, 1989).

[175]Marquette Inn, 79 LA 1259 (Flagler, 1982); Cameron Iron Works, 73 LA 878 (Marlatt, 1979).

[176]Meredith Corp., Meredith Printing Div., 78 LA 859 (Talent, 1982); United States Dep't of the Air Force, 76 LA 315 (Nicholas, 1981); Federal Compress & Warehouse Co. Wohl Shoe Div., 75 LA 217 (Howell, 1980); Marion Power Shovel Co., 69 LA 339 (McDermott, 1977); United Eng'g & Foundry Co., 37 LA 1095 (Kates, 1962).

In 1981, the Steelworkers and the Container Industry negotiated a provision in their master labor agreements that was labeled a "Justice and Dignity" clause. This was an effort by the parties to establish in discipline cases the basic right of an accused to be presumed innocent until proven guilty, and to avoid the serious financial and social losses an individual employee incurs while a grievance challenging the employer's disciplinary action is processed through the grievance and arbitration procedure. Accordingly, where the employer's refusal to keep a grievant on the job pending the outcome of the grievance violated the "justice and dignity" clause, the arbitrator ordered the grievant to be made whole for the days he was suspended even though the suspension was justified.[177] Similar provisions have subsequently been negotiated between other employers and employees in the steel and copper industry represented by the Steelworkers. Although the language varies between agreements, the clauses usually provide that an employee disciplined or discharged because of improper conduct will remain on the active payroll until the employee's grievance is concluded, unless the conduct presents an immediate danger to fellow employees or plant equipment because of fighting, theft, or a concerted refusal to perform assigned work.[178]

Where prejudice occurs because of management's violation of the contractual due process requirements, arbitrators usually sustain the grievance, at least in part.[179] When the employer impinges upon significant contract rights in the course of disciplinary proceedings, the arbitrator may set aside a discharge and order reinstatement with full back pay, even if just cause would otherwise have been found.[180] In one case, the arbitrator reinstated the grievant with back pay because of the employer's failure to issue a termination slip required under the collective bargaining agreement. The evidence convinced the arbitrator that the absences leading to discharge of the grievant were caused by health problems resulting from widespread racism in the workplace.[181]

---

[177]United States Steel Corp., U.S. Steel Div., 95 LA 610 (Das, 1990).

[178]U.S. Steel-Fairfield Works, 102 LA 652 (Dybeck, 1993); U.S. Steel Corp-Fairfield, 95 LA 610 (Das, 1990); U.S. Steel-Edgar Thompson Works, 95 LA 566 (Talarico, 1990); U.S. Steel-Lorain, 95 LA 7 (Talarico, 1990); Bethlehem Steel Corp., 94 LA 1309 (Henle, 1990). See also Gilliam, "Innocent Until Proven Guilty, The Union View, Arbitration: Promise and Performance," Proceedings of the 36th Annual Meeting, National Academy of Arbitrators, 77–84 (BNA Books, 1984); Hoffman, "The Management View," id. at 84–89.

[179]Tropicana Prods. Inc., 96 LA 212 (Abrams, 1990); Furr's Supermarkets, 95 LA 1021 (Rezler, 1990) (prolonged investigation); General Dynamics Convair Div., 95 LA 500 (Jones, 1990) (pervasive and blatant violations of due process provisions); Champion Spark Plug Co., 93 LA 1277 (Dobry, 1989) (failure to provide notice and use of stale disciplinary record); Montgomery Ward & Co., 80 LA 321 (Dobry, 1983); Plantation Patterns, Inc., 78 LA 647 (Dallas, 1982); Kaiser Steel Corp., 78 LA 185 (Lennard, 1982); Lake to Lake Dairy, 77 LA 452 (Pieroni, 1981).

[180]Purina Mills, 98 LA 504 (Jacobs, 1992).

[181]B-Line Sys., Inc. 100 LA 933 (Cohen, 1993).

In a case in which the employer committed numerous and egregious violations of the agreement, the employer was ordered to pay the union's reasonable expenses incurred in representing the grievant.[182]

## C. *Judicial Review of Arbitration Awards Concerning Industrial Due Process*[183]

Courts accept that arbitrators consider due process as a standard part of interpreting collective bargaining agreements which require just cause for discharge.[184] It is well settled that an arbitrator is not precluded from weighing considerations of fairness when reviewing the discharge penalty where the labor agreement contains a just cause provision.[185]

For example, in *Chauffeurs Local 878 v. Coca-Cola Bottling Co.,*[186] when the Eighth Circuit enforced an arbitration award reinstating an employee discharged for dishonesty who was not given an opportunity to tell his side of the story, it agreed that the just cause standard included both procedural and substantive considerations. The Sixth Circuit also found that determinations of procedural fairness are sufficiently integral to "just cause" to sustain arbitrators' decisions.[187] Similarly, an arbitration award reinstating an employee because the employer refused to provide the union or employee with the name of a witness prior to the arbitration hearing was enforced by the Ninth Circuit.[188]

Courts have enforced awards reinstating an employee who was denied union representation when confronted with disciplinary charges,[189] as well as those reinstating an employee who was not informed of all the charges until after the discharge.[190]

Some courts have vacated arbitration awards, reversing discharges because of due process violations where the court found public

---

[182]National R.R. Passenger Corp., 95 LA 617 (Simons, 1990).

[183]The general topic of confirmation and vacatur of awards is covered in Chapter 14.

[184]Paperworkers v. Misco, Inc., 108 S.Ct. 364 (1987); Stroehmann Bakeries, Inc. v. Teamsters Local 776, 969 F.2d 1436 (3d Cir. 1992).

[185]Eberhard Foods, Inc. v. Handy, 868 F.2d 890, 130 LRRM 2833 (6th Cir. 1989).

[186]613 F.2d 716, 103 LRRM 2380 (8th Cir.), cert. denied, 446 U.S. 988, 104 LRRM 2431 (1980).

[187]Bruce Hardwood Floors v. Carpenters Local 2509, 8 F.3d 1104, 144 LRRM 2622 (6th Cir., 1993); Eberhard Foods, Inc. v. Handy, 868 F.2d 890 (6th Cir., 1989); Johnston Boiler Co. v. Boilermakers Local 893, 753 F.2d 40, 118 LRRM 2348 (6th Cir., 1985); Anaconda Co. v. Machinists Dist. Lodge 27, 693, F.2d 35, 111 LRRM 2919 (6th Cir., 1982). See also Federated Dep't Stores v. Food & Commercial Workers Local 1442, 901 F.2d 1494, 134 LRRM 2162 (9th Cir., 1990).

[188]McClatchy Newspapers v. Typographical Union 46, 686 F.2d 731, 111 LRRM 2254 (9th Cir.), cert. denied, 103 S.Ct. 491 (1982).

[189]Anaconda Co. v. Machinists Dist. Lodge 27, 693 F.2d 35, 111 LRRM 2919 (6th Cir., 1982).

[190]Safeway Stores, Inc. v. Food & Commercial Workers Local 400, 621 F.Supp. 1233, 118 LRRM 3419 (D.D.C., 1985).

policy was violated. Public policies such as health and safety may be a basis for reversing a decision that reinstates an employee because of a due process violation. In *Iowa Electric Light & Power Co. v. Electrical Workers (IBEW) Local 204*,[191] the Eighth Circuit vacated an arbitration awarded reinstating an employee who defeated the interlock system controlling the doors of a nuclear power plant, where the arbitrator found the employee did not have notice the situation was as grave as claimed by the company. Using public policy considerations, courts have also overturned awards that based the reinstatement of employees who engaged in sexual harassment on due process grounds.[192]

## III. Progressive Discipline as an Element of Just Cause

Discipline is an adverse action taken by an employer against an employee because of the employee's behavior. Progressive discipline is a system of addressing employee behavior over time, through escalating penalties. The purpose of progressive discipline is to correct the unacceptable behavior of an employee. Employers impose some penalty less than discharge to convey the seriousness of the behavior and to afford employees an opportunity to improve. The discharge penalty is reserved for very serious incidents of misconduct and for repeated misconduct.

The concept of progressive discipline is based on the premise that both employers and employees benefit when an employee can be rehabilitated and retained as a productive member of the work force. The trained employee is seen as a valuable resource, making it economically prudent to attempt rehabilitation of a current employee.[193] The expected result of progressive discipline is that the employee will recognize he has engaged in unacceptable conduct and will correct his future behavior.[194]

---

[191]834 F.2d 1424, 127 LRRM 2049 (8th Cir., 1987).

[192]Stroehmann Bakeries v. Teamsters Local 776, 969 F.2d 1436, 140 LRRM 2625 (3d Cir., 1992) (recognizing the concept of industrial due process in an arbitration award that reinstated an employee accused of sexual harassment because the discharge decision was made without sufficient investigation, but overturning the award on public policy grounds because the arbitrator did not find that the harassment did not occur). See also Newsday v. Communications Workers Local 915, 915 F.2d 840, 135 LRRM 2659 (2d. Cir., 1990), cert. denied, 111 S.Ct. 1314 (1991) (award of reinstatement for failure to apply progressive discipline overturned because it violated public policy against sexual harassment in the workplace).

[193]Zack, "Just Cause and Progressive Discipline," in Labor & Employment Arbitration, Bornstein & Gosline, eds., 19–15 (Matthew Bender, 1994).

[194]Shop N' Save Warehouse Foods, Inc., 85 LA 494, 499 (Neumark, 1985).

Communicating employer expectations to employees with behavior problems before imposing discipline is an integral part of all discipline systems.[195] An employer must warn employees of the consequences of their actions and when their jobs are in jeopardy.[196] The imposition of even minor discipline sends a clear signal to the employee that he has stepped outside the boundaries of acceptable behavior. When warnings are not issued for lesser offenses, employees are denied the opportunity to correct their behavior. Many arbitrators are reluctant to uphold discipline when the employer imposes a suspension or discharge without having previously warned the employee, except in cases of serious misconduct.[197]

Employee problems fall into two broad categories: (1) behavior problems and (2) performance problems.[198] Behavior problems, if not remedied through appropriate nondisciplinary and progressive disciplinary action, generally lead to discharge. Performance problems may be more appropriately dealt with through nondisciplinary action alone, such as counseling, training, accommodation, or reassignment. This section addresses primarily behavior problems, only touching on performance problems. Chapter 6 contains a detailed discussion of performance problems.

## A. *Other Employer Communications Distinguished*

Not all employer comments on employee behavior are part of the progressive discipline system. Some employer commentary—such as counseling or instruction—puts employees on notice of the employer's expectations but does not constitute adverse action. Other commentary—such as performance evaluation or rating—may have an adverse consequence (e.g., an employee whose work performance is not deemed satisfactory does not get a "merit" increase in pay) but is still not considered discipline. The employer has a right to evaluate employee performance and to reward high performance, independent of its right to discipline employees for failures to perform. Counseling and evaluation are considered separately below.

*1. Counseling.* The objective of employee counseling is to change employee behavior and develop productive members of the

---

[195]Grinnell Corp., 92 LA 124 (Kilroy, 1989).

[196]Burlington N. R.R., 101 LA 144, 150 (Massey, 1993) (performance); Reynolds Metals, 99 LA 239 (Kahn, 1992); Man Roland, Inc., 97 LA 175 (Speroff, 1991).

[197]See, e.g., Carl Bolander & Sons Co., 100 LA 1, 3 (Reynolds, 1992); Valentec/Kisco-Olivette, 100 LA 71 (Fowler, 1992); Dyer's Chop House, Inc., 82 LA 198, 202 (Ray, 1984).

[198]Archer, Daniels, Midland Processing Co., 91 LA 9 (Cerone, 1988); GATX Terminals Corp., 91 LA 1162 (Baron, 1988).

organization.[199] Oral and written counseling sessions offer an employee the opportunity to correct behavior before the need for discipline arises and may preserve the employment relationship.[200] Oral counseling is sometimes not reported in an employee's personnel file. Oral counselings may be informal discussions between a supervisor and an employee, in which the employee is advised that certain behavior does not meet the employer's standards and that specified remedial actions are needed. In some work places this is called "instruction," to avoid any suggestion that the employee is being disciplined. Most employees respond favorably to informal counseling and are fully capable of avoiding or correcting their errors, especially when a supervisor points out that the employee is on the verge of harming her own interests.[201] Consequently, oral counseling is not generally considered discipline. Should oral counseling prove ineffective, however, a formal counseling session may follow.

A written memo detailing the oral counseling session may be placed in the employee's personnel record.[202] The session and written documentation are intended to provide the employee with fair notice of the employer's specific requirements. The written document lends formality to the session, thereby increasing its significance to the employee.[203]

Since counseling is usually a separate and distinct procedure from discipline,[204] documentation of a counseling session may be introduced into a disciplinary hearing only to meet the defense that the employee did not have notice of the rule violated or the nature of the infraction.[205] If the employer later attempts to use the counseling as the basis for disciplinary action, however, or as an impediment to promotion, the counseling may be found to have been a disciplinary action.[206]

---

[199]Gallaudet Univ., 95 LA 983 (Hockenberry, 1990).

[200]Jacksonville Elec. Auth., 100 LA 1018 (Byars, 1993) (counseling after employer determined that discipline was appropriate served no constructive purpose); Hill's Pet Prods., 92 LA 944 (Dilts, 1989) (noting that counseling may be in writing and is defined as giving opinion or advice for directing the judgment or conduct of another); Red Cross Blood Serv., 90 LA 393 (Dworkin, 1988).

[201]Kravit, "The Role of Counseling in the Disciplinary Process," 41 Arb. J. 60 (Dec. 1986).

[202]See, e.g., Boise Cascade Paper, 101 LA 1073 (Nicholas, 1993).

[203]Centennial One, Inc., 84 LA 89 (Mittelman, 1985).

[204]Pacific Bell, 92 LA 127 (Oestreich, 1989) (determining that employee had reasonable cause to believe that discussion with supervisor was for the purpose of investigation or discipline).

[205]Trendler Metal Prods., 101 LA 749 (Green, 1993) (according no weight to memorandum in arbitral just cause determination, but admitting to show employee's knowledge); Genie Co., 97 LA 542 (Dworkin, 1991) (determining that counseling is not discipline under the parties' agreement and was not to be considered in weighing the legitimacy of a discharge but only to prove that employee was on notice that employer considered his conduct to be a policy violation).

[206]Beverly Enters., 100 LA 522 (Berquist, 1993) (concluding that in a progressive system, written counseling is discipline when used to support just cause for termination); Port of Tacoma, 99 LA 1151 (Smith, 1992) (counseling letter used to support just cause for termination is discipline); Sacramento Air Logistics Ctr., 93 LA 470 (Hoh, 1989) (concluding that written

Other written notices may be issued to employees to advise them of rules, policies, or status. So long as the communications have no adverse impact on employees, arbitrators have not found them to be disciplinary in nature.[207] They do, however, provide the employee with notice of the employer's expectations.

*2. Evaluations.* An employer may conduct performance appraisals or evaluations of its employees to inform employees of perceived deficiencies and to allow them opportunities to improve performance.[208] Performance evaluations may be periodic reviews of all employees to determine whether work is being satisfactorily performed or may be specific reviews conducted in response to a perceived deficiency.[209] Arbitrators have found that unlike counseling, performance evaluations are not disciplinary even when later used as the basis for disciplinary action.[210] Performance evaluations are distinguished by their attempt to recognize good performance and behavior, as well as note any perceived deficiencies.

## B. Sources of Progressive Discipline

Some collective bargaining agreements specifically provide for progressive discipline and delineate its administration. General guidelines for progressive discipline may be set forth in the collective bargaining agreement, with the employer developing a specific policy within these guidelines. For instance, the collective bargaining agreement may establish the types of discipline that may be imposed, or may specify the sequence that must be followed. In many cases, however, the rules, including penalties, are unilaterally promulgated by the employer.[211]

Employer-implemented rules must be reasonable, communicated clearly to employees, and consistent with the collective bargaining

---

counseling is disciplinary in nature, despite company's express policy that written counseling is not disciplinary, because it could later be used to affect the employee adversely).

[207]Arch of Ill., Inc., 93 LA 1097 (Cohen, 1990) (finding that informational letter to employees informing them of their status as "irregular workers" during strike was not disciplinary); Columbia Bd. of Educ., 73 LA 382 (Perry, 1979) (finding that private conversation between director of vocational education program and teacher regarding employer's expectations under school's dress code was not form of discipline, since employer did not say that teacher's conduct was inappropriate and did not threaten penalty for violating dress code policy).

[208]Municipality of Anchorage, 101 LA 1127 (Carr, 1994).

[209]U.S. Dep't of Army, 88 LA 1200 (Nolan, 1987).

[210]Avondale Sch. Dist., 102 LA 1153 (Knott, 1994) (stating that it is not improper for an employer to take into consideration poor performance evaluations as demonstrating an employee's overall problems and failures in work responsibilities when determining the penalty to be assessed for a disciplinary infraction); City of Mentor, 94 LA 486 (Graham, 1990) (concluding that performance evaluation was itself not discipline even though as a result of the review the employer determined that discipline was justified). But see Los Angeles County Sheriff's Dep't, 83 LA 453 (Draznin, 1985).

[211]Zack, Grievance Arbitration, 58 (Lexington Books, 1989).

agreement.[212] In some cases arbitrators have refused to impose a rigid system of progressive discipline where none has been negotiated by the parties and the employer has no policy requiring a particular progression of penalties.[213] Even so, there is general consensus among arbitrators that just cause requires any penalty imposed be reasonable in view of the nature of the offense.[214] For this reason, many arbitrators will overturn discharge for a single, nonserious offense.

## C. Steps of Progressive Discipline

All progressive discipline systems use a series of steps, or disciplinary actions, which increase in severity. The generally accepted forms of discipline prior to discharge are oral warnings, written warnings, and suspensions.[215] Other types of discipline, such as wage deductions, are usually rejected by arbitrators because they are contrary to the principles of just cause.[216] In one case, an arbitrator rejected an employer's attempt to deduct cash shortages from the pay of employees on the basis that the deduction would reduce the wages set forth in the labor agreement.[217] Arbitrators are reluctant to find that an employer's withholding of monetary benefits is an appropriate form of discipline. For example, charging employees a $25 fee to replace a plastic time card has been found to be a disciplinary fine which cannot be imposed without regard to the disciplinary procedure and without considering whether the employee exercised reasonable care.[218] Withholding work[219] and denying overtime[220] have also been

---

[212]Denver Traffic Control Ctr., 99 LA 929 (Corbett, 1992); Wolf Mach., 72 LA 510, 513 (High, 1979). For discussion on consistency of rules with the collective bargaining agreement, see section entitled "Consistency With Collective Bargaining Agreement" in this chapter.

[213]"While concepts of corrective (in contrast to punitive) discipline have merit, it is an arbitrator's function to interpret collective bargaining agreements, not advise company and union what should be done in them. It is one thing to determine whether or not a contract permits discharging an employee under given circumstances. It is entirely another matter for an arbitrator to conclude that an employee's discharge violated a contract because of something not in the contract." Aro, Inc., 47 LA 1065, 1070 (Whyte, 1966). See also Curtis Mathes, 74 LA 171 (Goodstein, 1979) (10-day suspension upheld where arbitrator found he could not impose his own system of progressive discipline); Tex-a-Panel Mfg. Co., 62 LA 272 (Ray, 1973) (discharge sustained where contract contained no requirement of progressive discipline for poor work performance); Union Carbide Corp., 46 LA 195 (Cahn, 1966) (suspension not required before termination where progressive discipline not required by contract). Compare Thatcher & Sons, 76 LA 1278 (Nutt, 1981) (arbitrator upheld termination of an employee for engaging in an unsafe work practice, finding construction industry does not customarily use progressive discipline for this type of offense).

[214]R. E. Phelon, 75 LA 709 (Keefe, 1969).

[215]Delmarva Power & Light Co., 100 LA 457, 461 (DiLauro, 1992).

[216]Zack, "Just Cause and Progressive Discipline," in Labor & Employment Arbitration, Bornstein & Gosline, eds., 19–14 (Matthew Bender, 1994).

[217]Pepsi Cola Gen. Bottlers, 92 LA 1272 (Madden, 1989); For examples of other types of discipline disallowed by arbitrators, see City of Cincinnati, 80 LA 748 (Klein, 1983) (working on off days without pay); City of Boca Raton, Fla., 75 LA 706 (Davidson, 1980) (extra work without pay).

[218]Flexible Corp., 95 LA 1049 (Duda, 1990).

[219]Oliver Rubber Co., 82 LA 38 (Daughton, 1984).

[220]Grief Bros., 55 LA 384 (Markowitz, 1970).

considered improper forms of discipline. This section discusses the four most common steps of progressive discipline: oral warning, written warning, suspension, and discharge. Finally, this section looks at how demotion and transfer relate to progressive discipline and briefly examines alternatives to progressive discipline.

*1. Oral Warning.*   The imposition of an oral warning signifies that progressive discipline has begun. It may be difficult to distinguish disciplinary warnings from other communications between employers and employees, such as counseling, instructions, and evaluations, that do not constitute disciplinary action. Frequently, warnings are distinguished by including an explicit statement that a failure to improve may result in further disciplinary action. Oral warnings are used for minor offenses that do not disrupt the workplace to any great extent. Typical examples are tardiness, minor attendance violations, and minor safety violations.

As the oral warning is the first step in a process that can ultimately lead to termination, there must be a written record of the imposition of discipline. In one case, the arbitrator found that the employer's undocumented oral warnings could have been construed by grievant as "friendly advice" instead of discipline.[221] The oral warning documented in writing, or "written oral warning," is the lightest form of discipline. Since it is oral, it is less serious than a written warning. Since it is memorialized, it may later be used to show notice of rules. The memorialization usually includes the particulars giving rise to the oral warning, such as date, time, and nature of offense. The oral warning clearly notifies the employee that she has engaged in unacceptable behavior and that future misconduct will likely result in more severe discipline.[222]

*2. Written Warning.*   The next level of discipline is usually a written warning, although some employers begin progressive discipline with a written warning. Through the written warning, the employer notifies the employee that she has engaged in unacceptable behavior. Written warnings may be called reprimands. Reprimands are considered generally to be part of a discipline system,[223] and collective bargaining agreements often define reprimands as discipline.[224] The misconduct is likely to be more serious than that for

---

[221]Goshen Rubber, 99 LA 770 (Briggs, 1992).

[222]Koven, Smith & Farwell, Just Cause: The Seven Tests, 2d ed., 403–04 (BNA Books, 1992).

[223]See State of Ohio, 106 LA 914 (Feldman, 1996) (describing reprimands as part of a progressive discipline system); Napoleon Bd. of Educ., 74 LA 303, 305 (Roumell, Jr., 1980) (noting that "[a]rbitrators * * * generally supported the principle of progressive discipline, involving the use of reprimands, written reprimands and disciplinary suspensions prior to discharge").

[224]Johnson Controls World Servs., Inc., 105 LA 1194 (Poole, 1996) (determining that oral reprimand is not discipline under the contract); Mason & Hanger-Silas Mason Co., 106 LA 636 (Moore, 1996) (noting that contract defines reprimand as discipline); Genie Co., 97 LA 542 (Dworkin, 1991) (noting that under the contract, reprimands trigger every level of discipline).

which an oral warning would be given, either because of the nature of the offense[225] or because it is not the first instance of misconduct by the employee.[226] Depending upon the disciplinary system involved, a written warning may automatically follow after one or more oral warnings, even if the offenses are not of a similar nature. Typical offenses for which a written warning might be issued include failure to follow a supervisor's instruction, poor performance, and discourtesy to a customer.

The written warning generally includes a statement of the alleged conduct, including dates and times; a recitation of the specific rule or policy that was violated; an acknowledgment of receipt by the employee;[227] and an indication of the next level of discipline. The arbitrator may disallow use of a written warning from the employee's personnel file where receipt is denied by the grievant and cannot be proved by the employer.[228] Consequently, the employer will often ask the employee to sign the written warning or will indicate the employee's refusal to do so, to document that it was communicated to the employee.

Disagreements may occur as to whether certain types of written communications to an employee constitute discipline. Where a document merely informs the employee of his or her status (e.g., "This is your fifth absence in the last 6 months."), that he or she could potentially be subjected to discipline (e.g., "Our attendance system permits discipline after six absences in 6 months."), or where there is no impact on contractual rights (e.g., "In accordance with Article VI, Section 3 of the contract, after five absences in a 6-month period, employees will be required to bring a doctor's slip upon returning from any absence caused by illness."), the communication may not be discipline.[229]

Written and oral warnings are a significant factor in evaluating the propriety of more severe discipline for future offenses.[230] Warnings serve as notice that future conduct could result in more severe discipline. The fact that an employee has previously been warned has served as a critical factor in upholding more severe discipline, since

---

[225]Public Util. Dist. 1, 105 LA 332 (Henner, 1995). For example, written warning was the appropriate level of discipline for a 19-year employee with a clean record who was responsible for a property damage accident. City of Plymouth, 103 LA 424 (Berquist, 1994). Written reprimand was reduced to oral reprimand where grievant's conduct was not intentional.

[226]Midwest Coca-Cola Bottling Co., 94–1 ARB ¶ 4086 (Reynolds, 1993).

[227]Acknowledgments often state that the employee does not necessarily agree with the allegations in the warnings but is signing only to acknowledge receipt.

[228]Laidlaw Transit, Inc., 104 LA 184 (Concepcion, 1995).

[229]See Arch of Ill., 93 LA 1097 (Cohen, 1990) (grievance protesting the placement of an informational letter in a striker's personnel file was denied).

[230]Volz & Goggin, eds., Elkouri & Elkouri, How Arbitration Works, 5th ed., 931–33 (BNA Books, 1997).

the employee had notice and warning that conduct was unacceptable.[231] On the other hand, an employer's failure to provide counseling, oral warning, or written warning to an employee often results in the reversal of future disciplinary actions.[232]

*3. Suspension.* Suspensions are typically the next step following oral or written warnings in progressive discipline and may be imposed following one or more incidents of less serious misconduct for which the employer has issued warnings.[233] They result in the employee being removed from the work place for a designated period of time, in loss of pay, and sometimes in loss of seniority for the period of the suspension. The suspension places a blemish on the employee's employment record and, like warnings, can serve as a basis for more severe discipline in the future. Some progressive discipline systems establish a progression of suspensions prior to discharge, such as 1 day, 3 days, and 10 days. Other employers simply impose multiple suspensions of various lengths, depending on the offense. Yet another approach is to permit only one suspension as a final step before discharge. Whatever the employer's policy, the written notice of suspension generally states the consequences of further misconduct, notes the rule(s) violated, and includes an acknowledgment by the employee.

Some arbitrators emphasize that suspensions should be corrective or rehabilitative, not punitive. For example, one arbitrator observed: "Suspensions are corrective measures designed to rehabilitate a miscreant employee; to restore him/her to acceptable levels of production and/or behavior."[234] A suspension may be overturned or reduced if found to be unduly harsh or retaliatory, rather than corrective.[235] Some flexibility is available to the employer in adjusting the

---

[231]See Johnson Controls, 95 LA 182 (Dworkin, 1990) (discharge upheld where grievant was warned that his failure to improve his poor work quality would result in termination); Fairmont Gen. Hosp., 94 LA 1080 (Hewitt, 1990) (discharge upheld for poor performance where employee had been suspended, warned, and counseled about poor performance); Safeway Stores, 94 LA 983 (Knowlton, 1990) (checkstand employee properly suspended for improper conduct in checkout line where he had been warned about flamboyant and annoying conduct and counseled on customer relations).

[232]Heckett Div. of Harsco, 95 LA 195 (Nicholas, Jr., 1990) (discharge improper where employer failed to warn employees that misuse of steel plant property and working for their own benefit on company time was improper and cause for immediate termination); Carbonic Prods., 93 LA 189 (Gentile, 1989) (just cause did not exist to discharge two employees who fought in workplace where neither had prior warnings for the same offense).

[233]FKW, Inc., 104 LA 783 (Wray, 1995) (2-day suspension for tardiness proper where grievant had previously been given both oral and written warnings); Frito-Lay, Inc., 96–1 ARB ¶ 6180 (Murphy, 1995) (suspension was proper discipline for quarreling with coworker where employee had previously been given oral warning and suspension); Snappy Air Distrib. Prods., 104 LA 184 (Jacobowski, 1995) (1-day suspension proper for horseplay where employee had previously been given "stern" oral warning); City of Shaker Heights, Ohio, 96–1 ARB ¶ 6095 (Imundo, 1995) (suspension of 10 days proper for violating numerous rules, considering that employee had prior record of written reprimand and 3-day suspension).

[234]Red Cross Blood Serv., 90 LA 393, 397 (Dworkin, 1988).

[235]Id. (Dworkin reduced a 2-month suspension for negligence to 1 month, finding original penalty to be punitive, since, if correction was the goal, it is unlikely that the second month of the disciplinary layoff added any corrective influence to what was accomplished in the first).

length of the suspension to fit the situation. The length may vary depending upon the seriousness of the offense itself, the disciplinary practices of the employer, the past disciplinary record of the employee, and the existence of mitigating circumstances.[236] In some instances, a disciplinary suspension is appropriate for the first occurrence of misconduct that is serious but not flagrant enough to warrant immediate discharge.[237] It puts the employee on notice that her job is in jeopardy if she continues to engage in unacceptable behavior.

A number of specialized types of suspension are used in progressive discipline systems. They include: suspensions pending investigation, conditional suspensions, working suspensions, "decisionmaking leave," and indefinite suspensions. Each is discussed below.

Many employers place employees on suspension while they conduct an investigation of alleged misconduct. Depending on the result of the investigation, the employee could face discharge, a lesser disciplinary action, or reinstatement with back pay if the allegations prove unfounded. Employers must, however, conduct a prompt investigation to avoid imposing unduly on the employee's right to know his status.[238]

"Conditional" suspensions last until an employee meets some condition imposed by the employer. Arbitrators have upheld conditional or indefinite suspensions until undocumented employees corrected their social security numbers;[239] until "punk" or "new wave" grocery store baggers presented a more conventional appearance;[240] or until a driver salesman, who had a DUI and driver's license revocation, was able to drive legally.[241]

A suspended employee is absent for the period of suspension, requiring additional expense in the form of replacement overtime or training, and an employee returning to work after receiving an unpaid suspension may feel angry, creating an uncomfortable personal relationship between the employee and his supervisor. As a result, a type of discipline known as a "paper" or "working" suspension has developed.[242] When this level of disciplinary action is reached, the employee is advised in writing of the reasons for the disciplinary action, that the employee is receiving a suspension for the infraction, and that the employee will be working and paid during the suspension

---

[236]Public Util. Dist. 1, 105 LA 332 (Henner, 1995); City of Plymouth 103 LA 424 (Berquist, 1994).

[237]Lamar Constr. Co., 98 LA 500, 503 (Kanner, 1992); Grain Processing Corp., 92 LA 265, 270–71 (Hilgert, 1989).

[238]Furr's Supermarkets, 95 LA 1021 (Rezler, 1990) (employer violated contract permitting indefinite suspension pending completion of "reasonably prompt investigation" when it took 17 days to investigate alleged threats and abusive language; suspension reduced from 17 to 5 days); Allied Health Care Prods., 94 LA 178 (Cipolla, 1990) (discharge upheld, but employee receives 1 ½ days back pay because the employer failed to comply with the contractual provision requiring a predischarge suspension of up to 5 days to investigate).

[239]Acme Bldg. Maintenance, 88 LA 404 (McKay, 1986).

[240]Fisher Foods, 88 LA 1984 (Richard, 1987).

[241]De Beverage Co., 85 LA 891 (Gibson, 1985).

[242]Huberman, "Discipline Without Punishment," HBR July–Aug. 1964, 62.

period. The employee is further advised that the action is a next step in progressive discipline. If the unacceptable behavior is not corrected, further and more serious disciplinary action will follow. Suspensions of this type can serve the same purpose as an actual suspension if clear notice of the severity of the discipline is given to the employee. The psychological impact on the employee, however, may prove to be less significant than the embarrassment and wage loss of being barred from work. Working suspensions without pay have been deemed impermissible.[243]

A relatively recent form of suspension is the "decisionmaking leave." An employee who has demonstrated behavior or performance problems, and has received a variety of progressive disciplinary action but has still not conformed, receives written notice of being placed on a brief leave of absence, the purpose of which is to permit him to consider whether he desires to continue employment.[244] The decisionmaking leave focuses on the employee's recognition that his future behavior must comply with the employer's standards. The employee can decide either to return to work on the condition of meeting acceptable standards or to resign.[245]

Indefinite suspensions, in which there are no stated conditions for a return to work, have been equated with discharge or constructive discharge. Arbitrators evaluate these suspensions on that basis, imposing a higher standard of proof on the employer.[246] Some arbitrators have determined that indefinite suspensions are invalid, finding that a disciplinary layoff must be for a specific term, and the union and the employee are entitled to know its exact duration.[247]

Sometimes when there is just cause for discharging an employee—often for drug use—the employer will decide that the employee should be given a final opportunity for rehabilitation or correction so that otherwise satisfactory employment can continue. The employer, working with the union, may enter into a written "last-chance" agreement with the employee, affording a final opportunity to correct a behavior or performance problem.[248] The last-chance

---

[243]City of Cincinnati, 80 LA 748 (Klein, 1983) (employer may not cause police officer to lose pay for hours worked as a form of discipline, as managerial prerogatives do not permit employer to take away employee's contractual right to be paid for all hours worked); Missouri Power & Light Co., 80 LA 297 (Westbrook, 1982) (while employer could have suspended line crew for refusal to obey work order, it cannot withhold grievant's pay because the denial of contractual benefit is not an appropriate form of discipline).

[244]Southwestern Bell Tel. Co., 102 LA 531 (Nolan, 1994); Georgia Power Co., 100 LA 622 (Singer, 1993); Rohr Indus., 94 LA 1303 (Harkless, 1990); Shell Oil Co., 93 LA 273 (Allen, 1989).

[245]Allied Health Care Prods., 94 LA 178 (Cipolla, 1990).

[246]See Art Carved, Inc., 70 LA 869 (Kramer, 1977) (equating indefinite suspension to a discharge and imposing a clear and convincing standard of proof on the employer); Canteen Corp., 89 LA 815 (Keefe, 1987) (indefinite suspension constitutes a constructive discharge).

[247]Cascade Corp., 82 LA 313 (Bressler, 1984).

[248]See Chapter 8 for a discussion of last-chance agreements in drug cases, and Chapter 12 for limitations on the arbitrator's remedial authority under last-chance agreements.

agreement usually embodies a period of absence from work—frequently for rehabilitation—although an employee may be entitled to use earned leave to continue to be paid while off the job. Last-chance agreements vary with the employee problem being addressed. Typically they include provisions establishing the range of acceptable future conduct, specific rehabilitation and testing requirements, the duration of the agreement, and the consequences of failing to meet the behavioral or testing standards. Some agreements state that the employee may be terminated for any reason during the term of the agreement.[249] In the face of an arbitration provision in a collective bargaining agreement that conflicts with a last-chance agreement, courts have not always enforced an individual's waiver of arbitration.[250]

*4. Discharge.*    Discharge is the most extreme industrial penalty since the employee's job, seniority, and other contractual benefits and reputation are at stake.[251] It was once referred to as "industrial capital punishment," but at least one arbitrator has suggested that "a more accurate equivalent to discharge is permanent exile."[252] One arbitrator has distinguished discharge from all other forms of discipline.

> While arbitrators often speak of discharge as part of a disciplinary progression—a penalty which is a step above lesser penalties—the perception is flawed * * *. Discharge and suspension are separate and distinct penalties. Suspensions are corrective measures designed to rehabilitate * * *. Discharge on the other hand is the severance of an employment relationship. An employer has no legitimate interest in

---

[249]Naval Weapons Station Earle, 100 LA 1097 (Robinson, 1993); Genie Co., 97 LA 542 (Dworkin, 1991); Gaylord Container Corp., 97 LA 382 (Goodman, 1991); University of Mich., 96 LA 688 (Sugerman, 1991); Diesel Recon Co., 96 LA 1193 (Odom , 1991); Sime & Co., 96 LA 193 (Odom, 1990); Northrop Corp., Aircraft Div., 96 LA 149 (Weiss, 1990); Baltimore Specialty Steels, 95 LA 1191 (Strongin, 1990); U.S. Steel Corp., 94 LA 1109 (McDaniel, 1990); Atlantic Richfield Co., 81 LA 1193 (Heinsz, 1983); Hayes Int'l Corp., 81 LA 99 (Van Wart, 1983).

[250]The Third Circuit considered a last-chance agreement that provided for final determination of the appropriate penalty by the company's disciplinary committee, but did not address the standard for determining the underlying question of the employee's guilt. The disciplinary committee upheld the employee's dismissal after the employer found that he had violated the last-chance agreement. When the union sought to arbitrate the dismissal, the employer maintained that the employee had waived his right to arbitration under the last-chance agreement. The court disagreed, however, noting that the collective bargaining agreement had a broad arbitration clause that did not expressly exclude the last-chance agreement from arbitration. Adhering to the strong presumption of arbitrability, the court concluded that in the absence of an express exclusion, a last-chance agreement is arbitrable when the underlying dispute is arbitrable, unless the employer produces "strong and forceful" evidence to exclude from arbitration the underlying question whether the employee in fact violated the last-chance agreement. Steelworkers Local 1165 v. Lukens Steel Co., 969 F.2d 1468 (3d Cir., 1992). See also Smith v. ITT Standard, 834 F.Supp. 618 (E.D.N.Y., 1993). Cf. Tootsie Roll Indus., Inc. v. Bakery, Confectionery & Tobacco Workers Local 1, 832 F.2d 81, 126 LRRM 270 (7th Cir., 1987).

[251]Volz & Goggin, eds., Elkouri & Elkouri, How Arbitration Works, 5th ed., 905 (BNA Books, 1997).

[252]Schroeder, "Discharge: Is It Industrial Capital Punishment?" 37 Arb. J. No. 4, 65 (1982), cited in Volz & Goggin, eds., Elkouri & Elkouri, How Arbitration Works, 5th ed., 905 n. 102 (BNA Books, 1997).

whether or not a discharged employee ever achieves rehabilitation. Its sole purpose is to unburden the work force of an individual whose conduct has become intolerable. In other words, discharge is designed to abolish the employment relationship; disciplinary suspension is designed to improve it.[253]

The principles of just cause allow an employee to be terminated in two types of situations: a single incident of vary serious misconduct[254] or the final step in the progressive disciplinary process.[255] A single occurrence of some types of misconduct often warrants discharge in any employment environment. An employee who engages in conduct such as stealing, striking another employee, selling drugs on site, or working on a hazardous task under the influence of drugs or alcohol may be subject to discharge, even in the absence of a specific rule.[256] In these situations, some arbitrators reason that "there are certain standards of conduct which are so inherent in the employee/employer relationship that specific notice is unnecessary."[257] For other types of serious misconduct, the right of an employer to terminate an employee based on a single incident may depend upon the collective bargaining agreement, the rules of the employer, past practice, and other factors.[258]

The employer, however, is not rigidly bound to the application of progressive discipline in every situation. There is general agreement that summary discharge may be warranted for severe misconduct, such as theft or striking a supervisor,[259] as well as those types of misconduct that are specified by the parties as warranting summary discharge.[260] Nevertheless, there are many circumstances under

---

[253]Red Cross Blood Serv., 90 LA 393, 397 (Dworkin, 1988).

[254]Big Bear Stores, Inc., 103 LA 1149 (Bell, 1995) (employee properly discharged for stealing pack of cigarettes from employer's grocery store); Dravo Lime Co. Black River Div., 96–1, ARB ¶ 6067 (Imundo, 1995) (discharge proper for employee where drug test was positive for marijuana); Fine Host Inc., 96–1 ARB ¶ 6010 (Talarico, 1995) (employee who pocketed cash from beer sales was properly discharged).

[255]Midwest Coca-Cola Bottling Co., 94–1 ARB ¶ 4086 (Reynolds, 1993). However, suspension is not necessarily a prerequisite to discharge where adequate warning has been given. Merchants Fast Motor Lines, Inc., 94–1 ARB ¶ 4220 (Johnson, 1994). See also Dunlop Tire Corp., 92–2 ARB ¶ 8582 (Minn., 1992), where discharge was overturned because grievant was not found to be at the last step of progressive discipline.

[256]Koven, Smith & Farwell, Just Cause: The Seven Tests, 2d ed., 398–99 (BNA Books, 1992); Zack, Grievance Arbitration, 58 (Lexington Books, 1989).

[257]Hughes Mkts., 97 LA 912, 918 (Prayzich, 1991).

[258]International Paper Co., 101 LA 1106 (Yancy, 1993) (discharge for racial and sexual harassment upheld despite lack of prior discipline based on gravity of the offense); Goodyear Aerospace Corp., 86 LA 403 (Fullmer, 1985) (discharge for possession of firearm on employer's property).

[259]Lukes Steel Co., 101 LA 569 (Strongin, 1993) (employee summarily discharged for throwing a rock at a supervisor). See general discussion in International Harvester Co., 12 LA 1190 (McCoy, 1990).

[260]See discussion in Western Auto Supply, 71 LA 710 (Ross, 1978).

which arbitrators come to different conclusions.[261] Arbitrators are by no means uniform in their decisions on very similar facts.

By way of example, consider the offense of theft. While many arbitrators uphold summary dismissal, others look much more deeply and refuse to uphold the discharge. One such situation was faced by an arbitrator in a case in which an employee was found guilty of stealing two candy bars from his employer. The arbitrator converted the employee's discharge to a suspension without back pay, reasoning as follows:

> Let it be understood at the beginning that we accept the company's argument that it must control pilferage and theft of company product.
>    * * *
> While there is no doubt that dishonesty is dishonesty, regardless of the nature of the act, it can be argued that some acts of dishonesty are more serious than others. Is the theft of one dollar ($1.00) as serious as the theft of one thousand dollars ($1,000)? Is the theft of two candy bars as serious as the initial breaking of the package, or the theft of the product having greater value? Can it be argued that there is such a thing as gross dishonesty, which is more serious than just dishonesty?
> We do not wish to communicate the impression that theft or dishonesty may be excused and/or viewed as acceptable. It is not, regardless of the value of the product or item stolen. However, in arbitration law there is the belief that the punishment ought to fit the crime. This suggests that certain violations of work rules or contractual terms are best dealt with by verbal warning, while other violations are so severe that discharge on the first occurrence is justified. We are inclined to be persuaded, in this case, by the union's argument that the penalty, discharge, is too severe for the crime, theft and pilferage of two candy bars.[262]

The same spectrum of arbitral philosophy can be seen in sexual harassment situations. Many arbitrators will uphold the discharge of an employee found to have committed sexual harassment,[263] but several arbitrators have awarded reinstatement where the employee was not progressively disciplined[264] or was denied the opportunity to refute the charges.[265] Other arbitrators have awarded reinstatement

---

[261]Bistate Dev. Agency, 101 LA 427 (McGrady, 1993); Lee Stown Co., 102 LA 979 (Sergeant, 1994).

[262]PYA/Monarch Food Serv., 94 LA 575, 578–80 (Smith, 1990).

[263]American Protective Servs., 102 LA 161 (Gentile, 1994); Hughes Aircraft Co., 102 LA 353 (Bickner, 1993); George Koch & Sons, 102 LA 737 (Brunner, 1994); International Paper Co., 101 LA 1106 (Yancy, 1993); Lohr Distrib. Co., 101 LA 1217 (Fowler, 1993); Schlage Lock, 88 LA 75 (Wyman, 1988).

[264]Newsday v. Long Island Typographical Union, 915 F.2d 840 (2d Cir. 1990), cert. denied, 111 S.Ct. 7314 (1991).

[265]Stroehmann Bakeries v. Teamsters Local 776, 969 F.2d 1436, 140 LRRM 2625 (3d Cir.), cert. denied, 506 U.S. 1022, 141 LRRM 2984 (1992); Renton Sch. Dist., 102 LA 854 (1994).

where the employee was apologetic and had an otherwise unblemished record.[266]

There are other representative splits of arbitral authority regarding summary discharge. Employees found guilty of using intentional racial slurs and epithets often are summarily discharged,[267] although not all arbitrators would uphold such discharges.[268] Similarly, some arbitrators will uphold the summary discharge of an employee who brought a gun to work.[269] Others will not.[270]

One area where arbitrators usually, but not always, refuse to uphold the summary discharge of an employee concerns falsification of employment applications.[271] Some of the factors arbitrators examine in determining the appropriate penalty in such cases include the type of falsification, the time period between the misrepresentation and its discovery, the employee's job performance, how the falsification was discovered, and whether the employee would have been hired if the employer had known the truth.[272]

Where discharge is the final step in the progressive discipline process, the employee will usually have received several warnings and at least one suspension.[273] In some instances, an employee will have been put on notice that he can expect to be discharged for an additional incident of specified misconduct.[274] In cases commonly referred to as "last-straw" discharges, an employee engages in some misconduct that would not, by itself, be just cause for discharge. However, based on the accumulation of offenses, the employer decides termination is appropriate. This decision reflects the employer's conclusion that past efforts at rehabilitation have failed and there is no reasonable alternative to discharge. Arbitrators will uphold last-straw discharges when the employer has sufficient evidence to show that an employee's pattern of unsatisfactory conduct warrants discharge.[275]

---

[266]King Soopers, Inc., 101 LA 107 (Snider, 1993); Chrysler Motors v. Allied Indus., 959 F.2d 685 (7th Cir., 1992); Communications Workers v. South W. Elec., 882 F.2d 467 (10th Cir., 1981).

[267]American Standard Corp., 64 LA 15 (Lipsitz, 1974).

[268]Lockheed Aeronautical Sys., 101 LA 526 (Hoffman, 1993).

[269]City of New Haven, 101 LA 647 (Stewart, 1993). Cf. Lukes Steel Co., 101 LA 569 (Strongin, 1993) (employee summarily discharged for throwing a rock at a supervisor).

[270]Folsom Return to Custody, 101 LA 837 (Staudohar, 1993).

[271]Rubinstein, "The Use of Predischarge Misconduct Discovered After an Employee's Termination as a Defense in Employment Litigation," 24 Suffolk U.L.Rev. 1, 2 n.6 (1990) (citing cases). See Chapter 10.

[272]Id. See also Southern Cal. Edison, 101 LA 201 (Prayzich, 1993); Brinks, Inc., 79 LA 816 (Briggs, 1982); Kraft Foods, 50 LA 161 (Turkus, 1967); Tiffany Metal Prods., 56 LA 135 (Roberts, 1971). See full discussion at Chapter 7, in section entitled Falsification.

[273]When an employer relies on prior discipline to support its decision to discharge, the notice of termination must clearly inform the employee that the prior discipline is being relied upon as the basis for the severity of the discipline. See Zack, Grievance Arbitration, 121 (Lexington Books, 1989).

[274]Kimberly-Clark Corp., 82 LA 1090, 1095 (Keenan, 1984).

[275]Fairmont Gen. Hosp., 94 LA 1080, 1082–83 (Hewitt, 1990). See also Volz & Goggin, eds., Elkouri & Elkouri, How Arbitration Works, 5th ed. 925 (BNA Books, 1997).

Constructive discharge occurs when the employer, by statements or conduct, manifests an intent to terminate the employee's employment and the employee relies on these statements or conduct. The cases often focus on whether the employee reasonably believed that he was being terminated or whether the employee voluntarily quit. For example, an employer's statement that the employee must resign or be terminated has been deemed to be a constructive discharge.[276] An employee's refusal to comply with management's request to engage in conduct not required under the contract has also been considered a constructive discharge rather than a voluntary resignation.[277] An employee who tenders her resignation and then has a change of mind has been found to have been constructively discharged where her employer refused to allow her to withdraw her resignation but had taken minimal or no steps to replace her.[278] Other cases examine the circumstances surrounding an allegedly "voluntary resignation," such as the employee's mental state[279] or confrontational remarks from supervisors.[280]

*5. Demotion and Transfer as Alternatives to Progressive Discipline.* Placing an employee in a lower job classification or in a position involving lesser pay, status, skills, or benefits is a demotion. Arbitrators disagree as to whether demotions are an appropriate form of discipline and look to the contract language for guidance. Most arbitrators refuse to uphold demotions as disciplinary measures unless the labor agreement specifically allows for them since such disciplinary action would violate the employee's seniority rights.[281] Clauses providing that wage rates fixed by the contract will continue for the duration of the contract may also limit an employer's right to demote.[282] Still other arbitrators find that an employer may not use demotion as discipline if the contract provides for specified methods of discipline, but not demotion.[283]

[276]MacMillan Bloedel Containers, 92 LA 592 (Nicholas, Jr., 1989).

[277]Continental White Cap, 90 LA 1119 (Staudohar, 1988).

[278]Moss Supermarket, 99 LA 409 (Grupp, 1992).

[279]United Tel. Co. of Tex., 93 LA 1047 (Shieber, 1989) (employer constructively discharged grievant by accepting oral "I quit" as voluntary resignation; grievant made the statement during an unprovoked outburst resulting from a chemical imbalance caused by a failure to take high blood pressure medication; grievant later retracted the statement, explained his medical condition, and sought reinstatement as soon as he recovered, so the employer was not harmed by the purported resignation).

[280]Commodore Home Sys., Inc., 82 LA 395 (Schedler, Jr., 1984) (no constructive discharge even though a supervisor told the grievant her production was "killing him"; grievant had said she could not keep up, no one liked her, and she was quitting, and hit the time clock and drove home).

[281]Elkouri, supra note 275, at 783; American Nat'l Can, 95 LA 873 (Borland, 1990); Republic Steel Corp., LA 733 (Platt, 1955); Goodyear Atomic Corp., 25 LA 736 (Kelliher, 1955).

[282]Elkouri, supra note 275, at 780 n.664, at 566, citing National Vulcanized Fibre Co., 3 LA 259, 263 (Kaplan, 1946).

[283]Id. at 783 nn.678 & 679, citing American Steel & Wire Co., 6 LA 379, 382 (Blumer, 1946), and Reynolds Alloys Co., 2 LA 554 (McCoy, 1943).

Arbitrators frequently find that demotion is not a proper form of discipline for offenses that do not involve poor job skills.[284] Some arbitrators have found that demotions are proper disciplinary measures if the demotion is for a fixed period where an employee could have been subject to a disciplinary suspension.[285] Similarly, some arbitrators feel demotion is an appropriate disciplinary measure in lieu of discharge when the employee's conduct would have warranted termination.[286]

Transfers as a form of disciplinary action are generally examined under the same analysis as demotions. That is, arbitrators look to contract language, the purpose of the transfer, whether it is for a specific duration, and whether the employee could have been subject to discipline.[287] If the transfer is viewed as a disciplinary measure, it will be examined under the contractual just clause provision.[288]

## IV. Arbitral Concepts of Fairness

Arbitrators have both idiosyncratic and consensus ideas about what constitutes fairness in the workplace. Idiosyncratic notions of fairness may explain some otherwise inexplicable arbitral decisions, but they cannot be generalized and must remain, for that reason, unexplored in this text. What is far more important to the advocate or advisor is the consensus about fairness that is demonstrated in the vast majority of arbitral decisions dealing with making rules, enforcing rules consistently, imposing the appropriate penalty, and fairly administering the disciplinary system.

### A. *Making and Communicating Rules*

Arbitrators uniformly agree that an employer has the right to establish and enforce work rules, subject to the requirement that the rule must be reasonable[289] and rationally related to a legitimate

---

[284]Southern Cal. Rapid Transit Dist., 100 LA 701 (Brisco, 1992); Archer, Daniels, Midland Processing Co., 91 LA 9 (Cerone, 1988) (demotion improper discipline because it was for an indefinite duration and because it was a result of the grievant's attitude rather than his performance); National Metal & Steel Corp., 86 LA 217 (Rothschild, 1985) (demotion improper for "suspicion of still drinking").

[285]Libby, McNeil & Libby of Canada, Ltd., 74 LA 991 (O'Shea, 1980).

[286]Southwest Petro-Chem, Inc., 92 LA 493 (Berger, 1988).

[287]Denver Pub. Schs., 73 LA 918 (Meiners, 1979) (employer violated contract provision barring use of transfer as a disciplinary measure when it transferred a teacher as a result of an altercation between the teacher and a student).

[288]Communication Workers, 86 LA 1003 (Hockenberry, 1986).

[289]Volz & Goggin, eds., Elkouri & Elkouri, How Arbitration Works, 5th ed., 764 (BNA Books, 1997). See Texas Utils. Elec. Co., 90 LA 625 (Allen, 1988) (rule encouraging coworkers to report unsafe or hazardous conditions caused by use or possession of illegal drugs or alcohol was reasonably related to the safe, orderly, and efficient operation of the plant).

business objective.[290] The employer's ability to establish rules is also limited by the union's right to bargain under the National Labor Relations Act. Some collective bargaining agreements specifically reserve to the employer the right to make rules, while other collective bargaining agreements place limitations upon the right.[291] Absent any contractual restraints, the employer may implement reasonable work rules so long as they comply with the law and do not contradict the collective bargaining agreement.[292] One arbitrator sets forth the tests for reasonableness as follows:

> The tests of "reasonableness" which are most frequently invoked by arbitrators include whether the rule in question violates any part of the Contract; whether it materially changes a past practice or working condition; whether it is related to a legitimate business objective of management; whether it is arbitrary, capricious or discriminatory; and whether it is reasonably applied.[293]

In reviewing the reasonableness of a rule, arbitrators generally consider the content of the rule, the consistency of the rule with any negotiated agreement, and the notice given to employees, as well as the clarity and scope of the rule.[294]

*1. Content.*    A rule must be reasonably related to a legitimate business objective. An employer cannot regulate an employee's behavior outside the workplace unless the conduct or situation impacts the employer's operations.[295] If the activity to be regulated does not have the appropriate nexus to the workplace, the rule will not withstand arbitral review.[296] For example, a requirement that new hires live within 10 miles of the plant was not reasonably related to the efficient operation of a specialty wax facility.[297] On the other hand, the connection between some rules and operations is self-evident. Regular attendance, for instance, is necessary for productivity.[298] Similarly, safety

---

[290]Hill & Sinicropi, Management Rights, A Legal and Arbitral Analysis, 71 (BNA Books, 1986). See also Forest Hills Bd. of Educ., 93 LA 990, 993 (Heekin, 1989) (evaluates new smoking rule based upon whether it is reasonably related to a legitimate management interest). Further discussion on implementing rules can be found in Chapter 11.

[291]Hill & Sinicropi, Management Rights, A Legal and Arbitral Analysis, 65 (BNA Books, 1986).

[292]Industrial Finishing Co., 40 LA 670, 671 (Daugherty, 1963).

[293]Union Sanitary Dist., 79 LA 193 (Koven, 1982).

[294]Id.

[295]Wilcots, "Employee Discipline for Off-Duty Conduct: Constitutional Challenges and the Public Policy Exception," Lab. L. J. 3, 4 (Jan. 1995). See Chapter 9.

[296]See Bauer Bros., 48 LA 861, 863 (Kates, 1967) (Rule requiring safety glasses during lunch unreasonable); Pioneer Gen-E-Motors Corp., 3 LA 486, 488 (Blair, 1946) (assault of supervisor off site not related to workplace; "The proper and only authority over the personal lives of employees, once they leave their place of employment, is the civil authority.").

[297]Quaker State Corp., 92 LA 898 (Talarico, 1989).

[298]One arbitrator found management has a fundamental right to modify its attendance policy. General Foods Corp., 91 LA 1251 (Goldstein, 1988).

rules are needed to protect employees, avoid accidents, and provide a safe work environment.[299] What the rule actually says is the starting point for any analysis. For instance, a rule simply forbidding illegal activity may not be enforced because it is overbroad. One arbitrator held that a rule providing for termination upon criminal conviction did not justify indefinitely suspending an employee who was arrested on drug-related criminal charges.[300] Disciplinary action has been upheld, however, where an employee is convicted of criminal activity that has an adverse effect on the employer's operation. For example, a driver was properly discharged after arrest for driving under the influence off duty made him uninsurable.[301] Discharge has also been upheld where an employee engaged in conduct that exposed the employer to potential civil liability.[302]

The right of an employer to protect its business interests must be balanced against an employee's right to privacy and self-expression.[303] An employer cannot expect to have an arbitrator uphold a rule that regulates an employee's behavior outside of the workplace, unless the conduct or situation impacts the employer's operations.[304] If the activity to be regulated does not have the appropriate nexus

---

[299]Dyno Nobel, Inc., 104 LA 376 (Hilgert, 1995) (facial hair banned for employees wearing respirators); Gaylord Container Corp., 97 LA 382 (Goodman, 1991) (safety glasses); GSX Servs. of Cal., 96 LA 792 (Riker, 1991) (handling hazardous waste); Gold Kist, 94 LA 152 (Byars, 1990) (steel mesh gloves); Interstate Brands Corp., 94 LA 977 (Berger, 1990) (ear plugs); Bell Foundry, 92 LA 1214 (Prayzich, 1989) (operation of forklift); Hercules Inc., 91 LA 987 (Nolan, 1988) (handling asbestos).

[300]Babcock & Wilcox Co., 102 LA 104 (1994) (lack of nexus to workplace, no cited violation of work rules, and 30-year practice militated against suspension). For full discussion, see Chapter 6.

[301]Ernst Enters., 103 LA 782 (Doering, 1995). See also Jersey Shore Steel Co., 100 LA 489 (Goulet, 1992), where just cause existed to discharge a steel-mill employee who was arrested and pleaded guilty to delivery and possession of marijuana while off duty. But see Star Tran., Inc., 104 LA 641 (Baroni, 1995), where a bus operator was discharged after he pleaded guilty to a misdemeanor of injury to a child which occurred during a robbery. The robbery was a major news event in the city and the company discharged the bus operator on the grounds that the incident adversely affected the company's reputation. The arbitrator sustained the grievance and ordered reinstatement on the basis that the operator's off-duty involvement did not affect the company's reputation adversely since none of the news reports identified him as a company employee. While acknowledging a nexus between the employee's off-duty misconduct and his job duties as a bus operator, the arbitrator found the misconduct did not affect his job performance or his relations with coworkers.

[302]For example, the discharge of a janitor following a conviction for sexual misconduct was upheld due to the strong likelihood the employer would be held civilly liable in the event of further misconduct. College of St. Scholastica, 96 LA 244 (Berquist, 1991). See also King's Daughters' Med. Ctr., 96 LA 609 (Curry, 1991) (discharge upheld where physical therapist violated 20-minute rule for application of hot pack to patient, exposing hospital to possible suit).

[303]These rights are frequently implicated in disputes concerning off-duty conduct (or misconduct), drug and alcohol testing, dress and grooming, political activities, searches of employees' bags and lockers, bathroom use, fraternization and intermarriage, etc. See Chapter 9 for further discussion.

[304]Wilcots, "Employee Discipline for Off-Duty Conduct: Constitutional Challenges and the Public Policy Exception," Lab. L. J. 3, 4 (Jan. 1995).

to the workplace, the rule will not withstand arbitral review.[305] Even where employee rights are readily apparent, the interests of the employer may allow it to regulate employee conduct because of a nexus to the workplace. For example, a bus driver asserted the right to engage in an off-duty association activity (being Grand Dragon of the Ku Klux Klan). As a result, the outraged local community threatened a boycott if the driver were not fired. The competing constitutional consideration, in this case freedom of association, must be weighed against the employer's business interests. The arbitrator deferred to the employer's business interests and upheld the discharge.[306] Arbitrators have recognized the employer's interest in prohibiting personal activities at work and in banning potentially destructive public criticism.[307]

Some rules cover subjects that may not have been contemplated at the time of bargaining, but are necessary for the safe, orderly, and efficient operation of the plant. If this sort of rule is at issue, the employer's right to create the necessary rule will be upheld.[308] Even so, arbitrators may require prior discussion with the union before implementation. For example, an arbitrator suspended a new rule that restricted smoking and required a meeting with the union before imposing the rule.[309]

Arbitrators examine the substance of rules to determine whether they are necessary to the efficient, orderly, or safe operation of the business. For example, the employer has an interest in making sure its safety procedures are followed and its equipment is handled properly.[310] Arbitrators have reviewed the reasonableness of a safety rule by examining the asserted safety concerns and the business reason behind the rule.[311]

---

[305]See Bauer Bros., 48 LA 461, 463 (Kates, 1967); Pioneer Gen-E-Motors Corp., 3 LA 486, 488 (Blair 1946).

[306]Baltimore Transit Co., 47 LA 62 (1966).

[307]For example, a public high school's librarian received a written reprimand after sending members of a regional association of librarians an electronic-mail message that criticized curriculum changes proposed for the school and sought help in dealing with the problems she perceived. The arbitrator found the school librarian had no inherent authority to access an e-mail system in expressing personal opinions about the proposed curriculum plan, and her employer may prohibit the use of its equipment for purely personal activities without running afoul of any constitutional protections. The school district, however, lacked just cause for disciplining the librarian since it admittedly had no rules or regulations on using the system. Conneaut Sch. Dist., 104 LA 909 (Talarico, 1995). But see United Press Int'l, 94 LA 841 (Ables, 1990), where discharge of an investigative reporter for violating a ban on outside activity that created a conflict of interest was upheld because the potentially destructive public criticism of the employer was not in keeping with honorable relations with employers and employees.

[308]American Zinc Co. of Ill., 20 LA 527, 530 (Merrill, 1953).

[309]Acorn Bldg. Components, Inc., 92 LA 68 (Roumell, 1988).

[310]Gold Kist, 94 LA 152 (Byars, 1990) (operation of saw without steel mesh gloves); Bell Foundry, 92 LA 1214 (Prayzich, 1989) (negligent operation of forklift); Hercules Inc., 91 LA 987 (Nolan, 1988) (failure to follow safety procedures regarding handling asbestos).

[311]Volz & Goggin, eds., Elkouri & Elkouri, How Arbitration Works, 5th ed. (BNA Books, 1997); American Zinc Co. of Ill., 20 LA 527, 530 (1953); Hill & Sinicropi, Management Rights, A Legal and Arbitral Analysis, 71 (BNA Books, 1986).

The way arbitrators have evaluated rules prohibiting smoking, in light of the societal reevaluation of the factual predicate for banning or restricting smoking, illustrates how arbitrators apply the principle that a rule must be "reasonable." Arbitrators generally agree that management has the right to establish reasonable rules restricting or banning smoking, absent contractual limitations.[312] A smoking ban was found reasonable where management received substantial input from employees, including union members.[313] A no-smoking rule was deemed unreasonable where there was no evidence that smoking had caused injury to health or property at the company.[314]

However, in the process of balancing the various interests, at least one arbitrator has recognized the pain to addicts deprived of tobacco and found arbitrary and capricious a rule prohibiting smoking outdoors.[315] Where evidence is produced establishing the dangers of second-hand smoke, arbitrators have been willing to recognize a legitimate managerial interest in the prohibition of smoking as a safety concern.[316] Some arbitrators see the nexus between employee health and passive smoke as so well established that specific proof of harmful effects on health is not required to show the rule's reasonableness.[317]

Arbitrators are divided on whether smoking is a working condition that should be bargained for or that constitutes a past practice.[318] In one case, a longstanding practice of allowing smoking inside the plant made a new rule prohibiting smoking unreasonable.[319] An alternative view is that recent information regarding the harmful effects of smoke constitute a changed circumstance that makes an otherwise binding past practice no longer viable.[320]

---

[312]Peterson, "No Smoking! The Arbitration of Smoking Restricting Policies," Disp. Resol. J., 49 (Jan., 1995).

[313]Methodist Hosp., 91 LA 969 (Reynolds, 1988).

[314]Tokheim Corp., 96 LA 122 (Cox, 1990). See also Cross Oil & Ref. of Ark., 104 LA 757 (Gordon, 1995). In that case a refinery announced a new policy banning the use of any type of tobacco product on company time and provided for graduated penalties up to discharge for the third offense. Smoking had always been allowed at the facility, but had been limited to five outdoor areas for at least 20 years. The arbitrator sustained the grievance on the basis that the company had a long-established smoking practice and the company's affirmative obligation under the contract to provide for the health and safety of employees could not be invoked absent objective evidence of an abnormally dangerous condition.

[315]Honeywell, Inc., 92 LA 181 (Lennard, 1989).

[316]Central Tel. Co. of Nev., 92 LA 390 (Leventhal, 1990) (When an employer is on notice that a harmful toxic agent is present in the workplace, it is obliged to take immediate steps to eliminate that substance.). Wyandot, Inc., 92 LA 457 (Imundo, 1989) (smoking is a privilege that can be lifted when the health of co-workers is at stake; "smoking is a health hazard and a ban on smoking is a positive factor in maintaining a healthy workplace").

[317]Peterson, "No Smoking! The Arbitration of Smoking Restricting Policies," Disp. Resol. J., 47 (Jan., 1995).

[318]Id. at 49.

[319]Basler Elect. Co., 90-2 ARB ¶ 8354 (Caineswright, 1990).

[320]Lake County Sch. Bd., 93 LA 1103 (Bairstow, 1989). See also Dayton Newspapers, 91 LA 201 (Kindig, 1988) (no evidence that smoking in the workplace was a binding past practice).

*2. Consistency With Collective Bargaining Agreement.* If the employer makes a rule that violates or conflicts with the negotiated agreement, the employer may breach its duty to bargain.[321] In one case, the employer implemented a rule requiring employees to smoke only at lunch and break times, and only in designated areas outside the plants, even though smoking had been a negotiated working condition from 1947 to January 1, 1994. The arbitrator noted that specific provisions of the agreement permitted smoking in designated places at specified times and had been consistently interpreted over time. He held that management's responsibility in ensuring employees a safe and sanitary work environment is subject to compliance with the bargaining agreement and the law.[322] Similarly, where the parties' agreement articulated a smoking policy which had been in effect since 1978, the employer was not permitted to unilaterally adopt an overall policy creating a companywide smoke-free operation.[323]

Some collective bargaining agreements specifically require negotiating rules relating to working conditions, wages, and other benefits. In those cases the employer must negotiate with union representatives prior to implementing a new rule. In one case, the arbitrator recognized the propriety of a no-smoking policy where there was a recognized fire hazard, but suspended implementation of the policy for 2 weeks and required at least one good faith discussion of the policy with the shop committee as required by the contract.[324] In another case, the union challenged the company's right to promulgate additional details to existing work rules regarding wearing apparel. The union contended the company failed to bargain over new required uniforms and the method of paying for them. The arbitrator recognized management's right to promulgate work rules under such constraints as reasonableness, consistent application, and adequate discussion. However, he found that once the rules become a subject of mutual agreement, specific bargaining and agreement are required to alter them. He ruled that payment for the uniforms was a unilateral change in negotiated employees' wages.[325]

*3. Employee Notice of Rules.* Even if the arbitrator finds that a rule complies with the collective bargaining agreement and is for a lawful objective, the arbitrator may find the employees or the union were not adequately notified of the rule or the consequences of a

---

[321]See Central Tel. Co. of Va., 68 LA 957, 961 (Whyte, 1977) (management precluded from implementing attendance policy that did not excuse sickness or on-the-job injury where parties' agreement recognized such excused absences); Electrical Repair Serv. Co., 67 LA 173, 178 (Towers, 1976); Hill & Sinicropi, Management Rights, A Legal and Arbitral Analysis, 79 (BNA Books, 1986).

[322]PMI Food Equip. Group, 103 LA 547, 549 (Imundo, 1994).

[323]Hobart Corp., 103 LA 1089 (Millious, 1994).

[324]Acorn Bldg. Components, Inc., 89-1 ARB ¶ 8243 (Roumell, 1988).

[325]Mrs. Baird's Bakeries, Inc., 68 LA 773, 776 (Fox, 1977).

violation. While arbitrators agree that the employer may change plant rules to meet changed circumstances, the employer must provide sufficient notice to employees and the union. A rule will not be enforceable unless the employee has either actual or constructive notice of that rule.[326] Likewise, management must provide written notice of any changes to existing rules.

If a rule has not been adequately disseminated, disciplinary action may be set aside.[327] Actual notice may be achieved by a number of means, including orientation at the time of hire, bulletin board postings, payroll stuffers, employee meetings, or mailers.[328] There may be an implied obligation to read and be bound by rules posted or set forth in a rule book or handbook.[329] A collective bargaining agreement may set forth a required method of disseminating a new rule. In one case, direct notification was inadequate because the contract required that a copy be provided to the union's official representative and posted on the bulletin board.[330]

a. Unwritten and Unpublished Rules.   Arbitrators have recognized that it is not possible to specifically anticipate and prohibit all unacceptable conduct. Some conduct is so clearly harmful to the workplace that a reasonable employee would recognize it as prohibited. As one arbitrator stated: "Some forms of misconduct are so obviously wrong and unendurable that employees must know that they cannot retain their jobs if they do those things."[331] In a less serious case, the grievant who indicated he had loaded a basket of parts onto a truck but actually left them sitting on the dock was discharged for carelessness. Upholding the discharge, the arbitrator stated that even though there is no rule specifically prohibiting carelessness, conduct that is commonly recognized as an infraction may warrant discipline.[332]

Logical extensions of written rules or policies have also been permitted. For example, where the employer's policy prohibited sexual

---

[326]Labor and Employment Arbitration, Bornstein & Gosline, eds., 19-8 (Matthew Bender & Co., 1991). See also Delta Air Lines, 89 LA 408 (Kahn, 1987).

[327]See Iowa-Ill. Gas & Elec. Co., 84 LA 868 (Keefe, 1985) (rule applying greater penalty was not publicized); Great Plains Bag Corp., 83 LA 1281 (Laybourne, 1984) (rule requiring employees to be at work station at starting time unenforced for four years); Bekins Moving & Storage Co., 82 LA 642 (Daughton, 1984) (dissemination of rules not proven).

[328]In at least one instance, an arbitrator found that including notice with employee paychecks was not a sufficient method of dissemination. The employer was required to either publish clear rule or republish existing rule where practice had been to allow employees to go to their vehicles after punching in. Bayshore Concrete Prods. Co., 92 LA 311 (Hart, 1989).

[329]Labor and Employment Arbitration, Bornstein & Gosline, eds, 19-8 (Matthew Bender & Co., 1991).

[330]Bayshore Concrete Prods. Co., 92 LA 311 (Hart, 1989).

[331]Babcock & Wilcox, 102 LA 104, 107 (Nicholas, 1994). Accord Lockheed Eng'g Sciences Co., 101 LA 1161, 1164 (Neas, 1993). See also Burlington N. R.R., 90 LA 585 (Goldstein, 1987), where grievant's threat to kill company president violated implied covenants of good faith and fair dealing in individual employment contract.

[332]Genie Co., 97 LA 542 (Dworkin, 1991).

harassment, the rule logically extended to employees of the company's customers.[333]

When rules cannot be written down, the importance of applying the rule consistently is even more important. One arbitrator acknowledged common sense would dictate grievant's unsafe actions violated safety policies of the company, but reversed the discharge. The arbitrator indicated the discharge was not sustained because the policy had been inconsistently applied and the company had not made it clear that progressive discipline steps could be modified based on the severity of the infraction.[334] In another case, an employer's unwritten, unpublished, and uncommunicated policy that required employees returning from disability leave to submit to a drug test was refused enforcement.[335]

Where an established practice exists, management cannot use an unwritten, conflicting rule to justify disciplinary action. For example, an employee was discharged for failing to remove an offensive message from his hard hat. The arbitrator found just cause lacking because no rule existed about writing on hard hats, there was an established practice of allowing writing on hard hats, and co-workers who wore offensive messages were not disciplined.[336]

b. Clarity of Rules.   A rule must clearly and unambiguously establish the scope of prohibited conduct, as well as the consequences of violations, in order to be enforceable. Work rules may not be enforced if they are vague.[337] Arbitrary rules have also been overturned, as have overbroad rules.[338] Arbitrators have found rules to be unreasonable where they provide no clear guidance as to what is expected of employees.[339] For example, an arbitrator found a rule requiring employees to complete accident and safety reports "in a timely manner" to be impermissibly vague.[340]

Likewise, a rule requiring employees to perform their duties in a professional and workmanlike manner failed to delineate any prohibited conduct. The employee's discharge for an offensive answering machine message was without just cause because the employee had no notice that his conduct was prohibited.[341]

---

[333]Plain Dealer Publ'g Co., 99 LA 969 (Fullmer, 1992).

[334]Chase Brass & Copper Co., 90 LA 916, 922 (Bressler, 1988).

[335]Donaldson Mining Co., 91 LA 471 (Zobrak, 1988).

[336]Armco, Inc., 93 LA 561 (Strongin, 1989).

[337]Foote & Davies, 88 LA 125 (Wahl, 1986) (no just cause to discharge employee for reporting to work under the influence of intoxicants where no enforceable policy on blood testing, and employee worked satisfactorily for over an hour).

[338]See Maple Meadow Mining, 90 LA 873 (Phelan, 1988).

[339]See TransWorld Airlines 93 LA 167 (Eisler, 1989) (rule requiring performance of duties in professional and workmanlike manner provided no clear guidance as to what is expected of employees); Hoover Co., 77 LA 1287, 1290 (Strasshofer, 1982) ("a reasonable rule must be one which the employees can understand and comply with").

[340]Ideal Elec. Co., 98 LA 410 (Heekin, 1991). See also PMC Specialties Group, 97 LA 444 (High, 1991).

[341]TransWorld Airlines, 93 LA 167 (Eisler, 1989).

Rules that fail to differentiate between prohibited conduct and acceptable conduct are usually found to be unreasonable. For example, where an alcohol-use rule failed to differentiate between regular alcoholic beverages and medicines containing alcohol, the employer improperly discharged an employee who had a blood level of 0.27 from ingestion of cough medicine.[342] The arbitrator found no evidence that the parties intended to include medicines containing alcohol within the scope of the rule.[343] In a comparable case, the arbitrator found that differentiating between prohibited and company-approved reading material was difficult and an unreasonable application of the "management rights clause."[344]

## B. Consistency of Enforcement

Arbitrators recognize that proper discipline requires consistency in rule enforcement.[345] Consistency requires that rules be enforced evenhandedly and without discrimination. The level of discipline imposed must be based upon the nature of the offense and the disciplinary record of the employee. Consistency in applying a rule is also an important factor in determining whether employees have notice of the rule. Even a state law regarding the conduct may be insufficient where the employer has failed to consistently apply the rule. For example, an employee's suspension for failing to wear a seat belt on the job was overturned despite the fact that state law required all motor vehicle drivers and passengers to wear seat belts.[346] The employer did not consistently enforce the safety rule requiring seat belt use, and the arbitrator found the inconsistent application of the employer's rules inequitable.[347]

When the employer administers discipline in a consistent manner, employees have a clear understanding of the employer's expectations and the consequences of failing to meet them. Consistency of enforcement requires the following:

(1) The rule must be applied on a uniform basis to all employees subject to the rule.

(2) If an employer has been lax in enforcing a rule, adequate notice must be given to employees before the employer may begin stricter enforcement.

---

[342]Jefferson Smurfit Corp., 100 LA 1033 (Witney, 1993).

[343]Id.

[344]Jones Operation & Maintenance Co., 97 LA 670 (Statham, 1991). See also RMS Techs., Inc., 94 LA 297 (Nichols, 1990) (employer failed to provide objective standards for its prohibition against "racial, ethnic, or sexist" printed matter and took no action against other individuals who had brought in similar material); Hoover Co., 77 LA 1287, 1290 (Strasshofer, 1982).

[345]See United States Steel Corp., 40 LA 598 (Seitz, 1963) (suspicious circumstances did not prove wrongdoing); Wertheimer Bag Co., 33 LA 694 (Maggs, 1959).

[346]Montcalm County Rd. Comm'n, 94 LA 45 (Daniel, 1989).

[347]Id.

(3) All employees who engage in similar acts of misconduct should receive the same degree of discipline unless some reasonable basis exists for different treatment.

Each will be discussed below.

*1. Uniform Enforcement.*   Arbitrators find just cause lacking where the evidence shows the employer has been inconsistent or discriminatory in its enforcement of the work rules. For example, an arbitrator refused to uphold the discharge of an employee who reported for work under the influence of alcohol where the evidence showed that other employees who engaged in the same conduct were not punished.[348] In another case, an arbitrator set aside the discharge of an employee involved in a firearms transaction because the other employee involved in the transaction was not disciplined.[349]

Inconsistent treatment will not be found where the cases being compared are dissimilar. An employee of a telephone company was terminated for giving confidential information from a customer's account to a third party, for use in a custody fight. Another employee who had listened into conversations between her ex-husband and his girlfriend was disciplined but not terminated. The arbitrator held the discharge was for just cause because giving out confidential information for third-party use against a customer was a more serious offense than eavesdropping.[350]

*2. Lax Enforcement.*   When the employer establishes a rule but is lax in its enforcement, the implication is that it condones the conduct. Employees may be lulled into a false sense of security. Therefore, an employer may not suddenly begin enforcing a rule without giving clear notice of this intent to employees.[351] In one case, an employer's tolerance of the misconduct of an alcoholic employee over a 10-year period led the employee to believe his conduct was sanctioned by management.[352]

In another case, the failure to post a new rule that was at variance with a longstanding practice was a major consideration in overturning the discharge of a 30-year employee who was disciplined for leaving his work station without permission. The arbitrator said:

---

[348]Commercial Warehouse Co., 100 LA 247, 251 (Woolf, 1992).

[349]Southern Cal. Rapid Transit Dist., 82 LA 126 (Draznin, 1983). See also Wagner Castings Co., 89-2 ARB ¶ 8577 (Talent, 1989) (employer may not discharge only one of two employees who participated in altering a document submitted to company to support a request for sick leave).

[350]United Tel. Co. of Kan., 100 LA 541, 547 (Pratte, 1993).

[351]Champion Spark Plug Co., 93 LA 1277, 1284 (Dobry, 1989) (threatening a supervisor); Southern Cal. Edison, 89 LA 1129 (Collins, 1987) (falsification of records); Great Plains Bag Corp., 83 LA 1281, 1285 (Laybourne, 1984) (tardiness); Western Paper Box, 81 LA 917, 921 (Concepcion, 1983) (drinking alcoholic beverages on employer's premises).

[352]Eaton Corp., 99 LA 331, 336 (Lewis, 1992).

[T]he rules were never posted. True, [grievant] may have been apprised of the rule in question, but when management chooses to apply a rule rigidly to the point of meeting violation with discharge there should be no doubt in the minds of the employees and those enforcing the rules about the nature of the rule. This precaution had not been taken by management. The shortcoming is aggravated when one considers that the rule represented a change of a practice which had existed for many years. Sound industrial policy dictates that abrupt changes in rules should be accompanied by a gradual educational process.[353]

In order to begin to enforce a rule after a period of lax enforcement, an employer must provide clear notice to employees and the union.[354] Although some arbitrators have concluded that oral notice to union officials is adequate to advise employees of a change in enforcement policies,[355] the preferred practice is to provide clear and unambiguous written notice to the employees.[356] Similarly, an employer must notify employees when it decides to change or expand the scope of a policy that relates to discipline.[357]

The employer must have actual or constructive knowledge that a rule is being violated in order to be charged with lax enforcement. Testimony that certain conduct has occurred without punishment only begs the question. The fact that some employees have engaged in misconduct and have not been punished is not significant unless the employer had knowledge of the transgressions.[358] Arbitrators impute laxness of rule enforcement to the employer through the actions of its supervisors.[359] In cases where the misconduct is blatant, the employer may be presumed to have knowledge, even if it maintains it was unaware of the misconduct. As with any argument of constructive knowledge, the evidence must show a reasonably alert employer should have known of the conduct.[360]

Arbitrators consider whether the employer has condoned a work-rule violation in fashioning a remedy. For example, one arbitrator

---

[353]Joy Mfg. Co., 6 LA 430, 434 (Healy, 1946). See also Bethlehem Steel Co., 12 LA 167 (Seleckman, 1949).

[354]Genest-Midwest, Inc., 67-2 ARB ¶ 8569 (Allman, 1967) (employer owes duty to employees to put them on notice when it intends to impose discipline for behavior that has previously been tolerated); Fairbanks Morse, Inc., 47 LA 224 (Fisher, 1966) (an employer may engage in stricter enforcement of its absenteeism policy after notice is posted and the union is notified of the change).

[355]HBI Automotive Glass, 97 LA 121, 128 (Richard, 1991) (union officials advised in meeting that any future threats to supervisors would result in severe discipline).

[356]Engelhard Kaolin Corp., 96 LA 563, 566 (Galambos, 1990) (implementation of new substance abuse policy that clearly stated that old policy was discontinued).

[357]Kansas Power & Light Co., 87 LA 867, 872 (Belcher, 1986) (employer sought to expand "no-fault" absentee policy to include absences due to illness).

[358]Peabody Coal Co., 92 LA 658, 660 (Hewitt, 1989).

[359]General Tel. Co. of Cal., 86 LA 138 (Maxwell, 1985). See Eberele Tanning Co., 71 LA 302 (Sloan, 1978); Metro Contract Serv., Inc., 68 LA 1048 (Moore, 1977); Misco Precision Casting Co., 40 LA 87 (Dworkin, 1962).

[360]The concept of constructive knowledge is often encountered in sexual harassment cases. See Robinson v. Jacksonville Shipyards, Inc., 760 F.Supp. 1486 (M.D. Fla., 1991).

found that the employer's tolerance of a practice that was contrary to its rules because it derived a substantial financial benefit from that practice, constituted condonation of the work-rule violation, and provided an adequate foundation for reversal of a 5-day layoff.[361] Similarly, another arbitrator found that an employer's enforcement of a work rule only when a loss accrued to the employer as a result of the violation rose to the level of condonation.[362] The arbitrator wrote:

> The Company cannot, over a long period of time, condone a violation of a plant rule and then impose discipline when this known violation results in loss and inconvenience to the Company. * * * It cannot now take the position that it can sit back and know that the rule is consistently violated, and only impose punishment when some loss results to the Company.[363]

Along the same lines, another arbitrator refused to sustain a 1-day layoff of an employee who engaged in "horseplay" by throwing wrapped waste glass in the direction of a trash can where it was shown that such a work-rule violation was a recurring one that was known to management and never acted upon.[364] Furthermore, the failure of a supervisor to warn an employee of a work-rule violation when the supervisor caught the employee violating the rule on previous occasions was viewed as a mitigating factor against discharging the employee.[365]

*3. Unequal or Discriminatory Enforcement.* The penalty selected must be consisted with other penalties imposed for similar offenses, under similar circumstances. Arbitrators analyze situations where employees receive different disciplinary treatment for similar offenses by examining whether the employer had a valid reason for treating employees differently.[366] As stated by one arbitrator, "no departure from the consistent or uniform treatment of employees [occurs] merely because of variations in discipline reasonably appropriate to the variations in circumstances." Where disciplinary distinctions cannot be accounted for, just cause is lacking. For example, discharge for fighting was not appropriate where other employees guilty of fighting received only suspensions.[367]

---

[361]Alan Wood Steel Co., 3 LA 557 (Brandschain, Widdoes & Irvin, 1946).

[362]Allis-Chalmers Mfg. Co., 8 LA 177 (Kelliher, 1947). See also Norwich Pharmacal Co., 5 LA 536 (Shipman, 1946).

[363]Allis-Chalmers, at 180.

[364]Bay City Shovels, Inc., 20 LA 342 (Ryder, 1953).

[365]General Tel. Co., 86 LA 138 (Maxwell, 1985).

[366]For discussion on discrimination, see Chapter 13.

[367]Alan Wood Steel Co., 21 LA 843, 849 (Short, 1954). See also B-Line Sys., 94 LA 1047 (Fowler, 1990).

The primary factors that can be used to justify different treatment are differing circumstances and past disciplinary records of employees.[368] In one case, the discharge of an employee convicted of felony—aggravated drug trafficking—was distinguished from convictions for other felonies. The discharge was upheld because none of the other felonies was of a "heinous" nature and the employer had a consistent practice of not allowing drug traffickers to work in the plant.[369]

A range of disciplinary actions may apply to a certain offense, depending upon the degree of fault. For example, discharge for sexual harassment was proper because the grievant's acts were more serious than those of other employees who were merely suspended or demoted for sexual harassment.[370] In a case involving a sheriff's department, the arbitrator upheld a 3-day suspension for a deputy who damaged a patrol car, even though other deputies had been in automobile accidents without discipline. The arbitrator found the suspension was justified because of the greater degree of fault attributable to the grievant.[371]

In some circumstances, the department in which an employee works may result in a different level of discipline. The discharge of a press punch operator for drinking alcoholic beverages was upheld even though employees in other departments had received lesser discipline for the same offense. The arbitrator reasoned the discharged employee's misconduct was more serious because the punch press operator's position was one of the most dangerous jobs in the industry.[372]

Some arbitrators hold employees who act as union officials to a higher standard of responsibility than other employees. One such case involved a demonstration by employees who illegally occupied the district office of the employer. The arbitrator upheld the harsher penalties imposed on the union officials who participated in the demonstration, on the basis that they had an obligation to refrain from engaging in illegal behavior.[373] In another case, an arbitrator held that a union steward has a higher level of responsibility for following the collective bargaining agreement and can be disciplined when his conduct clearly violates the agreement.[374]

Arbitrators uphold differences in penalties based upon the length of an employee's service with the employer. Arbitrators generally

---

[368]For a discussion on the use of prior discipline in imposing progressive discipline, see section on Progressive Discipline earlier in this chapter.

[369]Standard Oil Co., 89 LA 1155, 1158–59 (Feldman, 1987).

[370]Fry's Food Stores of Ariz., 99 LA 1161 (Hogler, 1992). See also Price Bros. Co., 74 LA 748 (Laybourne, 1980) (discharge of grievant for his participation in a wildcat strike upheld even though other participants were not disciplined).

[371]Ramsey County Sheriff's Dep't, 100 LA 208 (Gallagher, 1992).

[372]Jehl Cooperage Co., 75 LA 901 (Odom, 1980).

[373]New Jersey Bell Tel. Co., 77 LA 1038 (Wolff, 1981).

[374]E. A. Norris Plumbing Co., 90 LA 462 (Christopher, 1987).

believe that an employee with long, satisfactory service deserves some additional consideration, especially if the penalty is discharge. In a case where an employer failed to give proper consideration to an employee with 20 years of service, a good record, and no discipline, the discharge was overturned.[375] Conversely, a short term of employment is sometimes viewed as a reason for refusing to mitigate a disciplinary penalty. The employer is not always required to consider length of service in deciding on penalties. Discharge is still appropriate for egregious misconduct, even where the employee has a lengthy record of satisfactory employment. For example, where an employee patronized a prostitute in a company vehicle and was convicted on a misdemeanor charge, discharge was upheld despite 20 years' service.[376]

## C. Appropriateness of the Penalty

Collective bargaining agreements usually do not limit the arbitrator's power to formulate remedies in discharge or discipline cases. The arbitrator, therefore, has the authority to order the remedy that he or she deems appropriate.[377] Most arbitrators will evaluate the discipline imposed by the employer to determine whether the penalty (or corrective measure) is excessive. Discipline may be considered excessive if it is disproportionate to the degree of the offense, if it is out of step with the principles of progressive discipline, if it is punitive rather than corrective, or if mitigating circumstances were ignored.

A few collective bargaining agreements specifically limit the arbitrator's authority to alter the discipline imposed by the employer. For example, one collective bargaining agreement provided that, with regard to discharges, "the arbitrator shall have jurisdiction only to determine if the employee committed the offense for which he was discharged." The arbitrator concluded that this language meant that an arbitrator was prohibited from considering the appropriateness of the penalty and from reducing or modifying it.[378] Absent contractual

---

[375]Ohio Dep't of Youth Servs., 97 LA 734, 738 (Bittel, 1991). See also Ball-Icon Glass Packaging Corp., 98 LA 1, 4–5 (Volz, 1991) (discharge of employee who struck supervisor set aside based, in part, on good work record of 20 years); but see Carolina Tel. & Tel., 97 LA 653 (Nolan, 1991) (discharge of 22-year employee for absenteeism upheld).

[376]Indiana Bell Tel. Co., 99 LA 756 (Goldstein, 1992). See also Chapter 12 on employment history.

[377]Minute Maid Co. v. Citrus Workers Local 444, 42 LA 864, 56 LRRM 2095 (5th Cir. 1964) (order of reinstatement with back pay enforceable even though contract did not expressly provide for back pay as a remedy); Mississippi Aluminum Corp., 27 LA 625 (Reynard, 1956).

[378]Consumers Oil Co., 77 LA 141 (Hill, 1981). See also Florida Wire & Cable Co., 63 LA 335 (1974); Sohio Chem. Co., 44 LA 624 (Witney, 1964) (contract provided that arbitrator may not award "compensation, damages, or other redress to any employee," but arbitrator held that he had authority to order employees who had improperly traded jobs to return to pretrade jobs).

limitations on the arbitrator's remedial authority, the arbitrator evaluates the appropriateness of the discipline imposed. As one arbitrator commented, "we are not brought in to try the facts, but to review the employer's judgment."[379]

Most arbitrators hesitate to reduce the penalty imposed by the employer if the penalty is consistent with that imposed in similar cases and there are no elements of discrimination, unfairness, or capricious or arbitrary action. But, as one arbitrator stated, "the examination of the penalty as it relates to the offense is an element of the just cause concept."[380]

In circumstances in which the parties have specifically negotiated that discharge is to be the penalty for designated conduct, the arbitrator is bound by the parties' contract and generally cannot deviate from the parties' bargain.[381] In reviewing other disciplinary matters, however, an arbitrator is free to review the penalty imposed by the company. As described by one arbitrator:

> In disciplinary matters, a penalty that is markedly too harsh for the offense is unreasonable and an abuse of managerial discretion. A penalty that flows from incomplete analysis of both the misconduct and the individual employee is arbitrary.[382]

Arbitrators have consistently held that an excessively harsh penalty for misconduct violates the requirement that discipline be imposed only for just cause. "Inherent in the right to discipline for just cause is the requirement that the form and degree of discipline be reasonable both as regards the basis for discipline and the penalties assessed * * * ."[383] In this respect, one arbitrator wrote:

> [C]onsideration has to be given to whether a lesser penalty will serve the employer's purpose, especially since discharge * * * makes it difficult, if not impossible, for a person to obtain other employment. Where the employee has a long record of service without any previous discipline, a lesser, but nonetheless severe, punishment will ordinarily preclude repetition of the offense and will adequately serve notice on other employees that dishonesty will not be tolerated.[384]

---

[379]Ross, "The Criminal Law and Industrial Discipline as Complex Systems: Some Comparative Observations: Discussion, Labor Arbitration: Perspectives and Problems," Proceedings of the 17th Annual Meeting, National Academy of Arbitrators, M.L. Kahn, ed., 144, 148–49 (BNA Books, 1964).

[380]Inland Container Corp., 91 LA 544, 548 (Howell, 1988). But see Stockham Pipe Fitting Co., 1 LA 160, 162 (McCoy, 1945).

[381]See Chapter 12.

[382]Clow Water Sys. Co., 102 LA 377, 380 (Dworkin, 1994).

[383]Merchants Fast Motor Lines, 103 LA 396, 399 (Shieber, 1994), citing Clow Water Sys. Co., 102 LA 377 (Dworkin, 1994).

[384]Yellow Freight Sys., Inc., 103 LA 731, 737 (Stix, 1994).

Arbitral power to modify discipline imposed by an employer was expressly confirmed by the Supreme Court in *Paperworkers v. Misco, Inc.*[385]

Beyond basic principles of progressive discipline, arbitrators believe the degree of discipline should be proportionate to the seriousness of the offense.[386] Stated another way, the penalty must "fit the crime."[387] In 1947, an arbitrator considering the reasonableness of discharging an otherwise good worker who "appropriated approximately one hour of company time for loafing and personal business" found the penalty did not "fit the crime" and observed:

> [P]erhaps the best [an arbitrator] can do is to decide what reasonable man, mindful of the habits and customs of industrial life and of the standards of justice and fair dealing prevalent in the community ought to have done under similar circumstances and in that light decide whether the conduct of the discharged employee was defensible and the disciplinary penalty just.[388]

Fifty years later there is still no set formula that arbitrators use to determine whether the penalty chosen by the employer should be upheld or rejected. Arbitrators consider a variety of factors in determining whether a penalty is excessive. Several of the most frequently cited considerations are the employee's intent and attitude, the likelihood of rehabilitation or repetition, emotional distress, and the employer's degree of fault.

When assessing whether discipline is excessive, arbitrators often consider the attitude of the employee. An admission of wrongdoing, an expression of remorse, or an offer of apology may lead to a finding that leniency was appropriate.[389] By contrast, when an employee avoids responsibility for his actions, the arbitrator may be less inclined to overturn a serious penalty. In *BHP Petroleum*, for example, the arbitrator upheld a discharge, citing, among other factors, the employee's tendency to blame others for his shortcomings.[390]

Similarly, the arbitrator may consider the willful or intentional nature of the misconduct in evaluating the appropriate degree of

---

[385]Paperworkers v. Misco, Inc., 484 U.S. 29, 126 LRRM 3113 (1987). See generally Chapter 14.

[386]Columbia Aluminum Co., 102 LA 274 (Henner, 1993). See also Appeal of Bruno, 31 Ed. Dep't Rep. 503 (1993) (discipline imposed upon tenured teacher must be proportionate to the offense).

[387]Lockheed Eng'g Co., 101 LA 1161 (Neas, 1993); City of Bridgeport, 101 LA 295 (Cain, 1993); PYA/Monarch Food Serv., 94 LA 575, 578–80 (Smith, 1990); Huntington Chair Corp., 24 LA 491 (McCoy, 1955).

[388]Riley Stoker Corp., 7 LA 764, 767 (Platt, 1947).

[389]King Soopers, Inc., 101 LA 107 (Snider, 1993); Frontier Airlines, Inc., 61 LA 304, 314, 319 (Kahn, 1973).

[390]102 LA 321 (Najita, 1993). See also lockheed Missiles & Space Co., 101 LA 804 (Gentile, 1993); King Soopers, Inc., 101 LA 107 (Snider, 1993); City of St. Paul, Minn., 101 LA 265 (Neigh, 1993). See also Appeal of BOCES, 32 Ed. Dep't Rep. 358 (1992); Communications Workers v. South W. Elec., 882 F.2d 467 (10th Cir., 1989).

discipline.[391] Discharge of an employee for breach of on-call obligations was held to be excessive when the employee's actions were merely negligent, created no demonstrable harm to the employer, and did not defy authority or undermine the employer-employee relationship.[392] In another case, in upholding a 3-day suspension, the arbitrator was influenced by the fact that the employee's conduct was a "fixed and premeditated intention" not to participate in an assignment that other employees were willing to perform.[393] Even where conduct was willful, however, the penalty may be excessive. In one case, a 4-week suspension was reduced to a 10-day suspension where a relief ticket agent failed to follow security procedures by conducting a passenger search, but previously had advised the manager that he would not conduct the search unless a law enforcement official was nearby, and the manager's answer had not been unresponsive.[394]

If rehabilitation is likely to be successful, or if treatment for a causative disorder is realistic, an arbitrator may reduce discipline. In one case a police officer who had been convicted of off-duty criminal sexual conduct with a 14-year-old girl was reinstated because he was remorseful and cooperative in treatment and evidence established a good prognosis for controlling his behavior.[395]

In another case the arbitrator held that the presence and possibility of recovery from the disease of alcoholism may be considered as mitigating factors and "properly taken into account in determining whether a penalty imposed for misconduct is appropriate."[396] Under the facts of that case, however, the arbitrator held that mitigation was inappropriate where the long-term employee's on-duty intoxication causing vehicular damage constituted serious misconduct, the employee had been urged for 5 years to seek treatment but did so only half-heartedly, and the evidence regarding prospects of the employee's rehabilitation was not persuasive.

Arbitrators also may reduce penalties if the employee's conduct was an isolated incident in an otherwise good work record. An arbitrator reduced a discharge to a 1-month suspension, finding that infractions that were isolated, off-duty occurrences without indication of recurrence did not warrant discharge. The arbitrator also noted that it was unlikely that the employee would repeat the misconduct.[397] By

---

[391]Anchorage Hilton Hotel, 102 LA 55 (Landeau, 1993); Western Auto Supply, 71 LA 710 (Ross, 1978).

[392]City of St. Joseph, 102 LA 179 (Gordon, 1993). See also Safeway Stores, Inc., 65 LA 1177 (J. Smith, 1975).

[393]Prindle Int'l, 61 LA 613 (Heilbrun, 1973). See also Glenn L. Martin Co., 6 LA 500 (Brecht, 1947) (employee reinstated where there was no intent to defy plant rule against running).

[394]Frontier Airlines, Inc., 61 LA 304 (Kahn, 1973).

[395]City of St. Paul, Minn., 101 LA 265 (Neigh, 1993). See also EG & G Mound Applied Techs., 102 LA 60 (Heekin, 1993).

[396]New Jersey Bell Tel. Co., 89-2 ARB ¶ 8381 (Nicolau, 1988). See also Lockheed Missiles & Space Co., 101 LA 804 (Gentile, 1993).

[397]City of Napa, 102 LA 590 (Knowlton, 1994).

contrast, another arbitrator upheld the discharge of the local union's "founding father" who had committed repeated violations, clashed with several customers, and "had shown no promise of responding favorably" to corrective discipline.[398]

Arbitrators may view an employee's extreme emotional distress at the time of the misconduct as a mitigating factor in the review of harsh discipline. A panel of arbitrators found that a 45-day suspension of an employee who processed and granted benefits for her own son was excessive in consideration of the fact that she had a good 10-year employment history, had relied upon her supervisor to review the form, and was under emotional distress at the time she processed the form.[399] Similarly, an arbitrator found that discipline was unwarranted for a station agent who allowed a passenger to board a plane without a search when the oversight occurred immediately after and was a direct consequence of the employee's involvement in a near-accident.[400]

If management also was at fault in the conduct leading to discipline, the arbitrator may find that a reduction of penalty is appropriate. In concluding that a school-bus driver had been improperly suspended for 10 days for leaving unruly students at a bus stop, the arbitrator found that the driver had brought the students' discipline problem to management's attention on several occasions but management had taken no action.[401] Similarly, an arbitrator held that discharge was too severe for an employee who had been involved in an on-premises, work-related fight immediately after working hours. The employer had known of the intended fight but merely alerted security and police and "sat and waited for all of the incidents to take place and then stepped in and imposed its discipline" instead of acting in the interest of good labor-management relations to avoid rather than contain the incident. The arbitrator held that, although discharge was justified, the fact that the company "was not entirely without blame in the incident" led him to award reinstatement without back pay.[402]

## D. *Fair Administration of the Progressive Discipline System*

Arbitrators have looked at certain "fairness" issues in the administration of the progressive discipline system when determining whether to uphold a particular discipline. While there is no unanimity

[398]Arden Farms Co., 45 LA 1124 (Tsukiyama, 1965).

[399]City of Bridgeport, 101 LA 295 (Cain, 1993).

[400]Frontier Airlines, Inc., 61 LA 304, 314, 319 (Kahn, 1973).

[401]Utica Community Schs., 64 LA 346 (Roumell, 1975). See also Chrysler Corp., 64 LA 700 (Alexander, 1975).

[402]Zinsco Elec. Prods., 65 LA 487 (Erbs, 1975).

on these specific fairness issues, they are important for the advocate or advisor to consider. These issues are the effect of passage of time, the accumulation of dissimilar offenses, challenges to prior discipline, and managerial discretion.

A question that occurs with some regularity is: How far back into an employee's record can an employer go in attempting to support the imposition of more severe forms of discipline? There is no clear-cut answer. Often, the employer's rules and the collective bargaining agreement are silent on this issue. In general terms, evidence of prior discipline is excluded when it took place so long ago as to be of little value in determining whether the current discipline was for just cause. The more serious the offense, the longer it will have an effect on future discipline.

Some collective bargaining agreements specifically address this issue by the use of a "wash out" clause, which prohibits using prior discipline as the basis for progressive discipline after a certain period has elapsed. However, even if no limitation is expressed in the collective bargaining agreement, arbitrators will generally recognize the decreasing impact of past offenses over time.[403]

A factor that is considered important by some arbitrators is the length of time an employee has had a discipline-free record.[404] A discipline-free record for a lengthy period of time is evidence the employee is attempting to comply with rules and is capable of being rehabilitated. In one case, an arbitrator held that three instances of discipline over a six-year period showed the employee was responding affirmatively to progressive discipline and therefore discharge for the fourth offense was not for just cause.[405]

Since the purpose of progressive discipline is to put employees on notice of improper behavior in order to give them a chance to correct their behavior, it is clearly proper to increase the severity of discipline where the employee has previously committed the same offense. The question, however, is whether an employee who engages in various types of relatively minor misconduct should receive increasingly severe levels of discipline. In answering this question, arbitrators will, of course, consider the collective bargaining agreement and the employer's rules. The nature of the prior violations, the discipline imposed, and the employee's response to the discipline will also be considered.[406] The nature of the notice given by the prior disciplinary warnings can be an important factor in addressing this issue.[407]

---

[403]Volz & Goggin, eds., Elkouri & Elkouri, How Arbitration Works, 5th ed., 927–29 (BNA Books, 1997). But see Regents of the Univ. of Mich., 91-1 ARB ¶ 8280 (Sugarman, 1991), where discipline based on 3-year-old last-chance letter was upheld.

[404]Basin Elec. Power Coop., 91 LA 443, 447 (Jacobowski, 1988) (employer failed to give proper consideration to 2 ¼-year period between occurrences). See also Zack, Grievance Arbitration, 121 (Lexington Books, 1989).

[405]Iowa-Illinois Gas & Elec. Co., 87-1 ARB ¶ 8103 (Voltz, 1986).

[406]Essex Indus. Chems., 88 LA 991, 993 (Cluster, 1987).

[407]Maryland Jockey Club, 99 LA 1025, 1028 (Farwell, 1992).

In one case, a truck driver had been given a suspension for reporting to work several hours late. Five months later, he parked his truck and slept for 25 minutes without notifying his employer. The employer discharged him, contending that the discipline for tardiness put him on notice that he should not have slept in his truck without informing the dispatcher. The arbitrator disagreed and determined tardiness was not sufficiently related to sleeping on the job to justify escalation of the penalty.[408] By contrast, another arbitrator held that written warnings for absenteeism, coupled with a suspension for insubordination, could be used to support a discharge for excessive absenteeism.[409] It is fair to say that as violations accumulate, arbitrators are likely to uphold heavier penalties, including discharge.[410]

Unless an employee is discharged for one incident of very serious misconduct, the termination decision must be based at least partially on prior discipline. Evidence of both prior discipline and final misconduct are necessary.[411] The employer must show that the employee had notice of the consequences of continued misconduct and that a reasonable attempt was made toward rehabilitation through the use of progressive discipline. An employee may challenge the use of prior discipline by denying the misconduct it addresses. If the prior discipline could have been grieved and was not, belated attempts to challenge the discipline at a subsequent arbitration will not be credited by most arbitrators.[412] Even so, some arbitrators believe an employee is less likely to use the grievance procedure when there are no immediate economic consequences, and will permit prior discipline to be challenged. This is a minority view which must be consistent with negotiated time limits applicable to most grievance procedures and equitable principles.[413] If the employee did not have the right to grieve the prior disciplinary actions, and the employer is using them to support its discharge decision, the employee generally has the right to present evidence that will refute the allegations contained in the prior disciplinary actions.

How much discretion does an employer have in deciding exactly what discipline to impose in a specific situation? In some cases, the collective bargaining agreement or work rules specifically delineate the amount of discretion available to the employer. An employer is generally assumed to have some flexibility to address the factual distinctions in unique situations, provided the discipline is carried

---

[408]Lady Baltimore of Mo., Inc., 95 LA 452, 455 (Westbrook, 1990).

[409]Union Oil of Cal., 91 LA 1206, 1209 (Klein, 1988).

[410]Koven, Smith & Farwell, Just Cause: The Seven Tests, 2d ed., 414 (BNA Books, 1992).

[411]Bornstein & Gosline, "Evidence in Arbitration," Labor and Employment Arbitration, 5–26 (Matthew Bender, 1994).

[412]Kimberly-Clark Corp., 82 LA 1090, 1094 (Keenan, 1984). See also Volz & Goggin, eds., Elkouri & Elkouri, How Arbitration Works, 5th ed., 926–27 (BNA Books, 1997).

[413]Overhead Door Co., 70 LA 1299, 1302 (Dworkin, 1978).

out in a just and equitable manner and provided the employer's actions are reasonable.[414]

In some limited circumstances, an employer may properly determine that based upon an employee's responses to progressive discipline, rehabilitation is impossible. In this situation, the employee may be terminated before completing all the steps that would normally be followed. The employer's action, however, must not be contrary to established rules.[415]

---

[414]Delmarva Power & Light Co., 100 LA 457, 461 (DiLauro, 1992). For further discussion of consistency, see section entitled Consistency of Enforcement in this chapter.

[415]Pratt & Whitney Aircraft Group, 91 LA 1014, 1018 (Chandler, 1988).

# Chapter 3

# Attendance

## I. Absence as a Cause for Discipline

There are as many reasons for absences as there are workers. Whether discipline will be sustained depends largely on the unique facts of the case. Some employers use "no fault" attendance programs,[1] while other employers have more traditional systems. Consequently, it is not possible for even the most exhaustive study of absenteeism to result in a "rule book" that will allow practitioners to determine whether just cause for discipline exists in any particular case. Careful review of the published arbitration awards and literature on absenteeism, however, reveals certain factors that are routinely considered by arbitrators in resolving such disputes. The following represent many of the common factors evaluated by arbitrators in determining whether absenteeism merits discipline. Other considerations, though, are the rights of employees under statutes such as the Family and Medical Leave Act and the Americans with Disabilities Act.[2]

### A. *Employers' Policies*

Many employers have established formal attendance policies setting forth the bases upon which discipline and discharge will be imposed. While such policies are usually written, some arbitrators have upheld unwritten policies as well.[3]

---

[1]For three examples of arbitrators refusing to uphold discipline under a no-fault system, see Wilderness Foods, 84-1 ARB ¶ 8242 at 4091 (Roumell, 1984); Metal Container Corp., 81-2 ARB ¶ 8610 (Ross, 1981); Kerotest Mfg. Co., 71 LA 744 (Blue, 1978).

[2]29 U.S.C. §2601 et seq. (1993) and 42 U.S.C. §1201 et seq. (1990). Both statutes are discussed in Chapter 13.

[3]E.g., Menasha Corp., 89 LA 1316 (Baron, 1987); Standard Prods. Co., 88 LA 1164 (Richard, 1987); Saginaw Mining Co., 81 LA 672 (Feldman, 1983).

A "no fault" attendance policy usually imposes specified "points" for certain occurrences and establishes progressive discipline based upon the number of points accumulated. Where such a "no fault" policy is established, however, the employer may find itself prohibited from seeking to reintroduce fault into the disciplinary equation.[4] Furthermore, arbitrators may require that the reasons for an employee's absence or mitigating circumstances be considered under a valid "no fault" policy.[5]

While adherence to a formal attendance policy does not necessarily ensure discipline will be upheld, many arbitrators have upheld discipline imposed under such a policy.[6] On the other hand, where the employer has implemented an attendance policy and then fails to follow its terms, arbitrators have overturned or reduced the discipline.[7]

The interplay between written attendance policies and just cause principles affects whether adherence to a written policy will be enough for an arbitrator to sustain the discipline imposed. The way arbitrators view this interplay is discussed below.

*1. Collectively Bargained Versus Unilaterally Imposed Policies.* While some attendance policies are collectively bargained, others are unilaterally imposed by the employer. Several arbitrators have affirmed the employer's authority to unilaterally adopt such a policy where the collective bargaining agreement expressly authorizes the employer to adopt reasonable work rules.[8] On the other hand, some arbitrators have declined to enforce attendance policies adopted without the union's involvement, particularly where they are contrary to an express provision of the contract or a past practice.[9]

---

[4]E.g., Dap, Inc., 84 LA 459 (Shieber, 1984).

[5]E.g., Robertshaw Controls Co., 94 LA 957 (Kilroy, 1990); All Am. Gourmet Co., 94 LA 361 (Stoltenberg, 1990); Associated Wholesale Grocers, Inc., 89 LA 1144 (Berger, 1987); ITT Power Sys. Corp., 84 LA 288 (Elkin, 1985); Sanyo Mfg. Co., 84 LA 169 (Nicholas, 1984); Indianapolis Rubber Co., 79 LA 529 (Gibson, 1982); Burns Int'l Sec. Sys., Inc., 78 LA 1163 (Kelliher, 1982).

[6]E.g., Westvaco Corp., 92 LA 1289 (Nolan, 1989); Marquette Tool & Die Co., 88 LA 1214 (Hilgert, 1987); Multiplex Co., 81 LA 625 (Smith, 1983); Gordon, L. & Son, Inc., 80 LA 560 (Barnhardt, 1983); General Metal & Heat Treating, Inc., 80 LA 7 (Wolle, 1982); Amoco Chems. Corp., 79 LA 89 (Byars, 1982); Carnation Co., 79 LA 679 (de Grasse, 1982).

[7]E.g., Master Builders, Inc., 92 LA 1021 (Curry, 1989); Inco Alloys Int'l, 91 LA 1237 (Kilroy, 1988); Kansas Power & Light Co., 87 LA 867 (Belcher, 1986); Dap, Inc., 84 LA 459 (Shieber, 1984); General Mills Fun Group, 72 LA 1285 (Martin, 1979); Air Reduction Co., 45 LA 280 (Morgan, 1965); F.H. Lawson Co., 43 LA 1031 (Kates, 1965); Commercial Steel Co., 39 LA 286 (Kates, 1962).

[8]E.g., Wire Rope Corp. of Am., Inc., 95 LA 126 (Moller, 1990); Philip Morris U.S.A., 94 LA 41 (Dolson, 1989); General Foods Corp., 91 LA 1251 (Goldstein, 1988); T. Marzetti Co., 91 LA 154 (Sharpe, 1988); B.F. Goodrich Co., 90 LA 1297 (McIntosh, 1988); Packaging Corp. of Am., 86 LA 753 (Smith, 1986); Lakeside, Ltd., 86 LA 601 (Bognanno, 1986); Atlantic Richfield Co., 86 LA 393 (Dunn, 1986); Regal Plastic Co., 86 LA 788 (Woolf, 1985); Webster Elec. Co., 83 LA 141 (Kindig, 1984); Giant Food, Inc., 79 LA 916 (Seibel, 1982); Union Tank Car Co., 77 LA 249 (Taylor, 1981); Lima Register Co., 76 LA 935 (Heinz, 1981); LeBlond Mach. Tool, Inc., 76 LA 827 (Keenan, 1981); Stroh Die Casting Co., 72 LA 1250 (Kerkman, 1979); Marley Cooling Tower Co., 71 LA 306 (Sergent, 1978); Park Poultry, Inc., 71 LA 1 (Cohen, 1978).

[9]E.g., Tyson Foods, Inc., 92 LA 1121 (Goodstein, 1989); Simpson Paper Co., 86 LA 503 (Leach, 1985); Southwest Forest Indus., Inc., 81 LA 1234 (Cromwell, 1983).

*2. Reasonableness of the Policy.*    Where the arbitrator concludes discipline is based upon a policy that constitutes an unreasonable exercise of management rights, discipline has been reduced or overturned. While the reasonableness of a policy is sometimes arbitrated upon adoption of the policy,[10] it is more commonly raised when the policy is applied to a particular employee.[11]

Thus, an employer's unilateral adoption of an attendance policy opposed by the union may present a procedural dilemma for the union. While some arbitrators have ruled a union may not challenge such a policy until an actual dispute arises following discipline of an employee,[12] others have opined that a union waives its right to challenge a policy by failing to grieve immediately upon its adoption.[13]

*3. Due Process Issues.*    A full discussion of due process is contained in Chapter 2. This discussion addresses only the specific due process elements related to absenteeism. Some arbitrators have overturned or reduced discipline where the employee was unaware that his absence would lead to the discipline.[14] Arbitrators have overturned discipline where an attendance policy has not been consistently followed.[15] In other cases, notice to the employee is relied upon by the arbitrator in upholding discipline.[16] Other arbitrators, however, have found just cause even where such notice had not been provided.[17]

---

[10]E.g., Cooper Indus., 94 LA 830 (Yarowsky, 1990); Primeline Indus., Inc., 88 LA 700 (Morgan, 1986); Cosmair, Inc., 80 LA 22 (Kerrison, 1982); Giant Foods, Inc., 79 LA 916 (Seibel, 1982).

[11]E.g., Philip Morris U.S.A., 94 LA 41 (Dolson, 1989); T. Marzetti Co., 91 LA 154 (Sharpe, 1988); Standard Prods. Co., 88 LA 1164 (Richard, 1987); Lakeside, Ltd., 86 LA 601 (Bognanno, 1986); Island Creek Coal Co., 86 LA 417 (Feldman, 1985); Dap, Inc., 84 LA 459 (Shieber, 1984); Indianapolis Rubber Co., 79 LA 529 (Gibson, 1982); Burns Int'l Sec. Sys., Inc., 78 LA 1163 (Kelliher, 1982).

[12]E.g., Wackenhut Servs., Inc., 91 LA 1343 (Hardbeck, 1988).

[13]E.g., Philip Morris U.S.A., 94 LA 41 (Dolson, 1989); Standard Prods., Inc., 88 LA 1164 (Richard, 1987); Lawrence Bros., Inc., 86 LA 1132 (Gibson, 1986). See Chapter 11 for discussion of when rules can be changed.

[14]E.g., Marathon Petroleum Co., 95 LA 906 (Barroni, 1990); Grinnell Corp., 92 LA 124 (Kilroy, 1989); Inco Alloys Int'l, Inc., 91 LA 1237 (Kilroy, 1988); Concrete Pipe Prods. Co., 91 LA 405 (Williams, 1988); Bumper Works, Inc., 87 LA 586 (Schwartz, 1986); Fred Rueping Leather, 83 LA 644 (Jacobowski, 1984); General Elec. Co., 74 LA 847 (Abrams, 1980); Niles, Shepard, Crane & Hoist Corp., 71 LA 828 (Alutto, 1978); Oglebay Norton Co., 82 LA 652 (Duda, 1984); Sprague Devices, Inc., 79 LA 543 (Mulhall, 1982); New Castle State Hosp., 77 LA 585 (Deitsch, 1981); Marley Cooling Tower Co., 71 LA 306 (Sergent, 1978).

[15]E.g., Robertshaw Controls Co., 94 LA 957 (Kilroy, 1990); Georgia-Pacific Corp., 93 LA 373 (Savage, 1989); Commercial Filters Div., 91 LA 25 (Bethel, 1988); Worcester Quality Foods, Inc., 90 LA 1305 (Roche, 1988); All Am. Gourmet Co., 88 LA 1241 (Zobrak, 1987); Nuodex, Inc., 87 LA 256 (Millous, 1986); Indian Indus., Inc., 86 LA 573 (Traynor, 1985); Meskur Indus., Inc., 85 LA 921 (Mikrut, 1985).

[16]E.g., Philip Morris U.S.A., 94 LA 41 (Dolson, 1989); West Penn Power Co., 91 LA 303 (Kindig, 1988); Copaz Packing Corp., 86 LA 46 (Seinsheimer, 1986); Island Creek Coal Co., 86 LA 417 (Feldman, 1985); Litton Microwave Cooking Prods., 84 LA 761 (Bognanno, 1985); Texas City Ref., Inc., 83 LA 923 (King, 1984); McGraw-Edison, 81 LA 403 (Role, 1983); Union Carbide Corp., 74 LA 681 (Bowers, 1980); Bethlehem Steel Corp., 74 LA 507 (Fishgold, 1980).

[17]E.g., Philip Morris U.S.A., 94 LA 41 (Dolson, 1989); Armstrong Rubber Co., 74 LA 362 (Williams, 1980).

Arbitrators have overturned or reduced discipline for absenteeism where the discipline administered was greater than the employer previously imposed in comparable circumstances.[18]

Some arbitrators have concluded that progressive discipline is "inherent in the concept of just cause."[19] Arbitrators holding such a view have overturned or reduced discipline or discharge where progressive discipline has not been followed[20] or have upheld discipline or discharge where progressive discipline has been followed.[21] Some arbitrators have upheld discipline or discharge for absenteeism even where progressive discipline has not been followed.[22]

*4. Conflicts Between Just Cause and the Employer's Policy.* Cases have raised the issue of whether the employer must prove just cause for discipline even if the employer strictly followed the terms of its attendance policy when imposing discipline. Some arbitrators have declined to address the issue of just cause in the presence of a properly adopted and applied policy,[23] while many arbitrators have upheld discipline under such policies, concluding that compliance with the employer's policy satisfies just cause standards.[24] Still other arbitrators, however, have held that compliance with an attendance policy does not relieve the employer from its burden of proving just cause based upon all of the factors discussed above.[25]

*5. Precedent.* An employer's decisions to bend its attendance policy for one employee may be regarded as a precedent that other employees expect to be followed.[26] Thus, an employee who took time off to bale hay on his farm expected an excused absence, since the

---

[18]E.g., Marathon Petroleum Co., 95 LA 906 (Baroni, 1990); Sterling Beef Co., 91 LA 1049 (Watkins, 1988); Commercial Filters Div., 91 LA 25 (Bethel, 1988); TRW, Inc., 90 LA 31 (Graham, 1987); Alpha Beta Co., 89 LA 804 (Kaufman, 1987); Inter-Pack Corp., 87 LA 1232 (Brown, 1986); American Mfg. Co., 82 LA 36 (Speroff, 1983). But see North River Energy Co., 88 LA 447 (Witney, 1988).

[19]Furry Mach., Inc., 89 LA 739, 744 (Goldstein, 1987).

[20]E.g., Inco Alloys Int'l, Inc., 91 LA 1237 (Kilroy, 1988); Master Builders, Inc., 91 LA 1021 (Curry, 1989); Calgon Carbon Corp., 88 LA 347 (Tharp, 1987); DeBrough Mfg. Co., 86 LA 1263 (Jacobowski, 1986); General Mills Fun Group, 72 LA 1285 (Martin, 1979); Bethlehem Steel Co., 72 LA 1036 (Aronin, 1979); Olin Mathiesen Corp., 49 LA 573 (Belshaw, 1967).

[21]E.g., Hughes Aircraft Co., 92 LA 634 (Richman, 1989); S.E. Rykoff & Co., 90 LA 233 (Angelo, 1987); Kaiser Aluminum & Chem. Corp., 87 LA 236 (Feldman, 1986); Shell Oil Co., 85 LA 769 (LeBaron, 1985); McGraw-Edison, 81 LA 403 (Role, 1983); Lucky Stores, Inc., 78 LA 233 (Darrow, 1982); Presbyterian Univ. Hosp., 77 LA 959 (McDermott, 1981); Allied Roll Builders, Inc., 71 LA 997 (Leahy, 1978); Sharon Steel Corp, 71 LA 737 (Klein, 1978); General Elec. Co., 71 LA 129 (Twomey, 1978).

[22]E.g., Eastern Airlines, Inc., 88 LA 223 (Dworkin, 1986).

[23]E.g., General Tire, Inc., 93 LA 771 (Groshong, 1989).

[24]See cases cited at supra note 5.

[25]E.g., Greater Baltimore Med. Ctr. 93-2 ARB ¶ 3566 (Feigenbaum, 1993); Webster Elec. Co., 83 LA 141 (Kindig, 1984); Park Poultry, Inc., 71 LA 1 (Cohen, 1978); S & S Corp., 62 LA 882 (Williams, 1973).

[26]TRW, Inc., 90 LA 31 (Graham, 1987).

employer allowed another employee to take excused time off to compete in a fishing tournament.[27]

The decisions in this area reflect the arbitrators' recognition that unions should be permitted to enforce prior discretionary decisions by the employer so that all employees receive equal treatment.[28] For instance, discipline was reduced where an employee who was absent for a period of three consecutive days received a written warning for each day and was terminated. Since the employer had never before handled absences in this manner the arbitrator reduced the discipline to a warning.[29]

Similarly, discipline was revoked because of the treatment received by other employees in *Lithonia Lighting Co.*[30] The collective bargaining agreement provided for excused absences to take children to the doctor for a recurring illness. Despite the exclusion of general illnesses such as colds or the flu, the employer generally excused absences for any illness, rather than just recurring illnesses. An employee was disciplined for taking time off to bring a child to the doctor for the flu. The arbitrator held that the employer had never followed the contract language and the discipline must be rescinded.

## B.  *The Employee's Work Record*

Whether absenteeism constitutes just cause for discipline is materially affected by whether an employee is a repeat offender. In numerous instances, arbitrators have upheld discipline for absenteeism based, in part, on the employee's history of attendance problems.[31] Conversely, arbitrators have overturned or reduced discipline where it was based on the employee's first offense or the employee's attendance record did not otherwise support the discipline.[32] Should the arbitrator conclude the employee's offense is sufficiently serious, however, even an unblemished attendance record may not insulate the grievant from discipline.[33]

---

[27]Bowman Transp., Inc., 79-1 ARB ¶ 8059 (Hon, 1978).

[28]Bentworth Sch. Dist., 88-2 ARB ¶ 8327 (Heekin, 1987); Phillips 66 Co., 88 LA 617 (Weisbrod, 1987); Inter-Pack Corp., 87 LA 1232 (Brown, 1986); Lithonia Lighting Co., 83-1 ARB ¶ 8217 (Williams, 1983); Penobscot Poultry Co., 72-2 ARB ¶ 8510 (Devino, 1972). But see Eastern Airlines, Inc., 88 LA 223 (Dworkin, 1986).

[29]Penobscot Poultry Co., 72-2 ARB ¶ 8510 (Devino, 1972).

[30]83-1 ARB ¶ 8217 (Williams, 1983).

[31]Union Oil of Cal., 91 LA 1206 (Klein, 1988); Philip Morris, U.S.A., 87 LA 975 (Flannagan, 1986); Island Creek Coal Co., 86 LA 417 (Feldman, 1985); Rockwell Int'l Corp., 86 LA 120 (Feldman, 1985); Amax Coal Co., 85 LA 225 (Kilroy, 1985); Cameron Iron Works, 85 LA 936 (Milentz, 1985); Champion Papers, Champion Int'l, Courtland Mill, 74 LA 623 (White, 1980); General Elec. Co., 74 LA 290 (MacDonald, 1979).

[32]E.g., Union Camp Corp., 91 LA 749 (Clarke, 1988); Menasha Corp., 71 LA 653 (Roumell, 1987); American Brass Co., 88 LA 161 (Fullmer, 1986); Shell Oil Co., 83 LA 787 (Allen, 1984); Safeway Stores, Inc., 79 LA 742 (MacLean, 1982).

[33]E.g., Howell Indus., Inc., 95 LA 1112 (Stoltenberg, 1990).

Arbitrators are less consistent when considering the relevance of an employee's disciplinary and work history for nonattendance issues in determining whether absenteeism constitutes just cause for discipline. Some arbitrators have relied on a disciplinary record for nonattendance transgressions in upholding the discipline of an employee for absenteeism.[34] Similarly, arbitrators have relied on an otherwise positive work record to mitigate discipline imposed for absenteeism.[35] A few arbitrators, however, have declined to rely on the employee's prior disciplinary record, on the grounds that it bears no relationship to discipline for absenteeism.[36]

## C. Mitigating and Aggravating Circumstances

In most absenteeism cases the central consideration is the reason for the employee's absence, or other mitigating circumstances. Generally, the less control the employee has over the circumstances causing his absence, or the more justification the employee has for his absence, the more likely the arbitrator will be to find there is no just cause for discipline. Of course, different arbitrators weigh such mitigating circumstances differently.

*1. Illness of Employee.* Usually, illness is covered in the collective bargaining agreement. Even if it is not, if the employee demonstrates a valid illness, arbitrators will often reduce or overturn discipline for absences caused by the illness. These cases may be affected by the Family Medical Leave Act (FMLA). Furthermore, employees with physical or mental conditions that rise to the level of a disability may be protected under the Americans with Disabilities Act (ADA).[37] In numerous cases, arbitrators have overturned or reduced discipline where the employee's absence was caused by illness beyond his control.[38] This is particularly true where the employee's absence is covered in whole or in part by contractual sick leave or other approved leave benefits.[39]

---

[34]E.g., Climate Control/McQuay, Snyder Gen. Corp., 89 LA 1062 (Cromwell, 1987); Witco Chem. Corp., 71 LA 919 (Light, 1978).

[35]E.g., S.E. Rykoff & Co., 90 LA 233 (Angelo, 1987); Rockwell Int'l Highway Brake & Trailer Axle Div., 88 LA 1092 (Morgan, 1987); Southwest Detroit Hosp., 82 LA 491 (Ellman, 1984).

[36]E.g., American Welding & Mfg. Co., 94 LA 340 (Duda, 1990).

[37]See Chapter 13 for discussion of statutes.

[38]E.g., Iowa-Illinois Gas & Elec. Co., 95 LA 553 (Volz, 1990); International Paper Co., 94 LA 409 (Mathews, 1990); Delta-Macon Brick & Tile Co., 92 LA 837 (O'Grady, 1989); Northrop Corp., 91 LA 231 (Weiss, 1988); Lever Bros. Co., 87 LA 260 (Traynor, 1986); Smith Meter Co., 86 LA 1009 (Creo, 1986); ITT Power Sys. Corp., 84 LA 288 (Elkin, 1985); American Mfg. Co., 82 LA 36 (Speroff, 1983); East Ohio Gas Co., 78 LA 71 (Michelstetter, 1982); Safeway Stores, Inc., 75 LA 430 (Winograd, 1980); Dwyer Instruments, Inc., 74 LA 668 (Greco, 1980); Babcock & Wilcox Co., 72 LA 1073 (Mullin, 1979); Park Poultry, Inc., 71 LA 1 (Cohen, 1978).

[39]E.g., American Brass Co., 88 LA 161 (Fullmer, 1986); Kansas City Power & Light Co., 87 LA 867 (Belcher, 1986); Rockwell Int'l Corp., 86 LA 120 (Feldman, 1985); Homestake Mining

Arbitrators, however, have concluded that even legitimate illness, if chronic, is no impediment to discipline.[40] In certain cases arbitrators have upheld discipline where the employee's absence was due to illness but other circumstances weighed in favor of discipline.[41]

a. Mental Illness.   Employees who are mentally incapacitated, and who are disciplined for absences, will often be treated leniently by arbitrators, especially if the employee is in a treatment program.[42] Several arbitrators have also reduced discipline on the basis that severe depression and post-traumatic stress disorder can be so debilitating that the employe is unable to even notify the employer of an absence.[43]

The arbitrator's decision in *Southern California Edison Co.*[44] is illustrative of this tolerance. A mentally ill employee was terminated for poor attendance and failure to notify management of his absences in advance. While he was absent, the employee was undergoing psychiatric care and the psychiatrist considered the employee totally disabled, instructing him not to work. Although the employer's policy required employees to notify management of any absence in advance, the employee's emotional illness or disability caused the arbitrator to reverse the discharge.

Seasonal depression has also been recognized as a mitigating factor for disciplinary purposes. In *General Mills Inc.*,[45] an employee was terminated for absenteeism caused by his seasonal depression during the spring and fall, which made it difficult for him to report to work during 1 to 2 weeks. The arbitrator ordered reinstatement since the condition caused the absences and the employee had few absences outside of this pattern.

In those cases where an employee has not sought treatment because he is so incapacitated that he does not recognize the illness, the absences are generally mitigated and the employee is given a

---

Co., 85 LA 29 (Gunderson, 1985); Kansas City Power & Light Co., 84 LA 393 (Kubie, 1985); Detroit Osteopathic Hosp., 83 LA 1308 (Daniel, 1984); SCM Corp., 83 LA 1186 (Speroff, 1984); Kansas City Gas & Elec. Co., 83 LA 916 (Thornell, 1984); Pantasote, Inc., 82 LA 665 (Seinsheimer, 1984); Armstrong Rubber Co., 78 LA 857 (Williams, 1982); Pickards Mather & Co., 76 LA 676 (Witt, 1981); United States Postal Serv., 73 LA 1174 (Garrett, 1979).

[40]E.g., Mallinckrodt, Inc., 95 LA 966 (Hilgert, 1990); Philip Morris U.S.A., 94 LA 41 (Dolson, 1989); Linn County, Iowa, 81 LA 929 (Sinicropi, 1983).

[41]E.g., Quarto Mining, 95 LA 1169 (Brunner, 1990); American Welding & Mfg. Co., 94 LA 340 (Duda, 1990); Mead Paper, Chilpaco Mill, 91 LA 52 (Curry, 1988); PPG Indus., Inc., 90 LA 1033 (Edelman, 1988); North River Energy Co., 88 LA 447 (Witney, 1987); Porritts & Spencer, Inc., 83 LA 1165 (Byars, 1984); Arch of Ill., Inc., 82 LA 625 (Hewitt, 1984); Plastomet Corp., 81 LA 700 (Roumell, 1983); Stokely Van Camp, Inc., 81 LA 677 (Schaffer, 1983); Monsanto Co., 76 LA 509 (Thomson, 1981); Union Carbide Corp., 74 LA 681 (Bowers, 1980); Ambac Indus., Inc., 72 LA 347 (Kuypers, 1979).

[42]Iowa-Illinois Gas & Elec. Co., 95 LA 553 (Volz, 1990); East Ohio Gas Co., 78 LA 71 (Michelstetter, 1982).

[43]Iowa-Illinois Gas & Elec. Co., 95 LA 553 (Volz, 1990); Southern Cal. Edison Co., 89-1 ARB ¶ 8149 (Horowitz, 1989); Western Airlines, 84-1 ARB ¶ 8026 (Randall, 1983).

[44]89-1 ARB ¶ 8149 (Horowitz, 1989).

[45]99 LA 143 (Stallworth, 1992).

chance to be rehabilitated.[46] Thus, a 28-year employee whose absences were caused by anxiety and depression, and who was unable to care for herself or act rationally, was not penalized for her failure to seek treatment until 2 weeks after her termination.[47]

Absences for general stress and other emotional problems do not evoke the same arbitral reaction. Discipline under these circumstances is more often upheld.[48] For example, an employee of a Manhattan museum was properly terminated for three absences despite her fear for "her personal safety due to the Three Mile Island accident in Harrisburg, Pennsylvania."[49]

b. Physical Illness.   Employees with a physical illness are often excused from absences, so long as the absence was necessary and the condition causing the absence is corrected, so the absences will not recur. For example, an employee who was absent or late in excess of 300 times in 4 years, and was out for 6 months for surgery, was not properly terminated since the absences were for a condition that was corrected by surgery.[50] Similarly, a 3-week absence due to a miscarriage was excused where the employer knew that the employee was having medical problems.[51] Six days of hospital time was also acceptable for an employee suffering from a spider bite.[52]

Conversely, injury from a dog bite did not excuse absences where the employee failed to report the absences.[53] And an employee was discharged for taking a day off to have a cyst removed when he was already on probation for excessive absences.[54] The arbitrator upheld the discharge on the grounds that the cyst had been present for approximately 8 months and it had not worsened at the time that the employee had it removed. Further, there was no reason why the employee could not have scheduled the doctor's appointment during nonwork hours.

Similarly, an employee who was absent because he was injured in a bar fight was properly disciplined since the failure to report to work was totally within the employee's control. The fact he was in the hospital emergency room did not absolve the employee of the responsibility for the circumstances which made it impossible for him to report to work.[55]

---

[46]Western Airlines, 84-1 ARB ¶ 8026 (Randall, 1983).

[47]James River Corp., 96 LA 1174 (McDonald, 1991).

[48]Union Carbide Corp., 88-2 ARB ¶ 8362 (Imundo, 1988).

[49]American Museum of Natural History, 80-1 ARB ¶ 8139 (Ludolf, 1980).

[50]Northrop Corp., 91 LA 231 (Weiss, 1988). See also University of Cincinnati, 89 LA 388 (Wren, 1987).

[51]Mission Indus., Mission Uniform & Linen Serv., 98 LA 688 (Weiss, 1991).

[52]Homestake Mining Co., 85 LA 29 (White, 1985).

[53]Sun-Maid Raisin Growers of Cal., 72 LA 133, (Weiss, 1979).

[54]Babcock & Wilcox Co., 69-1 ARB ¶ 8093 (Kates, 1968).

[55]Wyandotte Chems. Corp., 62-1 ARB ¶ 8325 (Miller, 1962).

Although most decisions excuse absences by genuinely sick employees, arbitrators have permitted terminations of employees who are chronically sick and cannot perform the job duties.[56] Even long-term employees are subject to termination if they are physically unable to maintain a normal work schedule,[57] especially if they refuse to seek treatment for medical problems.[58] A single illness after numerous other unexcused absences can also result in termination,[59] and discharge is appropriate for employees who lie about being sick when in fact they are healthy and simply on vacation.[60]

c. Work-Related Illness.    Absences caused by an injury on the job are deemed excused.[61] If, however, the employee is engaged in impermissible activities while on medical leave for an injury at work, the discharge may be upheld.[62] Terminations have also been sustained if there is no job that the employee can safely perform after experiencing a work-related injury.[63]

2. *Drugs, Alcohol, and Related Issues.*    There have been numerous cases where the employee's absenteeism is caused, in whole or in part, by addiction to alcohol or drugs. Arbitrators have taken different approaches to this difficult problem. Some arbitrators regard the situation as beyond the employee's control, as in cases of other illnesses, and therefore decline to find just cause for discipline.[64] Similar reasoning has at times been applied to other disorders, such as compulsive gambling.[65] While excessive absences for intoxication may

---

[56]Union Carbide Corp., 88-2 ARB ¶ 8362 (Imundo, 1988); Philip Morris U.S.A., 94 LA 41 (Dolson, 1989).

[57]Goodyear Tire & Rubber Co., 88 LA 745 (Dworkin, 1987) (23-year employee was properly terminated because she was physically incapable of working a normal schedule).

[58]Quarto Mining, 95 LA 1169 (Brunner, 1990).

[59]Stokely Van Camp, Inc., 81 LA 677 (Schaffer, 1983).

[60]La Crosse Lutheran Hosp., 73 LA 722 (McCray, 1979) (employee was in Las Vegas while on sick leave); General Tel. Co., of Ohio, 74 LA 1052 (Laybourne, 1980) (employee was at amusement part with his family while on sick leave).

[61]Kansas City Area Transp. Auth., 98 LA 57 (Cohen, 1991); cf. B-Line Sys., Inc., 100 LA 933 (Cohen, 1993) (discipline not warranted when employee was absent due to failing health caused by widespread discrimination and harassment at work); T. Marzetti Co., 91 LA 154 (Sharpe, 1988); ITT Power Sys. Corp., 84 LA 288 (Elkin, 1985) (reprimand was lifted against employee who was absent when she became ill after being exposed to toxic fumes in the workplace).

[62]Potash Co. of Am., 85 LA 559 (White, 1985).

[63]Mallinckrodt, Inc., 95 LA 966 (Hilgert, 1990); Excel Corp., 95 LA 1069 (Shearer, 1990). See also Mead Paper, 91 LA 52 (Curry, 1988).

[64]E.g., Westinghouse Elec. Corp., 95 LA 881 (Talarico, 1990); United States Steel Corp., 95 LA 462 (Das, 1990); Aeroquip Corp., 95 LA 31 (Steiber, 1990); United States Plywood Corp., 88 LA 275 (Mathews, 1986); Food Mktg. Corp., 88 LA 98 (Doering, 1986); Youngstown Hosp. Ass'n, 82 LA 31 (Miller, 1983); St. Joe Minerals Corp., 73 LA 1193 (McDermott, 1979). Cf. Eaton Corp., 94 LA 971 (Eisele, 1990)(discharge upheld, but employer required to reinstate employee should substance abuse problem be overcome).

[65]E.g., Phillips 66 Co., 88 LA 617 (Weisbrod, 1987).

justify discharge,[66] an employee's absence for treatment of alcoholism is frequently found excusable,[67] even if the employee cannot give notice of the absence.[68] While the state of being under the influence of alcohol does not serve as a legitimate excuse for absenteeism, or relieve an employee of responsibility for failing to be present at work, an employee who voluntarily enters a treatment program may be afforded some flexibility.[69] One arbitrator reasoned that by entering into a treatment program, the employee is taking positive steps to correct the drinking problem. Thus, corrective discipline by the employer is unnecessary as the employee is engaging in positive corrective behavior, and failure to impose the discipline will not encourage the employee to fall back into the drinking problem.[70]

Other arbitrators, however, decline to mitigate an employee's discipline on the basis of illness,[71] particularly when the absenteeism is especially severe or harmful to the employer's operations.[72]

One factor given particular emphasis in many cases is whether the employee has voluntarily come forward for assistance with his substance abuse or other personal problems. Where the employee comes forward seeking assistance before the employer seeks to impose discipline, some arbitrators consider such forthrightness an important factor mitigating the discipline.[73] Conversely, where the employee fails to seek treatment until after discipline has been imposed, some arbitrators refuse to consider the employee's belatedly seeking assistance as a factor mitigating discipline.[74]

Once an employee completes a treatment program, he has an obligation to notify his employer of the date he expects to return to

---

[66]Eaton Corp., 99 LA 331 (Lewis, 1992) (termination was proper of 29-year alcoholic employee who worked only 39 of last 55 scheduled days); Active Prods. Co., 68-1 ARB ¶ 8103 (May, 1967) (excessive absences for intoxication justify discharge where prior warnings have not deterred the absences).

[67]Growmark Inc., 100 LA 785 (Ver Ploeg, 1993); Atchison, Topeka & Santa Fe Ry., 87 LA 972 (Johnson, 1986); Damascus Steel Casting Co., 80-1 ARB ¶ 8188 (Duff, 1980) (employee's 5-day suspension for spending a month in a rehabilitation center for alcoholism was lifted); Warner & Swasey Co., Turning Mach. Div., 78-2 ARB ¶ 8370 (Siegel, 1978).

[68]Philip Morris U.S.A., 99 LA 1016 (Volz, 1992) (employee's discharge was reversed because he had no opportunity to notify the company that he had entered an out-of-town treatment center for alcoholism).

[69]Damascus Steel Casting Co., 80-1 ARB ¶ 8188 (Duff, 1980). Some state statutes specifically prohibit termination of an employee who is in a treatment program.

[70]Id.

[71]E.g., Goodyear Tire & Rubber Co., 92 LA 91 (Dworkin, 1988); Shell Oil Co., 90 LA 286 (McDermott, 1988); American Ship Bldg. Co., 81 LA 243 (Everitt, 1983); Johns-Manville Prods. Corp., 76 LA 845 (Kates, 1981); General Elec. Co., 72 LA 355 (Clark, 1978).

[72]E.g., Eaton Corp., 94 LA 971 (Eisele, 1990); General Dynamics, 79 LA 182 (Rule 1982).

[73]E.g., Wacker Silicones Corp., 95 LA 784 (Hodgson, 1990); Rockwell Int'l Highway Brake & Trailer Axle Div., 88 LA 1092 (Morgan, 1987); Cleveland Elec. Illuminating Co., 88 LA 781 (Morgan, 1987); Atchison, Topeka & Santa Fe Ry., 87 LA 972 (Johnson, 1986); Indianapolis Rubber Co., 79 LA 529 (Gibson, 1982); Warner & Swasey Co., 71 LA 158 (Siegel, 1978).

[74]E.g., Toledo Molding & Die Co., 88 LA 937 (Ipavec, 1987); Bemis Co., 81 LA 733 (Wright, 1983); Western Gear Corp., 74 LA 641 (Sabo, 1980). But see Aeroquip Corp., 95 LA 31 (Steiber, 1991).

work.[75] And if the employee fails the program, discharge for future alcohol-related absences can be proper.[76] Other addictions, such as gambling, are sometimes treated similarly to alcoholism.[77] For an in-depth discussion of substance abuse, see Chapter 6.

*3. Incarceration.* There is no single rule for determining when the employer can discipline an employee for absences caused by incarceration. Arbitrators consider the duration of the incarceration, the nature of the alleged act resulting in confinement, the impact of the absence on the employer's operations, and the grievant's service and employment record.[78] Certain arbitrators have viewed incarceration in the employee's favor and found there was no just cause,[79] particularly where the employee takes pains to notify the employer of his situation[80] or subsequently is exonerated of the alleged criminal offense for which he was incarcerated.[81] Other arbitrators have viewed this justification with less sympathy and have found such absence to be proper grounds for discipline.[82]

These factors were discussed at length in *Dickenson Press,*[83] which also contains a comprehensive survey of incarceration decisions. In *Dickenson Press*, the employee was stopped by the police because his muffler had dropped from his car. When the officers checked the employee's driver's license, they discovered that he owed a debt to a court-appointed lawyer and was in arrears in his child support. He was arrested. Three hours before he was to start work, he called his mother and asked her to inform his employer of the situation. The employee was incarcerated for 7 days. He was terminated upon his return to work.

The arbitrator reduced the discipline because the employee kept the company informed and had a reasonable work record. Further, the impact on the employer—paying some overtime and the failure to get some work completed—was no different than if an employee took a vacation. The employee was reinstated, but without back pay because he was responsible for the absence.

---

[75]American Ship Bldg. Co., 81 LA 243 (Everitt, 1983).

[76]Shell Oil Co., 90 LA 286 (McDermott, 1988).

[77]Phillips 66 Co., 88 LA 617 (Weisbrod, 1987).

[78]Dickenson Press, 93-1 ARB ¶ 3044 (Roumell, 1992); Warner-Lambert Co., 89 LA 265 (Sloan, 1987). See also McInerney Spring & Wire Co., 72 LA 1262 (Roumell, 1979).

[79]E.g., Plain Dealer Publ'g Co., 86 LA 1237 (Abrams, 1986); McInerney Spring & Wire Co., 72 LA 1262 (Roumell, 1979).

[80]E.g., Alpha Beta Co., 91 LA 1225 (Wilmoth, 1988).

[81]E.g., Owens-Illinois, Inc., 71 LA 1095 (Foster, 1978).

[82]E.g., U.S. Steel Corp., 95 LA 566 (Talarico, 1990); U.S. Steel Corp., 94 LA 1017 (McDaniel, 1990); Augusta Newsprint Co., 89 LA 725 (King, 1987); Seven-Up of Ind., 87 LA 691 (Murphy, 1986); American Inks & Coatings Corp., 87 LA 691 (DiLauro, 1986); Boeing Servs. Int'l, 75 LA 967 (Kramer, 1980); Dorsey Trailers, Inc., 73 LA 196 (Hamby, 1979); Bethlehem Steel Corp., 72 LA 210 (Sharnoff, 1979).

[83]93-1 ARB ¶ 3044 (Roumell, 1992).

Employees who were absent anywhere from several hours to 3 months have been reinstated for the reasons discussed in *Dickenson Press*.[84] Thus, in *Plain Dealer Publishing Co.*[85] a 3-month period of incarceration did not justify termination of a 14-year employee with an exemplary attendance record, even though the incarceration was for two counts of sexual battery of his sons. The arbitrator in *Plain Dealer Publishing* felt that the company had not suffered serious harm by the employee's absence and cited as additional factors that the company did not have a formal attendance policy and the employee had a good work history and an exemplary attendance record.

Conversely, an employee incarcerated for a short period of time, who willfully does not notify his employer of the absence, may be justifiably terminated. For instance, arbitrators have upheld terminations of employees who were absent for as few as 3 days since management was not notified of the incarceration.[86]

An employee who lied about a jail-related absence was found to have been properly terminated.[87] Even an employee who did not go to jail, but told his employer that he was in jail so that he could justify a day off, was subject to termination.[88] In one case an employee had someone call in sick for her when in fact she was in jail. But since she was in fact sick when she was in jail and for several days thereafter, just cause did not exist for discharge. The arbitrator noted there was no requirement that employees be at home or in the hospital to claim sick leave.[89]

The reason for incarceration is also relevant to some decisions. Factors considered by arbitrators are whether or not there is a connection between the employee's job duties, the subject of incarceration, and whether retaining the employee will adversely impact the company.[90]

---

[84]Id. Even one call notifying an employer that the employe will be absent for an indeterminate amount of time has been held adequate. GATX Terminals Corp., 90-1 ARB ¶ 8207 (Marcus, 1989).

[85]86 LA 1237 (Abrams, 1986).

[86]United States Steel Mining Co., Shawnee No. 51 Mine, 93-1 ARB ¶ 3198 (Rimmel, 1992) (discharge was warranted for employee who was absent for more than 5 days since he did not notify management of his incarceration); Crown Cork & Seal Co., 72 LA 613 (Daly, 1979) (termination was proper for an employee who failed to give notification of his 3-day absence due to incarceration for selling marijuana).

[87]GF Furniture Sys., 87 LA 500 (Klein, 1986) (employee was properly discharged for telling his employer that he was going to the hospital for tests when in fact he was going to jail).

[88]Quaker Oats Co., 86 LA 673 (Petersen, 1986).

[89]Memphis Light, Gas & Water Div., 88 LA 167 (Carter, 1987).

[90]GATX Terminals Corp., 90-1 ARB ¶ 8207 (Marcus, 1989) (termination not proper for an employee arrested for suspicion of kidnapping and aggravated rape as there was no connection between the arrest and the employee's job duties or obligations, and the reinstatement would not "subject the company to obloquy or loss of business"). See also Warner-Lambert Co., 89 LA 265 (Sloane, 1987) (discharge improper where employee jailed for possession of a loaded gun and a small amount of cocaine while off duty since the misconduct occurred off company premises and the business was not adversely affected). See generally Chapter 9 for a discussion of the required "nexus" between off-duty conduct and discipline.

Employees who are jailed for no fault of their own have been permitted to return to work without penalty,[91] unless the employee was absent for an excessively long period of time.[92] Further, some arbitrators decline to penalize employees for jail-time absences that could have been avoided by some action on the part of the employer.[93]

*4. Family Emergency.* Family emergencies often require an employee to take time off from work, and some emergencies may be covered under the FMLA.[94] Some arbitrators have reduced or overturned discipline based on such a justification,[95] while other arbitrators have rejected this defense in cases where either the employee has failed to prove the existence of the emergency or the arbitrator concludes the emergency was not sufficiently serious to justify the absence.[96] Taking a child or spouse to the doctor in an emergency usually results in an excused absence.[97] Even frequent absences for serious family problems may be excused. An employee's frequent absences to care for a child who exhibited threatening and potentially violent behavior did not justify termination.[98] The unavailability of child care may create a family emergency, thereby excusing the employee's absence.[99]

Family emergencies do not always create a valid excuse for absence. Where an employee was absent without notice to the employer for 3 weeks to be with a spouse who was injured in the Navy, discipline was upheld.[100] An employee who failed to report to work after expiration of a personal leave of absence was not excused, despite the fact that the employee was caring for a seriously ill child.[101]

---

[91]GATX Terminals Corp., 90-1 ARB ¶ 8207 (Marcus, 1989).

[92]U.S. Steel Corp. 95 LA (Talarico, 1990) (9 months). Cf. 3M Co., 72 LA 949 (Grabb, 1979) (despite acquittal and reversal on retrial of a life sentence, employee not entitled to reinstatement because of a poor work record and refusal to testify at the arbitration).

[93]McInerney Spring & Wire Co., 72 LA 1262 (Roumell, 1979) (jailed employee could have reported to work if the employer had signed the work release form; employer refused to sign the form so the employee's absences could not be held against him and, therefore, he was reinstated).

[94]See also Chapter 13.

[95]E.g., Jones Operating & Maintenance Co., 93 LA 239 (Schwartz, 1989); Mesker Indus., Inc., 85 LA 921 (Mikrut, 1985); Pennsylvania Power Co., 81 LA 850 (Bolte, 1983); Knauf Fiber Glass, 81 LA 333 (Abrams, 1983); County of Monroe, 72 LA 541 (Markowitz, 1979).

[96]E.g., U.S. Steel Corp., 95 LA 610 (Das, 1990); Wilte Hardware Corp., 94 LA 1161 (Hilgert, 1990); Rohm & Haas Tex., Inc., 91 LA 339 (McDermott, 1988); Derby Cap Mfg. Co., 87 LA 1042 (Imundo, 1986); Savanah Transit Auth., 86 LA 1277 (Williams, 1985); Fry's Food Stores, Inc., 71 LA 1247 (Randall, 1979).

[97]Mesker Indus., Inc., 85 LA 921 (Mikrut, 1985); Knauf Fiber Glass, 81 LA 333 (Abrams, 1983); Lithonia Lighting Co., 83-1 ARB ¶ 8217 (Williams, 1983); Southern Ohio Coal Co., 72-2 ARB ¶ 8516 (Dworkin, 1977).

[98]County of Monroe, 72 LA 541 (Markowitz, 1979).

[99]U.S. Steel Corp., 95 LA 610 (Das, 1990); Social Sec. Admin., 89-2 ARB ¶ 8611 (Feigenbaum, 1989) (unexpected unavailability of a regular as well as the backup child care provider constituted an emergency and entitled the employee to an excused absence).

[100]Safeway Stores, Inc., 81 LA 657 (Wilmoth, 1983).

[101]Witte Hardware Corp., 94 LA 1161 (Hilgert, 1990).

An unusual family emergency occurred in *Arch of Illinois Inc.*[102] An employee failed to report to work during a wildcat sympathy strike because he was receiving threats against himself, his family, and his property. The arbitrator felt the threats were serious and ruled against disciplining the employee.

*5. Attending Funerals.*   Many bereavement policies restrict the use of leave to deaths of immediate family members such as spouses, children, parents, and siblings. While restrictive policies may be necessary to limit the number of excused absences, they may not cover the death of individuals with whom the employee had a special relationship.[103]

Arbitrators frequently permit excused absences when an employee attends a funeral of a close relative even if that relationship was not covered in a bereavement policy. In *Hercules Powder Co.,*[104] the collective bargaining agreement provided for bereavement leave for funerals of the employee's parents or a person standing in the place of a parent, among others. The employee's stepfather died and the employee gave the proper notice to the company of his intent to attend the funeral. The employer refused to pay bereavement leave on the grounds that the stepfather did not stand in the place of a parent because he did not contribute to the employee's support or upbringing; they were simply friends. The arbitrator noted that some parents and children are friends and some are enemies. The employee was awarded the funeral leave pay.[105]

This exception may not appear to apply to funerals of nonfamily members. In *Derby Cap Manufacturing Co.,*[106] the arbitrator ruled that the employer had just cause to deny grievant bereavement pay for taking time off due to the death of a man with whom she had a long-term intimate relationship. Since the deceased did not qualify as a spouse under the company's bereavement leave policy, nor was he considered a spouse under state law, the employee's absence was unexcused.

A miscarriage was also held to fall outside of an employer's bereavement leave policy. In *Tate Andale,*[107] an employee was properly disciplined when he took time off from work to be with his wife who was in the hospital following a miscarriage. The employee requested

---

[102]93 LA 1097 (Cohen, 1990).

[103]Some questions regarding bereavement leave may now be governed by the FMLA.

[104]63-2 ARB ¶ 8612 (Marshall, 1963).

[105]See also Kay Screen Printing, Inc., 81-1 ARB ¶ 8179 (Davis, 1980) (discipline held improper for attending funeral of an uncle); Bell Fed. Credit Union, 89-1 ARB ¶ 8032 (Belcher, 1988) (no just cause for termination for attending funeral of a great-aunt). But see Lawrence Bros., Inc., 86 LA 1132, (Gibson, 1986) (employee properly disciplined for her absence to attend the funeral of her niece's daughter).

[106]87 LA 1042 (Imundo, 1986).

[107]90-2 ARB ¶ 8608 (Bernhardt, 1990).

bereavement leave as he had already exhausted his allowable vacation and personal days. While the arbitrator agreed the employee's loss would fit the general definition of bereavement, he found that a miscarriage did not qualify for bereavement leave under the collective bargaining agreement, which required a funeral and a death certificate. Further, the employee's situation was somewhat unsympathetic since his "real problem . . . is that he had used his leave imprudently." The outcome of this decision might have been different under a broader bereavement leave policy or for an employee with a better attendance record.

6. *Car Trouble.*   Car troubles are frequently cited as the reason for an absence and are a frequent subject of arbitration decisions. The decisions consistently apply the general rule that car trouble does not constitute an adequate justification for an absence.[108] Thus, a 7-day suspension was upheld where an employee missed 1 day of work due to alleged car problems.[109] The arbitrator focused on the employee's inadequate effort to have the car repaired or get to work by alternative means, such as borrowing another car, renting a car, asking for a ride, taking a taxi, or traveling by bus.[110]

Where an employee appeared to make a good faith effort at getting his car repaired, termination was held proper due to the employee's failure to follow the employer's notification policy for absences.[111] Even having the car stolen does not provide an excused absence.[112]

7. *Inclement Weather.*   The weather can make it almost impossible for an employee to travel to work. Many decisions find inclement weather is a mitigating factor, so that the employee is not penalized for an absence caused by extreme weather conditions. Even if main highways are open, impassable local roads can cause employees to get stuck in the snow or be unable to back out of a driveway. These conditions have been deemed an act of God and held to justify an employee's absence.[113] An employee's absence may also be excused if the local government instructs residents to stay home.[114]

While weather conditions often impact an entire community, there are frequent circumstances where one individual is subjected to worse conditions than others nearby. In *Napco Plastics Co.,*[115] the

---

[108]Regional Transp. Dist., 95 LA 248 (Snider, 1990); AT&T Techs., Inc., 89-2 ARB ¶ 8354 (Nathan, 1988); Rockwell Int'l Corp., 86 LA 120 (Feldman, 1985); Union Carbide Plastics Co., 63-1 ARB ¶ 8378 (Stein, 1963); Connors Works, Connors Steel Div., H. K. Porter Co., 61-2 ARB ¶ 8426 (Williams, 1961).

[109]Union Carbide Plastics Co., 63-1 ARB ¶ 8378 (Stein, 1963).

[110]Id.

[111]Connors Works, Connors Steel Div., H. K. Porter Co., 61-2 ARB ¶ 8426 (Williams, 1961).

[112]AT&T Techs., Inc., 89-2 ARB ¶ 8354 (Nathan, 1988).

[113]Environmental Elements Corp., 78-1 ARB ¶ 8230 (Milentz, 1978).

[114]U.S. Army Training Ctr. & Fort Leonard Wood, 74-1 ARB ¶ 8282 (McKenna, 1974).

[115]80-1 ARB ¶ 8278 (Shanker, 1980).

employer had occasionally declared snow days, but did not declare one on the day the grievant failed to come to work. The employee testified that the roads by her home had not been plowed. Despite her efforts to drive to work, she could not control her car or keep it from repeatedly skidding. The arbitrator held her absence excusable on the grounds that an employer should look to the weather conditions facing the individual employee. The arbitrator reasoned that individual employees would not abuse this approach since they lose a day's pay for such an absence, and they must demonstrate a good faith effort to make it to work.

Arbitrators have also excused absences due to personal emergencies caused by weather conditions. For example, despite an employee's poor attendance record, his final absence was caused by the need to repair a furnace during a cold spell and did not warrant termination.[116] In *Bowman Transportation, Inc.,*[117] a transportation worker who owned and lived on a 55-acre farm took time off without permission due to weather conditions to bale some hay that was recently cut. Despite the employer's contention that the need to take time off to take care of conflicting personal business is not an emergency, the arbitrator held that the need to bale hay was in fact an emergency and, therefore, the absences were excused.

A weather-related absence will not be excused, however, if the employee's responsibilities include working during weather emergencies. It has been held that U.S. postal workers were not excused from work due to poor weather conditions.[118] In *Marathon Petroleum Co.*[119] a refinery employee was disciplined for failing to report for his scheduled shift during a hurricane because he was moving his family inland. The arbitrator found that just cause existed for the discipline because part of the employee's job was to provide manpower during hurricane emergencies.

Despite the arbitral tendency to excuse absences due to weather conditions, an employer is permitted to enforce its attendance policy which specifically states that an absence due to transportation difficulties will not be excused.[120] Similarly, an employer has a right to impose penalties for absences due to weather conditions when calculating attendance bonus eligibility.[121]

---

[116]United Eng'g & Foundry Co., 69-2 ARB ¶ 8706 (Scheib, 1969).

[117]79-1 ARB ¶ 8059 (Hon, 1978).

[118]U.S. Postal Serv., 77-1 ARB ¶ 8052 (Fasser, 1977). Despite a record Cleveland snow storm, which was one of the worst since 1903 or 1913, the Postmaster attempted to deliver the mail. Approximately 60% of the letter carriers arrived for work. The others who did not arrive were allowed to consider the day as a day of paid emergency annual leave or a day of leave without pay. The employees grieved. The arbitrator held the Postmaster had the discretion to deny administrative leave under the Postal Manual.

[119]95 LA 906 (Baroni, 1990).

[120]Jenn-Air Corp., 80 LA 881 (Edes, 1983).

[121]Teleflex, Inc., 79 LA 1094 (Feldman, 1982).

8. *Employee Dishonesty.*  Arbitrators have been more inclined to find just cause for discipline where the employee attempts to deceive the employer about the true reason for his absence. Thus, arbitrators have upheld discipline in cases where the employee has given the employer false information as to the reason for the absence.[122] Several such cases have involved employees who attempted to conceal the fact that they were incarcerated.[123] Conversely, where the employer fails to prove the employee's dishonesty, the discipline or discharge has been overturned.[124]

9. *Failure to Notify Employer.*  Numerous cases have considered the employee's alleged failure to provide the employer with prompt notice of her absence, either as an aggravating circumstance or a separate offense. Some arbitrators have upheld discipline where the employee has failed to provide such notification,[125] particularly if the employer has an express policy requiring that absent employees call in.[126] On the other hand, some arbitrators have overturned or reduced discipline in such cases,[127] particularly where the employee was unable to call in,[128] made a good faith effort to contact the employer,[129] or reasonably believed there was no need to call in.[130]

---

[122]Safeway Stores, Inc., 93 LA 1147 (Wilkinson, 1989); Quaker Oats Co., 86 LA 673 (Peterson, 1986); Potash Co. of Am., 85 LA 559 (White, 1985); Chattanooga Gas Co., 83 LA 48 (Mullin, 1984); Bethlehem Steel Corp., 75 LA 1201 (Sharnoff, 1980); General Tel. Co. of Ohio, 74 LA 1052 (Laybroune, 1980); John Morrell & Co., 74 LA 756 (Stokes, 1980); West Penn Handling Equip. Co., 74 LA 37 (LeWinter, 1980); LaCrosse Lutheran Hosp., 73 LA 722 (McCrary, 1979).

[123]E.g., GF Furniture Sys., Inc., 87 LA 500 (Klein, 1986); Le-Bo Prods., Inc., 74 LA 1245 (Wray, 1980). But see ASC, Inc., 89 LA 258 (Ipavec, 1987).

[124]E.g., GF Furniture Sys., Inc., 87 LA 500 (Klein, 1986); Le-Bo Prods., Inc., 74 LA 1245 (Wray, 1980). But see ASC, Inc., 89 LA 258 (Ipavec, 1987).

[125]E.g., ARA Mfg. Co., 86 LA 719 (Brunner, 1985); Wellco, Inc., 85 LA 1003 (High, 1985); Atlantic Richfield Co., 84 LA 257 (Gibson, 1985); Safeway Stores, Inc., 81 LA 657 (Wilmoth, 1983); Champion Int'l Corp., 81 LA 1285 (Flannagan, 1983); FMC Corp., 74 LA 1185 (Doering, 1980); Armstrong Rubber Co., 74 LA 362 (Williams, 1980); Marmon Group, Inc., 73 LA 1279 (Bode, 1980).

[126]E.g., Arch of W. Va., 94 LA 503 (Feldman, 1990); West Penn Power Co., 91 LA 303 (Kindig, 1988); Presbyterian Univ. Hosp., 77 LA 959 (McDermott, 1981); Detroit Edison Co., 73 LA 565 (Lipson, 1979); Dorsey Trailers, Inc., 73 LA 196 (Hamby, 1979); Rheem Mfg. Co., 72 LA 1217 (Baron, 1979); Crown Cork & Seal Co., Inc., 72 LA 613 (Daly, 1979); Sun-Maid Raisin Growers of Cal., 72 LA 133 (Weiss, 1979).

[127]E.g., Fairbanks Morse Pump Co., 94 LA 1206 (Gordon, 1990); McCarthy's, Inc., 84 LA 799 (Nelson, 1985); Reliance Steel Aluminum Co., 79 LA 911 (Mathews, 1982); Redmar Plastics, Inc., 79 LA 351 (Eagle, 1982); Todd Pac. Shipyards, 76 LA 928 (Draznin, 1981); Electronic Enclosures, Wyle Co., 71 LA 214 (Hill, 1978).

[128]E.g., Armstrong Rubber Co., 78 LA 857 (Williams, 1982); Paxon Mach. Co., 74 LA 860 (Letson, 1980).

[129]E.g., Jefferson Smurfit Corp., 93 LA 423 (Bankston, 1989); Indian Indus., Inc., 86 LA 573 (Traynor, 1985); Corwin & Co., 81 LA 706 (O'Connell, 1983); Ideal Elec. Co., 77 LA 123 (Martin, 1981); Niagara Mach. & Tool Works, 76 LA 160 (Grant, 1981); St. Regis Paper Co., 72 LA 312 (Elkin, 1979); Borg-Warner Corp., 72 LA 184 (Allen, 1979); Monte Mart, Inc., 71 LA 70 (Randall, 1978).

[130]E.g., City of Rochester, 78 LA 758 (Miller, 1982); Sun-Maid Raisin Growers of Cal., 72 LA 133 (Weiss, 1979).

10. *Impact on the Employer's Operations.*   In some cases, arbitrators have weighed the impact of an employee's absenteeism on the employer's operations. Thus, arbitrators have found just cause for discipline based, in part, upon the harm or burden imposed on the employer by the employee's absenteeism.[131] Some arbitrators have overturned or reduced the discipline where there is no such impact or at least where the employer has failed to prove such impact.[132]

Even if individual absences are excused, however, the cumulative total of absences may provide a basis for discipline. As noted by one arbitrator: "'Even if the reasons offered for each individual absence seem proper, employees may be disciplined for excessive absenteeism, if the absences are so frequent as to render the employee's services of little or no value to the employer.'"[133]

## D. Absence Without Leave

Under certain circumstances, an employer may properly consider that an employee who fails to notify it that he will be absent has abandoned the job. In one such instance an employee properly called in sick but thereafter went to Europe for 1 month. The arbitrator concluded the employer acted properly in deeming the job abandoned when the employee failed to report for duty after being notified by mail that she must report her absence within 3 days.[134]

If the employer deems the employee to have voluntarily quit, as opposed to terminating the employee for absenteeism, arbitrators will consider whether the employee's actions manifested an intent to resign. In one case the employer's rules made it clear that an employee would be considered a voluntary quit if he failed to call in for 2 consecutive days. The employee called in the first day of a 3-day absence, but failed to call in on the second and third days. The arbitrator held that this call-in manifested a desire by the employee to maintain rather than abandon his job.[135] According to the arbitrator, after the grievant's sister telephoned his supervisor on the first day of absence and advised him the grievant was ill and unable to work,

---

[131]E.g., Mallinckrodt, Inc., 95 LA 966 (Hilbert, 1990); Mead Paper, Chilpaco Mill, 91 LA 52 (Curry, 1988); Augusta Newsprint Co., 89 LA 725 (King, 1987); Goodyear Tire & Rubber Co., 88 LA 745 (Dworkin, 1987); GF Furniture Sys., Inc., 87 LA 500 (Klein, 1986); Safeway Stores, Inc., 80 LA 735 (MacLean, 1983); Asarco, Inc., 74 LA 1024 (Bothwell, 1980); Hawaii Transfer Co., Ltd., 74 LA 531 (Tsukiyama, 1980).

[132]E.g., Excel Corp., 95 LA 1069 (Shearer, 1990); Delta-Macon Brick & Tile Co., 92 LA 837 (O'Grady, 1989); Warner-Lambert Co., 89 LA 265 (Sloane, 1987); Cleveland Elec. Illuminating Co., 88 LA 781 (Morgan, 1987); Morgan Adhesives Co., 87 LA 1039 (Abrams, 1986); Louisville Water Co., 77 LA 1049 (Volz, 1981).

[133]Georgia-Pacific Corp., Southern Pulp & Paper Div., 91-1 ARB ¶ 8150 at 3738 (Williams, 1990) (quoting BNA's Grievance Guide, 9th Ed., p. 26).

[134]Hubinger Co., 71 LA 1258 (Krinsky, 1979).

[135]Oscar Mayer & Co., 80-1 ARB ¶ 8139 (Ludolf, 1980).

there was no reasonable justification to conclude the grievant intended to quit his job.[136]

On the other hand, an arbitrator upheld terminating an employee for job abandonment when the employee refused to report to work in New York City for fear of the Three Mile Island nuclear accident in Harrisburg, Pennsylvania. The grievant made no attempt to discuss her decision to absent herself from work or to reveal her fears to her supervisor.[137]

*1. Duty to Investigate.* If the employer has a rule deeming an employee who is absent without notification to have voluntarily quit, arbitrators consider whether the employee who is absent was unable to provide such notification. Thus the employer may be obliged to make a reasonable investigation before deciding the employee should be deemed to have voluntarily quit.[138]

*2. Procedures for Reporting Absences.* When an employer amends existing notification rules, employees must be made aware of the change in policy. An employee who was discharged for failure to comply with his employer's rule, due to his absence for 3 consecutive days without notification, was reinstated. Because the new rule bore a superficial similarity to the old contract clause, the arbitrator held the employer must have an "in-depth" discussion with its employees when it promulgates a new rule regarding the reporting of absences.[139]

Where the employer had taken reasonable steps to make its policy clear, as evidenced by its uniform and nondiscriminatory application, the policy's longstanding duration, and the fact the employee had been terminated once before for a similar violation, an arbitrator sustained the employee's discharge for failing to report his absence for 3 consecutive workdays following the conclusion of an approved 10-day medical leave of absence.[140]

*3. Construction of Ambiguous Notification Rules.* An ambiguous contractual notification provision may lead an arbitrator to overturn the discipline because she concludes the employee was improperly advised of the rules. In one instance an employee was discharged for being absent for 3 consecutive workdays without notifying the company. The employee had notified the company only on the first day of his 4-day absence. Since the ambiguous language of the agreement could be interpreted to only require notification within the first 3 days of an absence of any length, the arbitrator held the employee

---

[136]Id. at 3646.

[137]American Museum of Natural History, 80-1 ARB ¶ 8071 (Turkus, 1979).

[138]Oscar Mayer & Co., 80-1 ARB ¶ 8139 at 3646 (Ludolf, 1980). See also Todd-Pacific Shipyards, 76 LA 928 (Draznin, 1981).

[139]Borg-Warner Corp., 72 LA 184 (Allen, 1979).

[140]ITT Gen. Controls, 76 LA 1258 (Bickner, 1981).

was never properly advised of the employer's notification requirement and reinstated the grievant.[141]

   4. *Mitigating Factors.*   Even when the notification policy is reasonable on its face, and an employee fails to strictly comply with its terms, arbitrators have sometimes set aside, or at least modified, discipline. The mitigating factors that arbitrators consider are discussed below.

   a. Reasons Beyond Employee's Control.   The general rule that an employee may be excused for not properly notifying the employer of his absence where that failure was the result of conditions beyond the employee's control was stated in *American Shipbuilding Co.*[142] There, an alcoholic employee was discharged due to absence for 6 consecutive workdays without notifying his employer following a 2-week absence for alcoholism treatment. While the discharge was sustained in arbitration, the arbitrator noted that the employee would have been excused from the reporting requirements if he had shown that he was unable to notify his employer for reasons beyond his control.

   In one case the company discharged an employee for "three days no contact" after it had suspended her for alleged undocumented alien status. The arbitrator ruled the company could not require the employee to report her absences, which were due to conditions beyond her control, where the company was aware she would be absent because it had suspended her.[143]

   There was a similar holding in a case where the employee was terminated for failing to report to work, without notification, for 3 consecutive days.[144] The arbitrator found just cause was absent since the employee had the sincere belief that he had been fired, and call-in applies only in cases in which the failure of the employee to be at work is not attributable to the company.[145]

   Where the arbitrator found the employee was not accountable for his actions due to mental illness and abuse of medication, he ruled that the employee was excused from reporting in.[146]

   Where an employee was denied sick leave when she failed to notify the company of her intended absence, the arbitrator held that her failure to notify was excused because she attempted to call 8 to 10 times within a half-hour period. She was unable to get through due to understaffed phone lines resulting from picketing of the office. Moreover, other employees who failed to notify were granted sick leave. The arbitrator noted that she made reasonable efforts to comply

---

[141]North Am. Philips Corp., 9 LAIS 1019 (Brooks, 1981).

[142]81 LA 243 (Everitt, 1983).

[143]Redmer Plastics, Inc., 70 LA 351 (Eagle, 1982).

[144]Design & Mfg. Corp., 9 LAIS 1126 (Edes, 1982).

[145]Id.

[146]Amoco Oil Co., 85-1 ARB ¶ 8003 (Dunham, 1984).

with company policy, and concluded that her failure to notify the employer of her absence was due to events beyond her control.[147]

An alcoholic employee who had a doctor's note that he had "blacked out" and this prevented his reporting to the employer was excused from his failure to notify the employer of a 5-day absence. He was reinstated, but without back pay.[148]

b. Inconsistent Application. An employee was terminated for being absent without notification when he traded shifts with another employee in violation of company policy. The arbitrator held that the employee's actions did not warrant termination, since (1) the company's operations did not suffer, (2) the actions showed no turpitude, and (3) other similar violations did not result in discharge, giving rise to an inference of discriminatory application of the policy.[149]

In a company that did not have a formal notification policy, an employee failed to call in during a 3-week absence. The employee was reinstated with back pay because the company was provided sufficient notification by the employee's sister and his wife. They called and told the grievant's supervisor that the employee would be out for the day and that he was under a doctor's care for an emotional condition. In reinstating the employee, the arbitrator considered other mitigating factors, including the lack of a fair investigation by the company as well as an inconsistent and discriminatory application of the company's informal notification procedure.[150]

Where an employee was terminated for a 3-day absence without supervisory permission, the employee was reinstated by the arbitrator because the employee was ill and had called in and left a message with a co-worker. The arbitrator held that while the grievant did not comply with the letter of the company policy, the evidence showed that leaving messages with co-workers had sufficed for other employees in the past and the supervisor had often accepted such messages as proper notification.[151]

c. Ambiguous Instructions. Where an employee was discharged, in part, for failure to notify his employer of his absence, that reason for discharge was overturned by the arbitrator. The company sent the employee a letter, after 3 weeks of absence, advising him he must obtain proper medical documentation before returning to work. The employee misunderstood the letter to mean he need not call in until he had obtained the documentation.[152]

d. Good Faith Attempt. A discharged employee who did not report for work and failed to notify her employer of her absence was

---

[147]Michigan, Department of Soc. Servs., 84-1 ARB ¶ 8104 (Dobry, 1983).

[148]Niagara Mach. & Tool Works, 76 LA 160 (Grant, 1981).

[149]Sahara-Nevada Corp., 80-2 ARB ¶ 8374 (Weiss, 1980).

[150]Dawson-Baker Packing Co., 80-1 ARB ¶ 8036 (Chalfie, 1979).

[151]Amax Nickel, Inc., 84-2 ARB ¶ 8525 (Allen, 1984).

[152]Asarco, Inc., 74 LA 1024 (Bothwell, 1980).

reinstated by the arbitrator because she made a good faith attempt to comply with the notification requirement. The arbitrator found that she had called a fellow employee, who agreed to work the grievant's shift but arrived to work one-half hour late. The arbitrator ruled that she "complied with the spirit of the call-in rule."[153]

A similar good faith exception was found where an employee was terminated for failing to report or call in for his shift. The arbitrator credited the employee's claim that he misread the new work schedule, thus causing his inadvertent absence. Because the new schedule was complex and differed significantly from its predecessor, the arbitrator found the grievant not culpable.[154]

## II. Tardiness and Leaving Early

Most arbitrators have concluded that progressive discipline is appropriate for eliminating tardiness.[155] One arbitrator cited the need for progressive discipline in overturning a termination for tardiness following a single written warning.[156]

Many arbitrators considered counseling an important tool for correcting tardiness.[157] As noted by one observer, an employer should utilize all reasonable and cost-effective corrective measures before discharging the chronically tardy employee.[158]

Arbitrators have furthermore recognized the appropriateness of due process and just cause principles in tardiness cases. Where an employer docked a teacher's pay and suspended the grievant without pay for one-half day, for example, the arbitrator held that under a contract requiring written notice of a teacher's "alleged delinquencies or inadequacies of performance," due process and just cause required notice to the teacher before tardiness could lead to the docking of pay or disciplinary action.[159]

Similarly, where an employer's policy established that 11 to 13 points would result in suspension and accumulation of 14 points would require discharge, an arbitrator concluded the employer was not authorized to terminate an employee for accumulating 12 points, without warning the employee that his next unexcused tardy would result in termination.[160]

---

[153]B & I Realty, Inc., 79-2 ARB ¶ 8333 (Sinclitico, 1979).

[154]U.S. Steel Corp., 84-1 ARB ¶ 8153 (Dybeck, 1983).

[155]Elk Mound Sch. Dist., 9 LAIS 2030 (Vernon, 1981).

[156]Sun Furniture Co., 71 LA 928, 929 (Szollosi, 1978).

[157]Kite, "Preventing Employee Tardiness," 46 Supervision, 14–15.

[158]Kennedy, "A Counseling Approach to Chronic Tardiness," 29 Supervisory Mgmt., 28 (Nov., 1984).

[159]Elk Mound Sch. Dist., 9 LAIS 2030 (Vernon, 1981).

[160]Metal Container Corp., 81-2 ARB ¶ 8610 (Ross, 1981).

## A. Defining "Tardiness"

What constitutes "tardiness" and which tardies should be excused are frequently arbitrated.[161] Late arrival to the workplace is the most obvious form of tardiness. Other forms of lateness have also been held to constitute tardiness. The lack of notice and the employer's inability to secure timely substitutes for tardy employees can have an adverse affect on operations.[162] There may be inefficient and disorderly plant operations, additional work burdens upon other employees, payment of overtime wages, loss of production, and customer dissatisfaction.[163] Tardiness may furthermore result in serious morale problems within the workforce.[164]

Returning late from lunch or break is commonly held to constitute a tardy under an attendance program.[165] Arbitrators have also held that leaving early for lunch[166] as well as leaving work early[167] are properly treated as tardies.

An employee's proximity to his work station may also be an important factor in determining whether the employee was tardy. In one case the arbitrator concluded that where a contract did not specify whether the workday begins at the time clock or the work station, an employee was unjustly discharged for tardiness because he failed to clock in before the beginning of his shift.[168] Also, where an employee was a few steps from her work station when she punched in, an arbitrator concluded discipline was not for just cause.[169]

## B. Factors Used by Arbitrators in Evaluating Discipline

Excuses for employee tardiness are varied.[170] Furthermore, the standards by which employers and arbitrators evaluate excuses for tardiness are often subjective and complex.

---

[161]Western Reserve Transit Auth., 9 LAIS 2010 at XI-2025 (Laybourne, 1981) (tardiness referred to as "sharking").

[162]Trojan Luggage Co., 76 LA 324 (A. Modjeska, 1981). See also General Elec. Co., 74 LA 290 (MacDonald, 1979); AMBAC Indus., Inc., 72 LA 347 (Kuypers, 1979).

[163]Western Lake Superior Sanitary Dist., 9 LAIS 2146 (Gallagher, 1982); Metal Container Corp., 81-2 ARB ¶ 8610 (Ross, 1981); Ohio Mach. & Mold Co., 76 LA 1066 (Young, 1981); Wolverine Aluminum Co., 74 LA 252 (Dobry, 1980).

[164]Kite, "Preventing Employee Tardiness," 46 Supervision, 14-15.

[165]Metropolitan Transit Auth., 82 LA 141 (King, 1984); Pacific Northwest Bell Tel. Co., 81 LA 297 (Gaunt, 1983); National Oats Co., 82-2 ARB ¶ 8561 (Smith, 1982); Rubber Workers Fed. Credit Union, 80-1 ARB ¶ 8288 (Owen, 1980).

[166]A.R.A. Mfg. Co., 73 LA 972 (Carter, 1979).

[167]Dyrotech Indus., Inc., 83 LA 337 (Leach, 1984); GAF Corp., 77 LA 947 (Weinberg, 1981).

[168]Pacific Air Motive Corp., 28 LA 761 (Jones, 1957).

[169]Rubber Workers Fed. Credit Union, 80-1 ARB ¶ 8288 (Owen, 1980).

[170]See Kite, supra note 157, at 73.

*1. Automobile Breakdowns and Inclement Weather.* Automotive and weather problems are often excuses for tardiness. Whether they will be accepted depends on the effort exerted by the employee to get to work, and the employee's attendance record. In a case where an employee was tardy due to a flat tire in one instance and then experienced problems with his car battery on another, the arbitrator concluded that since the grievant had taken reasonable steps to arrive at work as soon as possible and had called in to report his car problems, the employer improperly imposed discipline.[171] A mailroom clerk was suspended for unexcused absence upon failing to arrive at work due to a snowstorm. The arbitrator, however, upheld the discipline noting the grievant's record of tardiness and that she had represented to her employer she would be in later that day.[172]

On the other hand, where public transportation delays brought on by bad weather caused an employee to be late, the arbitrator found that the employer improperly warned the employee for tardiness. In the arbitrator's view, the extenuating circumstances created by inclement weather were beyond the grievant's control.[173]

*2. Oversleeping.* Oversleeping is rarely accepted as a valid excuse for tardiness. In various arbitration cases where employees claimed oversleeping was caused by adjustment problems due to a recent layoff, working overtime and family problems, failure of an alarm clock to go off, taking prescribed medication, and failure to hear the alarm clock, discipline was deemed appropriate.[174] In one case, however, where the grievant argued that he had worked excessive overtime and was suffering from delayed stress disorder due to military service in Vietnam, the arbitrator concluded the penalty of discharge was too severe.[175]

*3. Prior Record.* Arbitrators sometimes consider the employee's disciplinary record and how the employer has considered the record

---

[171]Western Lake Superior Sanitary Dist., 9 LAIS 2146 (Gallagher, 1982). See also Mor Flo Indus., Inc., 83 LA 480 (Cocalis, 1984), where arbitrator held that employee who was a passenger in a car that had a flat tire should not have been denied double-time premium.

[172]Board of Trustees, Boilermakers-Blacksmiths Nat'l Pension & Trust Fund, 84-2 ARB ¶ 8588 at 5539 (Thornell, 1984). See also Carnation Co., 9 LAIS 1156 (Axon, 1982), where arbitrator found that running out of gas was not an "unforeseeable emergency" and that grievant was not saved by the fact that he called in to report that he would be late; Naval Air Rework Facility, 72 LA 1266 (Mire, 1979), where employee failed to provide any evidence in support of alleged breakdown of his car.

[173]Kerotest Mfg. Corp., 71 LA 744 (Blue, 1978). See also Board of Trustees, Boilermakers-Blacksmiths Nat'l Pension & Trust Fund, 84-2 ARB ¶ 8588 (Thornell, 1984), discussed above where the grievant's excuse that a snowstorm prevented her from getting her car out of the driveway was not accepted by the employer or the arbitrator.

[174]Dyrotech Indus., Inc., 83 LA 337 (Leach, 1984); Southern Cal. Rapid Transit Dist., 10 LAIS 2001 (Rothstein, 1982); Ohio Mach. & Mold Co., 76 LA 1066 (Young, 1981); Metal Container Corp., 81-2 ARB ¶ 8610 (Ross, 1981). See also Des Moines Indep. Community Sch. Dist., 10 LAIS 2030 (Wyman, 1982); General Elec. Co., 74 LA 290 (MacDonald, 1979).

[175]Olin Corp., 80 LA 797 (Denson, 1983).

in imposing discipline.[176] There is no general rule about the number of tardies within a defined period which will support discipline for "excessive" tardiness. Arbitrators have upheld discipline for 2 instances of tardiness in 1 week combined with improper work performance,[177] 18 days of absenteeism and 59 times tardy in 1 year and 3 tardies out of 12 work days at the beginning of the next year,[178] and 4 occurrences of absenteeism, tardiness, and reporting to work station late within a 12-month period.[179] On the other hand, three instances of tardiness within a 14-month period were not excessive, due to the lack of notice to the employee that such a degree of tardiness was excessive.[180] Arbitrators may consider discipline for misconduct other than absenteeism or tardiness, when assessing the propriety of the penalty.[181]

Although a grievant's record of tardiness was below the departmental average, the arbitrator concluded the grievant's unwillingness to make adjustments in his schedule to end his propensity for tardiness justified discharge.[182] Also, where an employee suffered a long period of personal tragedy and tardiness, the arbitrator held that while he sympathized with the grievant's plight, his failure to improve was caused not by the personal tragedy but by a lack of attentiveness or caring.[183]

Finally, in a case where an employee had been warned, counseled and failed to attend an investigatory meeting to discuss his tardiness record, the arbitrator sustained the discipline. The arbitrator also concluded the grievant undercut his own credibility based upon an obvious falsification of an "Agreement for Modification of Support Order" offered in support of his testimony regarding domestic difficulties.[184]

In extreme cases, where corrective discipline has failed to correct persistent tardiness deficiencies, arbitrators have ruled that even minor tardiness can appropriately precipitate termination.[185]

*4. Miscellaneous Excuses.* Other excuses for tardiness that have not been accepted by arbitrators are family problems, being

---

[176]Board of Trustees, Boilermakers-Blacksmiths Nat'l Pension & Trust Fund, 84-2 ARB ¶ 8588 (Thornell, 1984).

[177]Trojan Luggage Co., 76 LA 324 (Modjeska, 1981).

[178]Dravo Doyle Co., 73 LA 648 (H. Jones, 1979).

[179]General Elec. Co., 74 LA 290 (MacDonald, 1979).

[180]Des Moines Indep. Community Sch. Dist., 10 LAIS 2030 (Wyman, 1982).

[181]Ferro Corp. Composites Div., 9 LAIS 1028 (Wilmoth, 1981).

[182]Goodyear Atomic Corp., 82-2 ARB ¶ 8490 (Strasshofer, 1982).

[183]Pacific Northwest Bell Tel. Co., 81 LA 297 (Gaunt, 1983).

[184]GAF Corp., 77 LA 947, 950 (Weinberg, 1981). See also Tech. Cast., Inc., 74 LA 732 (Lewis, 1980) (employee employed only 17 months repeatedly warned and counseled); General Elec. Co., 74 LA 290 (MacDonald, 1979) (employee offered no reasons, only "no apparent reason" for tardiness).

[185]Metropolitan Transit Auth., 82 LA 141 (King, 1984). See also Pacific Northwest Bell Tel. Co., 81 LA 297 (Gaunt, 1983).

delayed by trains, fraudulent claims of attendance at a court hearing, and "no apparent reason."[186]

*5. Inconsistent Application.* Arbitrators sometimes cite discrimination in setting aside discipline in tardiness cases. In one case an employer suspended an employee for 3 days because he left for lunch 10 minutes early. The employer did not impose discipline on two other employees who returned 1 to 4 minutes late from lunch. The arbitrator held that the employer discriminated against the grievant and sustained the grievance.[187] Likewise, where it was shown that other employees with tardiness problems were not subject to docking of pay, an arbitrator awarded the grievant all monies withheld from her salary.[188]

In other instances arbitrators have rejected discrimination allegations. In one case the arbitrator concluded there was insufficient evidence about the circumstances surrounding other employees' records to evaluate the grievant's record and determine whether the employer had discriminated against the grievant.[189]

*6. Errors in Timekeeping.* Errors in the employer's time clock are often resolved against the employer. In one case where a grievant claimed her tardiness was due to the error of the employer's time clock, the arbitrator held it was unreasonable to discipline the employee for tardiness of up to 2 one hundredths of an hour when the error of the time clock is of that magnitude.[190]

A different conclusion, however, was reached where the grievant made a similar claim of time clock inaccuracy. The arbitrator found that for 28 years the employer set the clock ahead 5 minutes. This did not contribute to the employee's tardiness since the grievant knew of the policy and had received extensive warnings regarding his tardiness.[191]

*7. Improvement.* Evidence of improvement in an employee's tardiness record, following counseling and warnings, may result in

---

[186]Metal Container Corp., 81-2 ARB ¶ 8610 (Ross, 1981). See also Gulf & W. Taylor Forge, 84-2 ARB ¶ 8561 (Nicholas, Jr., 1984); Pacific Northwest Bell Tel. Co., 81 LA 297 (Gaunt, 1983); GAF Corp., 77 LA 947 (Weinberg, 1981); General Elec. Co., 74 LA 290 (MacDonald, 1979).

[187]A.R.A. Mfg. Co., 73 LA 972 (Carter, 1979).

[188]Elk Mound Sch. Dist., 9 LAIS 2030 (Vernon, 1981).

[189]Goodyear Atomic Corp., 82-2 ARB ¶ 8490 (Strasshofer, 1982). See also Board of Trustees, Boilermakers-Blacksmiths Nat'l Pension & Trust Fund, 84-2 ARB ¶ 8588 (Thornell, 1984); Dyrotech Indus., Inc., 83 LA 337 (Leach, 1984); Southern Cal. Rapid Transit Dist., 101 LAIS 2001 (Rothstein, 1982); City of Allentown, 78 LA 809 (DiLauro, 1982); Pismo-Oceano Vegetable Exch., 75 LA 1232 (Hill, 1980); General Elec. Co., 74 LA 290 (MacDonald, 1979); Dravo Doyle Co., 73 LA 648 (Jones, 1979).

[190]Chromalloy Am. Co., 80 LA 720, 724 (Woolf, 1983).

[191]City of Allentown, 78 LA 809 (DiLauro, 1982). See also Dyrotech Indus., Inc., 83 LA 337 (Leach, 1984) (arbitrator did not accept grievant's excuse that the alarm had failed to go off or that he read the clock wrong).

arbitrators overturning subsequent discipline. Where attendance records evidenced a decrease in incidents of tardiness or where 120 days had elapsed without an employee incurring an unexcused tardy, arbitrators have held the employees demonstrated a propensity for rehabilitation and the discipline was overturned.[192] Discipline for tardiness has been overturned where the penalties were imposed too quickly to provide the employee an opportunity to improve or for the employer to consider whether there had been improvement in the employee's attendance.[193]

*8. De Minimis Doctrine.*    Some arbitrators have excused tardiness because being a few minutes late causes little harm. This doctrine was applied where an employee was denied double-time pay when he arrived at work 10 minutes late due to a flat tire. The arbitrator concluded the effect of the employee's lateness on production was de minimis and therefore sustained the grievance.[194] Likewise, where an employee was tardy 1 minute but was within a few steps from her work station, the arbitrator concluded her tardiness was de minimis.[195]

Arbitrators have rejected the de minimis argument when there was a known policy or a poor record. Where the union argued the grievant's tardiness of 4 minutes was de minimis due to the employer's practice of setting the time clock forward, the arbitrator sustained the discipline because the grievant knew of the practice.[196] Also, where the union argued the grievant was tardy only a few minutes many of the times she was disciplined, the arbitrator upheld the discipline because of the grievant's poor record.[197] Where the triggering incident of discharge was a 19-minute tardy, the arbitrator found that standing alone the late report to work would not justify discharge. When coupled with five other acknowledged violations of the rules, however, the discharge stood.[198]

Similarly, while the grievant's last three tardies were minor, the lateness was within a few weeks of an unauthorized leave and a warning by his foreman that he was nearing the "border line." This work history justified the company's action.[199]

---

[192]Wilderness Foods, 84-1 ARB ¶ 8242 (Roumell, 1984) (drop in points in point system); Metal Container Corp., 81-2 ARB ¶ 8610 (Ross, 1981) (120 days); Rubber Workers Fed. Credit Union, 80-1 ARB ¶ 8288 (Owen, 1980) (several months).

[193]Rubber Workers Fed. Credit Union, 80-1 ARB ¶ 8288 at 4292, 4293 (Owen, 1980).

[194]Mor Flo Indus., Inc., 83 LA 480 (Cocalis, 1984).

[195]Rubber Workers Fed. Credit Union, 80-1 ARB ¶ 8288 (Owen, 1980).

[196]City of Allentown, 78 LA 809 (DiLauro, 1982).

[197]Board of Trustees, Boilermakers-Blacksmiths Nat'l Pension & Trust Fund, 84-2 ARB ¶ 8588 (Thornell, 1984).

[198]Metropolitan Transit Auth., 82 LA 141 (King, 1984).

[199]General Elec. Co., 74 LA 290 (MacDonald, 1979).

Finally, an arbitrator concluded the de minimis rule of the Wage and Hour Division of the Department of Labor applied to payment of wages, and not to tardiness, as the union argued.[200]

*9. Notification.*   One factor that is often important in tardiness cases is whether employees have telephoned the employer and advised they will be late for work. In many cases, arbitrators have noted that had the employees called in, no punitive action would have been taken. Thus, where an employer discharged an employee for a number of shop-rule violations, including running out of gas and returning late, all without reporting in, the arbitrator upheld the discipline. He noted that the sensible thing to do would have been to call the plant, explain what happened, and return as soon as possible.[201]

In another case an employee was suspended for tardiness when his car broke down. The arbitrator stated the grievant failed to present any supportive evidence of the breakdown of his car or explain why he failed to reach the facility by telephone.[202]

Employees may be required to give the reason and anticipated duration for their tardiness. A contract stated that when employees are unavoidably detained from work they would not be disciplined, nor their service records interrupted, provided they notified the employer. The arbitrator held that the employer had the right to withhold work from an employee who did not give the reason for his inability to report to work at his regularly scheduled hour, but merely told his plant manger that he would not be in until 11:00 p.m.[203]

Despite notification, repeated or implausible excuses for tardiness will not prevent discipline. In one case where an employee was discharged for excessive tardiness, the arbitrator refused to accept as a mitigating circumstance that the employee always notified the employer of his absences. In view of the employee's poor attendance record, and his falsification of a document at the hearing, which cast doubt upon his credibility, notification was not enough.[204]

In another case, however, the arbitrator concluded the employer improperly discharged an employee for failing to obtain the supervisor's permission to be late. The rule required the employee call the plant and provide the reason for being late. The rule made no reference to the necessity for obtaining approval.[205]

---

[200]A.R.A. Mfg. Co., 73 LA 972 (Carter, 1979).

[201]Tech-Cast, Inc., 74 LA 732, 736 (Lewis, 1980).

[202]Naval Air Rework Facility, 72 LA 1266 (Mire, 1979). Board of Trustees, Boilermakers-Blacksmiths Nat'l Pension & Trust Fund, 84-2 ARB ¶ 8588 (Thornell, 1984). See also Southern Cal. Rapid Transit Dist., 10 LAIS 2001 (Rothstein, 1982).

[203]Oliver Rubber Co., 82 LA 38 (Daughton, 1984).

[204]GAF Corp., 77 LA 947 (Weinberg, 1981).

[205]Ad-Art, Inc., 80 LA 1021 (Hughes, 1983).

## C. Alternative Consequences

*1. Withholding Work as Discipline.*   A tardy employee may lose the right to work the remainder of the shift. One arbitrator stated that an employer could replace a tardy employee where the union and the company had agreed that a 15-minute tardiness, whether at the beginning of a shift or after lunch, gave the foreman the right to send the worker home.[206] Where an arbitrator considered alternatives available to an employer in addition to denying a work break to a tardy employee, the arbitrator reasoned the employer could preclude the employee from beginning work after that employee is almost 2 hours late.[207]

Withholding work as a disciplinary action may, however, raise just cause concerns. In a case where the grievants informed their employer they would be late due to a union meeting and the employer had previously refused them the right to attend the meeting, the arbitrator concluded that before the employer could replace the employees, it should have advised them that if they did not report on time, they would be treated as absent and replaced.[208]

*2. Withholding Wages and Benefits as Discipline.*   It is generally recognized employers have the right to dock pay for time not worked. Where the employee was more than one-half hour late reporting to work, the employer penalized the employee by withholding the 15-minute paid lunch period, which had been unilaterally granted as an incentive to report to work on time. Since the parties' agreement made no provision concerning paid lunch, the arbitrator found the employer was within its power to withhold the paid lunch period.[209]

Also, an arbitrator held an employee was not lulled into a false sense of security by an employer's consistent failure to dock his wages for tardiness of 5 minutes or less. The evidence showed that while the employer did not dock the employee for such increments, it nevertheless counted them in its attendance control program.[210]

In a case where an employer imposed upon a teacher a half-day wage deduction for the time the grievant was absent one morning, along with a half-day suspension without pay, the arbitrator held the

---

[206]Wolverine Aluminum Co., 74 LA 252 (Dobry, 1980).

[207]Aydin Raytor Corp., 82-1 ARB ¶ 8136 at 3641 (Mulhall, 1982). See also Oliver Rubber Co., 82 LA 38 (Daughton, 1984) (employer withheld work from an employee who did not give a reason for inability to report to work); Air Carrier Engine Serv., Inc., 81-2 ARB ¶ 8352 (Greene, 1980) (past practice required an employee to work a full 8 hours after arriving late before being entitled to pay at the overtime rate).

[208]Sugar Creek Packing Co., 10 LAIS 1249 at XI-1624 (Laybourne, 1983). See also Elk Mound Sch. Dist., 9 LAIS 2030 (Vernon, 1981) (where a teacher-nurse was refused work, the arbitrator made a distinction between punishment and business reasons).

[209]Winston Heat Treating Inc., 75 LA 961 (High, 1980).

[210]Dravo Doyle Co., 73 LA 648 (H. Jones, 1979).

docking constituted discipline and should be subject to the rules of just cause.[211]

3. *Withholding Overtime and Holiday Pay.*   No clear conclusion may be drawn from a review of the reported arbitration awards regarding whether an employee who is tardy and not allowed to work the remainder of the shift should be paid overtime or holiday pay. The facts vary greatly from case to case. In a case where an employee was 10 minutes late due to a flat tire while driving to work, the arbitrator concluded the employer's denial of double-time premium for Saturday work was unreasonable, because the provision was clearly meant as an incentive to encourage employees to report to work on time, and denial of the pay would defeat the purposes of the contract provision.[212]

Also, where a contract provided that overtime was to be paid for work in excess of 8 hours in any one working day, an arbitrator held that a tardy employee's overtime wages were to be computed beginning at the end of the 8 hours actually worked and not beginning at the end of his regularly scheduled shift. The company had a past practice of requiring an employee to work the full 8 hours prior to payment of overtime.[213] Where deductions were made from the holiday wages of automobile workers equivalent to the time the employees were late in reporting for work on the day before and/or after a 3-day holiday period, the arbitrator held the employer should have deducted salary only from one holiday and not from each holiday.[214]

## III.  Requiring Medical Examinations and Certifications

Absenteeism cases often involve issues of medical evidence.[215] For example, an employee who is discharged for excessive absenteeism may claim the absences are due to a medical condition that is beyond his control. An employee seeking to return to work may present a physician's certificate supporting his fitness for duty, while an examination by the company's physician indicates he continues to suffer from a medical disability. At times there may be conflicting medical evidence regarding a grievant's entitlement to contractual benefits for illness or injury such as sickness or disability leave. Where

---

[211]Elk Mound Sch. Dist., 9 LAIS 23030 at XI-2079 (Vernon, 1981).

[212]Mor Flo Indus., 83 LA 480 (Cocalis, 1984). See also Carborundum Co., 71 LA 802 (Millious, 1978), where the arbitrator held the holiday pay section was in conflict with the tardiness guidelines.

[213]Air Carrier Engine Serv., Inc., 81-2 ARB ¶ 8353 (Greene, 1980).

[214]Scott Mfg. Div. of Kysor Indus. Corp., 80-1 ARB ¶ 8225 (Render, 1980).

[215]See Chapter 11 for a complete discussion of how arbitrators view medical evidence and decide among conflicting medical opinions.

an employee's medical condition is at issue, there are often challenging questions about how to present, evaluate, and resolve medical disputes.[216]

## A. *Employer's Authority to Require Verification of Medical Status*[217]

Arbitrators have held the employer can require written verification of an employee's medical status where the employee claims entitlement to contractual benefits based upon a medical condition. The employer is entitled to verify whether an employee is too ill to work and, if so, for how long this condition is likely to continue. An arbitrator upheld the discharge of an employee who initially cited babysitter problems as grounds for absence and subsequently claimed she was ill. The employee was required to be examined by a company doctor and the arbitrator concluded just cause for discharge existed where the employee failed to keep appointments for medical examinations with the company doctor and failed to report for work after the doctor had certified her as being able to return to work.[218] Similarly, an employer can properly require appropriate written verification from employees who claim to be sick on the day before or after a holiday.[219]

Submitting a doctor's note does not automatically preclude the employer from requiring additional medical evidence. The employer, depending upon the circumstances, may be justified in seeking more detailed medical certification or even examination by a doctor.[220] In one case, the arbitrator reasoned that since the responsibility for obtaining reports regarding the grievant's condition rested with the employer and because the data sought either had already been provided or was otherwise not available in the time frame requested, and in view of the fact the grievant's doctor certified that returning to work would be dangerous to her health, the grievant's termination on the ground of insubordination for failure to comply with an order

---

[216]For a thought-provoking article advocating that arbitrators, with the consent of the parties, should engage in independent research regarding medical questions, see Zack & Zack, "Arbitrators and Medical Evidence," 39 Arb. J., 6 (Sept. 1984). See also Wilson, "Medical Evidence in Arbitration: Aspects and Dilemmas," 39 Arb. J., 11–18 (Sept. 1984).

[217]For further discussion of medical evidence, see Chapter 11.

[218]Pacific Tel. & Tel. Co., 81 LA 259 (Conners, Jr., 1983). See also Willoughby-Eastlake City Schs., 75 LA 21 (Ipavec, 1980); Atlantic Bldg. Sys., Inc., 80 LA 369 (Williams, 1983). Employer entitled to require written verification of employee's condition before granting sick leave: Northern Ind. Pub. Serv. Co., 74 LA 604 (Kossoff, 1980); American Hoechst Corp., 73 LA 1235 (Caraway, 1979). Accord Dayton-Rogers Co., 84-1 ARB ¶ 8083 (Flagler, 1984). Similarly, in Judson Park, Inc., 84 LA 210 (Dworkin, 1985), the arbitrator held a prior settlement agreement between the parties justified the employer's requirement to produce a medical release.

[219]Modine Mfg. Co., 83-1 ARB ¶ 8251 (Fitzsimmons, 1983). See also Rudin Mgmt. Co., 74 LA 189 (Talmadge, 1979) (employer may confirm sick leave claims by appropriate controls in the absence of specific contractual prohibitions).

[220]Aero Nuclear Corp., 10 LAIS 1206 (Creo, 1983), also found at 83-2 ARB ¶ 8424.

to obtain a medical certificate releasing her for duty was improper.[221] When the employer may properly require a doctor's note because it promises confidentiality, it must scrupulously honor employee's requests for confidentiality by limiting publication to persons involved in the administration of attendance and personnel programs.[222]

## B. *Elements of a Valid Doctor's Note*

Employers may require an acceptable, written verification of illness to grant an excused absence.[223] Where a back-to-work form was incomplete and unsigned, the employer's refusal to allow an employee to return to work was upheld.[224]

On occasion, there may be disputes over whether the employer properly rejected a medical excuse. Arbitrators have recognized that employers can question doctors' notes under certain circumstances. For example, an employee's absence was unexcused because he failed to call in, and his medical excuse consisted of a self-serving report to a nurse that he was vomiting and had diarrhea the evening before which caused him to oversleep. The arbitrator held the employee had not established good cause for not calling in.[225]

Even where the employer reasonably requires a doctor's excuse, an aspect of the requirement may be unreasonable. An arbitrator held the employer improperly suspended an employee for 1 day when he failed to produce a physician's statement within 48 hours of his return to work. The arbitrator found the company's 48-hour requirement was inconsistent and contrary to specific provisions of the agreement.[226] Where the employer discharged an employee for violating the rule requiring medical excuses to be provided within 3 days, the arbitrator found the rule overly harsh and converted the discharge into a disciplinary layoff.[227]

---

[221]Gillette Co., 79 LA 943 (Bard, 1982). For further discussion, see Chapter 7, section V.

[222]Saginaw Mining Co., 83 LA 741 (Duda, Jr., 1984). For an analysis of the employee's competing right to privacy, see the discussion entitled "The Employee's Right to Privacy" in this chapter.

[223]See Chapter 11 for a further discussion of medical evidence.

[224]Texas City Ref., Inc., 83-2 ARB ¶ 8450 (Taylor, 1983).

[225]Arch of Ill., Inc., 82 LA 625 (Hewitt, 1984). In Merck Sharp & Dohme, Div. of Merck & Co., 70-1 ARB ¶ 8115 (Duff, 1979), discipline was held appropriate where a medical excuse was obviously based upon inaccurate information supplied by the employee. See Chapter 11.

[226]Kansas City Area Transp. Auth., 76 LA 1267 (Eisler, 1981). See also Star-Kist Foods, Inc., 78 LA 801 (Weiss, 1982), where penalty of discharge was found to be too severe for an employee who waited longer than the 20-day period to submit the required doctor's statement certifying the cause for absence since there was no evidence anyone else had ever been discharged for such a delay. Discharge was sustained, however, in one case where an employee failed to produce a valid doctor's note to justify his absences until the second step of the grievance procedure. Southland Corp., 75 LA 1285 (Gray, 1980).

[227]Bendix Corp., 85-1 ARB ¶ 8008 (Flannagan, 1984).

## C. *Employer's Authority to Require Medical Examinations*

Employers may wish employees to undergo medical examinations for a variety of legitimate reasons. Arbitrators have long upheld the general authority of employers to require employees to take medical examinations provided the tests are for appropriate reasons, administered reasonably, and not otherwise restricted by the agreement.[228] Arbitrators commonly uphold the use of medical exams when an employee seeks to return to work following a lengthy absence from duty.[229] Similarly, arbitrators have upheld an employer requirement that employees provide particular medical records before being allowed to return to duty.[230]

While it is appropriate to require back-to-work physical exams, it may be unreasonable to place extreme time constraints upon the employee in completing the medical examination. In a case where the company's right to require a complete return-to-work physical examination of an employee was upheld, the arbitrator ruled the employee must be given a reasonable opportunity to complete the examination, in that case, 2 weeks.[231]

The results of required medical examinations may be evaluated by arbitrators for reasons other than simply deciding whether an employee is ill and unable to work. In one case an employee had been on sick leave for arthritis when the plant was shut down. Upon resuming operations, the company required supplemental documentation of the grievant's disability. The employee submitted proof of a different disability, pulmonary disease, and the company directed

---

[228]See, e.g., Rudin Mgmt. Co., 74 LA 189 (Talmadge, 1979), holding that in the absence of specific contractual prohibitions, the employer may test the veracity of the employee's claim of illness by asking the employee to submit a physician's statement certifying illness. See also Reynolds & Reynolds Co., 9 LAIS 1139 (Render, 1982) (employer allowed to direct an employee to submit to medical examination to substantiate her physician's report that she was disabled for purposes of disability insurance provided under the agreement); U.S. Assay Office, 80-1 ARB ¶ 8301 (Marcus, 1980) (mass physical examinations upheld); Public Serv. Co. of N.M., 82 ARB ¶ 8494 (McBrearty, 1982) (employer's right to arrange for medical exams of employees for the purpose of determining fitness did not include psychological testing because a psychological test was not a medical exam). Contra H.O. Canfield Co. of Va., 79-1 ARB ¶ 8261 (Ables, 1979) (suspension for insubordination was not sustained where an employee refused to obey an order to see a physician to verify his claimed illness). Accord National Steel Corp., 76 LA 103 (Roberts, 1981).

[229]In agreement with this view is one award that held that where an employee had been off the job for 16 months with a compensable injury, the company reasonably had the right to request an examination by the grievant's doctor and by its own doctor if deemed necessary. See Kansas Gas & Elec. Co., 11 LAIS 1291 (Thornell, 1984).

[230]Atlantic Bldg. Sys., Inc., 80 LA 369 (Williams, 1983).

[231]Peschke Packing Co., 79-2 ARB ¶ 8452 (Coyle, 1979). Care must also be taken in imposing deadlines for submitting "medical proof." For example, where an employee was terminated for failing to apply for medical leave within a period specified in the agreement, the arbitrator interpreted the agreement as only requiring "medical proof" sometime after the initial period of absence. Colt Indus., Quincy Compressor Div., 9 LAIS 1185 (Wright, 1982).

the employee be examined by its own physician, who found the employee was able to return to work. The arbitrator concluded the employee's continuing eligibility for sick leave must be related to the same disability.[232]

While requiring physical examinations is upheld when it is for appropriate reasons, administered reasonably, and not otherwise restricted by the agreement, an employee's inability to pass such a physical examination may not be an agreed-upon ground for termination.[233] One arbitrator found that the employer's right to administer physical examinations to employees returning from long-term layoffs does not create any new right to terminate, or decline to recall, an employee. The employer is still limited to those causes existing in other parts of the agreement.[234] Where the employer has a right to require medical information, failure to timely comply with reasonable requests for the information may be grounds for discipline, denial of contractual benefits, or a refusal to permit the employee to return to work. In one case, an arbitrator upheld the employer's refusal to permit an employee to return to work until the employee provided requested medical records supporting his fitness for duty.[235] There must, of course, be appropriate reasons for requiring the medical records before allowing an employee to return to work, or an arbitrator will not uphold the requirement.[236]

## D. Use of Employer's Physician for Medical Examinations

In order to satisfy legitimate questions about an employee's medical condition, the employer may ordinarily require examination by its own physician.[237] This must be distinguished, however, from attempts to preclude from consideration evaluations by other medical professionals. Attempts to reserve exclusive authority to determine employees' fitness for duty have been rejected. For example, where the company sought to require examination by the employer physician after returning from sick leave and to reserve to the company doctor

---

[232]Birmingham-Jefferson County Transit Auth., 9 LAIS 2047 (Schaffer, 1982).

[233]Morenci Rubber Prods., Inc., 9 LAIS 1220 (Dobry, 1982).

[234]Id.

[235]Accord Iowa Malleable Iron Co., 74 LA 858 (Carter, undated); Atlantic Bldg. Sys., Inc., 80 LA 369 (Williams, 1983); Lloyd Noland Found., Inc., 74 LA 1236 (Griffin, 1980). But see Gillette Co., 79 LA 953 (Bard, 1982) (addressing the employer's responsibility for obtaining reports regarding an employee's condition).

[236]U.S. Steel Corp., 83-2 ARB ¶ 8555 (Dybeck, 1983) (holding that conditioning the employee's return to work upon his authorization to release hospital medical records was improper since the facts did not give the employer sufficient cause to require their release).

[237]This ordinary right may, however, be restricted by the agreement. For example, in Consolidated Elec. Coop., Inc., 84-2 ARB ¶ 8461 (Heinz, 1984), the arbitrator held the company could not compel an employee to see a company doctor before seeing his own doctor where the employee had requested supplemental injury benefits and the contract only provided for compulsory company doctor examination in the case of sick leave.

exclusive authority to declare one fit for work, refusing a medical release from an employee's personal physician was declared improper.[238]

Like the right to require an examination, the use of a company doctor is not unrestricted. The requirement to see a company doctor must be founded upon sufficient information to raise a legitimate question of the employee's fitness for duty. Where an employee's own physician had unconditionally released him to return to work and the company subsequently required him to undergo an electroencephalogram based upon conversations with unqualified members of the grievant's family and a hospital employee, the arbitrator held the employee was entitled to all lost time due to the company's refusal to return him to work.[239]

Where an employee's return to duty is delayed while waiting for medical clearance, there is frequently a question of who should bear the economic burden. The cases are not consistent and appear to turn upon the reasonableness of the delay. Where an employee's promotion was delayed by a company medical officer who required repeated mental examinations of the employee, the arbitrator held the employee's promotion was improperly delayed and the employee was granted back pay.[240]

In another case, an employer sent an employee home in the belief the employee had a contagious skin disease. The employer required the employee to produce medical documentation that he did not have the disease before being allowed to return to work. The employee then presented medical evidence supporting his good health. The arbitrator held the employer was required to reinstate the employee with back pay for the time the employee was absent due to the employer's mistaken belief he had a contagious skin disease.[241] Similarly, an employer had to reimburse an employee for time lost due to the company doctor's unavailability to conduct an examination and issue a medical release.[242] Where an employee had obtained an unrestricted release to return to work but the company did not allow his return for over 1 month, the arbitrator held the employee's release created a presumption the employee could work and the company had to rebut this presumption with a determination by its own doctor. The company's delay in arranging for an examination of the employee was held to be unreasonable.[243] A contrary conclusion, however, was reached by another arbitrator who denied an employee's claim for

---

[238]Alofs Mfg. Co., 82-2 ARB ¶ 8452 (Daniel, 1982).

[239]Curtis Mathis Mfg. Co., 79-1 ARB ¶ 8164 (Carter, 1979).

[240]Naval Air Rework Facility, Norfolk, Va., 82-1 ARB ¶ 8224 (Tharp, 1982). The agreement limited the back pay to the period beginning 30 days after the grievance was filed.

[241]Fram Corp., 9 LAIS 1133 (Kates, 1982).

[242]Libby, McNeill & Libby, 10 LAIS 1012 (Strasshofer, Jr., 1982).

[243]Davey Expert Tree Co., 11 LAIS 1254 (Strasshofer, Jr., 1984); Accord West Carrollton Parchment Co., 80-1 ARB ¶ 8001 (Chalfie, 1979).

lost time due to the employer's requirement the employee obtain a second medical release from the employer's doctor.[244]

On the other hand, when the delay is attributable to the employee, the employer is not required to bear the economic loss.[245] Where the employee's doctor is the cause of the delay, it is attributed to the employee.[246] Where resort to a third, neutral physician was ordered, an arbitrator ruled the company was not liable for the employee's lost time in pursuing this procedure.[247]

## E.  The Employee's Right to Privacy

To sustain disciplinary action against an employee who refuses to give the employer access to the employee's medical records, the employer must demonstrate a need for the information that outweighs the employee's privacy interests. Whether there is a sufficiently compelling need for medical information is a fact-specific inquiry, determined on a case-by-case basis.

In *San Diego Transit Corp.,*[248] a bus driver refused to release to his employer the results of his Department of Motor Vehicles-mandated physical examination. The arbitrator upheld the employer's decision to discharge the employee for this refusal, despite the employee's objections to releasing the report because it was "private and confidential," reasoning as follows:

> First, * * * [t]he Company is obligated to provide safe, efficient public transportation, and the physical fitness of the operators is central to meeting that obligation. The Company has the right to obtain the results of the medical examination to confirm for its proprietary purposes that the operators are physically qualified to drive; and so long as the confidentiality of the examination results is guaranteed by proper record security, a fair balance is struck between the operators' right to privacy and the Company's right to know first hand whether the operators are physically qualified to drive. Second, for more than twenty years the Company has required and received from countless operators the written releases or the results of the medical examinations without resistance from the operators and apparently with the approval of the Union.[249]

---

[244]County of Kern, 11 LAIS 2155 (Tamoush, 1984).

[245]Kansas Elec. Co., 11 LAIS 1291 (arbitrator noted 3-month delay between grievant's requested reinstatement and his resumption of work seemed excessive, but much of the delay was attributable to the grievant's own failure to furnish requested medical information).

[246]Aero Nuclear Corp., 83-2 ARB ¶ 8424 (Creo, 1983), where the arbitrator held a delay caused by a doctor chosen by the grievant must be borne by the grievant and not by the employer.

[247]Peterson Spring Corp., 74 LA 744 (Keefe, 1980).

[248]96 LA 137 (Christopher, 1991).

[249]Id. at 138.

Thus, legitimate safety concerns and a long history of requiring the information without protest may be sufficient.

The arbitrator reached a different conclusion in *Morgan County Sheriff's Department*.[250] There, the arbitrator held that just cause did not exist to impose a 5-day suspension for insubordination upon a deputy sheriff who refused the department's requests to authorize the release of his private psychologist's records to the department's psychologist, although he did submit to an examination by the department's psychologist.

The arbitrator ruled that the employee's refusal to sign the release did not justify the disciplinary action, because the arbitrator found evidence that the psychologist did not "absolutely need" the requested records and the employee had a legitimate concern about further dissemination.[251]

Even where an employer can demonstrate a compelling need for medical information, it may be outweighed by the employee's privacy concerns if the scope of the medical authorization is not limited to the specific matter at issue. For example, in *Bondtex Corp.*,[252] an employer argued that it had just cause to discharge an employee who failed to sign a release granting the employer access to the employee's medical records. The employer's discharge decision was based on the employer's belief that it had the right to gain access to the information to determine whether, in fact, the employee had misrepresented his medical condition and prognosis at the time he was hired. Although sympathetic to the employer's desire to investigate whether the employee had falsified his records, the arbitrator sustained the grievance noting that the authorization form was "so lacking in specificity and so broad in its application and coverage as to cause any reasonably prudent person to think twice before signing what would amount to a license for a fishing expedition into his private affairs."[253] Significantly, the arbitrator intimated that if, indeed, the employer had drafted a medical authorization that clearly defined and limited the scope of the inquiry to the specific matters of concern, the discharge decision would have been upheld.[254]

Similarly, in *Fleming Foods West, Inc.*,[255] the arbitrator concluded that an employer's insistence that an employee suspected of moonlighting while on disability leave sign an open-ended, blanket medical-records release before returning to work was a violation of the collective bargaining agreement. The arbitrator noted that the unrestricted,

---

[250]98 LA 975 (Cohen, 1992).

[251]Id. at 978.

[252]68 LA 476 (Coburn, 1977).

[253]Id. at 478.

[254]Id.

[255]92 LA 168 (Seidman, 1989).

indefinite release converted the employer's otherwise reasonable request for medical documents into an unreasonable intrusion into the employee's private medical history.

In *Western Airlines,*[256] the arbitrator declined to uphold an employer's decision to keep an employee out of work when, in connection with a return-to-work physical examination after suffering an injury, he agreed to release his medical records to the company doctor but refused to release his medical records to the employer. Finding that the employee had complied with the collective bargaining agreement's return-to-work requirements by agreeing to an examination by the company doctor and by releasing his own doctor's medical records to that doctor and, further, finding that the collective bargaining agreement did not contain a requirement that medical records be released to the company, the arbitrator ordered the employer to make the employee whole.

When employers offer employees assistance for psychological problems through an employee assistance program (EAP) there may be privacy concerns. Arbitrators attach significance to whether the employer provides the employee with the opportunity to disclose his or her concerns confidentially to an in-house doctor or counselor through the EAP. Where the treating psychologist or psychiatrist was permitted to divulge information about the employee to the employer, without also allowing the employee a confidential means by which to express his concerns, arbitrators may be reluctant to uphold discipline against the employee on the ground that the employee's due process rights were violated.[257] These basic principles were upheld in a case where an arbitrator concluded the employer could require a physical examination when an employee was exposed to chemicals while working. The employer was entitled to aggregate all information required by law about the employee's ability to work. In recognition of the employee's right to privacy in medical information, however, the arbitrator specifically held that the employer may not obtain the diagnosis, or details of a specific nature, because that information is confidential.[258]

The employees' right to privacy was addressed in a case where the company sought detailed medical information from an employee's physician regarding the cause of an on-the-job injury. A contract provision gave employees the right to return to work with limitations upon furnishing physicians' statements authorizing them to return to work. The arbitrator held the employer's inquiry was restricted to

---

[256]74 LA 923 (Richman, 1980).

[257]City of Allentown, 100 LA 592 (DiLauro, 1992), (where employee confided in EAP's doctor, and this confidence was disclosed to the employer which resulted in employee's discharge, the discharge was in violation of the employee's due process rights).

[258]Williams Pipe Line Co., 78 LA 617 (Moore, 1982). See also Saginaw Mining Co., 83 LA 741 (Duda, Jr., 1984) (holding an employer must scrupulously honor confidentiality by limiting publication to persons involved in administration of attendance and personnel programs).

information regarding whether the physical limitation was permanent or temporary and, if temporary, for how long.[259]

## F. *Pyschological Examinations*

Arbitrators generally uphold an employer's demand that an employee submit to a psychological evaluation when there are grounds to suspect the employee is emotionally or mentally unable to perform the work or when there is reliable evidence to suggest a risk of self-harm or harm to others.[260] The decisions require "some cogent showing that the employee presents * * * a danger or is * * * incapable of performing his job * * *."[261] Indeed, as part of their award, some arbitrators have directed employees to undergo an examination as a prerequisite to gain reinstatement. For example, a school board that improperly reassigned a teacher accused of sexual misconduct, but that had reasonable grounds for believing his continued activity as a teacher posed unacceptable risks, was ordered by the arbitrator to renew its offer of psychological or psychiatric evaluation of the teacher.[262] The arbitrator then conditioned the teacher's return to his former position on his agreement to submit to the evaluation and on a finding that the teacher was emotionally fit to resume classroom teaching.[263]

In another case, where an employee committed an unprovoked assault on a co-worker and supervisor while suffering a brief psychotic episode, the arbitrator reduced the discharge to an unpaid leave of absence with instructions to get both a physical and a mental examination and present written release for work within 90 days of the examinations.[264]

---

[259]Magnode Prods., Inc., 71 LA 707 (Bressler, 1978).

[260]See Port of Tacoma, 96 LA 361, 364 (Latsch, 1991), quoting Standard Knapp Div., 50 LA 833, 835 (Cahn, 1968) (while an employer does not enjoy unlimited authority to order an employee to submit to psychological evaluation, " 'it must be said that when a substantial basis exists for concluding that an employee presents such a danger or by reason of mental impairment cannot properly perform his work, the Company may well be warranted in requiring the employee to submit to a psychiatric examination as a condition of his continued employment' "); City of Chicago, 97 LA 20 (Goldstein, 1990) (police department properly placed investigator on involuntary, unpaid medical leave so that he might undergo psychotherapy recommended as result of psychological evaluation, where co-workers' reports of grievant's aberrant behavior gave department reasonable grounds for ordering examination; medical leave was based on evaluator's finding that grievant was unfit for duty, and grievant was not discharged); IBP, Inc., 89 LA 41 (Eisler, 1987) (just cause existed for nondisciplinary discharge of employee who refused to submit to psychological evaluation after he ignored repeated requests of female co-worker, her relatives, and management to cease trying to contact her). But see U.S. Steel Corp., 54 LA 572 (Garrett, 1970) (employer that received "unofficial notification" that an employee had attempted suicide during a leave of absence was precluded from ordering the employee to submit to psychiatric evaluation before returning to work because the employer had failed to provide enough justification for its decision).

[261]Standard Knapp Div., 50 LA 833, 835 (Cahn, 1968).

[262]Summit City Bd. of Mental Retardation, 100 LA 4 (Dworkin, 1992).

[263]Id.

[264]U.C. Agric. Prods. Co., 89 LA 432 (Anderson, 1987).

This is not the same as an unlimited right to require medical examinations. Another arbitrator held that a public utility's right to arrange for medical exams of its employees at any time, to determine fitness for the job, did not include psychological testing because a psychological test is not a medical exam. The arbitrator held that management improperly suspended and later discharged a working foreman who refused on two occasions to take psychological tests following his collapse at work.[265] Another arbitrator held that where the basis for placing the employee on sick leave is emotional or psychiatric, the employer must obtain the opinion of a licensed psychiatrist.[266]

---

[265]Public Serv. Co. of N.M., 82-2 ARB ¶ 8494 (McBrearty, 1982).
[266]Boces, First Supervisory Dist., 82 LA 1269 (Sabghir, 1984).

# Chapter 4

# Job Performance Problems

## I. Introduction

Some employee behavior that leads to discipline is not evidence of straightforward misconduct or a breach of workplace responsibilities. Sometimes an employee is incapable of doing a particular job because of a lack of competence; an inability to work at an appropriate speed, skill level, or quality level; the loss of a qualifying certificate; or an inability to learn skills appropriate to a new job. Often, the employee is not at fault in the traditional sense. The employee did not intend to misbehave, she simply could not perform the required work. While an adverse employment action is imposed, and can be grieved through the disciplinary grievance system, the action is not taken to correct behavior. The employee may be trying as hard as she can but may be incapable of changing the behavior. Consequently, she cannot be kept in a particular job. There is, of course, always the possibility that the employer has obligations to accommodate the employee under the Americans with Disabilities Act.[1]

In some instances, the employee's behavior is negligent and the question for an arbitrator is whether the degree of negligence is so high that the employee should be treated as if the act were intentional. There is a continuum from negligent to intentional action with which arbitrators have struggled.

Finally, employees may fall asleep on the job or simply loaf. In both instances they are not performing the expected work. In the former, the employee may have been unable to stay awake because of some medical reason or may simply have decided to nap on the employer's time. In the latter case, the employee may be perfectly

---

[1]42 U.S.C. §12101 et seq. (1990).

capable of doing the job but deliberately takes too much time in doing it. The behavior discussed in this chapter differs from later discussions of refusals to perform work and misconduct because performance problems are often a mixture of inability, incompetence, and intentional misbehavior, which are all discussed below. As the discussion demonstrates, arbitrators may be uncomfortable calling an action "discipline" when the employee was doing all she could but could not meet reasonable expectations. Nevertheless, they uphold adverse job actions in recognition of the employer's need to have an effective workforce.

## II. Incompetence

Incompetence is often used generically to indicate unacceptable performance that may, in one arbitrator's words, be viewed as having the "dual connotation of unsatisfactory job performance and inability to acquire the skills necessary to perform adequately."[2] It encompasses: (1) "pure" incompetence, which is inherent inadequacy or ineptitude in performance; and (2) poor performance including intentional and negligent misconduct.[3] The meaning of "incompetence" in a specific case depends on the intent of the parties and the precise wording of the contract.

### A. "Pure" Incompetence

"Pure" incompetence, without any misconduct, is a comparatively rare topic in arbitration awards.[4] Usually, employers have a right to terminate employees who are unfit or unable to perform their jobs.[5] "Pure" incompetence implies that the parties thought the employee would be able to perform, the employee tried to perform, but the employee was unable to do so at even a minimum level of acceptability.[6] There is an inference that even the best effort of the employee

---

[2]Michigan Dep't of Mental Health, 82 LA 1311, 1316 (Girolamo, 1984), quoting Knight Newspapers, Inc., 58 LA 446 (Platt, 1972).

[3]Trendler Metal Prods., 101 LA 749, 753 (Greene, 1993) (" 'Employees are incompetent "when they are substantially deficient in their work . . . (or) when their effort and workmanship deteriorate to a point where they no longer keep up with the standard of performance of others in their classification," ' " quoting Republic Steel Corp., 25 LA 733 (Platt, 1955)).

[4]These cases are discussed in greater detail in Demotion for Inability to Perform in this chapter.

[5]Natco Ltd. Partnership, 102 LA 771 (Marcus, 1994) (applying arbitrary and capricious standard of review to nondisciplinary demotion); Southwestern Bell Telecom, 94 LA 199 (O'Grady, 1990); Michigan Dep't of Mental Health, 82 LA 1311 (Platt, 1972).

[6]Saginaw Bd. of Educ., 101 LA 194 (McDonald, 1993) (arbitrator refused to accept assertion of incompetence to classify an error in judgment).

would not be sufficient to meet the work requirements.[7] A charge of incompetence reflects an assessment by a qualified observer that the employee is incapable of improving. For this reason, "pure" incompetence may be as hard to challenge as it is to prove. In fact, the defense may rely not on assertions of competence, but on claims of contractual procedural violations.[8]

Arbitrators have upheld employer assertions that they are not required to retain an employee who cannot perform adequately.[9] Incompetence may be the basis for discharging employees who, for instance, have not passed a job competency test despite multiple opportunities to do so.[10] Demotions for incompetence have been justified on the ground that an employee's performance, though adequate at one time, has fallen below the standard required to hold the position "either because his own performance has deteriorated or, though it has not deteriorated, because the standard in his occupation has been raised by the greater ability of those around him."[11] The scarcity of cases may indicate that employees charged with incompetence are concerned about future employment possibilities and are not inclined to risk an arbitrator affirming their incompetence. In addition, instead of charging the employee with ineptitude and inadequacy of performance, other ways of characterizing the performance problem, either according to its origins or its results, may be used.

## B. Conduct as an Element of Incompetence

When a charge of incompetence is based upon an employee's production output, the behavior may be characterized as a failure by the employee to meet quality or quantity standards or negligent performance, which are both discussed later in this chapter.

---

[7]See, e.g., MacMillan Bloedel Packaging, Inc., 106 LA 33 (Holley, Jr. 1995).

[8]Clorox Co., 103 LA 932 (Franckiewicz, 1994).

[9]St. Regis Paper Co., 74 LA 896 (Harter, 1980). Even when employers voluntarily or contractually limit their ability to terminate professional employees, they may retain exceptions for incompetence or misconduct. See Rood v. General Dynamics Corp., 444 Mich. 107, 507 N.W.2d 591, 9 IER Cases 1155 (1993) (upholding discharge of plant physician under the terms of employee handbook).

[10]MacMillan Bloedel Packaging, Inc., 106 LA 33 (Holley, Jr., 1995); Burlington N. R.R., 101 LA 144 (Massey, 1993); Iowa Elec. Light & Power Co., 100 LA 393 (Pelofsky, 1993); Florsheim Shoe Co., 74 LA 705 (Roberts, 1980). But see Marathon Oil Co., 97 LA 1145 (Massey, 1991) (reinstating employee as not incompetent despite fact he failed qualification test because test was unreasonable).

[11]Ford Motor Co., Opinion A-30 (Shulman, 1943) (quoted in Volz & Goggin, eds., Elkouri & Elkouri, How Arbitration Works, 5th ed., 781 (BNA Books, 1997). See also City of Key West, 106 LA 652 (Wolfson, 1996) (noting that if a competent employee does not carry out his duties because of deliberate misconduct or improper attitude, then after an effort to correct the employee's misconduct, disciplinary measures that bear a reasonable relation to the gravity of the offense may be used; however, where the reason for poor performance is incompetence, demotion rather than discipline is in order) and cases cited.

Before there is discipline, however, there may be a challenge to an employer's procedures for evaluation, which is a matter of contract interpretation rather than discipline. Since performance appraisals can be criticized as subjective, disciplinary grievances often focus on procedural errors in conducting the appraisal or a lack of fairness in the appraisal.[12] Even when it appears that the poor performance is documented and the procedures have been followed, a grievant's past record of adequate work and lack of progressive discipline may be the basis for reinstatement with a last-chance warning despite negligent performance.[13] Some arbitrators have held that demotion may not be used as a form of discipline for negligence or a failure to perform in a particular instance, unless there is a specific contract provision allowing it.[14] Most arbitrators do not require specific contract language, however, when the demotion is for "pure" incompetence.[15] In fact, arbitrators disagree on whether demotion for "pure" incompetence is discipline or whether calling performance incompetent makes a demotion fall within a "for cause" provision.[16]

Requirements to maintain competency in one's professional field often underlie assertions of incompetence. Teachers are often discharged for "incompetence," which can include ineffective teaching skills, poor classroom management, inappropriate conduct, or failure to follow institutional rules about paperwork.[17]

---

[12]See Iverson v. Wall Bd. of Educ., 522 N.W.2d 188 (S.D., 1994) (holding that inclusion of subjective performance evaluations in a teacher's personnel file is not an arbitrary and capricious or unreasonable act by a school principal); Hertz Corp., 103 LA 65 (Poole, 1994) (noting that accuracy in productivity evaluations is important to employer and employee alike and that an arbitrator must evaluate the specifics of disciplinary action to ensure that the system was applied fairly). Note also that as of 1987 the Federal Labor Relations Authority determined that arbitrators should be permitted to review direct attacks on performance standards raised through grievance challenges to disciplinary action based on appraisals. Employees thus now can challenge the adverse action by questioning the standards on which the appraisal is based. Newark Air Force Station, 30 FLRA 616 (Katz, 1987).

[13]Western Auto Supply Co., 87 LA 678 (O'Grady, 1986); Ohio Valley Hosp. Ass'n, 79 LA 929 (Abrams, 1982).

[14]Thoroughbred Containers, 99 LA 400 (Volz, 1992); City of Pascagoula, 97 LA 799 (Hart, 1991). Courts also have recognized demotion as a form of discipline for misconduct that indicates a lack of judgment and thus potential incompetence. See Keen v. Penson, 970 F.2d 252 (7th Cir., 1992) (upholding a university professor's demotion for writing a letter to a student that reflected lack of judgment and thus incompetence).

[15]City of Pascagoula, 97 LA 799 (Hart, 1991); Rohm & Haas Tex., Inc., 92 LA 850 (Allen, 1989); Southwest Petro-Chem, Inc., 92 LA 492 (Berger, 1988); Thompson Bros. Boat Mfg. Co., 55 LA 69 (Moberly, 1970); Duquesne Light Co., 48 LA 1108 (McDermott, 1967)

[16]See Hertz Corp., 103 LA 65 (Poole, 1994), disagreeing with Orrville Prods., Inc., 88 LA 204 (Dworkin, 1987). See also Lukens Steel Co., 42 LA 252 (Crawford, 1963); Macomber, Inc., 37 LA 1061 (Updegraff, 1961).

[17]Johnson v. Francis Howell R-3 Bd. of Educ., 868 S.W.2d 191, 192–93 (Mo. App., 1994) (holding that "[f]ailure to maintain classroom discipline, provide adequate individualized attention to students, and provide prompt and accurate information about student performance was 'incompetence' under Teacher Tenure Act justifying termination of permanent teacher"); Little Rock Sch. Dist., 102 LA 666 (Allen, 1994); Phillips v. State Bd. of Regents of State Univ. & Community College Sys. 863 S.W.3d 45 (Tenn., 1993) (judicial approval of dismissal of tenured faculty for "capricious disregard of professional conduct" and other "inappropriate behavior"); MacKenzie v. Webster Parish Sch. Bd., 609 So. 2d 1028 (La. App. Cir., 1992) (discharge for poor evaluations and poor "classroom management techniques" not arbitrary or capricious);

Failure to meet new or ongoing standards of competence as set by co-workers or the pool of possible workers also may be used as a basis for discharge rather than demotion.[18] Many arbitrators will rescind the discipline if inadequate performance can be cured by additional training or supervision of the employee's work.[19] Even if the employee's inability to perform adequately has been shown, arbitrators may require the employer to also show that "the grievant cannot perform his job functions in the future."[20] Other arbitrators require the employer to prove the employee's lack of qualification by more than the normal preponderance of the evidence.[21] Finally, arbitrators have held that the employer must warn employees that their work is poor before disciplining them for incompetence.[22]

Generally, when discipline is imposed for "incompetence" in the form of a specific mistake, misdeed, or misjudgment, proof of the specific misconduct follows the normal requirements of just cause.[23] When incompetence is not based on a specific instance of misconduct but relates to a continuous pattern of activity (or inactivity), arbitrators examine whether the employer was arbitrary, capricious, or discriminatory in determining whether the employee was incompetent.[24]

---

See Jones v. Houston Indep. Sch. Dist., 805 F.Supp. 476 (S.D. Tex.), aff'd, 979 F.2d 1004 (5th Cir., 1992) (discharge for being an ineffective teacher upheld as not violating any "liberty interest"); Joseph F. Whelan Co., 273 NLRB 340, 118 LRRM 1040 (1984). Since "incompetence" is often found as a basis for discharge under teacher tenure statutes, behavior that might be categorized differently in other employment settings is called "incompetence" when teachers are terminated.

[18]KDFW-TV, 92 LA 806 (Allen, 1990) (upholding discharge of female weather anchor for unsuitability under contract clause allowing discharge for "other legitimate reasons" even though she was incompetent only in comparison to co-workers or people in similar positions).

[19]Peoples Natural Gas, 105 LA 37 (Murphy, 1995); Klauser Corp., 102 LA 381 (McCurdy, 1994) (recognizing a duty to train); Burlington N. R.R., 101 LA 144 (Massey, 1993) (requiring employer to set up a coordinated improvement plan for employee); Kerr-McGee Ref. Corp., 90 LA 829 (Allen, 1988) (recognizing a duty to train); City of Omaha, 86 LA 142 (Thornell, 1985).

[20]Michigan Dep't of Mental Health, 82 LA 1311 (Girolamo, 1984) (key in upholding discharge was finding of inability to acquire necessary skills). See also Featherlite Trailers of Iowa, 90 LA 761 (Schwartz, 1987); City of Omaha, 86 LA 142 (Thornell, 1985) (single act of negligent driving of fire truck not proof that grievant was incapable of doing the job); Ohio Valley Hosp. Ass'n, 79 LA 929 (Abrams, 1982).

[21]Asserting a standard of more than a preponderance but less than clear and convincing evidence, Arbitrator Harry Platt in Knight Newspapers, Inc., 58 LA 446, 451 (1972), said: "In a discharge case, where the asserted reason for the discharge is incompetence, the burden of proving an employee's unqualification is on the employer. To sustain that burden, the persuasive power of the employer's evidence must be such that the employee's unqualification emerges with forceful clarity."

[22]Burlington N. R.R., 101 LA 144 (Massey, 1993); GATX Terminals Corp., 91 LA 1162 (Baroni, 1988); Archer, Daniels, Midland Processing Co., 91 LA 9 (Cerone, 1988); Independent Sch. Dist., 88 LA 1168 (VerPloeg, 1987). See also Jones v. New York City Bd. of Educ., 592 N.Y.S. 2d 441, 189 A.D.2d 818 (App. Div., 1993) (upholding hearing panel finding that tenured teacher had sufficient warnings and opportunity to improve to provide adequate basis for dismissal for incompetence).

[23]See, e.g., Bonsall Union Sch. Dist., 103 LA 777 (Kaufman, 1994); City of Phoenix, 102 LA 879 (Wyman, 1994); Trendler Metal Prods., 101 LA 749 (Green, 1993).

[24]Natco Ltd. Partnership, 102 LA 771 (Marcus, 1994) (applying arbitrary and capricious standard of review to nondisciplinary demotion); Klauser Corp., 102 LA 381 (McCurdy, 1994); Cuyahoga Metro. Hous. Auth., 90 LA 616 (Bittel, 1988) (characterizing just cause determination

## III.  Failure to Meet Quality or Quantity Standards

Arbitrators recognize the employer's need to impose reasonable quality or quantity standards[25] and to raise standards over time in order to make operations more competitive or efficient.[26] Similarly, an employee's performance, though satisfactory in the past, may later be judged unsatisfactory either because the employee's performance has deteriorated or the performance of other employees has improved.[27]

Cases that arise from an employee's failure to meet quality or quantity standards may be regarded as incompetence cases, rather than negligence cases.[28] That is, an employee's consistent failure to meet quality or quantity standards is commonly regarded as evidence of the employee's basic inability to perform job duties and not the failure of an otherwise qualified and able employee to exercise reasonable care on the job.[29] The distinction between incompetent and negligent job performance is significant because it often determines the appropriateness of the employer's decision to terminate, demote, or transfer an employee rather than impose progressive discipline. Arbitrators reason that progressive discipline, intended to deter future infractions of rules or other misconduct, would serve no purpose for an employee whose work has been substantially deficient or who has been unable to keep up with the work of others in the job classification.[30]

If the basic competence of the employee is *not* at issue, discipline is generally permissible for failure to meet reasonable quality or quantity standards.[31] The inquiry in such cases is whether there was just cause to discipline the employee.[32]

---

in terms of fairness considerations); Featherlite Trailers of Iowa, 90 LA 761 (Schwartz, 1987); but see Kerr-McGee Ref. Corp., 90 LA 829 (Allen, 1988) (applying just cause standard to "pure" incompetence case).

[25]Hertz Corp., 103 LA 65 (Poole, 1994) (rejecting application of just cause standard of review to arbitrator's assessment of a productivity system); Coca-Cola Bottling Midwest, 100 LA 911 (Bognanno, 1993); cf. Trane Co., 103 LA 392 (Krislov, 1994) (applying "patently unreasonable or arbitrary" standard of review).

[26]E.g., Marathon Petroleum Co., 91 LA 824 (Grimes, 1988). See also section entitled Demotion for Inability to Perform in this chapter.

[27]Ford Motor Co., Opinion A-30 (Shulman, 1943) (quoted in Volz & Goggin, eds., Elkouri & Elkouri, How Arbitration Works, 5th ed., 781 (BNA Books, 1997).

[28]E.g., Dodge Cork Co., 8 LA 250 (Branochem, 1947); Machine Prods., Inc., 28 LA 245 (Hawley, 1956). See also Section A.

[29]See Republic Steel Corp., 25 LA 733 (Platt, 1955) (distinguishing negligence from incompetence). But see Laidlaw Waste Sys., 90 LA 570 (Clifford, 1987) (discharge upheld where employees may have been able to meet production standards but refused to do so); Avery Int'l Co., 90 LA 267 (Oberdank, 1987).

[30]See, e.g., Southwestern Bell Telecom, 94 LA 199 (O'Grady, 1990); Kerr-McGee Ref. Corp., 90 LA 829 (Allen, 1988); Cheyenne Pipeline Co., 59 LA 726 (Rentfro, 1972).

[31]Hertz Corp., 103 LA 65 (Poole, 1994); Trane Co., 103 LA 392 (Krislov, 1994); Kriklok Corp., 102 LA 183 (Frost, 1993).

[32]Coca-Cola Bottling Midwest, 100 LA 911 (Bognanno, 1993).

Discipline for failure to meet quality or quantity standards has been reversed, or mitigated, where the employer's standards were unreasonable or unreasonably applied. Thus, discipline or discharge may be inappropriate when the employer failed to provide employees with reasonable notice of the performance standard expected of them,[33] provided insufficient or inadequate training,[34] provided inadequate equipment or supervision,[35] assigned an unreasonable amount of work,[36] or had not imposed similar discipline when other employees failed to meet production standards.[37] Moreover, discipline for undisputed failure to meet quality or quantity standards may be overturned if the employer fails to establish that the disciplined employee was in fact the source of the problem. This can occur when the employee's finished work is mingled with that of other workers.[38]

# IV. Loss of Qualifying Status

## A. Driver's License

Employees who drive delivery trucks, service vehicles, buses, ambulances, and other vehicles on public roads must obtain and maintain valid operator's licenses that are appropriate to the vehicle operated and the state(s) in which the employee is employed. Failure to have the required current license renders the employee legally unable to perform driving duties. In such circumstances, employers have terminated, or assigned nondriving duties to, employees pending reissuance of the required license.

For example, the arbitrator in *King & American Ambulance Co.*[39] upheld the termination of an ambulance driver who had failed to maintain the necessary driver's license. Similarly, in *Frank Russell & Son Trucking Co.*,[40] the arbitrator upheld the discharge of a truck driver who had driven the employer's trucks while his license was suspended. In another case, the arbitrator upheld the discharge of an employee who had failed, within the requisite 90-day period following the merger of two trucking companies, to acquire his license and to satisfactorily complete instruction and tests to drive trucks.[41]

---

[33]Featherlite Trailers of Iowa, 90 LA 761 (Schwartz, 1987); L.F. Fails Mach. Co., 7 LA 935 (Copelof, 1947).

[34]Merchants Fire Dispatch, 12 LA 407 (Hayek, 1949); A. Gross Candle Co., 9 LA 61 (Lesser, 1947).

[35]McDonnell Aircraft Corp., 3 LA 158 (Klamon, 1946).

[36]Borden's Farm Prods. Co., 8 LA 593 (Feinberg, 1947).

[37]Marathon Oil Co., 97 LA 1145 (Massey, 1991).

[38]Tri-United Plastics Corp., 2 LA 398 (Brown, 1946); but see Consolidated Vultee Aircraft Corp., 9 LA 510 (Abernethy, 1948) (deferring to employer's judgment as to who was the responsible employee).

[39]87 LA 78 (Concepcion, 1986).

[40]89-1 ARB ¶ 8248 (Reilly, 1989).

[41]Merchants Fast Motor Lines, Inc., 90-2 ARB ¶ 8399 (Chumley, 1990).

Where there are special circumstances, however, arbitrators have reinstated employees discharged for lack of an operator's license. One arbitrator determined there was no just cause to discharge a grievant with a suspended driver's license because the employer failed to thoroughly investigate the grievant's lack-of-knowledge defense and did not consider the postdischarge reinstatement of the employee's license.[42] Reinstatement was also ordered where the employer mistakenly believed the grievant had lost his driver's license because his insurance had lapsed.[43]

## B. Security Clearance

Generally, if an employee is unable to obtain or maintain a required government security clearance, an arbitrator will uphold the resultant discharge. One arbitrator found, as a matter of public policy, that federal security regulations are superimposed on a collective bargaining agreement and permit termination of employees whose clearances for classified information are suspended.[44] In *Liquid Carbonic Corp.*,[45] the arbitrator reasoned that a just-cause defense had no application where security requirements were involved, and upheld a suspension where the employee had been denied security clearance for classified government defense work and other work was not available. Four employees in *Computer Sciences Raytheon*[46] were terminated for failure to timely obtain security clearances. The arbitrator denied their grievances, even though the employer had permitted the employees to work in secured areas while their clearances were pending.

An employee's inability to work on a military installation without government clearance was emphasized in *M & M Restaurants, Inc.*[47] The employee was a short-order cook whose security badge was revoked; consequently she was denied access to the cafeteria (located on the grounds of a naval gun factory) and could no longer report for work. Her employer said she could return to work as soon as she secured her badge. The union grieved, but the arbitrator found no evidence that the grievant had been discharged. The arbitrator noted that the actual grievance had been against not the company but the government, which had denied the employee physical access to her place of employment.

---

[42]Group W. Cable of Chicago, 93 LA 789 (Fischbach, 1989).
[43]Emery Air Freight, 83-1 ARB ¶ 8489 (Darrow, 1983).
[44]Wisconsin Tel. Co., 26 LA 792 (Whelan, 1956).
[45]22 LA 709 (Baab, 1954).
[46]99 LA 12 (Frost, 1992).
[47]29 LA 202 (Cayton, 1957).

## C. Insurance

Arbitrators have sustained terminations of employees whose poor driving records have caused insurers to refuse to provide their employers with liability coverage for them. In *Pal-Tex Transportation Co.,*[48] the arbitrator noted that the three employees discharged because they could not be insured knew that their offenses were cumulative and yet made no protests with the police at the times of their convictions. In another case, the arbitrator upheld the terminations of two parking valets because their uninsurability prohibited them from performing their valet driving duties and they turned down other jobs at the employer's facility.[49] Where insurance had been denied to an ambulance driver after an excessive number of driving violations and he was unable to secure alternative coverage, the arbitrator conditionally upheld the termination. He gave the grievant 45 days to meet insurability requirements or obtain insurance of his own, in which case he would be reinstated without back pay, seniority, or other benefits.[50] Similarly, in *Vindicator Printing Co.,*[51] the arbitrator held that the grievant would be eligible for reinstatement without back pay or benefits if, within 45 days, he could secure identical insurance coverage and pay any excess premium.

Arbitrators have overturned discharges or reduced penalties where employees who became uninsurable due to their poor driving record were given an adequate opportunity to contest their driving violations,[52] where the employer otherwise considered the employee's work record to be satisfactory,[53] where the employees had not been warned about their driving records,[54] where the employer had permitted and even encouraged "loose" driving practices,[55] and where contractual disciplinary procedures had not been followed.[56] In *International Business Services, Inc.,*[57] the employer, who contracted with the Federal Aviation Administration (FAA) to operate a parking lot at Washington National Airport, discharged an airport shuttle-bus driver because her driving record prevented the employer from insuring her through its new carrier. The arbitrator reinstated the employee, finding that the FAA had never demanded that the employer discharge the grievant and that the employer neither attempted to secure alternate insurance for the driver nor offered her nondriving

---

[48]77-1 ARB ¶ 8024 (Sartain, 1976).

[49]Highlands Inn, 86-1 ARB ¶ 8306 (Tamoush, 1986).

[50]Memorial Livery Servs., Inc., 79-1 ARB ¶ 8268 (Perry, 1979).

[51]88-2 ARB ¶ 8409 (Prusa, 1988).

[52]Brown-Graves Co., 86-2 ARB ¶ 8508 (Chattman, 1986).

[53]Wilshire Bedding Co., 77-1 ARB ¶ 8168 (Gentile, 1977).

[54]W. J. Bremmer, Inc., 64 LA 778 (Ferguson, 1976); Inland Lumber Co., 62 LA 1150 (Wilmoth, 1974).

[55]Orlando Transit Co., 60 LA 460 (Vadakin, 1973).

[56]Curtis Mathes Mfg. Co., 56 LA 274 (Autrey, 1971).

[57]98 LA 1116 (Bernhardt, 1991).

duties. As a general observation, the arbitrator said: "[A]rbitrators have recognize [sic] the reality that such insurance is necessary while at the same time requiring the Employer to go to some effort in order to preserve the employee's job."[58]

## D. Certification

Arbitrators customarily have found just cause for terminating or suspending an employee who fails to obtain required professional licenses or skill certifications. In *Bell Helicopter Textron*,[59] for example, a welder failed the test needed for certification of his ability to weld steel and aluminum. The arbitrator upheld the discharge, finding that the grievant had received ample training opportunity even though he had completed only 21 weeks of a 36-week program at the time of his termination. The employee had the option to seek qualification early, had done so, and had failed. In some circumstances, arbitrators have required employers to give employees additional opportunities to obtain necessary certification, for example, where the employee had insufficient time to qualify[60] or where an employee of long service could obtain an alternate certification that would allow continued employment.[61]

In *King & American Ambulance Co.*,[62] an ambulance driver was discharged for not having a state ambulance driver's license. The union argued that other employees who allowed their licenses to lapse were given written warnings, not terminated. The arbitrator held that the employer has the right to: (1) expect that an employee's licenses and certificates are current, and (2) act according to that presumption when making assignments. Consequently, employees have the responsibility to notify the employer when a license or certificate is lost or lapses. Since the grievant had previously been warned because her emergency medical technician's certificate lapsed, the loss of her ambulance driver's license was a second offense justifying discharge.

One arbitrator held that if the employer imposed discipline for loss of a license, it must be guided by how the licensing entity regards the employee's status. In *Riverside Osteopathic Hospital*,[63] a nurse was suspended when she produced a letter from the state's Board of Nursing instead of what the parties had agreed constituted appropriate proof of certification: the license itself or a canceled check. The letter stated that the nurse was licensed to practice, could continue

---

[58]Id. at 1119, citing Sandusky Dressed Beef Co., 69 LA 766 (Strasshofer, 1977); Inland Lumber Co., 62 LA 1150 (Wilmoth, 1974); and Orlando Transit Co., 60 LA 460 (Vadakin, 1973).

[59]74 LA 1139 (Shearer, 1980). See also Donaire v. NME Hosp., Inc., 65 EPD ¶ 43,214 (11th Cir. 1994).

[60]WBRE Radio, Inc., 59 LA 1249 (Seitz, 1972).

[61]Northwest Airlines, Inc., 53 LA 357 (Sembower, 1969).

[62]87 LA 78 (Concepcion, 1986).

[63]77 LA 418 (Kruger, 1981).

to practice while her license was being processed, and could use the letter as proof of licensure while waiting. The arbitrator found that the Board of Nursing had determined the grievant was properly licensed and the employer could not make its own determination.

# V. Negligence or Carelessness

Negligent or careless performance is a common ground for discipline and discharge. Arbitrators have upheld suspension or termination for a first offense, depending on the nature and severity of the misconduct, in cases of gross negligence or wanton disregard for the safety of persons or property. Where the alleged act of omission involves ordinary negligence or carelessness, however, arbitrators usually require the employer to apply the customary steps of progressive discipline, i.e., a reprimand or warning for a first offense and more severe corrective measures for repeated offenses.

## A. Defining and Distinguishing Ordinary and Gross Negligence

No single, comprehensive definition of "negligence" or "carelessness" is used by arbitrators because no one definition could possibly cover all occupations, industries, or circumstances. In addition, the distinction between "negligence" and "carelessness" in employee work performance is not significant.[64] Arbitrators generally consider "negligence" to be the failure to do what a reasonably prudent employee would have done, or not done, under the same or similar circumstances.[65] "Carelessness" is the absence of ordinary care and is often used to describe poor or substandard work performance that did not result from errors in judgment.[66] These cases are normally analyzed as unsatisfactory performance and subject to the ordinary steps of progressive discipline.

In contrast to mere errors of judgment, the term "gross negligence" denotes intentional or willful acts or omissions, in flagrant or reckless disregard of the consequences to persons or property.[67] Arbitrators also have found gross negligence in cases of wanton inattentiveness or indifference by employees to the foreseeable dangers or injurious results of their acts or omissions. In cases of gross negligence, the act or omission by the employee often justifies a suspension or discharge for a first offense. These distinctions are discussed below.

---

[64]Genie Co., 97 LA 542 (Dworkin, 1991).

[65]City of Plymouth, 103 LA 424 (Berquist, 1994).

[66]See, e.g., Southwestern Bell Tel. Co., 102 LA 531 (Nolan, 1994); General Mills, 102 LA 595 (Goldstein, 1993); Burlington N. R.R., 101 LA 144 (Massey, 1993); Ingalls Shipbuilding, 101 LA 683 (Koenig, 1993); Coca-Cola Bottling Midwest, Inc., 100 LA 911 (Bognanno, 1993); General Tel. Co. of Cal., 89 LA 867 (Collins, 1987).

[67]T.W. Recreational Servs., 93 LA 302 (Richard, 1989).

## B. *Typical Cases of Ordinary Negligence*

Arbitrators will sustain reasonable disciplinary action where it is shown employees did not exercise reasonable care in performing their duties or failed to do what a reasonably prudent employee would have done in the same or similar circumstances. Normally, an employee will receive a warning for first offenses involving ordinary carelessness or negligence. When careless or negligent performance continues after warnings, more severe disciplinary action may be justified. Disciplinary action has been sustained for ordinary negligence, or careless performance, in cases where a mechanic failed to perform safety procedures[68] and where a repairman negligently caused the loss of returned defective parts in his care.[69] Suspensions were sustained in these cases as progressive discipline because the employees had received prior warnings for careless or negligent performance. Other arbitrators have imposed or sustained demotions as the appropriate form of disciplinary action in cases involving negligent performance.[70]

Other typical examples of ordinary carelessness or negligence are a worker who produced defective cartons until the error was discovered several hours later,[71] an equipment operator who drove a sweeper over a tree,[72] a journeyman sprinkler fitter whose negligent installation caused damage that required the work to be redone,[73] a material handler who erroneously weighed and recorded metal used in the production of wire,[74] and a payroll clerk whose repeated carelessness resulted in large overpayments.[75] In all these cases the arbitrators sustained termination after progressive discipline because they found further progressive discipline could no longer reasonably be expected to prevent the employees from repeating their careless or negligent performance.

## C. *Factors in Proving Ordinary Negligence*

Arbitrators require employers to establish one or more of the following factors to sustain allegations of negligence or carelessness:

> (1) the employee had an obligation or requirement to perform the act or refrain from the act alleged to be negligent;[76]

---

[68]Peoples Natural Gas, 105 LA 37 (Murphy, 1995).

[69]Gates Chevrolet Co., 63 LA 753 (Coyle, 1974).

[70]Iowa Power Co., 97 LA 1029 (Thornell, 1991); Army & Air Force Exch. Serv., 90 LA 764 (Nelson, 1988); Sunshine Biscuits, 60 LA 197 (Roberts, 1973); American Radiator & Standard Sanitary Corp., 29 LA 167 (Duff, 1957).

[71]Champion Dairypak, 105 LA 462 (Allen, 1995).

[72]Bermuda Dunes Country Club, 104 LA 1082 (Darrow, 1995).

[73]Cosco Fire Protection, 91 LA 593 (Koven, 1988).

[74]Copperfield Bimettalics Group, 83 LA 1024 (Denson, 1984).

[75]Greyhound Lines, Inc., 67 LA 483 (Larkin, 1976).

[76]Gates Chevrolet Co., 63 LA 753 (Coyle, 1974); National Steel Corp., 54 LA 1174 (Krimsly, 1970) (written rule not required to sustain discipline).

(2) there was actual or potential damage to persons, property, or the company;[77]

(3) the act or omission was the actual or proximate cause of the damage;[78]

(4) the adverse consequences or damages were foreseeable;[79]

(5) the act or omission was unreasonable under the circumstances;[80]

(6) the employee was trained and capable of performing the act or omission alleged to be negligent;[81] and

(7) the employee knew or should have known of the disciplinary consequences of the act or omission.[82]

## D. Typical Cases of Gross Negligence

Arbitrators will sustain more severe disciplinary penalties for a first offense in cases where employees act in reckless or wanton disregard of the consequences of their actions. Arbitrators found there was just cause to terminate employees for gross negligence in cases where a service technician failed to perform critical safety tests,[83] a setup man caused an accident resulting in damages worth over $10,000 and a loss of 1 ½ days of production,[84] a grocery clerk failed to check the age of a purchaser of alcoholic beverages,[85] a process operator relit burners without first purging the furnace of fumes,[86] a hotel maintenance engineer left a burning candle in a dangerous area,[87] a collection representative mishandled collection accounts resulting in losses of $14,000,[88] a chemical worker failed to observe established procedures resulting in the collapse of a tank and loss of 400 gallons

---

[77]"There is not always a requirement for actual damage where the potential for damage was created by a negligent act or omission. The just cause test does not require the horse to escape before the employer can discipline an employee for leaving the barn door open and putting the employer at risk of losing the horse." S & J Ranch, 103 LA 350, 360 (Bogue, 1994). See also Interchecks, Inc., 88 LA 1279 (Weiss, 1987).

[78]Southwest Airlines, 93 LA 575 (Morris, 1989); Stauffer Chem. Co., 83 LA 272 (Corbett, 1984) (no proximate cause established).

[79]Alpac Corp., 68 LA 732 (Tanaka, 1977).

[80]Grand Blanc Community Schs., 97 LA 162 (Kerner, 1991).

[81]Cosco Fire Protection, 91 LA 593 (Koven, 1988); Hess Oil Virgin Islands, 72 LA 81 (Berkman, 1978).

[82]Vons Cos., 100 LA 297 (Ross, 1992); Rohm & Haas Tex., Inc., 92 LA 850 (Allen, 1989); Cosco Fire Protection, 91 LA 593 (Koven, 1988); Consolidation Coal Co., 85 LA 506 (Hoh, 1985); Copperfield Bimettalics Group, 83 LA 1024 (Denson, 1984); Gates Chevrolet Co., 63 LA 753 (Coyle, 1974).

[83]BHP Petroleum, 102 LA 321 (Najita, 1994).

[84]Trendler Metal Prods., 101 LA 749 (Green, 1993).

[85]Vons Cons., 100 LA 297 (Ross, 1992).

[86]Hess Oil Virgin Islands Corp., 91 LA 1284 (Hunter, 1988).

[87]Holiday Inns, Inc., 82 LA 597 (Concepcion, 1984).

[88]Municipality of Anchorage, 82 LA 256 (Hauck, 1983).

of hydrochloric acid,[89] a boiler operator failed to shut off a gas valve to a heater,[90] a speeding fuel delivery driver caused the truck to overturn and spill,[91] a crane operator backed into a wall at full speed,[92] a truck driver recklessly collided with another vehicle,[93] and a truck driver spilled a load of fuel by driving recklessly.[94]

Arbitrators have found gross negligence but reduced a termination to a suspension where a corrections officer's inattention resulted in an escape,[95] a district representative made errors in handling money that resulted in significant losses,[96] two aircraft mechanics were responsible for a collision involving a B-737 during pushback,[97] a forklift driver had an accident injuring another worker,[98] and a mechanic left bearings out of a rebuilt gearbox used in an aircraft engine.[99] Whether a suspension or termination is appropriate for gross negligence depends on the facts and circumstances surrounding the misconduct, the employee's prior record, the policies and practices of the employer, and a variety of other factors.

### E. Factors in Proving Gross Negligence

Where gross negligence is alleged, arbitrators rely on the same factors required to sustain allegations of negligence or carelessness as well as on a variety of factors to determine whether the severity of the alleged act or omission rises to wanton or willful misconduct warranting suspension or discharge for a first or second offense. They determine the following:

(1) whether the misconduct by the employee is habitual,[100] the employee is "accident prone,"[101] or whether the employee is likely to repeat the alleged act or omission;[102]

[89]Neville Chem. Co., 74 LA 814 (Parkinson, 1980).

[90]Hess Oil Virgin Islands, 72 LA 181 (Berkman, 1978).

[91]Standard Oil Co. of Cal., 65 LA 829 (Walsh, 1975).

[92]National Steel Corp., 54 LA 1174 (Krimsly, 1970).

[93]Curtis Mathes Co., 52 LA 145 (Merrill, 1968).

[94]Mobil Oil Corp., 51 LA 696 (Turkus, 1968).

[95]D.C. Dep't of Corrections, 105 LA 843 (Rogers, 1996) (upholding suspension).

[96]Dayton Newspapers, Inc., 103 LA 641 (Keenan, 1994) (termination reduced to suspension because errors were readily correctable through progressive discipline).

[97]Southwest Airlines, 93 LA 575 (Morris, 1989) (considering mitigating circumstances).

[98]Bell Foundry, 92 LA 1214 (Prayzich, 1989) (upholding suspension).

[99]Purex Indus., Inc., 81 LA 747 (Meiners, 1983) (upholding suspension).

[100]Sim-Kar Lighting Fixture Co., 99 LA 837 (Valentine, 1992); Municipality of Anchorage, 82 LA 256 (Hauck, 1983); W.C. Richards Co., 64 LA 382 (Kelliher, 1975) (company owes a duty to all its employees to maintain a safe place of work and because of the repeated safety violations by this employee, and his attitude and conduct, he jeopardized the safety of other employees in the plant).

[101]Georgia-Pacific Corp., 52 LA 325 (Hertz, 1968). But see Interstate Bakeries Corp., 38 LA 1109 (Frey, 1962).

[102]Holiday Inns, Inc., 82 LA 597 (Concepcion, 1984).

(2) the attitude of the employee;[103]

(3) the actual injury or damage sustained to persons or property;[104]

(4) the potential injury or damage that could have resulted from the negligent act or omission;[105] and

(5) the effect of the alleged negligence on co-workers or customers of the company.[106]

### F. Defenses to Discipline

If culpable negligence or carelessness is established, arbitrators have considered the following factors in defense or mitigation of the disciplinary action imposed:

(1) inadequate training[107] or lack of notice the act or omission is prohibited;[108]

(2) inadvertence or positive attitude by the employee;[109]

(3) supervisory acts or omissions that materially contributed to the alleged negligence;[110]

(4) co-workers' acts or omissions that materially contributed to the alleged negligence;[111]

(5) defective machinery or processes that caused or contributed to the alleged negligence.[112]

Arbitrators also consider the additional factors that are part of any just cause determination:

---

[103]BHP Petroleum, 102 LA 321 (Najita, 1994); Rohr Indus. Inc., 65 LA 982 (Lennard, 1975) (employee concealed the accident); Curtis Mathes Co., 52 LA 145 (Merrill, 1968); Mobil Oil Corp., 51 LA 696 (Turkus, 1968).

[104]Trendler Metal Prods., 101 LA 749 (Green, 1993); Gulf States Paper Corp., 97 LA 60 (Welch, 1991); Steel Branch Mining, 96 LA 931 (Roberts, 1991); Asarco Inc., 95 LA 1016 (Jewett, 1990); Bell Foundry, 92 LA 1214 (Prayzich, 1989); Municipality of Anchorage, 82 LA 256 (Hauck, 1983); Purex Indus., Inc., 81 LA 747 (Meiners, 1983).

[105]S & J Ranch, 103 LA 350 (Bogue, 1994); BHP Petroleum, 102 LA 321 (Najita, 1994); Hess Oil Virgin Islands Corp., 91 LA 1284 (Hunter, 1988); Mobil Oil Corp., 51 LA 696 (Turkus, 1968).

[106]Buick Youngstown Co., 41 LA 578 (Dworkin, 1963).

[107]Peoples Natural Gas, 105 LA 37 (Murphy, 1995). But see United Parcel Serv., Inc., 105 LA 637 (Nicholas, 1995) (negligent act not related to inadequate training).

[108]Central Tel. Co., 93 LA 185 (Hardbeck, 1989); Piggly Wiggly T-212, 81 LA 808 (Nelson, 1983); Servair Inc., 76 LA 1134 (D'Spain, 1981).

[109]Dayton Newspapers, Inc., 103 LA 641 (Keenan, 1994); Crown Divs. of the Allen Group, 103 LA 378 (Klein, 1994); Consolidation Coal Co., 85 LA 506 (Hoh, 1985); General Tel. Co. of Cal., 44 LA 669 (Prasow, 1965); Ingalls Shipbuilding Corp., 37 LA 953 (Murphy, 1961).

[110]See, e.g., Steel Branch Mining, 96 LA 931 (Roberts, 1991); Southwest Airlines, 93 LA 575 (Morris, 1989); Stauffer Chem. Co., 83 LA 272 (Corbett, 1984).

[111]Lawrence Paper Co., 96 LA 297 (Berger, 1991); Southwest Airlines, 93 LA 575 (Morris, 1989).

[112]Fruehauf Trailer Corp., 83 LA 462 (Storey, 1984).

(1) lack of an adequate investigation by management into the circumstances of the alleged negligence;[113]

(2) disparate treatment;[114]

(3) absence of progressive discipline;[115] and

(4) the length of an employee's service (which may constitute a mitigating factor in cases of gross negligence).[116]

## G. Penalties

Because disciplinary determinations are made on the particular facts and circumstances surrounding the alleged act of negligence, the practices of the parties, and the work history of the employee, there is no consistent pattern of specific disciplinary penalties being imposed for any particular act of negligence. Most reported cases of negligence apply the traditional steps of corrective discipline, i.e., warning, suspension, and discharge, as appropriate in the case. Not all arbitrators agree, however, that a demotion is an appropriate disciplinary sanction in cases of employee negligence.[117] Finally, in a few reported cases, employees have been required to reimburse their employers for lost or damaged materials.[118]

# VI.  Demotion for Inability to Perform

Generally, the term "demotion" is used to refer to the process of moving an employee to a position lower in wage scale or rank.[119] In many cases involving demotion, the characterization of the action as "disciplinary" or "nondisciplinary" determines whether it is contractually permissible and whether the employer must have complied with the contract's disciplinary procedures before imposing the measure.

---

[113]S & J Ranch, 103 LA 350 (Bogue, 1994).

[114]Central Tel. Co., 93 LA 185 (Hardbeck, 1989).

[115]Johnson Controls World Servs., Inc., 105 LA 1194 (Poole, 1996); Montcalm County Rd. Comm'n, 94 LA 45 (Daniel, 1989).

[116]D.C. Dep't of Corrections, 105 LA 843 (Rogers, 1996); Trendler Metal Prods., 101 LA 749 (Green, 1993); Iowa Power Co., 97 LA 1029 (Thornell, 1991); Bell Foundry, 92 LA 1214 (Prayzich, 1989); Hess Oil Virgin Islands Corp., 91 LA 1284 (Hunter, 1988).

[117]See, e.g., City of Omaha, 86 LA 142 (Thornell, 1985).

[118]See, e.g., United Parcel Serv., 105 LA 637 (Nicholas, 1995); Southeastern Pa. Transp. Auth., 88 LA 621 (Schwartz, 1986); U.S. Immigration & Naturalization Serv., 82 LA 836 (Fox, 1984). See also Cal. Lab. Code §2865 ("An employee who is guilty of a culpable degree of negligence is liable to his employer for the damage thereby caused to the employer.").

[119]Shawnee Local Bd. of Educ., 104 LA 682 (Weisheit, 1995) (distinguishing demotions from transfers).

Arbitrators often view demotion, like promotion, as related to the competence and qualification of the employee, and therefore non-disciplinary in nature.[120] In cases where arbitrators have determined that disciplinary action would serve no purpose, such as cases involving "pure" incompetence,[121] demotion has been upheld as management's right to assure efficient operations.[122] Thus, a demotion may be justified when the employee lacks the level of skill to perform the duties of the job classification,[123] the employee consistently fails to meet production standards,[124] the employee demonstrates a continual and persistent pattern of carelessness,[125] or the employee's carelessness endangers herself or co-employees.[126]

In cases involving demotions for ineptitude or incompetence, some arbitrators have ruled that the demotion must have been preceded by adequate warnings that performance was unsatisfactory.[127] Other arbitrators have not permitted demotions on the ground that the employer failed to demonstrate that the employee received sufficient training.[128] Further, where it is proved that the employee discharged or demoted for alleged incompetence was qualified for the job when hired, some arbitrators have ordered reinstatement on the ground that progressive discipline should have been imposed.[129] Other arbitrators, however, have ruled in similar cases that when an employee's once-satisfactory performance has deteriorated to the point of becoming unsatisfactory, it is within the employer's authority to

---

[120]Cavis Iron Works, 54 LA 1149 (Keefe, 1970).

[121]See section entitled Incompetence in this chapter.

[122]Natco Ltd. Partnership, 102 LA 771 (Marcus, 1994) (applying arbitrary and capricious standard of review to nondisciplinary demotion); Southwestern Bell Telecom, 94 LA 199 (O'Grady, 1990).

[123]Cosco Fire Protection, 91 LA 593 (Koven, 1988); Machine Prods., Inc., 28 LA 245 (Hawley, 1956); Dodge Cork Co., 8 LA 250 (Branochem, 1947).

[124]National Rolling Mills, Inc., 84 LA 1144 (DiLauro, 1985); Revlon, Inc., 82 LA 451 (Darrow, 1984); Package Prods., Inc., 83 LA 86 (Duff, 1984); Dodge Cork Co., 8 LA 250 (Branochem, 1947).

[125]GATX Terminals Corp., 91 LA 1162 (Baroni, 1988); Alfred M. Lewis, Inc., 81 LA 621 (Sabo, 1983). Note, however, that demotions and transfers are often deemed inappropriate as discipline for isolated acts of carelessness Checker Motors Corp., 95 LA 435 (Lipson, 1990).

[126]Iowa Power, Inc., 97 LA 1029 (Thornwell, 1991); National Rolling Mills, Inc., 84 LA 1144 (DiLauro, 1985).

[127]Parkin Printing Co., 76 LA 1075 (Robinson, 1981); San Antonio Air Logistics Ctr., 74 LA 486 (Coffey, 1979).

[128]Timex Corp., 63 LA 758 (Gruenberg, 1974); Hayes Int'l Corp., 61 LA 1295 (Nicholas, 1973).

[129]City of Key West, 106 LA 652 (Wolfson, 1996) (noting that if an employee has full capability of performing a job, but for reasons of deliberate misconduct and improper attitudes does not carry out his duties, then subsequent to an effort to correct the employee's misconduct, disciplinary measures that bear a reasonable relation to the gravity of the offense must be used; however, where the reason for poor performance is incompetence, demotion rather than disciplinary measures is in order) and cases cited; Neches Butane Prods. Co., 5 LA 307 (Carmichael, 1946) (survival of trial period is proof of initial qualification for job; cannot be discharged for lack of qualifications); Master Elec. Co., 5 LA 339 (Hampton, Chair, 1946).

demote the employee to the next-highest-ranking job within the employee's capabilities.[130]

Demotions are rarely permitted as a form of discipline unless specifically authorized by contract.[131] Demotions are viewed as a permanent disqualification from a particular job classification in contravention of valuable seniority rights.[132] Demotions have also been disallowed as a form of discipline on the ground that their unlimited duration amounts to an indeterminate sentence.[133] Demotions have therefore been revoked in cases where the imposition of progressive discipline would have been appropriate,[134] as in cases where deterioration of job performance grows out of personal misconduct. In those cases, disciplinary measures with the object of correcting misbehavior and restoring employee productivity are appropriate.[135] Discharge for poor performance may then be appropriate where the imposition of progressive discipline does not correct the employee's misbehavior.[136]

In cases involving nondisciplinary discharge for consistent failure to meet production standards or other incompetence, arbitrators have ordered the employee to be reinstated and demoted to the next-highest-ranking job within the employee's capabilities as a remedy.[137] This occurs most often when the employee has performed satisfactorily in a lower job classification.[138] But where there was no position into which an employee could be demoted, a discharge for failure to meet production standards has been upheld.[139]

## VII. Loafing and Extending Breaks

To loaf is to spend time in idleness, to lounge or loiter about.[140] An employer may view loafing as dishonesty or theft of company

---

[130]Duquesne Light Co., 48 LA 1108 (McDermott, 1967).

[131]Shawnee Local Bd. of Educ., 104 LA 682 (Weisheit, 1995); Mason & Hanger-Silas Mason Co., 96 LA 864 (Allen, 1991); Thompson Bros. Boat Mfg. Co., 55 LA 69 (Moberly, 1970). But see Ameron Corrosion Control Div., 66 LA 588 (Rill, 1976) (upholding disciplinary demotion under management rights clause).

[132]American Nat'l Can, 95 LA 873 (Borland 1990); Republic Steel Corp., 25 LA 733 (Platt, 1955); Goodyear Atomic Corp., 25 LA 736 (Kelliher, 1955).

[133]Trans World Airlines, 66 LA 1193 (Turkus 1976),

[134]Mason & Hanger-Silas Mason Co., 96 LA 1159 (Allen, 1991); Goodyear Atomic Corp., 25 LA 736 (Kelliher, 1955).

[135]See Duquesne Light Co., 48 LA 1108 (McDermott, 1967).

[136]City of River Rouge, 62 LA 121 (Keefe, 1974); Trans-Tel Corp., 71-1 ARB ¶ 8442, 4450 (Turkus, 1970).

[137]Klauser Corp., 102 LA 381 (McCurdy, 1994); Gulf State Utils. Co., 102 LA 470 (Massey, 1993) (revoking involuntary transfer out of seniority group in favor of demotion to lowest classification within group); Sunshine Biscuits, 60 LA 197 (Roberts, 1973); Federal Mach. & Welder Co., 5 LA 60 (Whiting, 1946).

[138]Thoroughbred Containers, 99 LA 400 (Volz, 1992); Marathon Oil Co., 97 LA 1145 (Massey, 1991); American Fuel Cell, 97 LA 1045 (Nicholas, 1991); Sunshine Biscuits, 60 LA 197 (Roberts, 1973).

[139]Marathon Petroleum Co., 91 LA 824 (Grimes, 1988).

[140]Black's Law Dictionary, 1085 (4th ed., 1968).

time.[141] Arbitrators treat loafing situations, including cases involving extended breaks, in a manner similar to other performance problems. The employer's work rules, past practice, and aggravating and mitigating factors interact to make the inquiry into loafing violations very fact-specific.

Arbitrators first ask whether a particular rule has been violated.[142] If the employer does have such a rule, the arbitrator will determine whether the rule is reasonable and whether it was reasonably applied.[143] Factors that arbitrators have considered in evaluating the reasonableness of the employer's application of a rule include whether there was appropriate notice or publication of the rule and whether it was uniformly applied,[144] whether a fair and impartial investigation was conducted,[145] and whether progressive discipline was applied.[146]

In general, arbitrators will uphold the suspension[147] or discharge[148] of an employee who has a history of loafing or abusing break time and who has been warned previously about similar violations. Even in the absence of a pattern or history of similar violations, an arbitrator may consider as an aggravating factor the cumulative effect of the loafing violation and other violations in upholding a discharge.[149]

On the other hand, in the absence of previous disciplinary action for violations of a similar nature, an employee's discharge will not

---

[141]John Brunner Co., 75 LA 1292 (Craver, 1981).

[142]Pottsville Area Sch. Dist., 91 LA 515 (Mayer, 1988) (suspension improper where no policy existed); but see Nestle Co., 81 LA 1263 (Feigenbaum, 1983) (absence of specific rule not relevant).

[143]Southwest Airlines Co., 87 LA 594 (Helburn, 1986) (finding reasonable the employer's rule since an employer "has the right to ask for a fair day's work in return for wages and benefits provided" and finding its application reasonable with regard to one discharged employee but unreasonable as to another).

[144]TYK Refractories Co., 96 LA 803 (Talarico, 1991) (disparate treatment of employees); Stocker & Sitler Operating Co., 74 LA 752 (Feldman, 1980) (noting that because the union did not challenge the reasonableness of the employer's rule, uniform application and appropriate publication would not be considered). See Chapter 10 for a full discussion of rules.

[145]TYK Refractories Co., 96 LA 803 (Talarico, 1991) (failure to conduct fair and impartial investigation); Lee C. Moore Corp., 84 LA 1166 (Duff, 1985).

[146]Sinternet Corp., 95 LA 978 (Richard, 1990) (upholding discharge where employee was progressively disciplined); St. Luke's Hosp., 93 LA 1241 (Johnson, 1989) (grievant was under final warning when discharged); Wheatland Tube Co., 84 LA 527 (Bowers, 1985) (upholding discharge where progressive discipline applied); M.S. Ginn & Co., 75 LA 341 (Merrifield, 1980) (overturning discharge where employer failed to provide warning to employee).

[147]Monarch Tile, 100 LA 1029 (Frost, 1993); Emerson Elec. Co., 83 LA 895 (Fitzsimmons, 1984); Library of Congress, 73 LA 1092 (Aronin, 1979); Consolidated Foods Corp., 43 LA 1143 (Klein, 1964); Caterpillar Tractor Co., 42 LA 710 (Davis, 1964).

[148]General Mills, 102 LA 595 (Goldstein, 1993); Temperature Indus. Int'l, 101 LA 352 (Fowler, 1993); Southwest Airlines Co., 87 LA 594 (Helburn, 1986); Wheatland Tube Co., 84 LA 527 (Bowers, 1985); Nestle Co., 81 LA 1263 (Feigenbaum, 1983). But see Gill Studios, Inc., 78 LA 915 (Goetz, 1982) (discharge improper for employee with prior warning for similar violation where employee not warned that discharge could result).

[149]Frito-Lay, Inc., 105 LA 761 (Gentile, 1995) (discharge appropriate when loafing considered in the aggregate); A.H. Belo Corp., 55 LA 469 (Rohman, 1970) (series of acts taken together justify discharge).

be upheld, as when the offense was minor and had not been the subject of previous disciplinary action, even where the employee was under a last-chance agreement,[150] where a first violation is charged and other related offenses are not sufficient to uphold the discharge,[151] where the employee's disciplinary record has been free of blemish for 4 years,[152] or where the employee had not been warned after being caught loafing on the first occasion.[153]

Arbitrators also consider relevant the employee's knowledge or intent. A suspension was upheld for an employee who departed from duty without permission and falsified a time log to cover the absence,[154] and discharge was proper where an employee should have known that a 2 ½-hour break was excessive.[155] An employee's discharge was overturned where she reasonably believed that she was clocked out and not extending her break;[156] a discharge was reduced to suspension where the employee's actions were done on "impulse;"[157] and a 5-day suspension was excessive where the two employees' extended break was inadvertent because neither had a watch.[158]

Finally, an arbitrator may consider the presence of mitigating factors and the employee's longevity in evaluating the appropriateness of discipline imposed. For instance, suspensions were overturned where the employer had condoned similar acts in the past.[259] A discharge was reduced to a suspension where the employee had worked for the company for 10 years and where the employee may not have heard the quitting bell, had no clock to check, and had a perfect 6½-year record of employment.[160]

---

[150]Northrop Corp., 96 LA 149 (Weiss, 1990).

[151]Mt. Sinai Hosp., 78 LA 937 (Graham, 1982).

[152]M. S. Ginn & Co., 75 LA 341 (Merrifield, 1980).

[153]Huber, Hunt & Nichols, 52 LA 965 (Kabaker, 1969).

[154]City of Cedar Rapids, 95 LA 1119 (Cohen, 1990).

[155]General Mills, Inc., 102 LA 595 (Goldstein, 1993).

[156]Southwest Airlines Co., 87 LA 594 (Helburn, 1986) (also upholding discharge of another employee for profound disregard of the rule).

[157]Western Auto Supply Co., 71 LA 714 (Ross, 1978).

[158]John Breuner Co., 75 LA 1292 (Craver, 1981).

[159]Pottsville Area Sch. Dist., 91 LA 515 (Mayer, 1988); J&J Register Co., 91 LA 2234 (Allen, 1988).

[160]Visador Co., 73 LA 578 (Seifer, 1979).

# Chapter 5

# Refusals to Perform Work
# or Cooperate

## I. "Work Now, Grieve Later"

The widely accepted general rule is "work now, grieve later."
The rule is based on a presumption that the parties to a collective
bargaining agreement intend to refer all their disagreements to the
grievance procedure and that no "self-help" is to be tolerated. An
early award, *Ford Motor Co.,*[1] is often cited as the leading authority
on the subject. The arbitrator wrote:

> Some men apparently think that, when a violation of contract seems
> clear, the employee may refuse to obey and thus resort to self-help
> rather than the grievance procedure. That is an erroneous point of view.
> In the first place, what appears to one party to be a clear violation may
> not seem so at all to the other party. Neither party can be the final
> judge as to whether the contract has been violated; * * *
> The only difference between a "clear" violation and a "doubtful" one is
> that the former makes a clear grievance and the latter a doubtful one.
> But both must be handled in the regular prescribed manner;
> * * * an industrial plant is not a debating society * * * [and] * * * produc-
> tion cannot wait for exhaustion of the grievance procedure.

### A. *Individual Refusals to Obey*

Typically, the "work now, grieve later" rule is invoked by arbitrators when an employee resists employer orders relating to a change
in the working environment. Where employees simply refuse to perform a job or accept a work assignment—rather than filing a grievance—arbitrators typically uphold discipline. There are an enormous

---

[1]3 LA 779, 780–81 (Shulman, 1994).

153

number of factual circumstances in which refusing to do ordered work results in an arbitrator upholding discipline. Some typical examples include suspension for refusing to do a job differently so as to aid a time study;[2] suspension for an employee who refused to wipe paint off of a new tractor's tires;[3] suspension for striking a foreman who had issued an order to perform a task, even though the employee had an injured arm;[4] termination on grounds of job abandonment for refusing to perform an assigned job after filing a grievance;[5] suspension for a driver who refused to allow another employee to drive his assigned truck;[6] suspension for an employee who refused to take another employee's place at an oven;[7] discipline of an employee who refused to work in a dyes shop;[8] suspension of an employee who refused to implement a new work procedure;[9] and a suspension for refusing to decorate with Christmas lights.[10]

## B. *Group Refusals to Obey*[11]

Arbitrators also support discipline when there is a group of employees involved in a work refusal. The discharge of an employee was approved when her protest over an assignment was believed by her foreman to be a group action, and she failed to state that she wanted to file a grievance.[12] Discharge was considered proper for an employee who instigated a walkout.[13] Suspension imposed by an employer was upheld even though the arbitrator determined that the employer had violated the agreement by setting up a separate plant to do bargaining unit work.[14]

## C. *Examples of Improper Refusals to Obey*

The "work now, grieve later" rule has been invoked in many situations. It is rarely the specific act ordered that determines whether the refusal is a disciplinable offense. Refusals leading to discipline have involved transfers;[15] changes in production standards and work-

---

[2]Armstrong Cork Co., 1 LA 574 (Guild, 1946).
[3]John Deere Tractor Co., 5 LA 561 (Updegraff, 1946).
[4]Continental Can Co., 6 LA 363 (Boyd, 1947).
[5]Dayton Malleable Iron Co., 8 LA 544 (Wardlaw, 1947).
[6]Safeway Stores, Inc., 51 LA 413 (Gillingham, 1967).
[7]J. Weingarten, Inc., 52 LA 301 (Autrey, 1968).
[8]American Cyanamid Co., 74 LA 15 (Friedman, 1980).
[9]Brinks, Inc., 76 LA 1120 (Rothman, 1981).
[10]City of Marshall, 96 LA 984 (Allen, 1991).
[11]Group refusals to obey may be protected conduct under the National Labor Relations Act. See Chapter 10.
[12]Triumph Explosives, Inc., 2 LA 617 (Killingsworth, 1945).
[13]Dresser Indus., Inc., 52 LA 978 (Bothwell, 1969).
[14]Lucky Stores, Inc., 56 LA 613 (Karasick, 1971).
[15]Cedars-Sinai Med. Ctr., 48 LA 1027 (Block, 1967); Great Atl. & Pac. Tea Co., 1 LA 63 (Albert, 1944); Ford Motor Co., 3 LA 779 (Shulman, 1944).

loads;[16] working through lunch;[17] reporting early;[18] reporting to a new location;[19] cleaning up;[20] backfilling the job of a suspended employee;[21] performing nonunit work or work that is "not my job;"[22] not taking a break when directed;[23] returning to a former job;[24] the appropriate use of the grievance procedure;[25] protesting a new method of time reporting;[26] excessive heat;[27] failure to report to work;[28] overtime work;[29] assaulting a co-worker;[30] attending meetings;[31] wearing or not wearing shirts;[32] submitting to drug tests;[33] undergoing physical examinations;[34] search of a lunch basket;[35] obtaining a medical certificate;[36] taking a personal leave;[37] following dress or grooming codes;[38] and displaying provocative messages on posters or clothing.[39]

---

[16]Legal Aid Soc'y, 81 LA 1065 (Nicolau, 1983); Republic Steel Corp., 34 LA 553 (Mittenthal, 1959); Skenandoa Rayon Corp., 18 LA 239 (Justin, 1952); Goodyear Clearwater Mills, 6 LA 117 (McCoy, 1947); National Mach. Co., 5 LA 97 (Klamon, 1946).

[17]Rock Hill Printing & Finishing Co., 16 LA 722 (Jaffee, 1951).

[18]Fitchburg Paper Co., 47 LA 349 (Wallen, 1966).

[19]Mountain States Tel. & Tel. Co., 47 LA 739 (Peck, 1966).

[20]United States Pipe & Foundry Co., 69 LA 732 (Jedel, 1977); United States Steel Corp., 48 LA 32 (Florey, 1966).

[21]Cyclops Corp., 56 LA 351 (Altrock, 1971).

[22]General Elec. Co., 73 LA 1273 (Maroney, 1979); Mark Twain Indus., Inc., 74 LA 441 (Stix, 1979); C. Schmidt Co., 66 LA 90 (McIntosh, 1976); Oberle-Jodre Constr. Co., 57 LA 1028 (Ipavec, 1971); Ford Motor Co., 3 LA 779 (Shulman, 1944).

[23]Fourco Glass Co., 84 LA 693 (Cantor, 1985).

[24]Georgia-Pacific Corp., 96 LA 201 (Allen, 1991).

[25]North Am. Aviation, Inc., 15 LA 652 (Aaron, 1950); Cragin Mfrs., 3 LA 746 (Cheney, 1946).

[26]Blaw-Knox Co., 3 LA 753 (Blair, 1946).

[27]Consolidated Packaging Corp., 52 LA 259 (Hertz, 1966).

[28]Memphis Light, Gas & Water Div., 98 LA 1123 (Goldman, 1992).

[29]Pacific Southwest Airlines, 62 LA 1189 (Gentile, 1974); International Paper Co., 60 LA 964 (Ray, 1973); Inmont Corp., 60 LA 1125 (Kelliher, 1973); BP Oil Co., 59 LA 976 (Oppenheim, 1972); Crescent Constr. Co., 55 LA 869 (Shieber, 1970); Pratt & Whitney, Inc., 53 LA 200 (Seitz, 1969); International Minerals & Chem. Corp., 49 LA 159 (Oppenheim, 1967); Quinn Wire & Iron Works, 44 LA 1016 (Moore, 1965); Bemis Bros. Bag Co., 44 LA 1139 (Stix, 1965).

[30]Southern Bell Tel. Co., 27 LA 557 (Blair, 1956).

[31]Valley Hosp. Ass'n, 97 LA 661 (Calhoun, 1991).

[32]City of Jamesville, 64 LA 783 (Schurke, 1975); Day & Zimmerman Inc., 44 LA 385 (Boles, 1965); Packaging Corp. of Am., 37 LA 338 (Teple, 1961); R. C. Allen Bus. Machs., Inc., 29 LA 404 (Howlett, 1957).

[33]Ethyl Corp., 95 LA 632 (Blum, 1990); Crescent Metal Prods. Inc., 91 LA 1129 (Coyne, 1989). For a more complete discussion, see Chapter 6.

[34]Carpenter Steel Co., 44 LA 1185 (Jerrison, 1965); Safeway Stores, Inc., 45 LA 663 (McNaughton, 1965).

[35]Freuhauf Corp., 49 LA 89 (Daugherty, 1967).

[36]Johnson Controls Inc., 92 LA 449 (Mayer, 1989).

[37]Briggs & Stratton Corp., 64 LA 1155 (Kossoff, 1975).

[38]Checker Cab Co., Inc., 62 LA 1107 (Fleischli, 1974); City of Detroit, 61 LA 645 (McCormick, 1973); Olin's, Inc., 41 LA 562 (Black, 1963).

[39]Armco Inc., 93 LA 561 (Strongin, 1989); True Temper Corp., 76 LA 1 (Duff, 1980); California Processors, Inc., 56 LA 1275 (Koven, 1971).

## D. *Legitimate Refusals to Obey*

The "work now, grieve later" principle does not apply to an employee's refusal to obey an order given by one who is not authorized to do so.[40] To be valid, the order must be by someone with appropriate authority, and the employee must understand that person to possess such authority. Other situations where refusals are acceptable are discussed later in this chapter.

## II. Insubordination: Refusals to Do Work Required by Superior

### A. *General Principles*

Generally, employees must follow orders given by a superior, although they may later challenge the propriety of the order through the established grievance procedure.[41] As one arbitrator put it: "[T]o permit employees to willfully disregard a direct order would result in chaos."[42] Insubordination is the refusal by an employee to work or obey an order given by the employee's superior. In most instances, any employee who refuses to work or obey now (and grieve later) is considered "insubordinate."[43] This basic definition, however, is subject to at least six qualifications.

First, an employee's refusal to work or obey must be knowing, willful, and deliberate.[44] Mere negligence in performing one's duties is not insubordination.[45]

Second, the order must be both explicit and clearly given, so that the employee understands both its meaning and its intent as a command.[46]

---

[40]New York Blower Co., 92 LA 433 (Belshaw, 1989) (clerk was not authorized to give assignments).

[41]The general rule, "Work now, grieve later," is discussed at the beginning of this chapter.

[42]When no specific protected activity is alleged, a charge of insubordination against an employee who is a union representative is generally treated no differently than a charge of insubordination against any other employee. Clark Equip. Co., 61 LA 1301 (Kossoff, 1974); Harley Davidson Motor Co., 61 LA 1103 (Edes, 1973). Arbitrators occasionally have held union representative employees to a higher degree of responsibility, indicating they should serve as an example to the others. E. A. Norris Plumbing Co., 90 LA 462 (Christopher, 1987); Ceco Corp., 71 LA 1148 (Caraway, 1978); Arden Farms Co., 45 LA 1124 (Tsukiyama, 1965). See Chapter 10 for a fuller discussion.

[43]Taft Broadcasting Co., 51 LA 665 (Bradley, 1978). See also Pinto Valley Copper Corp., 83 LA 1300 (Lennard, 1984).

[44]Fourco Glass Co., 84 LA 693 (Cantor, 1985); Chromalloy Div.-Oklahoma, 67 LA 1310 (Moore, 1977); Dayton Tire & Rubber Co., 65 LA 34 (Ipavec, 1975); Colgate-Palmolive Co., 64 LA 397 (Allen, 1975); Best-Ways Distribution Co., 55 LA 1056 (Block, 1970); Agrico Chem. Co., 55 LA 481 (Greene, 1970); National Carbide Co., 24 LA 804 (Warns, 1955).

[45]Hub City Jobbing Co., 43 LA 907 (Gundermann, 1964).

[46]Suntec Indus., 99 LA 105 (Stanton, 1992); P.P.G. Indus., Inc., 90 LA 479 (Sedwick, 1987); Pinto Valley Copper Corp., 83 LA 1300 (Lennard, 1984).

Third, the order given must be both reasonable[47] and work related.[48] The employee need not be on duty to be found insubordinate,
provided the employee's conduct injuriously affects his employer's
business.[49]

Fourth, the order must have been given by someone with appropriate authority, and the employee must have understood that person
to possess that authority.[50]

Fifth, the employee must be made aware of the consequences of
failing to perform the work or follow the directive. For example, an
employer improperly suspended an employee for insubordination because the employee took 2 days off to be with his child for her surgery.
The employer denied his request for leave, offered to allow the employee to use vacation time, but failed to tell him he would be disciplined if he took the days off.[51]

Finally, if practical, the employee must be given or have time
to correct his purportedly insubordinate behavior. For instance, a
discharge for insubordination was overturned where an employee
requested a different assignment after he was told at the end of his
shift that the next day he would be assigned to inventory duty. His
supervisor refused the request, commented on his poor attitude, and
discharged him. The arbitrator found the employee had not been
given an opportunity to report the next day and perform the job
assignment, nor the opportunity for sober reflection.[52]

## B. Specific Conduct Constituting Insubordination

Insubordination takes many forms. The most commonly recognized type of insubordination occurs when an employee refuses to do
work expected or requested by his supervisor. In these instances, an
employee usually resorts to "self-help"; i.e., instead of following the
regular grievance procedures for protesting a superior's directive, the
employee takes matters into his own hands. This employee self-help
runs directly counter to the general rule of "work now, grieve later"
and is itself considered insubordination.[53] The refusal is frequently

[47]Virgin Islands Tel. Corp., 101 LA 273 (Nicholas, 1993); Ermanco Inc., 101 LA 269
(Ellmann, 1993); Prestige Stamping Co., 74 LA 163 (Keefe, 1980).

[48]Georgia Power Co., 87 LA 800 (Byars, 1986).

[49]Inland Container Corp., 28 LA 312 (Ferguson, 1957). But see Midwest Mfg. Co., 97 LA
403 (Wright, 1991).

[50]Suntec Indus., 99 LA 105 (Stanton, 1992); Railway Carmen, 77 LA 694 (Thornell, 1981).

[51]Pinto Valley Copper Corp., 83 LA 1300 (Lennard, 1984). For the general proposition
that employees must be made aware of the consequences of failing to perform, see Suntec
Indus., 99 LA 105 (Stanton, 1992); Micro Precision Gear & Mach. Corp., 31 LA 575 (Young, 1958).

[52]Tension Envelope Corp., 99 LA 1208 (Bankston, 1992).

[53]Virgin Island Tel. Corp., 101 LA 273 (Nicholas, 1993); Washington Hosp. Ctr., 75 LA
32 (Rothschild, 1980); Hygrade Food Prods. Corp., 74 LA 99 (O'Neill, 1980); American Cyanamid
Co., 74 LA 15 (Friedman, 1980); Grand Junction Steel Fabricating Co., 58 LA 240 (Allen, 1972).

manifested by the employee leaving or staying away from work.[54] An unauthorized vacation may be considered an insubordinate absence.[55]

An employee may also be found insubordinate for using abusive language towards his supervisor[56] or for exhibiting a general attitude of defiance or disrespect.[57]

Employees generally do not have freedom to select with whom they will work. An employee's refusal to accept a work assignment on the grounds that the employee dislikes a co-worker with whom he is told to work can be insubordination.[58] An employee may refuse to follow an order, in some instances, because of privacy concerns. An employee's refusal to submit to a search, or a drug or blood test, may be insubordination if an employer reasonably believes that the employee is physically incapacitated, or that company property has been stolen, or that an employee has violated the law.[59] There are, however, numerous exceptions, as discussed in Chapter 6.

Arbitrators have sustained insubordination charges in the following circumstances: refusing to attend or interrupting a company meeting;[60] refusing to follow company dress code;[61] refusing to follow com-

---

[54]S.B. Thomas, Best Food Baking Group, 92 LA 1055 (Chandler, 1989) (employee left work upon finding truck not refueled); Air Express Int'l Corp., 81 LA 753 (Weiss, 1983) (employee left job without permission prior to finishing work); Arrow Lock Corp., 84 LA 734 (Nemaizer, 1985) (employee walked off job in response to alleged harassment from supervisor); H.J. Scheirich Co., 76 LA 723 (Lynch, 1981) (employee walked off job during work hours); Algoma Steel Corp., 73 LA 1256 (O'Shea, 1979) (employee left plant premises without permission); Louisville Tin & Stove Co., 41 LA 386 (Witnel, 1963) (employee absent without permission).

[55]Century Boat Co., 76 LA 699 (Keefe, 1981).

[56]City of Racine, 78 LA 627 (McCrary, 1982); Seattle Dep't Stores, 75 LA 6 (Beck, 1980); American Sugar Co., 52 LA 1228 (Whyte, 1969).

[57]Federal Correctional Inst., 75 LA 295 (Woodward, 1980); National Carbide Co., 24 LA 804 (Warns, 1955) (abusive or profane language; shop talk distinguished.)

[58]Lucky Stores, Inc., 101 LA 135 (Christopher, 1993); Griffin Pipe Prods. Co., 72 LA 1033 (Doyle, 1979).

[59]Folsom Return to Custody, Inc., 101 LA 837 (Staudohar, 1993) (refusal to permit vehicle search for contraband); GSX Servs. of Cal., Inc., 96 LA 792 (Riker, 1991) (refusal to take blood test to determine physical fitness); Bowater Carolina Corp., 92 LA 162 (Clark, 1989) (refusal to provide urine sample for drug test); Concrete Pipe Prods. Co., 87 LA 601 (Caraway, 1986) (refusal to consent to drug testing policy); Shell Oil Co., 84 LA 562 (Milentz, 1985) (refusal to permit search of car for drugs); Kraft Inc., 82 LA 360 (Denson, 1984) (refusal to permit search of person for drugs); Shell Oil Co., 81 LA 1205 (Brisco, 1983) (refusal to permit search of lunchbox for drugs); Prestige Stamping Co., 74 LA 163 (Keefe, 1980) (refusal to permit search for drugs); AMF/Harley-Davidson Motor Co., 68 LA 811 (Martin, 1977) (refusal to allow inspection of purse for stolen property); Colgate-Palmolive Co., 50 LA 441 (Koven, 1968) (refusal to allow fingerprints following theft suspicion); Safeway Stores, Inc., 45 LA 663 (McNaughton, 1965) (refusal to take physical exam to determine stamina for job).

[60]Ermanco, Inc., 101 LA 269 (Ellman, 1993); Valley Hosp. Ass'n, 97 LA 661 (Calhoun, 1991); Scovill, Inc., 84 LA 201 (Storey, 1985); American Can Co., 57 LA 1063 (Kerrison, 1971).

[61]Lloyd, Ketchum Oldsmobile, 77 LA 953 (Hilgert, 1981); National Park Serv., 72 LA 314 (Pritzker, 1979); Checker Cab Co., Inc., 62 LA 1107 (Fleischli, 1974); Day-Zimmermann, Inc., 44 LA 385 (Boles, 1965). But see Mitchell-Bentley Corp., 45 LA 1071 (Ryder, 1965).

pany safety policy;[62] entering or parking in a restricted area;[63] refusing to answer one's pager while on call;[64] reading on the job;[65] and refusing to raise the American flag.[66]

## C. Exceptions

Numerous exceptions to the "work now, grieve later" rule are recognized by arbitrators. Indeed, Arbitrator Shulman, who is generally credited with first discussing the rule, later ruled on specific situations in which it was acceptable for an employee to refuse to carry out an order from a supervisor. Thus, in *Ford Motor Co.,*[67] he awarded full back pay to two glaziers who refused to accept work as painters. The grievance was a "bald case in which a skilled tradesman was assigned to work wholly different from and unrelated to his classification * * *".[68] In fact, Arbitrator Shulman commented that nothing in his leading case "justifies the disciplinary action in this case" because "[t]hat opinion dealt primarily with production employees."[69]

In both cases, he was dealing with production and craft workers represented by the same UAW local union. The arbitrator said that the general rule could be applicable to skilled craftsmen if there was a "reasonable dispute" concerning whether or not particular work was within a skilled classification. But, he concluded, it cannot be applied in situations where there is no dispute that particular work is the work of a particular classification. A limited exception has been recognized where a skilled craftsman has been ordered to perform a job wholly unrelated to his craft and refuses.[70]

In *Pacific Mills,*[71] the arbitrator reinstated and made whole a production employee who had been discharged for allegedly being insubordinate when she withdrew her earlier temporary waiver of her seniority right and insisted on exercising her contractual seniority right to a particular job. The arbitrator found that the employee "had

---

[62]Chanute Mfg. Co., 99 LA 20 (Levy, 1992); Gwaltney of Smithfield, Inc., 81 LA 241 (Bernhardt, 1983).

[63]McDonnell Douglas Corp., 94 LA 585 (Woolf, 1989); Todd-Pacific Shipyards, 86 LA 171 (Draznin, 1985); Federal Mogul Corp., 69 LA 919 (Morgan, 1977); Baldwin Rubber Co., 22 LA 765 (Bowles, 1954).

[64]Champion Int'l Corp., 73 LA 921 (Rimer, 1979).

[65]Library of Congress, 73 LA 1092 (Aronin, 1979).

[66]Ralston Purina Co., 61 LA 14 (Krislov, 1973).

[67]3 LA 782 (Shulman, 1946).

[68]Id. at 783.

[69]Id.

[70]Atlantic Richfield Co., 70 LA 707 (Fox, 1978); Ironrite, Inc., 28 LA 394 (Haughton, 1956).

[71]2 LA 545, 548–49 (McCoy, 1946).

a legal right at any time thereafter to withdraw that waiver," and to assert her seniority and claim a particular job.

In *American Transformer Co.*,[72] a union steward's explanation to employees of their contract rights led the employees to disobey a foreman's order. The union steward was discharged for insubordination. The arbitrator ordered the union steward to be reinstated and made whole because he had "acted in accord with his responsibility as chief shop steward" and could not, therefore, be held to have been insubordinate. Thus, these arbitrators carved out the criminal or unlawful conduct safety and health, craft work, contractual "legal rights," and union rights as exceptions to the "work now, grieve later" rule. In time, further exceptions to the rule were recognized.

*1. Safety and Health.*   An employee is not obliged to follow an order that threatens the employee's health or safety.[73] Some arbitrators require that an actual threat exist, but the majority apply an objective standard to determine if the employee's safety or health-related fear was reasonable under the circumstances.[74] As one arbitrator noted:

> The fear of bodily harm to the employee or his family, or damage to his property, must be real, not something which could possibly happen. The fear of danger must be sufficient that a normal ordinary person would reasonably and conscientiously believe that peril was imminent.[75]

There is a line of cases in which the imposed discipline is set aside and the employees are made whole. In these cases arbitrators found both that the employee believed the work was unsafe and that the work probably was unsafe. A union steward who had advised a co-worker not to perform a task that both the steward and the co-worker believed unsafe was reinstated and made whole.[76] Eight em-

---

[72]1 LA 456–57, (Flink, 1945).

[73]See, e.g., USS-Fairless Works, 101 LA 380 (Neumeier, 1993) (use of equipment, despite order to the contrary, in order to remove a work hazard in an emergency situation); Beverly Enters., 100 LA 552 (Berquist, 1993) (refusal to lift patient because of back injury); Minnesota Mining & Mfg. Co., 85 LA 1179 (White, 1985) (refusal to work because of low visibility); Tenneco Oil Co., 83 LA 1099 (King, 1984) (refusal to report to work because of recent traumatic experience); T & J Indus., Inc., 79 LA 697 (Clark, 1982) (refusal to work in freezing conditions); United Parcel Serv., Inc., 78 LA 836 (McAllister, 1982) (refusal to write while walking); Halstead & Mitchell, 74 LA 946 (Odom, 1980) (refusal to stack materials too high); Checker Motors Corp., 61 LA 33 (Daniel, 1973) (refusal to operate machine and risk loss of fingers); United States Steel Corp., 55 LA 61 (Dybeck, 1970) (refusal to remove dust mask); Halstead Metal Prods., Inc., 49 LA 325 (Wagner, 1967) (abnormally dangerous work conditions); United States Pipe & Foundry Co., 48 LA 1349 (Coffey, 1967) (refusal to move overhead crane).

[74]Stockham Valve & Fittings, 102 LA 73 (Poole, 1993) (employee lacked physical capacity to follow work command); Ralph's Grocery Co., 101 LA 634 (Ross, 1993); Fulton Seafood Indus., Inc., 74 LA 620 (Volz, 1980); Sheller-Globe Corp., 60 LA 414 (Seidman, 1973); Laclede Gas Co., 39 LA 833 (Bothwell, 1962); LaClede Steel Co., 56 LA 407 (Volz, 1971) (employees properly refused to return to plant after evacuation due to bomb threat). For minority view, see Consolidated Edison Co., 61 LA 607 (Turkus, 1973).

[75]Fulton Seafood Indus., Inc., 74 LA 620, 623 (Volz, 1980), quoting Union Carbide Corp. 70-2 ARB ¶ 8536 (Stouffer, 1970).

[76]Copco Steel & Eng'g Co., 21 LA 410 (Parker, 1953).

ployees who had made several attempts to work in the cold before refusing to work at all were reinstated and made whole.[77] "Too cold" was also accepted in the case of an individual employee who was ordered to be made whole.[78] The discharge of an employee who refused to use an employer safety apparatus in favor of one of his own choosing was overturned (with a make-whole order) since both appliances met OSHA requirements.[79] A make-whole order was issued in the case of a worker who refused to perform a task within 24 hours of having sustained a severe injury in a hazardous situation.[80] The discharge of an employee who was known by the employer to previously have incurred back injuries was overturned (with a make-whole order) when the employee refused to perform a task involving heavy lifting.[81]

There is another line of case in which the claim of a threat to the employee's safety or health was accepted as both real and made in good faith, yet the remedy is less than a make-whole order. These cases generally exhibit complex fact situations in which the overall conduct of the grievant may have been questionable. Thus, full back pay has been denied where the grievant rejected helpful suggestions as to how to accomplish an ordered task;[82] the grievant failed to adequately explain his problem;[83] the employee engaged in a heated argument;[84] the grievant was just difficult to deal with;[85] and the condition, though uncomfortable, was not really "abnormally dangerous."[86]

In many cases in which the employee sought to defend the refusal to obey an order on the ground that it posed a threat to the employee's safety or health, the penalty imposed by the employer was upheld because the arbitrator concluded that no threatening condition existed.[87] In one case the penalty imposed was found to have been proper, but it was set aside because of the employer's delay in imposing the penalty.[88] In another case, the discharge of an employee was upheld on the ground that the refusal to work for safety reasons does not extend to group actions.[89] If an employee's refusal to work is based

---

[77]Muter Co., 47 LA 332 (Di Leone, 1966).

[78]T & J Indus., Inc., 79 LA 697 (Clark, 1982).

[79]Manistee Drop Forge Co., 62 LA 1164 (Brooks, 1974).

[80]Minnesota Mining & Mfg. Co., 85 LA 1179 (White, 1985).

[81]Beverly Enters., 100 LA 522 (Berquist, 1993).

[82]American Fork & Hoe Co., 5 LA 300 (Gilden, 1945).

[83]Goodyear Clearwater Mills No. 1, 8 LA 647 (McCoy, 1947).

[84]Pet Dealers Supply Co., 60 LA 814 (Fellman, 1973).

[85]United States Steel Corp., 55 LA 61 (Dybeck, 1970).

[86]Parker Co., 60 LA 473 (Edwards, 1973).

[87]Griffin Pipe Prods. Co., 72 LA 1033 (Doyle, 1979); Bethlehem Steel Corp., 65 LA 902 (Harkless, 1975); Waterford Sch. Dist., 61 LA 722 (Watkins, 1973); Sheller-Globe Corp., 60 LA 414 (Seidman, 1973); Fruehauf Trailer Corp., 48 LA 1291 (Kallenbach, 1967); Bauer Bros. Co., 48 LA 861 (Kates, 1967); Sealtest Foods, 47 LA 848 (Mullin, 1966).

[88]Gibson Refrigerator Div., 52 LA 663 (Keefe, 1969).

[89]Chrysler Corp., 63 LA 677 (Alexander, 1974).

upon mere personal preference or uncomfortable work circumstances, it does not fall within this exception. A mere assertion that one is exercising one's safety rights, absent specific identification of the danger, is insufficient.[90]

*2. Union Rights.* An exception has been recognized where an employee has been deprived of representation by a union official during a meeting with company officials, thereby interfering with the employee's proper use of the grievance procedure. The employee's legitimate refusal to participate in a discussion in the absence of union representation will not constitute insubordination. Before the right to union representation attaches, however, the employee must have a reasonable belief that some sort of disciplinary action will result from the meeting.[91]

A 1945 case recognized that a union steward could not be discharged for insubordination when the steward was carrying out his duty to advise employees of their contractual rights.[92] In another case that year, the discharges of three union stewards were overturned (with a make-whole order) when the arbitrator determined that the union steward had a contractual right to question the employer's assignment of employees to work outside of the plant.[93] A later decision explained that exceptions existed to the "work now, grieve later" rule. This time, in yet another *Ford Motor Co.* case,[94] the arbitrator set aside the suspension of a union chairman who was administering the grievance procedures as specified in the contract. The employer's disciplinary action had ignored "the duty of the Company to respect action falling primarily within the Union's domain."[95]

It has been held that a union steward cannot be discharged for refusing a supervisor's order to cease investigating a grievance.[96] Several cases hold that it is improper for an employer to interfere with the operation of the grievance procedure by not allowing a union steward to be present.[97] A union official who left work without permission in order to go to the union convention was discharged improperly

---

[90]Grain Processing Corp., 92 LA 265 (Hilgert, 1989) (sickness claim pretext to avoid work order); Peabody Coal Co., 87 LA 1002 (Volz, 1986); Fulton Seafood Indus., Inc., 74 LA 620 (Volz, 1980); Brockway Clay Prods. Co., 28 LA 37 (Duff, 1957).

[91]Pacific Bell, 92 LA 127 (Oestreich, 1989) (reasonable belief discussion was to be an investigatory interview); Allied Employers, Inc., 72 LA 437 (Peterschmidt, 1978); Illinois Bell Tel. Co., 63 LA 968 (Dolnick, 1974); Southern Cal. Edison Co., 61 LA 33 (Daniel, 1973); Food Employers Council, Inc., 40 LA 1100 (McNaughton, 1963); The Arcrods Co., 39 LA 784 (Teple, 1962); Valley Iron Works, 33 LA 769 (Anderson, 1960); Braniff Airways, Inc., 27 LA 892 (Williams, 1957). See Chapter 2 for a fuller discussion of *Weingarten* rights.

[92]Smith-Blair, Inc., 100 LA 344 (Goodstein, 1992); American Transformer Co., 1 LA 456 (Flink, 1945). See also Copco Steel & Eng'g Co., 21 LA 410 (Parker, 1953).

[93]Schick, Inc., 2 LA 552 (Stone, 1945).

[94]10 LA 213 (Shulman, 1948).

[95]Id. at 214.

[96]International Harvester Co.,. 16 LA 307 (McCoy, 1951).

[97]Southern Cal. Edison Co., 61 LA 453 (Block, 1973); Kimberley-Clark Corp., 55 LA 291 (Jaffee, 1970); Electronics Specialty Co., 52 LA 982 (Koven, 1969); Food Employers Council,

(and made whole) because the contract required the employer to grant a leave of absence in such circumstances.[98] Some cases have recognized the rights of the union in general, but grant less than full reinstatement because the actions of the union officials or members were somewhat less than perfect.[99]

There are other cases where the penalty imposed by the employer was upheld because the actions of the union officials went far beyond the bounds of what was considered to be reasonable by the arbitrator. Actions of union officials that have gone too far include countermanding supervisory orders or instructing employees not to work as directed by supervision;[100] physically interfering with supervision;[101] threatening, instigating, or engaging in a slowdown, work stoppage, or walkout;[102] leaving work to attend a union meeting;[103] belligerence when acting as an individual worker and not in the capacity of a union steward;[104] posting a bulletin board notice in violation of contractually prescribed procedures;[105] acting contrary to the requirements of the grievance procedure;[106] and testing the appropriateness of the employer's rules.[107] Indeed, there are cases that note that union stewards, as such, are held to a higher standard of conduct than are other employees.[108]

*3. Contract Rights.* Another exception exists where an employee refuses an order that directly conflicts with a clear right of the employee,[109] and the employee has no time to resort to the grievance

---

Inc., 40 LA 1100 (McNaughton, 1963); Valley Iron Works, 33 LA 769 (Anderson, 1960); Braniff Airways, Inc., 27 LA 892 (Williams, 1957).

[98]Dole Refrigerating Co., 96 LA 787 (Bowers, 1991). See also International Salt Co., 39 LA 238 (Mittenthal, 1962); Telex, Inc., 35 LA 873 (Kinyon, 1960).

[99]Greif Bros. Corp., 67 LA 1001 (Flannagan, 1976); Lind Constr. Co., 47 LA 369 (Conn. Bd., Summers, 1966); Elgin Instrument Co., 37 LA 1064 (Roberts, 1961); Southern Bakeries Co., 36 LA 440 (Dworet, 1960); United States Ceramic Tile Co., 31 LA 617 (Duff, 1958); Le Roi Mfg. Co., 8 LA 350 (Updegraff, 1947); Rhode Island Tool Co., 7 LA 113 (Healy, 1946).

[100]M.M. Mades Co., 14 LA 748 (Copelof, 1949); Commercial Pac. Cable Co., 11 LA 219 (Kerr, 1948); Nathan Mfg. Co., 7 LA 3 (Scheiber, 1947).

[101]Harley Davidson Motor Co., 61 LA 1103 (Edes, 1973); Borg-Warner Corp., 27 LA 148 (Dworkin, 1956).

[102]Lancaster Electro Plating, Inc., 93 LA 203 (Bressler, 1989); Bucyrus-Erie Co., 69 LA 93 (Lipson, 1977); Robertshaw Controls Co., 55 LA 883 (Seinshemer, 1970); McConway & Torley Corp., 55 LA 31 (Cohen, 1970); V.E. Anderson Mfg. Co., 43 LA 174 (King, 1964).

[103]Home Furniture Co., 50 LA 1140 (Porter, 1967).

[104]Franz Food Prods., Inc., 28 LA 543 (Bothwell, 1957).

[105]Cypress Gardens Citrus Prods., Inc., 50 LA 1183 (Christon, 1968).

[106]Shelby County Gov't, 100 LA 284 (Harvey, 1992); Danly Mach. Co., 51 LA 739 (Larkin, 1968); Fruehauf Trailer Co., 31 LA 1031 (Peterschmidt, 1958).

[107]Modine Mfg. Co., 60 LA 141 (Talent, 1973).

[108]E. A. Norris Plumbing Co., 90 LA 462 (Christopher, 1987); Atlas Chain & Mfg. Co., 32 LA 117 (Crawford, 1959); Monsanto Chem. Co., 27 LA 400 (Reynard, 1956); Nathan Mfg. Co., 7 LA 3 (Scheiber, 1947).

[109]Sheller Mfg. Corp., 34 LA 689 (McCoy, 1960) (employee rightly refused to alter time sheets, which reflect a definite right of the employee to proper pay); International Harvester Co., 16 LA 307 (McCoy, 1957) (order interferes with union's right to investigate and process grievance); Ford Motor Co., 10 LA 213 (Shulman, 1948) (same). However, recall that in Ford Motor Co., 3 LA 779 (1944), Arbitrator Shulman noted that there is no exception simply because

process. This behavior may not be insubordination because the principle of "obey now, and grieve later" presupposes an adequate relief under the grievance procedure. For instance, in one case the company had a specific contractual obligation to permit a designated employee to attend a union convention. The employee was designated, the company was informed of this, and the employee filled out the appropriate vacation request. Nevertheless, the company continued to refuse the vacation time, despite meetings with union officials, because of its production needs. The employee eventually went to the convention and was terminated. The contractual requirement could not have been enforced by an arbitrator before the convention under the time limits contained in the grievance procedure. Consequently, the arbitrator overturned the discipline.[110]

It has been found improper to discharge an employee for refusing a transfer in a situation in which the contract allowed employees to refuse to be transferred.[111] An employee was improperly suspended for taking his vacation after it had been cancelled because the vacation had been scheduled for months and the cancellation was too late.[112] An employee who refused to obey an improper work order, and was suspended for the remainder of the day, could not be suspended for refusing to obey the work order on the next day since by then it was clear the order was beyond the authority of supervision.[113] It was noted in one case that rather than suspending employees, the employer should initiate a grievance to test the limits of a provision allowing employees to refuse to do certain work.[114] Employees may refuse to change their time cards (and, accordingly, discipline for not doing so is improper) in order to protect their right to be paid properly.[115] It has been held that employees cannot be suspended for refusing to work overtime when the contract clearly states that employees cannot be compelled to work overtime.[116] In several cases, discipline was either set aside or reduced, where employees refused a work order as a test of their rights under the agreement.[117]

---

an order appears to violate the collective bargaining agreement. Shulman noted that "what appears to one party to be a clear violation may not seem so at all to the other party." Id. at 781. Thus, the general rule, "work now, grieve later." See also Goodyear Atomic Corp., 71 LA 619 (Gibson, 1978) (insubordination upheld where refusal to act was based on fact that order might violate contract right).

[110]Dole Refrigerating Co., 96 LA 787 (Bowers, 1991).

[111]Moore Enameling & Mfg. Co., 7 LA 459 (Abernethy, 1947).

[112]Bethlehem Steel Co., 11 LA 629 (Shipman, 1948).

[113]Dwight Mfg. Co., 12 LA 990 (McCoy, 1949).

[114]Kay Mfg. Corp., 13 LA 545 (Komaroff, 1949).

[115]Sheller Mfg. Corp., 34 LA 689 (McCoy, 1960).

[116]National Lead Co. of Ohio, 48 LA 61 (McCoy, 1966).

[117]Continental Pac. Lines, 54 LA 1231 (Feller, 1970); Loren Cook Co., 55 LA 429 (Coffey, 1970); Allied Maintenance Co. of Ill., Inc., 55 LA 731 (Sembower, 1970); United Tel. Co., 55 LA 862 (Duff, 1970).

*4. Other.*    An exception has been recognized where the employer directs the employee to engage in illegal or immoral behavior[118] or where the order might subject the employee to wrongful incrimination. For example, refusals to take a lie detector test have been held not to constitute insubordination because such tests have not attained a degree of reliability necessary to sustain a finding of guilt. Where there is no contractual obligation to comply and no binding past practice, constitutional and civil liberties attach.[119]

In proper circumstances, employees may not be disciplined for exercising their individual beliefs about worship, privacy, or patriotism, for example. This is not an entirely new development in the field of labor arbitration. In a case where an employee had yielded to the national emergency during World War II and as a show of his patriotism had not asserted his religious belief that he should not work on Sunday, the arbitrator set aside the post-war suspension of the employee for having refused to work on Sundays.[120] Sincerely held religious beliefs have led to the reduction of the penalty imposed by the employer in cases dealing with a refusal to sell lottery tickets[121] or to work on Good Friday.[122] Such beliefs, however, were of no avail to an employee who simply walked off the job several hours early on his Sabbath.[123]

There is a line of cases finding discipline to have been improperly imposed in circumstances where the employer's action conflicts with the individual's right to privacy.[124] Similar results have been achieved where the employer's actions have clashed with certain statutory rights.[125] Discipline that was imposed as a result of employee refusals to cease expressing their political beliefs was found to be improper.[126] Although a suspension was upheld because the employee had failed to state his reason for refusing to obey an order, the employee's firmly held moral belief that he should not raise and lower the American

---

[118]Kilsby Tubesupply Co., 76 LA 921 (Weiss, 1981); California Mild Producers, 65 LA 1139 (Gentile, 1975); Illinois Bell Tel. Co., 63 LA 968 (Dolnick, 1974); Temco Aircraft Co., 29 LA 693 (Boles, 1957); Rockhill Printing & Finishing Co., 16 LA 722 (Jaffee, 1951); Ford Motor Co., 3 LA 779 (Shulman, 1944).

[119]Buy-Low, Inc., 77 LA 380 (Dolnick, 1981); Cardinal Servs., Inc., 77 LA 213 (Millious, 1981); Art Carved, Inc., 70 LA 869 (Kramer, 1977); Town & Country Food Co., 39 LA 332 (Lewis, 1962). See Chapter 7 for a discussion of legal constraints on the use of polygraphs.

[120]Goodyear Tire & Rubber Co., 1 LA 121 (McCoy, 1945).

[121]Lucky Stores Inc., 88 LA 841 (Gentile, 1987).

[122]Bronx-Lebanon Hosp. Ctr., 90 LA 1216 (Babishkin, 1988).

[123]Oolite Indus., Inc., 77 LA 838 (Greene, 1981).

[124]Tribune Co., 93 LA 201 (Crane, 1989); Gem City Chems., Inc., 86 LA 1023 (Warns, 1986); Roth Pump Mfg. Co., 82 LA 1199 (O'Reilly, 1984); Scott Paper Co., 52 LA 57 (Williams, 1969).

[125]Bake Rite Rolls, 90 LA 1133 (DiLauro, 1988); EZ Communications, Inc., 91 LA 1097 (Talarico, 1988); Johnson Controls, Inc., 84 LA 659 (Imundo, 1985) (refusal to work in excess of statutorily imposed limits on hours worked not a cause for discipline).

[126]California Processors, Inc., 56 LA 1275 (Koven, 1971); Allegheny County Port Auth., 58 LA 165 (Duff, 1971).

flag caused an arbitrator to urge the employer to avoid the conflict in the future by not assigning the duty to the employee.[127]

In two cases in which employees bypassed the chain of command and took their complaints either to higher employer officials or to public officials, the discipline imposed by the employer was found to be improper.[128] Arbitrators who have considered the question of an ineffective remedy conclude that discipline is improper where compliance with the order would mean that the employees would have no effective remedy for the right that had been denied to them.[129]

In *San Diego Gas & Electric*,[130] three employees had been discharged for failing to comply with hair-styling rules. The arbitrator rejected the employer's claim that the employees had violated the "work now, grieve later" rule. He noted "that principle of arbitration was first developed by the highly revered Harry Shulman" in regard to orders to perform work functions. The rule was held inapplicable in a situation involving a "highly personal act."

These exceptions to the general rule must be distinguished from those situations in which the employer fails to demonstrate that all the requisite elements of insubordination have been met. Therefore, where the employee has not willfully disobeyed an order,[131] where the order given is unreasonable,[132] where the order has not been clearly communicated,[133] where the order is not work related,[134] where the employee is unaware of the consequences of ignoring the order,[135]

---

[127]Ralston Purina Co., 61 LA 14 (Kristov, 1973).

[128]Saucelito Ranch, 85 LA 282 (Draznin, 1985); Northwest Airlines, Inc., 58 LA 894 (Koven, 1972).

[129]Velva Sheen Mfg. Co., 98 LA 131 (Modjeska, 1991); Basic Aluminum Castings Co., 55 LA 1029 (Kates, 1970).

[130]57 LA 821 (Leonard, 1971).

[131]Lifetile Corp., 99 LA 672 (Bergeson, 1992).

[132]James River Corp., 101 LA 363 (Lewis, 1993) (employee ordered to write two five-page papers); Gem City Chems., Inc., 86 LA 1023 (Warns, 1986) (employee ordered to take drug test where no indication of drug problem existed); Defense Language Inst., 64 LA 498 (Modjeska, 1975) (employee told to write down answers about incident instead of communiating them orally); Dravo-Doyle Co., 54 LA 604 (Krimsly, 1970) (employee ordered to shave beard where contact with others was rare and beard posed no safety or production threat to customer relations); Toledo Scale Co., 1 LA 459 (Lehoczky, 1945) (employee told to report to supervisor every time he left office).

[133]Atlantic Southeast Airlines, 101 LA 515 (Nolan, 1993) (drug test requirement not common knowledge); Merryweather Foam, Inc., 98 LA 611 (Bittel, 1992) (policy concerning time off to prepare for grievance hearing unsettled); John W. Galbreath & Co., 85 LA 575 (Bolte, 1985) (policy on overtime scheduling not definite); Dart Indus., Inc., 67 LA 1178 (Gilroy, 1977) (policy on soft drinks in workplace unstated); General Refractories Co., 64 LA 1051 (McIntosh, 1975) (parking policy unclear); Boyce Mach. Corp., 48 LA 251 (Oppenheim, 1967) (policy regarding frolics unwritten); Lawrence Bros., Inc., 28 LA 83 (Davis, 1957) (dress code requirement not regularly followed).

[134]Burnham Corp., 76 LA 153 (McIntosh, 1981) (order related to simple housekeeping matter and not to safety or efficient operation of plant); South Cent. Bell Tel. Co., 59 LA 134 (Steward, 1972) (employee asked about off-duty conduct that had no effect on company).

[135]Signal Delivery Serv., Inc., 86 LA 75 (Weis, 1985); Golden Eagle Dist., Inc., 85 LA 279 (D'Spain, 1985).

or where the employer has tolerated similar behavior in the past,[136] discipline for insubordination may not be upheld.

## D. Discipline Imposed

There is a consensus among arbitrators that employers have the right to discipline employees who are insubordinate.[137] Discharge, however, is not the appropriate penalty in every case of insubordination.[138] An arbitrator hearing an insubordination case has the authority to ensure that the penalty imposed by the employer is appropriate, in light of all the circumstances. This authority to modify the penalty is inherent in the arbitrator's position, although it may be modified by contract language to the contrary.[139]

Typically, arbitrators uphold employer discipline for insubordination as long as the penalty is reasonable and not excessive, capricious, or discriminatory punishment.[140] For example, the penalty of discharge was found to be too severe for a crane operator who insisted on keeping a jug of water in his cab in violation of the rule prohibiting littering and loitering.[141]

Unless the first offense is egregious, progressive discipline is often required for insubordination.[142] In the area of patient care, or impact on an entire entity's production, however, first offenses may lead to termination.[143]

The most important mitigating factor that arbitrators normally consider is the employee's past work record. Where an employee has a long and exemplary work history, with little indication of past disciplinary problems, the arbitrator may reduce the penalty imposed.[144] Among other mitigating factors are the contributory fault

---

[136]Butler Aviation-Boston, Inc., 97 LA 477 (Avins, 1991); McCray Corp., 48 LA 395 (Witney, 1967); Ken-Wal Constr. Co., 30 LA 242 (Mueller, 1958); International Harvester Co., 13 LA 582 (McCoy, 1949).

[137]National Carbide Co. 24 LA 804 (Warns, 1955).

[138]Thomas Truck & Caster Co., 74 LA 1276 (Cohen, 1980); MGM Grand Hotel, 68 LA 1284 (Weiss, 1977).

[139]Prismo-William Armstrong Smith Co., 73 LA 581 (Jedel, 1979); Kaiser Sand & Gravel, 49 LA 190 (Koven, 1967); Michigan Steel Casting Co., 6 LA 678 (Platt, 1947).

[140]3M Co., 80 LA 926 (Gallagher, 1983); Lloyd Ketchum Oldsmobile, 77 LA 953 (Hilgert, 1981); Bauer Bros. Co., 23 LA 696 (Dworkin, 1954).

[141]Safeway Stores, Inc., 78 LA 394 (Jackson, 1982); American Cyanamid Co., 74 LA 15 (Friedman, 1980); Kast Metals Corp., 69 LA 1179 (Blackmar, 1977); Clopay Corp., 55 LA 453 (Jaffee, 1970).

[142]Vaco Prods. Co., 77 LA 432 (Lewis, 1981); Morton Frozen Foods, 61 LA 98 (Barnhart, 1973); A & M Metal Casket Co., 55 LA 835 (Altrock, 1970).

[143]Woman's Gen. Hosp., 74 LA 281 (Klein, 1980) (health care employee discharged for first offense of insubordination by refusing to tender critical care to patient); Viking Fire Protection Co., 74 LA 947 (Pollard, 1980) (employee's refusal to perform work stops company's entire production).

[144]Reynolds Metals Co., 78 LA 687 (Fasser, 1982); Pepsi Cola Bottling Co., 78 LA 516 (Keenan, 1982); Zapata Indus., Inc., 76 LA 467 (Woolf, 1981); Goodyear Atomic Corp., 71 LA

of the employee's supervisor,[145] whether the order was clearly given,[146] the employer's past treatment and tolerance of similar instances of misconduct,[147] the consequences of the employee's wrongful refusal,[148] whether the employee relied on the advice of his union steward or foreman,[149] and whether the employer acted in haste in making its disciplinary decision.[150]

Where the employee has already been given a second chance,[151] however, or where the employee was dishonest during the investigation of the insubordination,[152] the arbitrator is particularly unlikely to reduce the discipline that was imposed.

### E.  Burden of Proof

The employer has the burden of showing that all the factors mentioned above applying to the general rule of "work now, grieve later" have been met. Thus, the employer case would include showing the order was explicit, reasonable, work related, and communicated. The employer would also have to make some showing that the disobedience of a superior's order was willful and that the employee knew or should have known the consequences. It would then fall to the employee to show that her failure to obey falls into one of the recognized exceptions to the general rule or to present any mitigating factors.

## III.  Refusals to Work Overtime

Overtime assignments have two faces in the workplace. In some circumstances, overtime is a favored assignment to the employee because of the additional pay. In essence, overtime becomes an added

---

619 (Gibson, 1978); James C. Heinz Co., 54 LA 1026 (Leiken, 1970); National Lawyers Club, Inc., 52 LA 547 (Seidenberg, 1969); Chalfant Mfg. Co., 52 LA 51 (Nichols, 1968). Of course, an employee's short work history with the company may also affect the arbitrator's decision. See, e.g., Inglis Ltd., 67 LA 878 (O'Shea, 1976).

[145]Southern Gage Co., 74 LA 296 (Herrick, 1980); Kast Metals Corp., 61 LA 87 (Moore, 1973); Reynolds Metal Co., 17 LA 710 (Granoff, 1957).

[146]Sealtest Dairy Prods. Co., 35 LA 205 (Morvant, 1960).

[147]Keystone Steel & Wire Co., 78 LA 370 (Roomkin, 1982); Woodward's Spring Shop, Inc., 63 LA 367 (Pinkus, 1974); Ohio Steel Foundry Co., 36 LA 1088 (Dworkin, 1961); Bethlehem Steel Co., Inc., 12 LA 167 (Selekman, 1949).

[148]Library of Congress, 78 LA 784 (Rothschild, 1982); Hayes Aircraft Corp., 34 LA 450 (Flannagan, 1960).

[149]Associated Grocers of Cal., Inc., 80 LA 611 (Sartain, 1983); United Eng'g Co., 64 LA 1274 (Rule, 1975); United States Steel Corp., 51 LA 571 (Garrett, 1968).

[150]Triple L Enters., 70 LA 97 (Jeanney, 1978); St. Joseph Packaging, Inc., 68 LA 1366 (Moore, 1977).

[151]Algoma Steel Corp., 73 LA 1256 (O'Shea, 1979).

[152]Hygrade Food Prods. Corp., 74 LA 99 (O'Neill, 1980).

benefit of employment. Under other circumstances, overtime is seen as a burden on the employee, who may have personal obligations, or the overtime assignments may involve unfavorable tasks. Due to these opposing viewpoints, overtime can draw a discrimination claim from both ends: (1) when the individual believes he or she is being **denied** overtime assignments; or (2) when the individual believes he or she is being given **too much** overtime.

## A. *Management Rights Versus Personal Needs*

Unless there are specific restrictions by law or by agreement, management is generally considered to have the right to set work schedules, including overtime.[153] While past practice may affect the analysis of a situation, an employer who has previously sought voluntary overtime may require overtime as operational needs dictate.[154]

Arbitrators have balanced the rights of the employer to require overtime with the legitimacy of the employee's basis for refusing overtime.[155] Often the arbitrator reaffirms the "work now, grieve later" doctrine and acknowledges the employer's right to schedule overtime, finding that the employee has acted wrongly in presuming he could leave the workplace or not show up as scheduled without penalty. Next, the arbitrator evaluates the reason given by the employee for refusing the overtime assignment. This may result in altering or eliminating the discipline for refusal to work.[156]

## B. *Overtime Communications*

The appropriateness of a refusal to work case may depend upon the communications between management and the employee assigned to work overtime. If the type of overtime being called has a procedure spelled out in the collective bargaining agreement, it must be followed.[157] Short-notice calls of overtime, coupled with articulated reasons for not being able to work overtime, will cause the arbitrator to

---

[153]Volz & Goggin, eds., Elkouri & Elkouri, How Arbitration Works, 5th ed., 739 (BNA Books, 1997); McConway & Torley Corp., 55 LA 31 (Cohen, 1970); Michigan Seamless Tube Co., 48 LA 1077 (Keefe, 1967); Link-Belt Co., 48 LA 570 (Cayton, 1966).

[154]Elkouri, supra note 153, at 741.

[155]Keystone Steel & Wire, 94 LA 423 (Goldstein, 1990).

[156]Fieldcrest Cannon, Inc., 99 LA 776 (Giblin, 1992); Lear Seating Corp., 98 LA 194 (Ellmann, 1991); Phillips 66 Co., 93 LA 707 (Goodstein, 1989); FMC Corp., 92 LA 483 (Dworkin, 1989); Commercial Filters Div., 91 LA 73 (DiLauro, 1988); Green Bay Packaging, Inc., 87 LA 1057 (Gundermann, 1986); Ashland Chem. Co., 87 LA 318 (Seltzer, 1986); Quaker Oats Co., 84 LA 1085 (Newmark, 1985); Fred Rueping Leather, 83 LA 644 (Jacobowski, 1984); Norfolk Shipbuilding & Drydock Corp., 74 LA 1020 (Maggiolo, 1980); Pullman Trailmobile, 74 LA 967 (Ekstrom, 1980); Standard Shade Roller Div., 73 LA 86 (Dawson, 1979); Georgia Kraft Co., 71 LA 222 (Spritzer, 1978).

[157]Heckett, Div. of Harsco Corp., 94 LA 647 (Crane, 1990); Grocers Baking Co., 72 LA 59 (Daniel, 1979); National Hose Co., 73 LA 1048 (Robins, 1979).

focus on procedural issues.[158] Notice has two purposes: (1) to inform the employee of the need for overtime and the specific assignment of overtime; and (2) to notify the employee of the clear consequences for a refusal to work.

Refusal to work overtime is usually a species of insubordination. If a false reason is given by the employee for refusing the overtime assignment, the offense may be categorized as providing false information for company records. If the refusal is considered insubordination, the employer must inform the employee of this, give the employee a direct order, and advise the employee of the consequences for insubordination.[159] If refusals of overtime have previously been allowed due to conflicting needs of employees, and this employee provides a comparable reason, the employer may ultimately lose the case, despite giving a direct order, because the order is unreasonable.[160] Some arbitrators emphasize the importance of identifying the nature of the infraction and what communication took place with the employee.[161]

Procedures used in calling overtime can also be a focal point. In one case, an arbitrator reinstated employees who were discharged for refusing to show up for emergency Saturday overtime.[162] The calling of the overtime was deemed proper, but the arbitrator found a violation of due process under the collective bargaining agreement because the employer failed to "precisely" inform employees that all assigned employees were needed, that only limited excuses would be acceptable, and that an employee could be discharged for failing to report.

## C. Discipline Examples

An employee who refuses to work overtime because of an alleged breach of the labor agreement in assigning the overtime may ultimately prevail even when charged with insubordination.[163] Some arbitrators find an exception to the "work now, grieve later" rule situations where the labor agreement does not require the employee to work

---

[158]Keystone Steel, 94 LA 423 (Goldstein, 1990); Phillips 66 Co., 93 LA 707 (Goldstein, 1989); Xidex Corp., 73 LA 864 (Bornstein, 1979); Georgia Kraft Co., 71 LA 707 (Sprinter, 1978).

[159]Southern Champion Tray Co., 96 LA 633 (Nolan, 1991); Globe Tool & Eng'g Co., 83 LA 605 (Millious, 1984); Cyclops Corp., Tex-Tube Div., 78 LA 1067 (Marlatt, 1982); MacMillan Bloedel Particleboard, Inc., 72 LA 759 (Styles, 1979); Standard Shade Roller Div., 73 LA 86 (Dawson, 1979); Teleflex, Inc., 72 LA 668 (Chalfie, 1979); Parke-Davis & Co., 72 LA 622 (Keefe, 1979).

[160]Kaiser Aluminum & Chem. Corp., 92 LA 367 (Corbett, 1989); Parsons Contractors, 91 LA 73 (DiLauro, 1988); Norfolk Shipbuilding & Drydock Corp., 74 LA 1020 (Maggiolo, 1980); Pullman Trailmobile, 74 LA 967 (Ekstrom, 1980); Georgia Kraft Co., 71 LA 222 (Spritzer, 1978).

[161]Lear Seating Corp., 98 LA 194 (Ellmann, 1991).

[162]Phillips 66 Co. Rail Car Maintenance Ctr., 93 LA 707 (Goodstein, 1989).

[163]Id.

the overtime assignment or where the employee has an implicit or expressed option to refuse an overtime assignment.[164]

If the employer treats the matter as insubordination and terminates or suspends the employee, the employer may be required to make the employee whole if the discipline is overturned. On the other hand, if employees exercise their contractual rights and refuse legitimate overtime assignments, management may be allowed to fill overtime classifications with supervisory employees or perhaps subcontracted employees.[165]

An employee who does not make reasonable attempts to adjust his personal obligations and become available to work overtime runs the risk of discipline. In *Southern Champion Tray Co.*,[166] the employee knew that he would have to stay to fix a certain machine the following day. Although he had been told that it might involve overtime, he failed to make arrangements to have his son picked up at school or stay late at school. Because of a delay in getting a seal, the job took longer than expected. Despite a direct order, and without trying to make arrangements with the school, the employee left a short time before he would have finished the job. In addressing the union's defense, the arbitrator denied the grievance and stated:

> Accepting for sake of argument that an employee could legitimately leave work if necessary to protect a child it does not follow that every familial problem justifies disobeying direct orders. At the very least, the employee must try to satisfy his or her parental obligations without interfering with the employer's business.[167]

An employee who states a meritorious personal reason for not wanting to work presents a more difficult situation. The difficulty is twofold: (1) most employers understand an employee has a life outside the workplace, yet the employee has an obligation to be at work when assigned, not just when it is convenient; and (2) failure to work overtime has conflicting components of misconduct for refusing to work and simple absence. Discipline has been reversed where a direct order was not clearly given and the employer had allowed other employees to refuse overtime for various personal reasons. It was arbitrary, for example, to determine that an ill father-in-law was less important than a baseball game.[168]

---

[164]Stanray Corp., 48 LA 492 (Sembower, 1967). Cf. Anchorage, Alaska, 81 LA 829 (Thomas, 1983) (suspensions upheld for overtime refusal even though intent of contract to give employees discretion). National Lead Co. of Ohio, 48 LA 61 (McCoy, 1966); Hawaiian Airlines, 37 LA 275 (Burr, 1961); West Penn Power Co., 27 LA 461 (Begley, 1956).

[165]Aurora Casket Co., 96 LA 855 (Gibson, 1991).

[166]96 LA 633 (Nolan, 1991).

[167]Id. at 637.

[168]FMC Corp., 92 LA 483 (Dworkin, 1989); Tryco Mfg. Co., 83 LA 1131 (Fitzsimmons, 1984) (employees had not been disciplined on previous occasions for refusing overtime).

Illness or fatigue are also common reasons given by employees in refusing overtime. Illness resulting in an employee missing a scheduled overtime is treated like a regular attendance issue, especially if the employee has also missed a regular shift preceding the overtime assignment.[169]

The more difficult issue arises when mandatory overtime is called and the employee has worked the regular shift but now claims illness or fatigue in refusing the overtime.[170] If the employer clearly communicates the need for overtime and the penalty for refusing, and evaluates the employee's concern, disciplinary action has a better chance of being sustained. If the strenuous nature of the work or repetitive overtime assignments are the cause of the fatigue or illness, the employee has a stronger argument. An employee who is obviously too ill to work has a valid reason for refusing overtime.

The wrong penalty for a refusal to work, even if it is a more favorable penalty to the employee, can also cause a reversal of an employer decision. An arbitrator determined that it was inappropriate to refuse holiday pay to employees based upon their refusal to work overtime on the day before the holiday. While the infraction of refusing to obey a direct order would have justified discharge, withholding holiday pay was not appropriate.[171]


# IV.  Refusal to Work With Other Employees

## A.  General Rule

An employee who desires to challenge a directive to work with another employee generally must "work now, grieve later."[172] Consequently, in the typical instance where an employee resorts to self-help by refusing a work assignment involving contact with a particular co-worker, the arbitrator will find the employee insubordinate and sustain appropriate discipline. For example, in *U. S. Air Force Academy*,[173] the arbitrator upheld a written reprimand for a mechanic who refused to work with a fellow employee because the other employee had a hygiene problem, smoked, and was not very knowledgeable. The

---

[169]Quaker Oats Co., 84 LA 1085 (Newmark, 1985) (disciplined overturned); Parke-Davis & Co., 72 LA 622 (Keefe, 1979) (disciplined sustained; migraine headache); Teleflex, Inc., 72 LA 668 (Chalfie, 1979) (discipline sustained; tiredness).

[170]Kaiser Aluminum & Chem. Corp., 92 LA 367 (Corbett, 1989).

[171]Dillingham Mfg. Co., 91 LA 816 (Nicholas, 1988).

[172]See Ford Motor Co., 3 LA 779 (Shulman, 1944). But see discussion of exceptions, earlier in this chapter.

[173]97 LA 603 (Cohen, 1991). See also Oklahoma State AFL-CIO, 82 LA 657 (Yaney, 1984) (bookkeeper and computer operator for the Oklahoma state office of the AFL-CIO was properly discharged for openly engaging in AFL-CIO politics and being insubordinate to the newly elected state president).

grievant could have complained to his supervisor if, after accepting the assignment, any of these concerns developed into a threat to his health and safety.

## B. Exception for Unusual Health Hazard

In *Ford Motor Co.*,[174] the source of the "work now, grieve later" rule, the arbitrator tempered the harshness of the rule by providing an exception where the order would "involve an unusual health hazard." The primary focus where an employee refuses a work assignment with a co-worker has become whether the employee justifiably believed that the assignment involved a substantial risk to his or her health and safety. An employee may meet this burden by showing that a co-worker is unsafe. The employee cannot be disciplined for refusing to work with that employee.

For example, in *U. S. Plywood-Champion Papers, Inc.*,[175] the arbitrator found that certain truck drivers were improperly discharged for refusing to ride with a driver who was unsafe because: (1) the driver's record gave them ample reason to fear for their safety; (2) the company had never before disciplined employees for refusing to do work that they believed to be unsafe; and (3) the company's work rules stated that "safety should be your first consideration" and admonished employees not to take chances. Similarly, refusing to work with a co-worker who has threatened physical violence is not a disciplinable offense. For instance, an employer's discipline of the grievant was without cause where a co-worker pulled a knife during a dispute and slashed at the grievant.[176]

Arbitrators have imposed various evidentiary burdens in examining whether a work refusal was justified. In a minority of decisions,

---

[174]3 LA 779, 782 (Shulman, 1944) (not only may an employee refuse work with an employee who poses a health or safety threat, but the unsafe worker may be disciplined for hindering the employer's efforts to provide a safe workplace). See also Fox Chapel Auth., 95 LA 105 (Duff, 1990) (employer properly required a doctor's certificate before allowing an employee who was ill for more than 3 days to return to work, in part to protect other employees); Mercy Convalescent Ctr., 90 LA 405 (O'Grady, 1988) (employee with conjunctivitis in the right eye was properly made to stay away form work from March 26 to April 14 in order to prevent risk of infection to other employees); Weyerhauser Co., Shipping Container Div., 88-2 ARB ¶ 8494 (Shaw, 1988) (employee was properly discharged for assaulting a co-worker, although provoked).

[175]50 LA 115 (Jenkins, 1968). Amoco Tex. Ref. Co., 81-2 ARB ¶ 8504 (Taylor, 1981) (employer improperly suspended pipefitter for refusing to be suspended in a basket 200 feet off the ground where co-worker was inexperienced in operating the crane used to raise the basket). See also Grigoleit Co., 79-2 ARB ¶ 8612 (Lesar, 1979) (employee improperly given a "Warning Notice" and sent home where he refused to repair a wet, icy roof with only a deaf mute to assist him).

[176]Cidcomm, Inc., 79-2 ARB ¶ 8534 (Barsamian, 1979). Compare Arrowhead Containers, Inc., 90-1 ARB ¶ 8200 (Hoffmeister, 1984), where an employee was improperly discharged for insubordination and failure to get along with other employees following a threat on her life by a co-worker. Arbitrator Hoffmesiter ruled that the grievant, who had never been a problem employee in her 15 years with the company, deserved a "second chance" following the discharge of the other employee, who was the aggressor in their ongoing dispute.

the arbitrator has required only that the employee subjectively believe the assignment is unsafe.[177] Another minority view requires the employee to prove that the assignment posed an actual (objective) threat. [178]

The majority of arbitrators, however, require that the employee's belief regarding the risk of harm be reasonable.[179] As one arbitrator aptly summarized the rule:

> Indeed, the golden thread of reasonableness runs throughout arbitral decisions on safety and health matters. And the majority of arbitral thought holds that where a dispute arises regarding assigned work, and the subject employee truly believes that the performance of said work would create a serious health hazard to him, and a reasonable man could reach the same conclusion under like circumstances, the employee may refuse to comply with the work assignment."[180]

An employee who refuses to work with another employee might claim that the refusal is justified under the health and safety exception where the work assignment poses a threat of contracting a contagious disease.[181]

The limited arbitral experience with the issue suggests that employers will be held responsible for equipping employees to deal with the inevitable presence of AIDS in the workplace.[182] The only published arbitration award addressing the question whether an employee may refuse a work assignment based on fear of AIDS contagion is *Minnesota Department of Corrections*.[183] There, a correctional counselor refused to conduct "pat down" searches as the prisoners returned to their cell blocks from work, meals, and other activities. Prior to his refusal, the warden of the correctional institution circulated two memos—one to inmates and one to prison staff—stating that one of

---

[177]West Penn Power Co., 89 LA 1227 (Hogler, 1987); Lone Star Steel Co., 48 LA 1094, 1097 (Jenkins, 1967).

[178]3M Co., 80 LA 926 (Gallagher, 1983); Griffin Pipe Prods. Co., 72 LA 1033 (Doyle, 1979); Hercules, Inc., 48 LA 788 (Hopson, 1967); Wilcolator Co., 44 LA 847, 852 (Alteri, 1964).

[179]Northern Automatic Elec. Foundry, 90 LA 620, 623 (Poindexter, 1987); Amoco Oil Co., 87 LA 889 (Schwartz, 1986); Laclede Gas Co., 39 LA 833, 839 (Bothwell, 1962) ("The principle * * * is that an employee may refuse to carry out a particular work assignment, if at the time he is given the work assignment, he reasonably believes that by carrying out such work assignment he will endanger his safety or health. In such instance the employee has the duty, not only of stating that he believes there is risk to his safety or health, and the reason for believing so, but he also has the burden, if called upon, of showing by appropriate evidence that he had a reasonable basis for his belief"). See generally Volz & Goggin, eds., Elkouri & Elkouri, How Arbitration Works, 5th ed., 977–80 (BNA Books, 1997). See Insubordination: Refusals to Do Work Required by Superior in this chapter.

[180]Leland Oil Mill, 91 LA 905, 907 (Nicholas, 1988).

[181]Compare Mercy Convalescent Ctr., 90 LA 405 (O'Grady, 1988) with Fox Chapel Auth., 95 LA 105 (Duff, 1990) (arbitrators recognized that an employer must provide a safe workplace, including protecting employees from the threat of contracting contagious diseases).

[182]Minnesota Dep't of Corrections, 85 LA 1185 (Gallagher, 1985).

[183]Id.

the inmates had been recently diagnosed with "pre-AIDS" and urging the inmates to take precautions against the spread of AIDS such as refraining from homosexual activity, intravenous drug use, and sharing of personal items such as toothbrushes and cigarettes. The arbitrator reinstated the grievant, finding that two factors mitigated against discharge. First, by warning the inmates not to engage in casual contact such as sharing cigarettes and encouraging them to wash their hands, the warden contributed to the fear that AIDS could be transmitted through a pat down. Thus, the educational session that was held the same day was ineffective to dispel the fears of the staff. Second, the warden indicated in meeting with the grievant after his suspension that the grievant could return to work if he would conduct pat downs in the usual manner. The grievant stated that he would return to work if he could be permitted to wear gloves. The warden refused this request but honored it later in the day for other officers, demonstrating that the grievant's fears could have been accommodated. The arbitrator denied back pay, however, so that the grievant would not be rewarded for insubordination.

One commentator has argued on public policy grounds that arbitrators should adopt a subjective standard in arbitrations addressing refusals to accept work assignments involving exposure to HIV-infected individuals, unless the employer has adopted an AIDS-in-the-workplace policy and undertaken employee education measures aimed at dispelling unreasonable subjective fears of AIDS contagion.[184] Others contend that arbitrators should not protect those with AIDS or those who fear contracting it, but should only apply existing principles and the terms of the employment contract.[185]

## C. Exception for "Intolerable Affronts"

Where the actions of a co-worker pose an intolerable affront to another's personal dignity and emotional well-being, there is an exception to the "work now, grieve later" rule. In such instances, the employee may be justified in resorting to self-help and refusing to accept or continue a job assignment with the offending employee.[186] In one case the news director for a radio station was found to be justified in leaving her duties after hearing a joke regarding her supposed sexual promiscuity that had been played on the air.[187] The joke was the

---

[184]Squire, "Arbitration of Health and Safety Issues in the Workplace: Employees Who Refuse Work Assignments Because of Fear of AIDS Contagion," 44 Maine L. Rev. 315 (1992).

[185]Abrams & Nolan, "AIDS in Labor Arbitration," 25 U.S.F. L. Rev. 67 (1990).

[186]EZ Communications, 91 LA 1097 (Talarico, 1988).

[187]Id. See also Hermes Automotive Mfg. Corp., 87-2 Arb. ¶ 8471 (Roumell, Jr., 1987) (upheld the grievant's 1-week suspension but ordered that he be reinstated without back pay because the grievant's refusal to work with his supervisor was based, in part, on sexually oriented gesturing, joking, and touching; although these actions did not constitute sexual

culmination of an ongoing series of jokes and comments made by the two hosts of the station's morning program. When the grievant went on vacations, the hosts made fictitious reports that the grievant was having promiscuous sexual relations with various people at the vacation destinations. They also made various on-air comments suggesting that the grievant was having sex with large numbers of people, had sexually transmitted diseases, and was mentally unstable. The grievant repeatedly told the hosts that the comments were unwelcome and inappropriate. The arbitrator concluded that the grievant was justified in walking off the job rather than continuing to endure serious invasions of her personal rights and dignity: "other possible exceptions to the duty to obey orders exist under circumstances where the order commands the performance of an immoral act, or would humiliate the employee or invade some personal right which is considered inviolable."[188]

### D.  Off-Duty Conduct[189]

In a different vein, refusals to work with other employees are relevant to the inquiry of whether off-duty misconduct has a sufficient nexus to the workplace to justify discipline or discharge. In *W. E. Caldwell Co.,*[190] the arbitrator opined that in order for off-duty misconduct to bear a significant enough relationship to the workplace to justify disciplinary action, the conduct must:

(1)  harm the company's reputation or product;

(2)  render the employees unable to perform their duties or appear at work, in which case a discipline would be based on inefficiency or excessive absenteeism; or

(3)  must lead to the refusal, reluctance or inability of other employees to work with the employee in question.

Thus, where the employer can prove that the misconduct is severe enough to cause reluctance or refusal by others to work with the offending employee, discipline is appropriate. For instance, in *U. S. Immigration & Naturalization Service,*[191] the arbitrator found that

---

harassment under civil rights legislation at the time, largely because the victim was male, employer was estopped from placing the entire blame on the grievant where members of management had participated in, and even encouraged, the horseplay).

[188]EZ Communications, supra note 186, at 1100.

[189]See Chapter 9 for a full discussion of off-duty conduct.

[190]28 LA 434, 436–37 (Kesselman, 1957).

[191]90 LA 516 (Allen, 1988). See also West Monona Community Sch. Dist., 93 LA 414 (Hill, 1989) (school guidance counselor and junior high athletics coach properly discharged where he was convicted of vehicular homicide after traveling 80 miles per hour while intoxicated, wrecking his car, killing one student passenger, and permanently paralyzing another). The employer failed to carry its burden of demonstrating that off-duty misconduct affected the

an immigration detention officer was properly terminated after a party at which he publicly urinated twice, used offensive language, made insulting remarks, grabbed a female officer's behind and rubbed against her with sexual movements, and engaged in other outrageous behavior. The arbitrator found that the grievant's return to work would create low worker morale and that many employees would be reluctant to work with the grievant.

# V. Refusals to Cooperate in Investigations

As a general rule, an employee must cooperate with the reasonable investigations of his employer. An employer has the inherent right to conduct reasonable investigations regarding such matters as theft of company property or drug or alcohol use. Refusing to comply with the employer's reasonable request to permit searches or answer questions may be insubordination and subject the employee to discipline or discharge.[192] As the arbitrator said in *Illinois Power Co.*:[193]

> As a general rule in the area of labor relations, an employee cannot refuse to meet with an employer or to cooperate with the employer regarding legitimate work-related conduct. To do so is an act of insubordination, subject to disciplinary action up to and including discharge.[194]

---

ability of the grievant to work with other employees in City of New Hope, 89 LA 427 (Bard, 1987) (arbitrator found sexually explicit comments and sexual assault at employee picnic were a single, isolated act of misconduct; neither grievant's work record nor other conduct indicated a continuing threat; grievant was highly intoxicated at the time of the incident, and grievant and victim did not work in the same department). See also Iowa Pub. Serv. Co., 90-2 ARB ¶ 8530 (Murphy, 1990) (only evidence that other employees would not work with grievant because of his off-duty assaults on his ex-wife, her boyfriend, and his girlfriend was the refusal of the grievant's brother-in-law to clean shower rooms for fear of encountering the grievant); Government of the Virgin Islands, Dep't of Health, 91-2 ARB ¶ 8543 (Watkins, 1991) (more than 100 employees, the majority of whom were women, signed a petition urging the employer-hospital to reinstate the grievant, a security officer, after he was convicted of unlawfully kissing and fondling a woman whom he had pulled over for an alleged traffic violation while on duty as a part-time police officer).

[192]See Sauget Sanitary Dev. & Research Ass'n, 98 LA 1082, 1085 (Cipolla, 1992) ("There is a great deal of arbitral authority which indicates that discipline is appropriate in situations where employees refuse to cooperate with a Company's investigation of an incident which interfers (sic) with the Company's ongoing business"); Square D Co., 96 LA 541, 545 (Allen, Jr., 1991) ("Arbitrators have consistently upheld the right of employers to conduct reasonable searches of employees and their belongings in efforts to uncover stolen items and/or illegal drugs, especially where 'reasonable cause' suspicion is present."); Tampa Elec. Co., 83-2 ARB ¶ 8477 at 5124 (Crane, 1983) ("When employees are suspected of removing Company property, Management certainly has the right to conduct an investigation to identify the guilty parties and recover the stolen goods. It follows logically that employees can reasonably be required to cooperate in the investigation and to submit to a search of their belongings. It is a well established practice throughout industry to require employees to submit to searches when requested.").

[193]84 LA 586 (Penfield, 1985).

[194]Id. at 590.

This general right of the employer is limited in scope and constrained by the competing rights of the employee. Thus, while the employer's basic right to compel the reasonable cooperation of its employees in workplace investigations is rarely challenged, arbitrators are frequently faced with the issue of whether the employer went "too far."[195] A common objection is that the investigatory request relates to conduct outside the scope of the employer's regulatory authority. The competing concerns that arbitrators must balance are discussed below.

## A. *Requirement of Impact on Employer's Business*

The employer's right to investigate extends only to those matters which have a demonstrable nexus with its business.[196] The issue of a demonstrable effect on the employer's business most frequently arises in the "twilight zone" of the employee's off-duty activities.

In *King Co.*,[197] the arbitrator found that the employer failed to prove that an incident in which four co-employees pleaded guilty to vandalizing another employee's jeep was work related. He reasoned that "mere allegations" that the vandalism was related to problems at the workplace were insufficient to meet the employer's affirmative duty to prove a nexus between the off-duty conduct and its business, as were anonymous calls from persons expressing concern regarding the safety of the employer's operations. On the other hand, in *AT&T*[198] the arbitrator concluded "that there is a direct and clear relationship between Grievant's alleged off-duty misconduct and his work environment."[199] The arbitrator first noted:

> [T]he Company's rule making authority, derived from its inherent right to manage, is limited to promulgating rules which reasonably relate to the work environment or the Employer's business. An Employer has no right to govern the conduct of its employees generally where there

---

[195]The following discussion is intended to identify, but not exhaustively discuss, the issues that arise in the context of refusals to cooperate in investigations. These topics are more thoroughly developed in, among others, Chapter 2 (procedural protections available to the employee), Chapter 6 (drug testing), Chapter 9 (requirement that investigations be limited to those matters having a demonstrable effect on the employer's business), Chapter 11 (admissibility of evidence obtained through the investigatory process), and Chapter 13 (legislative limitations on the employer's investigatory rights). A thorough and insightful treatment of the issues raised in this discussion can be found in Hill & Wright, "Employee Refusals to Cooperate in Internal Investigations: "Into the Woods" With Employers, Courts, and Labor Arbitrators," 56 Mo. L. Rev. 869 (1991).

[196]See Chicago Pneumatic Tool Co., 38 LA 891 (Duff, 1961).

[197]89 LA 681 (Bard, 1987). This classic statement of the factors establishing work relatedness was first promulgated in W.E. Caldwell Co., 28 LA 434, 437–37 (Kesselman, 1957).

[198]102 LA 931 (Kanner, 1994).

[199]Id. at 938.

is no nexus or direct relationship to the employee's work or the health of the enterprise.[200]

Nonetheless, he found that the grievant's misconduct, depositing a counterfeit check and later withdrawing the proceeds, undermined the employer's trust in the grievant and therefore rendered him unfit to perform his duties as a building attendant.

## B. The Employee's Right Against Self-Incrimination

*1. Public Employees.*   When the employer is a public sector entity, another important limitation on the employer's investigatory right is the employee's right against self-incrimination, under the Fifth Amendment. The Fifth Amendment has direct application to public sector employers, who cannot compel employees to incriminate themselves under the threat of discharge. A public sector employer may, however, require an employee to cooperate in an investigation by first providing the employee with immunity (through an appropriate prosecutorial office) with regard to the compelled evidence. The U.S. Supreme Court has held that the Fifth Amendment protection against self-incrimination as extended to the states through the Fourteenth Amendment prevents *public* employers from requiring employees to make the Hobson's choice between incriminating themselves or forfeiting their employment.[201] The Court invalidated a New Jersey statute that recognized a public employee's right to remain silent but also mandated discharge of employees who refused to provide information relating to the execution of their public duties, finding the statute to be "the antithesis of free choice to speak out or to remain silent."[202]

In a subsequent case, the Supreme Court further developed the *Garrity* doctrine.[203] The Court held that a police officer could not be compelled to waive his constitutional right to remain silent under the threat of discharge, but noted in dicta that if the officer had immunity with respect to the use of his answers or the fruits thereof in a criminal prosecution and refused to answer questions narrowly relating to his performance of official duties, he could properly be discharged.[204] Later cases solidified the proposition that public employees can be compelled to respond to questions regarding the performance of their duties. The government can compel testimony of an

---

[200]Id. at 936.

[201]Garrity v. New Jersey, 385 U.S. 493 (1967).

[202]Id. at 497.

[203]Gardner v. Broderick, 392 U.S. 273 (1968).

[204]Id. at 278.

unwilling witness by granting the witness immunity from use of the compelled testimony in subsequent criminal proceedings.[205]

While the Fifth Amendment protects an individual from self-incrimination, it does not guarantee a public employee continued employment where he refuses to provide information relevant to his execution of public duties.[206]

2. *Private Employees.*   The Fifth Amendment is not directly applicable to private sector employers because it is a restraint on governmental action. There is a split among arbitrators about whether the constitutional protections should be applied in private sector arbitrations. Some arbitrators simply refuse to apply constitutional protections.[207] Other arbitrators believe that constitutional principles

---

[205]Kastigar v. United States, 406 U.S. 441 (1972). See City of Omaha, Neb., 90-1 ARB ¶ 8274 at 4346 (Rotenberg, 1990), where a police department employee refused to answer questions regarding her role in a murder. Arbitrator Rotenberg reasoned:

I conclude that at no time during the investigation conducted by the Employer did the Employer grant Grievant immunity from criminal prosecution based on Grievant's statements to be elicited in the proposed interviews. In the circumstances of this case and applying the law of the Supreme Court in *Lefkowitz* [Lefkowitz v. Turley, 414 U.S. 70 (1973)], I conclude that Grievant was not obliged to disclose any facts relating to her involvement in the shooting incident of July 1. Likewise, I conclude that her refusal to comply with the several ordrs [sic] from Sgt. [B] to submit to interview regarding her involvement in the July 1 shooting incident is privileged under the Fifth Amendment of the U.S. Constitution. It follows, and I conclude, that each of the threats or [sic] discipline and each act to implement these threats in reprisal for Grievant's withholding information and/or refusing to submit to interview regarding Grievant's involvement in the July 1 shooting incident is inconsistent with the Fifth Amendment of the U.S. Constitution and cannot stand.

See also Washoe County, Nev., 97 LA 393 (Concepcion, 1991), where a clerical employee was found not to be insubordinate in refusing to reveal how she had restricted access to the employer's computerized records. The grievant was told that such tampering constitutes a crime under Nevada law, and a district attorney was present during the alleged act of insubordination. Arbitrator Concepcion reasoned that the grievant could only be compelled to provide the information if "proper proceedings" were first executed, including an offer of immunity. Absent such proceedings, the grievant was not required to provide the requested information. "Put simply, where an employee cannot be compelled to answer question [sic], he or she cannot be considered insubordinate when he or she refuses to do so." Id. st 402. Finally, see United States Dep't of Treasury, 82 LA 1209 (Kaplin, 1984) (finding that a "notice to admit" sent to a federal employee was improper under the Fifth Amendment). Cf. Hamilton v. Waukesha County Area Vocational, Technical & Adult Educ. Dist., 118 LRRM 3197 (E.D. Wis., 1985), where a federal district court held that a public employer is not required to apprise an employee of his or her right to remain silent prior to questioning.

[206]This oft-cited principle was first stated in an award dealing with a private-sector employer, Simoniz Co., 44 LA 658, 663 (McGury, 1964):

We cannot say, in addition to the guarantee, that the person invoking the Fifth Amendment has the right to this advantage in a criminal proceeding, and also has a right to be completely free from any financial, social, or other possible loss which he may suffer, indirectly, as a result of exercising his constitutional right * * *

The Fifth Amendment does not guarantee that a person who invokes it will not be subject to any unfavorable inference and does not guarantee that a person who invokes it shall be continued in employment.

[207]See AT&T, 102 LA 931, 934 (Kanner, 1994) ("Grievant has no right under the Fifth Amendment against self-incrimination to refuse to answer questions by the Employer because of the pendency of his criminal trial. The Fifth Amendment protects citizens against answering self-incriminating questions propounded by the government, not by one's employer."); See

are properly part of the notions of fairness incorporated into just cause.[208]

Even among arbitrators who apply constitutional principles, there is a split on whether any evidentiary interferences can be drawn where a grievant, citing a Fifth Amendment privilege, refuses to testify on his own behalf. While some say they will not draw any inference,[209] as a practical matter the majority consider the grievant's refusal to testify as evidence that the testimony would have been unfavorable.[210]

While the Fifth Amendment to the United States Constitution protects individuals accused in criminal proceedings, it does not guarantee that employees who invoke the Fifth Amendment during an

---

Orthodox Jewish Home for the Aged, 91 LA 810, 815 (Sergent, Jr., 1988) ("The easy answer to [the grievant's constitutional] objections [to the administration of a polygraph examination] is simply that the constitution applies only to state action against an individual or property and it does not govern the voluntary relationship between an employer and employee * * *. Although compelling and useful in defining the issues raised in such cases, the analogy to constitutional law in labor arbitration is limited."); Simoniz Co., 44 LA 658, 663–64 (McGury, 1964) (grievant's exercise of Fifth Amendment rights does not preclude the employer from demanding honesty and cooperation or guarantee the grievant continued employment); Lockheed Aircraft Corp., 27 LA 709, 712 (Maggs, 1956) ("[T]he constitutional privilege against self-incrimination is available only against the Government.").

[208]In King Co. 89 LA 681 (Bard, 1987), Arbitrator Bard ruled that although constitutional protections may have limited application in labor arbitrations, the employee should not be punished for failing to cooperate in an investigation that might lead to his incarceration, especially where off-duty conduct is at issue. However, he "note[d] with the greatest possible emphasis that in this instance the employer has totally failed to satisfy its burden of proof on this issue, even if no Fifth Amendment issues were involved." Id. at 685. The award relied upon Arbitrator Whitley McCoy's reasoning in Exact Weight Scale Co., 50 LA 8, 8–9 (1967):

> I know of no principle, or decided case, upholding a company's right to compel an employee, under pain of discharge, to admit or deny a rule violation or other offense. Such a principle would contradict all our Anglo-American principles, particularly the one that a man is presumed innocent until he is proven guilty, and that the burden of proof is on the one alleging an offense.

An oft-cited private-sector award applying constitutional principles is Thrifty Drug Stores, Inc., 50 LA 1253 (Jones, Jr. 1968), where Arbitrator Jones viewed with skepticism the testimony of an employee who confessed to theft while under interrogation and threatened with discipline and implicated two co-workers. Finding no evidence corroborating the "compelled" testimony, he sustained the grievance. Both King Co. and Thrifty Drug Stores cited expansive language found in the U.S. Supreme Court's decision in Miranda v. Arizona, 384 U.S. 436, 467 (1966):

> [T]here can be no doubt that the Fifth Amendment privilege is available outside of criminal court proceedings and serves to protect persons in all settings in which their freedom of action is curtailed in any significant way from being compelled to incriminate themselves.

See also Hill & Wright, "Employee Refusals to Cooperate in Internal Investigations: 'Into the Woods' With Employers, Courts, and Labor Arbitrators," 56 Mo. L. Rev. 869, 892 n.131 (1991).

[209]American Int'l Aluminum Corp., 68-2 ARB ¶ 8591 (Sembower, 1968) (finding an "inescapable analogy" between a grievant's refusal to testify and the rule that a criminal defendant may not have his refusal to testify held against him); United Parcel Serv., Inc., 45 LA 1050 (Turkus, 1965).

[210]Representative awards include American Steel Foundries (Indiana Harbor Works), 94 LA 745, 747 (Seidman, 1990); Marathon Petroleum Co., 89 LA 716, 720, 723 (Grimes, 1987); Southern Bell Tel. & Tel. Co., 25 LA 270, 273 (McCoy, 1955). Owen Fairweather noted that "[i]n spite of the two views, however, the failure of the grievant to testify can be detrimental to his case. For example, a grievant's decision not to testify can leave damaging evidence

employer's investigation of infractions of work rules or policies will continue to be employed.[211] In fact, many arbitrators have concluded that an employer is under no obligation to continue to employ an individual who continuously frustrates the employer's legitimate investigation into allegations of serious infractions of policy.[212] One arbitrator upheld the termination of an employee for allegedly participating in stealing gas service from the employer where the employee refused to cooperate with the employer in its investigation.[213]

The arbitrator listed three factors for determining when an employer would have just cause for taking disciplinary action against an employee who failed to cooperate during an investigatory interview:

(1) If incident(s) took place during work hours while on a work assignment which relate to possible infractions of Company rules and/or policies.

(2) Where there is evidence suggesting the employee's involvement.

(3) When the employee refused to answer questions or otherwise cooperate in the legitimate investigation conducted by the Company.[214]

Unless the employer can demonstrate a compelling need for the information, arbitrators are reluctant to uphold discipline against employees who refuse to answer questions about off-duty activities. One arbitrator found an employer was not justified in suspending an employee for refusing to answer questions concerning her whereabouts on a Saturday.[215] The employer argued it was entitled to the information because it suspected the employee had made a false representation in requesting permission to take the day off from work. Finding in favor of the employee, the arbitrator explained that "the employment relationship does not carry with it an obligation to * * * throw one's private life open to the employer's questioning."[216]

In another case, an arbitrator refused to uphold the discharge of a county corrections officer who failed to notify management she planned to marry a state prison inmate because the employer failed to show that its interest in knowing about the marriage warranted an intrusion into the employee's personal life.[217] Citing the U.S. Supreme Court decision of *Loving v. Virginia*,[218] the arbitrator explained that

---

unrebutted." Fairweather's Practice and Procedure in Labor Arbitration, 3d ed., 282, Schoonover, ed. (BNA Books, 1991).

[211]Illinois Power Co., 84 LA 586 (Penfield, 1985).

[212]Id., quoting Arbitrator McGury in Simoniz Co., 44 LA 658, 663 (1964).

[213]Illinois Power Co., 84 LA 586 (Penfield, 1985).

[214]Id. at 590–91.

[215]South Cent. Bell Tel. Co., 59 LA 134 (Seward, 1972).

[216]Id. at 140.

[217]County of Napa, 102 LA 591 (Knowlton, 1994).

[218]388 U.S. 1 (1967).

"[i]n addition to guaranteeing the right to engage in intimate relationships without interference, the right to privacy also protects individuals from being unnecessarily forced to disclose information about such relationships."[219]

## C. Employee Protections

An employer's ability to require an employee's cooperation in an investigation is further constrained by statutes,[220] the parties' collective bargaining agreement, and the protections inherent in the just cause standard.

Limits on the company's ability to require cooperation in an investigation, coupled with popular misconceptions about constitutional rights in the private sector, may lead employees to be confused about whether they must comply with the employer's investigatory requests. Moreover, the employee's privacy interests and the potential for adverse consequences often make the employee reluctant to respond to the employer's demands. Arbitrators have required employers to inform the employee as to the consequences of refusing to cooperate in an investigation as a condition to effecting discipline or discharge.[221] As a matter of statutory law, an employer may not insist that the employee submit to investigatory procedures that violate federal or state statutes.[222] A contrary rule would obviously render the statutory protection meaningless.

Arbitrators look to the collective bargaining agreement to expand or constrict the employer's right to conduct reasonable workplace investigations. The parties' agreement on investigatory procedures

---

[219]County of Napa, 102 LA 591, 593 (Knowlton, 1994). The arbitrator acknowledged that the employer has a legitimate interest in knowing when a county correctional officer has a personal relationship with a county inmate. However, the arbitrator concluded that these concerns are not present when a county correctional officer is involved with someone incarcerated at another institution.

[220]See Chapter 13 for a discussion of related statutory rights.

[221]See Hill & Wright, "Employee Refusals to Cooperate in Internal Investigations: "Into the Woods" With Employers, Courts, and Labor Arbitrators," 56 Mo. L. Rev. 869, 908 n.211 (1991). For illustrations of the general rule that the penalty for employee misconduct must be clear before discipline can be sustained, see City of Berkeley, 93 LA 1161, 1165 (Riker, 1989) ("The charge for insubordination requires clear and specific instructions as well as an employee being told exactly what the penalty will be for refusing to comply," citing Micro Precision Gear & Mach. Corp., 31 LA 575, 579–80 (Young, 1958)) and Pacific Power & Light Co., 103 LA 824, 833 (DiFalco, 1994) ("The Union makes a good point when it asserts that the Grievant was not put on notice as to the consequences of his violation. Although this does not excuse the Grievant's conduct, nor cause the Company to fail to prove the violation, it does serve to mitigate the penalty imposed. An employee must be on clear notice of the rules that he has allegedly violated in committing an offense and most importantly, must have been warned about the consequences of his conduct."). Compare Shell Oil Co., 85-1 ARB ¶ 8290 (Bennett, 1985) (discharge upheld where grievant refused to allow a search of his pickup truck after being informed by department manager with significant past service in the union that such refusal would result in disciplinary action).

[222]See Chapter 13.

can provide clear notice of the employer's right to compel cooperation and the penalties for noncompliance in areas such as drug, alcohol, and psychological testing where such rights might otherwise be unsettled.[223]

Broadly speaking, arbitrators have required that investigations have a reasonable basis and be carried out in a fair, nondiscriminatory manner. While the elements of investigatory "due process" vary according to the facts of each case, such concerns have led arbitrators to rule, for example, that an employer must give notice prior to conducting searches that seriously impinge on privacy rights, such as random searches of purses and packages.[224]

## D. Searches and Testing

The conflict between the employer's right to have an employee cooperate in investigations and the employee's right to fair and reasonable procedures is most acute when the employer desires to conduct searches or administer tests.[225] The procedures may be highly

---

[223]Port of Tacoma, 96 LA 361, 362 (Latsch, 1991) (although the union cited numerous awards limiting an employer's ability to compel psychological testing, the employer's right was clearly provided without limitation by a negotiated collective bargaining agreement). But see Transit Mgmt. of Southeast La., Inc., 93-2 ARB ¶ 3429 (Massey, 1993) (although a clearly articulated policy covered drug testing, arbitrator examined employer's interests prior to concluding that the policy was reasonable and enforceable). See Bowater Carolina Co., 92 LA 162, 167 (Clarke, 1989) (agreement provided for 1 year of random drug testing as a condition to allowing grievant to return to work; hence, the arbitrator need not decide whether the requested urinalysis was reasonably related to the employer's business interests).

[224]See Ohio Dep't of Rehabilitation & Correction, 89 LA 865 (Duda, Jr., 1987) (5-day suspension for refusing to allow the employer to search a tote bag was reduced to a written reprimand where the employee had no notice of the search); Scott Paper Co., Southern Div., 69-2 ARB ¶ 8470 (Williams, 1969) (clear plant rule required for compelling search). Compare Shell Oil Co., 81 LA 1205 (Brisco, 1983) (employee could not refuse to permit the employer to search his lunchbox where he knew or should have known that such searches would be conducted); Aldens, Inc., 68-2 ARB ¶ 8814 at 5821–23 (Kelliher, 1968) (employee was discharged for refusing to allow a security officer to properly search her oversized purse; employer posted a sign discouraging employees from bringing large purses to work and reserving the right to inspect their contents. Arbitrator Kelliher reasoned that the employee should have expected to have her purse searched and that the employer did not need reasonable suspicion as inspections were limited to large purses, were routine, and were only about 20 per month in number.).

[225]It should be noted initially that the Fourth Amendment applies to government employers and, therefore, proscribes "unreasonable" searches and seizures. See Regional Transp. Dist., 94 LA 117, 123 (Hogler, 1989) (ruling that Fourth Amendment authorized routine drug tests, administered without a warrant, for employees in the transportation industry); Board of Educ. of the Sch. Dist. of the City of Pontiac, 93 LA 745 (Lipson, 1989) (school engineer's constitutional rights violated where administration searched his locker and removed a bag of marijuana from his sweat pants without reasonable basis).

Private employees are not bound by such restrictions, although the restrictions may become relevant if the search violates fundamental concepts of due process. A thoughtful review of arbitral awards addressing the applicability of the Fourth Amendment and the exclusionary rule barring the consideration of evidence obtained as the result of an unreasonable search can be found in Union Oil Co. of Cal., 99 LA 1137 (McKay, 1992), where Arbitrator McKay concludes that the Fourth Amendment concept of privacy does not apply to private employers but probably does apply to public employers.

intrusive to the employee's privacy interests and personal dignity and, in some cases, be of questionable probative value.[226] Arbitrators attempt to balance the employer's rights against the employee's rights of privacy and personal dignity in areas including random searches of purses, lockers, lunch boxes, or vehicles;[227] searches of the employee's person;[228] blood or urine tests to determine the presence of drugs or alcohol, administered randomly, periodically, or on the basis of reasonable suspicion;[229] polygraph testing;[230] and psychological testing.[231]

---

[226]See also section entitled Private Employees in this chapter.

[227]See Vulcan-Hart Corp., 86-1 ARB ¶ 8125 at 3539 (Bernhardt, 1986) (suspension upheld where employees refused supervisor's random request to search their lunch boxes as they left the plant, although they believed that the supervisor was joking); Aldens, Inc., 61 LA 663 (Dolnick, 1973) (grievance denied where employee refused search of automobile truck); Fruehauf Corp., 49 LA 89 (Daugherty, 1967) (denying grievance where employee refused to permit a search of his lunchbox); International Nickel Co., 50 LA 65 (Shister, 1967) (search of employee's locker proper given disappearance of company property).

[228]Champion Spark Plug Co., 77-1 ARB ¶ 8158 at 3691 (Casselman, 1977) (15-day suspension upheld where employee refused to permit a search under his sweater for a suspected bottle of alcohol; supervisor had "probable cause" to require search after observing grievant apparently place a bottle to his lips); Orgill Bros. & Co., 66 LA 307 (Ross, 1976) (refusal to permit body search when bulge observed in grievant's leg upon leaving plant supported discharge).

[229]One commentary concluded that where there is a reasonable basis, the employer may require the employee's submission to drug and alcohol tests. Hill & Wright, "Employee Refusals to Cooperate in Internal Investigations: "Into the Woods" With Employers, Courts, and Labor Arbitrators," 56 Mo. L. Rev. 869, 908–09 (1991). For illustrations of this principle, see GSX Servs. of Cal., 96 LA 792 (Riker, 1991) (employee properly discharged for refusing to take a blood test which was mandated by the employment contract); Regional Transp. Dist., 94 LA 117 (Hogler, 1989) (25-day suspension upheld for bus driver who refused to submit to drug test; employee's bizarre behavior in relieving another driver in the midst of his route provided justifiable basis for ordering test and employer's interest as a provider of transportation services was significant). For an award upholding the grievant's discharge after he spent a full day in a doctor's office "unable" to produce a urine sample and unwilling to be catheterized, see Bowater Carolina Co., 92 LA 162 (Clarke, 1989). For an award finding the employer's testing unreasonable, see Day & Zimmerman, 94 LA 399 (Nicholas, Jr., 1990) (requirement that employees be tested after returning from leaves of absence impermissibly attempts to regulate off-duty conduct).

[230]Arbitrators are in almost universal agreement that there is no right to administer polygraph examinations. See Glen Manor Home for the Jewish Aged, 81 LA 1178 (Katz, 1983), for a thorough review of such awards and commentaries reaching the same conclusion. Even where a labor contract authorizes the employer to conduct polygraph testing, some arbitrators have refused to uphold discipline based upon an employee's refusal to cooperate in the testing. See Buy Low, Inc., 77 LA 380, 385 (Dolnick, 1981) ("Since a union may not by collective bargaining contract waive an employe's right to refuse to submit to a polygraph test because it violates a clear underlying policy enunciated by courts and arbitrators on the efficacy of those tests, it follows that an employe's individual agreement to submit to such a test is, for the same reason, equally invalid."). As one arbitrator aptly observed, "[the] case clearly turns on the question of the reliability of the * * * [lie detector] tests." Bunker Ramo Corp., 76 LA 857, 861 (Hon, 1981) (after a lengthy review of arbitral decisions addressing the issue, Arbitrator Hon concluded that despite advances in the reliability of polygraph exams, they are still generally inadmissible as evidence at law and not a management prerogative in the arbitral setting). See Chapter 13.

[231]Gem City Chems., Inc., 86 LA 1023 (Warns, 1986); Standard-Knapp Div., 50 LA 833 (Cahn, 1968). See Port of Tacoma, 96 LA 361 (Latsch, 1991) (where discharge for refusal to submit to psychological testing was upheld because the collective bargaining agreement gave the employer the right to compel such testing without limitation, distinguishing awards ruling that the employer must demonstrate a "cogent" need for psychological testing, such as the

Although all these searches and tests may be permissible under proper circumstances, the employee's privacy interests cause arbitrators to examine the employer's actions with a heightened level of scrutiny. A consideration of all facts and circumstances is necessary to determine the reasonableness of requiring the search or testing in each particular case. Some specific examples will illustrate how arbitrators generally apply this balancing test.

In *Square D Co.*,[232] the employee was properly discharged for refusing to permit a search of his truck. The employer had reasonable suspicion for the search, based on the report of co-worker who saw the grievant conceal a copper bar in his apron. In *Dunes Hotel & Country Club*,[233] a hotel maid was properly discharged for insubordination. She was observed on a surveillance camera knocking a planted bottle of Qaaludes on the floor, out of view of the camera. She later refused to submit to a body search in a bathroom with curtains drawn and a female security officer observing. In *Transit Management of Southeastern Louisiana, Inc.*,[234] there was just cause for terminating an employee who refused to consent to a drug test. The test was ordered pursuant to a negotiated policy, there were compelling reasons for testing, and there were no mitigating circumstances.

---

inability of the employee to perform his job or a danger to other employees as a result of mental impairment, in the absence of contractual authorization).

[232]96 LA 541 (Allen, Jr., 1991).

[233](Burns, 1980).

[234]93-2 ARB ¶ 3429 at 5178 (Massey, 1993).

# Chapter 6

# Substance Abuse

## I. Introduction

Collective bargaining agreements have long provided for the discipline or discharge of employees under the influence of alcohol or drugs in the workplace. Shop rules frequently prohibit the use, possession, distribution, or sale of these substances at work. Increasingly, employers want to go beyond these proscriptions by requiring preemployment, postaccident, random, and reasonable suspicion drug testing, as well as drug testing as part of routine physical examinations. Some employers want greater latitude to discipline employees for off-premises and off-duty drug-related conduct.

While arbitrators are generally sympathetic with the goal of a drug-free workplace, they carefully evaluate the extent to which the employer's substance abuse program and its procedures are fair, consistent, accurate, and accommodate employee privacy rights. Absent an employer's clear and legitimate basis for requiring an employee to submit to a drug or alcohol test, an arbitrator will not hesitate in sustaining a grievance.[1]

## II. Work Rules/Policies Governing Alcohol and Drugs

### A. *Work Rules*

In drug and alcohol cases, most arbitrators require the work rule to be clear as to what conduct is prohibited and the penalties for breach of the rule. In cases involving use, possession, or distribution of illegal drugs, employers will often discharge an employee immediately, rather than follow an established progressive discipline proce-

---

[1]Denenberg & Denenberg, Alcohol and Other Drugs: Issues in Arbitration (BNA Books, 1991).

dure. If the work rules or past practice clearly establish that the employer has not used progressive discipline under such circumstances, most often the arbitrator will uphold the discharge. If the rule or past practice is not clear or specifically requires that progressive discipline be used, however, the arbitrator will probably reduce the termination to a penalty consistent with the progressive discipline procedure.[2] In *Abex Corp.*,[3] the employer had no rule against the use of marijuana in the workplace. Consequently, the arbitrator reduced a discharge to the penalty that would have been imposed for the first violation of the rule prohibiting the possession of alcohol in the workplace. A minority of arbitrators, noting the criminal aspect of drug use, possession, or distribution, find that such conduct warrants discharge unless there is a specific contrary policy.

In *Mississippi River Grain Elevator*,[4] the arbitrator upheld the discharge of two employees who were smoking marijuana at work. There was no express prohibition on the use of drugs, and the arbitrator rejected the union's argument that the employees should be given the penalty that would have been assessed if found to be drinking on the job. In rejecting this argument, the arbitrator noted: "I sanction the discharge from employment in this case on the ground that it is an implied condition of any collective bargaining agreement that, unless specifically stated to the contrary, there are some offenses which are so great that discharge from employment is the only appropriate penalty."[5] The more recent trend is for arbitrators to follow an employer's drug policy and the penalties delineated in the policy, unless the drug-related activity was especially serious, dangerous, or egregious. Most employers with drug and alcohol policies clearly spell out the penalties for violations of the policy. As with other types of cases, in drug cases arbitrators require that work rules be properly communicated to employees[6] and consistently enforced. Lax enforcement or inconsistent application of penalties will most likely result in reversal or modification of the penalty.[7]

## B. On-the-Job Use, Possession, or Sale

Typical work rules prohibit the use, possession, and sale of alcohol and drugs on the employer's premises.[8] These rules have been univer-

---

[2]National Car Rental Sys., Inc., 75 LA 518 (Zumas, 1989); Rohr Indus., 88 LA 703 (Ross, 1987); Warehouse Distrib. Ctrs., 90 LA 979 (Weiss, 1982).

[3]64 LA 221 (Rybolt, 1975).

[4]62 LA 200, 202 (Marcus, 1974). See also S.F. Kennedy-New Prods., 64 LA 613, 618 (McDermott, 1973).

[5]Mississippi River Grain Elevator, 62 LA 200, 202 (Zack, 1974).

[6]Maintenance Cent. for Seniors, 86 LA 288 (Roumell, 1985); Wautauga Indus., Inc., 78 LA 697 (Galambos, 1980); Swift & Co., 72 LA 513 (Renfro, 1979).

[7]Macmillan Bloedel Containers, 92 LA 592 (Nicholas, 1989); Delta Air Lines, 89 LA 408 (Kahn, 1987).

[8]The employer's obligation to bargain drug rules and governmental regulations are covered in Drug Testing, later in this chapter.

sally accepted as reasonable and often provide the foundation for employers' drug and alcohol policies and programs. The prohibition on drugs may be extended to cover employees on company business, regardless of their location.

*1. Use.* As a rule, arbitrators require the employer to produce substantial evidence when it charges an employee with use of drugs or alcohol at work. If the work rules contain a clear prohibition, arbitrators are likely to sustain the discharge or disciplinary action taken provided the evidence supports such action.[9] Discharge has been upheld even where the employee had a long and reputable service record. A 17-year employee with a good record was summarily discharged for drinking beer during a work break in violation of an explicit rule, and the arbitrator upheld the discharge.[10] Arbitrators have substituted lesser discipline for discharges involving use of drugs or alcohol on the job where there is insufficient proof or where progressive discipline was not properly followed.[11]

---

[9]Mason & Hangar-Silas Mason Co., 103 LA 371 (Cipolla, 1994) (employer's policy provided discharge for first offense of positive drug test, which had been enforced consistently for 10 years without challenge; employee had positive marijuana test); Union Tribune Publ'g Co., 93 LA 617 (McBreaty, 1989) (employee used methamphetamine and possessed marijuana); Kellogg Co., 93 LA 884 (Clarke, 1989) (just cause existed for marijuana use at work solely on basis of undercover agent testimony which arbitrator found was straightforward, detailed, and conformed with his reports to employer); Uniroyal Goodrich Tire Co., 93 LA 893 (Dworkin, 1989) (employee had red eyes, smelled of alcohol, and could not focus or communicate); Quaker Oats Co., 89 LA 1076 (Wright, 1987) (discharge proper for smoking marijuana where employee was observed in truck on company property lighting cigarette or other object a number of times and throwing napkins out of truck, where retrieved napkins were found to contain marijuana residue); Excel Corp., 89 LA 1275 (McDermott, 1987) (employee signed confession admitting use of marijuana and beer in company parking lot); Central Ohio Transit Auth., 88 LA 628 (Seinsheimer, 1987) (expert witness testified the high level of marijuana in blood and urine tests indicated employees had smoked marijuana on the job); St. Louis Paint Mfg. Co., 88 LA 1251 (Penfield, 1987) (employee sniffed chemical compound at work to get high in violation of company rule against such activity); Dietrich Indus., 88 LA 214 (Feldman, 1986) (discharge upheld for marijuana use at work; arbitrator accepted evidence from undercover agent); Exxon Chem. Ams., 87 LA 743 (Allen, 1986) (evidence supported employer's position employee smoked marijuana on company property); Intermountain Rural Elec. Ass'n, 86 LA 540 (Watkins, 1985) (employee exhibited signs of intoxication at work); American Cyanamid Co., 81 LA 630 (Fogelberg, 1983) (employees admittedly left fire brigade class without supervisor's permission and drank beer on company property during working hours); Champion Spark Plug, 68 LA 702 (Casselman, 1977) (employee had been seen drinking and had alcohol on his breath); Du-Co Ceramics Co., 63 LA 355, 356 (Wagner, 1974) (employee drinking on job in violation of plant rules subjecting employees to discharge for "bringing or consuming alcoholic beverages * * * onto plant premises").

[10]Drackett, Inc., 89 LA 99 (Ross, 1987).

[11]GTE Cal., 99 LA 196 (Richman, 1992) (discharge for drinking beer at lunch reduced to 2-week suspension in accordance with employer's drug and alcohol progressive discipline procedure); Keebler, 88 LA 183 (Belcher, 1986) (where truck driver brought open can of beer to company meeting, 5-day suspension reduced to written warning); Consolidation Coal, 87 LA 111 (DiLauro, 1986) (detection of marijuana odor insufficient to sustain discharge of two employees who were present where there was no other evidence of drug use); Owens Corning Fiberglass Corp., 86 LA 1026 (Nicholas, 1986) (discharge of employee improper where the action was based upon a former employee's uncorroborated statements that he had smoked marijuana with grievant and unsubstantiated statements of other employees that they had smelled marijuana); Baumfolder Corp., 78 LA 1060 (Modjeska, 1982) (discharge was without just cause in part because there was no allegation or showing that the grievant drank on premises).

Consuming alcohol in the company parking lot is typically considered drinking on company "property" and if the work rule is clear, discharges for such conduct will be sustained.[12] Other cases examine a somewhat expanded definition of company "property." Some work rules prohibit consumption not only on company property but also while driving or riding in a company-owned or leased vehicle. An arbitrator upheld the discharge of two employees who had two cold, opened beers in a company vehicle while delivering company products.[13] Discipline of an employee who drank during lunch was upheld because the employee was in charge of a city crane and responsible for its safe operations, even though the employee neither drank nor worked on any company "property."[14]

Whether an unpaid lunch hour is "company time," so that consuming alcohol violates a written company policy, is handled inconsistently by arbitrators. One arbitrator found a discharge improper since the employees were on their unpaid lunch period when they consumed alcoholic beverages. There was no sign of impairment when the employees returned to work. The arbitrator concluded unpaid lunches were time off from work, not "company time."[15] However, in several other cases discharge or lesser discipline was upheld for similar infractions.[16]

Discipline will not be upheld where the only basis is guilt by association. The fact that an employee is in a situation where drugs or alcohol are being used by another employee is not sufficient evidence to support discipline or discharge.[17] Where one of the employees is actually an undercover informant, if the testimony is credible, arbitrators have upheld discipline for use of drugs or alcohol on the job.[18]

---

[12]Schaefer-Alabama Corp., 70 LA 956 (LaValley, 1978) (employer had just cause to discharge employee who drank beer on parking lot, where plant rules subjected employees to immediate discharge for flagrant misbehavior that included drinking on company premises); AMF Lawn & Garden Div., 64 LA 988 (Wyman, 1975) (under plant rule forbidding employees to possess or drink liquor or any other intoxicating beverage while on employer's premises, penalty of discharge was not too severe for employee who consumed portion of can of beer in parking lot).

[13]Farm Stores, Inc., 81 LA 344 (Hanes, 1983).

[14]City of Milwaukee, 71 LA 329 (Maslanka, 1978).

[15]Kalamazoo County Rd. Comm'n, 88 LA 1049 (Lewis, 1987).

[16]City of Milwaukee, 71 LA 329 (Maslanka, 1978) (drinking during nonpaid lunch period warranted suspension where employee was responsible for city equipment); International Pipe & Ceramics Corp., 44 LA 267, 267 (Grant, 1965) (employee violated plant rule forbidding "drinking of alcoholic beverages during a lunch or dinner period during working hours on or off plant premises").

[17]Modine Mfg. Co., 90 LA 189 (Goldstein, 1987) (discharge based upon undercover investigator's uncorroborated testimony overturned; no proof shown employee smoked marijuana in car where others did).

[18]Kellogg Co., 93 LA 884 (Clarke, 1989) (just cause existed for marijuana use at work solely on basis of undercover agent testimony which arbitrator found was straightforward, detailed, and conformed with his reports to employer); Dietrich Indus., 88 LA 214 (Feldman, 1986) (discharge upheld for marijuana use at work; arbitrator accepted evidence from undercover agent).

*2. Possession.* When discipline is assessed for possession of alcohol or drugs on company property, the employer must have sound evidence linking the contraband to the employee. Arbitrators carefully evaluate the factual predicate for the discipline since they generally uphold discipline for possession.[19]

Arbitrators have upheld discipline or discharge for violation of the rule against possession when a drug or alcohol is found on the individual,[20] in the employee's locker,[21] near the employee's workplace,[22] in an employee's purse,[23] or in the employee's car on company property.[24] Even a small amount of liquor in a locker was sufficient for discharge of a long-service employee where the contract specified discharge for possession of intoxicants.[25] Similarly, discharge was proper where it was shown that an employee possessed a small amount of a prohibited substance in the workplace.[26] When alcohol was found in an employee's car in the company parking lot after the employer had declared a drug-free, alcohol-free, gun-free workplace, a discharge was sustained.[27]

The rule prohibiting possession of alcohol or drugs is not always limited to company property. The workplace is sometimes beyond the employer's physical facility. When employees operate company vehicles during the course of their employment, they are considered to be on company property.[28] Some employees are permitted to take company vehicles home and use them for personal matters. If they

---

[19]But see Philip Morris, Inc., 68-2 ARB ¶ 8773 (Volz, 1968) (arbitrator found that mere possession of alcohol on company premises, without the intent to consume the liquor on the property, did not establish cause enough to justify an employee's discharge; employee had kept the alcohol in the glove compartment of his automobile, but it was brought into the plant by another employee for that employee's use only; second employee's possession not considered to be possession by grievant for the purposes of discharge).

[20]Marathon Petroleum Co., 92 LA 471 (McDermott, 1989); Consumer Plastics Corp., 88 LA 208 (Garnholz, 1987); Valvoline Oil Co., 89 LA 209 (Brisco, 1987); Maverick Tube Co., 86 LA 1 (Miller, 1985); United States Metal Ref. Co., 78 LA 1334 (Stochaj, 1982); Bethlehem Steel Corp., 79 LA 1185 (Sharnoff, 1982); Jehl Cooperage Co., 75 LA 901 (Odom, 1980); General Elec. Co., 74 LA 25 (Spencer, 1979); United States Steel Corp., 62 LA 46 (Friedman, 1974).

[21]Quaker Oats Co., Stokely-Van Kamp, Inc., 96 LA 419 (Marcus, 1991); Burns Int'l Sec. Serv., Inc., 78 LA 1104 (Traynor, 1982); Sweetheart Cup Corp., 78 LA 274 (Eagle, 1982).

[22]General Elec. Co., 89 LA 375 (Seidman, 1987); Rust Eng'g, 85 LA 407 (Whyte, 1985); Dobbs Houses, Inc., 78 LA 749 (Tucker, 1982); Alcolac Chem. Corp., 55 LA 306 (Robertson, 1970).

[23]Marathon Petroleum, 92 LA 471 (McDermott, 1989).

[24]Safeway Stores, Inc., 88 LA 1317 (Staudohar, 1987); Emhart Packaging Group, 88 LA 51 (Rothschild, 1986); Goodyear Aerospace Corp., 86 LA 403 (Fullmer, 1985).

[25]Atlantic Steel Co., 50 LA 173 (Hebert, 1968).

[26]Dunlop Tire Co., 104 LA 653 (Teple, 1995) (termination of employee in possession of a small quantity of marijuana upheld; while the amount found was insignificant, that fact was considered irrelevant as any amount provided sufficient basis for discipline).

[27]Marathon Petroleum Co., 93 LA 1082 (Marlatt, 1989) (just cause existed to discharge employee who accidentally left a gun and alcohol in his car after a family gathering, where employer had made a well-publicized commitment to creating a drug-free, alcohol-free, gun-free workplace and exception for intent would render rule useless).

[28]Industrial Powder Coatings, 103 LA 519 (Statham, 1994); City of Kankakee, 97 LA 564 (Wolff, 1991); Farm Stores, Inc., 81 LA 344 (Hanes, 1983).

do so while drug impaired, they risk discipline.[29] The same prohibition of possession has been deemed to apply where an employee uses his personal car for company business[30] and where drugs are found in an employee's car returning home from work.[31]

In an unusual case, police had a tip that an employee was selling cocaine at the employer's plant. The employee was followed from his home to the plant, where he entered the plant parking lot, turned around, and parked in the street opposite the plant entrance. The employee was apprehended when he got out of his car. He was searched and 19 small bags of cocaine, clearly prepared for sale, were found on his person. He was arrested at 7:25 a.m. and his shift start time was 7:30 a.m. In sustaining the discharge, the arbitrator concluded that while the arrest thwarted the ability to carry out his clear intent, the employee intended to enter the plant with the drugs in his possession, an act violative of the rule against possessing drugs on company property.[32]

There also have been cases where the employee has contended unknowing possession. Some arbitrators have taken the position the employer must prove the employee knowingly possessed the prohibited substance, even where the policy or rule does not specifically require that the employee has knowledge of the drug or alcohol possession. Discharges for possession have not been upheld where the employer failed to show the employee knowingly brought alcohol or drugs onto company property,[33] where an employee unknowingly brought a whiskey bottle to work in her purse,[34] and where the evidence supported the employee's assertion that a whiskey bottle was planted on his car seat as part of a campaign of harassment.[35]

Similarly, possession was not substantiated where an employee claimed he knew nothing about a marijuana cigarette butt found in

---

[29]Motor Cargo, Inc., 96 LA 181 (Jones, 1990) (employee was arrested for drug use before he had an opportunity to operate the company vehicle; employee testified that he would have operated the vehicle the next morning, and evidence demonstrated that he would have still been impaired at that time).

[30]Potomac Elec. Power Co., 88 LA 290 (Fergenbaum, 1987) (discharge sustained where employee was stopped by police and marijuana was found in his car).

[31]Carter-Wallace, Inc., 89 LA 587 (Katz, 1987) (employer properly discharged employee for on-duty possession of narcotics when employee was arrested on way home from work and charged with possession of drugs).

[32]American Brass Co., 89 LA 1193 (Ahern, 1987).

[33]Poly Tech, Inc., 91 LA 512 (Gunderson, 1988) (discharge improper of employee alleged to have brought three cans of beer onto company premises, where employee claimed he had drunk beer off premises and cans were empty and employer failed to prove they contained beer); Kable Printing, 89 LA 314 (Mikrut, 1987) (discharge overturned when marijuana was found in employee's purse; while she admitted knowing it was marijuana, she later contended her brother had put it in her purse; arbitrator concluded the employer did not prove the employee knowingly possessed the marijuana); Braniff Airways, 73 LA 304 (Ray, 1979) (discharge unjustified when marijuana was found in airline attendant's portfolio she was carrying on company property; employee disclaimed any knowledge of how the drugs got there and no evidence was presented to show she knew how they came to be in her possession).

[34]Packaging Corp. of Am., 56 LA 856 (Anrod, 1971).

[35]Holcroft Co., 55 LA 907 (Keefe, 1970).

the back seat of his car, which had been used by others.[36] When an employee was found sitting in the back seat of another employee's car in the company parking lot and there was a lit marijuana cigarette in the front ashtray, the employer failed to link the cigarette to the employee. Furthermore, because there was no proof the employee brought the cigarette onto the premises or had smoked it, the discharge was overturned.[37]

There is also a strong contrary view that holds that intent is *not* an element to be proven to sustain discipline or discharge for violation of the rules against possession of drugs or alcohol in the workplace or on company property. In *Marathon Petroleum Co.,*[38] the union argued that the grievant should not be discharged because the violation was unintentional in that the liquor and firearms were left in the car after a family gathering. In responding to the union's argument that there should be an intent element to the rule, the arbitrator stated:

> At that point, then the Company rule becomes "no drugs, no alcohol, no guns, but with these exceptions: (1) you didn't intend to smoke the marijuana, (2) you didn't intend to drink the liquor, or (3) you didn't intend to shoot anybody." What sort of rule is that? Riddled with such loopholes it is no rule at all. Violations will only be determined after the fact, and the fact may be disaster of unimaginable proportions.[39]

*3. Sale or Distribution.*   Drug sale or distribution in the workplace constitutes a significant danger to employees because of the increased risk of on-the-job use and impairment. The workplace can be an ideal environment for the drug dealer as it provides a built-in customer base with little, if any, law enforcement surveillance. First-line supervisors seldom are equipped to detect drug distribution or sale since their responsibilities primarily are to concentrate on getting the work at hand done rather than policing drug activities.

When employees are disciplined for selling drugs, arbitrators can be expected to require a high standard of proof. While there is lack of unanimity among arbitrators as to the degree of proof necessary for the employer to prevail, in many instances arbitrators have determined the employer must meet the "clear and convincing" standard of proof.[40]

---

[36]Shell Oil, 87 LA 473 (Nicholas, 1986).

[37]Misco, Inc., 89 LA 137 (Fox, 1983).

[38]93 LA 1082, 1085 (Marlatt, 1989).

[39]Id. See also Burger Iron Co., 92 LA 1100, 1105 (Dworkin, 1989) ("notwithstanding the sale, or consumption of illegal drugs is not expressly prohibited by the plant rules, such conduct constitutes criminal behavior and is at variance with the proper deportment of an employee in the context of the employment relationship").

[40]Id.; Southern Cal. Permanente Med. Group, 92 LA 41 (Richman, 1989); General Portland, 62 LA 209 (Autrey, 1974); Kroger Co., 25 LA 906 (Smith, 1955). This requirement for a higher degree of proof is based on the view that a charge of committing a felony is injurious to an employee's prospects for future employment.

Drug dealing, by nature, is a furtive, clandestine activity. Consequently, employers have often had to resort to the use of undercover investigators to gather evidence sufficient to prove employees are engaging in the sale or distribution of drugs on company property.[41] In some cases the credibility or the expertise of the undercover agent has led the arbitrator to sustain drug-dealing discharges.[42] Conversely, arbitrators have been reluctant to uphold discharges in cases where the results of the agent's investigation amounted to hearsay evidence[43] or where they are based on uncorroborated testimony or reports of an investigator or otherwise deemed unreliable.[44]

## C.  On-the-Job Impairment

Impairment is an inability to do the normal tasks or duties of a job. Being "under the influence" is having a current level of a drug in one's bloodstream. Neither is shown by drug tests which measure metabolites created by prior drug use. It is possible to measure current

---

[41]Burger Iron Co., 92 LA 1100, 1106, 1107 (discharge of five employees for just cause where employer, through use of an undercover agent, discovered they were using, possessing, or selling drugs on company property; arbitrator held discharge was the proper deterrent given the potential profit in drug dealing); Aviall, Inc., 94 LA 721 (Sisk, 1990) (two employees properly discharged for selling marijuana and cocaine to undercover agent, despite his absence at the hearing; a major consideration was the public safety aspect of the employees' jobs, involving maintenance and rebuilding of jet aircraft engines for major airlines and the government); S.D. Warren Co., 89 LA 688 (Gwiazda, 1985) (discharge upheld where employee twice sold marijuana to undercover agent and urged him to smoke it at work); State Univ. of N.Y., 74 LA 299 (Babiskin, 1980) (just cause existed to discharge employee who sold amphetamines on campus to an undercover detective); S.F. Kennedy-New Prods., 64 LA 880 (Traynor, 1975) (four employees who company investigators found were using and distributing marijuana, mescaline, and PCP on company property to other employees were properly discharged).

[42]Cerro Corp., 69 LA 965, 965 (Griffin, 1977) (undercover agent testified he observed the employee distributing or using marijuana on six separate occasions on company premises; though agent's testimony was the only basis for discharge, the arbitrator considered him "a bona fide expert witness in the area of narcotics and controlled substance investigations"); American Air Filter Co., 64 LA 404 (Hilpert, 1975) (three employees distributed marijuana to undercover agent; his testimony was found credible whereas the employees' testimony was not).

[43]Southern Cal. Permanente, 92 LA 41 (Richman, 1989) (employer offered only inadmissible hearsay evidence to establish an agency relationship between the employee and a co-worker; employee admittedly told the investigator that he sold drugs in the past and could get drugs, and directed the investigator to a different employee who sold drugs to him, but no co-workers to whom drugs were delivered or sold were called as witnesses); Bamberger's, 59 LA 879 (Glushien, 1972) (where investigator did not testify, the employer's entire case rested upon the hearsay testimony of the supervisor to whom the agent reported).

[44]U.S. Borax, 84 LA 32 (Richman, 1984) (employee's discharge based solely on a single investigator's testimony; employer did not produce the marijuana agent claimed he bought from the employee; agent showed another employee the marijuana, but no one witnessed the transaction and agent's testimony was uncorroborated); Petibone Ohio Corp., 72 LA 1144 (Feldman, 1979) (agent testified he observed employees using and selling marijuana on numerous occasions, but no other evidence was produced to corroborate or substantiate his testimony and reports); General Portland, 62 LA 709 (Autrey, 1974) (discharges for possession overturned where there was no corroborating evidence to support investigator's testimony he witnessed five employees smoking and exchanging marijuana).

levels of blood alcohol to show that an employee is "under the influence." Although state law may provide a blood alcohol level that represents impairment for driving, it does not necessarily show an individual employee is impaired on the job, since tolerance and performance are individually determined. While there are tests for currently being under the influence of some drugs, they are rarely used.

Shop rules that prohibit employees from being impaired or under the influence of alcohol or drugs on the job are recognized as being reasonable and necessary to enable the employer to maintain an orderly, safe, and efficient operation. Determining whether an employee at work is, in fact, impaired or under the influence is the crux of many drug- and alcohol-related disciplinary arbitrations.

In alcohol cases, the evidence of on-the-job impairment most frequently is a supervisor's observations of the employee's behavior and appearance. In the main, arbitrators take the position supervisors are competent to assess whether an employee is impaired or under the influence as a result of their observations. Relatively few arbitrators will require alcohol tests to substantiate a supervisorial finding that an employee is under the influence.[45] Just as many states allow lay persons to opine that someone they observed was under the influence, most arbitrators accept a supervisor's conclusions that are based on actual observation. Most people have had enough experience observing intoxicated persons to know the symptoms.

In drug cases, however, symptoms of impairment or being under the influence often are not readily understood or apparent. Hence there is greater difficulty in determining when an employee is actually under the influence of drugs, even when drug tests are performed.[46] Employers frequently equate a positive drug test with impairment or being under the influence. Evidence of past drug use may remain in the employee's system for several days or even weeks after actual use. Because no correlation exists between a positive drug test and impairment, a positive drug test does not necessarily prove that an employee was under the influence of drugs at work.[47]

*1. Evidence of Impairment: Type.*    There are two types of evidence of impairment. An employee may exhibit observable physical signs of impairment such as slurred speech, red eyes, the odor of liquor, nystagmus, aberrant behavior, or a lack of coordination. An employee may also be tested to determine a level of blood alcohol. When the employee's blood alcohol level is measured, it can be compared against a state statutory standard. The statutory standard is a legislative determination of what level of blood alcohol makes an

---

[45]Northrop Worldwide Servs., Inc. 64 LA 742 (Goldstein, 1975).

[46]For an excellent discussion of drug testing, what it proves and does not prove, see Denenberg & Denenberg, "Drug Testing From the Arbitrator's Perspective," 11 Nova L. Rev. 371, 395–98 (1987).

[47]Dubowski, "Drug-Use Testing, Scientific Perspectives," 11 Nova L. Rev. 528 (1987).

individual "impaired" or "under the influence" for the purpose of driving an automobile.

Drug testing that shows the presence of drug metabolites is generally done by urinalysis. It does not show the current level of a drug in the employee's blood, but only that a drug has been metabolized. There are no comparable state statutory standards because drug metabolites can be found in the urine long after the effects of the drug have worn off. Because of the persistence of drug metabolites, and the fact that neither the drug dose nor the time of ingestion can be determined by urinalysis, even pharmacokineticists may have great difficulty testifying that an employee was "under the influence" or "impaired" while at work.

Consequently, the major factual problem with which arbitrators grapple is whether the employer has shown that the employee was impaired or under the influence of drugs or alcohol. Arbitrators are most persuaded in alcohol cases by evidence of objective physical manifestations of impairment or intoxication, and in drug cases by aberrant behavior, or outward abnormal appearance, combined with drug test results.

Discharge or discipline has been sustained where five witnesses described evidence of alcohol intoxication;[48] where a bus driver who refused an alcohol test behaved as if impaired;[49] where an employee's accident provided reasonable cause for a drug test that was positive for marijuana and cocaine;[50] where an employee submitted to urine and blood tests that revealed a blood alcohol level double the standard for presumptive intoxication under the state's motor vehicle act;[51] where an employee had a positive drug test after reinstatement on a last-chance basis because of a prior positive drug test;[52] where an employee's blood alcohol level exceeded state intoxication levels when tested 3 hours after reporting for work;[53] where a bus driver, whose admittedly poor judgment caused an accident, was impaired by marijuana;[54] where an employee was on duty under the influence of alcohol,[55] or marijuana;[56] where an employee had red eyes and a "laid-back" attitude and tested positive for marijuana;[57] where an employee, after an injury, was uncooperative, had a blank stare, and tested

---

[48]Dresser Indus., 99 LA 812 (Dee, 1992).

[49]Regional Transp. Dist., 94 LA 177 (Hogler, 1989).

[50]Morton Thiokol, 93 LA 434 (Allen, 1989).

[51]Performed Line Prods., Co., 88 LA 340 (Strasshofer, 1986).

[52]Thomas Steel Strip Corp., 87 LA 994 (Feldman, 1986); Indianapolis Power & Light Co., 87 LA 826 (Volz, 1986).

[53]Pittsburg & Midway Coal Mining Co., 91 LA 431 (Cohen, 1988).

[54]Regional Transp. Dist., 91 LA 213 (Goldstein, 1988).

[55]BASF Corp., 90 LA 460 (Daniel, 1987).

[56]Texas City Ref., 89 LA 1159 (Milentz, 1987).

[57]Orange County Transit Dist., 89 LA 544 (Brisco, 1987).

positive for marijuana;[58] where an employee tested positive for marijuana and an expert witness testified the level of marijuana in the employee's blood was sufficient to cause impairment;[59] where an expert witness testified that based upon the high level of marijuana determined by a urinalysis performed in conjunction with an annual physical given on company time, the employee was impaired when he provided the urine specimen;[60] where behavior and a drug test showed a bus driver was impaired by illegal drugs;[61] where an employee displayed erratic behavior and tested positive for marijuana;[62] where despite the absence of evidence of on-the-job impairment, the employee had a positive drug test;[63] and where a supervisor's reasonable observations were sufficient to find the employee impaired and provide grounds for administering a drug test, although no scientific evidence of the reliability of the positive drug test was provided.[64]

Some "under the influence" cases involve employees drinking during a lunch or dinner break. In one case the arbitrator sustained the discharge of an employee who had alcohol on his breath following his return from lunch break, became belligerent, and refused a sobriety test. The company rule permitted discharge for "drinking intoxicants on or off company premises and then returning to work."[65] Another arbitrator sustained a discharge under a plant rule that prohibited "drinking of alcoholic beverages during a lunch or dinner period during working hours on or off plant premises."[66]

*2. Evidence of Impairment: Degree.*   Where the physical manifestations or test results are less convincing, arbitrators are less likely to sustain discharges. In *U.S. Steel Corp.,*[67] the arbitrator would not accept a 0.062 percent blood alcohol as sufficient proof of being under the influence of alcohol, in light of evidence that the grievant worked the entire shift with no physical manifestations of impairment. Arbitrators have sustained grievances or reduced penalties where prescription medication could have exacerbated the effect of a small amount of alcohol;[68] where an employee had red watery eyes and a smell of beer but no other signs of intoxication;[69] where a foreman smelled alcohol on the employee's breath and the employee slipped

---

[58]Herlitz Inc., 89 LA 436 (Allen, 1987).

[59]Metropolitan Transit Auth., 88 LA 1247 (King, 1987).

[60]Amoco Oil Co., 88 LA 1010 (Weisenberger, 1987).

[61]Bi-State Dev. Agency, 88 LA 854 (Brazil, 1987).

[62]Consolidation Coal Co., 87 LA 729 (Hoh, 1986).

[63]Union Oil, 87 LA 297 (Boner, 1985).

[64]Roadway Express, 87 LA 224 (Cooper, 1986).

[65]Cal-Custom/Hawk, 65 LA 723, 724 (Ross, 1975).

[66]International Pipe & Ceramics Corp., 44 LA 267, 267 (Grant, 1965).

[67]95 LA 7 (Talarico, 1990).

[68]Loral Sys. Group, 94 LA 924 (Strasshofer, 1990).

[69]Fitzsimmons Mfg. Co., 92 LA 609 (Roumell, 1989).

on the floor;[70] where there was a dispute over whether the employee had alcohol on his breath, there was no impairment, and other outward signs could have been caused by anger;[71] where the only evidence was the smell of alcohol on the employee's breath;[72] where the employees were boisterous but did not have blood alcohol levels that met the state vehicle code standard for "under the influence";[73] where speech was incoherent but there were no other physical signs of impairment and evidence of alcohol on the employee's breath was disputed;[74] where a bus driver tested positive for marijuana following an incident but was never accused of causing an accident or being impaired or under the influence of drugs;[75] where aberrant behavior was minimal, no record of prior drug use existed, and the employer failed to prove the employee was intoxicated;[76] where the employee tested positive for marijuana but there was no evidence he used marijuana on the job or that it induced his aberrant behavior, which could be traced to his medications;[77] where the employee tested positive for marijuana but the "under the influence" standard could not be determined from the test;[78] where a railroad employee tested positive for marijuana after a collision but the level of metabolized marijuana was not dispositive of whether he was under the influence;[79] and where employees whose blood and urine samples tested positive for drugs did not exhibit behavior associated with being under the influence and the test results were not a reliable indicator of being under the influence.[80]

Where employees have safety-sensitive positions, employers often establish rules that forbid drinking within a certain period before reporting to duty. A truck driver's discharge was sustained because he reported to work within 3 hours after consuming several drinks, and that conduct both violated federal highway safety regulations and was contractual grounds for immediate termination.[81] In the air and ground passenger transportation industries, employers (and governmental regulators) establish work rules that prohibit drinking within a specified period before reporting to work. Some arbitrators, however, are reluctant to sustain discharges under these rules and impose lesser penalties where the infraction was minor or occurred

---

[70]Mercury Stainless, Inc., 91 LA 841 (Richard, 1988).

[71]General Dynamics Corp., 91 LA 539 (Marcus, 1988).

[72]Signal Delivery Serv., Inc., 86 LA 75 (Wies, 1985).

[73]General Felt Indus., Inc., 74 LA 973 (Carnes, 1979).

[74]Blue Diamond Co., 66 LA 1136 (Summers, 1976).

[75]Southern Cal. Rapid Transit Dist., 93 LA 20 (Christopher, 1989).

[76]Kroger Co., 88 LA 463 (Wren, 1966).

[77]United Techs. Ctr., 92 LA 829 (Williams, 1989).

[78]Bowman Transp., 90 LA 347 (Duff, 1987).

[79]Georgia Pac. Corp., 86 LA 411 (Clarke, 1985).

[80]Boone Energy, 85 LA 233 (O'Connell, 1985).

[81]Safeway Stores, Inc., 85-1 ARB ¶ 8180 (Tilbury, 1985).

many hours before reporting to work. Arbitrators have found discharge too harsh where a driver had two beers 2¼ hours before reporting to work,[82] where flight attendants violated a 24-hour rule (no alcohol 24 hours prior to flight),[83] and where a flight attendant violated a 12-hour rule.[84]

### D. Fitness for Duty

Plant rules commonly provide for, and arbitrators usually sustain, immediate discharge for reporting to work impaired or under the influence of drugs or alcohol. The rationale for these decisions is that employees have the duty to report for work psychologically and physiologically prepared to perform their assigned duties and to remain so throughout the workday.[85]

Discharges have been upheld where the employee's abnormal behavior was cause for a blood test that, an expert testified, indicated he was legally drunk when he reported to work;[86] where an employee subject to random testing tested positive for cocaine and PCP upon reporting for work;[87] and where an employee reported for work under the influence of alcohol and went to sleep on the job to improve his condition.[88] A suspension for reporting to work under the influence of alcohol was not upheld, however, where there was no evidence the employee was impaired and the employer had never defined "under the influence."[89]

There also have been cases in which discharge or discipline has been overturned where the employer charged an employee with violating a rule that had not been communicated,[90] where there has been lax rule enforcement,[91] and where the employer had been inconsistent in assessing the degree of discipline[92] or following progressive discipline.[93]

---

[82]Metropolitan Atlanta Rapid Transit Auth., 86 LA 334 (Statham, 1985).

[83]Northwest Airlines, Inc., 56 LA 836 (Wyckoff, 1971).

[84]Trans World Airlines, 38 LA 1221 (Wallen, 1962).

[85]Bornstein, "Drug and Alcohol Issues in the Work Place: An Arbitrator's Perspective," 39 Arb. J. 20 (1984).

[86]Southern Cal. Edison, 90 LA 960 (Draznin, 1988).

[87]Koppers Co., 91 LA 363 (Yarwosky, 1988).

[88]Nabisco Brands, Inc., 86 LA 430 (Cox, 1985).

[89]General Dynamics Corp., 91 LA 539 (Marcus, 1988).

[90]Maintenance Cent. for Seniors, 86 LA 288 (Roumell, 1985); Wautauga Indus., Inc., 78 LA 697 (Galambos, 1980); Swift & Co., 72 LA 513 (Renfro, 1979).

[91]MacMillan Bloedel Containers, 92 LA 592 (Nicholas, 1989).

[92]Delta Air Lines, 89 LA 408 (Kahn, 1987).

[93]Warehouse Distrib. Ctrs., 90 LA 979 (Weiss, 1982); Rohr Indus., 88 LA 703 (Ross, 1987); National Car Rental Sys., Inc., 75 LA 518 (Zumas, 1980).

### E. Off-Duty Conduct[94]

Most employees and arbitrators believe that the activities of an employee while not on duty or away from the workplace is of no concern to the employer. Under most circumstances, employers cannot assess disciplinary action based upon off-duty, off-premises conduct. However, when such off-duty or off-premises employee conduct adversely affects an employer's business or reputation, threatens the safety or well-being of employees, or makes the employee unfit or unavailable for work, there may be a sufficient interest by the employer to impose discipline.

Off-duty drug use, sale, or possession has often been found to fall within this exception, and to a lesser extent, off-duty alcohol use or abuse has also been found to be a proper basis for disciplinary action. The *key* element in such cases is the nexus between the off-duty, off-premises conduct and the employer's legitimate interests.

*1. Off-Duty Drug Use.*   There is general agreement among arbitrators that on-duty use of drugs is a legitimate concern of employers, and a sufficient basis for discipline. The same cannot be said for off-duty drug use. Some employers have established drug policies that require employees to be drug free whether on duty or off duty.[95] Employees have been disciplined for violating the off-duty use provision with mixed results. Arbitrators have upheld discharge of employees for off-duty marijuana use[96] and have overturned discharge for the same offense when the employer failed to prove that off-duty conduct affected the employee's work performance.[97] Employers also have attempted to discipline employees for off-duty drug use despite the absence of a policy or rule prohibiting such conduct. In most of these "no rule" cases, arbitrators have not sustained the discipline assessed. Discharge has been overturned where the employer could not prove the employee who tested positive for marijuana ever used it on the job,[98] and where the employee tested positive for marijuana and cocaine and admitted off-duty use and test results did not prove either were used at work.[99] Suspensions were overturned where four employees tested positive for marijuana or cocaine resulting from off-duty use but showed no functional impairment.[100] In one "no rule"

---

[94]The regulation of off-duty conduct in other contexts is discussed in Chapter 9.

[95]Ideal Elec. Co., 98 LA 410 (Heekin, 1991) (rule that prohibits sale or use of drugs and intoxicants off company property is facially reasonable, as employer has right to alcohol-free and drug-free work force when employees are on duty or when there is a close nexus to the job); Weyerhauser Co., 86 LA 182 (Levin, 1985).

[96]Marathon Petroleum Co., 89 LA 716 (Grimes, 1987); Georgia Power Co., 87 LA 800 (Byars, 1986).

[97]Crucible Materials Corp., 94 LA 540 (Harkless, 1989).

[98]Trailways, Inc., 88 LA 1073 (Goodman, 1987).

[99]Southern Cal. Gas Co., 89 LA 393 (Alleyne, 1987).

[100]Union Oil Co. of Cal., 88 LA 91 (Weiss, 1986).

case the arbitrator upheld the suspension of an employee who had a positive drug test, with no proof of on-the-job use, citing the employer's duty and right to provide a safe working environment.[101]

*2. Off-Duty Alcohol Use.* Because alcohol consumption is not illegal, off-duty use of alcohol without some exacerbating factor (arrest, fight, traffic accident, etc.) is typically not the subject of workplace discipline. As with other forms of off-duty conduct, arbitrators usually require the employer to establish some nexus between its interest as employer and the employee's off-duty drinking.[102] Discipline for off-duty drinking often occurs where an employee is convicted of driving while intoxicated. If the employee's job does not involve driving for the employer, arbitrators are unlikely to sustain the discharge.[103] Where the employee's job is to drive for the employer, arbitrators may[104] or may not[105] hold that off-duty driving under the influence is cause for discharge.[106] Even where the employee has his license to drive his personal vehicle suspended, if he retains his right to drive in his professional capacity an arbitrator may not uphold a discharge.

Arbitrators are more likely, however, to sustain discharges for off-duty driving under the influence when the employee is driving a company vehicle[107] or where work rules permit discharge for violations of criminal law.[108] Even without a driving-under-the-influence conviction, arbitrators uphold terminations when off-duty drinking habits cause work performance to deteriorate,[109] result in absence,[110] or cause the employee to commit offenses at the plant[111] or where the employer can show the off-duty drinking affects the employer's reputation.[112] For example, a discharge was upheld when an officer of the Ohio state highway patrol was convicted for driving under the influence.[113] The arbitrator found the incident harmed the employer's reputation, rendered the employee unable to perform his assigned duties, and led other employees to refuse or be reluctant to work with the grievant.

---

[101]Union Oil of Cal., 87 LA 297 (Boner, 1985).

[102]Ideal Elec. Co., 98 LA 410 (Heekin, 1991).

[103]U.S. Plywood Corp., 88 LA 275 (Matthews, 1986); Michigan City Sch. Corp., 91 LA 1244 (Eagle, 1989); Lamb Glass Co., 32 LA 420 (Dworkin, 1959).

[104]Pan Am World Servs., Inc., 86 LA 891 (Ferguson, 1986).

[105]L.F. Widmann, Inc., 99 LA 1173 (Dunn, 1992).

[106]J.F. Cassidy, Inc., 97 LA 801 (Oberdank, 1991).

[107]General Tire Serv., 52 LA 1279 (Todd, 1969).

[108]Cities Serv. Oil Corp., 41 LA 1091 (Oppenheim, 1963).

[109]Green River Steel Co., 49 LA 117 (Chalfie, 1967).

[110]Id.; American Airlines, Inc., 46 LA 737 (Sembower, 1966) (discharge justified when employee missed shift because he was in jail "sleeping off" his drunkenness).

[111]Inland Container Co., 28 LA 312 (Ferguson, 1957) (discharge justified when intoxicated off-duty employee entered plant and threatened fellow employee).

[112]Lockheed Aircraft Corp., 37 LA 906 (Roberts, 1961).

[113]Ohio, 94 LA 533 (Sharpe, 1990).

3. *Criminal Conviction as a Basis for Discipline.*   The sole basis for discipline may be off-duty conduct that led to an employee's criminal conviction. In discussing discipline based upon a criminal conviction, arbitrators will distinguish among offenses for which the employee was convicted. Where the employee is convicted of selling drugs, arbitrators tend to look more unfavorably upon the employee.[114] The employee may be found to be a corrupting danger to other employees even in the absence of a showing that any drugs were sold or used on the employer premises.[115] When an employee is selling drugs, the employer may not be required to demonstrate direct harm to its reputation or business in order to prevail at arbitration.[116] Not all arbitrators agree that a conviction for the sale of drugs standing alone permits an employer to terminate the employee,[117] although a conviction for drug use has been found to warrant termination.[118] This is particularly the case where an employer or industry has a current problem with employee drug use.[119]

A significant number of arbitrators will not sustain a discipline when the sole ground for the action is the employee's criminal conviction for the off-duty use of drugs. Without a nexus between that and the employee's ability to perform the job, or a showing that the conviction had an adverse impact upon the employer's business, the discipline will not be sustained.[120] As one arbitrator stated:

> Although felonious off-duty conduct is far more likely to be deemed just cause for discharge than is a misdemeanor, it is clear that a felony conviction is not, per se, a sufficient basis for the discharge of an employee. That is so, whether or not the employer has an announced policy to that effect.[121]

The split among arbitrators is even greater where there is no specific policy prohibiting the use of drugs at any time. It is more likely that the arbitrator will refuse to find the necessary nexus without the

---

[114]Hofman Ind., 273AAA9 (Stulberg, 1981); Joy Mfg. Co., 68 LA 697 (Freeman, 1977); National Steel Corp., 60 LA 613 (McDermott, 1973).

[115]Trane Co., 96 LA 435 (Reynolds, 1991).

[116]Delta Beverage Group, 96 LA 454 (Baroni, 1991) (arrest published in newspaper); Martin-Marietta Aerospace, 87 LA 695 (Aronin, 1985).

[117]Brockway Pressed Metals, Inc., 98 LA 1211 (Mayer, 1992); W. R. Grace & Co., 93 LA 1210 (Odom, 1989) (employer properly concluded that the employee was a dealer; nevertheless, employer could not show any nexus between that activity and employee's job).

[118]Jersey Shore Steel Co., 100 LA 489 (Goulet, 1992).

[119]US Air, Inc., 91 LA 6 (Ables, 1988) (an ongoing investigation into employee drug use at the airline provided the nexus between employee conduct and the job).

[120]Textron Lycoming, 104 LA 1043 (Duff, 1995); Schnuck Mkts., 102 LA 1016 (Suardi, 1994) (while recognizing how laudable a zero-tolerance policy might be, without a nexus to the workplace being shown, the discipline could not be sustained); Scott Paper Co., 100 LA 1113 (Carney, 1993).

[121]Hill & Kahn, "Discipline and Discharge for Off-Duty Misconduct: What Are the Arbitral Standards?" in Proceedings of the 39th Annual Meeting, National Academy of Arbitrators, 121, 152 (BNA Books, 1986).

existence of a zero-tolerance policy. This issue again arises most often in connection with criminal convictions for off-duty use. The absence of a rule, coupled with a failure by the employer to offer any evidence that the employee was impaired on the job, has been found to warrant overturning the discharge.[122] Other arbitrators have refused to affirm an employer's decision to terminate an employee unless the employer can demonstrate "a clear showing of 'adverse impact' on the Employer's enterprise."[123]

*4. Discipline Assessed While Criminal Charges Pending.* Where an employee was merely charged with a crime, an arbitrator held that the employer could not terminate the employee because it violates the employee's due process rights.[124] Another arbitrator overturned a discharge where there was no nexus between the employee's off-duty misconduct (sale of drugs) and his conduct on the job.[125] Conversely, it has been found that an employer is entitled to terminate an employee promptly in order to prevent the potential adverse impact of drug activity on its business interests.[126] An employer that has already disciplined an employee for drug use may not discipline that employee again if the employee is subsequently indicted for the same offense that led to the first discipline. The second discipline exposes that employee to double jeopardy.[127] An employee can be suspended pending the resolution of the criminal matter, but a rule providing for such suspension must also provide for back pay if the employee is ultimately acquitted.[128]

### F. Mitigating and Aggravating Circumstances in Alcohol-Related Discipline

Even where the arbitrator determines that an employee violated an alcohol-related work rule, mitigating factors will be considered in determining the fairness of the employer's disciplinary action. For example, arbitrators have been persuaded to mitigate a discharge

---

[122]Crucible Materials Corp., 94 LA 540 (Harkless, 1989).

[123]Brockway Pressed Metals, 98 LA 1211, 1214 (Mayer, 1992) (employee pleaded guilty to delivery of a controlled substance; employer was unable to demonstrate any adverse impact upon its business).

[124]Babcock & Wilcox, 102 LA 104 (Nicolas, 1994) (employer's policy and past practice was not to terminate employee based only on arrest).

[125]Lockheed Aeronautical Sys. Co., 92 LA 669 (Jewett, 1989).

[126]National Steel Corp., 60 LA 613 (McDermott, 1973).

[127]Southern Nuclear Operating Co., 102 LA 97 (Abrams, 1993).

[128]Vista Chem. Co., 92 LA 329 (Duff, 1989) (the promulgated rule stated that any employee charged with a drug-related crime would immediately be suspended; such a rule, the arbitrator noted, is seriously flawed without explicitly containing a provision for back pay).

where the employee consumed only a small amount of alcohol.[129] Arbitrators are also typically reluctant to uphold disciplinary actions for alcohol possession when the employer condones drinking through actual tolerance[130] or lax enforcement of a rule.[131] Where an employer had previously provided beer at meetings, the arbitrator overturned the suspension of an employee who brought his own beer to the meeting.[132] Similarly, arbitrators examine how the employer has treated like employees under similar circumstances in determining the propriety of alcohol-related disciplinary actions.[133] Arbitrators also require that an employer impose discipline when it first becomes aware of the alcohol-related offense. If the employer fails to do so, the discipline may be mitigated.[134] Similarly, where a supervisor who should have known the employee was intoxicated sent him out to operate a snow plow, he could not later be discharged for being under the influence.[135]

There are two distinct arbitral approaches to alcohol in the workplace. Some arbitrators take a straightforward approach. If the work rule was violated, properly assessed disciplinary action or discharge will be sustained. Other arbitrators view alcoholism as a disease that needs special attention and possibly intervention by the employer, and will take an approach that provides an opportunity for the employee to seek treatment and rehabilitation.

Arbitrators often consider mitigating a discharge when the employee has sought treatment for alcohol abuse. Thus, where an employee declined to disclose that his absence was for residential treatment of alcohol abuse, an arbitrator overturned the discharge.[136] An employee whose 6-day absence was for the residential portion of an alcoholism treatment program was reinstated.[137] It is not uncommon

---

[129]Marriott Host Int'l, 94 LA 862 (Rule, 1990) (restaurant improperly discharged bus person without written warning for consuming one vodka and orange juice while on duty; he was not drunk or impaired and there was no adverse publicity for the employer); McCormick & Baxter Creosoting Co., 55 LA 1274 (Jacobs, 1971) (discharge found to be too severe where, among other things, the employee only drank two bottles of beer).

[130]Commercial Warehouse Co., 100 LA 247 (Woolf, 1992).

[131]Riverview Supper Club, 82-2 ARB ¶ 8467 (Jacobowski, 1982); Golden Operations, CWC Casting Div. of Textron, Inc., 80-2 ARB ¶ 8543 (Ipavec, 1980) (discharge of employee who took a few sips of beer from the company's cabinet area was improper where management was aware of the concealment of beer and whiskey in the cabinet area, but failed to remove the liquor).

[132]Keebler Co., 88 LA 183 (Belcher, 1986).

[133]Youngstown Hosp. Ass'n, 82 LA 31 (Miller, 1983) (discharge improper when prior to discharge employer had knowledge of employee's alcohol dependence and employer had reinstated another employee with a similar problem).

[134]Montgomery Area Transit Sys., Div. of OMG, Inc., 100 LA 649 (Williams, 1993) (transit company improperly discharged bus driver after learning he had been convicted of off-duty driving under the influence, which was 6 months after driver told supervisor he had been drinking and had been arrested, where contract requires employer to take action within 5 days of knowledge of offense).

[135]City of Kankakee, 97 LA 564 (Wolff, 1991).

[136]Growmar, Inc., 100 LA 785 (Ver Ploeg, 1993).

[137]Phillip U.S.A., 99 LA 1016 (Volz, 1992).

for arbitrators to reinstate employees who have sought treatment for alcohol abuse subsequent to their termination.[138] Similarly, arbitrators may reinstate employees who have committed alcohol-related offenses on the condition that they enter treatment programs.[139] On the other hand, where the employer has permitted the employee to go through treatment and the treatment is ineffective, the arbitrator will often find the discharge proper.[140]

The foremost aggravating factor considered by arbitrators is employment in safety-sensitive positions. Arbitrators frequently uphold discharges for alcohol-related offenses by employees in safety-sensitive jobs because the activity impacts on the health and safety of the employee or his fellow employees.[141]

---

[138]Northwest Airlines, 89 LA 943 (Nicolau, 1984) (reinstatement of pilot who underwent alcohol treatment program); Ohio River Co., 83 LA 211 (Hewitt, 1984) (employer improperly discharged deckhand who admitted he had been drinking when he fell overboard, where grievant admitted that he had an alcohol problem, had joined and become an active participant in Alcoholics Anonymous, and had not had a drink since the accident); Thrifty Drug Stores, Inc., 56 LA 789 (Peters, 1971) (employer not justified in discharging employee who suffered relapse in his drinking problem following extended medical leave during which he enrolled in an alcoholism clinic); Armstrong Cork Co., 56 LA 527 (Wolff, 1971) (employee discharged due to alcohol-related absence is reinstated in part because he has joined Alcoholics Anonymous and regularly attended its meetings); Texaco Inc., 42 LA 408 (Prasow, 1963) (even though employee had been warned and suspended and was drunk and drinking on the job, discharge was too severe; employee was reinstated without back pay on basis of his long-term employment, and he had obtained medical help since his discharge and was involved in a rehabilitation program).

[139]Eaton Corp., 99 LA 331 (Lewis, 1992) (discharge of alcoholic employee for excessive absenteeism reduced to suspension and employee directed to attend Alcoholics Anonymous meetings and give supervisor written statement establishing such attendance); Morgan Adhesives Co., 87 LA 1039 (Abrams, 1986) (alcoholic who was discharged for poor attendance ordered reinstated without back pay on condition that he continue to attend Alcoholics Anonymous meeting regularly for 1 year); General Tel. Co. of Ind., Inc., 86-1 ARB ¶ 8012 (Winton, 1985) (employee who reported to work after imbibing reinstated on condition that he show proof of enrollment in a hospital-administered alcoholism program); Standard Packaging Corp., 71 LA 445 (Fogelberg, 1978) (alcoholic employee terminated for giving false reason for absenteeism reinstated provided he can demonstrate that his alcoholism can be controlled).

[140]Container Prods., 95 LA 1129 (Suardi, 1990) (just cause existed for discharge where employee violated reinstatement agreement by not continuing alcoholism treatment program); Bayou Steel Corp., 92 LA 726 (Chumley, 1989) (employee who had voluntarily participated in an employer-sponsored drug and alcohol treatment program was properly discharged for being intoxicated when he reported to work).

[141]Pittsburg & Midway Coal Mining Co., 91 LA 431 (Cohen, 1988) (coal miner whose blood alcohol exceeded state intoxication standards was properly discharged, since intoxicated employees in coal mining environment present significant hazard to themselves and co-workers); Cleveland Bd. of Educ., 90-1 ARB ¶ 8070 (Van Pelt, 1988) (school bus driver); Freeman United Coal Co., 82 LA 861 (Roberts, 1984) (roadgrader properly discharged when he operated machinery while intoxicated and careened off the road into a creek injuring himself and the grader); Asarco, Inc., 76 LA 163 (Grooms, 1981) (employer properly discharged alcoholic mineworker because even brief omission of mine safety practices can lead to serious injury or death of employee or other employees); Jehl Cooperage Co., 75 LA 901 (Odom, 1980) (employer properly discharged punchpress operator for having bottle of gin in dressing room, even though evidence was submitted of variations in kind and degree of penalty assessed for breaking alcohol-related rules, since punchpress operator's job is very dangerous); Day & Zimmerman, Inc., 75 LA 699 (Sisk, 1980) (employee who makes live ammunition at ammunitions plant properly discharged for reporting to work under the influence); Beatrice Foods, 73 LA 191 (Thornell, 1979) (forklift operator properly discharged for drinking during noontime break); City of Milwaukee, 71 LA 329 (Maslanka, 1978) (cranelift operator).

## G. Drug Testing

Drug testing has become the leading method employers use to detect drug use. Increased testing has caused an increase in employee concerns over their privacy rights[142] and raised questions about the legitimacy of the testing procedures themselves.[143]

*1. As a Subject of Bargaining.*   The National Labor Relations Board (NLRB) has held that drug testing of current employees is a mandatory subject of bargaining,[144] but that testing job applicants is not.[145] As with any mandatory subject of bargaining, a union may waive its right to bargain over the matter during negotiations. It can expressly agree to a drug-testing policy, or it can impliedly agree to testing by agreeing to the adoption of a broad management rights clause.[146] The NLRB has deferred to arbitration the question of whether a management rights clause permits the employer to unilaterally adopt a drug-testing policy.[147]

In evaluating unilaterally implemented drug-testing policies, arbitrators look to the past practice of the parties. If there has been a history of the employer unilaterally promulgating various work rules, a rule addressing drug testing can be unilaterally implemented.[148] Where there has been no clear past practice, arbitrators require employers to bargain with the union over the implementation of the policy before they will enforce it. Discipline has been set aside where the policy was not bargained by the parties.[149] This is true even if the employee tested positive for drugs.[150] To arbitrators who refuse to sustain discipline under unilaterally imposed policies, the implementation of a drug-testing procedure involves "a very significant alteration of working conditions."[151]

Although it has been argued that drug testing violates Fourth Amendment rights against unlawful search and seizure, Fourth Amendment safeguards have been found inapplicable in the private sector.[152] That is not the case in the public sector.[153]

---

[142]Vulcan Materials Co., 90 LA 1161 (Caraway, 1988).

[143]Shell Oil Co., 90 LA 286 (McDermott, 1988); Day & Zimmerman, Inc., 88 LA 1001 (Heinsz, 1987), Chase Bag Co., 88 LA 441 (Straffhofer, 1986).

[144]Kysor Indus. Corp., 307 NLRB 598, 140 LRRM 1127 (1992); Johnson-Bateman Co., 295 NLRB 180, 131 LRRM 1393 (1989).

[145]Star Tribune Div., 295 NLRB, 543, 131 LRRM 1404 (1989).

[146]Chicago Tribune Co. v. NLRB, 974 F.2d 933, 141 LRRM 2209 (7th Cir., 1992).

[147]Southern Cal. Edison Co., 310 NLRB 1229, 143 LRRM 1073 (1993).

[148]Stone Container Corp., 95 LA 729 (Nolan, 1990); Bay Area Rapid Transit, 88 LA 1 (Concepcion 1986); Gem City Chems., 86 LA 1023 (Warns, 1986).

[149]Utah Power & Light Co., 94 LA 239 (Winograd, 1990).

[150]Crown Zellerbach Corp., 87 LA 1145 (Cohen, 1986).

[151]Laidlaw Transit, 89 LA 1001, 1018 (Allen, 1987).

[152]Bistate Dev. Agency, 72 LA 198 (Newmark, 1979).

[153]Department of the Army, 92 LA 995 (Concepcion, 1989).

2. *As Federally Mandated.*   In various industries, such as truck-ing, the federal government has required employers to implement drug testing. Where the testing is mandated by the government, arbitrators have applied the governmental regulations regardless of whether the employer negotiated with the union first. Federal regula-tions supersede the duty to bargain, but only to the extent that specific requirements are mandated. Issues not specifically addressed by the regulations, such as discipline and rehabilitation, remain mandatory subjects of bargaining.[154]

3. *Testing Issues.*   If the testing policy is valid, there are three questions. Under what circumstances may the employee be tested? Was the testing procedure proper? What happens when an employee tests positive for the presence of a controlled substance?

a. When Employer May Test.   Drug testing is either for some cause (accident, reasonable suspicion) or random. There are some industries in which government regulations require testing and spec-ify that it shall be random.[155] Employer policies may provide for test-ing, but only when there is reasonable cause to believe the employee is using drugs. Arbitrators have been asked to address both when an employer may test employees and whether a particular test was justified under the specific facts.

i. Random Testing.   Some employers have policies that include a provision for random testing. These policies meet with mixed reac-tions from arbitrators. Unless there are very compelling circum-stances—a very dangerous workplace or a documented drug use prob-lem—arbitrators probably will not find random drug testing to be reasonable. Random testing has been found reasonable where the workplace is extremely hazardous and the employer is responsible for promoting and maintaining safe working conditions,[156] for bus drivers where safety is a major concern,[157] and for employees in a petroleum refinery[158] and a nuclear power plant.[159]

Random testing to improve safety is a legitimate concern when the employer has a particularly safety-sensitive business operation.[160]

---

[154]Amerigas, 102 LA 1185 (Marino, 1994) (employer was required to adopt the Department of Transportation regulations requiring random drug tests and was not permitted to adopt other policies that exceeded the DOT regulations without negotiating with the union over these additions); Columbia Gas of Ohio, 102 LA 85 (Cohen, 1993).

[155]In Columbia Gas of Ohio, supra note 154, the arbitrator noted the grievant, a pipe-fitter, held a safety-sensitive position subject to random drug tests pursuant to U.S. Department of Transportation regulations.

[156]Dow Chem. Co., 91 LA 1385 (Baroni, 1989). See also preceding section.

[157]S.C. Elec. & Gas Co., 91 LA 1385 (Baroni, 1989).

[158]Texas City Ref., 89 LA 845 (Boals, 1987).

[159]Arkansas Power & Light, 88 LA 1065 (Weisbrod, 1987).

[160]Day & Zimmermann, 94 LA 399 (Nicholas, 1990) (the highly explosive materials being produced at the plant is sufficient justification for a "stringent testing program").

In *Dow Chemical Co.*[161] the arbitrator in upholding a random drug test program stated:

> *Reasonableness of Random Testing:* The arbitrator is of the opinion that the Company's decision to implement random testing was a reasonable one, under the circumstances which existed in early 1987. Chemical plants are extremely hazardous work environments (as agreed to by both parties). The propensity for serious accidents is always present, and the Company has the responsibility, under Article XIV, of "promoting and maintaining safe . . . working conditions" within the plant. Evidence of a serious drug problem certainly did exist, and it appeared to be extensive throughout the plant at the time. The Company's conclusion that its "for cause" testing program was ineffective in identifying drug use among its employees, was a rational one. And, under the circumstances of increasing drug use, as indicated by the events of early 1987, the Company was acting reasonably in its decision to implement random testing among its hourly employees.[162]

However, random drug testing in hazardous workplaces, such as chemical plants, has not been universally upheld where the arbitrator found random testing required employees to give evidence against themselves[163] and where the employer failed to submit any evidence of special drug-related problems or evidence of drug-related accidents in the workplace.[164] Also, a random drug-testing policy was not sustained where an arbitrator believed random testing was an unwarranted, unjustified intrusion into the private lives of employees.[165] Random testing usually has been upheld as reasonable where it is part of a post-rehabilitation program or part of a last-chance agreement.[166]

ii. Reasonable Suspicion Testing.   Most policies call for testing when the employer has a reasonable basis, or probable cause, to believe that the employee is impaired on the job. Consequently, arbitrators have been asked to review the explanations of employers as to why the order for testing was given. These types of cases fall into two distinct categories: (1) cases in which the employee took the test and it turned out positive for a controlled substance; and (2) cases in which the employee refused to take the test and was disciplined, either for insubordination or because the policy specified discipline for refusal. The discussion of whether cause existed in the first place is the same in both categories, but the ultimate award may not be.

There is some question among arbitrators as to the standard to be used in ascertaining whether cause existed. Generally, "[a]rbitrators are not requiring employers to have sufficient evidence to support

---

[161]91 LA 1385 (Baroni, 1989).

[162]Id. at 1390.

[163]Vulcan Materials Co., 90 LA 1161 (Caraway, 1988).

[164]Day & Zimmermann, 88 LA 1001 (Heinsz, 1987).

[165]Boston Edison Co., 92 LA 374 (Nicolau, 1988) (random test of any employee seeking promotion was invalid).

[166]Koppers Co., 91 LA 363 (Yarowsky, 1988); General Elec. Co., 91 LA 400 (Allen, 1988).

a criminal indictment before they compel an employee to undergo a drug test."[167] Varying fact patterns have been reviewed by arbitrators when discussing reasonable cause. Where an employee has demonstrated a past pattern of drug use, coupled with certain symptoms caused by that use, testing can be ordered if those symptoms arise again.[168] Certainly, the smell of marijuana can provide a basis for ordering testing, especially when the employee appears to be hiding at the time.[169] A test also may be ordered when the employee's supervisor observes erratic behavior by the employee.[170] On the other hand, a news report followed by the employee's arrest without any other evidence has been found to be insufficient.[171] Many employers automatically require employees to submit to a test if they are involved in an accident.[172] Not all arbitrators believe that any accident, standing by itself, justifies testing.[173] Reasonable cause to demand a drug test may become evident in conjunction with a drug search. For example, in *Georgia Power Co.*[174] the arbitrator found the employer had reasonable basis for testing an employee after a trained search dog alerted twice on the employee's car while parked on company property and the employee admitted prior use of marijuana.

iii. Other Cause for Testing. Employers also have used preemployment physicals, workplace accidents or injury, return-to-work or periodic physicals, and return from extended absence as reasons for drug testing. Using accidents to trigger drug testing is a controversial issue in arbitration. Under some employers' programs, employees involved in accidents (usually those that cause or could have caused physical injury or substantial property damage) may be required to submit to testing. If a policy does not contain an unequivocal provision for postaccident testing, arbitrators probably will find the employer had no basis for demanding a drug test.[175] On the other hand, when accidents are combined with evidence of possible drug or alcohol use, or the accidents are very serious and appropriate provisions exist, an employer usually has a basis to demand a drug test.[176]

---

[167]Warehouse Distrib. Ctrs., 90 LA 979, 982 (Weiss, 1987).

[168]Delaware, 104 LA 845 (Gorman, 1993) (employee had recurring problem of failing to report to work without calling first; this same pattern was evident earlier when employee was using cocaine).

[169]Borg-Warner Corp., 99 LA 209 (Bethel, 1992) (employee was found in secluded area; there was a strong smell of marijuana).

[170]Coca-Cola Bottling Co., 97 LA 343 (Weckstein, 1991); Linde Gases of the Midwest, 94 LA 225 (Nielsen, 1989).

[171]Phillips Indus., 93 LA 1133 (Dills, 1989).

[172]Portland Police Bureau, 104 LA 647 (Henner, 1995).

[173]City of Texas City, 104 LA 534 (Allen, 1995); Stone Container Corp., 95 LA 729 (Nolan, 1990); Tribune Co., 93 LA 201 (Crane, 1989).

[174]93 LA 846 (Holley, 1989).

[175]Tribune Co., 93 LA 201 (Crane, 1989); Stone Container Corp., 91 LA 1186 (Ross, 1988).

[176]Regional Transp. Dist., 92 LA 213 (Goldstein, 1988); Boise Cascade Corp., 90 LA 105 (Hart, 1987); Corondelet Coke Corp., 81 ARB ¶ 918084.

Some employers have added drug and alcohol tests to annual or periodic physical examinations, or required them when employees return to work following extended absences, or as part of a licensing process such as the Department of Transportation's medical certification for truck drivers. These tests must be part of the negotiated testing policy because the right to require a physical examination does not necessarily include the right to require a drug or alcohol test.[177]

Where there is a requirement that employees returning from extended absence have to meet the employer's physical requirements, where all employees are required to take an annual physical exam, and where the inclusion of a drug and alcohol test as part of a physical exam has been found reasonable and nondiscriminatory, arbitrators have upheld provisions for testing.[178]

b. Testing Procedures.   Arbitrators require that testing procedures include the proper protocol to ensure the integrity of the sample, to protect the privacy rights of the employee, and to ensure the accuracy of the results. There are certain standards that a testing facility must maintain to ensure due process to the employee. The "procedures, quality, and credentials of a test lab is a key issue in drug testing."[179] Laboratory quality and reliability can be challenged. When a laboratory is fully licensed by a state and certified by various professional organizations, the challenges have not been accepted by arbitrators.[180]

Generally, test protocols require that the sample be subjected to two tests that produce positive results before an employee will be considered to demonstrate evidence of past drug use. Initially a preliminary screening test, usually an immunoassay, is administered. If this test is positive, some form of confirmation test, using a different method, is administered.

The most commonly used confirmatory test is the gas chromatography/mass spectrometry test. In almost every decision where the validity of the test results are the issue, the arbitrator has accepted the test results of a two-step procedure that includes GC/MS confirmation.[181] The U.S. Supreme Court noted the reliability of results when tests are conducted by an immunoassay screen followed by a

---

[177]California Rapid Transit Dist., 92 LA 995 (Concepcion, 1989); ITT Barton Indus., 89 LA 1196 (Draznin, 1987).

[178]Stanadyne, 91 LA 993 (Fullmer, 1988); Amoco Oil Co., 88 LA 1010 (Weisenberger, 1987); Alcan Aluminum Co., 88 LA 386 (Kindig, 1986).

[179]Westinghouse Elec., 99 LA 201, 208 (Allen, 1992) (employee properly refused test ordered by a customer of the employer, where the customer refused to offer any information on the quality or procedure for the lab that it utilized; employee offered to be tested at an independent facility).

[180]Valvoline Oil Co., 89 LA 209 (Briscoe, 1989) (lab was licensed by state of Illinois, the U.S. Drug Enforcement Administration, the Illinois Dangerous Drug Commission, the College of American Pathologists, and the Department of Health and Human Services).

[181]Sharpless Coal Corp., 91 LA 1065 (Stoltenberg, 1988).

GC/MS confirmation.[182] Arbitrators have held that an employee who tests positive on a screening test must be given a more reliable confirmatory test before he can be disciplined.[183] Similarly, a termination will not be upheld where the employee has been given two of the same tests, and one shows a positive and the other a negative result.[184]

In addition to the type of test and the reliability of the lab, the employer must demonstrate an unbroken chain of custody.[185] When there is a mix-up in the documentation that is supposed to record the chain of custody, or no documentation exists to support that chain, the arbitrator may question the integrity of the sample and sustain the grievance.[186] It is not necessary for the employer to prove test results by calling the lab individual who performed the test analysis as a witness if the test is performed by an independent lab and there is no actual evidence of tampering.[187] The same is true if the lab and testing procedures are governed by federal regulations.[188]

A drug-testing policy can be invalid on its face if the procedures are deemed unfair. For example, a policy that requires the employee to be observed by another while giving a urine sample has been found to be an unwarranted invasion of the employee's privacy.[189] Where there are extreme safety threats, however, observed collection may be approved. In *Arkansas Power & Light*,[190] observed urine collection was approved in a nuclear power plant. Similarly, if the agreement spells out certain procedures and those procedures are violated, the test and the results can be voided.[191]

c. Effect of Positive Test.  There has been little agreement among arbitrators as to whether a positive drug test standing by itself is a legitimate reason to discharge or discipline an employee. Most arbitrators discuss the necessity for a nexus between the positive test and the employer's business. The basic rule that an employee's off-duty conduct is of no concern to the employer is balanced against the right of the employer to maintain a drug-free workplace. Not all arbitrators have agreed upon where that balance is struck.

---

[182]Skinner v. Railway Labor Executives Ass'n, 109 S.Ct. 1402, 130 LRRM 2857 (1989).

[183]Day & Zimmermann, 94 LA 399 (Nicholas, 1990).

[184]Southern Cal. Rapid Transit Dist., 101 LA 10 (Gentile, 1991).

[185]Delaware, 104 LA 845 (Gorman, 1995); Valvoline Oil Co., 89 LA 209 (Briscoe, 1987).

[186]Phoenix Transit Sys., 89 LA 973 (Speroff, 1987) (inconsistent chain of custody documents); Day & Zimmerman, 88 LA 1001 (Heinsz, 1987) (no chain of custody documentation).

[187]United Parcel Serv., 101 LA 589 (Briggs, 1993); Valvoline Oil Co., 89 LA 209 (Briscoe, 1987).

[188]Bethlehem Steel Corp., 102 LA 1211 (Doeken, 1993).

[189]Sharpless Coal Corp., 91 LA 1065 (Stoltenberg, 1988).

[190]88 LA 1065 (Weisbrod, 1987).

[191]Chevron, U.S.A., 95 LA 395 (Riker, 1990) (the collective bargaining agreement required employees to get regular physical exams, including a drug test, with the results of the exams to be kept confidential; the lab gave the results to the employer when an employee tested positive; subsequent discipline set aside).

It is helpful to look at the views of scientists to understand why there is disagreement over the sufficiency of a positive test result as the sole ground for termination. Leading scientists agree that "[t]esting does only one thing. It detects what is being tested. It does not tell us anything about the recency of the use. It does not tell us how the person was exposed to the drug, it doesn't even tell us whether it affected performance."[192] Arbitrators naturally ask, "What is the nexus to the job?" It may be that the drug and alcohol policy itself spells out the nexus. For example, the employer and the union may agree that a positive test result is automatically considered job impairment. Even if the policy does not equate a positive test result to impairment, it can still be a sufficient basis to justify discipline. If the employer is engaged in a highly hazardous activity, has adopted a drug-free workplace policy, and clearly informs employees they will be subject to discipline or discharge if there is evidence of drug use in the employee's system while he or she is at work, a positive test result has been held sufficient for termination.[193]

Another possible explanation for arbitrators differing on this subject is the nature of the employer's business. Arbitrators are more likely to find a nexus between the drug use and the workplace in inherently dangerous fields, even when there is no showing that the employee was impaired while at work.[194] In addition, where the public safety is involved, a positive test result alone will often suffice as a basis for termination.[195] One arbitrator found that employer concern for employee safety and the nature of the drug problem in society is of such importance that it justifies a policy that discourages any use of drugs on or off duty. Thus, discipline was upheld for a positive test result alone.[196] This is a minority view.

It is unlikely that most arbitrators will sustain a termination on the basis of a positive test result alone where the employer policy prohibits employees only from being impaired on the job.[197] Where an employee manifests no symptoms of being under the influence at work and there is no announced policy that *any* positive test result can support discipline, arbitrators refuse to enforce a termination.[198]

---

[192]Denenberg & Denenberg, "Employee Drug Testing and the Arbitrator: What Are the Issues?" 42 Arb. J. 26 (June, 1987).

[193]Mason & Hangar-Silas Mason Co., 103 LA 371 (Cipolla, 1994) (employer operated a nuclear facility; given the nature of the business and the policy adopted by the employer, no showing of a nexus between the test result and the job was required).

[194]Dravo Lime Co., 105 LA 54 (Imundo, 1995) (employer was a mining company; consequently, safety was paramount).

[195]Southern Cal. Rapid Transit, 96 LA 20 (Gentile, 1990); Mayflower Contract Servs., 91 LA 1353 (Petermann, 1988).

[196]Vista Chem. Co., 99 LA 994, 997 (Baroni, 1992) (drug policy "should not be undermined by application to narrow interpretation suggesting that correlation between use and impairment is paramount").

[197]Dial Corp., 99 LA 176 (Gordon, 1992).

[198]Georgia Pac. Corp., 86 LA 411 (Clarke, 1985).

To prevail, the employer must introduce evidence of impairment on the job in addition to the positive test result.[199]

d. *Refusing a Drug Test Order.*[200]   The general rule is "work now, grieve later," but there are exceptions. If the employee is protesting an unwarranted invasion of privacy, winning an arbitration will not protect the employee from an unwarranted invasion of privacy.[201] Some arbitrators will not sustain discipline of an employee who refuses to submit to a drug test where the employer fails to prove it had a reasonable belief that the employee was impaired[202] or where the refusal is a reasonable protest against invasion of the employee's privacy.[203] Other arbitrators feel that any alleged invasion of privacy does not supersede the basic premise that one must obey first and grieve later. They may, however, mitigate the penalty.[204]

It is possible for an employer to waive its right to challenge a refusal to take a drug test. For example, where an employee was unable to provide a urine sample and was told to go home and try again the next day, the employer could not discipline the employee for refusing to give a sample.[205]

## H. Employee Assistance Programs

In order to encourage employees with drug and alcohol problems to seek assistance, many employers have developed employee assistance programs (EAPs). These programs allow employees to obtain help for their problem before it is too late for them to save their jobs or themselves. Many employer drug policies specifically state that if employees voluntarily enter the program before testing positive or being accused of impairment, discipline will not be assessed.[206]

An employer's obligation to accommodate employees who have performance problems due to drugs will be reduced where it has an EAP available which preserves employee confidentiality.[207] The absence of an EAP may persuade an arbitrator to overturn or stay a

---

[199]Universal Frozen Foods, 97 LA 1113 (Downing, 1991); United Techs. Carrier, 92 LA 829 (Williams, 1989).

[200]See Chapter 7 for a discussion of test falsification.

[201]See Chapter 7 for a discussion of cooperating in testing.

[202]Pioneer Flour Mills, 101 LA 816 (Bankston, 1993); Tribune Co., 93 LA 201 (Crane, 1989).

[203]Utah Power & Light, 94 LA 233 (Winograd, 1990); Gem City Chems., Inc., 86 LA 1023 (Warns, 1986); Union Plaza Hotel, 88 LA 528 (McKay, 1986).

[204]Pepsi-Cola Bottling Co., 93 LA 520 (Randall, 1989) (failure to prove a reasonable basis for the test warranted lowering the penalty from termination to a suspension).

[205]Moore-Handley, Inc., 102 LA 813 (Grooms, 1994).

[206]Columbia Gas of Ohio, 102 LA 85 (Cohen, 1993).

[207]Southern Cal. Permanente Med. Group, 92 LA 41, 46 (Richman, 1989) (employer failed to establish employee was selling drugs at the workplace; arbitrator did find employee was a drug user who should be treated "no better and no worse than any other drug user under the policy adopted by the Employer"); Kimberly-Clark Corp., 92-1 ARB ¶ 8270 (Strozdas, 1991).

termination until the employee has had the opportunity to participate in a rehabilitation program.[208] The employee's willingness to participate is, of course, a necessary condition.[209]

An employer may believe that an employee has a problem even if the employee denies that a drug or alcohol problem exists. The employer may then seek to direct the employee to obtain help, notwithstanding the employee's denial. Some arbitrators have held that when the employer can establish that the employee has used drugs, the employer can require the employee to enter the EAP as a condition of continued employment.[210] Other arbitrators have held the employer must not only prove that the employee used drugs, but also that the employee was impaired on the job or had a serious drug problem that required rehabilitation.[211]

Some employees argue that the existence of an EAP precludes discipline until they have been offered assistance. Unless the rules of the workplace provide for the employer to offer help,[212] the employer normally is not required to offer it.[213] Some policies do provide that the employer is required to offer help, but only when it can be shown that the employee is a good candidate for rehabilitation.[214] Absent that showing, discipline can be imposed.[215] Of course, the employer is required to treat its employees equally. Thus, when the employer has engaged in disparate treatment toward employees, the refusal to permit an employee to participate in an EAP in lieu of discipline can be challenged.[216] Where an employee refused an offer of rehabilitation, however, discharge was appropriate as the employer had no duty to, and indeed could not, make the employee enter rehabilitation.[217]

*1. Discipline of Employee Enrolled in an EAP.*   When employers offer employees assistance for psychological problems through an EAP

---

[208]Aeroquip Corp., 90-2 ARB ¶ 8550 (Stieber, 1990).

[209]Trane Co., 90-1 ARB ¶ 8113 (Redel, 1990).

[210]Southern Cal. Permanente Med. Group, 92 LA 41 (Richman, 1989).

[211]Crucible Materials Corp., 94 LA 540 (Harkness, 1989).

[212]Industrial Power Coatings, 103 LA 519 (Statham, 1994) (company had promulgated a rule that required the employer to offer the use of its EAP when it is reasonable to do so; burden was upon the employer to show that it was not reasonable in the particular case, and it failed to do so; fact that the employee did not acknowledge that he had an alcohol problem was not a sufficient basis upon which to deny help).

[213]Burger Iron Co., 92 LA 1100 (Dworkin, 1989); Performed Line Prods. Co., 88 LA 340 (Strasshofer, 1986).

[214]Thermo Eng'g Corp., 102 LA 612 (Dworkin, 1993) (employee had an attendance problem; treatment counselor testified that it could not be said that the employee's attendance would improve with treatment).

[215]Burns Aerospace Corp., 104 LA 1210 (Smith, 1995) (employer policy allowed the employer to discipline an employee who failed an alcohol test or to offer rehabilitation, and, interestingly, the company had only implemented a drug-testing policy; arbitrator held that a drug policy includes the use of alcohol).

[216]Welch Foods, 96 LA 962 (Feldman, 1991); Metropolitan Transit Auth., 93 LA 477 (Allen, 1989).

[217]Penwalt Corp., 86 LA 686 (Daniel, 1986).

there may be privacy concerns to which arbitrators attach significance if the employer does not permit the employee to confidentially disclose concerns to an in-house doctor or counselor through the EAP. Where the treating psychologist or psychiatrist was permitted to divulge information about the employee to the employer, without also allowing the employee a confidential means to express his concerns, the arbitrator was reluctant to uphold discipline against the employee on the ground that the employee's due process rights were violated.[218]

What happens when the employee slips while enrolled in the program? Where the employee has repeatedly failed to improve after several attempts at treatment, discipline will be sustained by an arbitrator.[219] Similarly, where the employee willfully refuses to follow the treatment program prescribed, a termination will be upheld.[220] Conversely, the discharge of an employee who missed only two counseling sessions in nine months was reduced to suspension.[221]

*2. The Employer's Right to Discipline an Addict or Alcoholic Who Has Voluntarily Sought Rehabilitation.* If the employee has sought help but has also committed an otherwise terminable offense, an arbitrator may be inclined to mitigate a discharge. One arbitrator posed four questions that should guide other arbitrators:[222]

1. What is the point at which the employee with an alcohol abuse problem no longer meets the basic requirements of the job?

2. Is the employee with an alcohol abuse problem entitled to one last chance to be rehabilitated before discharge?

3. What should be the relationship between an employee assistance program (EAP) and discipline of an employee with an alcohol abuse problem?

4. If management had "just cause" to discharge an employee with an alcohol abuse problem on the date of termination, may an arbitrator consider evidence of post-discharge rehabilitation as grounds for reinstatement?[223]

---

[218]City of Allentown, 100 LA 592 (Di Lauro, 1992) (where employee confided in EAP's doctor, and this confidence was disclosed to the employer which resulted in employee's discharge, the discharge was in violation of the employee's due process rights.)

[219]Eaton Corp., 94 LA 971 (Eiselo, 1990) (employee failed four treatment programs).

[220]Sterling Chems., 93 LA 953 (Taylor, 1989) (employee tested positive for drugs while in the treatment program as well as refusing to follow scheduling treatment).

[221]Exxon Co. U.S.A., 101 LA 997 (Sergent, 1993).

[222]Bornstein, "Getting to the Bottom of the Issue: How Arbitrators View Alcohol Abuse," 44 Arb. J. 46 (1989).

[223]Id. Arbitrator Bornstein also noted that arbitrators have developed three different approaches to answering these questions. Some believe that employees with an alcohol or drug problem should be treated no differently than any other employee. To them, alcoholism is volitional and should be treated as such. They believe no more leniency should be given to employees who are alcoholics than is given to any other employee. The second group believes that alcoholism is partly a disease and partly volitional. Rehabilitation will be considered by them, but only if sought before discharge. The last group of arbitrators treat alcoholism strictly as a "treatable disease" and consider postdischarge conduct relevant. Under this approach, as

Initially, the arbitrator must determine whether there is a relationship between an employee's drinking or drug problem and his problems at work. If there is a correlation, no mitigation is warranted.[224] If there is a connection, when must the employee seek help for this attempt at rehabilitation to be considered? Employees who seek help before they are discharged are viewed more favorably by arbitrators than employees who wait until after they have been discharged.[225] Most arbitrators will grant employees the necessary time, without facing discipline, for them to obtain the help they need for their problem. They must do so prior to being discharged. Under this theory, alcoholism or drug addiction is treated as a correctable disease.[226]

   *3. The Effect of Postdischarge Rehabilitation.*   Whether arbitrators will consider postdischarge rehabilitative efforts by terminated employees is an area of considerable controversy. Employers often are precluded from presenting evidence about postdischarge conduct on the basis it was not known at the time of termination and therefore was not a factor in the decision to terminate the employee. In the same vein, it is argued that employee conduct subsequent to discharge should not be given any consideration when it is positive. In cases involving substance abuse, postdischarge attempts at rehabilitation are sometimes considered in the context of determining whether the termination should be upheld.[227] The fact that the employer could not have known or considered the after-the-fact events remains relevant to the issue of remedy.

   There are two schools of arbitral thought. One school of arbitrators contend that "[n]o subsequent rehabilitation by the grievant can undermine the propriety of the Employer's decision to discharge nor does it vest the arbitrator with authority to second guess that decision."[228] This school may ask the employer to grant the employee clemency, but assert that there is no arbitral power to order it.[229]

   The second school of thought holds that postdischarge rehabilitation should be considered. The theory is that "[t]he prime purpose of industrial discipline is not to inflict punishment for wrongdoing, but

Arbitrator Bornstein observed, the fact that the employee obtained successful treatment for the disease removed the cause for termination, namely, alcoholism, which then enabled the employee to return to work.

   [224]Thermo King Corp., 102 LA 612 (Dworkin, 1993); Goodyear Tire & Rubber Co., 92 LA 91 (Dworkin, 1989).

   [225]Growmark, Inc., 100 LA 785 (Ver Ploeg, 1993); Toledo Molding & Die Corp., 88 LA 937 (Ipavec, 1987).

   [226]Bornstein, "Getting to the Bottom of the Issue: How Arbitrators View Alcohol Abuse," 44 Arb. J. 46 (1989).

   [227]Chrysler Corp., 40 LA 935 (Alexander, 1963); Texaco Inc., 42 LA 408 (Prasow, 1963).

   [228]Duquesne Light Co., 92 LA 907, 911 (Sergent, 1989).

   [229]P.H. Glatfeler Co., 103 LA 879 (Singer, 1994).

to correct individual faults and behavior and to prevent further infractions." To these arbitrators, therapy fulfills that function and should be considered.[230]

Not all arbitrators agree that there is a hard and fast rule that postdischarge rehabilitation should always or should never be considered. The particular facts of the case, for example, whether the employee has been given a prior chance, may affect that question.[231] Arbitrators who believe that postdischarge conduct is relevant are in the minority.[232] Most believe that only predischarge rehabilitation should be a factor.

## I. Last-Chance Agreements

*1. Purpose and Elements.* A last-chance agreement, as the name describes, provides the employee a final opportunity for rehabilitation instead of discharge for using alcohol or drugs.[233] As one arbitrator described such agreements:

> Last chance agreements ordinarily remove elements of just cause from an individual's job protections. They provide an employer a guarantee that an undesirable employee can be discharged if s/he does not improve. They are what they say they are—one *last* chance. They are bargained for and approved by unions when the probable alternative is an employee's dismissal. Last chance agreements are useful to bargaining units and employers alike. They save jobs for the present and (hopefully) lead to revitalization of an employee's compliant and productive performance.[234]

Another arbitrator noted the value to society that is served by last-chance agreements:

> Last Chance Agreements are supported as a matter of public policy. They serve a useful social function of salvaging the employment of employees whose jobs would otherwise be lost. Many times, the impact of a "Last Chance" Agreement will have sufficient shock value to rehabilitate an errant employee. If arbitrators did not enforce Last Chance Agreements, employers would cease to enter them, and the beneficial, social purpose which they serve would be lost to society generally and to members of the bargaining unit specifically.[235]

---

[230]Ashland Petroleum Co., 90 LA 681 (Volz, 1988); Texaco, Inc., 42 LA 408 (Prasow, 1963).

[231]Ocean Spray Cranberries, 105 LA 148 (Dichter, 1995).

[232]Atlantic Southeast Airlines, 101 LA 511 (Nolan, 1992); Pittsburgh & Midway Coal Co., 91 LA 431 (Cohen, 1988).

[233]See Chapter 12 for a general discussion of last-chance agreements.

[234]Genie Co., 97 LA 542, 545 (Dworkin, 1991).

[235]Porcelain Metals Corp., 73 LA 1133, 1138 (Roberts, 1979).

Last-chance agreements vary considerably in their terms, but those used in alcohol and drug cases have the following common elements:[236]

(1) The employee promises to refrain from use or abuse of alcohol, drugs, or both.

(2) The employee promises to participate in an employee assistance program or other rehabilitation program (e.g., Alcoholics Anonymous) and comply with program requirements.

(3) The employee agrees to submit to alcohol or drug screening randomly or under certain circumstances. Failure to do so constitutes a violation of the last-chance agreement.

(4) The employee agrees to maintain satisfactory performance and attendance.

(5) The employee understands that violation of any of the terms will result in immediate discharge.[237]

*2. Role of Arbitrator and Validity of Last-Chance Agreements.* Where the penalty for violation of the agreement has been specified, the role of the arbitrator is to determine only whether the grievant violated the last-chance agreement. As one arbitrator noted:

> The question of appropriate penalty is settled by the agreement of the parties, and usual constraints, such as progressive discipline or mitigating circumstances, need not be weighed by management and cannot be introduced by the Arbitration Board (footnote omitted).[238]

The Sixth Circuit Court of Appeals concluded that an arbitrator had exceeded his authority by reinstating an employee who had admittedly violated a last-chance agreement; the arbitrator had concluded that the penalty of discharge was too severe.[239] The court held that since the penalty of discharge had been established in the last-chance agreement, the arbitrator had no authority to amend the terms of that agreement.[240]

---

[236]See cases cited in notes 239 and 240, infra; see also Elkouri & Elkouri, Resolving Drug Issues, 106-08 (BNA Books, 1993).

[237]An example of a comprehensive last-chance agreement appears in General Elec. Co., 91 LA 400 (Allen, 1988). In that case, the arbitrator upheld the discharge on the basis that the employee violated a number of the terms of that last-chance agreement by not remaining drug free, by not participating continuously in treatment, and by missing work. See also Denenberg & Denenberg, Alcohol and Drugs: Issues in the Workplace, 139–41 (BNA Books, 1983).

[238]Linde Gases of the Midwest, 94 LA 225, 231 (Nielsen, 1989). See also University of Mich., 96 LA 688 (Sugerman, 1991).

[239]Bakers Local 326 v. ITT Continental Baking Co., 749 F.2d 350, 117 LRRM 3145 (6th Cir., 1984).

[240]Id. This principle was reaffirmed by the Sixth Circuit in Ohio Edison Co. v. Ohio Joint Council, 947 F.2d 786, 138 LRRM 2823 (6th Cir., 1991).

Some last-chance agreements provide that any violation of the terms deprives the employee of the right to resort to the grievance/arbitration procedure in the collective bargaining agreement. In one case, the employer asserted that the discharge was not substantively arbitrable. The arbitrator concluded the employee had not waived his right to grieve and arbitrate whether he was guilty of the misconduct, despite language in the last-chance agreement that "any future misconduct will result in discharge without recourse through the grievance procedure."[241] Similarly, an arbitrator found that a discharge was arbitrable even though the last-chance agreement authorized termination for its violation "without recourse to the grievance procedure." The arbitrator noted that an employee has a fundamental contractual right to grieve and be confronted in arbitration with the evidence against him and be given the opportunity to contest that evidence.[242] He found that the right to grieve and arbitrate was such a fundamental right that it could not be relinquished.[243]

The Third Circuit Court of Appeals found the issue of whether an employee violated a last-chance agreement was an arbitrable issue, despite a provision in the last-chance agreement that neither the employee nor the union had recourse to the grievance/arbitration procedure to protest the penalty. The court noted this language did not clearly and unambiguously describe the issue or issues to be excluded from arbitration. Accordingly, the provision did not act as a waiver of the employee's right to grieve and arbitrate whether the last-chance agreement was violated.[244]

On the other hand, one arbitrator found the entire last-chance agreement invalid because it provided that a violation of its terms would result in discharge without resort to "grievances, claims, arbitration or lawsuit."[245] The arbitrator concluded that the right to grieve and arbitrate whether the employee violated the last-chance agreement was so fundamental that the employer's attempt to take away that fundamental right warranted invalidating the entire last-chance agreement. The grievant was reinstated with full back pay.

Where the union has not been signatory to a last-chance agreement executed by the employer and the employee, arbitrators have judged the agreement valid.[246] Another arbitrator concluded that a

---

[241]Hendrickson Turner Co., 101 LA 919, 920 (Dworkin, 1993).

[242]Kaydon Corp., 89 LA 377 (Daniel, 1987).

[243]Compare Gaylord Container Corp., 97 LA 382 (Goodman, 1991) (arbitrator found he lacked jurisdiction to hear grievance, although he also found that the employee had admitted to violating the last-chance agreement).

[244]Steelworkers v. Lukens Steel Co., 969 F.2d 1468, 140 LRRM 2757 (3d Cir., 1992). See also National Steel Corp., 88 LA 457 (Wolff, 1986) (employer need only prove the agreement was violated and not that the penalty was appropriate).

[245]Monterey Coal Co., 96 LA 457 (Feldman, 1990).

[246]Columbia Gas of Pa., 102 LA 513 (Duff, 1994); Exxon Co. U.S.A., 101 LA 997 (Sergent, 1993); Container Prods., Inc., 95 LA 1129 (Suardi, 1990).

union may not contest in arbitration the validity of a return-to-work agreement that subjected the grievant to periodic drug tests where the union had previously withdrawn a separate grievance over this agreement.[247]

Another factor central to the validity of a last-chance agreement is its duration. One arbitrator held that last-chance agreements must terminate within sensible time limits since an indefinite term would be "manifestly unreasonable."[248] Although he noted that last-chance agreements are entitled to arbitral deference, the arbitrator held that such agreements are not without constraints and must be scrutinized before being enforced.

3. *Majority View.*   As aptly stated by one arbitrator:

> The sole question to be decided is whether the grievant violated the last chance agreement and if that is answered in the affirmative, then the discharge must be upheld.[249]

In that case, the last-chance agreement required the employee with an admitted drug dependency to undergo drug screening any time the employer requested. After the employee tested positive for drugs in violation of the last-chance agreement, the discharge was upheld. In rejecting the union's argument that the employee need not submit to testing outside of working hours, the arbitrator stated:

> The agreement of the parties is clear and exact. It says "at any time." If it had meant otherwise, such could have been stated. When an employer is concerned with the complete resolution of a problem of drug dependency such a commitment would be entirely reasonable since the purpose is not merely the capacity of the individual to perform his work adequately but his overall physical condition. While such may not be an appropriate condition of employment imposed upon regular employees, by agreement of the parties including the employee, it may certainly be an individual condition of employment and is entitled to enforcement.[250]

The view of the majority of arbitrators ruling on last-chance agreements in substance abuse cases is to uphold the discharge if the employee violated the agreement. This is so where the employee fails a drug test,[251] fails to take a drug or alcohol test,[252] fails to follow

---

[247]Ethyl Corp., 95 LA 632 (Blum, 1990).

[248]Ohio Dep't of Highway Safety, 96 LA 71, 77 (Dworkin, 1990).

[249]Kaydon Corp., 89 LA 377, 378 (Daniel, 1987).

[250]Id. at 379.

[251]Baltimore Specialty Steels Corp., 95 LA 1191 (Strongin, 1990) (employee tested positive for drugs); Koppers Co., 91 LA 363 (Yarowsky, 1988) (employee tested positive for drugs); Indianapolis Power & Light Co., 87 LA 826 (Volz, 1986) (employee tested positive for drugs).

[252]Ethyl Corp., 95 LA 632 (Blum, 1990) (employee refused to undergo second drug test where prior test was faulty); Linde Gases of the Midwest, 94 LA 225 (Nielsen, 1989) (employee refused to submit to alcohol test).

the rehabilitation program,[253] actually uses drugs,[254] arrives at work under the influence,[255] or fails to come to work because of drug use.[256]

*4. Exceptions to Majority View.* Where arbitrators have not upheld the discharge in those substance abuse cases involving a last-chance agreement, they have done so primarily for two reasons: either the employer failed to prove that the last-chance agreement was violated or the last-chance agreement was found to be invalid or not properly communicated to the employee.[257] Failures of proof can involve involuntary changes of rehabilitation programs,[258] de minimis violations of the agreement,[259] behavior not covered by the agreement,[260] unreasonable employer requests for testing,[261] and absence of proof that the employee actually used drugs.[262] The paucity of these cases is a reflection that most arbitrators are inclined not to disturb a last-chance agreement for other than compelling reasons. Many arbitrators feel that failure to give effect to the bargain reached between the parties would discourage employers from entering into such agreements in the future—a socially undesirable result.[263]

*5. Miscellaneous.* One issue presented by last-chance agreements is whether they create precedent that an arbitrator will conclude obligates the employer to enter into such agreements with all

---

[253]Union Carbide Corp., 97 LA 1079 (Bittel, 1991) (employee did not follow prescribed course of treatment); Diesel Recon Co., 96 LA 1193 (Odom, 1991) (employee used drugs while on rehabilitation program); Simetco, Inc., 96 LA 193 (Odom, 1990) (employee missed counseling sessions).

[254]Toledo Bd. of Educ., 96 LA 808 (Duda, 1991) (employee used drugs and violated other provisions of last-chance agreement); Ohio Dep't of Highway Safety, 96 LA 71 (Dworkin, 1990) (employee intoxicated at work); Federal Aviation Admin., 93 LA 41 (Allen, 1989) (employee consumed alcohol while on rehabilitation program); Inland Container Corp., 91 LA 544 (Howell, 1988) (employee discharged for alcohol abuse); General Elec. Co., 91 LA 400 (Allen, 1988) (employee used drugs and missed counseling sessions).

[255]National Steel Corp., 60 LA 613 (McDermott, 1973) (employee under influence of alcohol at work).

[256]United States Steel Corp., 87 LA 973 (Neyland, 1986) (employee failed to report to work and admitted drinking the prior night).

[257]Duro Bag Mfg. Co., 101 LA 433 (Stanton, 1993) (last-chance agreement invalid); Monterey Coal Co., 96 LA 457 (Feldman, 1990); Food Mktg. Corp., 88 LA 98 (Doering, 1986) (employee did not sign last-chance agreement, and it was not delivered to him in a manner designed to communicate its seriousness).

[258]Food 4 Less Supermarkets, 102 LA 817 (Grabuskie, 1994) (employee's involuntary discharge from one rehabilitation program and subsequent enrollment in another program did not violate last-chance agreement); United States Steel Corp., 94 LA 1109 (McDaniel, 1990) (employee's involuntary removal from an agreed-upon rehabilitation program and subsequent voluntary enrollment in another program complied with the spirit of the last-chance agreement).

[259]Exxon Co. U.S.A., 101 LA 997 (Sergent, 1993) (missing two counseling meetings in 9 months was not unreasonable).

[260]U.S. Steel-Lorain, 95 LA 7 (Talarico, 1990) (last-chance agreement referred only to drugs and not alcohol use).

[261]Freuhauf Corp., 88 LA 366 (Nathan, 1986) (since the company's order to take a drug-screening test was unreasonable, the employee was reinstated without back pay, even though the employee openly admitted violating the last-chance agreement to remain drug free).

[262]Jim Walters Resources, 95 LA 1037 (Roberts, 1990) (company failed to prove employee used drugs).

[263]See Porcelain Metals Corp., 73 LA 1133, 1138 (Roberts, 1979).

other employees who engage in a particular offense. In one case an arbitrator held that an employee discharged for poor attendance should have been given a last-chance agreement since other similarly situated employees in that company had been.[264] The prior settlement agreements on their face did not specify that they were without precedent. Accordingly, the arbitrator held that the employee was improperly denied a last-chance agreement based on his poor attendance. In another case, a similar conclusion was reached. The employee's discharge was overturned since he had not been given a last-chance agreement which had been given to other employees who were found to have been intoxicated on the job.[265] There is no indication in that case that the prior last-chance agreements noted they were nonprecedential. It is an open question whether last-chance agreements, which on their face state that they are without precedent, will be found by arbitrators to be nonprecedential when such agreements are routinely entered into with employees.

In another unusual case the arbitrator found that the company improperly denied reinstatement to an employee after a long-term disability on the basis that the employee had refused to sign an extension of a last-chance agreement.[266] The employee had worked for only 2 weeks of the last-chance agreement's 6-month probationary period before going on disability. Even though the employee refused to sign the last-chance agreement, the union agreed to extend it. Notwithstanding, the employer required the employee to sign it and when the employee refused, reinstatement was denied. The arbitrator reinstated the grievant noting that the company acted unreasonably, particularly in light of the union's concession that the last-chance agreement could be extended and would be binding even without the employee's signature.[267] As a general rule, all parties concerned, including the employee, the union, and the company, sign last-chance agreements.[268]

## J. Termination of the Employer's Duty to Accommodate

The employer's duty to accommodate a drug or alcohol problem varies with the type of work the employee does, the type of workplace, the employee's length of service, the employer's rule, and the availability of assistance.[269]

The danger associated with the employer's workplace is inversely related to the employer's duty to accommodate—the greater the danger, the less the duty to accommodate. Thus, a welder in a petroleum

---

[264]TRW, Inc., 90 LA 31 (Graham, 1987).

[265]Navistar Int'l Corp., 88 LA 179 (Archer, 1986).

[266]Pacific Rim Packaging, 97 LA 457 (Fields, 1991).

[267]Id.

[268]See BASF Corp., 90 LA 460, 462 (Daniel, 1987).

[269]For the employer's obligation to accommodate under the American with Disabilities Act, see Chapter 13.

complex is entitled to less accommodation that a clerk in an insurance company.[270] Similarly, the employee's job is a major factor in considering the extent to which an employer may be obliged to accommodate a drug or alcohol dependency problem. An employer's duty to accommodate an airline pilot may be less than its duty to an employee assigned to custodial duties.[271] In many instances it is the combination of job and workplace that determines the degree of accommodation required. A custodian in a chemical plant may be entitled to less accommodation than a custodian in an office.[272]

Arbitrators may give greater consideration to the obligation to accommodate when the employee has long job tenure.[273] Length of service, however, is not a guarantee of continued employment.[274] Similarly, an employee with a good work record is likely to be extended a greater opportunity to overcome the dependency problem.[275] This weighing of the "equities" reflects the application of the just cause standard, even where the employer has promulgated specific rules regarding drug or alcohol infractions.[276]

Although employers' rules may not differentiate among types of drugs used, arbitrators often consider the specific drug when deciding what accommodation is appropriate.[277] If a drug is illegal, arbitrators

---

[270]Dow Chem. Co., 90-1 ARB ¶ 8112 (Baroni, 1989) (discharge of employee, a boilermaker/welder at a large petrochemical complex, upheld; employee twice tested positive for marijuana in random drug tests within a period of several months and arbitrator was not persuaded that proof of actual impairment on the job was a necessary fact to support termination).

[271]Delta Airlines v. Air Line Pilots, 686 F. Supp. 1573, 127 LRRM 2530 (N.D. Ga., 1987), aff'd, 861 F.2d 665, 130 LRRM 2014 (11th Cir., 1988), cert. denied, 493 U.S. 871, 132 LRRM 2623 (1989) (reinstatement of pilot by arbitrator overturned); Delta Airlines, 89 LA 408 (Kahn, 1987).

[272]Sterling Chems., 93 LA 953, 958 (Taylor, 1989). The arbitrator noted that "[a] drug abuse policy, particularly in a chemical plant fraught with danger, is both reasonable and is a generally accepted employment standard." The arbitrator distinguished the particular work environment as a factor in assessing the reasonableness of a drug policy.

[273]Virgin Islands Water & Power Auth., 93-2 ARB ¶ 3332 (Lubic, 1993).

[274]Eaton Corp., 94 LA 971 (Eisele, 1990), where termination of 25-year employee was upheld even though the union argued that postdischarge events should be considered. The union stressed that after discharge the employee's depression and alcoholism were properly evaluated and treated so that recovery was a real possibility, but the arbitrator rejected the union's argument, despite employee's years of service, noting:

> Whatever value the union's argument has it would be more credible if this were the grievant's first participation in a treatment program rather than his fifth. However, the argument is probably questionable under the best of circumstances because the courts have not looked with favor or [sic] arbitrators' decisions which find just cause for discharge and then turn around and order some form of reinstatement.

Id. at 974, footnote omitted.

[275]Loral Sys. Group, 94 LA 924, 928 (Strasshofer, 1990) (among the mitigating circumstances noted by the arbitrator was the following: "no prior formal discipline for this type of offense * * *").

[276]Chattanooga Gas Co., 92-1 ARB ¶ 8180 (Howell, 1991) (arbitrator found reasonable a company policy providing for discharge of an employee whose drug test was positive; arbitrator observed that the employee had the right to file a grievance on the basis the discharge was not for just cause).

[277]Spencer, "The Developing Notions of Employer Responsibility for the Alcoholic, Drug-Addicted or Mentally Ill Employee: An Examination Under Federal and State Employment Statutes and Arbitration Decisions," 53 St. John's L. Rev. 659 (1979).

support less employer tolerance for the misbehavior.[278] The fact that
an employee has been found a "user" of illegal drugs does not, however,
justify discharge.[279] A nexus between the illegal substance and the
workplace must be established. In contrast, alcohol abuse is more
often considered a disease susceptible to treatment. Since alcohol is
legal it evokes a greater tolerance among arbitrators, and they are
more likely to require accommodation.[280]

The duty to accommodate is subservient to a reasonable and
necessary employer rule. If the rule sets forth the circumstances in
which termination will occur, arbitrators focus on the rule and the
circumstances evidencing a violation.[281] Violation of an employer rule
for which there is a specific penalty brings into play the just cause
standard.[282] For instance, if a rule provides working under the influence will result in discharge, an arbitrator is likely to sustain the
discharge if a clear violation is shown.

Arbitrators recognize that employees who have substance abuse
problems often "slip."[283] When an employee's continued pattern of
behavior shows improvement, an arbitrator may be persuaded that
continued accommodation is warranted.[284] The previously discussed
factors are, of course, relevant.

At some point the employer may tell the employee that its efforts
to accommodate him will not continue indefinitely. The basic question
then becomes whether the employee was given a fair opportunity to
pursue rehabilitation and whether the employee had been given fair
warning of the consequences of continued errant behavior.[285]

---

[278]Kansas City Cold Storage, 94 LA 783 (Madden, 1990) (employer denial of sick leave
for drug treatment of cocaine addict upheld even though the employer had granted sick leave
for alcohol abuse treatment; arbitrator found the distinction associated with legal and illegal
substances not arbitrary).

[279]Aeronca, Inc., 93 LA 782, 789 (Doering, 1989) (arbitrator found employee was not a
"dealer" in providing marijuana to an undercover agent; company rules provided that user gets
a second chance whereas a seller does not, and in this instance arbitrator ruled "the grievant
should be given a one-time, in-between, last chance remedy—namely, a reinstatement without
backpay * * *").

[280]Atchison, Topeka & Santa Fe Ry., 87 LA 972 (Johnson, 1986); Youngstown Hosp. Ass'n,
82 LA 31 (Miller, 1983).

[281]Southern Cal. Rapid Transit Dist., 93 LA 20 (Christopher, 1989) (no just cause to
discharge a bus driver who tested positive for marijuana after an incident involving an elderly
pedestrian; employee not accused of causing the accident; arbitrator found employee not having
caused the accident a mitigating factor with regard to imposing discharge and ruled:

> The District shall have the right to test the grievant for a controlled substance at the
> time the grievant is reinstated. If the test result is negative, the grievant shall be returned
> to his former position of bus operator. If the test result is positive, the grievant shall be
> placed in the EAP and be subject to the Program's procedures and requirements.

Id. at 24.

[282]Linde Gases of the Midwest, 94 LA 225 (Nielsen, 1989).

[283]Thrifty Drug Stores Co., 56 LA 789 (Peters, 1971).

[284]Cleveland Elec. Illuminating Co., 88 LA 781 (Morgan, 1987).

[285]American Synthetic Rubber Corp., 73-1 ARB ¶ 8070 (Kesselman, 1973).

# Chapter 7

# Dishonesty and Disloyalty

## I. Introduction

Among the most serious forms of employee misconduct are acts of dishonesty. Intent is a critical component when employees are disciplined for such actions. When there is clear intent to steal or defraud, many arbitrators take an unwavering strict approach, concluding that if the employer-employee bond of trust has been breached, no mitigating factors can or should lessen the penalty. Some arbitrators will consider mitigating factors such as the value of what was taken, the employee's prior employment record, length of service, harm to the employer, motivation of the employee, or attempts to deny the act.

Many actions that involve dishonesty fall within the broad concept of theft, ranging from the outright taking of property to the falsification of documents for personal gain. In other cases, the dishonesty may involve not a taking but some other act of intentional falsehood that compromises employer-employee trust. Finally, there are actions that compromise the employee's duty of loyalty to the employer.

## II. Theft

### A. Elements of Theft

Theft in the workplace, often called "misappropriation," may take a variety of forms. Examples of actions often considered to constitute theft include "grazing" in retail food stores,[1] recording and seeking

---

[1]Dierbergs Mkts., Inc., 93 LA 1113 (Yarowsky, 1989).

wages for time not worked,[2] and making personal phone calls on company time using company phones.[3]

Regardless of the form of the alleged theft, arbitrators commonly use a four-pronged test to resolve disciplinary cases involving these allegations.[4] To support the discipline or discharge of an employee for theft, an employer must establish and prove by accurate, reliable, and credible evidence[5] the following elements:

    (1) The goods belonged to the employer, another employee, a customer, or a member of the public;

    (2) The employee exercised control over the goods, engaged in "asportation" (the carrying away or removal of an item from the place in which it had been deposited), or converted the goods to her own use;

    (3) The goods were taken without the express or implied consent or authorization of the person who could have given such consent or authorization; and

    (4) The goods were taken with an "intent to steal or animus furandi," which is the "intent to deprive the owner of his property permanently."[6]

These four elements are an adaptation of the common law definition of theft, which requires that there be some "intentional wrongdoing." As used in the context of employee relations, "intent to steal" is present when the employee, for personal gain, "knowingly and willfully" takes something belonging to another without permission, direct or implied. The terms "knowing and willful" serve to distinguish an act of theft from situations in which the employee exercised poor judgment, made an inadvertent error, was excusably ignorant, committed a good faith mistake, had implied permission, or intended to borrow and return.[7] The "knowing and willful" character of an action may be either express or implied and may be established through the employee's actions or words. Thus, the determination that an employee had the requisite "intent to steal" often turns on credibility.[8]

## B. Progressive Discipline and Mitigation

Although progressive discipline customarily is an element of just cause, when the issue is theft, arbitrators usually do not require

---

[2]Acme Mkts., Inc., 86-1 ARB ¶ 8094 (DiLauro, 1985).

[3]Pacific Tel. & Tel. Co., 83-2 ARB ¶ 8571 (Oestreich, 1993).

[4]Imperial Glass Corp., 61 LA 1180 (Gibson, 1973). See Vaughn, "Theft," in Labor & Employment Arbitration, Bornstein & Gosline, eds., §24.03 (Matthew Bender, 1988 & 1995 Supp.) (the most comprehensive analysis of theft cases in the arbitral forum); Koven, Smith & Farwell, Just Cause the Seven Tests, 2d ed., 161–62, 245 (BNA Books, 1992).

[5]Southern Cal. Edison Co., 61 LA 803, 807 (Helbling, 1973).

[6]Imperial Glass Corp., 61 LA 1180, 1183 (Gibson, 1973).

[7]Adapted in part from Bornstein & Gosline, eds., Labor & Employment Arbitration, at 24-17 and 18, n.4 (Matthew Bender, 1988).

[8]See Thrifty Drug Stores Co., 50 LA 1253 (Jones, 1968).

progressive discipline. These offenses tend to warrant summary discharge because the act, conduct, or behavior involved is inimical to employer-employee trust. Even where an immediate discharge is appropriate, however, a thorough and fair investigation is still required.

Some arbitrators take the strict position that "theft is theft" and that mitigating circumstances are irrelevant if the elements of theft, particularly the "intent to steal," have been shown. Where significant mitigating factors are present, however, other arbitrators may not accept the propriety of summary discharge.[9] Among the traditional mitigating factors considered in theft cases are a good, discipline-free work record;[10] long service;[11] and minimal value of the item taken.[12] In addition, if the employer has not consistently applied and administered relevant company policy, an arbitrator may find that discharge was too severe.[13]

Examples of cases in which the value of the item stolen was held to be irrelevant are *Tri-City Nursing Center*[14] and *Greyhound Food Management.*[15] In *Tri-City,* the arbitrator upheld a discharge based upon the theft of one onion, and in *Greyhound,* the arbitrator upheld a discharge involving the theft of a 58-cent can of orange juice. In each case, the employer had a clear, consistently enforced policy that acts of theft or pilferage were unacceptable in any degree. In *Tri-City,* the arbitrator noted that imposition of a penalty of suspension for minor theft but discharge for major theft is "putting a price-tag on theft," enabling pilferage to become rampant.

Often, the relatively minor value of the stolen goods combined with a long and good service record will lead an arbitrator to modify the degree of discipline administered.[16] In *Hawaiian Telephone Co.,*[17] however, the grievant, a 28-year employee discharged for the theft of $1.10, gave inconsistent, evasive, implausible testimony and thus was discredited by the arbitrator. The arbitrator upheld the discharge and concluded that, notwithstanding the employee's good record and the small sum involved, leniency was not appropriate in view of the

---

[9]See Bornstein & Gosline, eds., Labor & Employment Arbitration, at 24-28 & 29 n.3 (Matthew Bender, 1988).

[10]Western Insulated Wire Co., 45 LA 972 (Jones, 1965); Memphis Compress Co., 44 LA 897 (Murphy, 1965).

[11]Alfred M. Lewis, Inc., 85-2 ARB ¶ 8594 (Gentile, 1985).

[12]Kroger Co., 71 LA 989 (Heinsz, 1978).

[13]Iowa-Illinois Gas & Elec. Co., 85-1 ARB ¶ 8274 (Keefe, 1985). See Bornstein & Gosline, eds., Labor & Employment Arbitration (Matthew Bender, 1988).

[14]84-1 ARB ¶ 8289 (Keefe, 1984).

[15]89 LA 1138 (Grinstead, 1987).

[16]Holiday Mkts., Inc., 77 LA 648 (McKay, 1981) (a package of cigarettes); Peoples Gas Light & Coke Co., 44 LA 234 (Drake, 1965) ($10 worth of building materials). See Spartan Stores, Inc., 33 LA 40 (Howlett, 1959) (2¢ worth of crackers); Pabst Brewing Co., 29 LA 464 (Gilden, 1957) (five beers); Chrysler Corp., 24 LA 549 (Wolff, 1955) (a pair of coveralls).

[17]43 LA 1218 (Tsukiyama, 1964). See Manhattan Brand Food Prods., 62 LA 405 (M. Ross, 1974) (ham pilfered in lunch bag over a 12-year period); Kane Transfer, Inc., 63 LA 858 (Seibel, 1974) (can of Spam).

grievant's incredible denial and complete failure to follow company procedures.

In some cases, arbitrators have considered the minor value of the item stolen not as a mitigating factor, but as evidence that the "intent to steal" was not present. In these cases, the arbitrator concluded that it is unlikely the grievant would have taken the unreasonable action of putting his job in jeopardy for an item of so little value.[18] Removal of an item in such situations may be attributed to poor judgment, lapse in memory, or some similar justification.

## C. Work Rules Concerning Theft

· Arbitrators generally hold that an employee does not need a rule to tell her that stealing is wrong and is a dischargeable offense.[19] In so-called "scrap" cases, however, a stated policy may be necessary. These cases involve the discipline for theft when the employee has removed items that the employer has discarded as being of no value to the company. Arbitrators look for a consistently enforced policy that has been clearly communicated to employees concerning the disposition or removal of scrap or waste.[20] Relevant policies often restrict or prohibit employees from using or borrowing company equipment or sampling company products.

## D. Presumptions in Theft Cases

Two evidentiary presumptions are common in analyzing theft or pilferage cases: (1) the presumption of innocence, which precludes any presumption of an "intent to steal";[21] and (2) the presumption that the possession of goods, including items in an employee's automobile, lunchbox, locker, or home indicates that the possessor stole the items.[22] Both presumptions are rebuttable.[23]

## E. Circumstantial Evidence as Proof of Theft

Circumstantial evidence may be sufficient to support a finding of just cause for discharge in theft cases, but arbitrators who apply

---

[18]See Bornstein & Gosline, eds., Labor & Employment Arbitration (Matthew Bender, 1988).

[19]A.O. Smith Corp., Kankakee Works, 76 LA 592 (D. Cohen, 1981); Portsmouth Naval Shipyard, 76 LA 373 (Hoban, 1981).

[20]See Great Atl. & Pac. Tea Co., 77 LA 133 (Amis, 1981) (employee consumed perishable item to be discarded); Emge Packing Co., 61 LA 250 (Getman, 1973).

[21]Safeway Stores, Inc., 55 LA 1195, 1203 (Jacobs, 1971).

[22]Schoonoven, ed., Fairweather's Practice and Procedure in Labor Arbitration, 3d ed., 240–41 (BNA Books, 1991).

[23]See Bornstein & Gosline, eds., Labor & Employment Arbitration, at 24-17 & 18, nn. 76-81 (Matthew Bender, 1988). For a discussion of quantum of proof, see Chapter 14.

a higher standard of proof in theft cases may be reluctant to sustain termination based on circumstantial evidence alone. The definition of circumstantial evidence in this context is the same as in other types of cases.[24] A brief but precise definition was provided in *Soule Steel Co.*,[25] an often-cited arbitral decision:

> Circumstantial evidence is that type of evidence which, without going directly to prove the existence of a fact, gives rise to a logical inference that such fact does exist. Great latitude is allowed in admitting circumstantial evidence where the circumstances are such that direct evidence is lacking.[26]

In *Max Factor & Co.*,[27] a co-worker observed the grievant secreting company products on her person. This was reported to a plant guard, who in turn reported it to a supervisor. The supervisor told the guard to recover the items from the grievant, which the guard did. When the items were recovered by the guard, only the grievant and the guard were present. The stolen products were returned to the processing line and the grievant was discharged. The grievant denied that any theft took place and challenged the guard's testimony that the items were recovered from her. In upholding the termination, the arbitrator relied on the testimony of the guard, the supervisor, and the co-worker who initially had observed the grievant. The arbitrator did not credit the grievant's testimony and concluded that there was sufficient circumstantial evidence to prove the grievant's guilt, even though the company could not produce the stolen items.

# III. Falsification

## A. Introduction

When an employee intentionally falsifies company records, submits a false claim, or alters employment-related tests,[28] employer-employee trust is impaired. When the employee engages in these activities to gain some economic or personal benefit from the employer, these acts are considered serious offenses akin to theft.[29] When an employee is found to be willfully dishonest in this context, arbitrators

---

[24]For a discussion of circumstantial evidence in general, see Chapter 14.

[25]85 LA 336 (Richman, 1985).

[26]Id. at 343.

[27]61 LA 886 (Jones, 1973).

[28]Falsification of employment applications is addressed in Falsification by Applicants in this chapter.

[29]W. R. Grace & Co., 86 LA 999, 1003 (Galambos, 1986), citing Elkouri & Elkouri, How Arbitration Works, 4th ed., 655 (BNA Books, 1985).

uphold stiff penalties, including discharge,[30] although some will consider mitigating circumstances.[31] In contrast, when discipline relates to innocent or inadvertent misrepresentations that are not intended to deceive and cause no loss to the employer, arbitrators tend to view discharge or other severe discipline unfavorably.[32]

## B. Types of Records Falsified

*1. Time Records.* Time-record falsification is one of the most frequent falsification problems. It can also be one of the most difficult to defend since in many situations it is the employee's own responsibility to record her time on the job.[33] Arbitrators have not hesitated to uphold discharge or discipline where employees were found to have intentionally falsified their own time card[34] or a co-worker's.[35] Moreover, because this type of falsification is considered an act of theft, even small discrepancies will often subject the grievant to discipline.[36]

Most cases in which the arbitrator has reduced a penalty imposed by the employer for alleged time-card falsification involve either mitigating circumstances[37] or the employer's failure to prove that the time-card discrepancy was the product of an intentional act as opposed to carelessness.[38]

*2. Business and Production Records.* A wide variety of cases involve alleged falsification of business or production records. They

---

[30]W. R. Grace Co., 86 LA 999, 1003 (Galambos, 1986), citing Kroger Co., 44 LA 915, 917 (Reid, 1965).

[31]Southern Cal. Edison, 89 LA 1129, 1138 (Collins, 1987).

[32]Straits Steel & Wire Co., 91 LA 1058, 1061 (Elkin, 1988).

[33]Schmidt Co., 62 LA 14, 18 (Atwood, 1974) (where the arbitrator upheld the discharge stating that employees who clock in and out have a duty to exercise due care to see that they punch their time cards properly so that only actual time worked is recorded).

[34]Timken Co., 88-1 ARB ¶ 8056 (Duda, 1987); National Elevator Indus., Inc., 86-2 ARB ¶ 8574 (Concepcion, 1986); Fleming Cos., 85-2 ARB ¶ 8618 (Shearer, 1985); Georgia Pac. Corp., 85-1 ARB ¶ 8311 (White, 1985); Foremost-Gentry, 84-1 ARB ¶ 8239 (Concepcion, 1983); First Nat'l Supermarkets, Inc., 84-1 ARB ¶ 8106 (Johnson, 1983); Group W Cable, Inc., 83-2 ARB ¶ 8610 (Thornell, 1983); Michigan Wheel Div. of Dana Corp., 82-1 ARB ¶ 8190 (Daniel, 1982); Federal Mogul Corp., 80-2 ARB ¶ 8616 (Martin, 1980); T & A Thrifty Marts, Inc., 76-2 ARB ¶ 8612 (Ipavec, 1976).

[35]Kaiser Found. Hosp., 94 LA 725 (Kaufman, 1990) (although discharge too severe, discipline still warranted for an employee who punched a co-worker's time card at quitting time when the co-worker left work 15 minutes early).

[36]Alofs Mfg Co., 89 LA 5 (Daniel, 1987) (written reprimand upheld where union president failed to record 1 hour and 15 minutes of union business on time card); Golden Eagle Distribs., Inc., 85 LA 279 (D'Spain, 1985) (where arbitrator found that discipline was warranted for employees who left the employer's premises for 6 minutes without clocking out).

[37]GTE N., Inc., 96 LA 692, 695 (Feldman, 1991) (discharge too severe for employees who left 3 minutes earlier than they represented on their time cards, where facts indicated employees thought they were complying with company policy).

[38]Carbide Corp., 100 LA 763 (Felice, 1993); Valentec/Kisco-Olivette, 100 LA 71 (Fowler, 1992); Snyder Gen. Corp., 99 LA 1108 (Bard, 1992) (where just cause did not exist to discharge grievant who printed later times on his time card after he had punched out, since employer could not prove that grievant knew that he would be credited with extra time); Southern Cal. Carton, 88 LA 591 (Scholtz, 1986).

include inflating or deflating production statistics,[39] claiming other employees' production rates,[40] falsifying customer invoices,[41] falsifying customer orders,[42] reporting work done on a day on which it was not performed,[43] falsely reporting cash transactions,[44] making fictitious passenger reservations,[45] falsifying patient records,[46] and falsifying personnel records.[47]

The most serious of these cases involve deliberate theft from the employer or injury to the employer's business or customer relations.[48] Cases involving theft often exact the toughest penalties. Even where theft is not involved, discipline has been upheld where the company proved its records were falsified by an employee on whom it depends to accurately keep its records. The arbitrator takes the view that a company is entitled to expect honest and accurate versions of daily transactions from the employees whom they have entrusted with that work.[49]

*3. Medical and Insurance Records.*   The usual effect of the falsification of medical records is to secure some benefit to which the employee would not ordinarily be entitled.[50] In this situation, the conduct is considered theft. In *Southwestern Bell Telephone Co.,*[51] an employee was accused of falsely listing her live-in boyfriend as her "husband" on medical and dental insurance forms. The arbitrator upheld the discharge, noting that the grievant's falsification not only secured almost $900 in medical benefits for her boyfriend but also obligated the company to pay approximately $2,000 in premiums for this additional coverage.[52]

---

[39]Contel of Mo., Inc., 92-1 ARB ¶ 8143 (Fowler, 1991); Madison Furniture Indus., 88 LA 804 (King, 1987); Thomas Indus., Inc., 83 LA 418 (Feigenbaum, 1984); Brunswick Corp., 51 LA 1296 (Duff, 1969); Cannon Elec. Co., 28 LA 879 (Jones, 1957).

[40]Pacific Bell, 86 LA 1156 (Oestreich, 1986); H.R. Terryberry Co., 65 LA 1091 (Hillman, 1975).

[41]Farmer Bros., Co., 93-1 ARB ¶ 3144 (Christopher, 1992).

[42]Ameripol-Synpol Co., 100 LA 896 (Nicholas, 1993); Leaseway, Transco Serv., 96 LA 823 (Concepcion, 1991).

[43]Carrier Corp., 89-1 ARB ¶ 8188 (Wilmoth, 1989).

[44]Interstate Brands Corp., 97 LA 293 (Canestraight, 1991); Western Airlines, Inc., 83-2 ARB ¶ 8341 (Koven, 1983).

[45]Frontier Airlines, 82 LA 1283 (Watkins, 1984).

[46]Youngstown Hosp. Ass'n, 83-1 ARB ¶ 8015 (Klein, 1982).

[47]Brunswick Corp., Defense Div., 88-2 ARB ¶ 8450 (Duff, 1988).

[48]Akro Corp., 85-2 ARB ¶ 8429 (Morgan, 1985); Dana Corp., 83-1 ARB ¶ 8212 (Abrams, 1983); Fox Indus., Inc., 82-1 ARB ¶ 8068 (Leahy, 1981) (where grievant was a piece-rate employee, discharge was upheld when grievant falsified his piece count so as to increase wages).

[49]Western Airlines, Inc., 83-2 ARB ¶ 8341 (Koven, 1983). See also Federal Mogul Corp., 81-1 ARB ¶ 8140 (Lipson, 1980).

[50]Falsification of doctor's certificates for sick leave is addressed below.

[51]95 LA 46 (Massey, 1990).

[52]See also Bi-State Dev. Agency, 96 LA 1090 (Cipolla, 1991); Panhandle E. Pipeline Co., 88-1 ARB ¶ 8021 (Yarowsky, 1987); Southwest Detroit Hosp., 82 LA 491 (Ellmann, 1984); Columbus & S. Ohio Elec. Co., 84-1 ARB ¶ 8009 (Perry, 1983).

4. *Reimbursement Forms.* Intentional falsification of reimbursement forms for personal gain is essentially a form of theft, and arbitrators treat it that way.[53] Although discharge is a common penalty imposed for this type of offense,[54] arbitrators may not find it appropriate in all cases. In *Saunier-Wilhelm Co.,*[55] the grievant was discharged for falsifying approximately $50 worth of hotel and meal receipts for himself and his wife, who accompanied him on the trip against the employer's orders. The discharge was reduced to reinstatement without back pay because it was a first offense in 20 years and the conduct did not result in serious harm to the company. While the arbitrator specifically denounced the falsification of the reimbursement form, he stated that, under these circumstances, discharge was not warranted.[56]

5. *Safety Records.* Arbitrators treat the health and safety of both the workforce and the community at large as vital considerations. Accordingly, falsifications that may adversely affect these populations will not be readily excused. In *W.R. Grace Co.,*[57] the arbitrator found that the employer properly discharged the grievant for concealing and tampering with chemical emissions records on the same day that two residents of the surrounding community were sent to the hospital for exposure to the emissions. The arbitrator stated that since chemical emissions are of great public concern, falsification of such vital information constitutes a serious offense and represents just cause for strong discipline.[58]

In *Town of Southington,*[59] the arbitrator upheld a discharge for falsification of fire inspection logs for local businesses. The arbitrator also held, however, that in light of the grievant's long and dedicated service with the town, the effective date of the discharge would be delayed by 2 months so that the grievant's pension could be fully vested.

---

[53]Cadillac Prods., Inc., 76-2 ARB ¶ 8541 (Forsythe, 1976).

[54]Internal Revenue Serv., Nashville Dist., 82-1 ARB ¶ 8266 (Render, 1982); Super-Valu Stores, Inc., 74 LA 939 (Evenson, 1980); Cadillac Prods., Inc., 76-2 ARB ¶ 8541 (Forsythe, 1976).

[55]77-2 ARB ¶ 8378 (LeWinter, 1977).

[56]See also Amoco Oil Co., 93 LA 1021 (Allen, 1989); Toledo Scale Co., 77-1 ARB ¶ 8190 (Eisenberg, 1977); Headquarters, Sacramento Air Logistics Ctr., McClellan Air Force Base, 76-2 ARB ¶ 8466 (Staudohar, 1976) (arbitrator agreed with employer that mechanic who falsified expense vouchers, but lacked criminal intent, was properly suspended for 3 days). Cf. Potlach Corp., 82 LA 445 (Kapsch, 1984) (discharge upheld since grievant's intent was to receive reimbursement for hunting boots that grievant stated were safety boots).

[57]86 LA 999 (Galambos, 1986).

[58]See also Vulcan Chems., 93-2 ARB ¶ 3591 (Yarowsky, 1993) (discharge warranted where employee falsified his safety inspection log to cover up not making his inspection rounds; had he made his rounds, he more than likely would have discovered a leak that eventually resulted in 7,600 gallons of toxic waste spilling into the surrounding area).

[59]100 LA 67, 70 (Halperin, 1992).

## C. Factors Considered in Falsification Cases

In determining whether an employer has proven falsification or whether a reasonable penalty has been imposed, arbitrators analyze a variety of factors. Some of the more frequently considered factors are intent, motivation, effect of the falsification, and clarity and consistency of the company's policy. A combination of factors, rather than one particular factor, often determines the outcome in a given case. This is especially true in the mitigation analysis, in which arbitrators may rely upon several factors that, taken together, merit a reduction in a penalty imposed by the company.[60]

*1. Intent.* In falsification cases, the employer generally must show that the employee intentionally engaged in the misconduct in question.[61] Where the employer is able to show this, the discharge or discipline is more likely to be upheld absent mitigating circumstances.[62] A finding of intent may be based on a variety of factors, such as a grievant's admission that he knowingly falsified a company record;[63] a grievant's attempt to conceal information during a subsequent company investigation;[64] a grievant's extensive knowledge of the employer's production system, making a mistake highly unlikely;[65] and a grievant's implausible, incredible, or contradicted testimony.[66]

On the other hand, intent was not found where the grievant unwittingly submitted a record that had been falsified by another person;[67] where the grievant lacked the mental capacity to understand the company procedure that he falsified;[68] and where the grievant

---

[60]See, e.g., Public Serv. Co. of N.C., Inc., 92-2 ARB ¶ 8552 (Holley, 1991) (discharge was too severe since falsified 401(k) form was confusing and employee had 21 years of solid service); Carrier Corp., 89-1 ARB ¶ 8188 (Wilmoth, 1988) (discharge was too severe since grievant had no notice that infraction could result in discharge and he had a solid 5-year record).

[61]See Carbide Corp., 100 LA 763, 767 (Felice, 1993) (discharge not appropriate where no evidence of intent to defraud or deceive the company); Morrell & Co., 74 LA 756, 763 (Stokes, 1980) (grievant falsified company records; intent is shown through grievant's actions).

[62]See, e.g., Southwestern Bell Tel. Co., 95 LA 46, 49 (Massey, 1990) (discharge for falsification of company medical forms upheld where employee demonstrated requisite intent to defraud the company); Pacific Bell, 86 LA 1156, 1159 (Oestreich, 1986) (suspension upheld where employee knew that his actions, falsifying sales records to take credit for co-workers' sales, were wrong, and his actions to conceal the falsification demonstrated intent).

[63]Batesville Casket Co., 80-1 ARB ¶ 8066 (Seinsheimer, 1979).

[64]Union Camp Corp., 83-1 ARB ¶ 8095 (Dunn, 1982) (during company investigation of their use of funeral leave, employees stated that their deceased great-grandmother was their deceased grandmother).

[65]Madison Furniture Indus., 88 LA 804, 808 (King, 1987) (employee's 6 years of experience with the employer's incentive system indicated a knowing inflation of her production record).

[66]Morrell & Co., 74 LA 756 (Stokes, 1980); Brunswick Corp., 51 LA 1296, 1298 (Duff, 1969) (grievant's denial that she deliberately inflated her production count is rejected in light of credible testimony of employer witnesses).

[67]Continental Baking Co., 85-2 ARB ¶ 8561 at 5303 (Seidman, 1985) (no intent to deceive where grievant's daughter falsified doctor's note without the knowledge of grievant).

[68]Southern Cal. Carton, 88 LA 591, 593 (Scholtz, 1986) (no proof of intent to deceive with regard to irregularities in punched time cards in light of grievant's limited intellectual capacity).

was innocently confused.[69] An employer's failure to prove intent may result in a reduction of the penalty imposed[70] or a finding that no discipline was appropriate.[71]

   *2. Motive.*   An employee's motive for engaging in falsification often is an important factor in an arbitrator's review of discipline or discharge. Where an employee is found to have deliberately falsified a document for financial gain, severe discipline generally is upheld.[72] Motive also can be an important factor in determining whether the alleged falsification has taken place. In *Frontier Airlines,*[73] the arbitrator was presented with circumstantial evidence that the grievant, an airline reservation agent, made false reservations for fictitious passengers. In upholding the discharge, the arbitrator concluded: "Only the grievant had a motive for wanting Flight 27 to appear closed: to assure that there would be space available for his family."[74]

   Conversely, a lack of financial or other personal motivation often is a significant factor when grievances are sustained. In *Dunlop Tire & Rubber Corp.,*[75] the arbitrator rejected the company's contention that the grievant intentionally aggravated his on-the-job leg injury to enhance his worker's compensation claim. The arbitrator concluded that the grievant had no motive to aggravate the injury because he still was working and the alleged aggravation, a cut or scratch in the scar tissue, could not have affected his worker's compensation benefits. Similarly, in *Kaiser Foundation Hospitals,*[76] the arbitrator reduced a discharge to a suspension for a grievant who had punched another employee's time card, not for personal gain, but out of sympathy for the employee who had to leave work early to take his mother to the hospital.

   In *Thomas Industries, Inc.,*[77] the penalty of discharge was found to be too severe where the grievant falsified a production record to

---

[69]Schulze & Burch Biscuit Co., 100 LA 948, 954 (Goldstein, 1993) (sequence of events demonstrates that grievant may have been confused about her entitlement to unemployment benefits).

[70]See, e.g., Carbide Corp., 100 LA 763, 767 (Felice, 1993) (discharge was reduced to a suspension without pay for employee who failed to accurately fill out his time sheets but employer failed to prove intent to defraud); Arkansas Okla. Gas Corp., 96 LA 704 (Allen, 1989); Marine Corps Air Station, 82 LA 28, 31 (Nolan, 1983), (discharge reduced to a 10-day suspension for carelessness where, despite suspicion that employee intentionally falsified warehouse order records, the employer failed to establish intentional conduct).

[71]Sumter Elec. Coop., Inc., 82 LA 647, 649 (Maxwell, 1984) (discharge inappropriate where no proof of grievant's intent to falsify use of leave time).

[72]See, e.g., Brammer Mfg. Co., 83-2 ARB ¶ 8541 at 5407 (Talent, 1983) (discharge upheld where grievant withheld information pertaining to her unemployment compensation benefits claim, to secure higher unemployment benefits than she was entitled to receive).

[73]82 LA 1283 (Watkins, 1984).

[74]Id. at 1288.

[75]64 LA 1099, 1104 (Mills, 1975).

[76]94 LA 725, 727 (Kaufman, 1990).

[77]83 LA 418, 421 (Feigenbaum, 1984).

reflect fewer pieces than he actually produced. The arbitrator concluded that the grievant was not motivated by personal monetary gain, but, rather, he misstated his production output to protest a temporary production standard that the grievant believed was too high.[78]

A lack of motivation to achieve personal gain, however, will not guarantee a grievant a favorable decision. In *Farmer Brothers Co.*,[79] the arbitrator upheld a discharge of a route sales representative who recorded incorrect prices on invoices to help a distressed, long-time customer of the company. The arbitrator concluded that, although a lesser penalty might have been an acceptable alternative to discharge, the company's judgment as to the appropriate penalty should not be disturbed because "the grievant violated the trustworthiness required of his outside, unsupervised work."[80]

*3. Effect of the Falsification.*   In deciding falsification cases, arbitrators often will consider the effect that the falsification had on the employer's business[81] or on the grievant's fellow workers.[82] Where the loss is minor, this factor in some cases may lead to mitigation of the penalty.[83] Arbitrators often reject arguments of de minimis harm, concluding that the employee's honesty, trustworthiness, and reliability are at issue, not the loss to the employer.[84]

A significant adverse effect on the company, however, sometimes will be weighed as evidence in support of the discipline or discharge of the employee. In *W. R. Grace & Co.*,[85] the proofs showed an employee tampered with chemical emission records that would verify why fumes, which caused at least two local residents to be hospitalized, were inadvertently emitted from the plant during the employee's shift. The arbitrator, finding that discharge was appropriate, stressed the serious nature of chemical emissions and noted that a fine had

---

[78]Id. Although the arbitrator reinstated the grievant, he did so without back pay because of the intentional falsification.

[79]93-1 ARB ¶ 3144 (Christopher, 1992).

[80]Id. at 3790. See also Interstate Brands Corp., 97 LA 293 (Canestraight, 1991) (route salesman who failed to properly record cash transactions on his customer sheet was not reinstated where, although no dishonesty with intent to steal was proven, he admitted falsifying the sheets; arbitrator found it absurd to reinstate grievant because his sales records would be unreliable); Atlanta Linen Serv., 85 LA 827 (Slatham, 1985).

[81]W. R. Grace & Co., 86 LA 999, 1000 (Galambos, 1986).

[82]See, e.g., Central Chevrolet Co., 86-1 ARB ¶ 8012 at 3051 (Nolan, 1985) (employee must be protected from a false charge of sexual harassment which can subject the individual to ridicule, social stigma, or perhaps to the destruction of a career); Brunswick Corp., 51 LA 1296, 1298 (Duff, 1969) (the grievant's inflation of her production count was unfair to other employees who appeared comparatively less competent).

[83]Straits Steel & Wire, 91 LA 1058, 1061 (Elkin, 1988) (grievant falsified a doctor's note to add a second day of illness; arbitrator reduced the penalty, noting that the grievant's conduct had minimal impact on the company).

[84]Cadillac Prods., Inc., 76-2 ARB ¶ 8541, at 6792 (Forsythe, 1976).

[85]86 LA 999, 1000 (Galambos, 1986).

been levied against the company due to its inability to gather sufficient facts to report the incident in a timely manner to the proper government agency.

4. *Clarity and Consistency of Company Policies.*   Where the employer relies upon a policy that prohibits the falsification at issue, arbitrators often will consider the clarity of the policy and the consistency with which it is enforced. Arbitrators are unlikely to reduce a penalty for a proven instance of falsification when other employees were given the same penalty for that conduct.[86] Conversely, if the employer has permitted other employees to act as the grievant has without discipline, the discipline often will be set aside.[87]

5. *Contract Language.*   Although most falsification cases deal with general principles of management rights and employee honesty, some cases will turn on specific contract language. In *H & H Plastics Co.,*[88] the arbitrator acknowledged the grievant's good record but upheld discharge for falsification of a leave request, citing a contract provision that expressly provided for discharge where an employee gives a false reason for obtaining a leave of absence. Similarly, in *Trevathan v. Newport News Shipbuilding,*[89] the U.S. Court of Appeals for the Fourth Circuit upheld enforcement of an arbitration award that concluded that a contractual provision prohibiting falsification of company records extended to cheating on a requalification test.

On the other hand, discipline or discharge may not be upheld if the collective bargaining agreement supports the employee's conduct. For example, where a legitimately ill employee called in sick but did not disclose the fact that she was in jail during the first day of her sick leave, the arbitrator rejected the employer's claim that under the agreement the employee could qualify for sick leave only if otherwise available for work and at home or in a hospital while ill.[90] The sick leave provisions of the contract did not impose a requirement that the employee be otherwise available to work.

6. *Employee's Record.*   Discharge and other severe penalties for falsification may be reduced when the employee has a long and relatively unblemished work record.[91] Where the dishonesty is serious—

---

[86]Farmer Bros. Co., 93-1 ARB ¶ 3144 (Christopher, 1992) (where employer fired five other employees for the same offense, arbitrator ruled that grievant was on notice that his actions would result in discharge).

[87]Ameripol-Synpol Co., 100 LA 896, 899 (Nicholas, 1993); Carbide Corp., 100 LA 763, 766 (Felice, 1993); Memphis Light, Gas & Water Div., 88 LA 167 (Carter, 1987).

[88]85-1 ARB ¶ 8271 (Kaufman, 1984).

[89]944 F.2d 902, 139 LRRM 3000 (table), text at Westlaw 91-2005 (4th Cir., 1991), aff'g 752 F.Supp. 698, 139 LRRM 2990 (E.D. Va., 1990).

[90]Memphis Light, Gas & Water Div., 88 LA 167, 175 (Carter, 1987).

[91]Ameripol-Synpol Co., 100 LA 896 (Nicholas, 1993) (arbitrator chided employer for discharging employee without considering his good work record); Town of Southington, 100 LA 67 (Halperin, 1992) (10 years warrants mitigation for falsification of inspection records); Public Serv. Co. of N.C., Inc., 92-2 ARB ¶ 8552 (Holley, 1991) (21 years of service mitigates fraudulent

and especially where the grievant's job requires trustworthiness—the grievant's prior record has been given little weight.[92]

In some situations, a grievant's long service record can work against her when error or ignorance is offered as justification for the alleged falsification. In *Madison Furniture Industries*,[93] the arbitrator reasoned that because the grievant had a full 6 years on the job under the same production system, the grievant had unlikely made an error. Therefore, her discharge for falsification was upheld.[94]

*7. Grievant's Candor.* Arbitrators often will consider whether the grievant tried to hide or cover up an alleged falsification. Where the grievant has been completely forthright about the conduct and has cooperated with the company's investigation, arbitrators have found this a mitigating factor.[95]

Arbitrators also have been sensitive to a grievant's candor or lack thereof at the arbitration hearing itself. Because the underlying charge is one of dishonesty, arbitrators have considered testimony that involves implausible explanations or obvious attempts to cover up as further evidence of the employee's untrustworthiness.[96]

---

401k withdrawal); Straits Steel & Wire, 91 LA 1058 (Elkin, 1988) (5 years of good work was sufficient to mitigate penalty for false medical note); Continental Baking Co., 85-2 ARB ¶ 8561 (Seidman, 1985) (25 years of good service was a factor in reduction of discharge for using a falsified doctor's note); Sumter Elec. Coop., Inc., 82 LA 647 (Maxwell, 1984), (11 years mitigates falsification of vacation time); Saunier-Wilhem Co., 77-2 ARB ¶ 8378 (LeWinter, 1977) (20 years of service mitigates falsification of travel voucher); Headquarters, Sacramento Air Logistics Ctr., McClellan Air Force Base, 76-2 ARB ¶ 8466 (Staudohar, 1976) (arbitrator would have mitigated penalty due to good record but 3-day suspension was already lenient enough). See also Brunswick Corp., 51 LA 1296, 1298 (Duff, 1969) (2-week suspension, although stiff, upheld where grievant falsified her production count for a second time within a short period and she already had been counseled and suspended for the first incident).

[92]Contel of Mo., Inc., 92-1 ARB ¶ 8143 (Fowler, 1991) (grievant's 16 years with the company of no avail in reversing discharge where grievant deliberately falsified sales records and company's employee award programs were operated on the honor system); Western Airlines, Inc. 83-2 ARB ¶ 8341 (Koven, 1983) (where falsification involves records of cash transactions, even 14½ years of good service will not mitigate discharge for employees who regularly handle these transactions).

[93]88 LA 804, 808 (King, 1987).

[94]Accord Leaseway, Transco Serv., 96 LA 823, 828 (Concepcion, 1991) (grievant's testimony that he thought he ran an entire order and did not intentionally check unselected items on the order sheet as selected is discounted and discharge upheld where, inter alia, employee had worked for company for approximately 7 years and was very familiar with the procedures of the job).

[95]See, e.g., Ameripol-Synpol Co., 100 LA 896, 900 (Nicholas, 1993) ("if he had offered some flimsy excuse or otherwise attempted to frustrate Company's investigation, your Arbitrator would view him in a different light altogether"); Arkansas Okla. Gas Corp., 96 LA 704 (Allen, 1991) (grievant's full cooperation was given great weight in arbitrator's holding that grievant committed a mistake rather than a falsification by inappropriately listing his ex-wife on insurance form); Kaiser Found. Hosp., 94 LA 725, 727 (Kaufman, 1990) (in reducing discharge to suspension arbitrator noted that grievant had cooperated with a company investigator and that the grounds for his discharge were based solely on admissions to the investigator); Thomas Indus., Inc., 83 LA 418 (Feigenbaum, 1984) (discharge converted to suspension where, inter alia, grievant was completely honest about what he had done).

[96]Super-Valu Stores, Inc., 74 LA 939, 944-45 (Everson, 1980) (grievant found guilty of lying and dishonesty when he continued to cover up the falsification of company records during an investigation of the matter).

## D. Filing False Claims

*1. Sick Leave.* When an employer alleges that an employee falsely reported he was ill to secure paid leave to which the employee would not otherwise be entitled, arbitrators frequently uphold the discipline regardless of the employee's reason for using the leave.[97] In *GF Furniture Systems,*[98] however, the arbitrator found significance in the reason the employee falsely claimed he was sick. The grievant had called in sick because he was afraid he would lose his job if he told his employer the truth, which was that he had been incarcerated for vehicular homicide. The arbitrator stated that he would be inclined to consider this reason as a mitigating circumstance if the grievant had not had a dismal record of reprimands and suspensions.[99]

Where an employee falsifies a doctor's written sick leave certifications to obtain time off with pay, arbitrators will be inclined to uphold the penalty.[100] The penalty often will not be upheld if the employer fails to prove intent to defraud[101] or if the employee has a legitimate doctor's excuse but the illness is questioned.[102]

Falsely asserting a family illness to secure time off with pay generally is treated the same as falsification of the employee's own medical condition. Thus, the arbitrators upheld discharges in *Dynair Services,*[103] where the grievant had falsely claimed an illness in the family so that he could work at another job, and in *F. W. Schumacker*

---

[97]Yamaha Musical Prod., 86-1 ARB ¶ 8282 (Keefe, 1986) (employee claimed he was sick so he could go hunting); La Crosse Lutheran Hosp., 73 LA 722 (McCrary, 1979) (employee claimed she was sick so that she could visit Las Vegas).

[98]87 LA 500 (Klein, 1986).

[99]Id. at 506.

[100]See, e.g., Morrell & Co., 74 LA 756 (Stokes, 1980); Standard Brands, Inc., 78-1 ARB ¶ 8043 (Millious, 1978).

[101]See, e.g., Continental Baking Co., 85-2 ARB ¶ 8561 (Seidman, 1985) (employee, discharged for unknowingly submitting a medical excuse forged by her daughter, was reinstated because she had 25 years of good service and employer could show no fraudulent intent); Riviera Kitchens, 80-1 ARB ¶ 8161 (Draper, 1980) (grievant was discharged for falsification when she submitted a doctor's note that was actually written by the doctor's nurse; the arbitrator reinstated the grievant with full back pay since grievant made no misrepresentation as to the source of the note); AP Parts Co., 77-2 ARB ¶ 8584 (Howlett, 1977) (arbitrator found discharge was too severe for an employee who altered his return-to-work date on his medical certification since the employee received no pay for the extra time off).

[102]Western Rubber Co., 83 LA 170 (Cohen, 1984) (grievant was legitimately sick and under a doctor's care and this was not a case where an employee calls in sick at one job so that he can report to a second job; rather, the employee was attempting to work both his day and evening jobs because of his family's deteriorating financial condition, but his medical condition became more serious later in the day when his shift with the employer started). See Flying Tigers Line, Inc., 91 LA 647 (Concepcion, 1988); Clark Oil & Ref. Corp., 79 LA 1181 (Franke, 1982) (grievant reinstated without back pay since no doctor had released grievant to return to work in spite of determination that grievant had misrepresented the facts of his condition); Louisiana Pac. Corp., Norton Plant, 82-1 ARB ¶ 8026 (Kates, 1981).

[103]91 LA 1261 (D'Spain, 1988).

& Co.,[104] where an employee falsely asserted a family illness so that she could extend her vacation.

Falsification related to other forms of leave, such as personal, vacation, and bereavement leave, receive similar analysis. In *Plough, Inc.,*[105] the grievant requested and received permission to go home early to deal with an emergency with his water heater. The company accused him of lying about the reason when it learned that he attended a union training class later the same day. The arbitrator held that the company failed to establish its claim of falsification because it did not prove that the grievant did not have an emergency at home. Of significance was a company policy that an employee who leaves work cannot return for the remainder of the shift. Thus, the arbitrator reasoned that the employer could not assume the employee had lied simply because he later attended the class.[106]

In a twist on the classic "my grandma died" falsification, three grievants in *Union Camp Corp.*[107] were given 3-day suspensions for falsely claiming that their great-grandmother, whose funeral they attended with pay, was their grandmother. The arbitrator upheld the suspension, finding that the grievants deliberately misrepresented their relation to the deceased for the purpose of receiving leave to which they were not entitled.

Although the more common occurrence is the improper use of sick leave as a substitute for vacation leave,[108] in *Sumter Electric Cooperative, Inc.,*[109] the grievant used vacation leave while he was sick. The employer discharged the grievant for falsification, but the arbitrator, sustaining the grievance, noted that the company allowed unused vacation leave to be used as sick leave and that the grievant had not acted deceptively, having recorded his time off as "personal-sick."

*2. False Workers' Compensation and Unemployment Benefits Claims.*   In addition to the general concern of dishonesty, false workers' compensation or unemployment claims have an adverse impact on the employer's business and premiums rates, which may be considered in arbitration of related discipline. In *Dunlop Tire & Rubber Corp.,*[110] an employee suffered an on-the-job leg injury and missed almost 3 months of work. He returned to light duty, then subsequently

---

[104]87-2 ARB ¶ 8573 (Rocha, 1987). For the same result in a similar case, see H & H Plastics Co., 85-1 ARB ¶ 8271 (Kaufman, 1984).

[105]80 LA 1005 (Flannagan, 1983).

[106]Id. at 1008.

[107]83-1 ARB ¶ 8095 (Dunn, 1982); cf. Union Carbide Corp., 81 LA 864 (White, 1983) (discharge was too severe for grievant who claimed uncle was grandfather to obtain leave for 3 days instead of 1 day).

[108]F. W. Schumacher & Co., 87-2 ARB ¶ 8573 (Rocha, 1987); Yamaha Musical Prod., 86-1 ARB ¶ 8282 (Keefe, 1986); La Crosse Lutheran Hosp., 73 LA 722 (McCrary, 1979).

[109]82 LA 647 (Maxwell, 1984).

[110]64 LA 1099 (Mills, 1975).

missed additional work time because his injury would not heal. The employer discharged the employee, contending that the employee was a malingerer and had aggravated his injury to obtain larger workers' compensation benefits. The arbitrator ordered the employee reinstated with full back pay, citing equivocal medical testimony, lack of proof that the employee had intentionally aggravated his injury, and the lack of motive (the employee was working for most of the period in question and would not have enhanced his workers' compensation benefits by any significant amount).[111]

False unemployment claims also affect the company's premium. The arbitrator in *Bramer Manufacturing Co.*[112] upheld the discharge of a temporarily laid-off employee who failed to report to the state unemployment office that she was working 40 hours per week in her second, previously part-time job. In *Schulze & Burch Biscuit Co.*,[113] the arbitrator reinstated an employee who had been accused of receiving unemployment benefits at the time she was receiving disability benefits. The company failed to prove intent to defraud because of the grievant's limited understanding of the English language and the confusing set of circumstances in which the grievant was laid off, on strike, laid off, then laid off for her disability.

*3. False Sexual Harassment Claims.* In recent years, sexual harassment has become a major issue in the workplace, raising a variety of issues associated with discipline for charges that ultimately are shown to have been false. In *Central Chevrolet Co.*,[114] the arbitrator was called upon to balance the competing interests between the allegedly harassed employee, the alleged harasser, and the employer. The grievant claimed that throughout a 1-year period her supervisor propositioned her and made suggestive remarks. The employer discharged the grievant for making a false claim, and the grievant alleged she had been discharged in retaliation for raising the sexual harassment claim. The arbitrator noted that employees should be encouraged to bring their concerns of sexual harassment to their employers and should not be punished for doing so. He said, however, that employers and individuals must be protected from false claims because of the employer's expense in investigating them and the possible destruction of the accused's career.

The arbitrator in *Central Chevrolet* held that he would reconcile these competing interests by first discerning "[i]f the Employer demonstrated that a fair and thorough investigation revealed no evidence

[111]Id. at 1104. See also Western Auto Supply Co., 96 LA 644, 647 (Hilgert, 1991) (discharge for filing false workers' compensation claim based, in particular, on the testimony of two co-workers who disputed the claim that the injury occurred on the job); United States Sugar Corp., 82 LA 604 (Hanes, 1984).

[112]83-2 ARB ¶ 8541 at 5407 (Talent, 1983).

[113]100 LA 948 (Goldstein, 1993).

[114]86-1 ARB ¶ 8012 (Nolan, 1985).

to support the Grievant's charges."[115] If so, the company's initial burden of proving just cause would be met and the grievant's assertion of retaliation would be regarded as an affirmative defense on which she bore the burden of proof. The grievant could satisfy this burden by showing that she made the charges of harassment in good faith and in reliance on some tangible evidence.[116] The arbitrator reasoned that by using this analysis, any doubt would be resolved in favor of the grievant so as not to discourage legitimate claims of sexual harassment. Applying this analysis, the arbitrator concluded that the company had met its burden of proof while the grievant failed to meet hers.[117]

In *King Soopers, Inc.,*[118] the grievant was a male supervisor who was fired for alleged sexual assault on a female store clerk. The arbitrator found the allegations were without merit and reinstated the supervisor. The arbitrator ordered the company to ensure that the female store clerk, who filed the false claim, was never allowed to work in the same store as the grievant.

*4. Other False Claims.*   In *Public Service Co. of North Carolina, Inc.,*[119] the company discharged the grievant for making a false claim for the purpose of obtaining a withdrawal from his 401(k) account. The arbitrator agreed with the company that the grievant had falsely claimed that he needed the money for his mother's medical treatment when, in fact, he wanted it to make repairs on his house. Notwithstanding that the money in the 401(k) plan actually belonged to the grievant, the arbitrator observed: "There is no doubt that public trust and accurate reports from employees are vital to the Company's interest.* * * [and t]he Company has a right to demand accurate information* * *."[120] The arbitrator mitigated the discharge to reinstatement without back pay on the basis of the grievant's 21 years with the employer and the unclear rules and procedures associated with the 401(k) plan.

## E. Test Falsifications

*1. Drug Testing.*   The most common cases involving falsification or tampering with drug tests involve allegations that the employee has provided the tester with an adulterated testing sample or a sample

---

[115]Id. at 3052.

[116]Id.

[117]See also Furr's, Inc., 88 LA 175 (Blum, 1986); Regional Transp. Dist., 87 LA 793, 798-99 (Vernon, 1986) (where arbitrator used a similar balancing analysis, but stated that discharge would not be upheld since there was little adverse impact on the employer or the accused).

[118]100 LA 900 (Sass, 1993).

[119]92-2 ARB ¶ 8552 (Holley, 1991).

[120]Id. at 5580.

from someone else.[121] In *Litton/Ingalls Shipbuilding*,[122] the grievant was discharged when she provided an invalid specimen for testing. Since the specimen was cold, the employer assumed that it was someone else's and that the grievant had smuggled it in for the test. The grievant offered immediately to give another sample, but her request was denied. The arbitrator reinstated the grievant, stating that the company's assumption was not conclusive proof of wrongdoing by the grievant and that the employer should have permitted the grievant to give another example.

By contrast, in *Alta Bates Hospital*,[123] the grievant admitted, after the fact, to substituting another individual's urine for her sample, and the arbitrator sustained the discharge. The grievant testified that she spilled her sample and was afraid that if she told the truth it would be assumed she was lying to cover up drug use. Although the arbitrator did not discredit this story, he upheld the discharge, finding the grievant's dishonest act gave rise to just cause. The arbitrator noted that the grievant was required to be tested under a "last-chance" agreement and had a great interest in making certain she did not violate her employer's trust.[124]

*2. Polygraph Tests.*   Although polygraph tests are not common in the workplace and are frequently prohibited under collective bargaining agreements and applicable statutes, the alleged falsification of a lie detector test arose in *Washtenaw County Sheriff's Department*.[125] A deputy sheriff volunteered to take a polygraph test after he was accused of theft. When the polygraph report was unfavorable, he falsified the results to indicate that he had no knowledge of the theft. Although the test was voluntary, the arbitrator held that, by falsifying the results and attempting to conceal and cover up, the deputy compromised his future credibility as a police officer.[126]

*3. Job Qualification Testing.*   Falsification during job qualification testing generally occurs when someone is applying for employment. The result is a refusal to hire the prospective employee, rather than an arbitrable discharge. Occasionally falsification occurs when an employee is attempting to transfer to another job or when the current job requires continuing certification. In *Trevathan v. Newport News Shipbuilding*,[127] the U.S. Court of Appeals for the Fourth Circuit

---

[121]For a further discussion, see Chapter 8.

[122]97 LA 30 (Nicholas, 1991).

[123]87 LA 719 (Rothstein, 1986).

[124]Id. at 721.

[125]84-2 ARB ¶ 8521 (Daniel, 1984).

[126]Id. at 5283-84 (because of the employee's long service with the county the arbitrator offered the grievant the option of resigning or taking a job in a nonlaw enforcement position after a disciplinary suspension).

[127]944 F.2d 902, 139 LRRM 3000, text at Westlaw 91-2005 (4th Cir., 1991), aff'g 752 F.Supp. 698, 139 LRRM 2990 (E.D. Va., 1990).

enforced an arbitrator's ruling that falsification of a qualification test, where potentially unqualified employees would not be retested for 1 year, was a serious offense that justified discharge under the terms of the contract.

4. *Quality Assurance Testing.*   Falsification of quality assurance tests has a substantial impact on the employer because a company's reputation rests on the quality of its product or service. In *Batesville Casket Co.,*[128] the company discharged an employee for falsifying quality assurance tests on caskets. The grievant allegedly indicated the caskets had been tested for air tightness when they had not. The arbitrator agreed that discipline was appropriate but reduced the discharge to reinstatement without back pay because of the grievant's 11 years of service and because the employer had entrusted quality control not to quality control employees, but to production employees who were subject to supervisory pressure to meet production goals.[129]

# IV. Falsification by Applicants

## A. *Introduction*

As a general principle, arbitrators agree that discipline is warranted when the evidence supports a finding that an employee falsified an employment application or other documents attendant to the initial employment processes, such as a medical history form. Falsification in this context generally falls into either of two types: willful acts of "commission" and deliberate acts of "omission." "Commission" occurs when an employee knowingly provides incorrect information to an inquiry. "Omission" occurs when an employee knowingly withholds information or provides answers that intentionally are incomplete, thus misrepresenting and misleading an employer. Arbitrators often are called upon to distinguish between such deliberate and willful acts of either "commission" or "omission" that involve an intent to defraud and situations where no intent to defraud is manifested. These situations include lapses of memory, oversights, inadvertent errors, poor judgment, or good faith misunderstandings as to how to answer.

## B. *Pledge of Truthfulness*

In administering discipline for false information provided in the application or hiring process, employers often cite the "caveat-pledge,"

---

[128]80-1 ARB ¶ 8066 (Seinsheimer, 1979).
[129]Id. at 3308.

which traditionally precedes the signature block where the employee executes the employment application. These provisions customarily incorporate at least three elements: (1) an acknowledgement that truthfulness is required, (2) an affirmation that truthful answers must be provided, and (3) an acknowledgement that termination is the probable and possible consequence if truthful answers are not provided. Two examples illustrate the common content of such statements. In *Morton Thiokol*[130] the arbitrator reported the "caveat-pledge" as follows:

> [A]ll information provided by me is true and correct to the best of my knowledge. I understand omissions and misrepresentations may be cause * * * for subsequent dismissal.[131]

In *Kraft Foods*[132] the "caveat-pledge" stated:

> I hereby affirm that my answers to the above are true and correct and that I have not knowingly falsified or withheld any facts in this application. *It is understood that false statements will be sufficient cause for dismissal from the employ of Kraft Foods.*[133]

## C. *Approaches to Evaluating Falsified Application Cases*

There are several lines of arbitral analysis for determining whether discharge is appropriate for falsification of an employment application. Certain core components are consistent elements in each approach. In 1968 in *Kraft Foods*,[134] the employee had falsely answered "no" to two questions about a prior injury. This falsification was discovered 34 months later, during which the grievant's employment had been satisfactory. In reinstating the employee without back pay, the arbitrator stated that he was impressed with the satisfactory service by the employee, was troubled by the length of time between the falsification and discovery, and was not persuaded that the employment relationship should be considered annulled on the basis of the "caveat-pledge."[135]

The arbitrator in *Kraft* set forth a checklist of factors that he found to be "especially important, controlling and decisive"[136] in application falsification cases. The factors, based "on a synthesis of all the

---

[130]85 LA 834 (Williams, 1985).

[131]Id. at 835.

[132]50 LA 161 (Turkus, 1967).

[133]Id. at 161–62 (emphasis added).

[134]Id.

[135]Id. See Wine Cellar, 81 LA 158 (Ray, 1983), and discussion of annulment theory in The Punishment and Annulment Theories in this chapter.

[136]Supra note 132, 50 LA at 166.

reported cases," are often cited in arbitration awards as the "*Kraft-Nine Factors*."[137] They are:

(1) The nature and character of the offense, defect or injury concealed;

(2) The number of matters concealed;

(3) The date when the concealed matters occurred in relation to the falsification;

(4) The reason why the falsification would have precluded the hiring ab initio, and whether that reason has remained valid;

(5) The time that elapsed between the falsification and the discovery;

(6) The performance of the employee between the date of falsification and date of discovery;

(7) The reason for the discovery;

(8) The employer's motivation in discharging based on the falsification; and

(9) Special considerations involving safety, national security and the like.[138]

Two years after the decision in *Kraft,* the arbitrator in *Thornsen Manufacturing Co.*[139] formulated a simplified, threefold test. Discharge for falsification of an application will be upheld if all three following factors are shown: (1) the falsification was deliberate as well as material; (2) the employer acted with dispatch on discovery of the falsification; and (3) the employer evaluated any mitigating circumstances that might justify an employee's conduct, such as lapse of memory or misunderstanding the questions.

Another approach was set forth in the 1971 decision in *Tiffany Metal Products Manufacturing Co.*[140] Since its publication, the case has been cited frequently with strong approval by arbitrators in discharge cases involving falsifications of employment applications and ancillary documents.[141] The test is especially useful when distinguishing falsifications that are willful and deliberate from those that are the result of inadvertent errors, oversights, and poor judgment. In *Tiffany,* the arbitrator articulated the following fourfold test or guideline,

---

[137]Salt River Project Agric. Improvement & Power Dist., 91 LA 1193, 1195 (R. Ross, 1988); Morton Thiokol, Inc., supra note 130; Brink's Inc., 79 LA 816, 822-24 (Briggs, 1982); Eaton Corp., 73 LA 367, 371 (Atwood, 1979).

[138]Kraft Foods, 50 LA 161, 166 (Turkus, 1967).

[139]55 LA 581 (Koven, 1970). See also Eaton Corp., supra note 137.

[140]56 LA 135 (R. Roberts, 1971).

[141]See Peoples Gas Sys., Inc., 91 LA 951 (Sergeant, 1988); V.A. Med. Ctr., 91 LA 588 (Howell, 1988); Utility Trailer Mfg. Co., 85 LA 643 (Brisco, 1985); Owens-Illinois, 83 LA 1265 (Cantor, 1984); Wine Cellar, 81 LA 158 (Ray, 1983); Huntington Alloys, Inc., 74 LA 176 (Katz, 1980); Cerro Copper Prods., Co., 76 LA 520 (Richardson, 1981); National Vendors, 67 LA 1043 (Edelman, 1976).

known as the *"Tiffany* test," for analyzing the propriety of discharge for the falsification of an employment application:

    (1) Was the misrepresentation deliberate or wilful?

    (2) Was it material to the employment at the time it was made?* * *

    (3) Was it material to the employment at the time of discharge? * * *

    (4) [Did] the employer act promptly and in good faith?[142]

In 1985, the arbitrator in *Morton Thiokol, Inc.,*[143] expanded on the *Tiffany* test, reaffirmed but modified the *Kraft*-Nine Factors, and articulated his own seven-factor analysis for evaluating application falsification cases. The factors are:

    (1) The nature and character of the offense, defect or injury concealed;

    (2) The presence or absence of an intent to defraud, which can be indicated by the deliberate nature and seriousness of the omissions;

    (3) The date the concealed matter occurred in relation to the falsification;

    (4) The effect the concealed information would have had on the hiring decision;

    (5) The elapsed time between the falsification and the discovery of the falsification;

    (6) The employee's performance between the date of falsification and date of discovery; and

    (7) The promptness of the employer's action after discovery of falsification.[144]

In *Morton Thiokol,* the arbitrator upheld the discharge, finding that the employee had deliberately omitted listing a former employer in the prior-employment segment of the application; the employer would not have hired the employee if that information had been truthfully presented; and the employer acted almost immediately upon learning of the falsification, even though 31 months had elapsed.[145]

## D. The Punishment and Annulment Theories

Two theories generally are advanced to justify discharge of an employee who has falsified an application: the "punishment" theory and the "annulment" theory.[146]

---

[142]Tiffany, supra note 140, at 140.

[143]85 LA 834 (Williams, 1985).

[144]Id. at 837–40.

[145]Id.

[146]Wine Cellar, 81 LA 158 (Ray, 1983). See also Borg-Warner Corp., 12 LA 207 (Kelliher, 1949) (falsification prevented employer from obtaining information from prior employer).

The annulment theory is based on the premise that the "original contract of employment" has been annulled or is voidable because of the intentional misrepresentation of a material fact. False assumptions were created and relied upon to establish the employee's initial employment status. The annulment theory is linked to the "caveat-pledge" statement under which the employee affixed his or her signature to the application. The punishment theory rests on the premise that the penalty of discharge is appropriate for the intentional and deliberate falsification of the employment application. This punishment, however, may be modified based on the *Tiffany* factors and any general considerations that may have an impact on the level of discipline administered.

In *Kraft Foods* the arbitrator wrestled both with the 34-month gap between falsification and discovery and with the application of the annulment and punishment theories. The arbitrator's comments in this benchmark arbitral decision are instructive:[147]

> Plainly, there comes a time when a discharge for falsification of an employment application becomes a penalty * * * rather than a ground per se for * * * rescission of the employment status. There comes a time when an employee has demonstrated * * * his continued employment will not give rise to the matter or event against which the employer's exclusion policy was directed * * *.
>
> How long a period of demonstrated satisfactory employment does it require * * *?
>
> The answer, of course, must vary from case to case depending upon all the facts and circumstances. * * * [P]rior concealment of falsification may lose its cogency and vitality as the basis of an annulment * * * of the employment relationship in the face of demonstrated satisfactory attitude, conduct and job performance as distinguished from the right to invoke disciplinary action therefor.[148]

### E. The Duration of Time Between Falsification and Discovery

Arbitrators attribute varying levels of significance to the time that elapses between the falsification and its discovery. In *Huntington Alloys, Inc.*,[149] the arbitrator upheld a discharge for falsification of an employment application when the discovery was made almost 8 years after the falsification. In *National Vendors*,[150] the arbitrator reinstated an employee when the discovery was made more than 4 years after the falsification. In both cases, the arbitrators reaffirmed and relied on the *Tiffany* test.

---

[147]Kraft Foods, 50 LA 161 (Turkus, 1967).
[148]Id. at 166.
[149]74 LA 176 (Katz, 1980).
[150]67 LA 1043 (Edelman, 1976).

Historically, a 1-year statute of limitations was applied to application falsification cases. This rule was based on a 1945 decision in *Ford Motor Co.*[151] where arbitrator concluded that to go beyond such a period would be unduly and unjustly harsh and unreasonable. It became a "rule of thumb" to some early arbitrators, but others applied it as an alternative[152] or gave it recognition, but did not accept it.[153]

A few years later, the arbitrator in *Kraft Foods* concluded that "[t]he preponderant number of reported decisions, however, have not adopted the one year statute of limitations promulgated in the Ford Motor Co. opinion."[154] In *Anaconda American Brass Co.*,[155] the arbitrator expressed the view that "[t]here is no way to fix a statute of limitations other than in relation to the circumstances of the particular case."[156] The contemporary arbitral rationale follows this approach.

Although modern cases revisit the "1-year rule,"[157] the prevailing contemporary approach to the impact of the duration of time between falsification and discovery is simple and direct: the longer the time between falsification and discovery, the more likely it becomes that the arbitrator will be persuaded by extenuating or mitigating circumstances and will apply a modified version of the punishment theory for the falsification. The materiality of the falsification may have an influence, but, as the second and third inquiries of the *Tiffany* test indicate, the impact may have been different at the time of the falsification than at the time of discovery.[158]

In *Utility Trailer Manufacturing Co.*,[159] relying on the application of the *Tiffany* test, the arbitrator found that an employee who had falsified information about his back condition should be discharged even though the discovery of the falsification was 23 months later. In reaching this conclusion, the arbitrator explained how he balanced the factors relative to the time between falsification and discovery:

> [T]he company had a right to rely on the accuracy of the Grievant's statements on the application form and on the medical history form,

---

[151]Ford Motor Co., Opinion No. A-184 (Shulman, 1945) (Chamberlain, Cases on Labor Relations, 1949, pp. 466 ff.), cited in Kraft Foods, 50 LA 161, 165 (Turkus, 1967); Quaker Oats Co., 36 LA 889 (S. Jaffee, 1961).

[152]Aviation Maintenance Corp., 8 LA 261 (Aaron, 1947).

[153]Bell Aircraft Corp., 17 LA 230 (Shister, 1951).

[154]Kraft Foods, 50 LA 161, 165 (Turkus, 1967).

[155]46 LA 559 (Altieri, 1965). See Salt River Project Agric. Improvement & Power Dist., 91 LA 1193, 1196 (R. Ross, 1988), in which Anaconda Am. Brass Co. is cited and quoted.

[156]46 LA at 562.

[157]See Ferro-Alloys Corp., 59 LA 255 (Keltner, 1972) (5½ years of satisfactory service following falsification; employee reinstated); Ward Mfg. Co., 46 LA 233 (Seinsheimer, 1966) (employee with 2-year clean record after falsification had omitted prior prison record; employee reinstated); Niagara Frontier Transit Sys., Inc., 26 LA 575 (Thompson, 1957) (nondisclosure of conviction and other charges, but 10 years of satisfactory service after falsification; employee reinstated).

[158]See Salt River Project Agric. Improvement & Power Dist., 91 LA 1193, 1195 (R. Ross, 1988).

[159]85 LA 643 (Brisco, 1985).

and the delay did not prejudice the Grievant in any way. The Company took action promptly once the facts were known. Its failure to investigate at an earlier time in reliance on those statements should not preclude appropriate disciplinary action.[160]

In addition to the duration of time between the falsification and discovery, another period that may be relevant is the time that has elapsed between the date of discovery and the date on which disciplinary action was administered.[161] The longer this period, absent justification, the greater the likelihood that the administered discipline will be modified under the punishment theory.

### F. Mitigating Circumstances

As illustrated by the first prong of the *Tiffany* test ("Was the misrepresentation deliberate or willful?"), falsification alone often will not support discharge. While an arbitrator may find that information on an employment application or medical history forms is neither truthful nor accurate, discipline nonetheless may be reduced under the punishment theory when the arbitrator finds no intent to defraud or mislead.[162] Where intent has not been established, arbitrators have accepted lapses of memory, oversights, inadvertent errors, good faith misunderstanding as to how to answer a question, or poor judgment[163] as justification for either reduction or negation of the administered discipline.

In *Salt River Project Agricultural Improvement & Power District,*[164] the arbitrator upheld the discharge of an employee who had

---

[160]Id. at 645.

[161]V.A. Med. Ctr., 91 LA 588 (Howell, 1988) (employer needs to act with reasonable promptness after discovery that a false statement was made on the employment application). In V. A. Med. Ctr. the arbitrator cited to Tiffany (at 592-93), Wine Cellar (at 591), and Huntington Alloys, Inc. (at 591) (employee answered "no" to question as to convictions when the answer should have been "yes").

[162]See Kaiser Steel Corp., 64 LA 194 (Roberts, 1975) ("no" to conviction question; however, employee understood it had been "dismissed", no showing of willful and deliberate falsification); Caterpillar Tractor Co., 36 LA 1439 (Young, 1991) (no intent to mislead employer regarding prior back problems). Compare with Peoples Gas Sys., Inc., 91 LA 951 (Sergent, 1988) ("no" to workers' compensation claim; intentional concealment found; discharge sustained); Cerro Copper Prods. Co., 76 LA 520 (Richardson, 1981) (did not reveal prior injuries; intent to conceal found); Farmland Foods, Inc., 64 LA 1260 (McKenna, 1975) ("no" to back problem; intentional concealment found; discharge sustained); Chanslor-Western Oil Co., 61 LA 113 (Meiners, 1973) ("no" to back trouble; intentional concealment found; discharge sustained).

[163]Owens-Illinois, 83 LA 1265 (Cantor, 1984) (confusion between "treatment" and "tests" in medical context); Gold Kist, Inc., 77 LA 569 (Statham, 1981) (signed application, but did not personally complete it); Norandex, Inc., 71 LA 1169 (Feldman, 1978) (did not think "fiancee" was a "relative"); National Vendors, 67 LA 1042 (Edelman, 1976) (did not understand he had a back problem); American Stevedoring Corp., 65 LA 801 (Davis, 1975) ("sincerely believed" a written proclamation and restoration of rights removed conviction); Hoffman Indus., Inc., 61 LA 929 (Duff, 1973) (employee did not reveal degrees for a "blue collar" position).

[164]91 LA 1193 (R. Ross, 1988).

been convicted as a drug dealer but had not revealed this in his employment application. After reviewing in detail a number of arbitral decisions,[165] the arbitrator concluded that the nature of the unrevealed conviction, when balanced with the "unwarranted risks which could prove detrimental" by this employee's "regular, continuous and constant contact" with this particular employer's employees, customers, and the public at large justified upholding the termination.[166] The approach in *Salt River Project,* however, may be contrasted with other arbitral rationales as illustrated in *Ryan Aeronautical Co.:*[167]

> Without in any sense minimizing the obligation of the employee to answer questions properly asked by his prospective employer, [the arbitrator] believes that to allow even substantial false statements in applications to be used forever as absolute and complete cause for discharge is to prevent an employee from reforming his life and from building better than he may have built before.* * *
>
> [T]he good employee who is discharged after some time is likely to suffer a much heavier penalty than the one who is refused employment in the first instance. * * * Increasing seniority, advancing age and accumulative good behavior may all place the employee in a good position where discharge for a nefarious act becomes a penalty of growing severity. In a sense the falsifier deserves the extra penalty because of his dereliction, and up to point his misconduct should outweigh the burden of the increasing severity of the results of his own acts, but it does seem as if a man should at some time be relieved from such very heavy penalties for all except the most heinous of crimes.[168]

The foregoing rationale is consistent with that found in *Kraft Foods,*[169] where the arbitrator expressed the view that "'the principle of a statute of limitations is well recognized even though it means that the mere lapse of time thus enables a guilty person to escape what otherwise would be regarded as just punishment.'"[170] Other arbitrators faced with similar issues have used analogous reasoning to determine that discharge of the errant employee was too severe in light of all the circumstances of a particular case.[171]

In two cases presenting relatively novel circumstances, arbitrators upheld discharges. In one an employee claiming to be "functionally illiterate" falsified his medical forms at the time of employment

---

[165]Id. at 1195–96.

[166]Id. at 1196.

[167]29 LA 182 (Spaulding, 1957).

[168]Id. at 185–86.

[169]50 LA 161 (Turkus, 1967). For additional discussions of the duty of loyalty, see Finkin, "Employee's Duty of Loyalty: An Arbitral-Judicial Comparison," in Arbitration 1993: Arbitration and the Changing World of Work, Proceedings of the 46th Annual Meeting, National Academy of Arbitrators, Gruenberg, ed., 200 (BNA Books, 1994).

[170]50 LA at 165, quoting Ford Motor Co., Opinion No. A-148 (Shulman, 1945) (Chamberlain, Cases on Labor Relations, 1949, pp. 466 ff.).

[171]Ferro-Alloys Corp., 59 LA 255 (Keltner, 1972); Niagra Frontier Transit Sys., Inc., 26 LA 575 (Thompson, 1957).

but understood the need for truthfulness.[172] In the other an employee claimed that he answered the questions untruthfully due to "divine inspiration" and "on the advice of his doctor."[173]

## V. The Duty of Loyalty: Disparaging the Employer[174]

Employers have a right to expect loyalty from their employees. This includes employees doing their best to enhance rather than endanger the best interests of the employer.[175] It has been generally recognized that "[t]he relationship between an employer and employee is, in reality, a two-way street in that the employer has certain responsibilities toward his employee who, in turn, has obligations—including loyalty—to his place of employment."[176] As one arbitrator rhetorically inquired, "Can you bite the hand that feeds you, and insist on staying for future banquets?"[177]

### A. The Duty

The two seminal arbitration decisions most clearly defining disloyalty, the factors that should be considered, and the probative value ascribed to those factors are *Los Angeles Herald-Examiner*[178] and *Zellerbach Paper Co.*[179] Arbitration decisions subsequent to these, in one way or another, are based on one or more of the factors established by these decisions.

In *Los Angeles Herald-Examiner*,[180] the arbitrator chronicled the factors arbitrators consider when determining whether an employee's conduct rises to the level of dishonesty or disloyalty permitting discipline:

the type of business; the nature of the employment; the degree of public visibility; the extent of the responsibility for the offensive acts of the person allegedly disloyal; the significance of any public policy affected by the conduct; the foreseeability of adverse economic impact on the employer; actual impact; whether, and to what degree, malice or carelessness motivated the conduct; the privilege of the employee to engage

---

[172]Mor-Flo Indus., 89 LA 762 (King, 1987).

[173]U.S. Steel, 74 LA 354 (Simpkins, 1980).

[174]For additional discussions of the duty of loyalty, see Finkin, supra note 169.

[175]Los Angeles Herald-Examiner, 49 LA 453, 464 (Jones, 1967).

[176]San Diego Gas & Elec. Co., 82 LA 1039, 1041 (Johnston, 1983).

[177]Forest City Publ'g Co., 58 LA 773, 783 (McCoy, 1972).

[178]49 LA 453, 464 (Jones, 1967).

[179]75 LA 868 (Gentile, 1980).

[180]49 LA at 453 (Jones, 1967).

in self-expression or in the pursuit of economic or psychological self-interest; the confidentiality of the material disclosed; the relevance of the disclosure to the expected job functions of the employee; the extent of authority or confidence reposed in the employee by the employer.[181]

Subsequently, in *Zellerbach Paper,* the arbitrator indicated that the following related factors should control whether discipline is appropriate:

(1) Was the act or conduct expressed orally or in writing? * * *

(2) Was the act or conduct directed toward persons within the private organization or outside the organization? * * *

(3) If the act or conduct was directed toward a customer or competitor of the organization, did it directly or indirectly cause damage to the business (competitive position or image) or interfere with the advantageous relations between the organization and the customer or competitor (loss of business opportunity)? * * *

(4) If the act or conduct was directed to a governmental enforcement agency, did the employee exhaust internal avenues of redress or correction (also were these "avenues" reasonably accessible and usable) or was the act or conduct directed to the exercise of a legal right protected by one or more of the applicable laws? * * *

(5) Were the statements (either oral or written) known to be or reasonably held by the employees making the statements to be "true", "false" or "undetermined" at the time they were made? * * *

(6) Was the "tone" or actual language of the statements (either oral or written) malicious[,] slanderous, inflammatory, disruptive, or [did it place] the company in a position of ridicule or disrepute? * * *

(7) Were there "substantial personal rights of expression and citizenship" involved?" * * *

(8) Did the employer condone the act or conduct in the past and did the company's policies adequately place the employee on notice of the possible and probable consequences if the act or conduct is carried out?[182]

---

[181]49 LA at 464. See also Union-Tribune Publ'g Co., 51 LA 421 (Jones, 1968).
[182]75 LA at 875-77.

## B. Decisions Upholding Discipline

Applying these factors, an arbitrator upheld an employer's written reprimand of an employee who published an article in a newspaper alleging the employer's nuclear power plant had an atrocious safety record, although the employee's actions were entirely without malice and reflected her personal thoughts regarding nuclear power. The action was not in the best interest of sound employer-employee relationship, and other ways were available to vent her feelings regarding nuclear power and weaponry.[183]

In *Southwestern Electric Power Co.*,[184] the arbitrator upheld discipline for filing a lawsuit against the employer and five company officials in an effort to injure the company's business or reputation. The arbitrator found that the employee's actions were a direct affront to managerial authority in a manner that adversely affected the employer-employee relationship; the actions were vengeful and spiteful, and the employee did not exhaust all internal remedies.

Another arbitrator found that an airline properly discharged a flight attendant for sending 14 unauthorized, unsigned messages through the in-house computerized communication system. The messages disparaged management, discredited the company, or otherwise could be considered objectionable by reasonable people. The messages were widely disseminated throughout the system, a repeated misuse of company property.[185]

In *Monarch Machine Tool Co.*,[186] the arbitrator found a 20-day suspension properly imposed by the employer for an employee "joke," written on the bottom of a posted newspaper clipping, that this employer "builds junk," because the comment was malicious and the grievant had a record of prior discipline.

A city employee was properly suspended for 3 days for writing a letter to the newspaper referring to the head of his employment group as "the head inquisitor for his section." The letter publicly disparaged the department, policies, and personnel, and the comment did not rise to the level of a legitimate public concern." The employer had previously warned the grievant that further disciplinary action would be taken if he repeated the issuance of disrespectful comments about the chief financial officer.[187] In another case, a journalist who published a book based on his work as an investigative reporter about his employer's financial difficulties, bankruptcy, management, and

---

[183]San Diego Gas & Elec. Co., 82 LA 1039 (Johnston, 1983).

[184]84 LA 743 (Taylor, 1985).

[185]Eastern Air Lines, 90 LA 272 (Jedel, 1987).

[186]82 LA 880 (Schedler, Jr., 1984).

[187]Los Angeles Harbor Dep't, 84 LA 860 (Weiss, 1985).

ownership was properly discharged. The journalist went beyond analyzing and reporting current events to commenting on them in a derogatory fashion highly critical of the employer's conduct.[188]

A discharge was upheld in *Southwestern Electric Power Co.,*[189] where an employee filed a lawsuit against the company and five officials for injuries sustained when an aerial bucket being used to replace a street light malfunctioned, causing him to be suspended in midair. The grievant avoided internal remedies that were available to resolve the dispute, and the arbitrator concluded that the employee filed the action to damage the company's business or reputation. In *San Diego Gas & Electric Co.,*[190] the arbitrator upheld a written reprimand for an engineer who published a newspaper article attributing a poor safety record to a unit at the employer's plant. The arbitrator found that grievant did not act out of malice but merely expressed her personal opinion.[191]

## C. Decisions That Modify Discharge

In *Washoe County,*[192] an employee was terminated for making statements to the news media against his department, its management, and the employer's sexually transmitted disease program. The arbitrator reduced the penalty and, addressing the balance that must be struck, said that neither the employer's right to conduct its business in an orderly fashion nor the employee's free speech rights are absolute. The employer's right "hinges on the requirement for loyal employees who usually keep adverse comments about the organization 'within the family'."[193] The arbitrator also observed that neither the employee nor the employer made an effort to resolve the matter and concluded that the failure to resolve the matter was a shared responsibility which justified modifying the action taken by the employer.

In *Borg-Warner Corp.,*[194] the employer improperly discharged an employee for violating rules prohibiting wasting time during working hours and giving false testimony to company management. The employee distributed a cartoon reflecting employee reaction to a proposed memorandum on working conditions.

In *Oklahoma Fixture Co.,*[195] just cause did not exist to discharge a carpenter for disloyalty after he asked a company customer whether

---

[188]United Press Int'l, 94 LA 841 (Ables, 1990).
[189]84 LA 743 (Taylor, 1985).
[190]82 LA 1039 (Johnson, 1983).
[191]Id. See also United Press Int'l, supra note 187.
[192]75 LA 1033 (Boner, 1980).
[193]Id. at 1034.
[194]77 LA 443 (Kaufman, 1981).
[195]98 LA 1178 (Allen, 1992).

it was getting fixtures from his employer at a lower price in light of layoffs and wage cuts. The grievant was honest and forthright, had no history as a malcontent or troublemaker, and there was no direct evidence of a negative impact on the company.

## D. *Decisions That Found No Penalty*

In *Town of Plainville,*[196] the arbitrator considered the following factors in finding that a public employee whistleblower should not be disciplined: significance of activity exposed; employee's motives; whether information given is true, and if not, the employee's "state of mind" regarding the truth of such information; means chosen by the employee to communicate his information or allegations; the potential or actual harm to the employer; and the employee's right to engage in self-expression.

In *Hopewood Foods, Inc.*[197] a stocker/cashier was discharged because he had criticized management and disagreed with corporate policies at the annual company shareholders' meeting. The employee had been representing his mother, who owned 49 percent of the company's common stock. The employer argued that this ownership made the grievant a part of management; therefore, the company did not have to establish just cause for termination. The arbitrator rejected this assertion but noted that the grievant's comments would have warranted discharge under most circumstances. They did not in this instance, however, because the grievant was not acting as an employee but as a representative of a stockholder.

---

[196]77 LA 161 (Sacks, 1981).
[197]74 LA 349 (Mullin, Jr., 1979).

# Chapter 8

# Workplace Misconduct

## I. Introduction

There is a wide variety of workplace misconduct for which employees are disciplined. It is often said that labor arbitration is extremely fact specific, and this is especially true when it comes to discipline for workplace misconduct. It is impossible to cover every act of misconduct; consequently, this chapter cannot be exhaustive.

## II. Health and Safety Violations

The Occupational Safety and Health Act[1] has been interpreted by the United States Supreme Court as requiring an employer to eliminate significant harm, but not to require absolute safety.[2] Because an employer is legally required to provide for the safety of its employees, it may properly promulgate and enforce safety rules.[3] Employees who are concerned about their own safety must be permitted to raise questions concerning hazards.[4] Where an employee has a legitimate fear of imminent danger, the employee may properly refuse to follow a management order.[5] Other refusals to follow safety rules, however, may constitute insubordination.[6]

---

[1]29 U.S.C.§651 et seq.

[2]Industrial Union Dep't v. American Petroleum Inst., 100 S.Ct. 2844 (1980).

[3]Niagara Mohawk Power Corp., 74 LA 58 (Markowitz, 1980).

[4]Reserve Mining Co., 55 LA 648 (Sembower, 1970).

[5]T&J Indus., 79 LA 697 (Clark, 1982). See also Whirlpool Corp. v. Marshall, 100 S.Ct. 883 (1980).

[6]Chanute Mfg. Co., 92-2 ARB ¶ 8452 (Levy, 1991). See also Chapter 5 on other refusals.

257

Safety rules may be unilateral or negotiated. If they are unilateral, they must be reasonable and enforced in an unbiased manner.[7] In addition, if a substantial change is made in a rule previously agreed to by the union, that change must be negotiated.[8] Substance abuse by an employee can pose potential safety concerns, and that topic is covered in Chapter 6.

While the damage caused by a safety violation may be a factor in determining penalty, the employer cannot rely solely on the severity of the accident to establish culpability. For instance, where safety violations committed by the chief lineman led to the death of another employee, but the procedures the chief lineman followed were a matter of regular practice, no suspension was justified.[9]

As with other rules, an employee may not be disciplined if he is not given notice that a task requires following certain safety rules. For instance, an employer did not have just cause to discharge an employee for not wearing a face shield while pumping chemicals, where the supposed rule was not known by the employee, and no documents had been distributed to employees communicating the rule.[10] If the rule is not uniformly enforced by supervisors, then the employee may be entitled to a lesser penalty, if any.[11] It may be improper to punish an employee if the employer has condoned the violation.[12] And if supervisors treat employees disparately, the penalty may be reduced.[13]

While smoking in the workplace is often a matter for negotiations, where safety is clearly the basis for prohibiting smoking, as where there are highly flammable materials, the employer can promulgate a rule and discipline employees for violating it. The rule, however, must be reasonable in light of the actual circumstances. For instance, a company could not impose a no-smoking rule in an area containing

---

[7]See Capital Bldg. Maintenance Servs., 100 LA 887 (Concepcion, 1993). See also Doe Run Co., 95 LA 705, (Heinz, 1990); Allied Chem. Corp., 74 LA 412 (Eischen, 1980).

[8]Curwood, Inc., 96 LA 506 (O'Grady, 1991).

[9]Choptank Elec. Coop., 87-2 ARB ¶ 8553 (Bernhardt, 1987).

[10]Cone Mills Corp., 104 LA 833 (Nolan, 1995); Smurfit Recycling Co., 103 LA 243 (Richman, 1994) (discharge improper where violated rule was posted in lunchroom, but not in employee's department, and where rule was posted only in Spanish, and employee only knew English).

[11]National O Ring, 97 LA 600 (Cloke, 1991) (suspension reduced to written warning where enforcement of safety rule was not uniform).

[12]Ideal Elec. Co., 98 LA 410 (Heekin, 1991) (rule against making safety devices inoperative is modified by adding phrase "without any form of management involvement" in order to prevent injustice to employee because of improper directive).

[13]Iowa Power, Inc., 97 LA 1029 (Thornell, 1991) (demotion of working foreman was too severe where grievant's record is no worse than another working foreman who was involved in equally serious accident but disciplined with lesser demotion than grievant); Straits Steel & Wire Co., 96 LA 798 (Mackraz, 1991) (discharge for alleged safety rule violation reduced where other violators of rule received warnings or suspension, and co-worker who committed similar violation 3 months later was not disciplined); Excel Corp., 95 LA 1069 (Shearer, 1990) (termination improper where employer failed to disprove that grievant was only employee ever terminated under similar circumstances).

hazardous materials, when the area was already heated by a gas-fired heater with a constant pilot burning.[14]

## III. Accidents

Involvement in an accident on the job may, in some circumstances, be cause for employee discipline.[15] Whenever an accident occurs, the first question is whether the accident was preventable and is chargeable to the employee.[16] Arbitrators may require a thorough investigation in which the grievant is given an opportunity to explain the circumstances.[17] In any discipline for accidents, the employer has the burden of proving that its decision to discipline the employee was justified: that the employee was culpable.[18]

If the facts reveal that the accident was preventable, then discipline is proper. Generally, unless the accident is extremely serious, progressive discipline is appropriate.[19] For instance, in *Jefferson Smurfit Corp.*,[20] an employee had been given a warning regarding his high injury rate. After the employee was involved in another accident following the warning, the employee was given a 3-day suspension. The employee was finally terminated following a subsequent accident.[21] The arbitrator found that the prior discipline put the employee on notice that he could be terminated if his reckless and negligent conduct continued.[22] Given the system of progressive discipline, termination was a proper form of discipline.[23]

In addition to the preference for progressive discipline, the range of discipline upheld by arbitrators varies greatly depending upon the individual case. Arbitrators have imposed or upheld discipline ranging from written warnings[24] to terminations[25] for involvement in an accident. For instance, an arbitrator found that discharge was proper discipline for an employee who was terminated, according to employer policy, after causing two traffic accidents in a 3-year period.[26] To the contrary, another arbitrator reduced to a 30-day suspension

---

[14]Van Waters & Rogers, 102 LA 609 (Feldman, 1993).

[15]See Jefferson Smurfit Corp./Container Corp. of Am., 98 LA 357 (Ipavec, 1992).

[16]Mead Paper, 91 LA 52 (Curry, 1988).

[17]Union St. Bus Co., 102 LA 976 (Sweeney, 1994).

[18]A.Y. McDonald Mfg. Co., 95 LA 803 (Fogelberg, 1990).

[19]Oil Transp. Co., 89-2 ARB ¶ 8443 (Carter, 1989).

[20]Jefferson Smurfit Corp./Container Corp. of Am., supra note 15, at 359.

[21]Id.

[22]Id. at 359–60.

[23]Id. (this was true regardless of the fact that no one was injured in the accident that led to discharge).

[24]A.Y. McDonald Mfg. Co., 95 LA 803 (Fogelberg, 1990).

[25]Griffin Indus., 97 LA 370 (Modjeska, 1991).

[26]Id. at 370.

an employer's discharge of an employee for numerous traffic accidents.[27] In that case the arbitrator found it important that the employer had a progressive scheme of discipline and that the grievant may not have been given proper instructions on the operation of his truck and was thus not solely responsible for the property damage.[28]

Similarly, an arbitrator reduced the penalty from a final written warning to a mere written warning in a case where it was not clear that the accident was solely the employee's fault, and there was evidence that the employer's rules had been unequally enforced.[29] In another case that emphasizes the importance of individual facts, an arbitrator found that an employee who had been an incumbent automotive mechanic for more than 17 years should not be demoted despite a few instances of carelessness resulting in accidents.[30] The arbitrator found that while the employee engaged in wrongdoing, the few incidents in the course of employment did not prove that the employee was incapable of performing the job as required by the collective bargaining agreement.[31]

Because accidents may result in liability claims, employers can require that all incidents involving property damage or personal injury, even if minor, be reported. Failure to report such incidents may be a reason for discipline. Rules that require the reporting of accidents may be strictly enforced, provided the enforcement is consistent.[32] The eventual penalty for failure to report an accident can be discharge.[33] Damage to property can indicate the extent of the employee's negligence, but some arbitrators have found the loss must be significant before an arbitrator will sustain a discharge.[34] When the loss is significant, but the penalty of discharge is not warranted for other reasons, the award of back pay may be reduced.[35]

Rules established in 1988 require postaccident drug testing in various transportation industries.[36] Employers who are subject to the Drug-Free Workplace Act of 1988[37] must implement a program and must clearly communicate the program and penalties, including the availability of employee assistance programs. Under the 1988 rules, discharge is not required if an employee tests positive for drugs.[38]

---

[27]Steel Branch Mining, 96 LA 931, 935–36 (Roberts, 1991).

[28]Id.

[29]A.Y. McDonald Mfg. Co., 95 LA 803 (Folberg, 1990).

[30]USS-Minnesota Ore Operations, 98 LA 251 (Peterson, 1991).

[31]Id. at 254.

[32]Browning-Ferris Indus., 88 LA 773 (Belcher, 1987); Merchants Fast Motor Lines, Inc., 81 LA 869 (Marcus, 1983).

[33]ATC/Vancom, Inc., 102 LA 249 (Cipolla, 1993).

[34]Hinckley & Schmitt, 73 LA 654 (Goldberg, 1979).

[35]Steelworkers, 92-2 ARB ¶ 8378 (Marino, 1992).

[36]53 Fed. Reg. 47,002 (Nov. 21, 1988).

[37]Pub. L. No. 100-690, Title V, Subtitle D, 41 U.S.C. §§ 701-07, 54 Fed Reg. 4,946 (Jan. 31, 1989).

[38]Von's Cos., 106 LA 740 (Darrow, 1996); Pacific Offshore Pipeline Co., 106 LA 690 (Kaufman, 1996).

## IV. Sleeping on the Job

Sleeping on the job is often a direct violation of company rules or patently contrary to the company's best interests.[39] Employees generally know that some sort of discipline will follow if they are found asleep during working hours.[40] There is no general consensus on the propriety and amount of discipline to be imposed in any specific sleeping situation. This lack of consensus exists because there are a number of mitigating and aggravating factors that may affect the outcome in any case.[41] In addition, usual considerations such as progressive discipline, fair warning of the rule and its consequences, longevity, and nondiscriminatory treatment among similarly situated employees will also apply to sleeping violations.[42]

In the earliest reported sleeping-on-the-job decisions, proof of sleeping was the sole consideration.[43] The burden of proof was simple: if the employer could prove the employee was sleeping, discharge was justified.[44] Employees were held to a strict standard where proof of sleep was established. Employee explanations and the arbitrariness of the sanction were irrelevant.

The analysis employed in sleeping-on-the-job cases has evolved over time. Although proof of sleep remains a component of the modern analysis, arbitrators now consider a number of additional factors in determining whether there is "just cause" for discharge. One of the

---

[39]Summary of Labor Arbitration Awards, American Arbitration Ass'n, Report No. 369-10 (Brown, Dec. 15, 1989).

[40]Todd Shipyard Corp., 81 LA 955, 957 (Letter, 1983) (grievant admitted knowledge of the rule); Washington Nat'l Airport, 80 LA 1018, 1020 (Everitt, 1983) (inattention to duty is like sleeping).

[41]Southwestern Eng'g Co., 95 LA 1006 (Suardi, 1990) (raising several issues that are important in the decision-making process: safety and productivity concerns, culpability, and mitigating factors that will affect the imposition of discipline); Basin Elec. Power Coop., 91 LA 443 (Jacobowski, 1988) (reproducing the employer's documentary checklist for determining whether there is sufficient evidence of sleeping; no reported ill effects on his job or performance, no reports of problems of safety, malfunction, or uncompleted duties; he was alert and not startled when approached and performed satisfactorily before and after, had not arranged an intentional sleep and was still at his work station; incident was not part of a continuing pattern or repeated sequence of prior infractions and warnings); Georgia-Pacific Corp., 88 LA 244 (Byars, 1987) (arbitrator found that sleeping away from the duty station, a poor work record, and prior sleeping discipline were the primary factors in terminations for sleeping); Nabisco Brands, Inc., 86 LA 430 (Cox, 1985).

[42]Olin Corp., 86 LA 1096 (Seidman, 1986) (addressing due process concerns based on analysis found in Enterprise Wire Co., 46 LA 359 (Dougherty, 1966) (set forth seven principles for due process in disciplinary cases)).

[43]Consolidated Vultee Aircraft Corp., 10 LA 844, 847 (Aaron, 1948) ("The only question to be determined by the Arbitrator is whether [the grievant] was actually sleeping on the job.").

[44]Pet, Inc., 83 LA 468 (1984) (no clear proof of sleep, reinstated); Washington Metal Trades, Inc., 80 LA 1 (Keltner, 1982) (no proof of sleep, reinstated); General Dynamics, 58 LA 1240 (Ansell, 1972) (employee sleeping on break, issue was whether they could combine coffee/lunch break, issue was not "proof of sleep"; no proof of sleep, reinstated); Amerada Hess Corp., 58 LA 295 (Kerrison, 1972) (no proof of sleep, reinstated).

earliest decisions reflecting this shift in the analysis was *Esso Standard Oil Co.,*[45] where the arbitrator held that proof of sleep was not the sole question to be considered. The arbitrator examined the grievant's past work record and weighed his duties against the reasonableness of the punishment, concluding that a 2-week suspension was justified.

There are three factors arbitrators typically use in deciding whether to uphold a disciplinary penalty in sleeping-on-the-job cases. First, arbitrators examine whether the employer has established and consistently applied a workplace rule against "sleeping on the job." Second, they consider mitigating factors, including the work record of the employee and the reasons why the employee fell asleep. Third, arbitrators consider the impact on the safety of other workers, and on the employer's property and business interests. Arbitrators balance the rule, the mitigating circumstances, and the impact on other workers and the business to decide appropriate sanctions for sleeping on the job.

## A. *Workplace Rules and Enforcement*

The first factor reviewed in any sleeping violation is whether the employer maintains a specific work rule prohibiting sleeping on the job. If the employer has specific rules, the more narrowly the sleeping policy is defined, the more influential the rule becomes.[46] Not all arbitrators require a specific rule.[47] In addition, contractual provisions, company rules, and prior disciplinary actions can define the appropriate penalty for sleeping violations and put the employee on notice of the penalty.[48]

Where the employer's work rules are not specific, sleeping on the job may be considered under the employer's general rules of conduct. An employee's inattention to his or her job can be classified as simple job neglect,[49] falsification of company records,[50] knowing destruction

---

[45]19 LA 495, 498 (McCoy, 1952). See also James Vernor Co., 20 LA 50, 53 (Bowles, 1953) (requiring reasonable uniformity in the enforcement of penalties).

[46]Valentec/Kisco-Olivette, 100 LA 71, 74 (Fowler, 1992) ("[i]f the Company had in place a policy calling for discharge based upon sleeping during one's shift the position of the Company would be much stronger").

[47]Boise Cascade Paper Group, 86 LA 177, 178 (Marlatt, 1985) (stating that "[w]hile the Company's work rules do not define what are 'intolerable infractions,' there is little doubt that sleeping on the job could be considered such an infraction under appropriate circumstances").

[48]Scott Paper Co., 99 LA 624 (Byars, 1992); Monsanto Co., 98 LA 710 (Kubie, 1992); Thorn Apple Valley, 98 LA 183 (Kanner, 1991); Southwestern Eng'g Co., 95 LA 1006 (Suardi, 1990); American Welding & Mfg. Co., 94 LA 340 (Duda, 1990).

[49]Scott Paper Co., 99 LA 624 (Byars, 1992) (negligent job performance); Georgia-Pacific Corp., 88 LA 244 (Byars, 1987) (neglect of job duties); Boise Cascade Paper Group, 86 LA 177 (Marlatt, 1985) (malingering).

[50]Valentec/Kisco-Olivette, 100 LA 71 (Fowler, 1992); Scott Paper Co., 99 LA 624 (Byars, 1992) (company charge that sleeping is dishonesty); Southwestern Eng'g Co., 95 LA 1006, 1010 (Suardi, 1990) ("sleeping has been likened to a theft of Company property").

of company property,[51] failure to produce the allotted production quota, or loss of critical production capacity.[52] This neglect can be much more serious where the employee was performing safety-related duties.[53] The objective characteristics of the employee's actions—location, timing, and culpability—are decisive factors in determining the level of discipline to be imposed.[54]

Given the seriousness of discharge, arbitrators generally require employers in sleeping-on-the-job cases to prove: (1) the existence of a clear workplace rule; (2) consistent enforcement of that rule, and (3) knowledge of the penalty to be imposed.[55] Where rules and penalties governing sleeping on the job have not been made clear, arbitrators may sustain the grievance or reduce sanctions. In one such case, the absence of a workplace rule was cited, among other factors, as reason to reinstate an employee who had been found sleeping hidden behind equipment.[56] Similarly, an employee who fell asleep during paid break time was reinstated where the company rule was unclear as to whether this conduct was prohibited.[57] Thus, while some arbitrators discount the need for a workplace rule,[58] most consider it an important factor in determining the appropriate discipline.[59]

---

[51]Todd Shipyard Corp., 81 LA 955 (Letter, 1983) (careless disregard for the safety of human life); New York Wire Mills Corp., 76 LA 232 (LeWinter, 1981) (serious neglect of job duties and responsibilities); New Castle State Hosp., 74 LA 365 (Witney, 1980) (resident neglect); FMC Corp., 73 LA 705 (Marlatt, 1979) (may result in delayed or defective shipments); Federal Prison Sys., 72 LA 1230 (Rule, 1979) (inattention to duty).

[52]Monsanto Co., 98 LA 710 (Kubie, 1992) (grievant fell asleep and failed to "drop a batch" of calcium requiring the entire plant to be shut down for several hours). See also Consolidation Coal Co., 99 LA 945 (Dissen, 1992); New York Wire Mills Corp., 76 LA 232 (LeWinter, 1981).

[53]Todd Shipyard Corp., 81 LA 955, 957 (Letter, 1983) (critically important for fire watch to remain alert "to guard against the extreme danger that fire poses to human life" and equipment); Mantua Chem. Terminal, 79 LA 732 (Mitrani, 1982) (employee found sleeping while working at oil refinery was properly discharged).

[54]Vought Corp., 81 LA 1200 (Stephens, 1983) (sleeping location could be seen from supervisor's desk); Weber Truck & Warehouse, 79 LA 738 (Levin, 1982) (sleeping at the beginning of the shift in hidden location); Federal Prison Sys., 72 LA 1230 (Rule, 1979) (meditating at his duty station).

[55]Purex Corp., 38 LA 313 (Edelman, 1962) (discharge upheld primarily because of consistent practices); Kawneer Co., 30 LA 1002, 1006 (Howlett, 1958) (absence of clear, published work rule militates against discharge decision); Wade Mfg. Co., 21 LA 676 (Maggs, 1953) (early case requiring adequate notice of rules).

[56]Colorado-Ute Elec. Ass'n, 86 LA 243 (Sass, 1985) (arbitrator also noted disparate treatment as reason to sustain the grievance).

[57]EG & G Mound Applied Techs., 102 LA 60 (Heekin, 1993).

[58]Packaging Corp. of Am., 76 LA 643 (High, 1981) (presence of rule against sleeping on the job is not necessary to support discharge of employee who sleeps on the job).

[59]Georgia-Pacific Corp., 88 LA 244 (Byars, 1987) (written policy in place, however, past practice did not adequately forewarn employees of policy); Colorado-Ute Elec. Ass'n, 86 LA 243, 246 (Sass, 1985) ("There are many reported arbitration decisions wherein a penalty of discharge has been upheld for [intentional "sleeping on the job"], * * * particularly where there is a clear rule and/or practice calling for discharge in such circumstances. Where the rules or practices do not clearly call for discharge, however, the penalty is usually something considerably less severe."); Lear Seigler, Inc., 79-2 ARB ¶ 8443 (Kossoff, 1979) (no clear rule, unintentional, discharge reduced to suspension); Kawneer Co., 30 LA 1002 (Howlett, 1958) (no clear rule, discharge improper); Minnesota Mining & Mfg. Co., 29 LA 528 (Horlacher, 1957) (no clear rule,

Even where there is a clear rule in place, sanctions may be subject to challenge where there is evidence of disparate treatment.[60] In many cases, grievants have successfully challenged their penalty by pointing out inconsistencies in the application of sleeping-on-the-job penalties.[61] For example, where employees had typically not been discharged for sleeping on the job, the arbitrator reinstated a grievant caught dozing in a back room despite a published rule requiring discharge for sleeping on the job.[62] Also, where employees found hiding away from their work stations were typically discharged, a grievant caught sleeping at his work station was reinstated. The arbitrator noted that past practices resulted in sending "mixed signals" to the grievant regarding the consequences for sleeping on duty.[63]

In sum, arbitrators will consider whether the employee has been adequately informed of the consequences of sleeping on the job. Although generally not determinative, the requirements of a clear work rule and consistent application of that rule are two factors that have become part of the analysis. The relative weight given these factors depends on the individual arbitrator and the totality of the circumstances.

## B. Proving an Employee Is Actually Asleep

In any sleeping case, the arbitrator must consider whether the employee was actually asleep. Several key factors are the environment (darkness or secluded location), the employee's appearance or condition (eyes closed, lying in prone position, no movement, no reaction

---

no fair notice, company condoned sleeping on break, reduced to suspension); Wade Mfg. Co., 21 LA 676 (Maggs, 1953) (although prior warning, no clear rule, 27-year employee reinstated). See also Snow, "Deciding an Arbitration Case: The Evolution of Arbitral Principles in 'Sleeping on the Job' Decisions," 2 Widener J. Pub. L. 491 (1993).

[60]James Vernor Co., 20 LA 50, 53 (Bowles, 1953) ("It is proper for the Arbitrator to make inquiry into the actual practice under the contract; that is, whether the express terms of the contract have been observed in practice or whether violations have been condoned so frequently that employees have been lulled into a sense of false security that the Company would wink at a violation without penalty.").

[61]Federal Bureau of Prisons, 91-2 ARB ¶ 8385 (Kessler, 1991) (no fair notice, disparate treatment, reinstated with pay); Essex Indus. Chems., Inc., 88 LA 991 (Cluster, 1987) (inconsistent enforcement, first offense, reinstated); Ridge Crest Convalescent Ctr., 87-1 ARB ¶ 8086 (DiLauro, 1986) (disparate treatment, reinstated); Phoenix Steel Corp., 44 LA 745 (Crawford, 1965) (inconsistent enforcement, first offense, unintentional, reinstated with pay); Douglas Aircraft Co., 27 LA 137 (Gaffey, 1956) (disparate treatment, insufficient proof of sleep, reinstated with pay); Linde Air Prods. Co., 23 LA 436 (Shister, 1954) (prior warnings but disparate treatment led arbitrator to reduce discharge to suspension without pay and reinstatement).

[62]Crawford County Jail Guards, 88-2 ARB ¶ 8622 (Talarico, 1988) (arbitrator refused to uphold the discharge without consistent application or a more explicit announcement of a new administration's intention to enforce the rule).

[63]Georgia-Pacific Corp., 88 LA 244, 247 (Byars, 1987) ("employees could have easily interpreted the Company's past action as indicative of a policy to discharge an employee caught sleeping away from his duty station but to take a less harsh action against anyone caught sleeping at his duty station," discharge was inappropriate).

when supervisor approaches), and employee surprise or disorientation when the supervisor makes contact. Ultimately, both direct and circumstantial evidence have been accepted by arbitrators to verify whether the employee was asleep. If an employee is found in a dark area away from his or her specific job duties, there is a strong inference that the employee was sleeping.[64] However, if there is no direct evidence that the employee is sleeping, the employee's mere presence in a dark room may not be sufficient.[65]

Another relevant factor is the employee's appearance or his actions. According to one arbitrator, it is not necessary to prove that the employee is clinically or medically sleeping; it is sufficient that the employee's outward appearance reasonably exhibits sleeping behavior.[66] Where the employee's outward, objective appearance indicates that she is sleeping, arbitrators appear to accept the employer's evaluation. Where an employee is found with his eyes closed for long periods of time, there is a strong inference of sleeping.[67] Where the employer did not see whether the employee's eyes were closed though, there may be no inference.[68] Lying down with a make-shift pillow can be persuasive.[69] The employee's prone position is often combined with evidence of a bed or lying in a remote location.[70] There can, however, be a legitimate explanation for an employee's lying in a prone position, such as illness or resting during a break.[71]

Evidence that an employee did not move for an extended period may support the inference of sleeping.[72] That an employee is startled when the supervisor touches or approaches the employee may be an additional indication of sleeping.[73] Of course, the most telling evidence

---

[64]Kaiser Aluminum & Chem. Corp., 90 LA 1053 (Runkel, 1988) (sleeping was flagrant because grievant did not merely doze off, but found a dark place and made a bed and deliberately went to sleep); Essex Indus. Chems., 88 LA 991 (Cluster, 1987) (employee was found in the dark with his eyes closed); Olin Corp., 86 LA 1096 (Seidman, 1986) (emkployee found in basement area where light bulb had been unscrewed was considered to be sleeping).

[65]City of Cleveland, 71 LA 1041 (Siegel, 1978) (employee found in dark room, lying on table; could have been watching TV instead of sleeping, although awkwardly).

[66]General Elec. Co., 74 LA 115, 116–17 (King, 1979). See also Consolidation Coal Co., 99 LA 945 (Dissen, 1992) (evidence that damage to the train rails in the mine could only have occurred if the grievant's locomotive ran in place for at least 15 minutes, generating significant amounts of smoke and noise is sufficient circumstantial evidence to show that he must have been asleep for that period).

[67]Id. (emkployee who was found sitting with his arms folded on his knees and his head lying on his arms).

[68]City of Cleveland, 71 LA 1041 (Siegel, 1978).

[69]Mantua Chem. Terminal, 79 LA 732 (Mitrani, 1982) (employee found lying down on two occasions during the shift with a jacket rolled up as a pillow was sufficient to show that the employee was sleeping).

[70]Georgia-Pacific Corp., 88 LA 244 (Byars, 1987).

[71]City of Cleveland, 71 LA 1041 (Siegel, 1978).

[72]Scott Paper Co., 99 LA 624 (Byars, 1992) (employee observed in crane for 30–45 minutes without moving); Basin Elec. Power Coop., 91 LA 443 (Jacobowski, 1988) (employee seen unmoving, with the only visible eye closed, for over 10 minutes).

[73]Basin Elec. Power Coop., 91 LA 443 (Jacobowski, 1988) (employee was startled when supervisor and others opened the door to the room in which the employee had been sitting).

of sleep is where the supervisor must awaken the employee.[74] Certain facts may counter the inference created by the outward appearance that the employee is sleeping. Employees have defended against sleeping charges by claiming that they were resting their eyes[75] or practicing transcendental meditation during a break period.[76]

## C. Aggravating and Mitigating Circumstances

Once the arbitrator has determined that the employee was in fact either inattentive to his duties or was sleeping on the job, the next step is to review the circumstances. Even if the employer does not have a specific rule requiring termination or suspension for every sleeping violation, there may be sufficient aggravating circumstances to warrant discipline. The most common aggravating circumstances are intentional acts (nesting, repeated violations, deliberate neglect of duty), loafing, loss of production, harm to equipment, and creation of a safety hazard.[77]

Nesting is making a bed or creating a place conducive to sleeping, often in a secluded area, and strongly exhibits an intent to sleep.[78] Arbitrators find that nesting is a deliberate neglect of job duties, and sleeping may be imputed to the employee.[79] Conversely, where an employee is found at a lunch table or a work station, the inference that the employee is neglecting job duties is weaker because the employee is not deliberately hiding from supervision or duties.[80] The reason for this distinction between locations is that in many cases it demonstrates intent.[81] Hiding for the purpose of sleeping is egregious because it shows an intent beyond simple nesting; the employee must

[74]Southwestern Eng'g Co., 95 LA 1006 (Suardi, 1990) (employee found lying on a board wrapped with foam and with a foam pillow, the supervisor had to awaken the employee); Basin Elec. Power Coop., 91 LA 443 (Jacobowski, 1988) (employee was observed with his head leaned back and eyes closed and the supervisor had to awaken him upon entering the room).

[75]City of Cleveland, 71 LA 1041 (Siegel, 1978).

[76]Federal Prison Sys., 72 LA 1230 (Rule, 1979) (grievant seen with his eyes closed for at least 3 minutes claimed that he practiced transcendental meditation and was totally conscious and alert during the entire period).

[77]Oshkosh Truck Corp., 81 LA 1009 (Cox, 1983).

[78]Kaiser Aluminum & Chem. Corp., 90 LA 1053 (Runkel, 1988); Colorado-Ute Elec. Ass'n, 86 LA 243 (Sass, 1985).

[79]Pet, Inc., 83 LA 468, 471 (Schedler, 1984) ("The Company has the right to expect a fair day's work for a fair day's pay; and, in the absence of extenuating circumstances, sleeping on duty is not allowed.").

[80]Southwestern Eng'g Co., 95 LA 1006 (Suardi, 1990) (employee sleeping in work area); Basin Elec. Power Coop., 91 LA 443 (Jacobowski, 1988) (employee dozed off at computer terminal); Page, Akulian & Harkins, 89 LA 821 (Koven, 1987) (sleeping at her desk); Vought Corp., 81 LA 1200 (Stephens, 1983) (sleeping in sight of supervisor's desk); New Castle State Hosp., 74 LA 365 (Witney, 1980) (presence in day room in work area).

[81]Georgia-Pacific Corp., 88 LA 244 (Byars, 1987).

leave his work duties to seclude himself.[82] Arbitrators express special disfavor with deliberate hiding.[83]

Depending on the grievant's intent, sleeping on the job may be characterized as a form of theft or fraud against the employer. Thus, evidence of deliberate conduct may provide justification for discharge.[84] As stated in one regularly cited decision:

> One who deliberately seeks out a secure hiding place to avoid detection and proceeds to deny management of his services wilfully and maliciously is not the same as one who through circumstances of his work or other situations falls inadvertently to sleep without the intention of defrauding management.[85]

Following these distinctions, the majority of cases where discharge is upheld contain some evidence of evasive or deliberate conduct.[86] In one such case, the arbitrator upheld the discharge of an employee found asleep in a hidden location away from his work station.[87] In another, the discharge was upheld where the employee was caught sleeping in a prone position on a bench away from his job.[88] Again, discharge was upheld where the employee was found sleeping in an area rumored to be a hiding place for employees.[89] From these and other cases, it is clear that location can be critical to the determination of intent.[90]

One arbitrator made an intensive study of sleeping cases and found that "in the majority of cases where discharge is upheld by the arbitrator it is because the employee was found sleeping away from his duty station."[91] Thus, arbitrators generally focus on the intentional

---

[82]Nabisco Brands, Inc., 86 LA 430 (Cox, 1985).

[83]Colorado-Ute Elec. Ass'n, 86 LA 243 (Sass, 1985).

[84]Phillips Lighting Co., 93-1 ARB ¶ 3149 (Goodstein, 1992) (second offense, prior warning, intentional, discharge upheld); Rohr Indus., 78 LA 978 (Sabo, 1982) (clear rule, intentional, discharge upheld).

[85]Crown Cork & Seal Co., 64 LA 734, 737 (Stilwell, 1975).

[86]Kimberly-Clark Corp., 92-1 ARB ¶ 8299 (Berkeley, 1992) (discharge upheld on "nest" theory where the grievant had prepared a place to sleep); Gold Bond Bldg. Prods., 84-2 ARB ¶ 8533 (Bennett, 1984) (discharge upheld where grievant found sleeping in prepared bed away from work station); American Art Clay Co., 77 LA 1143 (Madden, 1981) (employee discharged who left work station to sleep in car).

[87]Weber Truck & Warehouse, 79 LA 738 (Levin, 1982) (discharge upheld where employee found asleep in hidden area—second incident in 3 months).

[88]Mantua Chem. Terminal, Inc., 79 LA 732 (Mitrani, 1982).

[89]Nestle Co., 81 LA 1263 (Feigenbaum, 1983).

[90]Thorn Apple Valley, Inc., 98 LA 183, 187 (Kanner, 1983) ("Such lack of concealment denotes no specific attempt to steal time from the Company by not working."); Vought Corp., 81 LA 1200, 1202 (Stephens, 1983) (management failed to consider location of grievant "which was certainly not one which would have been selected by an employee who had a history of successfully eluding management for several hours," employee reinstated).

[91]Georgia-Pacific Corp., 88 LA 244, 247 (Byars, 1987).

nature of the sleeping.[92] As discussed below, though, the mitigating factors of illness, fatigue, or medication effects may undercut the presumption in these cases.

Arbitrators have ruled that there is no requirement that the job neglect cause actual loss to the employer.[93] On the other hand, where there is no loss as a result of the sleeping, there may be no prejudice to the employer.[94]

Assuming there is a clear and consistently enforced work rule, discharge is still not automatic for an employee caught sleeping.[95] Arbitrators will consider mitigating factors specific to individual employees before rendering judgment.[96] The employee's intent, past work record, and other special circumstances are considered in determining whether the sanction is appropriate.

Central to this part of the analysis is the issue of culpability. From the earliest reported decisions, arbitrators have assessed the moral offensiveness of the grievant's acts. As one arbitrator wrote:

> Instances of "sleeping on the job" may be assigned to at least three classes. First, there may be cases of illness or of loss of sleep for a very meritorious reason by some employee who thereafter unintentionally and against his will "nodded" or briefly fell asleep while trying to work. Second, an employee may neglect to sleep while off duty because [of] some personal activity of gambling or some other kind of "party" and because of neglecting his sleep while off duty, may give way to the necessity of sleeping during working hours. In a third class, could be put the situation where the employee deliberately and with premeditation as proved by his making advance arrangements, seeks a remote place on the premises of the employer where he thinks he will be undiscovered and there deliberately prepares to sleep and does do so.[97]

---

[92]Colorado-Ute Elec. Ass'n, Inc., 86 LA 243, 247 (Sass, 1985) (the employee's excuse did not justify "going behind the control panel in the motor control center and lying down on a bed of rags"); Western Auto Supply Co., 71 LA 710, 715 (Ross, 1978) ("hiding out clearly constitutes 'willful idleness' and * * * it involves a deliberate and intentional act to avoid work while at the same time deceiving the Company"). See also American Welding & Mfg. Co., 94 LA 340 (Duda, 1990); Georgia-Pacific Corp., 88 LA 244 (Byars, 1987); Mantua Chem. Terminal, Inc., 79 LA 732 (Mitrani, 1982); Inspiration Consolidated Copper Co., 72 LA 1275 (Thompson, 1979); Crown Cork & Seal Co., 64 LA 734, 737 (Stilwell, 1975) ("[o]ne who deliberately seeks out a secure hiding place to avoid detection and proceeds to deny management of his services wilfully and maliciously is not the same as one * * * falls inadvertently to sleep without the intention of defrauding management").

[93]Thorn Apple Valley, Inc., 98 LA 183, 188 (Kanner, 1991) ("sleeping on the job does result in loss of money from the Company for time not worked notwithstanding Grievant's lack of intent and notwithstanding no substantial prejudice to the Company's production needs"); Contico Int'l, 93 LA 530 (Cipolla, 1989).

[94]Lady Baltimore of Mo., Inc., 95 LA 452 (Westbrook, 1990).

[95]Consolidation Coal Co., 99 LA 945, 950 (Dissen, 1992) ("[t]he great wealth of arbitral authority entered by both parties shows that discharge has not been accepted as a uniformly valid penalty in instances of employees found sleeping on the job").

[96]State of Ohio, 97 LA 1206, 1210 (Rivera, 1991) ("[a] mandatory penalty which does not permit factors specific to the particular employee to be considered is facially unjust").

[97]Collins Radio Co., 30 LA 121, 122 (Updegraff, 1958).

Arbitrators have tended to find a lack of intent where the employee is in his work area,[98] has performed most or all of his work,[99] has not neglected his duties,[100] or where the period of sleeping is extremely short or occurs during a break or lunch period.[101] Arbitrators have generally considered an employee's illness or inattention due to the effect of a prescription medication as mitigating factors that may excuse sleeping violations.[102] Where illness or prescription medicine has contributed to the employee's sleeping, arbitrators generally reduce the discipline imposed by the company.[103]

In one case, the arbitrator set out the following determinants of culpability:

The culpability of employees who are found sleeping depends upon such factors as whether they are caught in a "nest," whether they have

[98]New Castle State Hosp., 74 LA 365, 367 (Witney, 1980) ("it cannot be held that the Petitioners neglected the residents because they were in the dayroom and not in the office").

[99]Basin Elec. Power Coop., 91 LA 443 (Jacobowski, 1988) (no evidence or challenge that he had neglected any duties or caused any problems); Essex Indus. Chems., Inc., 88 LA 991, 994 (Cluster, 1987) ("nothing to do but wait for his next batch of material to be delivered;" although he was told to sweep work area, there was no real evidence that work area was abnormally dirty); New Castle State Hosp., 74 LA 365 (Witney, 1980) (no duties were unfinished).

[100]Lady Baltimore of Mo., Inc., 95 LA 452, 454 (Westbrook, 1990) ("neither the twenty-five minute nap nor Grievant's failure to call in when he pulled off to sleep caused the failure to deliver groceries to two customers"); Essex Indus. Chems., 88 LA 991, 994 (Cluster, 1987) ("He had nothing to do but wait for his next batch of material to be delivered."); Georgia-Pacific Corp., 88 LA 244, 246 (Byars, 1987) ("Even if the Grievant had not admitted being asleep, the evidence was clear and convincing that he was asleep and was neglecting his duties."); Colorado-Ute Elec. Ass'n, 86 LA 243, 246 (Sass, 1985) ("he was clearly neglecting his duties"); Boise Cascade Paper Group, 86 LA 177 (Marlatt, 1985). See also Todd Shipyard Corp., 81 LA 955, 957 (Letter, 1983) ("proper performance of the Fire Watch work assignment mandates that the employee in the job be alert at all times").

[101]Georgia-Pacific Corp., 88 LA 244 (Byars, 1987) (finding more usual that the distinction between intentional and unintentional sleeping is implied, rather than written). If an employee sleeps on an unpaid lunch break, there is, of course, no offense because the employee is off duty; Maui Pineapple Co., 86 LA 907, 910 (Tsukiyama, 1986) ("[t]he brevity of his repose may have been a mitigating consideration if it were Grievant's first offense"); Oshkosh Truck Corp., 81 LA 1009, 1011–12 (Cox, 1983) (the employee's "sleep was of relatively short duration and did not extend beyond the typical 10 minute toilet break").

[102]Thorn Apple Valley, Inc., 98 LA 183 (Kanner, 1991) (questioning low blood sugar as cause); Southwestern Eng'g Co., 95 LA 1006 (Suardi, 1990); American Welding & Mfg. Co., 94 LA 340 (Duda, 1990) (questioning medication cause); Page, Akulian & Harkins, 89 LA 821 (Koven, 1987) (narcolepsy); Texas Int'l Airlines, Inc., 78 LA 893 (Dunn, 1982) (physical pain); Suburban Mfg. Co., 77 LA 1200, 1203 (Rimer, 1981) ("suspension of consciousness was health-related and not an act intended to receive pay for time not worked during an unauthorized rest period"); New York Wire Mills Corp., 76 LA 232 (LeWinter, 1981) (arthritis and hypertension); Norfolk Naval Shipyard, 76 LA 18 (Bowers, 1980) (stomach-gallbladder); City of Iowa City, 72 LA 1006 (Sinicropi, 1979) (eating disorder-obesity).

[103]Page, Akulian & Harkins, 89 LA 821 (Koven, 1987) (employer knew that the grievant had narcolepsy and was prone to falling asleep); Boise Cascade Paper Group, 86 LA 177 (Marlatt, 1985) (grievant came to work instead of staying home sick because of company need and attendance policy); Texas Int'l Airlines, Inc., 78 LA 893 (Dunn, 1982); City of Iowa City, 72 LA 1006 (Sinicropi, 1979) (arbitrator would normally consider evidence of illness but city had attempted to work with employee as to illness). See also cases of insufficient evidence of illness: Maui Pineapple Co., 86 LA 907 (Tsukiyama, 1986) (no supporting evidence of medication problem); Vought Corp., 81 LA 1200 (Stephens, 1983) (no evidence of illness).

deliberately left their work station and hid themselves in an effort to rest, *whether the falling asleep was inadvertent in an area they had a right to be in (such as falling asleep in the lunchroom),* what type of past disciplinary record they have, whether circumstances associated with their work contributed to the drowsiness and whether they were sleeping while on duty.[104]

Again, a distinction is drawn between those who inadvertently doze off and those who are caught intentionally trying to avoid work. Evidence of illness or medication causing drowsiness mitigates against deliberate intent and culpability. For example, discharge was inappropriate where an employee passed out due to an allergic reaction to medication.[105] Arbitrators may treat this issue as an affirmative defense. Consequently, the burden of proof rests with the grievant. Challenges to discipline will fail where the grievant is unable to provide adequate proof of illness or the impact of medication. In sum, whether there is evidence that the employee's conduct is unintentional or aberrational, arbitrators will consider mitigating factors when evaluating the appropriateness of sanctions for sleeping on the job.

Beyond an assessment of present intent, arbitrators also consider the past work record of the employee as a mitigating factor. Where there is a troubled work record, arbitrators may be more willing to uphold a strict sanction.[106] The employer's failure to consider a good past work record, however, may result in reinstatement.[107] Even where the employee's conduct created a safety hazard, an arbitrator may factor in the employee's good work record and conclude that sanctions should be reduced.[108] In short, both present and past conduct factor into the determination of the appropriate sanction.

A final mitigating factor in sleeping cases is whether the employer used the sleeping charge as a pretext for some other alleged or perceived problem.[109] Where a supervisor suspended a union steward for a brief sleeping violation, the arbitrator found the supervisor was

---

[104]Oshkosh Truck Corp., 81 LA 1009, 1011 (Cox, 1983) (employee who inadvertently fell asleep in bathroom stall while on break reinstated) (emphasis in original).

[105]Suburban Mfg. Co., 77 LA 1200 (Rimer, 1981); Lockheed Aircraft Corp., 55 LA 1058 (Cahn, 1970).

[106]Compare Southwestern Eng'g Co., 95 LA 1006 (Suardi, 1990) (7-year employee with good work record reinstated where discharged for falling asleep at work station); Riverway Harbor Serv., 84-1 ARB ¶ 8293 (Heinsz, 1984); Todd Shipyard Corp., 81 LA 955 (Letter, 1983); Hayes Int'l Corp., 80 LA 1313 (Traynor, 1983); Packaging Corp. of Am., 76 LA 643 (High, 1981); New York Wire, 76 LA 232 (LeWinter, 1981); General Elec. Co., 74 LA 115 (King, 1977); FMC Corp., 73 LA 705 (Marlatt, 1979); City of Iowa City, 72 LA 1006 (Sinicropi, 1979); Capital Steel Corp., 70 LA 121 (Potter, 1978).

[107]Olin Corp., 86-1 ARB ¶ 8248 (Seidman, 1986) (employee improperly terminated in that company failed to consider his conscientious work record). See also Chapter 12 for further discussion of work record as a mitigating factor.

[108]Consolidation Coal Co., 99 LA 945 (Dissen, 1992) (discharge reduced to suspension where a worker with a 14-year record of conscientious service inadvertently fell asleep at his work station).

[109]Lady Baltimore of Mo. Inc., 95 LA 452 (Westbrook, 1990).

motivated by the grievant's union activity and not the sleeping violation.[110]

### D. Safety

When sleeping on the job creates hazards for co-workers or business interests, proof of sleep alone may be sufficient to uphold a discharge. The need to maintain a safe working environment may not require a work rule and may outweigh mitigating factors.[111]

Concern for safety is always a factor, but where other employees are exposed to physical harm, proof of sleep is often determinative. For example, where the grievant fell asleep aboard a ship while on fire watch, which posed a great risk of fire, the arbitrator upheld the discharge despite the grievant's good work record and lack of intent.[112] On the other hand, where the sleeping violation poses no threat to business productivity or worker safety, discharge may be seen as excessive and the penalty reduced.[113]

The theory of deterrence has been used to justify discharge in cases where risk of harm exists but is not imminent. In one such case, the grievant had been employed for 5 years without incident and fell asleep in his work area when he had no duties to perform, but the arbitrator upheld the discharge on the grounds that it would deter others, an important assurance for a chemical plant.[114]

## V. Fighting and Threats[115]

### A. Fighting

Arbitrators have defined fighting as a physical attack or struggle involving the exchange of blows, or a strike by one upon another with

---

[110]State of Ohio, 97 LA 1206 (Rivera, 1991).

[111]Capitol Area Transp. Auth., 77-1 ARB ¶ 8170 at 3744 (Brown, 1976) ("[e]mployers do not have to publish rules that prohibit conduct so clearly wrong that common sense would dictate that the employer would regard such acts as misconduct").

[112]Texas Utils. Generating Co., 84-2 ARB ¶ 8470 (McDermott, 1984) (medication no excuse where leaking fuel caused hazard); Todd Shipyard Corp., 81 LA 955, 957 (Letter, 1983) ("[t]here are certain forms of misconduct which—considered alone—warrant termination without regard to elements of past record"); Packaging Corp. of Am., 76 LA 643, 644, 648 (High, 1981) (need for established work rule eliminated where employee misconduct exposes other employees and property to harm).

[113]Essex Indus. Chems., Inc., 88 LA 991 (Cluster, 1991) (conduct inconsequential, discharge reduced to suspension); Linde Air Prods. Co., 23 LA 436, 438 (Shister, 1954) ("[T]he offense of sleeping [on duty] would obviously have far more serious implications had the Company suffered any loss in production; or had [the grievant] left an operation in progress; or had he abandoned running equipment; or had he abandoned a post calling for his continuous presence * * *.").

[114]Velsicol Chem. Corp., 61-2 ARB ¶ 8314 (Petree, 1961).

[115]For a discussion of violence in the workplace, see Dennenberg, R. & S. Braueam, "Dispute Resolution and Workplace Violence," 51 Disp. Resol. J., 6 (1996).

an intent to harm or injure.[116] Employers have an obligation to provide for the safety of their employees, which includes protecting them from violence by other employees.[117] Employees who engage in fighting can be disciplined or discharged for their misconduct.[118] Arbitrators have upheld the discharge of an employee after a first offense for fighting.[119] Arbitral authority also supports the discharge of all employees who are actively involved in a fight.[120]

Discipline for fighting, even immediate discharge, is not contingent on a workplace rule expressly prohibiting the conduct.[121] Certain types of conduct are so inherently improper that no published rule is necessary to prohibit them in order to make them subject to discipline.[122] Arbitrators take a number of factors into consideration when deciding whether discipline is justified.[123]

*1. Provocation by Words or Gestures.* An employee who responds to the words or gestures of a fellow employee with violence becomes an aggressor and may be disciplined for his actions.[124] When one participant is a provocateur, and the other the aggressor, blame for the altercation must be shared equally.[125] Provocation may, however, be a mitigating factor in determining the severity of discipline.[126] Harmless or playful banter is unlikely to be sufficient provocation to justify the exchange of blows.[127]

The mitigating factor of provocation cannot be used, however, if the employee has had time to cool off.[128] Discipline is usually only mitigated if the employee's response is immediate.[129]

---

[116]Ohio Masonic Home, 94 LA 447, 450 (Volz, 1990); Interstate Brands Corp., 83 LA 497, 501 (Richman, 1984); ACF Indus., 79 LA 650, 652 (Cohen, 1982); Swainsboro Printing & Finishing Co., 56 LA 322, 323 (Williams, 1971); Shuler Axle Co., 51 LA 210, 214 (Dworkin, 1968).

[117]Missouri Rolling Mill Corp., 88 LA 1179, 1181 (Newmark, 1987).

[118]Marion Power Shovel Div., 82 LA 1014, 1016 (Kates, 1984); Mead Corp., 79 LA 464 (Williams, 1982).

[119]Missouri Rolling Mill Corp., 88 LA 1179 (Newmark, 1987); Marco Mfg. Co., 84 LA 134 (Richman, 1985).

[120]Tecumseh Corrugated Box Co., 90 LA 837 (Fullmer, 1988); Missouri Rolling Mill Corp., 88 LA 1179 (Newmark, 1987); Alvey, Inc., 74 LA 835, 838 (Roberts, 1980).

[121]City of Masillon, 92 LA 1303 (Elkin, 1989).

[122]Id. at 1305.

[123]Sunshine Biscuits, Inc., 89 LA 1183, 1186 (Madden, 1987).

[124]Mobay Chem. Corp., 74 LA 1113 (Weitzman, 1980).

[125]Bimex Corp., 99 LA 1012, 1015 (Flaten, 1992).

[126]Marin Honda, 91 LA 185 (Kanowitz, 1988); Olin Corp., 90 LA 1206, 1213 (Fitzsimmons, 1988); Reynolds Metal Co., 84 LA 367 (Gibson, 1985). Compare General Elec. Co., 73 LA 1248 (King, 1979) (no provocation found where grievant struck co-worker after being called a "flunky").

[127]Eagle Ottawa Leather Co., 82 LA 493, 494 (Jason, 1984).

[128]Alvey, Inc., 74 LA 835 (Roberts, 1980).

[129]Scranton Sewer Auth., 94 LA 920, 923 (Zirkel, 1990); Alvey, Inc., 74 LA 835 (Roberts, 1980) (discharge reduced to suspension for employee who was provoked by racial slurs; grievant was not completely absolved because grievant retained sufficient possession of his faculties to invite the other employee to step outside first).

*2. Name Calling and Racial Slurs.*    One common form of provocation that may mitigate an employee's discipline for fighting is name calling or racial slurs.[130] Racially derogatory comments can foreseeably provoke a person to use physical violence towards another employee. If the provoked employee had sufficient time for the "blood to cool" before engaging in physical violence, however, the provocation may not excuse the employee's subsequent physical violence against another employee.[131]

*3. Shop Talk Distinguished From Provocation.*    While verbal provocation may mitigate culpability for a fight resulting from that provocation, if the alleged provocation is mere shop talk, there is no mitigation of the discipline.[132] Shop talk is defined as "words and expressions normally used by employees in their day to day conversations in the shop."[133] Language that is directed at a specific individual or which the speaker knows is offensive to a particular employee goes beyond shop talk. That language may constitute "fighting words" and may serve to mitigate an employee's discipline for responding with violence to those words.[134]

*4. Past Disciplinary Record.*    Arbitrators often rely on a grievant's lack of a prior disciplinary record to justify reducing a penalty imposed by the employer for fighting.[135] Arbitrators also consider an employee's length of service in conjunction with their disciplinary record in determining the severity of the discipline for fighting.[136]

*5. Physical or Mental Impairment of Employee.*

a. **Drugs or Alcohol.**    Normally, intoxication does not mitigate discipline imposed for an employee's violent conduct because intoxication on the job is an additional disciplinary offense.[137] If the employee's

---

[130]McDonnell Douglas Space Sys., 92 LA 1107 (Herring, 1989) (discharge reduced to 10-day suspension for grievant who pushed co-worker where grievant was provoked by repeated racial slurs); State of Ohio, 91 LA 957 (Duda, 1988); G. Heilman Brewing Co., 83 LA 829 (Hilgert, 1984) (employer improperly discharged black employee who swung metal bar at co-employee who frequently had abused grievant with racial remarks and walked toward grievant with clenched fists).

[131]Alvey, Inc., 74 LA 835, 838 (Roberts, 1980).

[132]General Tire, 93 LA 345, 348 (Flannagan, 1989).

[133]Id.

[134]Id.

[135]Nabisco Brands, Inc., 96 LA 139 (Dworkin, 1991) (5-day suspension for fighting reduced to written warning in part due to employee's good work record); Reynolds Metal Co., 84 LA 367 (Gibson, 1985); (discharge reduced to 30-day suspension for employee who punched group leader where employee had no prior disciplinary record); Marion Power Shovel Div., 82 LA 1014 (Kates, 1984); Toledo Edison Co., 84 LA 1289 (Duda, 1985) (employee's 17-year clean record with employer was one factor that justified reducing penalty for fighting from discharge to suspension); Borg-Warner Corp., 22 LA 589, 596 (Larkin, 1954).

[136]Genuine Parts Co., 79 LA 220, 225 (Reed, 1982) (discharge of grievant with no disciplinary record upheld following fight with motorist; employee had less than 2 years seniority, which made it impossible to determine whether grievant would act in similar manner again.) See also Chapter 12.

[137]Imperial Clevite, Inc., 81 LA 1083 (Hill, 1983).

intoxication that led to an altercation was due to the employer providing alcohol at an office function, however, mitigation may be warranted.[138]

b. *Mental Illness.* When a grievant's violent or offensive behavior results from a mental illness, and is likely to continue, the employee may be subject to loss of employment (due to his disability), even though he may not be discharged for disciplinary reasons.[139] Altercations resulting from a short-term mental illness, such as a nervous breakdown, may mitigate an employee's penalty for violent conduct.[140]

*6. Self-Defense.* A nonaggressor in a fight may receive more lenient discipline or escape discipline, if it can be shown that after the fight began the nonaggressor merely defended herself.[141] In such a case, the employee can rely on the "well established right of reasonable self-defense."[142] One arbitrator held:

> It is a fundamental law of nature and of common and statutory law, that a person may use force to protect himself against the aggressions of another. Such protective acts however must be defensive, not retaliatory. As soon as the assailant desists, there can be no further need for defense.[143]

Even where "the non-aggressor may not be entirely free from blame, it is generally held that the non-aggressor may receive a lesser penalty than the aggressor."[144] A plea of self-defense may be used to justify an employee's participation in a fight if the defender had a reasonable belief that his assailant intended to do him bodily harm.[145] It is not necessary for the danger that gave rise to the belief actually to have existed. It is sufficient that the person resorting to self-defense reasonably believed in the existence of such a danger; a reasonable, albeit mistaken, belief is sufficient.[146]

---

[138]AFG Indus., 87 LA 1160 (Clarke, 1986).

[139]City of Hollywood, 94 LA 457 (Richard, 1989); Babcock & Wilcox Co., 75 LA 12 (Duff, 1980) (employer justified in terminating employee due to continued schizophrenic condition that caused him to verbally and physically assault co-workers).

[140]Marion Power Shovel Co., 69 LA 339 (McDermott, 1977).

[141]Central Die Casting, 102 LA 969 (Briggs, 1994); Allied Bendix Aerospace, 90 LA 109 (Flannagan, 1987); Coca-Cola Bottling Co., 83 LA 1173 (Bickner, 1984); U.S. Stove Co., 82 LA 965 (Rothschild, 1984); ACF Indus., 79 LA 650, 653 (Cohen, 1982); Shuler Axle Co., 51 LA 210 (Dworkin, 1968); Bethlehem Steel Co., 26 LA 874 (Seward, 1956); Consolidated Vultee Aircraft Corp., 11 LA 152 (Hepburn, 1948).

[142]ACF Indus., supra note 141, at 653, quoting Consolidated Vultee Aircraft, 11 LA 152 (Hepburn, 1948).

[143]Allied Bendix Aerospace, supra note 141, at 111.

[144]ACF Indus., supra note 141, at 653, citing Columbus Coated Fabrics Corp., 26 LA 638 (Stouffer, 1956), Robertshaw-Fulton Controls Co., 15 LA 372 (Marshall, 1950); Goodyear Clearwater Mills, 8 LA 647 (McCoy, 1947); see also Central Die Casting, supra note 141.

[145]Allied Bendix Aerospace, supra note 141.

[146]Id.

A plea of self-defense, however, will not excuse an employee's actions unless the reaction time between the provocation and the attack is practically instantaneous.[147] In weighing a claim of self-defense, arbitrators also examine whether the grievant had an opportunity to withdraw from an attack before using physical violence. Where retreat is virtually impossible and the grievant has good reason to fear injury, physical violence may be used in self-defense.[148]

*7. Violence Against Management and Nonemployees.* It is a commonly accepted principle that supervisors must be protected from abusive, threatening, and insubordinate acts by employees.[149] Striking or threatening to strike a supervisor warrants discipline.[150] The level of discipline imposed on employees for assaulting supervisors generally depends on the level of violence used by the employee. If an employee verbally accosts a supervisor due to the pressures of the job, a penalty less than discharge may be appropriate if the conduct does not constitute a threat of violence. For instance, a discharge for swearing at a supervisor was reduced to a 2-week suspension because the supervisor repeatedly interrupted the grievant who was attempting to meet quota.[151] An apology may further mitigate the seriousness of the offense. Where an employee made an obscene gesture at the supervisor as a result of job-related stress, the discharge was reduced to a 3-day suspension because the employee's actions were not a threat of violence and the employee apologized to the supervisor.[152]

When employees fight with nonemployees there is a different problem. One arbitrator upheld the discharge of a delivery driver who made a sudden stop to avoid a collision, causing the driver behind her to honk her horn. The delivery driver pursued the other driver to a parking lot and provoked a fight. Even though the delivery driver did not strike the first blow, discharge was appropriate because the grievant pursued the matter "instead of using one of many opportunities to avoid the confrontation. There simply was no justification for * * * the Grievant passing her delivery point" and following the vehicle.[153]

---

[147]U.S. Stove Co., 82 LA 965, 969 (Rothschild, 1984). See also Scott Paper Co., 66 LA 471, 473 (McLeod, 1976).

[148]Kaiser Found. Health Plan, 73 LA 1057 (Herring, 1979).

[149]Alumax Aluminum Corp., 92 LA 28, 31 (Allen, 1988).

[150]See also Kennecott Copper Corp., 52 LA 822 (Roberts, 1969); Pacific Tel. & Tel. Co., 40 LA 664 (Koren, 1963); Ross Gear & Tool Co., 35 LA 293 (Schmidt, 1960).

[151]Alumax Aluminum Corp. Tyrone Hydraulics, 75 LA 672 (Murphy, 1980) (discharge of intoxicated employee for kicking foreman reduced to suspension; employee apologized and did not mean to demean his foreman).

[152]Mead Packaging Co., 74 LA 881 (Ziskind, 1980).

[153]Genuine Parts Co., 79 LA 220, 224 (Reed, 1982). See also Piedmont Publ'g Co., 97 LA 739 (Nolan, 1991) (grievant discharged for fighting with independent hauler who refused to move his truck from employer's loading dock); Ohio Masonic Home, 94 LA 447 (Volz, 1990) (discharge set aside where employee involved in altercation with former girlfriend in employer's parking lot).

## B. *Threats of Violence*

Threatening a co-worker may be grounds for discipline or discharge if the person threatened has reason to fear for his safety.[154] Whether a specific statement is a threat depends on the context, the way the words are used, and the circumstances existing at the time the words are used.[155]

Lack of perceived dangerousness in an alleged threat may result in discharge being overturned.[156] Where a certified nurse's aide threatened to kill herself and several other employees if medical tests demonstrated she had cancer, the arbitrator found no just cause for discharge, despite a rule establishing threats as a major violation warranting immediate discharge. Though the arbitrator determined the grievant was guilty of making the statements, he overturned the discipline because witnesses did not see the threats as serious, there was no evidence that the grievant was disposed to violence, the employer failed to give the grievant an opportunity to explain her conduct, and the grievant had a good work record.[157] Conversely, a discharge was upheld where a co-worker perceived the threat to shoot as serious, due largely to the grievant's extensive history of abusive behavior suggesting a strong propensity for violence.[158]

Calling someone a "flunky," for example, is not considered a threat.[159] When one employee, soliciting for a union, told another employee, "Big Daddy will get you" for refusing to join the union, the arbitrator held that the employee could have reasonably believed he was threatened and discipline was warranted.[160] The statement "I hope the truck blows up when you start it," made by a bargaining unit member to another employee driving a tanker truck following a month long strike, constituted a threat due to the circumstances existing at the plant.[161]

Where a threat is specific and is in the speaker's power to carry out, arbitrators will not hesitate to impose discipline, up to and including discharge.[162] One arbitrator upheld the discharge of a white employee who threatened an older and smaller black employee for using

---

[154]See also Olin Corp., 103 LA 981 (Fowler, 1994); Paragon Cable Manhattan, 100 LA 905 (Dreizen, 1993); Emery Air Freight Corp., 94 LA 1023 (Feldman, 1990); Elastomeric Prods., Inc., 94 LA 610 (Cantor, 1990); J & L Specialty Prods. Corp., 94 LA 600 (Duda, 1990); Emery Indus., Inc., 72 LA 110, 112 (Gentile, 1979).

[155]Emergy Indus., Inc., 72 LA 110, 110 (Gentile, 1979).

[156]Concord Extended Care, 94-1 ARB ¶ 4069 (Stallworth, 1993).

[157]Id.

[158]The arbitrator observed: "The history of the grievant is ample evidence that his threats might not be mere empty words, but could actually result in violence. * * * This justified a real fear that his anger and resentment of his fellow employee * * * could result in a tragedy." Metal-Matic, Inc., 94-1 ARB ¶ 4183 at 3897 (Jacobowski, 1994).

[159]General Elec. Co., 73 LA 1248 (King, 1979).

[160]Babcock & Wilcox Co., 75 LA 716 (Johnston, 1980).

[161]Emery Indus., Inc., 72 LA 110 (Gentile, 1979).

[162]Walker Mfg. Co., 60 LA 645 (Simon, 1973).

a vending machine that was the subject of a union boycott.[163] The arbitrator found that racist threats against one's life cannot be considered a joke or a norm of conduct.

The more specific and credible the threat, the graver the misconduct. Another arbitrator upheld the discharge of an employee who threatened to rape a co-worker's wife if he did not join the union. It was not necessary to determine whether the grievant was joking when he made the remark, because the effect of the remark—as opposed to the grievant's intent—sufficiently intimidated the co-worker.[164]

Finally, an arbitrator upheld a 2-week suspension of an employee for threatening to cause bodily harm to employees who had made racial slurs to the grievant. The arbitrator held that threats of physical violence cannot be condoned, and it was the employee's responsibility to inform the employer of racial slurs, not to take justice into his own hands.[165]

# VI. Abusive, Profane, or Other Inappropriate Language

Workplace friction can easily be induced by speech. Disciplining employees for the language they use necessarily raises constitutional concerns. Limiting expression runs counter to guarantees of "free speech" found in the First Amendment (in the public sector) or implicit in the concept of ordered liberty, which is ostensibly protected in all workplaces.[166] In reviewing abusive or profane language and determining whether it is permitted or protected, arbitrators generally look to the type of statement made, its setting, the identities of the speaker and recipient, the consequences resulting from the statement, and the justification (if any). In some situations they review issues of constitutional or statutory protection.

## A. Type of Statement

Those employee statements usually censured relate to threats, provocations, profanity, and racial epithets.[167]

---

[163]Id.

[164]Napa Hawaiian Warehouse, Inc., 42 LA 490, 493 (Tsukiyama, 1963).

[165]LTV Aerospace Corp., 65 LA 195 (Moore, 1975).

[166]While constitutional guarantees are relevant only to public sector cases, arbitrators have long applied principles of free speech and due process to the private sector. Furr's Supermarkets, 95 LA 1021 (Rezler, 1990); United Grocers, Inc., 93 LA 1289 (Snow, 1990).

[167]Other forms of verbal expression may be found to be abusive. Charles Todd Uniform Rental Serv. Co., 77 LA 144 (Hutcheson, 1981) (discharge of a driver-salesman for preaching his religious faith to customers upheld).

*1. Threatening and Provocative Statements.*   Because of fears of workplace violence, threats and provocations are increasingly condemned. As the arbitrator reasoned in *Georgia Power Co.*:[168]

> I can identify no utterance that an employee can make that is more serious than a threat upon the life of a co-worker. Furthermore, an unanswered threat upon the life of a superior introduces the additional grim specter of a breakdown in discipline within the organization.[169]

Lesser threats of violence have also been deemed just cause for discharge. In *Elastomeric Products Inc.*,[170] the arbitrator found that the female grievant "terrified [her] supervisors" by her oral hostility. Consequently, he determined she must be held "responsible for the nature of [her] actions," and sustained the discharge. Similarly, in *Greyhound Lines, Inc.*,[171] the arbitrator easily affirmed the discharge of a bus driver for threatening bodily harm to a passenger.

Any ambiguity or vagueness in the nature of the statement necessarily reduces its negative import. Casual asides, mutterings, and the like may not be cause for discipline. Doubts are generally resolved in favor of the employee. In *Everfresh, Inc.*,[172] an employee's comment that he intended to "take care" of his supervisor was determined not to convey the requisite intent to threaten his supervisor with physical harm. Moreover, if management provokes a threatening or profane exchange with an employee, the employee is often found not culpable.[173]

*2. Profanity.*   Issues of profanity or obscenity are no easier for arbitrators. As a threshold matter, some arbitrators will distinguish between "foul" language and "abusive" language. In *Foothills Care Center, Inc.*,[174] a licensed practical nurse employed by a nursing home rudely responded to a visitor's inquiry by saying "How the hell should I know, I just came on duty." She was terminated for using "abusive language." The arbitrator reasoned:

> [T]he Union is correct when it argues that foul language is not necessarily abusive, and abusive language need not be foul. The two are not the same.
>
> This premise is easily illustrated. For instance, if Grievant had said, "Oh, damn, I dropped a glass", she has used foul, but not abusive, language.

---

[168]100 LA 622 (Singer, 1993).

[169]Id. at 630.

[170]94 LA 610 (Cantor, 1990).

[171]79 LA 422 (Larkin, 1982).

[172]99 LA 1038 (Allen, 1992).

[173]General Dynamics, 100 LA 180 (Francis, 1992); Leland Oil Mill, 91 LA 905 (Nicholas, Jr., 1988).

[174]80 LA 1046 (Cohen, 1983).

On the other hand, if Grievant had said to the visitor, "You fool, why are you bothering me? Any idiot could see that I am busy. Get out of my way so that I can do my work." This would be abusive language, and yet not one foul word or expletive has been used.[175]

Profanity must necessarily be considered in context. As the arbitrator reasoned in *Freightliner Corp.*:[176]

Profanity towards management generally is upheld as grounds for discipline. However, except where employees have consistently used such abusive language even in the face of repeated warnings to cease, arbitrators generally will not sustain a discharge for profanity alone.

Similarly, mere cursing or the use of obscene and vulgar language in and of itself is not sufficient basis for discipline of an employee according to many decisions. Much depends on the manner and spirit of its use, the exact language used, the extent to which profanity is used and/or tolerated in this particular plant, and in the community at large.[177]

*3. Racial Epithets.* Tolerance for abusive language has its limits. Contemporary standards abhor racial bigotry, and expressions of racial opprobrium are universally condemned. For example, the discharge of an employee for referring to his manager as a "nigger" was quickly affirmed.[178] Similarly, in *Pfizer Pigments*,[179] a supervisor greeted a black employee with the words "What is up, Ace?" The employee reacted with profanities and threats and for those reasons was terminated. The arbitrator held that the supervisor's greeting was a racial slur that provoked the employee. The discharge was reduced to a 1-week suspension.

## B. Setting

Arbitrators regard it as self-evident that a statement must be evaluated according to its setting. Whether a statement was made on or off duty, in private or public, or on the shop floor as opposed to in a grievance proceeding or at the bargaining table is significant in determining whether an arbitrator will sustain discipline.[180] Further, a statement made at a steel mill is reviewed differently from the same expression made by a kindergarten teacher. In order for off-duty

---

[175]Id. at 1048–49.

[176]95 LA 302, 311 (Tilbury, 1990).

[177]Id. at 311 (footnotes omitted). For a good general analysis discussing numerous other cases, see Alumax Aluminum Corp., 92 LA 28 (Allen, Jr., 1988).

[178]Host Int'l, 94 LA 492 (Talarico, 1990).

[179]95 LA 519 (Garnholz, 1990).

[180]See, e.g., Burton Mfg. Co., 82 LA 1228 (Holly, Jr., 1984).

remarks to be sanctionable, there must be a nexus to the employment relationship.[181]

When the speaker is a union steward or representative, the rules of engagement change. A union steward engaging in union activity is accorded far more latitude than is given a regular employee.[182]

Language that constitutes acceptable discourse among fellow employees may be unacceptable when addressed to supervisors or third parties. Supervisors are entitled to a certain modicum of respect, and the maintenance of reasonable decorum and order in the workplace requires at least minimal deference to authority. As one arbitrator held: "What may be shop talk between hourly paid employees is not the same level of conduct as insulting a supervisor * * *."[183]

The standards tighten when employees involve third parties. Profanity directed toward patients is not tolerated, even when provoked.[184] Verbally abusing customers is usually cause for suspension, if not discharge.[185] Indeed, placing obscene drawings in an area where they *might* have been viewed by the company's customers constituted just cause for discharge.[186]

Employee utterances can have both intended and unintended results. The employee who invites another employee to fight intends a physical altercation and, should one ensue, must be held accountable. Even if no such intent is openly manifested, but violence was a reasonable or foreseeable result, then the employee may be held accountable.[187]

More recently, cases addressing whether an employee's speech constitutes sexual harassment have become more common. Profanity or obscenity directed to or about female personnel may give rise to a hostile work environment and, if it does, may subject the speaker to appropriate discipline.[188]

## C. Defenses

There are two basic defenses for an employee's use of abusive or profane language. One defense can be provocation, especially when

[181]Keeble Co., 92 LA 871, 873 (Roumell, Jr., 1989).

[182]Hobard Corp., 75 LA 907, 909 (Curry, Jr., 1980). See Chapter 10 for a further discussion of discipline for union stewards.

[183]Acra Elec. Corp., 94 LA 767, 770 (McMillen, 1990).

[184]Veterans Admin. Med. Ctr., 76 LA 412 (Pastone, Jr., 1981).

[185]H. E. Miller Oldsmobile, 81 LA 1112 (Westbrook, 1983).

[186]Alumax Extrusions, Inc., 81 LA 722 (Miller, 1983).

[187]See, e.g., Stedman Mach. Co., 85 LA 631 (Keenan, 1985).

[188]GTE Cal., Inc., 103 LA 343 (Grabuski, 1994); Santa Cruz Transit Dist., 103 LA 167 (Pool, 1994). See Chapter 13 for a further discussion of sexual harassment.

the instigating conduct or remarks are made by supervision.[189] The response must be in proportion to the provocation.[190]

The other justification for using certain language is that it is mere shop talk. That is, the language is commonly accepted (if not condoned) in the workplace, and it should not subject the employee to discipline. Certainly, in many workplaces the casual use of profanity is the norm. With the increasing concern about sexual harassment in the industrial workplace, however, it is likely that the accepted norms will change.[191]

What is permissible shop talk, absent objection from a fellow employee, largely depends upon the nature of the employment. In *City of Minneapolis*,[192] a 911 emergency operator was given a 2-day suspension for using a series of four-letter words while referring to various callers. None of the remarks were actually made to customers. The arbitrator found that 911 operators often deal in highly stressful situations, and that expletives serve the purpose of venting and stress relief. Given that the employer acknowledged that some profanity was acceptable, the arbitrator decided that a logical line could not be drawn between acceptable and unacceptable profanity, and upheld the grievance.[193]

Along the same lines is the decision of the arbitrator in *Argonne National Laboratory*.[194] There, a janitor was given 3 days off for abusive and profane language. The arbitrator had "no doubt that [the] Grievant engaged in loud, profane complaints about his job," but found that such conduct did not have the result of actually impeding his work performance or otherwise being disruptive or insubordinate. The suspension was set aside.[195]

## D. Legally Protected Speech

In the public sector, employees enjoy the First Amendment guarantee of freedom of speech. In the private sector, the National Labor Relations Act (Act) gives wide latitude to remarks made within the context of activity protected by Section 7 of the Act, specifically including remarks made during labor negotiations or grievance processing by union representatives. Finally, some arbitrators will extrapolate principles derived from *Linn v. Plant Guard Workers*,[196] where the

---

[189]See, e.g., General Dynamics, 100 LA 180 (Francis, 1992); Pfizer Pigments, 95 LA 519 (Garnholz, 1990).

[190]94 LA 521 (Chandler, 1990).

[191]See Chapter 13 for a discussion of sexual harassment.

[192]101 LA 1006 (Daly, 1993).

[193]Id. at 1008.

[194]95 LA 543 (Wolff, 1990).

[195]Id. at 551. See also Yankee Screw Prods., 95 LA 909 (Kanner, 1990).

[196]383 U.S. 53, 61 LRRM 2345 (1966).

Supreme Court recognized that exaggerated rhetoric is commonplace in labor disputes, and that principles analogous to those under the First Amendment apply.[197]

In First Amendment cases, arbitrators follow the standards set forth in *Connick v. Myers*,[198] and evaluate whether the employee's speech addressed issues of public concern and, if so, balance the speech against the government's interest in efficient operations. Often arbitrators do not find the challenged speech to be constitutionally protected.[199]

The safe harbor for strong language afforded by the Act was expressed by an arbitrator[200] who borrowed his analysis from the NLRB:

> Offensive, vulgar, defamatory or opprobrious remarks uttered during the course of protected activities will not remove activities from the Act's protection unless they are so flagrant, violent, or extreme as to render the individual unfit for further service.[201]

In another case, a warehouse employee (the union president) was given a 1-day disciplinary layoff for telling the warehouse manager that the manager was a "f_____ liar."[202] An unfair labor practice charge was filed, then deferred to arbitration.

The arbitrator listed the following factors as relevant to whether the speech was protected by the Act:

> (1) the place of the discussion, i.e., in an office or conference room or on the production floor; (2) the subject matter of the discussion, i.e., whether it pertained to grievances, negotiations, or administration of the contract or to some unrelated matter; (3) the nature of the employee's outburst, i.e., relevant to argumentation of the subject matter or extraneous name calling, screaming, obscene gestures; (4) whether the outburst was, in any way, provoked by an employer's unfair labor practice, i.e., refusing to respond to questions, to process grievances, to allow the Union official to talk or carry on the responsibilities of his office.[203]

---

[197]U.S. Dep't of Navy, 75 LA 889 (Aronin, 1980). The Board led by Chairman William Gould has expressly adopted the *Linn* formulation. See KBO, Inc., 315 NLRB 570, 147 LRRM 1233 (1994).

[198]461 U.S. 138, 1 IER Cases 178 (1983).

[199]U.S. Dep't of Labor, 96 LA 5 (Feigenbaum, 1990); County of Monterey, 93 LA 841 (Riker, 1989); City of Los Angeles, 84 LA 860 (Weiss, 1985). Contra Department of the Air Force, 90 LA 1065 (Cohen, 1988) (employer sought relief against a newspaper publication of a union's alleged false and misleading statement; reasoning that to do so would constitute a "prior restraint" in violation of the First Amendment, the arbitrator denied the employer's grievance).

[200]United Cable Television Corp., 92 LA 3 (Koven, 1988), citing Dreis & Krump Mfg. Co., 221 NLRB 309, 90 LRRM 1647 (1975).

[201]92 LA at 9, quoting Dreis & Krump Mfg. Co., supra note 199. See also KBO, Inc., 315 NLRB 570, 147 LRRM 1233 (1994).

[202]Trans-City Terminal Warehouse Inc., 94 LA 1075, 1079 (Volz, 1990).

[203]Id. at 1078. Accord Yankee Screw Prods., 95 LA 909 (Kanner, 1990).

# VII.  Firearms or Weapons in the Workplace

Arbitrators generally disapprove the possession of weapons at work. One arbitrator noted that the harsh disciplinary action many employers take against employees using or possessing firearms in the workplace is justified. He wrote:

> Firearms have no place in an industrial setting and lives have been lost by the tragedies following hasty resort to their use following arguments. While it may be true that "Guns don't kill people, people do", it is also true that "People without guns don't use guns to kill people".[204]

## A.  What Constitutes a Weapon

Any object, including ordinary materials and tools available in the workplace, may be a weapon when used to threaten or inflict bodily injury.[205] Arbitrators confront a difficult problem when disciplinary action is taken against an employee for possession of a weapon in the workplace when that weapon is also used by the employee as a tool. For example, if an employee must be use a knife as part of her job, she may unintentionally gesture with it during an altercation. Absent evidence of any intent to harm or threaten anyone, the employee is guilty only of carelessness and bad judgment, and the penalty of discharge usually is not warranted.[206] An arbitrator reduced a discharge to a suspension for a meat cutter who waved a boning knife near the face of a co-worker during a dispute. The arbitrator found that the grievant had a knife in his hand because he was working with it and not for the purpose of injuring or threatening a fellow employee.[207] A power screwdriver used in the workplace, however, may constitute a deadly weapon if it is held in a menacing manner. Brandishing it at a co-worker may be grounds for discharge.[208]

An arbitrator upheld the discharge of an employee who brandished a knife at a security guard. The grievant used the knife in the plant. The arbitrator ruled, however, that it was immaterial the

---

[204]Goodyear Aerospace Corp., 86 LA 403, 405 (Fullmer, 1985).

[205]Southern Iron & Equip., 65 LA 694 (Rutherford, 1975) (upholding discharge for attacking supervisor with a piece of iron).

[206]Chatham Supermarkets, Inc., 71 LA 1084, 1088 (Roumell, 1978). See also Weather-Proof Co., 50 LA 199 (Graff, 1967) grievant suspended for 1 day for slashing co-worker's hand with knife used by grievant in her job; no intent to harm demonstrated); Hillbro Printing Co., 49 LA 173 (Mead, 1967) (discharge reduced to suspension where the arbitrator ruled that grievant, who was holding a knife as part of his work, did not mean to threaten foreman with knife when he made a hand gesture toward foreman).

[207]Chatham Supermarkets, Inc., 71 LA 1084 (Roumell, 1978).

[208]System Sensor, 102 LA 622, 626 (Doering, 1994).

employee had authority to carry a knife for use as a tool. The "significant factor was that [the grievant] threatened to use the instrument as a weapon, not a tool, and the threat was effective."[209]

## B. *Using or Threatening to Use a Weapon*

As one arbitrator said, "[b]y any possible standard of workplace conduct, an attack with a deadly weapon is intolerable; indeed, it ranks at the top of any list of industrial offenses."[210] Threatening to use a weapon is often as serious an offense as actually using a weapon. A threat is made when an employee holds a weapon ready for use and causes others reasonably to believe that they are in danger.[211] Threatening a fellow employee with a deadly weapon is justified only if an employee has no other way to defend himself against an imminent threat of serious bodily injury.[212] Employers are justified in taking threats seriously because they may provoke violent reactions from employees who feel threatened. It is irrelevant if the weapon used to make the threat is actually capable of working.[213]

Due to the extreme danger of injury posed by firearms, merely showing a gun may constitute a threat. Whether a threat can legitimately be inferred, however, depends on the circumstances of the particular case.[214] Even if the grievant displayed the weapon as a joke, if the reactions of co-workers evidence a fear that the threat of use was real, a threat may be inferred.[215]

---

[209]Certainteed Corp., 78 LA 1290, 1294 (Madden, 1982).

[210]Piedmont Publ'g Co., 97 LA 739, 741 (Nolan, 1991). See also United States Steel Corp., 58 LA 694 (Kreimer, 1972) (discharge of grievant, who stabbed co-worker with a knife, upheld); International Harvester Co., 50 LA 766 (Doyle, 1968) (employer properly discharged grievant who discharged pistol at a fellow employee).

[211]Nitec Paper Corp., 75 LA 1 (Goodman, 1980) (discharge of grievant for pulling a knife on a fellow employee, holding it to his stomach, and threatening to cut the employee to pieces sustained); Mobil Oil Corp., 73 LA 993 (Rose, 1979) (10-day suspension of an employee who pulled a knife on another employee upheld; employee, by his actions and language, had created a threat of physical harm to the other employee).

[212]Navy Exch., 52 LA 1142 (Williams, 1969) (5-day suspension of grievant, who displayed a knife to a fellow employee who had physically attacked grievant, overturned where grievant only displayed knife in an attempt to fend off unprovoked attack); Pride Packing Co., 48 LA 1092 (Jones, 1967) (discharge upheld where arbitrator found grievant did not have justification to display knife in self-defense because he had not done everything possible to avoid a potential physical confrontation).

[213]Flexible Materials, 101 LA 408 (Oberdank, 1993) (discharge of a grievant who pointed an empty gun at a co-worker's head as a joke was upheld).

[214]See also T.K. Valve & Mfg., Inc., 73 LA 241 (Helburn, 1979) (shop steward's discharge, for displaying handgun to fellow employees and showing them how to load it, upheld because steward's previously unfriendly relationship with employees led arbitrator to conclude that conduct was reckless and threatening); Owens-Corning Fiberglas Corp., 54 LA 419 (Reid, 1970) (employee reinstated who brought loaded gun into plant to show co-workers; conduct was foolish and dangerous but did not warrant discharge).

[215]Flexible Materials, 101 LA 408 (Oberdank, 1993).

## C. Level of Discipline

There is ample precedent supporting an employer's right to establish and enforce rules prohibiting the possession of weapons on an employer's premises.[216] The rules may be necessary to provide a safe workplace and maintain reasonable and necessary precautions for safeguarding the health and safety of employees.[217] Arbitrators are not hesitant to uphold the discharge of employees who bring weapons to the workplace in violation of such rules.[218]

Workplace rules prohibiting the possession of weapons on the employer's property may also apply to weapons stored in an employee's vehicle on the property.[219] Even if an argument could be made that language contained in such workplace rules implies that the rules apply only to carrying a weapon on one's person as opposed to being stored in a vehicle,

> common sense suggests that a loaded revolver—even one carried and left lying in a vehicle—comes under the general prohibition in the rule, subject to the penalty set forth.[220]

Lack of consistent enforcement of the rule may serve to mitigate the discipline imposed on an employee who brings a weapon to work.[221] Generally, having a gun in a vehicle in the parking lot, absent a specific threat, is viewed as less serious than carrying a gun into the

---

[216]City of New Haven, 101 LA 646, 648 (Stewart, 1993); Marathon Petroleum Co., 93 LA 1082 (Marlatt, 1989); Gardner-Denver Cooper Indus., 76 LA 26 (Witney, 1980); Brodie Indus. Trucks, 50 LA 112 (Teele, 1968).

[217]Marathon Petroleum Co., 93 LA 1082 (Marlatt, 1989), quoting Gardner-Denver Cooper Indus., 76 LA 26 (Witney, 1980).

[218]Indianapolis Pub. Transp. Corp., 98 LA 557, 565 (Doering, 1991); Marathon Petroleum Co., 93 LA 1082 (Marlatt, 1989); Van Wold-Stevens Co., 79 LA 645, 648–49 (Flagler, 1982); Transit Authority of River City, 79 LA 508 (Staudter, 1982); Curtis Mathes Mfg. Co., 70 LA 628 (Brown, 1978). But see Amerada Hess Corp., 77 LA 139 (Donoghue, 1981) (discharge of employee who possessed a starter's pistol on employer's premises, in violation of workplace prohibition of firearms, reduced to 30-day suspension; pistol was not considered a firearm because it was incapable of firing).

[219]Indianapolis Pub. Transp. Corp., 98 LA 557 (Doering, 1991) (discharge upheld for employee who reported to work with a handgun left in plain view in his pickup truck in the employer's parking lot). See also Goodyear Aerospace Corp., 86 LA 403 (Fullmer, 1985) (discharge of employee upheld who, in violation of workplace rule prohibiting the possession of firearms in the workplace, carried a weapon in his vehicle onto the employer's premises).

[220]Indianapolis Pub. Transp. Corp., 98 LA 557, 564 (Doering, 1991).

[221]Luxfer USA, Ltd., 102 LA 783 (Kaufman, 1994) (discharge reduced to suspension for employee who had a loaded gun in his car in employer's parking lot, notwithstanding workplace rule permitting summary discharge for possession of weapons; employer had been lax in enforcing rule, including allowing a foreman to sell guns in the employer's parking lot, and, therefore, could not discharge first person caught with a weapon at work after the employer decided to enforce the rule); Griffin Pipe Prods. Co., 70 LA 1231, 1232 (Boyd, 1978) (discharge reduced to suspension for employee who brought gun to work, in violation of workplace rule, because employer had made no effort to enforce rule against other individuals who possessed weapons at work). But see Marathon Petroleum, 93 LA 1082 (Marlatt, 1989) (discharge upheld and inconsistent enforcement argument rejected where employer had consistently enforced rule for 2 years prior to incident involving grievant).

plant. If the rule lacks specificity, or is not clearly communicated, discipline for violating the rule may be problematic.[222]

Even when there is a rule prohibiting possession of weapons in the workplace, arbitrators differ as to whether an employer has to prove that the employee intended to bring the weapon to the workplace or intended to use the weapon in the workplace to cause harm. One view is that rules prohibiting weapons in the workplace are absolute and should be enforced even if the employee did not intend to bring the weapon to work or to use the weapon to harm others. The fundamental purpose for having such rules is to keep all weapons out of the workplace because of their inherently dangerous nature.[223] Others maintain that intent is relevant. One arbitrator held that in order to sustain a discharge for violating a rule prohibiting possession of weapons in the workplace, there has to be "a clear showing that Grievant intended to bring a weapon on the premises and did this deliberately.* * * Intent must be given some weight in enforcing this or any rule."[224]

Even where there is not a specific workplace rule prohibiting employees from possessing weapons on an employer's premises, the employer may still discipline employees who bring unauthorized weapons into the workplace.[225]

## VIII. Horseplay

Arbitrators often distinguish horseplay from misconduct, based upon intent. Horseplay is generally characterized as conduct that is without malice, is playful, childish, or impulsive. One arbitrator defined horseplay, by reference to *Webster's Ninth New Collegiate Dictionary*, as "rough and boisterous play."[226] Where the horseplay is intended to injure a fellow worker, however, it is misconduct. Horseplay has the potential for physical injury or property damage. It

---

[222]U.S. Immigration & Naturalization Serv., 77 LA 1033, 1037 (Winton, 1981) ("[the employer] is almost asking for trouble in the way it allows employees to handle either Service owned firearms or personally owned firearms [in the course of employment]").

[223]Gardner-Denver Cooper Indus., 76 LA 26 (Witney, 1980). See also Marathon Petroleum, 93 LA 1082 (Marlatt, 1989) (arbitrator held that if employer was required to determine whether the grievant intended to cause harm, rule would be useless because actual violations could not be determined until after a weapon actually was used); Goodyear Aerospace Corp., 86 LA 403 (Fullmer, 1985) (discharge is appropriate even where the weapon is left in an employee's vehicle inadvertently); Van Wold-Stevens Co., 79 LA 645 (Flagler, 1982) (discharge of employee who placed weapons in employer's van upheld, even though grievant claimed he forgot the weapons were among possessions he carried into the van).

[224]Atlantic Steel Co., 79 LA 163, 166 (Goodman, 1982) (discharge reduced to suspension where grievant unintentionally brought vehicle to work with a gun in the glove compartment).

[225]Ross-Meehan Foundries, 55 LA 1078, 1080 (King, 1970); Brown & Williamson Tobacco Corp., 50 LA 403, 412 (Willingham, 1968).

[226]Eagle-Picher Indus., Inc., 101 LA 473, 475 (Staudohar, 1993).

becomes misconduct when there is injury or damage as the result of "an intentional act of wrongdoing."[227] It is rare for an employee to be discharged for horseplay that has resulted in unintentional injury, embarrassment, or damage to property. Employees are readily discharged for fighting or other intentional acts resulting in damage.

When analyzing a horseplay case, it is important to consider the following questions:

1. Was the conduct intentional or accidental?[228]
2. Was there a risk of injury or damage to other employees or company property?[229]
3. Was the workplace atmosphere generally conducive to playful acts?[230]
4. Did the employee react with regret or remorse for the injury or damage he or she caused?[231]

## A. Intentional or Accidental Conduct

The key factor in a horseplay case is whether the conduct involves an intentional act of wrongdoing. If an arbitrator is convinced an employee engaged in such wrongful conduct, severe discipline such as discharge likely will be upheld. If an arbitrator is convinced that either the conduct was unintentional or the result was unintended, severe discipline is unlikely to be upheld.

This distinction was highlighted in a case where a production line employee engaged in horseplay by sliding a hot bottle down the production floor past his foreman and to another employee who picked it up and was slightly burned. The arbitrator found the behavior

---

[227]Flat River Glass Co., 76 LA 946, 951 (Newmark, 1981).

[228]Id. at 955 (employee's "misconduct, however, while admittedly 'stupid' was not intentional * * * a grievant merely guilty of innocent, mischievous horseplay could and should be punished but not necessarily discharged"); Hess Oil Virgin Island Corp., 93 LA 581, 584 (Chandler, 1989) (evidence showed that the employees were intentionally fighting and not merely engaged in a "pre-arranged test of strength").

[229]Russer Foods, 75 LA 305, 306 (Grant, 1980) (setting a fellow employee's shoe on fire as a "hot-foot" gag is potentially dangerous); Kroger Co., 75 LA 290, 291 (Berns, 1980) (pouring lighter fluid on fellow employee's apron and then setting it on fire violated reasonable safety rule).

[230]Monsato Chem. Intermediates Co., 75 LA 592, 596 (Penfield, 1980) (employer's obligation "to maintain 'a workplace free from fears of threats and intimidation'" was reason to uphold a 30-day suspension of two male employees who used physical restraint on a female employee); Clay Equip., 73 LA 817, 819 (Carter, 1979) (employee who threw pie at consultant was reinstated because pranks were common event at the plant and the employee misunderstood distinction "between good clean fun * * * and the mindless throwing of a pie").

[231]Tyrone Hydraulic, Inc., 75 LA 672, 681 (Murphy, 1980) (employee, who obviously respected foreman, apologized to foreman he kicked after employee had been drinking); Southeast Container Corp., 69 LA 884, 887 (Seidenberg, 1977) (employee who "readily confessed to his transgression" had this considered when deciding upon punishment).

"stupid but not intentional" and reduced the discharge to a 2-week suspension.[232] In contrast, an arbitrator reinstated an employee even though the horseplay injured a co-worker, but denied back pay because the act was found to be done intentionally and with malice.[233] Specifically, the grievant pulled out the co-worker's chair because she was angry with her, which constituted malice.[234] A 35-year-old employee who injured the back of a 63-year-old employee, by carrying her over his shoulder and running the length of the plant, had his discharge sustained by an arbitrator.[235]

A number of discharges have been overturned where horseplay resulted in unintentional consequences. For example, in *Hamady Brothers, Inc.*,[236] a discharge was overturned where an employee had challenged two other employees to a race from an upper floor to the time clock, and during the race slid a door into a display case and broke a mirror. The grievant was charged with willful destruction of company property, an offense which, if proven, would undeniably constitute cause for discharge. The arbitrator found that by definition the word "willful" implies an act that is done deliberately, carefully thought out, done on purpose, and done in an unhurried manner. Consequently, he declined to uphold the discharge.[237] In another case the contention that the grievant's conduct in breaking a glass window was "willful destruction of company property" was not supported by the evidence. The grievant committed a serious offense when he threw an empty soft drink can at another employee, who earlier had thrown a rubber ball at him. The can hit and broke the glass window of a door, but the damage resulted from horseplay and was not willful. According to the arbitrator, the evidence showed that the requisite element of "intent" was lacking.[238]

In *Fisher Electronics, Inc.*,[239] a discharge was reduced to a 10-week suspension without pay in order to impress upon the grievant that employees have an obligation to "conduct themselves as mature individuals, rather than as light-hearted juveniles." The employee had moved a supervisor's chair as she was about to sit down, which showed a lack of judgment, but not malice.[240]

---

[232]Flat River Glass Co., 76 LA 946 (Newmark, 1981). See also U.S. Internal Revenue Serv., 77 LA 19 (Edes, 1981) (1-day suspensions of IRS agents who "mooned" a group of women in the garage of a restaurant/bar overturned).

[233]Federal-Mogul Corp., 91 LA 1402 (Nathan, 1988).

[234]Id.

[235]Muskin, Inc., 89 LA 297 (DiLauro, 1987); S.P. Drug Co., 44 LA 730 (Kornblum, 1965); Geigy Chemical Corp., 33 LA 819 (Murphy, 1959).

[236]57 LA 1097 (Roumell, 1972).

[237]Id. at 1099.

[238]Ozite Corp., 59 LA 1153, 1154 (Sergent, 1972) (even though grievant hit and broke a window of a door, "damages resulted from horseplay and was not willful").

[239]44 LA 343, 346 (Buckwalter, 1964).

[240]Id. at 346.

## B. Risk of Injury or Damage

The question of whether the employee intended any wrongdoing is sometimes outweighed by the risks the behavior presents to maintaining a safe workplace. An arbitrator upheld the discharge of an employee who lit toilet paper and set off the fire detection unit.[241] One arbitrator emphasized the employer's legitimate interests in maintaining a safe workplace free of unnecessary risks caused by misconduct of employees:

> The Arbitrator acknowledges, as does the company, and union, that management is under a continuing obligation to safeguard its employees, furnish a safe place to work, and protect its property and operations from the hazards and dangers of fire. The willful setting of a fire, or the application of heat to a fire detection unit so as to trigger the alarm system constitutes a serious, and grave form of misconduct. Whether such act is engaged in deliberately, with the intent to cause damage, or, whether the employee's behavior is in the nature of a "prank", or horseplay, such conduct cannot be condoned. Management is empowered, and obligated to take prompt and effective action to eliminate such dangers, and guard against recurrence, including appropriate discipline for engaging in such conduct where supported by sufficient proof, and evidence of just cause.[242]

In this arbitrator's view, the paramount factors are safety and the elimination of danger, rather than whether the employee intended the consequences of his or her acts.

In another case, an arbitrator upheld the discharge of an employee who exploded a cherry bomb in the employees' locker room in a chemical plant, causing damage to another employee's eye.[243] The employee's actions were found to have jeopardized the safety of the plant and other employees. Similarly, a meat cutter's discharge was upheld where the grievant had ignited the apron of a co-worker while the co-worker was using a knife to trim meat.[244] An employer properly discharged an employee who, during a coffee break, placed a lit cigarette in the pocket of a co-employee and intentionally started a fire under a co-employee's chair.[245]

An arbitrator upheld the discharge of an employee who was angry about being hit by a piece of hard rubber thrown by other employees and retaliated by placing lit cigarettes in back pockets of employees who (1) operated a machine with moving blades, and (2) entered a

---

[241]Abbott & Co., 76 LA 339 (Dworkin, 1981).

[242]Id at 343.

[243]Geigy Chem. Corp., 33 LA 819, 823–24 (Murphy, 1959).

[244]Kroger Co., 75 LA 290 (Berns, 1980).

[245]Russer Foods, 75 LA 305 (Grant, 1980). See Midland Ross Corp., 65 LA 1151 (Dallas, 1975) (30-day suspension appropriate for employee who exploded a firecracker at work station before Christmas holiday).

spray booth where combustible materials were present.[246] The arbitrator reasoned that the conduct involved a high risk of serious injury to others and could not be considered mere "horseplay."[247]

## C. Defenses

*1. Horseplay Tolerated.*   A common mitigating factor is that horseplay generally is tolerated or condoned in the workplace. A related factor is that similar conduct should result in similar discipline. If the arbitrator concludes that supervisors also engaged in or tolerated horseplay, significant discipline is unlikely.

In one case, the arbitrator found discipline appropriate because the act was not horseplay but racial harassment.[248] Nevertheless, the arbitrator concluded that discharge was excessive, in part, because "race-based teasing or taunting" had been tolerated in the workplace.[249]

Discharge is likely to be reduced to lesser discipline if horseplay is common in the workplace. Even where a co-worker was injured, where the co-worker has been a horseplay participant in the past and the grievant did not intend harm, the arbitrator reinstated a discharged grievant.[250] Some arbitrators reason that horseplay is a fact of industrial life and that less serious horseplay does not warrant exception to progressive discipline.[251]

*2. Contrition.*   Some decisions appear to turn on the reaction of the disciplined employee in response to the conduct in question. Arbitrators consider whether the disciplined employee admits his conduct, seems to genuinely regret that it occurred, and is contrite. These characterizations of postincident behaviors appear to be used as another means of determining whether the employee truly intended the consequences of his or her actions.[252]

---

[246]Decar Plastics Corp., 44 LA 921 (Greenwald, 1965).

[247]Id. at 923.

[248]Customized Transp., Inc., 102 LA 1179, 1181 (Stallworth, 1994).

[249]Id. at 1184.

[250]Eagle-Picher Indus., Inc., 101 LA 473 (Staudohar, 1993) (reinstatement of grievant who punched female co-worker, coworker had been active participant in horseplay, horseplay common in plant); Lee Clay Prods. Co., 40 LA 788 (Dworet, 1963) (discharge reduced to suspension where two employees engaged in horseplay and one's nose was broken, and since supervisors participated and encouraged horseplay); Ventoura Corp., 30 LA 132, 137–38 (Davis, 1958).

[251]Southeast Container Corp., 69 LA 884 (Seidenberg, 1977) (machine crew member smeared red ink over a handle on the press machine on the same day the general foreman held safety meeting to discuss horseplay; Gindy Mfg. Co., 58 LA 1038, 1040 (Handsaker, 1972) (discharge overturned where employee squirted fire extinguisher at a fellow employee in violation of a plant rule, but horseplay "widespread" and even involved supervisors); Erwin Mills Inc., 51 LA 225, 226–27 (Altrock, 1968) (reinstated employee finding conduct was provoked, was horseplay and took "[a]rbitral notice" that horseplay exists in any factory).

[252]Flat River Glass Co., 76 LA 946, 951 (Newmark, 1981) (discharge overturned where younger employee apologetic, contrite, "scared," and felt guilty).

Even though the horseplay resulted in damage and even recognizing the safety considerations in the airline business, one arbitrator set aside a discharge based on the following factors: (1) the employee's act of moving a co-worker's cart was spontaneous and the resulting damage caused to an airplane's fuselage, when the cart rolled into the plane, was unexpected; (2) the puncture in the skin was small, a 2-inch by 5-inch hole, and took only 4 to 5 hours to repair; and (3) the employee immediately and continually recognized the seriousness of his offense and apparently was genuinely contrite.[253]

# IX. Failure to Meet Grooming or Appearance Standards

Outside the workplace, individuals have significant control over their personal appearance. Even where an individual's appearance is offensive to prevailing community sentiment, the law may protect the right to dress as one chooses as a form of self-expression.[254] At the workplace, however, such freedom can be limited. Individual autonomy may at times give way to management's right to control what employees wear and how they look. Whether promoting health and safety, or advancing a favorable public image, employers often maintain appearance and grooming standards. Violating these standards can be considered misconduct and may lead to discipline. Repeated violations may lead to discharge. Third-party complaints, discussed below, also are sometimes the basis for discipline.

When arbitrators should limit the employer's authority to impose restrictions on employee appearance is a difficult issue. Arbitration decisions and federal cases reveal an unsettled area of law, marked by intense conflicts rooted in personal conviction.

## A. Arbitral Principles

The prevailing principle among arbitrators is that an employer has the right to enforce reasonable appearance standards designed to achieve legitimate business interests. Even where there is no specific provision in the collective bargaining agreement, arbitrators generally agree that the employer has the right to discipline employees who fail to meet reasonable dress and grooming requirements.

Arbitrators recognize two general justifications for imposing "appearance" standards on employees.[255] First, grooming standards

---

[253]Braniff Airways, Inc., 28 LA 453, 455–56 (Boles, 1957).

[254]Cohen v. California, 403 U.S. 15 (1971) (court held as constitutionally protected the wearing of a jacket imprinted with the legend "Fuck the Draft" in a courthouse corridor).

[255]County of Cattaraugus, 77 LA 1027, 1029 (Denson, 1981) (upheld requirement of wearing pink and white uniforms for nurse's aides; decision based on long history of wearing particular uniforms (past practice); arbitrator does note that the circumstances would be differ-

may be designed to promote health and safety. For example, a rule that prohibited pilots from growing beards was upheld because of the potential for interference with breathing devices.[256] If the rule is not reasonably related to its stated purpose, however, an arbitrator may find enforcement of such a rule would violate an employee's individual rights.[257] Where food contamination was at issue, an arbitrator upheld the discharge of an employee who had grown sideburns beyond company regulations.[258] Even where a dress code was opposed on religious grounds, the arbitrator permitted the employer to "give greater weight to safety considerations" and refused to allow the employee to return to work unless she complied with the dress code.[259]

The second type of permissible rule is one that protects or advances the employer's public image. As explained by one arbitrator, "[the employee] is the personification of the Company to those persons who observe him and so it is essential that he project an appropriate image by maintaining a pleasing personal appearance."[260] Whether it is to convey an impression of cleanliness,[261] trustworthiness,[262] or to promote a sense of unity and spirit among employees, protecting the company's public image is accepted as a legitimate reason for grooming rules.

There are many cases where sanctions stemming from image-based grooming rules have been upheld.[263] Arbitrators are receptive to these rules when the employee has direct contact with the public and where the business is highly dependent upon a favorable public

---

ent if there were a health/safety issue, but the evidence does not indicate such a situation); Dravo-Doyle, 54 LA 604, 606 (Krimsly, 1970) ("[t]he Company has the right to require its employees to cut their hair and shave *when long hair and beards can reasonably threaten the company's relations with its customers or other employees, or a real question of safety is involved* * * *.") (emphasis added).

[256]Pacific Southwest Airlines, 77 LA 320 (Jones, 1981). But see Union Carbide Corp., 82 LA 1084, 1087–88 (Goldman, 1984) (no-beard rules unreasonable where employees' use of oxygen equipment was not normally required).

[257]See Fisher Foods, Inc., 88 LA 1084 (Richard, 1987); Missouri Pub. Serv. Co., 77 LA 973, 976 (Maniscalco, 1981) (rule found to be improper; employer failed to demonstrate relationship between public attitude and rule; arbitrator recognizes rule of "legitimate business reasons" but maintains it is not found in this case). See RobertShaw Controls, 55 LA 283, 287 (Blak, 1970).

[258]Kellogg Co., 55 LA 84, 88 (Shearer, 1970).

[259]Colt Indus., 71 LA 22 (Rutherford, 1978) (safety rule required all employees, including women, to wear pants; grievance based on religious grounds denied).

[260]Southern Bell Tel. & Tel. Co., 74 LA 1115, 1116 (Duff, 1980). See also Pepsi Cola Gen. Bottlers, 55 LA 663, 666 (Volz, 1970) (employee who deals with the public or who solicits sales has an added responsibility for presenting a pleasing appearance).

[261]Albertsons, Inc., 102 LA 641 (Darrow, 1994) (a grocery store chain was permitted to maintain a rule against beards and long hair on drivers to project a pure and clean image).

[262]Pacific Southwest Airlines, 77 LA 320 (Jones, 1981). But see Union Carbide Corp., 82 LA 1084, 1087–88 (Goldman, 1984) (no-beard rule unreasonable where employees' use of oxygen equipment was not normally required).

[263]Fisher Foods, Inc., 88 LA 1084 (Richard, 1987); Mister A's Restaurant, 80 LA 1104, 1005 (Christopher, 1983) ("Companies providing service to the public have the right to protect their image."); Southern Bell Tel. & Tel. Co., 74 LA 115, 116 (Duff, 1980) (upheld rule prohibiting coin-telephone collectors from wearing shorts while on duty).

image, both of which are matters subject to proof at the hearing.[264] For example, where two grocery store packers showed up for work with "punk" haircuts, the arbitrator upheld the employer's decision to refuse the employees work until they could present a more conventional appearance.[265] In support of his decision, the arbitrator noted the special attention the "packers" receive working in public view, often the first and last employees seen by customers.[266] Where a restaurant rule required waitresses to have blond hair or wear blond wigs, the arbitrator denied the employee's challenge, explaining that "companies providing a service to the public have the right to protect their image."[267] On the other hand, where an employee does not deal with the public, it is less likely the rule will be upheld.[268]

As with all workplace rules, appearance restrictions must be clear and consistently applied.[269] Moreover, even where the rule is consistently applied and based on a legitimate purpose, there still must be a reasonable relationship between that purpose and the employer's action.[270]

While it is clear that all appearance regulations must be reasonable, the standard arbitrators apply is not susceptible of easy analysis.[271] In some decisions what is reasonable is determined by outside factors. In *Page Airways of Michigan,*[272] the arbitrator wrote:

> As fashion styles and public concerns change, rules and regulations * * * will continue to be tested and challenged as being unreasonable. And, each case will have to be determined on the facts peculiar to it.[273]

Thus, a no-beard rule was found unreasonable in a community where beards were common,[274] and a dress rule was found outdated.[275] In other cases, the employer's purpose in promulgating the rule is

---

[264]Arrow Redi-Mix Concrete, Inc., 56 LA 597, 601 (Fleischi, 1971) ("If the nature of the business is such that its sales are highly sensitive to the image portrayed, the balance tends to weigh heavily in favor of the Employer." The arbitrator found that the rule was not reasonably related to legitimate employer interest.).

[265]Fisher Foods, Inc., 88 LA 1084 (Richard, 1987).

[266]Id. at 1084.

[267]Mister A's Restaurant, 80 LA 1104, 1105 (Christopher, 1980).

[268]Computer Science Co., 87 LA 1302 (Marlatt, 1986) (rule requiring employees to wear suitable business attire found unreasonable as applied to computer technicians who did not deal with the public and had little contact with other employees).

[269]Fisher Foods, Inc., supra note 265, at 1084.

[270]Mister A's Restaurant, supra note 267.

[271]Fisher Foods, Inc., 88 LA 1084, 1089 (Richard, 1987) ("Arbitrators are sharply divided with regard to the burden and standard of proof required to establish the existence of those elements necessary to give rise to the Employer's right to regulate employee appearance for the sake of image.").

[272]69 LA 141 (Rinaldo, 1977).

[273]Id. at 144.

[274]Frito-Lay, Inc., 81-2 ARB ¶ 8562 (Forsythe, 1981).

[275]Oxford Nursing Home, 75 LA 1300, 1301 (Wolff, 1980) (20-year-old dress code prohibiting pant suits).

accepted, but the arbitrator considers whether that purpose can be achieved without a grooming rule. Where sanitation was the employer's concern, an arbitrator found that wearing hairnets could accomplish the purpose without requiring employees to cut their hair short.[276] Similarly, an arbitrator found that caps would allow long-haired employees to work safely with machinery without requiring them to cut their hair.[277] Finally, in some cases the employer simply fails to prove there is any legitimate reason for the rule. Where the employer could not show any basis for its assertion that prohibiting drivers from wearing mirror sunglasses would increase ridership or promote customer returns, discipline was overturned.[278] Similarly, a no-beard rule could not be enforced for male flight attendants when the employer was unable to show any effect on business.[279] Arbitrators have provided employees with considerable protection from rules that are arbitrary, capricious, overly broad, or otherwise not rationally related to the employer's stated objective.

## B. Constitutional Law

The United States Constitution protects individuals employed by governments from state action that infringes on their individual rights. While constitutionally based protections of individual freedom have little impact on the private employer, public employees have some constitutional protection of personal autonomy in the workplace. Public employees disciplined for failure to meet dress or grooming standards have attempted to challenge their employer's action as an unconstitutional infringement of liberty interests protected by the Fifth and Fourteenth Amendments.[280]

Although courts have made some statements regarding the existence of such a liberty interest, in practice little has materialized. For example, the Supreme Court upheld a police department's elaborate regulation of hair length, denying the argument that it violated protected liberty interests.[281] Similarly, where a police officer was reprimanded for wearing a stud-type earring, the court deferred to the judgment of the police department without a showing of adverse

---

[276]Roskam Baking Co., 79 LA 993 (Beitner, 1982).

[277]Challenge-Cook Bros., 55 LA 517 (Roberts, 1970).

[278]Milwaukee Transp. Serv. Inc., 77 LA 807, 813 (Jones, 1981).

[279]Pacific Southwest Airlines, 73 LA 1209, 1213 (Christopher, 1979).

[280]Kelly v. Johnson, 96 S.Ct. 1440, 1443 (1976) ("[W]hether the citizenry at large has some sort of 'liberty' interest within the Fourteenth Amendment in matters of personal appearance is a question on which this Court's cases offer little, if any, guidance. We can, nevertheless, assume an affirmative answer for purposes of deciding this case * * *."). See also Pence v. Rosenquist, 573 F.2d 395 (7th Cir., 1978) (holding that suspension of school bus driver for refusal to shave violates due process in the absence of some other justification).

[281]Kelly v. Johnson, 96 S.Ct. 1440, 1446 (1976) (Powell, J., concurring).

impact on police effectiveness.[282] Thus, unlike some arbitration decisions that require the employer to make an initial showing of reasonableness, the constitutional analysis places the burden on the employee to prove that the employer has acted irrationally.

Even where fundamental rights such as speech and the exercise of religion are at stake, employer managerial interests have consistently prevailed. For example, the Supreme Court held that the principle of religious neutrality should outweigh the free exercise of religion where a teacher attempted to wear traditional Sikh clothing in the classroom.[283] Even where no competing constitutional value was at stake, the Supreme Court has limited protection for free exercise of religious dress.[284]

### C. Civil Rights Statutes

Civil rights statutes have provided the primary source of legal challenge to dress and grooming rules in the workplace.[285] Unlike the constitutional protections, civil rights laws reach into the private sector. Most significantly, Title VII of the Civil Rights Act of 1964 prohibits discrimination by both public and private employers.

Under Title VII, courts have generally permitted employer dress and grooming rules that do not significantly discriminate or show preference to one sex, race, or religion over another.[286] Dress codes may distinguish between men and women on the basis of "commonly accepted social norms"[287] or "generally accepted community standards of dress and appearance."[288] Thus, in a Ninth Circuit case, the court upheld the dismissal of a male employee for failing to wear a tie even though no such requirement existed for females.[289]

Title VII does prohibit two types of employer appearance regulation as sexually discriminatory. First, where grooming requirements are applied to one sex and not the other or where they impose a greater burden on one sex than the other,[290] employer action may be

---

[282]Rathert v. Village of Peotone, 903 F.2d 510 (7th Cir.), cert. denied, 498 U.S. 921 (1990).

[283]Cooper v. Eugene Sch. Dist., 723 P.2d 298 (Or., 1986), appeal dismissed, 480 U.S. 942 (1987).

[284]Goldman v. Weinberger, 106 S.Ct. 1310, 40 FEP Cases 543 (1986) (appearance regulation that prevented an Air Force officer from wearing a yarmulke as required by the Orthodox Jewish faith upheld).

[285]See Chapter 13 for a full discussion.

[286]Fountain v. Safeway Stores, Inc., 555 F.2d 753, 95 LRRM 3106 (9th Cir., 1977); Barker v. Taft Broadcasting, 549 F.2d 400 (6th Cir., 1977).

[287]Carroll v. Talman Fed. Sav. & Loan of Chicago, 604 F.2d 1028, 1032 (7th Cir., 1979), cert. denied, 100 S.Ct. 1316 (1980).

[288]Id.

[289]Fountain v. Safeway Stores, Inc., 555 F.2d 753, 95 LRRM 3106 (9th Cir., 1977).

[290]Sprogis v. United Airlines, 444 F.2d 1194 (7th Cir.), cert. denied, 92 S.Ct. 536 (1971) (unlawful to impose requirements that are based on immutable sex characteristics or that affect constitutionally protected activities such as child-rearing which pose obstacles to one gender).

rendered unlawful. Under this doctrine, a bank violated Title VII by requiring female employees to wear a uniformlike "career ensemble," while permitting men to wear any customary business attire.[291]

Second, the statute prohibits grooming requirements based on impermissible stereotypes. For example, it is well settled that an employer violates Title VII by requiring employees to wear a uniform that subjects them to sexual harassment.[292] While the dress or grooming code may not discriminate on the basis of gender, it may violate Title VII where it creates a disparate impact on the basis of religion or race. In one case, the court held that an African-American employee was unlawfully discharged because his "Afro" haircut did not comply with the company dress code.[293]

## X. Conduct and Speech Toward Third Parties

Employers commonly attempt to regulate not only employee conduct toward fellow employees and supervisors, but also conduct directed toward other individuals and entities with whom the employer does business. Those covered by such policies may include contractors and other service providers who come to the employer's premises, customers, and clients, both at their own premises and at the employer's place of business.

### A. *Obligations Toward Those in the Employee's Care*

Employers have disciplined employees whose misconduct is directed toward students, patients, and inmates. Misconduct in these areas can be especially troubling because of the nature of the relationships, especially for patients who may depend entirely upon employees for their well being.[294] For instance, expressions of profanity and disgust directed at a patient by a nursing home employee were deemed verbal abuse and grounds for discipline.[295] Alleged threats, however,

---

[291]Carroll v. Talman Fed. Sav. & Loan of Chicago, 604 F.2d 1028 (7th Cir., 1979).

[292]EEOC v. Sage Realty Corp., 507 F.Supp. 599 (S.D.N.Y., 1981) (discharge held to be a violation of Title VII wherein a lobby attendant who refused to wear uniform that was revealing and sexually provocative caused her to be sexually harassed).

[293]EEOC Dec. No. 71-2444, 4 FEP Cases 18 (1971).

[294]Hillhaven Corp., 91 LA 451 (McCurdy, 1981) (nursing home aide was properly suspended after being observed wiping patients noses in a rough manner and speaking in a rude fashion); Eau Claire County Insts., 53 LA 350 (Harrison, 1969) (employee was suspended for striking a mentally ill patient).

[295]War Memorial Hosp., 89 LA 1166 (Borland, 1987); Veterans Admin. Med. Ctr., 76 LA 412 (Pastore, 1981) (swearing at patients scheduled for surgery). For an in-depth review of abuse, see Bittel, "Abuse by Caretakers: Arbitral Views on Discipline," 50 Disp. Resol. J., 66 (1995).

must be understood in context. Not all questionable verbal exchanges will result in discharge.[296]

Employees who physically abuse patients, students, and inmates are also subject to discipline. An employee who strikes such a person is almost always discharged.[297] Where an employee had continued contact with a student who filed a complaint against him, the arbitrator upheld a reprimand.[298] Further, nonpunitive reassignment to another wing of the hospital was deemed an appropriate response to inconclusive complaints that a hospital worker engaged in sexual misconduct.[299] The decisions make clear that an employee has a heightened duty of care in dealing with dependent people and that abuse of any kind simply will not be tolerated and may ultimately lead to discharge.[300] In addition to misconduct, a failure to provide a high level of care may also give rise to discipline for negligence.[301]

Discipline has been upheld against school employees based upon student charges of harassment. For example, a written reprimand was upheld after a college security officer continued to contact a female student (who had filed a sexual harassment claim against him) despite a clear warning to refrain from doing so.[302] The suspension of a community college teacher was upheld after he refused to answer charges of unprofessional conduct filed by numerous female students, despite the fact that he had been given ample notice of the student charges and reasonable time to answer them.[303]

## B. Obligations Toward Customers and Third Parties

*1. Harassment.* An employee's conduct found to constitute physical or verbal abuse of customers or other third parties is evaluated as harassment. Actions that constitute harassment for disciplinary

---

[296]Palmer Terrace Nursing Ctr., 82 LA 1179, 1181 (Kosoff, 1984) (discharge deemed too severe a punishment for nurse's aide who told aged, infirm resident "If you continue to give me problems, I will gladly kick your ass."); Foothills Care Ctr., Inc., 80 LA 1046, 1049 (Cohen, 1983) (discharge was improper after a nurse answered a patient's request for a cane with "Oh, hell, I'm busy").

[297]Ambassador Convalescent Ctr., Inc., 83 LA 44 (Lipson, 1984) (discharge appropriate where employee struck patient); Park Geriatric Village, 81 LA 306 (Lewis, 1983) (discharge of nurse's aide appropriate where she wrestled with frail, elderly patient and tried to take her cane from her).

[298]Vermont State Colleges, 100 LA 1193 (McHugh, 1993) (security officer continued to contact female student who had filed a sexual harassment charge against him).

[299]Motion Picture & Television Fund, 92 LA 833 (Gentile, 1989).

[300]Doctors Hosp. of Manteca, 98 LA 1019 (Riker, 1992) (just cause to discharge nurse who, while on strike, made a statement about a patient's condition, even though the nurse did not reveal the patient's name, because hospital employees have a heightened duty to maintain client's privacy interest).

[301]Cf. Bisbee Hosp. Ass'n, 79 LA 977 (Weizenbaum, 1982) (employer failed to show negligent infliction of injuries by employee to a nursing home resident who was injured while being bathed).

[302]Vermont State Colleges, 100 LA 1193 (McHugh, 1993).

[303]Pima Community College, 76 LA 1133 (Cherry, 1981).

purposes include "familiar" instead of "businesslike" behavior,[304] and "inappropriate" personal remarks.[305] Even consensual relationships with third parties may lead to employee discipline.[306] Where supported by competent evidence, the discharge of an employee for serious abuse or neglect of a customer, patient, or other third party will be supported almost without exception.[307]

Where there is no evidence of physical abuse, or where the incident is minor and isolated, a decision to discharge the employee is likely to be reduced to a suspension or reversed entirely. For example, suspensions for alleged use of excessive force have been vacated where the evidence did not substantiate the charge.[308]

One of the most common forms of a third-party complaint against an employee involves the harassment of customers. Discipline has been imposed when an employee engages in inappropriate physical conduct, such as striking a customer in response to being struck.[309] Physical conduct meriting disciplinary action includes damaging property. For example, an employee was discharged for placing obscene drawings on a door that could be seen by employees and customers.[310] Another employee was discharged for damaging a subcontractor's cherry picker by attempting to hot wire it.[311] A striker who damaged the truck of a third party who failed to honor a picket line

---

[304]Memphis Light, Gas & Water Div., 100 LA 291 (Caraway, 1993) (suspension pending reinstatement appropriate discipline where customer filed a sexual harassment complaint against employee who had tendency to be familiar instead of businesslike with female customers).

[305]Cub Foods, Inc., 95 LA 771 (Gallagher, 1990) (just cause existed for discharge of grocery store clerk where, after a previous warning and suspension for such behavior, he made an inappropriate remark to female customers on three occasions).

[306]See, e.g., National R.R. Passenger Corp., 95 LA 617 (Simons, 1990) (90-day suspension, and not discharge, appropriate discipline for a sleeping car attendant charged with violating rule requiring that he act in a professional manner toward the public where he engaged in consensual sexual intercourse with a female passenger).

[307]See Beaver Local Bd. of Educ., 106 LA 1084 (Fullmer, 1996) (discharge of a school bus driver for slapping a disruptive student); Lutheran Senior City, 102 LA 79 (Millious, 1994) (discharge of senior city employee for abuse toward resident upheld where grievant admitted that she verbally abused resident); Montana State Hosp., 99 LA 551 (McCurdy, 1992); Chicago Transit Auth., 97 LA 367 (Cox, 1991) (bus driver discharged for stabbing); Southern Cal. Rapid Transit Dist., 96 LA 1113 (Gentile, 1991) (discharge of bus driver for standing on hood of car and screaming at owner); City of Houston, 95 LA 1193 (Morris, 1990) (discharge for excessive force by police officer resulting in death); Hillhaven Corp., 91 LA 451 (McCurdy, 1988) (suspension for patient abuse upheld); Park Geriatric Village, 81 LA 306 (Lewis, 1983); Delaware River Port Auth., 76 LA 350 (Raffaele, 1981).

[308]City of Redwood City, 98 LA 306 (Riker, 1991) (suspension rescinded for police officer who used force on handcuffed prisoner). See also City of Louisville, 94 LA 243 (Volz, 1989) (discharge reduced to suspension for verbal and physical abuse of patient); Palmer Terrace Nursing Ctr., 82 LA 1179 (Kossoff, 1984) (reinstatement of discharged employee who verbally abused nursing home resident).

[309]A. Finkl & Sons Co., 90 LA 502 (Wolff, 1988); Johnson Controls, Inc., 85 LA 594 (Garnholz, 1985); San Diego Transit Corp. 83 LA 224 (Gentile, 1984); Alumax Extrusions Corp., 81 LA 722 (Miller, 1983).

[310]Alumax Extrusions Corp., 81 LA 722 (Miller, 1983).

[311]Johnson Controls, Inc., 85 LA 594 (Garnholtz, (1985).

was suspended.[312] Telling "offensive" jokes to customers, a seemingly minor offense, has been deemed a sufficient basis for employee discharge in certain circumstances.[313] Employees who preached their religious beliefs to customers have been subject to discipline, based on the theory that the practice alienated some customers.[314] Sexual harassment and propositioning of third parties also gives rise to discipline.[315]

Suspension or discharge is typically upheld where there has been prior disciplinary action, or if the conduct has been repeated or was particularly egregious, even when the harassment takes place away from the employer's work site. For example, an arbitrator upheld the decision to suspend indefinitely a utility company account investigator after a third complaint of sexual harassment of customers was filed against the employee.[316] Discharge of a grocery store employee for offensive personal remarks to female customers on three separate occasions was sustained where the employee had previous warnings and suspensions for similar behavior and the complaining customers refused to continue shopping at the company's store.[317] The discharge of a delivery man was also upheld after he continuously made "sexual propositions" and engaged in other forms of "customer abuse" for several years, and some stores where the employee delivered company products had barred him from the stores.[318] A driver-salesman who persisted in preaching his religious faith to customers even after the employer had suspended him because of loss of customers was found to have been discharged for just cause,[319] as was a telephone company outside repair technician who made obscene and harassing telephone calls to customers.[320]

Arbitrators have overturned or modified disciplinary action where the pattern of harassment was not significant or the harassment was not so egregious as to support discipline. For example, an airport operations agent was improperly discharged for discourtesy

---

[312]A. Finkl & Sons Co., 90 LA 502 (Wolff, 1988).

[313]Pittsburgh Press Club, 89 LA 826 (Stoltenberg, 1987) (where waiter in private club repeatedly made offensive jokes to club guests after being warned against such behavior, discharge was appropriate).

[314]Charles Todd Uniform Rental Serv. Co., 77 LA 144 (Hutcheson, 1981).

[315]Plain Dealer Publ'g Co., 99 LA 969 (Fullmer, 1992) (just cause existed to discharge newspaper distribution manager for sexually harassing married gas station clerk); Nabisco Foods, Inc., 82 LA 1186 (Allen, 1984) (discharge proper where deliveryman made sexual propositions and engaged in other forms of sexual abuse toward customers) and cases cited therein. For further discussion, see Chapter 13.

[316]Memphis Light, Gas & Water Div., 100 LA 291 (Caraway, 1993) (finding persuasive the fact that customer complaints were voluntarily submitted and that the grievant had engaged in a pattern of being "familiar" with female customers).

[317]Cub Foods, Inc., 95 LA 771 (Gallagher, 1990).

[318]Nabisco Foods Co., 82 LA 1186 (Allen, 1984).

[319]Uniform Rental Serv., Co., 77 LA 144 (Hutcheson, 1981).

[320]Southern Bell Tel. & Tel. Co., 75 LA 409 (Seibel, 1980).

to a patron who had confronted the agent for smoking in a nonsmoking area. The agent did not start the confrontation, did not exacerbate it, and could not have diffused the situation.[321] Discipline was reduced for a fire inspector who was discourteous to daycare center operators, even though he had acted improperly and had a long disciplinary record, because the city did not follow the steps of the progressive discipline system.[322] A hospital nursing assistant was terminated after a patient's mother complained that the employee commented on the patient's body in a sexual manner and gave the patient his telephone number. The patient and her mother did not testify and the nursing assistant was reinstated after providing a plausible and consistent explanation for the course of events.[323] A city employee who was discharged for whistling at and soliciting conversation from employees and clients of a Planned Parenthood office was ordered reinstated because the employee's work record was generally unblemished and the discharge could not be supported on the basis of the offensive conduct alone.[324]

2. *Discourtesy to Customers: "Tone and Manner" Complaints.* Discipline for discourtesy to customers or other third parties depends upon the pattern and severity of the conduct. Discipline will usually be upheld only if the employee violated a particular work rule, if the employee was engaged in a pattern of discourteous behavior, if the employee had previously been disciplined, or if the conduct was egregious. A discharge was upheld where a hospital nurse was repeatedly rude in her relations with the hospital staff, patients, and a patient's family, even after repeated warnings and disciplinary action.[325] Discharge was upheld for an 18-year telephone company service representative who was the subject of 12 "tone and manner" complaints from customers or supervisors in the 11 months prior to her discharge, even though she consistently received high performance appraisals. She had been warned repeatedly regarding the complaints and was given progressive discipline after each complaint, and her appraisals mentioned tone and manner problems.[326]

Discharge for discourtesy to a customer has been upheld in the absence of a pattern of discourteous behavior if a specific work rule is violated and the employee's conduct is highly offensive or poses a

---

[321]Broward County Aviation Dep't, 106 LA 1153 (Richard, 1996).

[322]City of Lawton, 104 LA 686 (Allen, 1995).

[323]University of Minn., 93 LA 1041 (Neigh, 1989). See also San Antonio, Tex., 94 LA 147 (McKee, 1989) (police officer who was suspended based on citizen's complaint of unprofessional conduct was reinstated after citizen failed to testify and no other witnesses appeared).

[324]City of Rochester, 82 LA 217 (Lawson, 1984).

[325]University Med. Ctr., 99 LA 406 (Seidman, 1992).

[326]Southwestern Bell Tel. Co., 102 LA 531 (Nolan, 1994). See also General Tel. Co., 87 LA 989 (Armstrong, 1986) (just cause existed to discharge telephone operator for his "tone of service," where operator's courtesy ratings were below office average and customers had complained about his attitude).

threat to the employer's business. For example, a discharge was upheld where a car mechanic responded to a customer's threat to take his car elsewhere by saying: "I don't give a f _____ where you take it for service."[327] Another employee was properly discharged for cursing at three occupants of a car after they complained that he parked a truck too close to them.[328]

Even if an employee is discharged primarily for reasons other than discourtesy, the employee's discourteous conduct is a permissible consideration in the employer's decision. The relevance of an employee's discourtesy is heightened where the employee was on notice of the complaints and was provided with an opportunity to respond.[329] Where the employee's discourtesy is less severe, suspension or other discipline may be appropriate. For example, just cause existed to suspend a telephone operator who was convincingly identified by a customer as having addressed the customer in a rude manner. The customer's own rudeness did not give the employee a license to behave similarly, and the company had counseled the grievant for similar misconduct.[330]

In the absence of a pattern of discourteous behavior, or in the absence of minimally offensive conduct, the employer's discharge or discipline for employee discourtesy will not be upheld. For example, the suspension of a restaurant waiter, because of the manner in which he had handled customers who were unhappy with the location of their table in restaurant, was overturned as inappropriate.[331]

*3. Third-Party Complaints of Other Employee Misconduct.* Discipline or discharge also has been upheld for theft from customers, disclosure of confidential information, poor service, and poor appearance of employees. Theft from customers is a clear example of employee conduct that directly affects the customer and leads to discipline. Discipline has been upheld, including termination, even for petty theft from a customer.[332]

---

[327]See also H.E. Miller Oldsmobile, 81 LA 1112, 1113 (Westbrook, 1983). Grey Eagle Distribs., Inc., 93 LA 24 (Canestraight, 1989) (just cause for discharge of union steward existed after he cursed at women in a parked car); cf. Rustco Prods. Co., 92 LA 1048 (Watkins, 1989) (discharge of delivery driver barred from customer's premises because of racial epithets and vulgar language reduced to suspension because language deemed not an extremely serious offense under the contract).

[328]Grey Eagle Distribs., Inc., 93 LA 24 (Canestraight, 1989).

[329]Anchorage Hilton Hotel, 102 LA 55 (Landau, 1993).

[330]American Tel. & Tel. Co., 98 LA 102 (Byars, 1991). See also Internal Revenue Serv., 92 LA 233 (Lang, 1989) (tax examiner properly disciplined for being discourteous and putting incoming calls on hold, even though employee did not violate specific code of conduct).

[331]Wine Cellar, 81 LA 158 (Ray, 1983). See also Dane County, Wis., 97 LA 221 (Flaten, 1991).

[332]State of Minnesota, 95 LA 995 (Gallagher, 1990) (discharge of state employee upheld for petty theft); Cincinnati Gas & Elec. Co., 90 LA 841 (Katz, 1988) (discharge reduced to suspension for theft of soft drinks).

Disclosure of confidential information relating to customers is generally a ground for discipline, including termination of employment. The issue most commonly arises in the context of confidential patient information.[333] Discharge also has been upheld where a telephone company service representative disclosed confidential customer information to a litigant in a child custody dispute.[334]

Complaints based on poor service have consistently led to sustainable disciplinary actions. Arbitrators have upheld a discharge where an employee of a home-delivery meal service failed to deliver meals to senior-citizen customers,[335] and a suspension based upon complaint letters from customers.[336] However, discipline has not been sustained when the employer failed to follow the disciplinary procedure set out in a collective bargaining agreement[337] or where the standard used to justify the discipline was too high to include customer complaints.[338]

Finally, decisions to discipline employees based upon their physical appearance and grooming have been upheld based upon customer complaints in conjunction with a uniformly applied work rule. For example, a decision to ban a bearded employee from the workplace was upheld after the employee drew customer complaints and the employer applied a policy it had consistently followed in the past.[339] Where the discipline is not based on customer complaints, however, the analysis is different. A decision to discharge employees from their bakery positions for refusal to cut their long hair was not upheld where the employer had based the discipline on a newly issued grooming code,[340] and a no-beard rule was found to be unreasonable where there was no uniform industry ban on beards, the company was not responding to customer complaints, and the company allowed long hair and moustaches.[341]

---

[333]Doctors Hosp. of Manteca, 98 LA 1019 (Riker, 1992) (discharge for public disclosure of diagnosis and condition of undisclosed patient in hospital at union strike rally); Michigan Dep't of Soc. Servs., 96 LA 46 (Grinstead, 1990) (just cause existed to discipline social services employee who admittedly disclosed to relative that client had AIDS).

[334]United Tel. Co. of Kan., 100 LA 541 (Pratte, 1993).

[335]Bay County Div. on Aging, 98 LA 188 (Daniel, 1991).

[336]Safeway Stores, Inc., 94 LA 983 (Knowlton, 1990).

[337]Wolf Baking Co., 83 LA 24 (Marlatt, 1984) (employer improperly discharged route salesman because of customer's irritation with grievant where employer failed to give warnings as required under contract).

[338]Interstate Brands, 97 LA 675 (Ellmann, 1991) (just cause did not exist to discharge route salesman under rule concerning "unsatisfactory performance").

[339]Aslesen Co., 74 LA 1017 (Fogelberg, 1980).

[340]Roskam Baking Co., 79 LA 993 (Beitner, 1982).

[341]Fairmont-Zarda Dairy, 106 LA 583 (Rohik, 1995).

# Chapter 9

# Off-Duty Conduct

## I. Introduction

An employer's right to question an employee's conduct is generally limited to behavior that occurs while the employee is on duty. Once an employee is off duty and away from the workplace, there is a presumption that the employee's private life is beyond the employer's control.[1] As one arbitrator put it over a half century ago:

> We can start with the basic premise that the Company is not entitled to use its disciplinary power for the purpose of regulating the lives and conduct of its employees outside of their employment relation * * *. What the employee does outside the plant and after working hours is normally no concern of the employer. If the employee commits no misconduct in the plant or during his working hours he is not subject to disciplinary penalty * * *.[2]

In other words, the boundary between the employer's interests and those of the employee shifts significantly when the employee goes off duty. The jurisdictional line between an employee's conduct on and off the job has been compared to the line

> between the kinds of conduct which the community may legitimately attempt to influence, and the kind which is strictly the individual's business, off bounds to the government.[3]

---

[1]See Chapter 8; Hill & Wright, Employee Lifestyle and Off-Duty Conduct Regulation (BNA Books, 1993).

[2]Opinion A-132, Ford Motor Co. & UAW-CIO (Shulman, 1944).

[3]Kadish, "The Criminal Law and Industrial Discipline as Sanctioning Systems: Some Comparative Observations," Proceedings of the 17th Annual Meeting, National Academy of Arbitrators, 125, 131, Kahn, ed. (BNA Books, 1964), cited and expanded upon in Hill & Kahn, Discipline and Discharge for Off-Duty Misconduct: What Are the Arbitral Standards? Proceedings of the 39th Annual Meeting, National Academy of Arbitrators, 121, 121–22, Gershenfeld, ed. (BNA Books, 1987).

The line dividing the employer's legitimate interests from the employee's right to privacy is difficult to draw.

After setting forth the "basic premise" quoted earlier, the arbitrator concluded that

> the jurisdictional line which limits the Company's power of discipline is a functional, not a physical line. [The Company] has power to discipline for misconduct directly related to the employment.[4]

The standard that has evolved in this area is a response to the question: When is misconduct "directly related" to employment? Although some believe that each determination is unique—"In determining whether there is a 'nexus', each incident must be carefully examined and the conclusion based upon the merits of that case *and that case alone * * *"[5]— arbitrators' decisions in this area are usually consistent with the reasoned, interest-based analytical framework described in this chapter.[6]

## II. The "Workplace Nexus" Standard: Relevance and Notoriety

An employer can discipline an employee for off-duty misconduct where the arbitrator finds what is often called a "workplace nexus." There must be some connection between the off-duty misconduct and the employer's interests that legitimizes the employer's decision to take disciplinary action.[7]

### A. *The Accepted Standard*

The general rule is that an employer cannot discipline an employee for off-duty conduct. An early attempt to categorize the exceptions to this general rule asserted that discipline may be imposed if the employee's conduct: (1) harms the employer's business, (2) adversely affects the employee's ability to perform his or her job, or (3) leads

---

[4]Opinion A-132, Ford Motor Co. & UAW-CIO (Shulman, 1944). See Lakeside Jubilee Foods, 95 LA 358, 363 (Berquist, 1990).

[5]St. Paul Pub. Sch. Indep. Sch. Dist. 625, 101 LA 503, 506 (Imes, 1993) (emphasis added).

[6]See Abrams & Nolan, "Toward a Theory of 'Just Cause' in Employee Discipline Cases," 85 Duke L.J. 594 (1985).

[7]The employer's ability to regulate employees' off-duty conduct may also be limited by statute. See, e.g., Section 201-d of the New York State Labor Law, which with certain limited exceptions bars employers from terminating or otherwise discriminating against employees on the basis of their (1) legal political activity, (2) legal use of products (e.g., alcohol and tobacco), or (3) legal recreational activities.

other employees to refuse to work with the offender.[8] Put another way, abstaining from off-duty actions that have one of those three effects is part of the employee's obligation to provide satisfactory work.[9]

An employer can impose discipline for off-duty conduct by establishing the conduct's relevance or notoriety. Off-duty conduct is relevant when the conduct relates to and harms the employer's business. Off-duty conduct is notorious when, although not otherwise relevant, it becomes so widely known and is so deplorable that it harms the employer's business interests.

## B. Harm to the Employer's Business

Harm is usually defined as actual business loss or damage to the employer's reputation.[10] Arbitrators usually examine the amount of adverse publicity and embarrassment to the employer, and the likelihood that the employer will lose business or suffer other adverse consequences if the employee is not disciplined. The mere showing that the employee has been arrested or involved in some misconduct as a matter of public record is insufficient.[11]

In determining whether an employer can discipline an employee because of the notoriety of the off-duty misconduct, the extent to which the publicity surrounding the conduct has connected the employee to the employer in the public mind is a crucial element. In one case, an employee was arrested for manufacturing illegal drugs in his home. At his co-defendant's trial, which received comprehensive media coverage, the employee admitted to volunteering his house as the location of the drug lab (for which he was paid $6,000 in cash) and to buying raw materials for the manufacturing operation. His name was widely published, as were photographs of his house. But because his employer's name was never mentioned, the decision to discharge the employee was overturned by the arbitrator.[12]

---

[8]W. E. Caldwell Co., 28 LA 434, 436–37 (Kesselman, 1957). Arbitrator Kesselman's formulation became widely accepted and is often cited, not always with attribution. See, for examples of the application of that standard to the employer's proof, Giant Eagle Mkts. Co., 101 LA 581, 583 (Zobrak, 1993); Virgin Islands Dep't of Health, 97 LA 500, 502 (Watkins, 1991); City of Bridgeport, 97 LA 327, 331 (Freedman, 1991).

Another useful formulation with a slightly different nuance is: "An employer is not prevented from disciplining its employees for off-duty conduct which *involves or affects the employer-employee relationship.*" American Airlines, 68 LA 1245, 1247 (Harkless, 1977) (emphasis added).

[9]State of Ohio, 94 LA 533, 537 (Sharpe, 1990), citing Abrams & Nolan, supra note 6.

[10]Inland Container Corp., 28 LA 312, 314 (Ferguson, 1951).

[11]See Cases cited supra note 8.

[12]Mobil Oil Corp., 95 LA 162 (Allen, Jr., 1990). Accord Valley Bell Dairy Co., 71 LA 1004 (Hunter, Jr., 1978).

In one case, an employee pleaded guilty to charges of breaking and entering his estranged wife's home with intent to commit murder and of attempting to burn down another house belonging to her. Since the press coverage of the case had identified him as one of the employer's bus drivers, the arbitrator upheld his discharge, commenting that "the very nature" of the employer's business and the employee's job responsibilities were such that the employer would "lose the confidence of the public" if it continued to employ the grievant.[13]

Another bus driver, who had been publicly identified as the acting Grand Dragon of the local Ku Klux Klan, and whose statements had been widely publicized, was discharged for his Klan activities. The arbitrator found that "his activities [were] not mere words, but action contrary to the rights of a large segment of the population."[14] He found that a threatened boycott of the bus company by its numerous African-American customers, and the possibility of violence, justified the driver's dismissal.

When the employer alleges that the misconduct is relevant to and harms its business, it must usually show that the harm is either inevitable or actual. In one case, a manager was dismissed after being arrested and charged with cocaine possession. In upholding his discharge, the arbitrator noted:

> The connection between the facts * * * and the extent to which the business is affected must be reasonable and discernible. They must be such as could logically be expected to cause some result in the employer's affairs. * * *
> The * * * [grievant was] Manager of a community center * * *, a position requiring great contact with the community, when success is based on leadership and trust attributes. The Facility Manager works with senior citizens and youth groups * * *.[15]

In this case the arbitrator believed the cocaine arrest inevitably diminished the leadership and trust the facility manger could command. Where the employee is not in a highly visible "leadership" position, and in the absence of evidence of drug use or of an effect on job performance, drug possession itself is probably not a sufficient basis for discharge.[16]

The operative element is not the mere fact that a crime, serious or not, was committed. Rather, it is the crime's relevance to the employer. Even major felonies can be found irrelevant. In the case of an employee who had assaulted his ex-wife and her boyfriend, the arbitrator found that the employer was not justified in discharging

---

[13]Trailways Southeastern Lines, Inc., 81 LA 712 (Gibson, 1983).

[14]Baltimore Transit Co., 47 LA 62, 66 (Duff, 1966).

[15]Wayne State Univ., 87 LA 953, 957 (Lipson, 1986).

[16]See St. Paul Pub. Sch. Indep. Sch. Dist. 625, 101 LA 503, 506 (Imes, 1993); City of Bridgeport, 97 LA 327, 331 (Freedman, 1991). See Chapter 6 for further cases on drug policies.

the grievant because he had little contact with customers or the public, his misconduct had not become widely known, and his relationship with co-workers was unaffected.[17] On the other hand, the discharge of a university employee was upheld when he had been arrested for selling amphetamines on campus while off duty.[18]

In the noncriminal context, arbitrators have long been reluctant to enforce discipline against employees for sexual activities that do not adversely affect the employer. An unmarried employee who was dismissed in 1948 for becoming pregnant was ordered reinstated. The arbitrator cited "the lack of interdependence between M.S.'s conduct dealing with the living of her private life and her job as a visual inspector."[19] "The particular misdeed complained of in this case has no relevance to the nature of M.S.'s job duties or her job performance."[20]

In *Ralphs Grocery Co.*,[21] a homosexual employee gave a party at his home. The entertainment included a lesbian performance. The arbitrator refused to uphold his discharge, finding no relevance to the workplace in the conduct at the party or in his homosexual status. "Management's disapproval alone does not satisfy the contractual standard of 'good cause.' "[22]

An employer's drug-free-workplace policy has generally been found insufficient, in and of itself, to support the dismissal of an employee convicted of (off-duty) possession of marijuana.[23] Similarly, an employee's admission during a routine medical examination that he had smoked marijuana (off duty) every day for many years was not found to be sufficient cause for discharge.[24] When the work is extremely hazardous, however, it may be easier to justify discipline.[25]

A written and acknowledged employer policy that explicitly extends beyond the workplace to forbid off-duty involvement with illegal drugs, and identifies the employer interests at stake, is likelier to influence an arbitration's outcome than any exhortations at the hearing. Arbitrators, however, have held employers strictly to the terms of their policies. For example, in a case where the company's work

---

[17]Iowa Pub. Serv. Co., 95 LA 319, 322–24 (Murphy, 1990).

[18]State Univ. of N.Y., 74 LA 299 (Babiskin, 1980).

[19]Crane Co., 12 LA 592, 596 (Gilden, 1949).

[20]Id. at 595. Accord Allied Supermarkets, Inc., 41 LA 713 (Henthal, 1963).

[21]77 LA 867 (Kaufman, 1981).

[22]Id. at 871.

[23]Scott Paper Co., 100 LA 1113 (Caraway, 1993). An employee's drug and alcohol use or abuse alone, without proof of further impact on the employer, is not sufficient. Schnuck Mkts., Inc., 102 LA 1016 (Suardi, 1994); Eagle Point Sch. Dist., 100 LA 496 (Wilkinson, 1992); City of Evanston, 95 LA 679 (Dilts, 1990).

[24]Crucible Materials Corp., 94 LA 540 (Harkless, 1989). The parties agreed that the employee's job was "potentially hazardous" and that "it was imperative that [the grievant] not be impaired at work." The arbitrator nonetheless found that the employee's termination lacked just cause, on the grounds that the employer had no rule prohibiting off-duty drug use and that there was no evidence that the grievant had ever been impaired while on duty. Id. at 544–45.

[25]Jersey Shore Steel Co., 100 LA 489 (Goulet, 1992).

rules stated that off-duty use of illegal drugs was "unacceptable" because "it can affect on-the-job performance," a pronouncement that off-duty drug use was "unacceptable" did not justify discharge.[26] The arbitrator found that the employer had to prove that the grievant's on-the-job performance had been affected. In a case where the work rule provided for discharge for "conviction" of a drug-related felony, and the charges against the employee had been dropped because he cooperated with the police, the arbitrator reinstated the employee.[27] In a case where the employer's policy specifically stated, "It is not our intent to mandate morality but to take appropriate action when conduct appears to impact job performance or bring public discredit to the Company, Union or employees," the arbitrator held the employer to the limitations in the policy.[28]

Although arbitrators generally agree that actual harm, not mere speculative harm, to the employer must be established in order to support discipline, the line between actual and speculative harm is not always easy to draw. Indeed, it may be that effective advocacy and the arbitrator's own views are more significant than the specific misconduct that leads to discipline.

The employer of a meter reader who entered customers' houses as part of his job duties was not required to prove actual harm in order to justify discharging him.[29] The arbitrator, finding that the grievant's off-duty conduct made him "a potentially unsafe employee," held that the general rule limiting the employer's reach into employees' private lives did not cover off-duty activities "likely to damage the business or reputation of the employer or impair plant discipline."[30] In another case, a chemical-plant employee's arson conviction was enough to justify his termination.[31] The arbitrator found "as a *fact* that there is a high potential for possible harm and reasonable prudence * * * justifies barring Grievant from Company premises."[32] When a college employee was arrested for fifth degree assault in a domestic dispute, the employer learned that several years before the

---

[26]Schnuck Mkts., Inc., 102 LA 1016, 1021–22 (Suardi, 1994).

[27]Mobil Oil Corp., 95 LA 162 (Allen, Jr., 1990). Similarly, an employee found with $250,000 worth of marijuana in his home had his indefinite suspension overturned in arbitration, on the ground that plant rules provided for termination "only upon conviction, not upon arrest or indictment." Babcock & Wilcox Co., 102 LA 104, 109 (Nicholas, Jr., 1994).

[28]Scott Paper Co., 100 LA 1113, 1116 (Caraway, 1993).

[29]Gas Serv. Co., 39 LA 1025 (Granoff, 1962).

[30]Id. at 1028. Arbitrator Granoff's award is dated and atypical in its condemnation of unconventional behavior.

[31]Occidental Chem. Corp., 97 LA 585 (Duff, 1991). The grievant had been convicted of setting fire to an apartment building 3 weeks after taking out an insurance policy on it. (Since he was sentenced to serve 3 to 9 years in prison for the deed, his inability to come to work could have sufficed as ground for discharge.)

[32]Id. at 588 (emphasis added). Arbitrator Duff continued: "The crime * * * presents a clear danger of repetition of an incendiary act in the working environment where flammable and explosive chemicals are always present." Id.

employee was hired, he had pleaded guilty to an assault on two women. The arbitrator reluctantly found discharge justified because the college had many female students and staff members.[33]

In another case, a hospital maid was discharged after she was caught shoplifting at a department store. The arbitrator upheld the discharge on the ground that the off-duty conduct raised serious doubts as to the grievant's suitability as an employee.[34] Sixteen years later, however, the same hospital terminated a nurse for the very same off-duty transgression, and another arbitrator reduced the penalty from discharge to suspension.[35] He found that "[t]he present record contains no proof of actual detriment or harm, or * * * proof from which detriment * * * [could] be * * * reasonably discerned."[36] The arbitrator in the earlier case had apparently found such proof in the fact of the criminal conviction itself, coupled with the employer's vulnerability to employee theft.[37]

It is difficult to reconcile such inconsistent results when the relevant facts are so similar. The arbitrator in the 1988 case acknowledged the earlier award, but distinguished it on the ground that the arbitrator in the 1972 case had failed to consider the now-traditional three-part standard.[38] Yet the 1972 award had set out the standard,[39] adding that "arbitral opinion on this subject appears clear,"[40] before going on to deny the grievance.

The fact that the risk to the employer was speculative did not seem to concern the arbitrator in the 1972 case, who noted that the employer had not contended that the employee ever stole anything at work. While allowing that "[i]t might be true that the grievant would never have taken anything from a patient, the hospital, or her fellow employees," he held that the hospital was not required to give her the benefit of the doubt, because the "grievant had indicated by her conduct a proclivity toward theft."[41]

In another case, an arbitrator took a contrary view of the inference an employer can draw from off-duty theft.[42] He reinstated an airline

---

[33]College of St. Scholastica, 96 LA 244 (Berquist, 1991). Despite finding that the grievant was "not an employee who can be trusted and would be safe" and who presented "an unreasonable risk of harm to persons at the College," (id. at 252), and that the college had presented no evidence of any adverse effect on the institution, "such an adverse effect is reasonably foreseeable," id. at 254; Arbitrator Berquist concluded that had the college not been the sort of institution it was, he "undoubtedly would have sustained the grievance," id.

[34]Fairmont Gen. Hosp., 58 LA 1293 (Dybeck, 1972).

[35]Fairmont Gen. Hosp., 91 LA 930 (Hunter, Jr., 1988).

[36]Id. at 934.

[37]He referred to the risk to hospital property, the property of other employees, and particularly "the personal property of the patients," adding: "The evidence establishes that in recent years there has existed a serious theft problem at the Hospital." 58 LA at 1295.

[38]W. E. Caldwell Co., 28 LA 434 (Kesselman, 1957).

[39]Fairmont Gen. Hosp., 58 LA 1293, 1294 (Dybeck, 1972).

[40]Id. at 1295.

[41]Id. at 1296.

[42]American Airlines, Inc., 68 LA 1245 (Harkless, 1977).

employee convicted of shoplifting—notwithstanding the well-settled relevance of employee dishonesty in the airline industry—arguing: "It does not follow * * * that the grievant would repeat a dishonest act of theft on the job."[43] The arbitrator also offered as justification for reinstatement the fact that nothing in the grievant's employment history before her conviction indicated that she was dishonest.[44]

## C. An Employee Unable to Work

It can be argued that when an employee is jailed for off-duty misconduct, the ground for discharge is absenteeism,[45] not the misconduct. Serving a jail sentence will not justify an extended absence from work. One can also view such cases as falling within the exception that when off-duty conduct affects the employee's ability to perform his job, the employer can impose discipline. As one arbitrator explained:

> [A]t the time the decision was made to discharge Mr. G—, he had been sentenced to serve sixty days in jail. This meant that the company, in order to keep him * * *, had to decide either to do without him for two months, or find * * * a temporary replacement * * *. [T]here are no mitigating or special circumstances here that would require the company to keep Mr. G— on the payroll.[46]

The reason a discharge is proper in such cases, the arbitrator continued, is not because of the crime the employee has committed, "but rather * * * that through the employee's own actions, he has made it impossible to fulfill his obligation [to] report to work."[47]

The usual rule can occasionally be overlooked, as in the case of a bus driver with a clean record who was jailed for 2½ weeks, and who tried to use his accrued sick leave to cover his absence, but was nonetheless discharged. Because the reasons behind his incarceration had no relevance to his ability to perform his job, he was returned to work.[48]

---

[43]Id. at 1247–48.

[44]"[I]t does not appear that the grievant previously in more than four years of employment had given management cause to question her honesty." Id. at 1248. The result in this case might reflect skillful advocacy on the part of union counsel.

[45]See Chapter 5.

[46]McInerney Spring & Wire Co., 72 LA 1262, 1265 (Roumell, 1979), quoting from his own unpublished decision in Jackson Products.

[47]Id. Having stated the theory, however, Arbitrator Roumell found it inapplicable to the grievant in the case before him. In Chicago Pneumatic Tool Co., 38 LA 891 (Duff, 1961), the arbitrator concurred in the employer's argument that an imprisoned grievant was "not now * * * able to go to work and * * *, under the circumstances, [the employer was] under no obligation to hold his job open for an indefinite period of one to twenty-four months * * *." Id. at 893.

[48]Metropolitan Transit Auth., 98 LA 793 (Allen, Jr., 1992).

One arbitrator offered a list of factors to consider when determining whether discharge is appropriate in such cases:

> (1) applicable language in the parties' agreement; (2) the length of the employee's incarceration; (3) the reasons for the incarceration (*i.e.*, arrest versus conviction); (4) the seriousness of the conduct leading to the employee's arrest; (5) the disciplinary action taken; (6) the employee's work and disciplinary record; and (7) the effect of the employee's absence on the employer and other employees.[49]

He also suggested that the same consideration applied where the question was whether an employee had a right to an unpaid leave of absence in order to serve a jail sentence. In such a case, however, less "fault" on the employee's part would be needed to justify the denial of a leave than to justify a discharge.

## D. *Refusal of Other Employees to Work With the Grievant*

If the employer can prove that co-workers will not work with the grievant, discharge can be sustained even where the relationship between the offense and the employer's interests is otherwise tenuous. *Robertshaw Controls Co.,*[50] a case often cited for this proposition, involved an employee who volunteered as a Scoutmaster when off duty. When he was charged with sodomy and corrupting the morals of children, his employer discharged him. He subsequently pleaded guilty. The arbitrator noted:

> Arbitrators are reluctant to sustain discharges based on off-duty conduct of employees unless a direct relationship between [the] conduct and employment is proved. Discretion must be exercised, lest Employers become censors of community morals.[61]

Nonetheless, the arbitrator found discharge appropriate in this case because co-workers, some of whose children had been in the grievant's Scout troop, refused to associate with the employee after his conviction. The arbitrator commented:

> A business enterprise by its nature requires collaboration, accord and reasonable harmony among employees. The technical and administrative sides of an enterprise cannot function correctly if the human side of the business is disrupted with conflict.[52]

---

[49]Sperry Rand Corp. 60 LA 220, 222 (Murphy, 1973).

[50]64-2 ARB ¶ 5611 (Duff, 1964), citing Chicago Pneumatic Tool Co., 38 LA 891, 893 (Duff, 1961).

[51]64-2 ARB at 5613.

[52]Id. Similarly, discharge of an employee convicted of incest was upheld, because there was evidence that fellow employees would no longer work with him. Lone Star Gas Co., 56 LA 1221, 1227 (Johannes, 1971). The arbitrator in that case also cited "the adverse publicity which the Company received."

The employer must show that co-workers will not collaborate with the offending employee. The employer's mere expectation that they may not is insufficient. In one case, an Ohio state trooper had an off-duty automobile accident and was subsequently convicted of driving under the influence of alcohol. In upholding the discharge, the arbitrator noted that "[n]o state trooper currently working for the State has been convicted of DUI" and that both the employee's supervisor and his co-workers testified to fellow troopers' adverse reaction to his conviction.[53] In another case, a hospital security guard was sentenced to 3 months in jail for kissing and fondling a stranger when he was off duty. Defending the employee's discharge at the arbitration hearing, the hospital contended that the employee was a threat to its largely female staff but could not name anyone who viewed him as a threat. The union, on the other hand, produced a petition signed by 115 employees, most of them women, urging his reinstatement. The arbitrator overturned the discharge.

## III. "Workplace Nexus" in the Public Sector: Public Trust

Although arbitrators apply the "workplace nexus" test in both private and public sector cases, it often appears easier for a *public* employer to dismiss an employee for off-duty misconduct. Both arbitrators and the courts have tended to protect the government employer's reputation and mission, citing the public trust.

Cases often involve employees working in law enforcement and public safety. For example, a police officer was found to have given his insurance carrier false information when he submitted a claim for damage to his personal boat. The arbitrator held that despite the fact that his conduct was off duty and unrelated to his work, there was just cause to terminate him.[55] The arbitrator found that the grievant had "intentionally caused an incident report to be generated

---

[53]State of Ohio, 94 LA 533, 538–39 (Sharpe, 1990). See also Haskell of Pittsburgh, Inc., 96 LA 1208, 1210 (Sergent, 1991).

[54]Virgin Islands Dep't of Health, 97 LA 500 (Watkins, 1991). See also Giant Eagle Mkts. Co., 101 LA 581, 583 (Zobrak, 1993); Scott Paper Co., 100 LA 1113, 1117 (Caraway, 1993); Lakeside Jubilee Foods, 95 LA 358, 366 (Berquist, 1990); Mobil Oil Corp., 95 LA 162, 168 (Allen, Jr., 1990).

In International Paper Co., 52 LA 1266, 1269 (Jenkins, 1969), an employee slashed his foreman with a knife during an off-duty argument in a tavern and was convicted of assault and battery. The arbitrator, unpersuaded that plant operations would be disrupted if he ordered the employee reinstated (it was "not too serious an offense"), sustained the grievance.

In Gould, Inc., 76 LA 1187 (Boyer, Jr., 1981), the grievant listed his supervisor's home with a real estate agent and then ordered a load of dirt dumped in the supervisor's driveway. The arbitrator converted the employee's dismissal to a suspension, on the ground that these practical jokes, while "serious," had no significant impact at the workplace.

[55]City of Stamford, 97 LA 261 (Pittocco, 1991).

for the sole purpose of perpetrating a fraud on [the insurance company]." He cited approvingly the City's argument that the act involved "moral turpitude," violated "the public trust," and cast doubt on the officer's credibility.[56]

Courts have been similarly strict. In *Core v. City of Traverse City*,[57] the court upheld the discharge of a city firefighter who was charged with violating a conservation law and had admitted to lying to an investigating officer. It found that his actions amounted to obstruction of justice, were "detrimental" to public trust, and "damaged the prestige of the department."[58] In *Puzick v. City of Colorado Springs*,[59] the court upheld the discipline of a police sergeant who initiated an off-duty sexual relationship with a probationary officer, because of the affair's potential impact on duty assignments, command and control, and promotion opportunities. In *Fabio v. Civil Service Commission*,[60] the court upheld the discharge, for conduct unbecoming, of a police officer who arranged for a fellow officer to have sex with his wife. In *Fleischer v. City of Signal Hill*,[61] a police officer was terminated when it was discovered that as an adult, he had had sexual relations with a 15-year-old girl. The court found that the illegality of his conduct, which "adversely affects [the] department's morale and community reputation," barred his claim for violation of his constitutional right to privacy.[62] In *Pechacek v. Minnesota State Lottery*,[63] the court upheld the denial of unemployment benefits to a lottery official who had been discharged after being convicted of sexually abusing his stepdaughter, on the ground that the felony conviction,

> job related or not, of a lottery employee affects the credibility of and reduces public confidence in the integrity of the Lottery, [and] even though for off-duty and off-site conduct, reflects * * * gross misconduct which interfered with and substantially affected his employment.[64]

The more extreme cases can be viewed either as disregarding relevance when the off-duty offense has little or no bearing on the employee's job responsibilities or as adopting the broadest possible view of relevance: almost no misconduct is irrelevant, because public servants are expected to be above reproach.

---

[56]Id. at 262.

[57]89 Mich. App. 492, 280 N.W.2d 569 (1979).

[58]Id., 280 N.W.2d at 571.

[59]680 P.2d 1283 (Colo. Ct. App., 1983).

[60]30 Pa. Comm. 203, 373 A.2d 751 (1977).

[61]829 F.2d 1491 (9th Cir., 1987).

[62]Id. at 1499.

[63]497 N.W.2d 243 (Minn., 1993).

[64]Id. at 246.

The application of that view has by no means been restricted to law enforcement personnel. A substance-abuse counselor was suspended after she pleaded guilty to driving under the influence of alcohol.[65] In upholding her suspension, the arbitrator highlighted government's role in law enforcement:

> [T]he interest of the [public] employer is particularly great in holding forth the image of employing law-abiding personnel, and most such employers have specific rules with respect to off-duty conduct.[66]

An unstated element underlies the phrase "holding forth the image": in the public sector, the "notoriety" threshold can be very low. A private sector employer must identify specific adverse effect, while the public sector employer is often presumed to have been injured when an employee strays, even when off duty.

A cogent argument for only narrowly subjecting public employees to a different standard than private sector employees was put forth by one arbitrator when he reinstated a department of public works employee who had been discharged after pleading guilty to off-duty possession of illegal drugs:

> The City does have certain unique qualities which must be upheld in its public dealings, but the Grievant does not fit into the group in which these qualities rest. Police officers should be free of criminal taint. Firemen should be void of the tinge of pyromania. Controllers and treasurers should be free of the suspicion of embezzling tendencies. Although these examples are not exhaustive, those people not falling within these job classifications should not be required to show any greater virtues than anyone else not so employed. City service, in and of itself, does not deprive men of the normal inadequacies and failures to which all of human nature is entitled.[67]

So stated, the standard is in fact no different: the off-duty misconduct must be relevant and must meet one of the three tests set forth in *W. E. Caldwell Co.*[68]

Sometimes the standard applied goes even beyond "law abiding." A nonteaching school employee stopped and offered a young female student a ride in his car. She refused his repeated requests and ultimately sought refuge in a nearby home.[69] In upholding his discharge, the arbitrators held that

> due to the sensitive nature of the school-student relationship, [school] employees must maintain an aura of respect about themselves. They

---

[65]Polk County, Iowa, 80 LA 639 (Madden, 1983).
[66]Id. at 642.
[67]City of Wilkes-Barre, 74 LA 33, 36 (Dunn, 1980).
[68]28 LA 434 (Kesselman, 1957).
[69]North Haven Bd. of Educ., 59 LA 99 (Purcell, McDonough, Sirabella, 1972).

must be above suspicion and guard themselves, particularly against involvement in any unfavorable student contact.[70]

Arbitrators will sometimes treat public employees no differently than they would have treated private sector workers charged with the same misconduct. Two intoxicated Internal Revenue Service employees "mooned" several women in a parking lot. When word of the prank reached their employer, they were suspended for 3 days.[71] In sustaining their grievance, the arbitrator described a standard for the public sector that was in fact no different from the private sector standard (as he himself, in closing, acknowledged):

> [T]he * * * standard to be applied in judging the conduct of employees in public service takes into realistic account the fallible nature of the human condition which results * * * in conduct which * * * [violates] moral and legal codes. It recognizes, quite properly, that however much an employer may be wont to enforce such codes and condemn their transgression, he is entitled to do so *only to the degree that there is a direct and demonstrable relationship between the illicit conduct and the performance of the employee's job or the job of others.* * * * Such limitations have long been recognized in respect both to private and public employers.[72]

## IV. The Nexus Requirement in Federal Sector Cases

The nexus requirement in federal sector cases is both broader and narrower than the nexus test discussed in this chapter: broader because the requirement applies to all misconduct (whether on duty or off), and narrower because it is applied in conjunction with the statutory requirement that an adverse personnel action against a federal employee must advance the "efficiency" of the federal service.[73]

In one case, the government terminated a clerical employee who had an otherwise satisfactory work record, after he was convicted for the second time of sexual offenses against a minor.[74] The arbitrator reinstated him, finding that the government's case failed both the applicable federal sector test and the "nexus" test:

> There must be a clear and direct relationship demonstrated between the articulated grounds for an adverse personnel action and either the employee's ability to accomplish his or her duties satisfactorily or some other legitimate government interest promoting the "efficiency of the service." [*Doe v. Hampton*, 566 F.2d 265, 272 (D.C. Cir. 1977)] [T]he

---

[70]Id. at 100.

[71]Internal Revenue Serv., 77 LA 19 (Edes, 1981).

[72]Id. at 21–22 (emphasis added).

[73]5 U.S.C. §7513(a).

[74]Social Sec. Admin., 80 LA 725 (Lubic, 1983).

SSA must directly prove by a preponderance of the evidence the nexus between the Grievant's off-duty sexual activities and [their] effect upon the efficiency of the service. Absent [such] a nexus, the Court held in *Doe v. Hampton*, the adverse action must be condemned as arbitrary and capricious.[75]

Federal sector jurisprudence has evolved into a complex system of shifting burdens to address the requirement that a federal agency establish that an employee's misconduct affected its "efficiency." This jurisprudence, developed under the decision of the Merit Systems Protection Board and the federal courts' review of those decisions, is unique to federal sector cases.[76]

---

[75]Id. at 728. See also Hoska v. Department of Army, 677 F.2d 131 (D.C. Cir., 1982).

[76]For an excellent analysis of the subject, see Broida, A Guide to Merit Systems Protection Board Law and Practice, 13th ed., 1239 ff. (1996).

# Chapter 10

# Union Activities

Discipline for participation in union activities may violate Section 7 or Section 8 of the National Labor Relations Act.[1] This chapter is concerned with arbitral responses to discipline, not whether the specific discipline would be unlawful under the Act.

## I. Participation in Unlawful Concerted Activities

Many collective bargaining agreements contain clauses that prohibit employees from engaging in strikes during the term of the agreement. Employees who participate in a strike may be disciplined or discharged if the strike violates the contract and the employees acted in concert.[2] Where employees did not come to work after an impasse in negotiations, the arbitrator would not sustain discharges under the no-strike clause.[3]

Discharge has been upheld for a variety of work stoppages in violation of no-strike clauses, including an employee's refusing to work and encouraging another to do the same,[4] a work stoppage to

---

[1]29 U.S.C. §§157, 158 (a).

[2]See Smith-Blair, Inc., 100 LA 344 (Goodstein, 1992) (no concerted activity where union steward advised employee that he did not have to report to work, since the employee did not contrive with steward not to report); Mead Corp., 95 LA 638 (Madden, 1990) (no concerted activity occurred to justify discharge where two workers left the plant on "personal business"; one had informed employer of the employee's refusal to work, but the other was unaware of the first employee's action); Madison Hotel, 69 LA 411 (Bernhardt, 1977) (employer failed to establish strike occurred, where there was no evidence that employees walked off the job in protest).

[3]Dan's Mkt., Inc., 72 LA 706 (Harter, 1979).

[4]Berc Bldg. Maintenance Co., 76 LA 487 (Pritzker, 1981).

protest an employee's suspension,[5] the refusal to obey an order not to leave the plant,[6] and the refusal to work mandatory overtime.[7]

Neither the length of the walkout nor the employee's reason for leaving work affects the employer's ability to impose discipline under a no-strike clause. For example, discipline has been imposed where employees acted in concert to leave a plant when the air conditioning failed and the temperature rose,[8] employees staged a 1-day walkout to honor a deceased co-worker,[9] employees refused to clock in because they had a "union problem" they wanted to discuss,[10] and where employees, at the union's request, refused to fill out a job analysis questionnaire.[11]

Inciting others to participate in an illegal work stoppage can be sufficient justification for discipline. Arbitrators have upheld discharges for distributing leaflets that said: "Strike Or Go Under,"[12] for trying to convince others to participate in a strike,[13] for instigating a walkout,[14] and for trying to persuade other employees not to cross a picket line.[15] The employer must, of course, prove the employee actually engaged in the persuasive activity.[16] Discharge, however, may be too severe a penalty, depending on the kind of incitement involved. For instance, where a union officer directed an employee not to fill in on a job that had been removed from the bargaining unit, the arbitrator overturned the discharge.[17]

Failure to report to work because of an alleged illness may be cause for discipline where the timing or circumstances indicate that it is actually a concerted work stoppage. For instance, an arbitrator found that employees who called in sick or alleged "personal reasons" for not reporting to work, after the company's only black foreman had

---

[5]National Mine Serv. Co., 69 LA 966 (Amis, 1977).

[6]Clinton Corn Processing Co., 71 LA 555 (Madden, 1978).

[7]Thermal Science, Inc., 85 LA 1017 (Nitka, 1985).

[8]South Cent. Bell Tel. Co., 71 LA 174 (Wolff, 1978) (suspension).

[9]S&S Corp., 64 LA 609 (Whyte, 1975) (suspension).

[10]Walt Disney World Co., 62 LA 789 (Oppenheim, 1974).

[11]Tappan Appliance Group, 64 LA 1269 (Knee, 1975) (suspension).

[12]Huron Forge & Mach. Co., 75 LA 83 (Roumell, 1980).

[13]SCA Servs., Inc., 66 LA 1073 (Mayer, 1976).

[14]Southern Ohio Coal Co., 66 LA 446 (Lubow, 1976).

[15]Warner & Swasey Co., 65 LA 709 (Walter, 1975).

[16]See Arch of Ill., Inc., 93 LA 1097 (Cohen, 1992).

[17]Mark Twain Marine Indus., Inc., 73 LA 551 (Guenther, 1979). See Transport Body Serv., 65 LA 894 (Raffaele, 1975) (no discharge where an employee advocated a strike to other employees when his previous offenses had been met with only verbal warnings); United States Steel Corp., 65 LA 15 (Garrett, 1975) (discharge too severe a penalty where pickets induced trainees not to attend class, even though this action was in violation of a court order restraining employees from engaging in strike, picketing, or in any other manner interfering with operations).

been demoted, were properly suspended.[18] Concerted work slowdowns can also result in discipline where they are prohibited by the contract.[19] The employer must show that a slowdown occurred,[20] was intended,[21] or was otherwise established by the evidence.[22] Some arbitrators, however, have found discharge too severe a penalty for a slowdown,[23] and some have found even the shortest suspensions too severe.[24]

A "stay-in" or sit-down strike, where employees remain on company property when they are not scheduled to work, has been found to be an appropriate subject for discipline. For example, in *Chrysler Corp.*,[25] the arbitrator approved the discharge of some, but not other employees where they had different reasons for remaining on plant property during a scheduled vacation time. Discharge was appropriate for an employee who physically attacked two guards and was arrested, and for employees who refused to leave the plant, even though they had stated a concern over their safety. Discharge was found not appropriate for employees who were not present when the first group of employees was told to leave, as well as for those who were told by the guards they could not leave, who were prevented from leaving, who entered to see what was happening and then left, or who left after unsuccessfully attempting to persuade the strikers to leave.

Picketing one's employer can be cause for discharge.[26] On the

---

[18]Longview Fibre Co., 69 LA 1182 (Mueller, 1977). See East Ohio Gas Co., 62 LA 90 (Edes, 1973) (suspension approved for 11 employees who called in sick on the day the promotion of a black employee to a supervisory position became effective).

[19]Walgreen Co., 100 LA 468 (Shieber, 1992) (discharge appropriate where the contract allowed discharge for participating in a work slowdown "in any way" and each grievant engaged in a concerted act of soliciting co-workers to work at a slower pace than they wanted to); Toshiba Am., Inc., 78 LA 612 (Flannagan, 1982) (discharge upheld where the employees performed the same job at an acceptable level in previous years and offered no reason for not performing acceptably thereafter).

[20]KHD Deutz of Am., 88 LA 1230 (Donnelly, 1987) (discharge overturned where there was no evidence of actual slowdown); Premier Indus., Inc., 81 LA 183 (Murphy, 1983) (2-week suspension too severe for urging production slowdown that did not occur).

[21]Pantry Pride Enters., Inc., 79 LA 883 (Carson, Jr., 1982) (burden of proof not met where employee told others not to work so fast or hard).

[22]Associated Wholesale Grocers, Inc., 89 LA 227 (Madden, 1987) (suspension of steward who ordered slowdown overturned where the evidence was tenuous and insufficient to overcome the greater latitude accorded a steward in the performance of his duties).

[23]Midcon Fabricators, Inc., 68 LA 1264 (Dugan, 1977) (discharge too severe where employees refused 1 hour of overtime each day after employer provoked the action by violating contract); Stevens Air Sys., 64 LA 425 (Stashower, 1975) (discharge too severe for member of union shop committee for telling three co-workers to slow down their production).

[24]Library of Congress, 62 LA 1289 (Rothman, 1974) (2 weeks too severe); Chromalloy Am., 61 LA 246 (Hon, 1973) (5-day layoff too severe). But see General Shale Corp., 80 LA 375 (Cromwell, undated) (3-day suspension appropriate where the contract prohibited slowdown).

[25]63 LA 677 (Alexander, 1974).

[26]Alladin Indus., Inc., 61 LA 896 (Hilpert, 1973).

other hand, picketing the parent company[27] or another company[28] during nonworking hours has been rejected as cause for discharge. Discipline has been upheld where the picketing involved illegal secondary activity[29] or an unauthorized strike,[30] and where the employee was honoring the picket line of another union.[31] Collusion with the organizers of the picket line may also make discipline appropriate.[32]

The discipline meted out to employees must be rationally related to that given other participants in the unlawful or questionable activity. Arbitrators often reduce the discipline where other employees received different punishment for the same or lesser activity. For instance, an arbitrator overturned the discharge where only 1 of 15 foremen was fired for participating in an illegal strike.[33] Differential discipline has been found appropriate where it is based on different levels of perceived employee involvement.[34] An employer has been permitted to discharge fewer than all participants where a rational basis exists for selecting those discharged.[35] For example, a discharge was upheld for one employee and not others where the breach of the no-strike clause was the fifth offense in 6 months for that employee. However, the discharge of four employees for promoting an illegal strike was reduced to a suspension where a proper investigation would have revealed equal or more active involvement by others.[37]

Discipline of union leaders for unlawful strikes is appropriate depending upon their degree of involvement in the illegal activity. For example, one arbitrator disapproved the suspension of union officials who cooperated with management in ending a strike, and of a union trustee who played no part in contract administration or negotiations, but upheld the discharge of an employee who coordi-

[27]Redfield Co., 69 LA 1024 (Aisenberg, 1977) (discharge not upheld for picketing parent company during nonworking hours in protest of the discharge of other employees).

[28]Kessler Coals, Inc., 69 LA 630 (Dyke, 1977) (discharge not justified for employees picketing another employer 10 miles away where stranger pickets appeared at first employer to force temporary closure of the first employer).

[29]Pacific Tel. & Tel. Co., 67 LA 45 (Barsamian, 1976).

[30]Pacific Tel. & Tel. Co., 80 LA 1151 (Alleyne, 1983).

[31]Universal Foods Corp., 79 LA 783 (Evenson, 1982).

[32]Ohio Educ. Ass'n, 94 LA 595 (Goldsmith, 1990) (4-day loss of pay upheld for refusal to cross picket line where the picketing would not have occurred had the grievant not given advance notice to the striking union to schedule the dates).

[33]Rust Eng'g Co., 89 LA 1296 (Gallagher, 1987). See Redfield Co., 65 LA 887 (Bardwell, 1975) (5-day suspension reduced to 3 days for followers of the illegal strike where the leader received a 5-day suspension); Monongahela Power Co., 64 LA 1210 (Blue, 1975) (4-day suspension of local union president who refused to cross picket line not upheld where two other employees who also refused received only a 2-day suspension).

[34]Super Valu Stores, Inc., 86 LA 622 (Smith, 1986).

[35]Rust Eng'g Co., 89 LA 1296 (Gallagher, 1987).

[36]Nottawa Gardens Corp., 90 LA 24 (Bendixsen, 1987). See Phillip Morris, USA, 66 LA 626 (Beckman, 1976) (discharge justified even where union maintained that employer imposed varying discipline on other participants).

[37]Homer Laughlin China Co., 67 LA 1250 (Jones, 1977).

nated pickets, discouraged other employees from returning to work, and took other illegal actions.[38]

Discipline has been upheld against union officials at all levels of the local, including local presidents,[39] shop stewards,[40] and executive board members.[41] Discipline against these officials has been reversed, however, where the employer had the opportunity to seek recourse from the union.[42]

## II. Strike Misconduct

Arbitrators have been more lenient in upholding discipline for misconduct that occurred during a lawful strike. For example, arbitrators have reduced discipline where employees placed nails in the path of or under employee cars,[43] threw objects,[44] held weapons,[45] or

[38]Koehring Co., 69 LA 459 (Boals, 1977).

[39]Dravo Corp., 68 LA 618 (McDermott, 1977) (discharge of local president approved for instigating and leading illegal work stoppage while on leave). See Quanex Corp., 96 LA 1007 (Poindexter, 1990) (discharge of one of the main leaders and agitators of illegal walkout proper); Coca Cola Co., 65 LA 165 (Crane, 1975) (sustaining refusal to rehire union representative who caused work stoppage).

[40]St. Francois County, 69 LA 102 (Elbert, 1977) (shop steward discharged for role as leader of illegal public employee strike). See Bucyrus-Erie, 69 LA 93 (Lipson, 1977) (discharge of steward approved where he parked car to block entrance to plant; discipline of group spokesman not approved because he did not block gate); Herrud & Co., 66 LA 682 (Keefe, 1976) (stewards' discharge approved where they announced they were "sticking with the people" and defied directives to return to work); Thiokol Corp., 63 LA 633 (Rimer, Jr., 1974) (discharge of safety steward for causing walkout approved, even where safety concerns led to action).

[41]Clinton Corn Processing Co., 71 LA 555 (Madden, 1978) (discharge of union executive board members approved where they were in forefront of illegal work stoppage; discharge of executive board member who left before discussion of action on work stoppage not upheld because employer failed to prove misconduct). But see Consolidation Coal Co., 78 LA 473 (Ruben, 1982) (suspension of mine health and safety committee member who refused to leave an area he was inspecting found improper where member was acting in scope of his official duties).

[42]Abex Corp., 68 LA 805 (Richman, 1977).

[43]Washington Scientific Indus., Inc., 67 LA 1044 (O'Connell, 1976) (no discharge for placing nails under employee cars); J.R. Simplot Food Co., 64 LA 1061 (Collings, 1975) (discharge inappropriate for distributing nails because the employer was "contributorily negligent" for operating the plant during a strike).

[44]See Carlisle Corp., 87 LA 103 (Feldman, 1986) (discharge for throwing rocks into parking lot and placing tacks in driveway during strike overturned and employee reinstated without back pay because no damage was done); Fourco Glass Co., 83 LA 327 (Hewitt, 1984) (discharge for throwing Molotov cocktail overturned where memorandum of agreement stated that there would be no discharge for picket line actions); American Standard, Inc., 79 LA 601 (Levin, 1982) (discharge for rock throwing which damaged guardhouse reduced to suspension, where conduct did not injure and no intent to injure); Charter Int'l Oil Co., 75 LA 929 (Milentz, 1980) (discharge for throwing steel ball bearings through a window reduced to 6-month suspension).

[45]See Georgia-Pacific Corp., 87 LA 188 (Gibson, 1986) (discharge reduced to suspension without pay for carrying toy gun near picket line where employee did not injure, attempt to injure, damage property, or point gun); Super Valu Stores, 80 LA 606 (Talent, 1983) (discharge reduced to reinstatement without back pay for possession of unloaded rifle in vicinity of picket line). But see County Line Cheese Co., 80 LA 717 (Grohsmeyer, 1983) (discharge allowed for possession of clublike weapon in hip pocket on picket line).

committed other property damage.[46] Discharge has been approved,
however, for theft during the course of an unlawful strike.[47] Physical
violence has warranted dismissal,[48] but not where the violence was
provoked[49] or where the employer felt the company had to meet a
higher burden of proof in a criminal case.[50] While mere verbal threats
from the picket line have been held insufficient for discharge,[51] racial
slurs have been cause for discharge.[52] Discharge for violation of strike
settlement agreements is often upheld,[53] and other poststrike activity
may also provide a basis for discipline.[54]

---

[46]A. Finkl & Sons Co., 90 LA 502 (Wolff, 1988) (discharge reduced to suspension where
employee damaged third-party truck whose driver failed to honor picket line; action was spontaneous, not directed at co-worker or employer, and employee was already penalized by criminal
prosecution). See McDonnell-Douglas Astronautics Co., 74 LA 726 (Hardy, 1980) (discharge
overturned for spraying liquid on cars passing through plant gate); General Tel. Co., 69 LA
351 (Bowles, 1977) (discharge reduced to 5 months' loss of pay for kicking truck since little
damage was done and it was not disruptive of employer operations). But see Clow Corp., 90
LA 969 (Cohen, 1988) (discharge appropriate for throwing red liquid on car).

[47]Tribune Star Publ'g Co., 78 LA 1153 (Katz, 1982).

[48]General Tel. Co., 69 LA 351 (Bowles, 1977) (discharge appropriate when employee
assaulted supervisor; discharge approved of another employee who repeatedly kicked and
struck supervisor).

[49]Reynolds Metal Co., 84 LA 367 (Gibson, 1985) (discharge reduced to 30-day suspension
for striking group leader after he called employee "son of a bitch," berated and harassed him
for several minutes, and invited him to come over so he could kick his ass); General Tel. Co.,
69 LA 351 (Bowles, 1977) (discharge for striking a security guard who charged the picket
line where pickets were sitting on chairs obstructing the entrance overturned and employee
reinstated with loss of 6 months' pay).

[50]Scott Meat Co., 69 LA 223 (Berger, 1977).

[51] American Standard Inc., 79 LA 601 (Levin, 1982) (discharge reduced to 15-day suspension where the threats were in response to company official's obscene comments); Western Die
Casting Co., 70 LA 391 (Koven, 1982) (discharge too severe a penalty for making driver of
moving fork lift flinch by opening fists close to his face and making obscene remarks). But see
Interstate Food Processing Corp., 83 LA 501 (Chandler, 1984) (discharge upheld for threats of
harm, property damage, and blocking plant entrance).

[52]Geauga Co., 87 LA 394 (Feldman, 1986) (discharge upheld where employee called appli-
cant "black bitch," "welfare nigger," and "black scab"); Honeywell Information Sys., 70 LA 985
(Berkman, 1978) (discharge for shouting "scab" at persons crossing picket line reduced to 1-
month suspension). Cf. Doctors Hosp. of Manteca, 98 LA 1019 (Riker, 1992) (discharge approved
for nurse who, at union strike rally, made statement reported by papers about dehydrated and
comatose patient, where hospital policy was that "at no time" was a patient diagnosis or
condition to be discussed); Lag Drug Co., 68 LA 706 (Kelliher, 1977) (discharge upheld for
profane language and racial slur directed at company vice president); H&L Tooth Co., 66 LA
1020 (Van Delden, 1976) (discharge upheld for streaking, mooning, and racial slurs).

[53]San Francisco Newspaper Agency, 87 LA 537 (Gentile, 1986) (discharge of union steward
approved where settlement agreement provided for immediate discharge if another work stoppage occurred at his direction); Orton/McCullough Crane Co., 62 LA 345 (Seidman, 1974)
(discharge upheld where settlement agreement provided for "immediate discharge" for violation
of company rule).

[54]See Chromalloy Am. Corp., 72 LA 838 (Cohen, 1979) (discharge reduced to a suspension
for the use of abusive language and threats and wearing a T-shirt with objectionable language
following the return to work after a strike); La Crosse Tel. Co., 65 LA 1077 (Mueller, 1975)
(suspension upheld for "staring at" replacement workers in attempt to intimidate them).

# III. Refusals to Cross Picket Lines

The imposition of discipline for refusing to cross a picket line raises significant issues. The refusal, sometimes referred to as a "sympathy strike," may constitute protected activity under Section 7 of the Act or impact provisions of the parties' contract. In many instances the contract will either permit employees to refuse to cross a picket line or prohibit them from doing so. As a result, arbitrators tend to apply a "totality of circumstances" test in determining whether the imposed discipline should be sustained. This test includes an analysis of the specific language contained in the parties' agreement; any reasonable employee safety concerns; any impact the refusal may have had upon the employer; and the traditional concepts of notice, disparate treatment, and excessive discipline.

## A. *Contractual Rights and Obligations*

Discipline imposed as the result of a refusal to cross a picket line has been overturned by arbitrators where there is a specific contractual right for employees to engage in this conduct.[55] Discipline for refusing to cross a picket line has also been held to violate contractual antidiscrimination provisions that protect membership in or engaging in activity on behalf of a union.[56] While contract language may vary, it is likely to be construed narrowly. Where employees sought to "honor" a picket line by refusing to load a truck going to the picketed customer, the arbitrator upheld their suspensions.[57] Similarly, where the picket line was not authorized by the union, the employer could discipline employees who refused to cross it.[58]

In the absence of a contractual right to refuse to cross a picket line, unions and employees run the risk of violating contractual no-strike provisions. Under these circumstances, discipline is generally upheld.[59] On the other hand, some arbitrators have concluded that a

---

[55]GTE N. Inc., 94 LA 1033 (Witney, 1990) (disciplinary letter overturned where the no-strike clause did not cover sympathy strikes and no one who had honored a picket line had received a letter during the 16 years the clause was in effect); But see Denver Hilton Hotel, 79 LA 1017 (Goodman, 1982) (replacement of worker approved where contract allows refusal to cross legally approved picket line of the union and line was put up by another union); Beaumont Concrete Co., 76 LA 228 (Gentile, 1981) (discharge overturned under contract provision barring discharge for upholding union principles, including refusing to cross a picket line); Atlantic Farms Mkt., 70 LA 752 (Weiss, 1978) (employer could not refuse to rehire employee where the contract said it was no violation to refuse to cross a picket line).

[56]Sears, Roebuck & Co., 35 LA 757 (Miller, 1960)

[57]Alfred M. Lewis, Inc., 50 LA 553 (Meiners, 1968).

[58].Central Stone Co., 98 LA 41 (O'Grady, 1991).

[59]Pacific Tel. & Tel. Co., 80 LA 1151 (Alleyne, 1983) (suspensions sustained where grievant violated no-strike clause by honoring another union's unauthorized picket line); Union Carbide Corp., 46 LA 265 (Teple, 1965) (discharge of union chairman and steward upheld for sanctioning

refusal to cross a picket line does not constitute a "strike" or a "concerted plan for absence from work" within the meaning of the contract and, accordingly, have overturned the discipline imposed.[60]

Discipline has also been set aside where an employer violated a "no-strike no-lockout" provision by refusing to schedule employees for work who had either honored the picket line or declined to promise not to honor the line.[61] Under the terms of the parties' contract, the employer's conduct constituted an impermissible lockout and constructive suspension of its employees.[62]

## B. *Other Factors*

In addition to analyzing the contract language, arbitrators examine the totality of circumstances involved in picket line cases and weigh the interests of both the employer and the employee. These include whether employees have legitimate safety concerns. Although a technical violation of a no-strike provision may occur by refusal to cross a picket line, the employee's refusal will be deemed justified and the discipline will be reversed where the refusal is based upon a reasonable fear of violence.[63] On the other hand, discipline will be sustained where the facts indicate that the claimed fear of harm was unreasonable.[64] For example, in *Hess Oil & Chemical Corp.,*[65] where

---

of work stoppage, as well as two other employees for engaging in it); Regent Quality Furniture, Inc., 32 LA 553 (Turkus, 1959) (union violated no-strike provision when its members honored picket line of another union that shared the same work locale). See also Monongahela Power Co., 64 LA 1210 (Blue, 1975); Michigan Consol. Gas Co., 54 LA 41 (McIntosh, 1969); Sealright Co., 53 LA 154 (Belcher, 1969); Gulf Coast Motor Lines, Inc., 49 LA 261 (Williams, 1967).

[60]Vermont Structural Steel Corp., 60 LA 842 (Hogan, 1973); Arkansas La. Gas Co., 42 LA 626 (Quinlan, 1964).

[61]Allied Employers Inc., 84 LA 5 (Kienast, 1984).

[62]Id.

[63]West Penn Power Co., 89 LA 1227 (Hogler, 1987) (suspension overturned where refusal to cross picket line was based on reasonable safety considerations); Manitou Constr. Co., 61 LA 727 (Williams, 1973) (discharge overturned where grievants had face-to-face confrontation with huge pickets, one of whom was known to have often carried a gun); Newark Morning Ledger Co., 61 LA 693 (Hill, 1973) (discharge overturned where grievants refused to cross another union's picket line that was put up by men the grievants or their young children knew); Joseph T. Ryerson & Son, Inc., 41 LA 52 (Lynch, 1963) (discharge overturned where employees refused to cross another union's picket line, where employees had no guarantee of their personal safety); Serrick Corp., 32 LA 994 (Davis, 1959) (discharge found to be excessive, but back pay not awarded, where reasonable concern for safety on first day was established, but was not established on subsequent days when police were present). But see Canton Drop Forging & Mfg. Co., 78 LA 1189 (Teple, 1982) (suspension appropriate where workers feared bodily injury and property damage, since the discipline did not violate the LMRA).

[64] Monongahela Power Co., 64 LA 1210 (Blue, 1975) (suspension upheld where picket line was peaceful); Bowman Transp. Inc., 62 LA 1264 (Hon, 1974) (discharge approved where there was no imminent danger); Aro, Inc., 47 LA 1065 (Whyte, 1966) (just cause for discharge where no violation or threat of violation associated with picket line); Pennsylvania R.R. Co., 45 LA 522 (Seidenberg, 1965) (2-day suspension of employee who refused to cross two silent pickets at employer's gate upheld where there was nothing to justify employee's alleged fear of harm to himself or his family); Pilot Freight Carriers, 22 LA 761 (Magge, 1954) (discharge upheld where refusal not based on fear of violence or, if it was, fear was not reasonable).

[65]45 LA 826 (Hoel, 1965).

a union other than that of the grievant was conducting informational picketing, the arbitrator noted the "peaceful nature" of the picketing in sustaining the grievant's discharge for refusing to cross the picket line.

Arbitrators may also consider whether the employee was on notice that failure to cross the picket line would result in discharge or discipline. For example, in *Hess Oil & Chemical Corp.*,[66] the discharge of an employee was upheld where the grievant had twice been given specific notice that he would be discharged if he did not report for work and the grievant's own union had advised its members to ignore the picketing. In *McKesson & Robbins*,[67] an employee was reinstated because the employer failed to provide a written warning notice stating the consequences of improper conduct prior to the actual termination, as required by the contract.

Arbitrators also consider the impact of the refusal on the employer's business operations. Where employees were suspended for 2 days for refusing to cross a picket line at an employer's customer, the arbitrator determined that because there was no emergency or urgency to the particular job, the discipline should be reversed.[68]

Discipline may also be mitigated if it subjects the grievants to disparate treatment. For example, an arbitrator ordered the employer to remove a warning letter (describing an employee's refusal to cross a sister union's picket line) from the grievant's personnel file, where no other employee engaging in the same conduct had received such a letter in 16 years.[69] In *Monongahela Power Co.*,[70] the arbitrator reduced the local union president's 4-day suspension to the same 2 days received by other employees who refused to cross the picket line, because there was no essential difference between their conduct. Moreover, where discipline is justified and yet deemed excessive, it may be reduced.[71]

## IV. Discipline of Stewards and Other Union Officials

The rights and duties of union stewards and officials in the workplace are derived from three sources: (1) federal, state, and local

---

[66]Id.

[67]37 LA 847 (McConnell, 1961).

[68]Arkansas La. Gas Co., 42 LA 626 (Quinlan, 1964).

[69]GTE N., Inc., 94 LA 1033 (Witney, 1990).

[70]64 LA 1210 (Blue, 1975).

[71]Continental Oil Co., 69 LA 399 (Wann, 1977) (3-day suspensions reduced to 1 day because employees were faced with moral dilemma of losing pay for not working and honoring another union's picket line); Newark Morning Ledger Co., 61 LA 693 (Hill, 1973) grievants reinstated without back pay because, among other reasons, their refusal to cross may have been genuine act of conscience, and as part-time employees they may not have known of new no-strike provision in contract).

statutes;[72] (2) the collective bargaining agreement;[73] and (3) provisions implied by law because of the nature of the relationship between the parties and the past practices they have developed in the course of administering their labor agreement.[74]

## A. *Discipline of Union Officials for Activity Undertaken on Behalf of the Union or Its Members*

A union steward or official serves in two capacities: first, as a bargaining-unit employee receiving pay or wages; and second, as a designated representative for the union in what are commonly referred to as union activities.[75] When the union representative is acting in an official capacity, negotiating grievances or engaging in collective negotiations, the union representative and the company have been described as "equals."[76] Thus, arbitrators have recognized that, while acting on behalf of the union, "[a] union representative must be able to do his job properly, without fear of retaliation of any kind for the performance of his proper role" and that "[m]ere zealousness can never justify punishment and a steward is certainly entitled to be wrong in issues that he presses on behalf of his constituents."[77] A union representative may be discharged or disciplined, however, for certain actions he engages in on behalf of the union.

*1. Abusive or Harsh Language.*   The discharge of union representatives for profanity used during labor-management meetings generally has been overturned by arbitrators.[78] As one arbitrator described:

> Arbitrators carefully uphold the right of Union representatives to speak freely at Company-Union meetings. I can find no decision where

---

[72]29 U.S.C. §§ 157, 158(a), 159.

[73]State of Ohio Dep't of Health, 97 LA 310 (Dworkin, 1991); Butler Paper Co., 91 LA 311 (Weiss, 1988); U.S. Dep't of Army Headquarters XVIII, 81 LA 852 (Merrifield, 1983); Pease Co., 67 LA 941 (Volz, 1976).

[74]Rocky Mountain News, 100 LA 1218 (Cohen, 1993); Sharples Coal Co., 91 LA 1317, 1322 (Volz, 1988) ("it has become well recognized that management must exercise its inherent or reserved powers reasonably. But this principle also applies in appropriate cases to the other party to the bargain, namely, the Union."); Hiram Walker & Sons, Inc., 80-1 ARB ¶ 3880 (Volz, 1977).

[75]General Elec. Co., 43 LA 838 (Kornblum, 1964). See also Ethyl Corp., 96 LA 255 (Caraway, 1991), quoting CECO Corp., 71 LA 1148 (Caraway, 1978) (describing twofold role of union steward as being charged with protecting the rights and interests of the employees as to their work jurisdiction and safe working conditions, as well as with carrying out the collective bargaining agreement.

[76]Owens-Illinois, Inc., 73 LA 663 (Witney, 1979).

[77]E.A. Norris Plumbing Co., 90 LA 462, 465 (Christopher, 1987).

[78]Kaiser Eng'rs, Inc., 63 LA 1051 (Cabe, 1974) (finding employer's discharge of union steward for using profane language during argument at company-union meeting not justified). See Chapter 11.

discipline of an employee for words spoken as a Union representative to a Company official at a Company-Union conference, has been upheld. While the Grievant's words were harsh and unnecessary, they were spoken in the course of the Grievant's performance of his duties as a Union representative, and they were not intended to be personally abusive toward the Supervisor. During the meeting, the Company and Union representatives met as men of equal stature for the purpose of discussing the business at hand, rather than as superiors and subordinates. The very nature of the collective-bargaining process is that an employee who is designated as a Union representative must be free to discuss Union matters as though he were not a Company employee. Otherwise, an employee would be inhibited in the performance of his duties as Union representative, by fear of discipline for the use of strong language.[79]

However, arbitrators have refused to excuse union representatives who combine profanity with physical threats against company representatives or supervisors.[80]

*2. Acts of Intimidation and Harassment.*   A union officer has a responsibility to assist in the creation of a safe and secure work environment. Acts of a local union officer "in intimidating, harassing, and threatening employees, especially those of a smaller physical size, about joining the Union, whether or not done on Company time,"[81] are viewed as a serious disciplinary offense for which the employee may be discharged. Similarly, acts of harassment and intimidation of co-employees by a union officer that go beyond permissible dissent by a union officer justify that officer's discharge.[83]

*3. Insubordination and Self-Help.*   An acceptable level of conduct is expected of a union officer, whether performing work directly for the employer or while engaged in union activity. While it is commonly recognized that union officials can and should be zealous in the execution of official duties, they should not be so zealous that their conduct amounts to insubordination.[84]

Recognizing the distinction between zealousness and insubordination, one arbitrator upheld the discharge of a union representative who ignored orders of her supervisors to return to her post because she thought she had been asked by some employees to represent

---

[79]Ormet Corp., 54 LA 363, 365 (Williams, 1970) (employer not justified in imposing written warning and 3-day suspension on union steward who, among other things, told a company spokesman that he was a "no-good bastard").

[80]Prince George's County, Md., 69 LA 917 (Ables, 1977) (upholding suspension of union steward for use of foul language and threats of physical violence against a management official); Boston Edison Co., 52 LA 841 (Murphy, 1969) (ordering 120-day suspension of union steward who threatened supervisor and used foul language).

[81]Hoosier Panel Co., 61 LA 981, 983 (Volz, 1973).

[82]Id.

[83]Potlatch Corp., 72 LA 583 (Leeper, 1979).

[84]See Chapter 7 for a detailed discussion of insubordination.

them when they were directed to report to the office. The arbitrator explained that "a union representative * * * may not be disciplined for zealousness in conducting the union's business but at the same time, that union representative may not disregard directives given by management."[85]

Where the union officer is engaged in work for the employer, the relationship between the officer and her supervisor should be sufficiently relaxed so that in case of a disagreement, the officer's position may be explained to the supervisor. Once the supervisor issues a direct order, however, it is the duty of the representative to obey it as given and continue any protest through the grievance procedure as any other employee would have to do.[86]

Arbitrators have found that "[s]elf-help is no more proper for union officials than other employees if there is a way to protect the Union's rights without disobeying a direct management order."[87] In fact, some arbitrators hold union representatives to the "obey now, grieve later" rule even more strictly than other employees since the representative is responsible for carrying out the provisions of the contract to the letter and setting the example for other employees.[88]

The use of self-help by union representatives has been excused, however, where there is a legitimate question of health and safety[89] or where there is no "reasonable method of protecting the union right involved except by self-help because immediate action was required or repeated attempts to persuade management to abide by the contract and respect the union right involved were unsuccessful."[90]

For example, in *Velva Sheen Manufacturing Co.*,[91] the arbitrator found discipline was not warranted where a union steward was representing herself and could not perform her job assignment and grieve at the same time. In that case, the grievant had filed a previous grievance on her own behalf a few months earlier, to which the employer responded that it would abide by the collective bargaining agreement. The arbitrator found that "[p]erforming the job assignment and grieving later would provide [the grievant] no remedy,

---

[85]Shelby County Gov't, 100 LA 284, 290 (Harvey, 1992).

[86]American Hoechst Corp., 68 LA 517 (Purcell, 1977) (upholding suspension of two stewards who engaged in self-help by refusing to return to work from a union business meeting when ordered to do so by a supervisor); Harley Davidson Motor Co., 61 LA 1103 (Edes, 1973) (upholding 2-week suspension of union representative who engaged in self-help rather than obey an order of his foreman and then utilize the grievance procedure).

[87]General Tel. Co. of Ind., 79 LA 225, 230 (Kossoff, 1982).

[88]E.A. Norris Plumbing Co., 90 LA 463 (Christopher, 1987); CECO Corp., 71 LA 1148 (Caraway, 1978).

[89] Harley Davidson Motor Co., supra note 86, at 1107. Cf. AIRCO, Inc., 62 LA 432 (Simon, 1974) (upholding discharge of steward based in part on his refusal to drive a truck and claiming that it was not safe when in fact it was).

[90]General Tel. Co. of Ind., 79 LA 225, 230 (Kossoff, 1982), citing Dynamic Mfrs., Inc., 36 LA 1193 (Maguire, 1960); International Harvester Co., 16 LA 307 (McCoy, 1950); Ford Motor Co., 10 LA 213 (Shulman, 1948).

[91]98 LA 131 (Modjeska, 1991)

except perhaps another promise. Given her belief that the company was ignoring its last promise, such a remedy would have appeared unsatisfactory."[92]

*4. Solicitation of False Testimony From Co-Workers.* While a union representative has a protected right to present grievances, discipline is appropriate if she attempts to do so by soliciting false testimony from co-employees.[93]

*5. Absences to Engage in Union Activities.* While a union representative has a protected right under the NLRA to represent grievants in grievance meetings,[94] the representative cannot do so at a time or in a manner that exceeds his contractual right to do so. Many contracts permit union representatives to spend working time—without loss of regular pay—in meetings with representatives of management or investigating grievances.[95] Arbitrators apply a reasonableness test when determining whether the nature of a particular union activity is an appropriate basis for absence such that the union representative should be paid for his time. Arbitrators also consider whether an undue burden on the employer's operation will result.[96]

A union officer who leaves her position to represent a grievant or conduct union business in violation of the contract may be subject to discipline or discharge. For example, in *Kaiser Aluminum & Chemical Corp.,*[97] the agreement permitted union officers to conduct business at the plant on company time because of schedule conflicts, provided there was little or no interference with plant operations. The union officer left his worksite in contravention of a direct order of his supervisor not to do so at that time. The arbitrator upheld the company's formal warning and three-day suspension of the official for insubordination, finding that the officer disobeyed an order and could have delivered the grievance during his next break.

Similarly, in *Ethyl Corp.,*[98] the arbitrator upheld a 4-day suspension for insubordination where a union representative left his job without the permission of his supervisor to attend a meeting between an employee and the company. The contract permitted union representatives to leave their jobs only to attend a grievance meeting, investigate grievances, or meet with company representatives at the request of or by agreement with the company. No grievance had been filed and the representative had been specifically ordered to return to work.

---

[92]Id. at 133.

[93]All Am. Nut Co., 61 LA 933 (Block, 1973).

[94]29 U.S.C. § 159(a).

[95]E.A. Norris Plumbing Co., 90 LA 463 (Christopher, 1987); General Tel. Co., 79 LA 225 (Kossoff, 1982); Pease Co., 67 LA 941, 944 (Volz, 1976).

[96]Sharples Coal Co., 91 LA 1317 (Volz, 1988); Pease Co., 67 LA 941 (Volz, 1976).

[97]90 LA 856 (Thompson, 1988).

[98]96 LA 255 (Caraway, 1991).

Where the agreement covers job-related injuries and requires the employer to maintain workers' compensation insurance, a union official is considered to be engaged in a union activity while being interviewed by a workers' compensation investigator.[99] Even though getting a labor agreement signed by the operators or owners of a facility relates directly to the maintenance of the union as an entity and thus is a union activity, discipline was upheld where the absence from work was for an unreasonable period of time.[100]

Poll watching during elections has been found to be a "union activity" requiring that a union representative be given an excused absence for union business.[101] Poll watching, however, is not considered a union activity when it is the personal decision of an employee to be helpful to the candidacy of a friend or relative.[102]

6. *Contract Interpretation.*   At least one arbitrator has refused to permit discipline of a union representative based on her correct interpretation of a labor agreement for a union member, where that interpretation caused an employee not to report to work for overtime.[103]

## B. *Disciplinary Immunity for Behavior Engaged In on Behalf of the Union*

Arbitrators have generally recognized that "union representatives have some immunity, though it is by no means unlimited, against punishment by the employer for their actions in performing their union duties."[104] Indeed, as one arbitrator observed:

> No one today would seriously question that the right of the Union Steward to do his job properly must be protected. He must be allowed to operate without fear of retaliation in the performance of that role, and that mere militancy or zealousness on his part will not justify punishment, nor can a Steward be limited to the language of polite society in fulfilling his role. On the other hand, Management cannot function properly if employees who are also Union Stewards can with

---

[99]Sharples Coal Co., 91 LA 1317 (Volz, 1988) (union representative engaged in union activity under the collective bargaining agreement when responding to workers' compensation fund investigator, but grievance denied because it was not reasonably necessary to take off a shift where interview could have been arranged during nonworking hours and interview should not have taken more than 1 or 2 hours). Cf. Consolidated Foods, 88 LA 1148 (Gundermann, 1978) (representation by a union at a workers' compensation hearing did not constitute official union business because employee rights regarding workers' compensation are statutory and not dependent upon or related to the collective bargaining relationship).

[100]Sharples Coal Co., supra note 99, at 1323.

[101]Id.

[102]Id. at 1322.

[103]Smith-Blair, Inc., 100 LA 344 (Goodstein, 1992).

[104]Maxwell Air Force Base, 97 LA 1129, 1133 (Howell, 1991).

impunity verbally insult and abuse members of Management with whom they come into contact as Stewards.[105]

Thus, arbitrators have repeatedly concluded "that union officials are not entirely immune under the 'protected union activity' concept; not all conduct is permissible. It is a case by case determination."[106]

Arbitrators tend to look at four factors in trying to separate protected and nonprotected conduct.[107] One factor is the place where the allegedly insubordinate act occurred, e.g., "in an office or conference room or on the production floor."[108] Private outbursts are less likely to affect management's right to maintain order and respect and are thus less likely to result in a finding of just cause for any discipline than are outbursts on the production floor.[109]

The second factor relates to the subject matter of the discussion giving rise to the incident. The more an incident relates to "grievances, negotiations, or administration of the contract," the more likely it is to result in a finding of immunity.[110] Indeed, "the parties [do not] have to be discussing the merits of a particular grievance for the protection to be in effect."[111]

Nevertheless, there are limits to this rule. For example, in *United Cable Television Corp.,*[112] the arbitrator refused to find a letter posted by a steward on a union bulletin board fully protected. The letter did not advance the union's position on a pending grievance, but sought to undermine a "deal" that already had been struck between the union and the employer. Thus, the steward's conduct "was motivated to prevent the Company and the Union from 'burying the hatchet.'"[113]

A third factor is a comparison of the employee's conduct with the issue at hand, i.e., whether the employee's conduct sufficiently related to the matter under discussion or was wholly unrelated and included "extraneous name calling, screaming, obscene gestures," and the like.[114] Conduct that is initially related to "protected activity," and thus protected, may lose its immunity if it continues beyond a reasonable point. For example, in *Kay-Brunner Steel Products,*[115] the arbitrator sustained a discharge of an alternate steward who had been repeatedly ordered to return to work, finding that, "[t]he Grievant had

[105]Hobart Corp., 75 LA 907, 909 (Curry, 1980).

[106]Maxwell Air Force Base, 97 LA at 1136.

[107]Trans-City Terminal Warehouse, Inc., 94 LA 1075, 1078 (Volz, 1990) (reciting the four factors while citing Atlantic Steel Co., 245 NLRB 814, 102 LRRM 1247 (1979)).

[108]94 LA at 1078.

[109]Burton Mfg. Co., 82 LA 1228, 1235 (Holley, Jr., 1984) (noting that "the threats and the name-calling incident were not observed by co-employees"); Owens-Illinois, Inc., 73 LA 663, 668 (Witney, 1979) (reversing discharge of steward where "meeting was behind closed doors").

[110]Trans-City Terminal Warehouse, Inc., supra note 107, at 1078.

[111]Southern Ind. Gas & Elec. Co., 85 LA 716, 720 (Nathan, 1985).

[112]92 LA 3 (Koven, 1988).

[113]Id. at 10.

[114]Trans-City Terminal Warehouse, Inc., supra note 107, at 1078.

[115]78 LA 363 (Gentile, 1982).

knowledge of the Agreement by virtue of his Union activities and thus could have filed a grievance challenging" the employer's conduct.[116] The arbitrator was persuaded by the fact that no grievance was pending and the grievant had ignored at least four orders to return to work, at least one of which warned him that "if he does not go back to work, I'm going to exercise my right to terminate him."[117]

A final, and perhaps the most important, factor is whether the employee's conduct was in any way provoked by the employer.[118] In addressing this issue, arbitrators determine whether the employer was "refusing to respond to questions, to process grievances, to allow the Union official to talk or carry on the responsibilities of his office."[119]

## C. Conduct of Union Official While in Capacity of Bargaining Unit Employee

Upon the completion of a union representative's involvement in union activities, the representative returns to regular work status and the protective cloak of a union steward or officer is removed. The officer then becomes subject to the same supervisory authority as any other employee.[120]

A union official who fails to distinguish his union representative capacity from his employee obligations may be subjected to discipline.[121] For example, in *Andrews Furniture Industries, Inc.*,[122] the union steward became so disrespectful that the arbitrator reinstated him only after a long suspension without pay.

To ensure rank-and-file employees of continuous representation, the union should be consulted before a union steward is dismissed, especially where the contract provides for notice and consultation with the union prior to the steward's discharge.[123]

---

[116]Id. at 367.

[117]Id. at 365.

[118]Trans-City Terminal Warehouse, Inc., supra note 107, at 1078.

[119]Id.; Army & Air Force Exch. Serv., 105 LA 332, 336 (Shieber, 1995) (noting that "[t]here was no provocation by management that provided any reasonable basis for Grievant's statements").

[120]Turco Mfg. Co., 74 LA 889 (Penfield, 1980); Calmar Inc., 51 LA 766 (Turkus, 1968); General Elec. Co., 43 LA 838 (Kornblum, 1964).

[121]Turco Mfg. Co., supra note 120, at 895 (upholding suspension and discharge of union officer in part based upon his abuse of his privilege as a union official).

[122]50 LA 600, 603–04 (Volz, 1968).

[123]Sauer, Inc., 100 LA 191 (Franckiewicz, 1992).

Chapter 11

# Evidentiary and Procedural Considerations

## I. Application of Legal Rules of Evidence

Generally, legal rules about the admissibility of evidence are not strictly observed in labor arbitration proceedings.[1] This general principle applies in discharge or disciplinary cases, as in the arbitration of any other issue.[2]

This relaxed standard is articulated in Rule 28 of the Voluntary Labor Arbitration Rules of the American Arbitration Association:

> The parties may offer such evidence as is relevant and material to the dispute, and shall produce such additional evidence as the arbitrator may deem necessary to an understanding and determination of the dispute. An arbitrator authorized by law to subpoena witnesses and documents may do so independently or upon the request of any party. The arbitrator shall be the judge of the relevance and materiality of the evidence offered and conformity to legal rules of evidence shall not be necessary. All evidence shall be taken in the presence of all of the arbitrators and all of the parties except where any of the parties is absent in default or has waived the right to be present.

At least one arbitrator has interpreted Rule 28 of the American Arbitration Association Voluntary Labor Arbitration Rules to mean that arbitrators may not exclude evidence as incompetent, but are

---

[1]Volz & Goggins, eds., Elkouri & Elkouri, How Arbitration Works, 5th ed., 403 (BNA Books, 1997); Fairweather's Practice and Procedure in Labor Arbitration, 3d ed., Schoonhoven, ed., 298 (BNA Books, 1991).

[2]Cub Foods, Inc., 95 LA 771 (Gallagher, 1990); Associated Cleaning Consultants, 94 LA 1246 (Lubow, 1990).

empowered to evaluate the "relevancy and materiality" of the evidence.[3] This approach means that everything is received unless it is of so little probative value that it can be eliminated without impairing the proof of the issues.

The liberal interpretation of the rules of evidence does not mean an arbitrator will accept gross and prejudicial hearsay. For example, a transportation company dispatcher testified to receiving a call from a man whose sister-in-law said her mother was pushed down the steps of a bus by the grievant.[4] That testimony was rejected as worthless. This arbitral flexibility in handling evidence has been confirmed by tripartite discussion panels of the National Academy of Arbitrators.[5]

While arbitrators may not strictly apply legal rules of evidence, "the good sense" of those rules is regularly used in evaluating evidence, if not in excluding it outright.[6] As one arbitrator observed at the suggestion the rules of evidence do not apply in arbitration, "Don't bet on that."[7]

According to one arbitrator, two widely different approaches have developed over the years in connection with rulings by arbitrators on objections to the receipt of evidence:

> Bill Simkin—probably one of the most accomplished and successful arbitrators of this century—is not an attorney and tends to discourage all objections. When the first such objection arises before him, he is likely to remind the parties that he is not a lawyer but that presumably they selected him to hear their case because they had some idea that he knew how to evaluate evidence. Thus he advises the parties that he is ready to take into evidence everything that is offered and decide later whether the evidence is of any real value in determining the issues.
>
> A radically different approach was developed by former Senator Wayne Morse of Oregon, during the period that he served as Impartial Chairman for the Pacific Coast Maritime Industry and the ILWU in the late 1930s. Wayne, dean of the Oregon Law School at the time, ran his hearings very much in the manner of a judge—ruling on objections to hearsay, leading questions, secondary evidence, and relevance in much the same way as one would have expected in federal district court.[8]

Few modern arbitrators follow either approach. Rather, the prevailing view gives the parties a relatively free hand in presenting

---

[3]Lever Bros. Co., 82 LA 164, 167 (Stix, 1983).

[4]Bloch, "The Applicability of Legal Rules Including Evidence," in Labor Arbitration: A Practical Guide for Advocates, Zimny, Dolson, & Barreca, eds., 121 (BNA Books, 1990), citing unreported case.

[5]Problems of Proof in Arbitration, Proceedings of the 19th Annual Meeting of NAA, 149–50, 163, 296 (BNA Books, 1967).

[6]Wirtz, "Due Process of Arbitration," in The Arbitration and the Parties, Proceedings of the 11th Annual Meeting of NAA, 1, 13 (BNA Books, 1958).

[7]Bloch, supra note 4.

[8]Garrett, "Anatomy of the Arbitration Hearing," in Labor Arbitration: A Practical Guide for Advocates, Zimny, Dolson, & Barreca, eds., 112, 115–16 (BNA Books, 1990).

relevant evidence.[9] The weight of the evidence is then determined by the arbitrator when studying the case.

## II. Procedural Issues

### A. *Quantum of Proof*

The quantum of proof is the amount of evidence needed to establish the elements of the case. It is "the quantity of proof required to convince a trier of fact to resolve or adopt a specific fact or issue in favor of one of the advocates."[10] "Preponderance of the evidence," "clear and convincing evidence," and evidence "beyond a reasonable doubt" are the three standards, in ascending order of difficulty of proof.

There is a divergence of opinion among arbitrators as to which standard of proof applies in disciplinary proceedings. In most discipline cases in which the degree of proof is stated, it is that the employer must establish its case by a preponderance of the evidence.[11] When theft is involved, however, many arbitrators conclude that, because the alleged act is of a criminal nature and involves moral turpitude, a standard higher than preponderance of the evidence should be used. Thus, many arbitrators adopt the standard of beyond a reasonable doubt.[12]

Additionally, in falsification cases, arbitrators disagree as to what the standard of proof should be.[13] The typical falsification case involves dishonest conduct—lying, cheating, or fraud—and, therefore, many arbitrators believe a more stringent quantum of proof (such as proof beyond a reasonable doubt) is necessary. Again, this is because the actions alleged constitute a crime or an act of moral turpitude.[14]

### B. *Calling the Grievant as an Adverse Witness*

The approach arbitrators take to procedural issues is far less structured than in a court of law. In a discharge or discipline case

---

[9]Volz & Goggin, eds., Elkouri & Elkouri, How Arbitration Works, 5th ed., 403, 409–10 (BNA Books, 1997); Fairweather's Practice & Procedure in Labor Arbitration, 3d ed., Schoonhoven, ed., 298 (BNA Books, 1991).

[10]Hill & Sinicropi, Evidence in Arbitration, 2d ed., 32 (BNA Books, 1987).

[11]See id. at 38–39.

[12]For "beyond a reasonable doubt" standard: Dockside Mach. & Boilerworks, 55 LA 1221 (Block, 1970); Atlas Freight Lines, 39 LA 352 (Koven, 1962); Great Atl. & Pac. Tea Co., 63-1 ARB ¶ 8027 (Turkus, 1962). For "clear and convincing" standard: Mastic Corp., 86-1 ARB ¶ 8217 (Nathan, 1986); Day & Zimmerman, Inc., 63 LA 1289 (Stratton, 1974); Kroger Co., 25 LA 906 (R. Smith, 1955). For preponderance standard: Babcock & Wilcox Co., 78-2 ARB ¶ 8544 (Dworkin, 1978). For a high level of proof, but moving somewhat away from a "beyond a reasonable doubt" standard: Armour-Dial, Inc., 76 LA 96 (Aaron, 1981).

[13]Brammer Mfg. Co., 83-2 ARB ¶ 8541 at 5402 (Talent, 1983) ("It has never been definitely resolved by the arbitral community."); Super-Valu Stores, Inc., 74 LA 939, 942 (Evenson, 1980) ("There is far less agreement among arbitrators regarding the quantum of proof required in discharge cases.")

[14]Super-Valu Stores, Inc., supra note 13, at 942.

where no supervisor is a party or witness to the underlying circumstances, the employer often calls the grievant as its first witness. Unions argue that this tactic is an inappropriate effort by the employer to circumvent its burden of proof. There is marked disagreement among the arbitrators and commentators on this issue.[15]

At the 19th annual meeting of the National Academy of Arbitrators, a Chicago area tripartite committee concluded it is generally unwise and undesirable to encourage calling witnesses from the opposition except in unusual cases, as where the grievant knows best what happened. Otherwise, the arbitrator should rule that the grievant may not be called to testify at the outset of a discharge or discipline matter.[16]

A New York tripartite committee reporting to the same meeting reached a different conclusion. It found it permissible for a party to call witnesses from the opposing side and to treat them as a hostile witness, but warned that the arbitrator should assume responsibility for ensuring that direct examination is proper and that the witness is protected against unfair tactics.[17]

Some arbitrators contend the employer should be permitted to call the grievant or any other adverse witness, so long as there is no contrary contractual mandate or mutual practice that forbids it.[18] This view is based on the perception of the grievant as the one seeking a remedy and invoking the arbitration process.[19]

The positions of arbitrators on this issue may be classified as follows:[20]

1. Any person present at the arbitration hearing may be called.

2. Neither side may call as a witness a person from the other side.

3. Persons may be called as witnesses for the other side, except grievants in Disciplinary Cases.

4. Under certain limited circumstances the Grievant in a disciplinary case may be called by the employer, but there must be a clear basis for such.[21]

---

[15]Jones, in Problems of Proof in Arbitration, Proceedings of 19th Annual Meeting of NAA, 99 (BNA Books, 1967). See also "Procedural Rulings During the Hearing: V. Witnesses From Opposing Sides; VI. Medical Affidavits," in Arbitration 1982: Conduct of the Hearing, Proceedings of the 35th Annual Meeting of NAA, 157–64. (BNA Books, 1983).

[16]Jones, in Problems of Proof in Arbitration," Proceedings of the 19th Annual Meeting of the NAA, 99 (BNA Books, 1967).

[17]Id. at 301.

[18]"Procedural Rulings During the Hearing: V. Witnesses From Opposing Sides," in Arbitration 1982: Conduct of the Hearing: Proceedings of the 35th Annual Meeting of NAA, 161 (BNA Books, 1983). Accord Tectum Corp., 37 LA 807 (Autrey, 1961).

[19]Procedural Rulings, supra note 18.

[20]These positions were described in Rohm & Haas Tex., 91 LA 339 (McDermott, 1988).

[21]Id. at 343.

## C. *Improperly Procured Evidence*

Evidence obtained by a search of the employee's person, locker, desk, or automobile, by clandestine surveillance or by other means that may arguably violate employee rights, raise a different sort of problem.[22] Labor advocates have stressed the individual's right to privacy and human dignity, while management advocates have emphasized the need to effectively investigate the facts, arguing that the employment relationship involves relinquishing certain rights. This tension has been particularly evident where security is involved.[23]

Arbitrators have admitted testimonial or documentary evidence obtained through a nonconsensual search, so long as the methods employed are not excessively shocking to the conscience of a reasonable person. In one case, an arbitrator accepted the search of an employee's lunchbox where it was inside his open locker, and the employee had been seen in a limited access area and in possession of parts he did not need. The arbitrator found the intrusion on the employee's privacy acceptable and supported by reasonable cause.[24] In another case, grievant lost a wallet with a zippered compartment containing marijuana. Although the wallet's owner could have been identified from cards and papers in the exposed section of the wallet, the marijuana was admitted because the search was not conducted in contemplation of prosecution.[25]

Although arbitrators have articulated different reasons, the majority do not apply the exclusionary rule of criminal law. They distinguish between state action and searches or confiscations of evidence by private employers, noting that the focus of the Fourth Amendment of the U.S. Constitution is on governmental, not private action.

Where an employer obtained evidence from the sheriff's department as a result of a potentially illegal search of the grievant's

[22]See generally Volz & Goggins, eds., Elkouri & Elkouri, How Arbitration Works, 5th ed., 454–58 (BNA Books, 1997).

[23]"Problems of Proof in Arbitration," Proceedings of the 19th Annual Meeting of NAA, 105–06, 129–34, 138–239 (BNA Books, 1967); Super Mkt. Serv. Corp., 89 LA 538 (DiLauro, 1987) (installation of closed circuit TV without bargaining with union ruled improper because of susceptibility to abuse, notwithstanding history of pilferage); Eico, Inc., 44 LA 563 (Delaney, 1965) (TV cameras on production floor violated maintenance of conditions clause in collective bargaining agreement). Compare Colonial Baking Co., 62 LA 586 (Elson, 1974) (installation of closed circuit TV in production area solely for security reasons in high crime area held proper as management right); Cooper Carton Corp., 61 LA 697 (Kelliher, 1973) (use of TV equipment a legitimate exercise of management's right to direct the working force); FMC Corp., 46 LA 335, 338 (Mittenthal, 1966) (right to monitor room with TV camera upheld where employer believed material losses were through theft).

[24]American Welding & Mfg. Co., 89 LA 247, 252 (Dworkin, 1987). Compare Campbell Soup Co., 2 LA 27, 31 (Lohman, 1946) (evidence inadmissible where obtained through search of grievant's locker and purse without disclosure to employee of reason for investigation).

[25]Rust Eng'g Co., 85 LA 407, 410 (Whyte, 1985).

residence, the arbitrator found it could be used to justify termination. He held that evidence garnered in conflict with "the concept of privacy" or the exclusionary rule is admissible except where the employer's conduct was lacking in any reasonable cause or otherwise violated fundamental concepts of due process or fair play, circumstances that were not present before him.[26] Where the employer lacked reasonable cause for a search, an arbitrator held that drugs found in the search had to be excluded. Other arbitrators have taken a similar view.[27]

Arbitrators have not favored objections to incriminating evidence because it was improperly procured by entrapment or improper surveillance.[28] But the use of recordings or transcriptions made without the knowledge of a party has received a mixed reception, as has the use of evidence obtained from a closed-circuit television camera.[29]

The results of a blood-alcohol test were admitted in a discharge arbitration, despite the fact that they were not admissible in the drunk-driving criminal proceeding against grievant.[30] Blood and urine test results were likewise received in evidence where the employees authorized the testing, even though they were told failure to cooperate would compel the conclusion that they were using drugs and they would then need to prove otherwise.[31] Where the collective bargaining agreement authorized drug and alcohol testing, a trucking company was permitted to introduce test results disclosing the presence of marijuana metabolites.[32] The weight of arbitral authority is that

---

[26]Union Oil Co. of Cal., 99 LA 1137, 1150 (McKay, 1992).

[27]Kerr McGee Chem. Corp., 90 LA 55 (Levin, 1987) (cocaine found in grievant's van excluded because there was no reasonable cause to suspect grievant was a drug dealer so there was no basis for the search). But see Georgia Power Co., 93 LA 846 (Holley, 1989) (car search by drug detection dog led to grievant's drug test and ultimate discharge; arbitrator upheld discharge, noting employer had properly told employees they would be subject to search if their vehicles were on company property and to drug testing if the drug detection dog alerted on their vehicles); American Welding & Mfg. Co., 89 LA 247 (Dworkin, 1987) (search of employee's lunchbox); Hennis Freight Lines, 44 LA 711 (McGury, 1964) (evidence of theft of company property previously suppressed in criminal proceeding received in evidence in arbitration as justification for discharge).

[28]Volz & Goggin, eds., Elkouri & Elkouri, How Arbitration Works, 5th ed., 403–10 (BNA Books, 1997); Fairweather's Practice and Procedure in Labor Arbitration, 3d ed., Schoonhoven, ed., 300 (BNA Books, 1991).

[29]Needham Packing Co., 44 LA 1057, 1080 (Davey, 1965) (transcript of tape-recorded phone conversation not received in evidence where party against whom it was offered was unaware of recording, and other evidence of conversations between parties was based on present recollection only). But see A. Finkl & Sons Co., 90 LA 1027, 1029 (Wolff, 1988) (videotape showing physical activity of grievant received in evidence against grievant discharged for falsely claiming disability); Associated Grocers of Colo., Inc., 82 LA 415, 418 (Smith, 1984) (tape-recorded admissions of grievant and fellow employee held "most reliable evidence" of what was said about alleged theft); Sun Drug Co., 31 LA 191, 194 (Marcus, 1958) (tape recording admitted in discharge case held not to be "entrapment" and legality of information-gathering process held to be for "other authorities").

[30]Georgia-Pacific Corp., 100 LA 713 (Hockenberry, 1993).

[31]Boone Energy, 85 LA 233 (O'Connell, 1985).

[32]Roadway Express, 87 LA 224 (Cooper, 1986).

employees may not be compelled to submit to random drug testing under a unilaterally implemented program.[33]

### D. Missing Witnesses

The failure of a party to call a witness available to it gives rise to a presumption that the witness's testimony would be adverse to the position of the party who could have called him.[34] Some arbitrators apply this presumption to the failure of a grievant to appear and testify at the hearing of his own grievance.[35] Others express the view that no such inference should be made. This latter view is based on an analogy to the privilege against self-incrimination in criminal cases. While the majority of arbitrators find no place for this privilege in arbitration, a minority give some deference to the privilege.[36]

## III. Validity of Work Rules

In some cases, specific work rules are the product of negotiations between labor and management. More often, however, work rules are unilaterally promulgated by the employer. Even in the absence of specific contractual language authorizing the employer to make work rules, arbitrators generally hold that the employer has the managerial prerogative to establish work rules. Work rules established by the employer, however, must not conflict with the collective bargaining agreement and must be reasonably related to the safe and efficient operation of the business.[37] The management rights clause in the

---

[33]Reported decisions upholding challenges to drug-testing programs include Gem City Chems., Inc., 86 LA 1023 (Warns, 1986); Capital Area Transit Auth., 69 LA 811 (Ellman, 1977); Boise Cascade Corp., 12 Daily Lab. Rep. A-4 (BNA, Jan. 20, 1987, Kagel). Compare Boone Energy, 85 LA 233 (O'Connell, 1985), where the arbitrator found no violation despite lack of contractual support for drug testing. The arbitrator in Ohse Foods, 100 LA 809 (Eisler, 1993), received evidence of contractually supported drug tests, but set aside a discharge because the tests were administered 65 hours after the grievant sustained an on-the-job injury. For an in-depth discussion of drug testing and related issues, see Chapter 6.

[34]Autodynamics, Inc., 99 LA 705, 707 (Kanner, 1992); Southern Cal. Permanente Med. Group, 92 LA 41, 45 (Richman, 1989).

[35]Marathon Petroleum Co., 89 LA 716 (Grimes, 1987); Republic Airlines, 83 LA 127 (Seidman, 1984).

[36]Marathon Petroleum Co., 89 LA 716, 720, 723 (Grimes, 1987) (failure of grievant to testify held against him by arbitrator in sustaining discharge for inability to cease use of controlled substances); Republic Airlines, Inc., 82 LA 127 (Seidman, 1984) (discharge upheld because grievant charged with unauthorized possession of another's paycheck refused to testify to rebut company case, despite prior acquittal of criminal charge by jury). But see City of Omaha, 90-1 ARB ¶ 8274 (Rotenberg, 1990) (discharge for refusal to submit to interrogation about homicide in building owned by grievant rescinded because refusal was exercise of Fifth Amendment privilege).

[37]Acorn Bldg. Components, 92 LA 68, 71 (Roumell, 1988); Aro, Inc., 47 LA 1065, 1069 (Whyte, 1966); Industrial Finishing Co., 40 LA 670, 671 (Daugherty, 1963).

collective bargaining agreement and the residual rights doctrine of managerial authority are often cited by arbitrators as providing the employer with the authority to make and amend rules.[38] When the employer establishes or changes work rules, it is required to provide adequate notice to employees.[39]

The employer's right to make and enforce work rules usually includes the right to make changes in the rules. In one case, an employer unilaterally implemented an attendance policy, which remained in effect for a lengthy period. The employer and the union never engaged in any negotiations concerning the policy. Later, the employer rescinded the policy and implemented a new one. The matter went to arbitration and the arbitrator found that the employer's action in implementing the new rules was proper.[40] Conversely, if the employer negotiates changes with the union, it can lose the right to amend the rules. In one case, the employer unilaterally implemented an attendance control program. Subsequently, it engaged in negotiations with the union, which resulted in modifications to the program. The program changes were ratified by the union. Later, the employer attempted to change some of the negotiated rules. In this case, an arbitrator held that the employer had no right to unilaterally make changes in the program after it had negotiated with the union.[41]

An employer generally has the right to implement a new rule that prohibits conduct that the employer has previously allowed, as long as the employer has a rational basis for enacting the rule. In one case, a new rule prohibiting the use of radios on the shop floor was upheld, based on safety considerations, even though the employer had permitted the use of radios for over 10 years.[42] However, an arbitrator in another case found that a rule prohibiting all smoking in a manufacturing plant was not a valid exercise of management rights, as smoking had always been permitted in the facility and the areas where smoking had been permitted were well ventilated. Additionally, the union had previously successfully challenged a rule prohibiting smoking in a break room.[43]

Arbitrators sometimes conclude that certain types of rules cannot be enforced unless they are negotiated with the union. Rules that are considered invasive of individual privacy or those that attempt to regulate off-duty conduct are carefully scrutinized by arbitrators.

---

[38]Mississippi Power & Light Co., 92 LA 1161 (Taylor, 1989) (collective bargaining agreement does not require rules to be negotiated; therefore, the making of rules is the sole prerogative of management); Wyandot, Inc., 92 LA 457 (Imundo, 1989) (collective bargaining agreement gave management the authority to both create new rules and modify existing rules).

[39]Englehard Kaolin Corp., 96 LA 563, 566 (Galambos, 1990); Kansas Power & Light Co., 87 LA 867, 872 (Belcher, 1986).

[40]B.F. Goodrich Co., 90 LA 1297 (McIntosh, 1988).

[41]Tyson Foods, Inc., 92 LA 1121, 1125 (Goodstein, 1989).

[42]Motor Appliance Corp., 106 LA 484 (Suardi, 1996).

[43]Basler Elec. Co., 94 LA 888 (Canestraight, 1990).

Several arbitrators have found that management does not have the right to unilaterally impose a random drug-testing policy.[44] One arbitrator found that an employer could not unilaterally require that cash shortages be deducted from employees' wages.[45] In another case, a residency requirement that served no appreciable purpose was held to be unenforceable.[46]

## IV. Timing: When Rules Can Be Challenged

Rules that are unilaterally promulgated by an employer may be challenged by the union on the ground that they violate the collective bargaining agreement or are arbitrary, discriminatory, capricious, or unreasonable.[47] Arbitrators have also held that a rule must lend itself to fair and equal application.[48] For example, a company established a rule that imposed discipline for reporting to work in an impaired state. An arbitrator found the rule to be unreasonable because it did not make an exception for the unintentional impairment caused by the ingestion of a prescription drug.[49] In another case, a rule that prohibited the wearing of rings in a smelting plant was found to be unreasonable in its application to employees who routinely wear safety gloves. Further, there was no evidence that the wearing of rings had caused any accidents.[50]

Many arbitrators have held that the union does not have to wait until a rule is enforced prior to filing a grievance.[51] One arbitrator stated that "the union is at all times authorized to challenge either a specific rule, or its application in a particular case."[52] Even if no employee has been disciplined or discharged, the union may properly file a grievance alleging that a conflict exists between the rule and the collective bargaining agreement.[53] However, in one case where the union challenged a whole set of new plant rules, the arbitrator found that the collective bargaining agreement and past practices

---

[44]Phelps Dodge Copper Prods. Co., 94 LA 393 (Blum, 1990) (implementation of random drug tests goes beyond residual powers of company); Utah Power & Light Co., 94 LA 233, 239 (Winograd, 1990) (drug-testing policy affects expectations of privacy, thus input from employee's bargaining representative is required to balance interests).

[45]Pepsi-Cola Gen. Bottlers, 92 LA 1272 (Madden, 1989).

[46]Quaker State Corp., 92 LA 898, 902 (Talarico, 1989).

[47]Schien Body & Equip. Co., 69 LA 930, 935–36 (Roberts, 1977).

[48]Hoover Co., 77 LA 1287, 1290 (Strasshofer, 1982).

[49]Anheuser-Busch, Inc., 95 LA 495 (Miller, 1989).

[50]Doe Run Co., 95 LA 705 (Heinsz, 1990).

[51]Linde Co., 34 LA 1, 5–6 (Schmidt, 1959) (Employees should not have to risk a disciplinary penalty in order to find out whether a work rule is a proper exercise of management prerogative).

[52]Babcock & Wilcox, 60 LA 778, 782 (Dworkin, 1972).

[53]Bucyrus-Erie Co., 69 LA 970, 974 (Johnson, 1977).

prevented a challenge to the rules until an employee had actually been disciplined or discharged.[54]

Some arbitration decisions that find that a union may challenge rules prior to their enforcement are based upon the industrial relations principle of "work now, grieve later." These decisions state that since an employee is required to obey any promulgated work rule, the union should have the right to file a grievance to test the propriety of the order. In this way, an employee does not have to risk discipline in order to determine whether a rule is unenforceable.[55] However, in some situations, a determination of the validity of a rule may have to wait until it is known how the employer will enforce it.[56]

Rules that result from negotiations between labor and management are generally not subject to challenge in the same manner as employer-promulgated rules. That is, they may not be challenged until they are actually applied. However, in applying any work rule, whether negotiated or unilaterally implemented, the employer is required to meet the "just cause" standard for discipline.

## V. Discipline in the Absence of Explicit Work Rules

Although specific contract rules or plant rules[57] serve to place the employee on notice of the potential disciplinary consequences of her conduct,[58] discipline in the workplace does not depend upon the existence of either. Arbitrators have upheld discipline in the absence of explicit rules.[59] Whether discipline will be upheld in the absence of a rule depends on the type of employee conduct for which discipline was imposed.

### A. Adverse Effect on Business

While many businesses are dependent upon goodwill, public image, public trust, and a good reputation, employers often do not promulgate employee conduct rules that address these business needs.

---

[54]Dial Corp., 90 LA 729, 735 (Hillgert, 1988).

[55]Ross Clay Prods. Co., 64-1 ARB ¶ 8315 at 4171 (Kabaker, 1963).

[56]ARA Mfg. Co., 84 LA 856, 859 (Lilly, 1985) (rule that prohibited loud conduct, abrasive comments, and a disrespectful attitude toward management not invalid as written).

[57]Arbitrators have consistently held that the employer can unilaterally establish reasonable plant rules, so long as they do not conflict with the law or the collective bargaining agreement. Plant rules are typically embodied in employee handbooks or posted rules.

[58]See Hill & Sinicropi, Evidence in Arbitration, 2d ed., 25–26 (BNA Books, 1987); Lithonia Lighting Co., 85 LA 627, 629 (Volz, 1985); Enterprise Wire Co., 46 LA 359, 363–65 (Daugherty, 1966).

[59]Volz & Goggin, eds., Elkouri & Elkouri, How Arbitration Works, 5th ed., 884–88 (BNA Books, 1997).

Yet in the absence of such rules many arbitrators have sustained discipline or even discharge on these grounds. For instance, an arbitrator held that just cause existed to discharge a grocery store employee for making inappropriate comments to a female customer on three occasions. The employee had been warned, counseled, and suspended in the past for similar behavior.[60] In another case, the arbitrator found the employer properly discharged an employee following an incident in which he parked a truck in a public parking lot so close to a car occupied by three women as to hinder their departure, and then cursed the women when they complained. Although the contract did not prohibit the use of abusive language toward the general public in the list of dischargeable offenses, the termination was warranted since the employee's conduct adversely affected the public image that the company and distributor had spent millions to create.[61] In another driving case, the arbitrator held that the employer properly discharged a delivery driver who, after a near accident with the company truck, pursued the matter by following the other driver to a parking lot and provoked a confrontation. The arbitrator reasoned that the employee must perform duties almost totally unsupervised and even in the absence of a written rule, the employee should know that the company cannot tolerate delivery drivers engaging in physical confrontations with the general public.[62]

## B. Dishonesty and Disloyalty[63]

Even in the absence of explicit work rules, employers are owed trust and honesty from their employees. A breach of that trust can be a basis for discipline. For instance, in *Arizona Bank*[64] the bank properly discharged a branch operations specialist for unsatisfactory performance. The employee failed to report three instances in which tellers gave co-workers lunch money from their cash drawers without

---

[60]Cub Foods, Inc., 95 LA 771 (Gallagher, 1990).

[61]Grey Eagle Distribs., 93 LA 24 (Canestraight, 1989).

[62]Genuine Parts Co., 79 LA 220 (Reed, 1982). See also Rustco Prods. Co., 92 LA 1048 (Watkins, 1989) (arbitrator reduced penalty from discharge to suspension for delivery driver who used racial epithets and vulgar language on dock of employer's customer; misconduct did not rise to a level considered "extremely serious" and routinely accepted by arbitrators as a basis for termination since employer did not lose customer or suffer damage to its business relationship). See Central Blood Bank of Pittsburgh, 69 LA 1031 (Amis, 1977). (employer was justified in discharging blood bank van driver for verbally abusing driver of another vehicle during accident; Blood Bank was dependent upon good will and trust for its existence and could ill afford public embarrassment).

[63]See Chapter 7 for a fuller discussion.

[64]91 LA 772 (Fine, 1988).

receiving appropriate exchanges. An employer has a reasonable expectation that an employee will not take kickbacks[65] or eavesdrop.[66]

## C. Invasion of Privacy[67]

Arbitrators have also found discipline warranted where an employee violated management's reasonable expectation of privacy,[68] created an unsafe workplace,[69] or was impaired by drugs or alcohol.[70]

## D. Absenteeism[71]

Arbitrators have consistently upheld terminations of employees for excessive absenteeism when they have violated an established plant rule.[72] On the other hand, in one recent decision the arbitrator found that because the employer did not have an absenteeism policy, it lacked just cause to discharge an employee for excessive absenteeism caused by the employee's diabetic condition.[73] The arbitrator held that in the absence of an absenteeism policy, it is difficult to define excessive absenteeism since the employer has an obligation under the

---

[65]United States Steel Corp., 94 LA 1065 (Das, 1990). There was just cause to discharge two maintenance department expediters who received money and goods paid by Vendor X totaling in excess of $10,000. The only service performed by the grievants for Vendor X was to use their positions as expediters to send motors from the plant to be prepared by Vendor X. The arbitrator found neither grievant reasonably could have believed that this arrangement was compatible with their obligations as employees.

[66]Claridge Prods. & Equip., 94 LA 1083 (Goodstein, 1990). Just cause to discharge employee who bugged the contract office in order to obtain information that was adverse to supervisors would help grievant combat scheduled transfer.

[67]See also Chapter 5.

[68]Press Democrat Publ'g Co., 93 LA 969 (McKay, 1989) (arbitrator found that while there is no general expectation of privacy that would prohibit grievant from entering the computer basket of his supervisor, grievant had no legitimate reason for pulling up the document—which proposed to discipline another employee—or making a copy of the document).

[69]Hess Oil Virgin Islands Corp., 91 LA 1284 (Hunter, 1988). Arbitrator Hunter upheld the discharge of a process operator who attempted to relight burners without first purging furnace of fumes, causing an explosion that extensively damaged the furnace and resulted in a 6-week downtime. See Mead Paper, 91 LA 53 (Curry, Jr., 1988), where the arbitrator found that the employer properly discharged an accident-prone employee as an individual unsuitable for work in paper mill. The employee sustained 10 times as many injuries as fellow co-workers and had been absent almost one-quarter of his 18 years of employment, and this pattern was likely to continue.

[70]Union-Tribune Publ'g Co., 93 LA 617 (McBrearty, 1989) (grievant properly discharged for on-duty ingestion of methamphetamine and possession of marijuana).

[71]See also Chapter 3.

[72]Westvaco, Va., Folding Box Div., 92 LA 1289 (Nolan) (employer properly discharged employee for attendance program that applied to all employees); Hughes Aircraft Co., 92 LA 634 (Richman, 1989) (discharge of 2-year employee who had received progressive discipline for excessive absenteeism under attendance program was warranted).

[73]Thrifty Cos., 103 LA 317 (Staudohar, 1994).

Americans with Disabilities Act to take the employee's handicapping condition into consideration.

## E. *Termination Based on Artistic or Business Judgment*

Discharge does not always have to be based upon misconduct or incompetency. Employers may exercise subjective judgment in discharging employees in some industries. For example, in the broadcasting industry, arbitrators have found an inherent right of management to exercise judgment about the suitability of employees as on-air personalities. An arbitrator held that the "special nature of the broadcasting industry and the subjective evaluations of the listener taste involved in such a determination" precluded him from substituting his judgment for that of management. He found that the broadcaster was discharged because management wanted a more "brisk type" of delivery and the grievant's voice was too "mild and mellow."[74] Similarly, an arbitrator found that a news director had exercised his subjective judgment in good faith based upon reasonable factors when he removed the grievant. The news director worked to change the image of the individual in the news anchor position so that the company could appeal to younger audiences and attract more advertisers. The decision was based, to a great extent, on ratings and consulting reports. Other decisions in the broadcast industry accept good faith judgment as a basis for termination.[75]

## VI. Medical Evidence[76]

Medical evidence is often used to show the physical capability of terminated employees for continued employment,[77] or the physical condition, illness, or injury of a disciplined employee. Despite the lack

---

[74]Taft Broadcasting Co., 64 LA 211 (Goetz, 1974).

[75]KDFW-TV, 94 LA 806 (Allen, 1990) (television station's discharge of a female weather anchor for "unsuitability" reasons did not violate contract where management was permitted to relieve employees from duty for "other legitimate reasons"; employee was removed to strengthen news team and ratings and company presented adequate evidence that it made a reasoned and "business necessity" decision. See Cosmos Broadcasting of La., Inc., 68 LA 1332, 1338 (Taylor, 1977) (employer must be accorded "discretion and flexibility in terminating the services of on-air personalities" in an industry where rightly or wrongly ratings are a measurement of the viewing audience); WFMJ Broadcasting Co., 52 LA 995 (Hertz, 1969) (broadcasting industry distinguished from mass production industry in which performance could be judged based on quantity produced or efficiency; standards used in evaluating broadcasting personnel were subjective).

[76]Issues of obtaining medical evidence are covered in Chapter 5.

[77]For a comprehensive discussion of the admissibility of medical evidence, the resolution of conflicts in such evidence received from two or more physicians, the weighing of such evidence by arbitrators, and the use of doctors' "slips" or certificates, see generally Volz & Goggin, eds., Elkouri & Elkouri, How Arbitration Works, 5th ed., 464–68 (BNA Books, 1997).

of opportunity for cross-examination, arbitrators commonly receive testimony from doctors in the form of written reports, statements, or affidavits.[78]

When both sides have submitted medical evidence and the doctors do not agree, many arbitrators give greater weight to the employer's medical evidence, provided it acted in good faith, pursuant to good faith medical advice.[79] In assessing the relative significance of medical evidence, many considerations play a role. For instance, a relatively old or "stale" diagnosis may be viewed as unreliable.[80] These considerations are discussed below.

## A. *Evaluating Conflicting Medical Evidence*

In many cases the arbitrator is faced with conflicting medical evidence. One arbitrator divided this evidence into two types: (1) conflicts in medical facts, and (2) conflicts in medical opinion:

> By medical *fact,* I mean objective data gathered by some recognized laboratory or clinical procedure, or by some accepted process of empirical measurement, for example, weight, temperature, pulse rate, blood pressure, or conditions such as a fracture, swelling, sugar in the urine, and dilation of the pupils. Medical *opinion,* on the other hand, consists of conclusions and implications drawn by a doctor from a given set of medical facts. The pertinent difference is that an *opinion,* even though objectively given, is not susceptible to the same kind of beforehand tests and proofs which apply in a search for *facts.*[81]

The arbitrator asserts that when arbitrators are faced with the problem of resolving conflicting medical evidence, they should be guided by the following principles:

> 1. Conflict in medical *fact,* as opposed to medical opinion, is generally susceptible to resolution by approved methods of observation or some laboratory or clinical procedure. When an arbitrator is unable to resolve an important conflict in fact to his satisfaction, he should make every effort to persuade the parties to engage a third qualified medical expert to ascertain the facts and report his findings.

---

[78]Volz & Goggin, eds., Elkouri & Elkouri, How Arbitration Works, 5th ed., 464 n.298 (BNA Books, 1997); Illinois Cement Co., 99 LA 481 (Koenig, 1992); Pacific Bell, 91 LA 653 (Kaufman, 1988); East Ohio Gas Co., 91 LA 366, 371 (Dworkin, 1988).

[79]Volz & Goggin, eds., Elkouri & Elkouri, How Arbitration Works, 5th ed., 465 (BNA Books, 1997), and cases collected at n.301.

[80]See East Ohio Gas Co., 91 LA 366, 373 (Dworkin, 1988); Northshore Gas Co., 40 LA 37, 43-44 (Sembower, 1963).

[81]Miller, "The Use of Experts in Arbitration: I. Expert Medical Evidence: A View From the End of the Table," in Arbitration and Social Change, Proceedings of the 22nd Annual Meeting, NAA, 135, 137 (BNA Books, 1970).

2. Conflict in medical *opinion,* as opposed to medical fact, is not generally susceptible to objective resolution by referral to a third expert, where the opposing opinions are each shown to be supported by a recognized body of medical authority. The arbitrator must then look to resolution of the case by application of appropriate standards of equity and fairness rather than force himself into choosing between two apparently legitimate schools of medical thought.

3. The arbitrator need not defer to the opinion of a medical witness whose judgment on the matter goes beyond the scope of his professional expertise. In accepting such evidence, the arbitrator should recognize its limitations and weigh it accordingly in deciding the issue before him.[82]

Actual conflicts in medical opinion must be distinguished from breakdowns in communications between the parties. For example, in one case the company was unaware of conflicting medical opinion about the employee's fitness for duty until the date of the arbitration hearing. The arbitrator held the employee should reapply for his position and make himself available for examination by the company doctor pursuant to the agreement.[83] Where an employee's doctor certified him as disabled, but an impartial doctor certified him as able to return to work, the company's termination of the employee was held improper. The company failed to establish that it communicated the impartial doctor's determination, or its conclusiveness (pursuant to company policy), to the employee.[84]

Finally, where the employer is not actually faced with conflicting medical information, but nevertheless seeks additional medical records regarding an employee's ability to return to work, the employer may be found to have violated the agreement. In a case where there was no conflict between the company doctor and the employee's doctor regarding the employee's ability to return to duties, an arbitrator held the company cannot require release of additional medical information. The mere disbelief of the employee by the company does not justify such a demand. The arbitrator held the employee properly submitted to the company doctor's physical examination as required under the agreement and the company's suspension of the employee thereafter was improper.[85]

## B. *Principles Used in Evaluating Medical Opinions*

A review of awards involving medical issues shows that a number of principles have evolved to assist arbitrators in resolving conflicts in

---

[82]Hill & Sinicropi, Evidence in Arbitration (BNA Books, 1980).
[83]Transportation Mgmt. of Tenn., Inc., 82 LA 671 (Nicholas, Jr., 1984).
[84]Kramer Trenton Co., 77 LA 680 (Flounders, 1981).
[85]Roth Pump Mfg. Co., 82 LA 1199 (O'Reilly, 1984).

medical opinions. These principles have been adopted from guidelines used by arbitrators to resolve conflicts in testimony in other types of cases.

*1. Qualifications.*   The background and training of one witness may be more relevant to the questions at issue than that of the other witness. If the training or specialty of one witness is particularly pertinent to the medical issues in the particular case, the arbitrator may tend to give greater weight to the testimony of that witness. For example, where an employee was discharged for insubordination, the arbitrator held the company's position, based upon a nurse's notes from a conversation with the grievant's psychiatrist, did not supersede the psychiatrist's own written report and the grievant was reinstated.[86]

*2. Apparent Reliability.*   Where a doctor's note simply parroted the employee's statement without any independent findings, the arbitrator held such doctors' notes are worth very little and do not suffice to overcome other evidence casting doubt upon the employee's claimed sickness or injury.[87] An employee was not entitled to paid sick leave for a hearing loss in one ear where his doctor's recommendation was unspecific and did not state the employee was unable to perform his duties as a French instructor.[88] On the other hand, where a doctor's report was prepared by a member of a hospital's staff and gave no diagnosis, the arbitrator ruled the note was sufficient medical documentation upon which the employee had a right to rely.[89]

Since a doctor's report submitted on behalf of an employee may be found unreliable based upon objective criteria, it follows that a doctor's report provided by an employer should be held invalid for similar reasons. Thus, in one case, an unsigned and erroneous doctor's report was held insufficient to support the employer's termination of a disabled employee.[90]

*3. Personal Testimony Versus Written Evidence.*   Arbitrators recognize it is not always possible, due to scheduling problems and

---

[86]Tenneco Oil Co., 83 LA 1099 (King, 1984). See also Boces, First Supervisory Dist., 82 LA 1269 (Sabghir, 1984), holding that where the basis for the employer's determination of unfitness is emotional or psychiatric, the employer must obtain the opinion of a licensed psychiatrist.

[87]Island Creek Coal Co., V.P. No. 2 Mine, 84-2 ARB ¶ 8316 (Mittelman, 1984). Accord City of Vineland, 10 LAIS 2105 (Hammer, 1983). See also Anaconda Aluminum Co., 85-1 ARB ¶ 8059 (Volz, 1983), upholding a company's refusal to allow an employee to return to work in spite of her physician's release where the employee was wearing an ankle brace. The arbitrator further held, however, that the company must allow the employee the opportunity to demonstrate her ability to work or to be examined by a company physician.

[88]New Brighton Area Sch. Dist., 84 LA 350 (C. Duff, 1985).

[89]Flint Osteopathic Hosp., 11 LAIS 1050 (Ellmann, 1983). See also Cabell-Huntington Hosp., 83-1 ARB ¶ 8121 (Kindig, 1983); Newport News Shipbuilding & Dry Dock Co., 77 LA 1236 (Garrett, 1981).

[90]City of Stamford, 12 LAIS 2062 (Pittocco, 1985).

expense, to present medical evidence in the form of direct testimony. Since they are classic hearsay, doctors' "slips" are subject to considerable suspicion.[91] They may be impeached when they are shown to have been given "as a favor," without true medical attention, or otherwise lack reliability. For example, where a grievant developed a pronounced limp after 45 minutes on the job, the employer properly disregarded his return-to-work slip and sought a second opinion.[92]

Despite hearsay objections, arbitrators have generally accepted doctors' written certificates. Where medical opinion lies at the very heart of the dispute, however, there is no guarantee such documentary evidence will be given as much credit as it would be were the doctor to testify in person.[93] The direct testimony of the medical expert, however, subject to cross-examination, is generally stronger evidence than a written document.

*4. Degree of Contact With Employee.* Where the employee has been observed by a doctor over a long period of time, the expert medical testimony of that doctor will usually be given greater weight than if the doctor's testimony is based upon a single evaluation. This criteria will usually give an advantage to the employee's personal physician, who is in a better position to render opinions based upon long-range observation.

In one case involving a conflict between the opinions of two doctors regarding the grievant's fitness for duty, the arbitrator resolved the dispute by giving greater weight to the opinion of the employee's doctor, because his report was more complete and specific and he had treated the employee for a much longer period of time.[94]

Likewise, in a case where there was a conflict between the opinion of the employee's doctor and the company's doctor, the arbitrator resolved the conflicting evidence by giving greater weight to the testimony of the doctor who had more contact with the employee. The two doctors disagreed over the nature of the employee's seizures and as to what restrictions should be placed on his duties. The arbitrator held the opinion of the employee's doctor, which was based upon

---

[91]See Bloch, "The Applicability of Legal Rules Including Evidence," in Labor Arbitration: A Practical Guide for Advocates, Zimny, Dolson, & Barreca, eds., 120, 129 (BNA Books, 1990). See also Volz & Goggin, eds., Elkouri & Elkouri, How Arbitration Works, 5th ed., 468 (BNA Books, 1997), and cases collected there at nn. 316–317.

[92]Pretty Prods., 96 LA 169, 172 (Bittel, 1990). See also Valvoline Oil Co., 96 LA 925 (Cipolla, 1991) (release from grievant's orthopedic surgeon properly disregarded pending a second opinion, where employer had legitimate safety concerns and traditionally sent long-term absentees for an examination by company doctor).

[93]See also Spang & Co., 82 LA 342 (Joseph, 1985) (holding that in the face of conflicting medical evidence and the employee's doctor not being available for cross-examination, there was no way of determining whether the doctor would have testified that there was no undue risk of reinjury if the employee resumed heavy lifting duties).

[94]Armstrong Rubber Co., 10 LAIS 1236 (Williams, 1983) (report from company doctor was much more complete than the statement by the employee's doctor and therefore given greater weight).

prescribed laboratory and clinical procedures, should supersede the company doctor's opinion which was based primarily upon medical opinion. The arbitrator further held the company has a duty to consider all relevant and reliable medical evidence in making termination decisions.[95] As the arbitrator noted:

> On the other hand it would appear that the Company's conclusions were based primarily on medical opinion—an opinion which was based upon implications drawn from a given set of medical facts. The key point is that the Company's opinion was not based on laboratory or clinical procedures. In fact, and most damaging to the Company's case, at no time did its medical staff examine W___ and apply certain medical tests and proofs which were necessary to support its conclusions, or in the alternative to engage a third qualified medical expert to ascertain the facts and report his findings.[96]

Similarly, an arbitrator found unreasonable a company's determination that an employee was not physically fit to return to work where the opinions of the employee's doctor and the company's doctor were in conflict and the company's doctor did not make an adequate examination or perform tests to establish minimum medical facts.[97]

While the opinion of the employee's doctor is usually given greater credence, that is because of the doctor's familiarity with the employee, as reflected in the report. Where the employee's doctor does not provide a report that shows this familiarity, it may carry less weight than the company doctor's report.[98]

5. *Knowledge of Job Requirements.*   The testimony of the grievant's physician about the employee's medical condition is generally given greater weight than the company physician's testimony. Conversely, the company doctor's testimony concerning the physical and mental demands placed upon the employee by a particular job environment usually carries more weight. This evidence is often crucial in cases involving the grievant's ability to do a physically demanding job. As one arbitrator observed:

> The proper use of this power will be evident if the facts in a particular case show that management's action was taken in good faith, was based on reasonably adequate medical testimony and evidence, and was not taken against a background that would indicate a discriminatory purpose. If these facts exist, there is a presumption of validity that favors

---

[95]Mobil Oil Corp., 81 LA 1090 (Taylor, 1983). Accord Town of Berlin, 80-2 ARB ¶ 8478 (Emerzian, 1980).

[96]Mobil Oil Corp., 81 LA 1090, 1094–95 (Taylor, 1983).

[97]Chicago Transit Auth., 84 LA 279 (Fletcher, 1985). This decision thus places the burden on the employer, in determining that an employee is not fit to return to duty, to make an adequate examination and administer tests to establish medical facts or otherwise be held liable for back pay during the period the employee is off work.

[98]Environmental Elements Corp., 82-1 ARB ¶ 8072 (Dunn, 1981).

the plant physician's medical testimony. This presumption arises out of the fact that the plant physician has a knowledge of both the employee's health and the job conditions.[99]

*6. Interests of the Physician.*   Occasionally, the arbitrator will disregard a doctor's opinion because there is evidence suggesting the doctor's opinion is biased. In one case the employer properly refused sick pay to an employee who did not provide adequate medical evidence of her disability. The arbitrator noted that while the employee submitted a memo from her personal physician stating she was disabled, the same physician had previously provided a statement to the effect the employee was capable of performing the job during the same period of time.[100]

*7. Chiropractic Evidence.*   Arbitrators have exhibited a good deal of individuality regarding the weight afforded chiropractic testimony and related evidence. In one case, an arbitrator concluded the company improperly terminated an employee as the result of 2 days of "unexcused absence." According to the arbitrator, the company wrongfully deemed the absences unexcused because the employee produced a note from his chiropractor's son, who was also a chiropractor. The arbitrator concluded that since the company had previously accepted a chiropractor's note verifying an illness, it should have accepted the notes in issue as verification of illness.[101] In another case, the arbitrator upheld a grievance where the employer categorically rejected as inadequate proof of illness a chiropractor's verification of unfitness for duty, holding past practice bound the company to accept suitable chiropractic certificates.[102]

In a similar light, one arbitrator even held spiritual treatment by a church pastor qualified the employee for sickness and accident benefits for the time she was absent from work for skin poisoning. Although the payment of these benefits depended upon treatment by a fully qualified physician, the company had accepted statements from the employee's pastor on two prior occasions. Thus, the arbitrator found the benefits payable.[103]

---

[99]International Shoe Co., 14 LA 253, 255 (Wallen, 1950), quoted in A. Wilson, "Medical Evidence in Arbitration: Aspects and Dilemmas," 39 Arb. J. 11 (Sept., 1984). Arbitrators have likewise been reluctant to hold employers responsible for good faith errors in diagnosing employee ailments. See Miles Labs., Inc., 83-1 ARB ¶ 8052 (Light, 1982).

[100]International Shoe Co., 14 LA 253 (Wallen, 1950), quoted in A. Wilson, "Medical Evidence in Arbitration: Aspects and Dilemmas," 39 Arb. J. 11 (Sept., 1984). Arbitrators have likewise been reluctant to hold employers responsible for good faith errors in diagnosing employee ailments. See Miles Labs., Inc., 83-1 ARB ¶ 8052 (Light, 1982).

[101]Boise Cascade Corp., 77 LA 28 (Fogelberg, 1981). Similarly, where an employer accepted a chiropractor's statements for medical insurance purposes, an arbitrator held it was unreasonable not to receive such statements for attendance purposes. Haws Corp., 81-2 ARB ¶ 8381 (Garman, 1981). Contra Champion Int'l Corp., 81-1 ARB ¶ 8218 (Johnson, Jr., 1981).

[102]Consolidation Coal Co., 83 LA 1158 (J. Duff, 1984). Contra Fran Jom, Inc., 75 LA 97 (Siegel, 1980), holding that the term "physician," as used in a sick-leave provision, meant medical doctor.

[103]Minnesota Mining & Mfg. Co., 81-2 ARB ¶ 8326 (Maslanka, 1981).

   8. *The Neutral Medical Examiner.*   Where conflicting medical evidence is presented, many arbitrators have upheld the use of a neutral medical opinion as determinative of the medical issue. In one dispute, the arbitrator ruled the conflict between two doctors' opinions regarding the physical condition of an employee with respect to sickness and accident benefits should have been resolved, pursuant to the agreement, by a third, neutral doctor.[104] Similarly, an arbitrator held that resorting to a third, neutral doctor's opinions was controlling where the employee's physician and the company's physician were in disagreement regarding the question whether the employee was permanently disabled within the meaning of a disability retirement provision.[105]

   Resort to a neutral physician has been ordered even where not required by the agreement. Thus, in one case, while not specified in the agreement, an arbitrator, after finding that just cause did not exist for the grievant's discharge, ordered as a remedy that the parties select a "mutually acceptable and suitable expert medical source or facility" and have the grievant undergo examination to determine whether he had sufficiently recovered from his injury to return to work.[106]

   The neutral medical opinion must still meet the normal requirements for reliability. In a case where the contract required a third, neutral doctor's opinion which would be "final," an arbitrator weighed the neutral doctor's opinion. The arbitrator concluded the doctor's report did not meet the contractual standard of finding the grievant "not able to safely perform the required work," since it was unspecific with respect to the job under scrutiny and used the phrases "moderately heavy lifting" and "excessive bending," which did not give the parties a standard they could apply to each job in question.[107]

   A neutral doctor's opinion may not resolve the dispute. For instance, in a case where the company and employee doctors disagreed over when an employee could have returned to work, the neutral doctor was unable retroactively to determine when the employee had previously recovered. Consequently, the arbitrator resorted to the employee's previous admissions in an EEOC hearing regarding when she was able to return to work to resolve the dispute, since this evidence did not conflict with the neutral doctor's opinion.[108]

---

   [104]Kelsey-Hayes Co., 83 LA 21 (Keefe, 1984). See also Peterson Spring Corp., 74 LA 744 (Keefe, 1980) (use of a third, neutral physician where the grievant's ability to return to work following treatments for coronary heart disease was in question); Dwyer Instruments, Inc., 74 LA 668 (Greco, 1980) (employer could have cleared up any questions regarding a grievant's medical condition by referring grievant to a third doctor in accordance with past practice).

   [105]Armstrong Rubber Co., 76 LA 749 (Williams, 1981). See also Turbodyne Corp., 80 LA 846 (Stevens, 1983); Greyhound Lines, Inc., 10 LAIS 1154 (Kelliher, 1983); Armstrong Rubber Co., 74 LA 362 (Williams, 1980).

   [106]Alton Packaging Corp., 83 LA 1318 (Talent, 1984).

   [107]Manufacturing Co., 82 LA 614 (Ray, 1984).

   [108]Teledyne Monarch Rubber, 83-2 ARB ¶ 8544 (Ipavec, 1983).

Conflicting medical opinions may arise between an employee's doctor and the company insurance carrier's doctor. In one case the employee's doctor had given the employee a restricted release to return to work, but the company would not reinstate the grievant until he was given an unrestricted release. A disability insurance carrier doctor, however, had earlier given the grievant a full release for the purpose of disability benefits. The arbitrator held the contract provided for the use of a third-party doctor in such instances and ordered the parties to submit the issue of the grievant's disability to a third-party doctor. The company was to provide back pay if it was shown the grievant was not disabled at the time he attempted reinstatement.[109]

## VII. Handwriting Analysis

Handwriting analysis (graphology) has emerged as one of the areas where arbitrators will rely upon the opinion of an expert to determine how much weight to give to evidence.[110] For example, in *Schlage Lock Co.,*[111] the arbitrator concluded that the evidence establishing the grievant as the author/writer of an anonymous note concerning a co-worker and an anonymous letter to the co-worker's husband was "overwhelming." The arbitrator's conclusion was based in large part on the fact that two acknowledged handwriting and document analysis experts provided an "elaborate and thorough analysis of the note and letter with company-provided exemplars of the grievant's handwriting."[112]

Arbitrators do not, however, require that both parties concur on the qualifications of a document examiner before accepting the evidence. To the contrary, arbitral authority suggests that so long as the examiner (1) is qualified by the arbitrator as an expert, (2) renders an opinion that is within the state of the art of the examiner's field of expertise, and (3) establishes that the examiner's methodology is sound and the analysis in-depth, comprehensive, and clear, the examiner's testimony will be persuasive and credited by the arbitrator.[113]

---

[109]Milgram Food Stores, Inc., 12 LAIS 1060 (Thornell, 1984).

[110]Schlage Lock Co., 88 LA 75, 77 (Wyman, 1986) ("As a complete novice in the art, skill, science, craft, profession—or whatever appellation appropriately describes the activity of those whose work involves establishing or authenticating whether or not a written, typed or printed specimen of language is attributable to a specific person—the arbitrator's indoctrination into the process by the specialists was sufficient for him to conclude that they are involved in something considerable [sic] more exact than occult. He was, in fact, convinced that the handwriting experts were quite capable of reaching incontestable conclusions.").

[111]Id.

[112]Id. at 77. The arbitrator also was influenced by the fact that the union-retained handwriting consultant was not put on the witness stand by the union.

[113]Id.

Where the document examiner is qualified as an expert, the examiner's conclusive determination will be accorded great weight when it corroborates testimonial or other evidence presented at the hearing. In *Protection Technology Los Alamos*,[114] the testimony of a police captain, together with the corroborating testimony of a handwriting specialist, persuaded the arbitrator that the grievance was untimely, since the initials on the grievance were made by someone other than the police captain.

Where persuasive handwriting analysis evidence is not refuted, arbitrators tend to place greater reliance on the conclusions reached by the handwriting expert.[115] On the other hand, where a document examiner concludes that the results of an examination are "inconclusive," many arbitrators will view the document in question in the light most favorable to the party challenging the authenticity of the document. This is especially true in discharge cases.[116]

## VIII. Circumstantial Evidence

In a discharge or discipline case, the most convincing evidence is often the testimony of an eyewitness who can affirm, "I saw what happened." In many cases, however, no such direct evidence is available. Where the discharge is for theft, instigation of a strike, sabotage, or tampering with company equipment, circumstantial evidence will almost always be the only evidence available. Where there are no eyewitnesses, the arbitrator must draw inferences to identify the culprit.[117]

Evidence is circumstantial when an inference needs to be made from the facts presented in order to establish a relevant fact.[118] In both civil and criminal judicial proceedings, circumstantial evidence is admissible, at least in the absence of direct, eyewitness evidence.[119]

---

[114]104 LA 23 (Finston, 1994).

[115]Peninsular Steel Co., 88 LA 391, 392 (Ipavec, 1986) (the assertion that the grievant has African-American friends does not refute the results of the handwriting analysis which conclusively established the grievant as the author of the portion of the note reading "Go to hell, neger [sic]"; Schlage Lock Co., 88 LA 75 (Wyman, 1975) (the failure of the union to put its retained handwriting consultant on the witness stand to dispute the findings of the company's consultants also persuaded the arbitrator that the grievant authored the documents in question).

[116]Mississippi Power Co., 90 LA 220 (Jewett, 1987) (because the results of an examination of the grievant's handwriting were inconclusive, the arbitrator declined to hold him accountable for endorsing the document in question, reinstated the grievant, and ordered that he be made whole in every respect).

[117]See Koven, Smith & Farwell, Just Cause: The Seven Tests, 2d ed., 270–71 (BNA Books, 1992), for general discussion of such cases.

[118]Derine v. Delano, 272 Ill. 166, 179, 111 N.E. 249 (1916); 31 C.J.S. Evidence §2 (1964).

[119]31A C.J.S. Evidence §161 (1964).

Arbitrators generally regard circumstantial evidence as fully admissible, and evaluate its weight. A tripartite panel reporting to the 19th annual meeting of the National Academy of Arbitrators concluded that circumstantial evidence may have as much probative value as testimonial or direct evidence. The panel recommended that it be received and considered in the context of all evidence offered and given such weight as it may deserve.[120]

A second panel reporting to this meeting viewed circumstantial evidence quite positively, stating:

> Since "direct" evidence may be falsified due to the commission of perjury by witnesses, it is not necessarily more probative than circumstantial evidence. Indeed, the latter may be more reliable than so-called "direct" evidence to the degree that close reasoning by inference in a particular situation may actually weave a tighter factual web often less subject to the diversion of doubts of credibility than is true where reliance must be had solely on the "I seed him do it" kind of direct evidence.[121]

Arbitrators have exhibited substantial agreement with these panel reports in published awards.[122]

# IX. Credibility

When two witnesses having personal knowledge of the facts testify in conflict, the arbitrator must address witness credibility. It is quite common in discharge and discipline cases for the grievant's version of events to differ markedly from that of his supervisor. If there is no other corroboration for either witness, how is the arbitrator to resolve the question?

[120]Problems of Proof in Arbitration, Proceedings of the 19th Annual Meeting of NAA, 98 (BNA Books, 1967).

[121]Id. at 192.

[122]Southwestern Bell Tel. Co., 84 LA 583 (Penfield, 1985) (suspension of computer operator for entering disruptive and unauthorized commands upheld on circumstantial evidence that grievant had access to work station and no one other than grievant had the necessary skill or access at time of entry of commands); Soule Steel Co., 84 LA 336 (Richman, 1985) (discharge rescinded where circumstantial evidence established co-employee was operator of crane that fell); Wisconsin Dep't of Health & Soc. Servs., 84 LA 219, 223 (Imes, 1985) ("In order for the Employer to meet the burden of proof that the grievant was guilty of patient abuse, however, the evidence must be credible enough to sustain the conclusion arrived at on the basis of the circumstantial evidence."); American Motors Corp., 52 LA 709 (Keefe, 1969) (discharge for theft upheld where employee had company property in his locker, was seen placing pail of salable liquid in locker, and refused to permit inspection of his thermos at plant gate); Lone Star Steel Co., 48 LA 949 (Jenkins, 1967) (determination of company that eight disciplined employees engaged in illegal concerted work stoppage upheld without direct evidence where arbitrator found circumstances of call-ins of absence for purportedly legitimate reasons to be circumstantially pretextual); Brown Shoe Co., 16 LA 461 (Klamon, 1951) (gambling discharge approved despite inability of supervisor to observe grievants who were overheard in dice game on company premises during working hours and grievants could not account for their whereabouts, having previously been warned twice about shooting dice on company time).

One arbitrator took the position that the supervisor must be believed because the employee has a vested interest in protecting his job, whereas the supervisor has nothing to gain or lose.[123] This viewpoint has been cited and followed in numerous cases.[124]

This approach is not universally accepted, however, and has been flatly rejected by some arbitrators.[125] A less mechanical and more analytical approach to the question of credibility can be found in more recent awards. One arbitrator proposed a checklist for evaluating the reliability of the witness and the testimony:

1. **The demeanor of the witness.** Does the witness appear nervous and hesitant or confident and unflinching?

2. **The character of the testimony.** Is the testimony specific and detailed or evasive and conclusionary? Are there inconsistencies present? Is there anything to impeach the witness's perception? Does the witness's recollection of the matter appear precise or does he appear confused regarding facts he initially remembered? [Is there substantiating documentation?]

3. **The self-interest of the witness.** Is there any reason why the outcome of the arbitration would benefit the witness and therefore bias his testimony or motivate him to lie?[126]

Another arbitrator has proposed a similar, but more extensive list of criteria, including:

(1) The relative strength of [witness] recollections, (2) consistency [over time], (3) consistency with prior statements made * * * in other forums, (4) evident bias or prejudice, (5) evident motivations to misrepresent known facts, (6) obvious emotional stress during examination, (7) other evident feelings * * * that would ordinarily impair a careful and accurate response to questions asked, (8) refusals to respond without acceptable reasons or evident evasiveness in responses given, (9) the quality of testimony considered in its entirety, (10) corroborating testimony of other witnesses, (11) the reasonableness of testimony considered in its entirety and in relation to other credible testimony offered, and (12) any other factors which, in the opinion of the Arbitrator, tend to strengthen or weaken the credibility or reliability of testimony.[127]

---

[123]Ford Motor Co., 1 ALAA 67244, 67620 (1954). See also Stessin, Employee Discipline, 44 (BNA Books 1960); Koven, Smith & Farwell, Just Cause: The Seven Tests, 2d ed., 272–73 (BNA Books, 1992).

[124]See Maui Pineapple Co., 86 LA 907, 909 (Tsukiyama, 1986); Motor Transp. Co., 76 LA 958, 960 (Talent, 1981); Lake Orion Community Sch., 73 LA 707, 710 (Roumell, 1979); Riley-Stoker Co., 63 LA 581, 584 (Shister, 1974); United Parcel Serv., Inc., 66-2 ARB ¶ 8703 (Dolson, 1966); Western Condensing Co., 37 LA 912, 914 (Mueller, 1962).

[125]See Cincinnati Paperboard Corp., 93 LA 505, 510 (Dworkin, 1989). Critics of the Shulman rationale consider self-interest of the grievant to be only one factor to be weighed in determining the overall issue of credibility. See Mittenthal, "The Search for Truth: II. Credibility—A Will o'-the-Wisp," in Truth, Lie Detectors, and Other Problems in Labor Arbitration, Proceedings of the 31st Annual Meeting of NAA (BNA Books, 1979).

[126]Parsons Contractors, 91 LA 73, 76 (DiLauro, 1988).

[127]Safeway Stores, 96 LA 304, 310 (Coyle, 1990).

While these checklists have not been widely adopted by other arbitrators, when testimony is deemed unreliable, it is usually because of one or more of these factors. Some arbitrators have refused to sustain a grievance where the disciplinary action was based solely on the unsupported testimony of an undercover agent.[128] But where the undercover agent is particularly credible because of the accuracy of his testimony and his past experience, the arbitrator may uphold the discipline imposed.[129]

## X. Res Judicata and Collateral Estoppel Effect of Other Proceedings

### A. *General Principles*

When an issue presented to a labor arbitrator has been previously litigated in another forum, the arbitrator must determine the effect of the prior decision.[130] The other forum may have been a criminal court, civil court, administrative agency, or another labor arbitration proceeding. When a decision has been made by another tribunal prior to the labor arbitration, the arbitrator may invoke the legal concepts of res judicata and collateral estoppel to determine the proper effect to give prior decisions. The underlying purpose of these doctrines is to foster judicial economy by not requiring a party to repeatedly litigate an issue or claim that has already been decided.[131] It is important to note, however, that these concepts are not necessarily applied in labor arbitration to the same extent that they are applied in the court system, since the basis and purpose of the two systems differ. Labor arbitration is based upon the collective bargaining agreement. Thus, an intervening change in the relevant contract language may permit arbitration of a claim that is identical to one previously decided. Part of the purpose of labor arbitration is to provide a forum for disputes that would otherwise interfere with workplace efficiency. Consequently, notions of "judicial economy" may be secondary to workplace efficiency or labor-management relations. Since the parties bear the cost of arbitration, "judicial economy" is a less compelling principle. A dispute that might be barred in litigation may nonetheless be arbitrated.

---

[128]Pacific Bell, 87 LA 313 (Schubert, 1986); A.R.A. Mfg. Co., 83 LA 580 (Canestraight, 1984); Pettibone Ohio Corp., 72 LA 1144 (Feldman, 1979).

[129]Consumer Plastics Corp., 88 LA 208 (Garnholz, 1987).

[130]See Chapter 14 for discussion of judicial treatment of inconsistent arbitral awards as well as the effect of prior arbitration decisions.

[131]Aircraft Workers Alliance, 99 LA 585, 596 (Sharpe, 1992).

## B. Res Judicata[132]

The purpose of the doctrine of res judicata is to prevent the relitigation of a claim that has been finally litigated in a previous proceeding involving the same parties. Due to the preclusive effect of res judicata, its application is limited to cases where the parties, issues, and causes of action are identical. Additionally, the prior decision must have been a final determination on the merits of the case.[133] Res judicata has been described as a "judicial doctrine universally recognized which forbids retrial of matters which have been previously definitely settled by a binding decision."[134]

Res judicata may also apply to prevent the litigation of a claim that could have been made in an earlier action but was not raised at that time.[135] Res judicata mandates that parties present in one action all claims for relief arising out of the same transaction. Conversely, if a claim for relief is presented that could not have been litigated in a previous proceeding, res judicata cannot be applied.

One concept used to decide whether res judicata is properly applicable to a claim is to determine whether rights established in the first action would be destroyed or impaired by the prosecution of the second action. If these previously established rights would be destroyed or impaired, res judicata is applicable to the subsequent proceeding.[136]

In labor arbitration, res judicata is raised most often where one party argues that the claim being asserted in a case has been finally decided in a prior arbitration. The concept of voluntary labor arbitration requires that issues that have been resolved in arbitration not be overturned in later proceedings, unless some compelling reasons exist for overturning the earlier decision.[137] Where the elements of res judicata are met, some arbitrators adopt a prior arbitration decision, even if they believe the first decision is incorrect, so long as they do not believe the first decision is clearly erroneous.[138]

---

[132]Res judicata should not be confused with the doctrine of stare decisis, which provides that a case decided on similar facts, but with different parties, may have persuasive value as precedent. Stare decisis is a legal concept that is not strictly applicable in labor arbitration but may be effectively used, in appropriate circumstances, to illustrate that a particular theory has been accepted by other arbitrators. See Safeway, Inc., 104 LA 102, 107 (Nelson, 1994).

[133]Webster Cent. Sch. Dist., 80 LA 1138 (Brand, 1983).

[134]Timken Roller Bearing Co., 32 LA 595, 597 (Boehm, 1958).

[135]See Aircraft Workers Alliance, 99 LA 585, 596 (Sharpe, 1992), citing Moore's Federal Practice and Procedure, ¶¶ 0.410[1], 0.441[2], at pp. 359, 729.

[136]Webster Cent. Sch. Dist., 80 LA 1138 (Brand, 1983).

[137]Mead Corp., 43 LA 391, 394 (Halley, 1964). See also Wolverine Aluminum Corp., 74 LA 252, 255 (Dobry, 1980) (arbitrator must give consideration to prior arbitration decisions based on same agreement if on point, even though arbitrator is not technically bound by prior decisions).

[138]Hoosier Energy Rural Elec. Coop., Inc., 80 LA 1146, 1148 (Seidman, 1983).

In one case, an employee was discharged for falsifying the extent of her work-related injury. At the hearing on her discharge, the arbitrator admitted evidence of threats that the employee allegedly made to co-workers, even though the threats were not directly related to her discharge. The arbitrator's award reinstated the employee without back pay. The employer complied with the award and reinstated the employee. However, shortly thereafter, the employer discharged her on the basis of the threats, which had been made prior to the first arbitration. In the second arbitration hearing, the employer argued that the first decision was not res judicata because the first arbitrator's award did not state that the threats were the reason for discharge. The second arbitrator rejected this argument and found that the first arbitration award was res judicata. The arbitrator found that the requirements of res judicata were met, in that the cases involved the same parties, the same or an intrinsically related offense, and the same facts. In addition, the arbitrator noted that there was no evidence of any changed circumstances.[139]

### C. *Collateral Estoppel*

Collateral estoppel is a legal doctrine that precludes the relitigation of a specific issue that has been decided in a prior action between the parties.[140] If a factual issue has been litigated and decided, collateral estoppel prevents the relitigation of the issue at a later time in another proceeding.[141] In order for collateral estoppel to apply, the issue determined in the first action must have been essential to that judgment and must have been determined by a valid and final judgment.[142]

The doctrine of collateral estoppel can be applied based on a final judgment made in either a prior arbitration decision or in another type of proceeding. In general, arbitrators are reluctant to apply collateral estoppel unless the circumstances clearly warrant the application of the doctrine and the application would not unduly prejudice either party.

In one case, an arbitrator refused to give collateral estoppel effect to the finding of another arbitrator, even though both cases involved the same union and employer. The employee in the later case had

---

[139]Rohm & Haas Tex., 106 LA 275 (Caraway, 1996). See also W.R. Grace & Co. v. Rubber Workers Local 759, 652 F.2d 1248, 107 LRRM 3251 (5th Cir., 1981), aff'd, 461 U.S. 757, 113 LRRM 2641 (1983).

[140]Bayshore Concrete Prods. Co., 92 LA 311, 315 (Hart, 1989) (arbitrator refused to apply collateral estoppel where the first arbitration involved a different union, reasoning that the employees in the second case would be denied due process because they had not been represented by their own union in the first arbitration).

[141]Aircraft Workers Alliance, 99 LA 585, 599 (Sharpe, 1992).

[142]Fairweather's Practice and Procedure in Labor Arbitration, 3d ed., Schoonhoven, ed., 233 (BNA Books, 1991).

been discharged for theft and, in the related criminal prosecution, evidence of items found in the grievant's trunk was excluded, due to a violation of criminal procedure. In a prior case involving the same employer and union (but a different employee), an arbitrator had concluded that criminal law exclusionary rules were applicable to the workplace. The second arbitrator refused to follow the ruling of the previous arbitrator as to the exclusion of evidence. He concluded that the prior decision was clearly erroneous on this issue, as it was contrary to established legal and arbitral principles, which provide that exclusionary rules of criminal law do not automatically apply in arbitration proceedings.[143]

## D.  Effect of Determinations of Administrative Tribunals

Occasionally, an administrative agency will render a final decision on an issue that is in dispute in an arbitration hearing. This occurs most frequently with claims for unemployment compensation, discrimination, and workers' compensation. Arbitrators usually do not consider findings or decisions of administrative agencies as having either res judicata or collateral estoppel effect.

When an employee is discharged, he or she will often apply for unemployment compensation benefits. A state agency must determine whether an employee was discharged for just cause, based on the applicable state statute. A finding that an employee was discharged for just cause will result in a denial of unemployment compensation benefits, either for a fixed period of time or until requalification requirements are met.

Often, the same evidence is presented to both the state unemployment compensation tribunal and the labor arbitrator. However, arbitrators have universally refused to give res judicata or collateral estoppel effect to decisions of unemployment compensation tribunals.[144] In addition, some states have enacted statutes that prohibit the use of unemployment compensation determinations in other proceedings.[145]

---

[143]Alden's, Inc., 61 LA 663, 666 (Dolnick, 1973).

[144]Grinnell Corp., 92 LA 124, 127 (Kilroy, 1989); Bon Secours Hosp., Inc., 76 LA 705, 709 (Feldesman, 1981) (decision by unemployment compensation appeals referee not binding because union was not a party to the hearing and the collective bargaining agreement was not considered by the referee). See also "Discipline, Discharge, External Law and Procedure—Roundtable Discussion," in Arbitration 1995: New Challenges and Expanding Responsibilities, Proceedings of the 48th Annual Meeting of NAA, Najita, ed., 227, 249 (BNA Books, 1996).

[145]Anderson Clayton Corp., 105 LA 807, 812 (Herring, 1995) (unemployment compensation decision may not be used in arbitration proceeding pursuant to California Unemployment Insurance Code §1960). See, for example, Ohio Revised Code §4141.28(S), which states, in part: "No * * * decision [concerning unemployment compensation benefits] * * * shall be given collateral estoppel or res judicata effect in any subsequent * * * arbitration proceeding * * *."

The union usually is not a party to the unemployment compensation proceedings, and the statutory definitions found in the various state unemployment compensation statutes are not equivalent to the "just cause" standard found in collective bargaining agreements. As stated by one arbitrator: "While judicial statements of the meaning of the just cause statutory standard have a familiar ring to contract readers, that standard comes from a different jurisprudential source."[146] The arbitrator also points out that res judicata is not applicable as the parties could not have obtained all the relief through the unemployment compensation proceedings that they could attain through arbitration.[147]

Arbitrators apply similar reasoning in refusing to give res judicata or collateral estoppel effect to decisions of workers' compensation and employment discrimination tribunals. One arbitrator found that a decision of a workers' compensation tribunal, which concluded that the grievant was 56 percent disabled, was not determinative of his physical capacity to work. The arbitrator noted that, although the same issues were present, one finding was not determinative of the other.[148] In a case where the EEOC found that the employer had not discriminated against the grievant, the arbitrator concluded that the finding was not binding. The arbitrator reasoned that the EEOC decision was based on public law, while the arbitrator's decision must be based on the terms of the collective bargaining agreement, and the collective bargaining agreement did not provide that EEOC determinations were controlling.[149]

## E. Criminal Proceedings

When an employee has been disciplined or discharged for an infraction that also results in criminal charges, the outcome of the criminal case is often offered as evidence at the labor arbitration hearing. While most arbitrators will allow the introduction of evidence of criminal proceedings, the result of a criminal charge is seldom accepted as conclusive evidence of the issue before the labor arbitrator. Because criminal law requires that charges be proven "beyond a reasonable doubt," most arbitrators will give limited collateral estoppel effect to a criminal conviction by accepting the conviction as evidence that a certain offense has been committed. However, the issue of

---

[146]Aircraft Workers Alliance, 99 LA 585, 596 (Sharpe, 1992).

[147]Id.

[148]Zellerbach Paper Co., 68 LA 69, 71 (Stashower, 1977). See also Kaiser Steel Corp., 68 LA 192, 195 (Christopher, 1977).

[149]American Fuel Cell & Coated Fabrics Co., 97 LA 1045 (Nicholas, 1991).

whether just cause for discipline exists remains to be determined by the arbitrator. In making a just cause determination, the arbitrator will consider the criminal conviction, along with other evidence presented at the arbitration hearing. For example, an arbitrator found that a grievant's conviction on a misdemeanor charge of sexual misconduct was not sufficient evidence to disqualify him from employment as a police officer.[150]

In a similar vein, arbitrators will consider the circumstances surrounding a guilty plea to determine the proper weight to give to the plea. In one recent case, a grievant argued that she was innocent, but pleaded guilty to petty theft in order to obtain a more favorable judgment that would help her to obtain other employment. The arbitrator rejected her explanation, concluding that she knew what she was doing when she entered the plea of guilty. In addition, the arbitrator found that the evidence presented at the hearing showed that she was guilty.[151]

Arbitrators do not regard an acquittal on criminal charges as conclusive evidence of innocence. The burden of proof required in a criminal trial generally exceeds the burden required in labor arbitration. Therefore, arbitrators will usually make their own determination of guilt by considering the evidence presented at the hearing, even though the same evidence was also presented in a trial that resulted in an acquittal on the criminal charges.[152] The arbitrator's decision will be based on the evidence presented at the arbitration hearing, rather than upon a conclusion reached in the criminal justice system. The same reasoning applies when criminal charges are dismissed or when the government decides not to prosecute a case.[153]

An additional reason for not giving binding effect to the outcome of a criminal case is that the strict rules of evidence found in criminal proceedings are not applicable to labor arbitration.[154] Therefore, evidence that could not be used in the criminal trial may be presented to an arbitrator. For example, an arbitrator found that the failure to advise the grievant of his *Miranda*[155] rights does not prevent enforcement of a work rule prohibiting possession of drugs.[156]

---

[150]City of St. Paul, Minn., 101 LA 265 (Neigh, 1993); see also King Co., 89 LA 681, 687 (result of criminal proceedings not binding on arbitrator).

[151]Albertson's, Inc., 106 LA 166, 170 (DiFalco, 1996).

[152]AT&T, 102 LA 931, 933 (Kanner, 1994) (acquittal of grievant on criminal charges will not be given any cognizance by arbitrator); United Parcel Serv., 67 LA 861 (Lubow, 1976).

[153]City of St. Petersburg, 104 LA 594, 596 (Thornell, 1995); Dannon Milk Prods., 76 LA 133 (Kramer, 1980).

[154]Aldens, Inc., 61 LA 663, 667 (Dolnick, 1973) (arbitrator is not prohibited from considering evidence that was rejected by criminal court on the basis that it was illegally obtained).

[155]Miranda v. Arizona, 384 U.S. 436 (1966).

[156]Dunlop Tire Corp., 104 LA 653, 659 (Teple, 1995).

## XI. New Evidence

Sometimes evidence is offered at an arbitration hearing that had not been disclosed at the earlier stages of the grievance process.[157] Whether it will be accepted depends on the "need for all the facts relevant to the case, the need to protect the integrity of the grievance procedure, [and] general notions of fairness."[158]

New evidence generally presents itself in one of two forms. First, there is evidence existing at the time of discharge but not discovered until after the discharge. The grievance investigation may reveal facts existing, but unknown to the employer, at the time of discharge. This is called after-acquired evidence. The second form of new evidence, postdischarge conduct, does not exist at the time of discharge. The evidence is truly new in that it relates to occurrences after the discharge. Arbitrators use similar considerations to decide whether after-acquired or postdischarge evidence will be accepted.

Some contracts prohibit evidence presented for the first time at the arbitration hearing from being admitted; others limit investigation after initial discharge or require listing all reasons supporting discharge in a dismissal letter.[159] In the absence of an applicable contractual provision, the treatment of after-acquired evidence is left to the arbitrator's discretion.

### A. After-Acquired Evidence

After-acquired evidence often relates to résumé or application fraud, but it can involve any other employee conduct prior to the discharge that is not discovered until after the discharge. After-acquired evidence often is not directly related to the reasons for discharge. For example, the employee may have been discharged for absenteeism, but the employer wants to present after-acquired evidence of application fraud. Employers argue that if they had been aware of this after-acquired evidence, they would never have hired the employee in the first place. Or they would have immediately discharged the employee upon learning of the evidence. Because after-acquired evidence often will not be directly related to the reasons for discharge, arbitrators have demonstrated reluctance to allow the use of such evidence in a hearing on the discharge.[160]

---

[157]See Volz & Goggins, eds., Elkouri & Elkouri, How Arbitration Works, 5th ed., 414–19 (BNA Books, 1997) for a discussion of failure to reveal evidence before the hearing.

[158]Id. at 414.

[159]Id. at 416.

[160]Giant Eagle Mkts. Co., 101 LA 581 (Zobrak, 1993) (evidence of application fraud by failing to list two prior convictions for felonies not considered in discharge for matters related to drug sale because charge of falsification was not raised in termination letter).

After-acquired evidence is frequently raised as a defense to liability in employment discrimination cases. In *Summers v. State Farm Mutual Automobile Insurance Co.,*[161] the employee alleged discriminatory discharge on the basis of age and religion. The employer asserted the discharge was for an unprofessional attitude. During trial preparation, the employer learned the employee falsified documents, after having been previously disciplined for such conduct. The Tenth Circuit upheld the district court's grant of summary judgment for the employer, asserting that after-acquired evidence of fraud "preclude[s] the grant of any present relief or remedy."[162]

In *McKennon v. Nashville Banner Publishing Co.,*[163] the Supreme Court considered whether an employee discharged in violation of the Age Discrimination in Employment Act is barred from all relief if the employer later discovers evidence that would have led to a lawful, legitimate termination. The Court held that the after-acquired evidence was not a complete bar to relief. If the employer can prove the severity of the act would have led to discharge, the after-acquired evidence will usually bar front pay and reinstatement, while allowing back pay from the date of unlawful discharge to the date the evidence was discovered.

The application of the doctrine of after-acquired evidence in a labor arbitration was addressed in *Lenox Hill Hospital.*[164] The discharged employee had also sued under the federal civil rights laws. In that suit the employer discovered that the employee had been discharged from a previous employer. This contradicted the employee's statements on her employment application at Lenox Hill. The employer asked the arbitrator to deny any remedy to the employee and dismiss the grievance based on after-acquired evidence of application fraud.

The arbitrator denied the employer's motion based on arbitral jurisdiction to dispose only of disputes arising out of grievances as defined by the collective bargaining agreement. Application fraud was not part of the conduct for which the employee was discharged and not part of the matter grieved.

> [I]t is not within the authority of this Arbitrator to require the Union to submit to arbitration a matter, which it can be stated with certainty it never agreed to arbitrate, namely adjudication of a dispute concerning the dismissal of an employee for alleged misconduct, which misconduct was not part of the charge against the employee, nor part of the cause for the employee's discharge, and which was not a part of the matter grieved.[165]

[161]864 F.2d 700, 708, 48 FEP Cases 1107 (10th Cir., 1988).
[162]Id.
[163]115 S.Ct. 879, 66 FEP Cases 1192 (1995).
[164]102 LA 1071 (Simons, 1994).
[165]Id. at 1074.

It can be argued, however, that once the employer learns of the after-acquired evidence, another dischargeable offense may occur which may give rise to another grievance proceeding.[166]

After-acquired evidence is more likely to be admitted in arbitration when it is directly related to the dischargeable offense.[167] Such evidence may be discovered during the investigation in connection with the grievance. "As a general rule * * * an employer may investigate further to substantiate facts known to exist at the time of dismissal to support action already taken, as long as an entirely new charge is not added and the discharged employee is given an adequate opportunity to contest [the evidence]."[168] A distinction has been made between evidence gathered after the discharge that supports the reason given for discharge and evidence gathered after a discharge to add an entirely new offense.[169]

When after-acquired evidence is discovered, timing may be a factor in determining whether it will be admitted.[170] The employer cannot know of application fraud and hold it over the employee's head as a potential ironclad excuse for discharge.[171] Indeed, such evidence is not truly after-acquired.

An employer may also be held to a certain level of diligence in investigation before being allowed to use after-acquired evidence. For instance, disciplining an employee and then increasing the penalty after discovering additional evidence that existed when the first penalty was imposed may meet arbitral disapproval for failure to investigate adequately.[172]

## B. Postdischarge Conduct

Postdischarge conduct is new evidence in every sense of the word. It occurred after the discharge. Often the effect of such evidence is

---

[166]Giant Eagle Mkts. Co., 101 LA 581 (Zobrak, 1993) (after-acquired evidence forms separate and independent basis for discharge). See also Alco Chem. Corp., 92 LA 1159 (Groshong, 1989) (postdischarge conduct case; recent instances of misconduct should go through normal grievance procedure).

[167]Growmark, Inc., 100 LA 785 (VerPloeg, 1993) (after-acquired evidence offered by employee admitted where it went to reason for employee's failure to report to work resulting in discharge).

[168]Vermont Dep't of Soc. Welfare, 86 LA 324, 327 (Kemsley, Chair, 1986) (postdischarge conduct case stating evidence adding new offense would violate collective bargaining agreement requiring reasons for discharge to be stated in dismissal letter).

[169]Id.

[170]Southern Minn. Sugar Coop., 90 LA 243 (Flagler, 1987) (offering after-acquired evidence at hearing deprived employee of opportunity to mount fully researched defense).

[171]Weber Truck & Warehouse, 79 LA 738 (Levin, 1982) (time to act was when discovery was made; improper for the employer to continue to hold it over employee's head once it decided to retain him).

[172]Gulf States Paper Corp., 97 LA 60 (Welch, 1991) (no evidence had been secreted or withheld or was unobtainable). But see Utility Trailer Mfg. Co., 85 LA 643 (Brisco, 1985) (23 months to discover false application does not constitute a waiver of employer's right to take action once facts known).

similar to that of after-acquired evidence: to support the discharge
or otherwise limit the employee's remedy. Postdischarge conduct can
also be used by the employee to assist the employee's case.

As a general rule, when evaluating just cause for discipline, arbitrators restrict themselves to considering information that was available to the employer when it imposed its penalty.[173] "The only relevant evidence are the facts which the person making the discharge was in possession of at the time he acted."[174]

Despite the general rule, some arbitrators have held that simply because a party's proof may be "characterized as post-discharge evidence does not preclude its admissibility or lessen its credibility."[175] Postdischarge conduct can sometimes independently justify termination and render the employee unfit for reinstatement.[176] In these cases, the conduct involved is sometimes so closely related to the event resulting in discharge as to be an "extension of that event."[177]

Postdischarge conduct may not be considered to determine the appropriateness of the discharge, but may still be admitted on the issue of reinstatement[178] or some other remedy sought by the employee.

Postdischarge conduct is often an issue in drug- or alcohol-related discharges. The parties seek to submit evidence of the employee's rehabilitation or additional use of drugs or alcohol. Alcohol and drug cases are often an exception to the general rule that postdischarge evidence is not considered relevant.[179] The postdischarge evidence in these cases generally addresses the feasibility of reinstatement.

[173]Davidson Transit Mgmt., Inc., 99 LA 924 (Hart, 1992); Georgia Pac. Corp., 93 LA 754 (Ipavec, 1989).

[174]Borden's Farm Prods., 3 LA 607, 608 (1945).

[175]Group W Cable of Chicago, 93 LA 789, 797 (Fischbach, 1989) (postdischarge evidence closely intertwined with employee's contractual due process rights and management's duty to fully investigate alleged offense leading to discharge). See also AT&T, 102 LA 931 (Kanner, 1994) (allowing subsequently discovered evidence as opposed to subsequently discovered grounds for discharge; employer limited to grounds set forth at time of discharge).

[176]Bib Bear Stores, 90 LA 634 (Ross, 1988) (employee's misconduct following arbitrator's award of reinstatement made further employment intolerable and justified discharge).

[177]Atlantic Southeast Airlines, Inc., 101 LA 511, 514 (Nolan, 1992) (citations omitted).

[178]Davidson Transit Mgmt., Inc., 99 LA 924 (Hart, 1992) (postdischarge evidence considered on remedy of reinstatement and back pay).

[179]See Atlantic Southeast Airlines, Inc., 101 LA 515 (Nolan, 1993) (holding no just cause for original discharge but subsequent act of misconduct ended right to reinstatement and back pay from that point); Atlantic Southeast Airlines, Inc., 101 LA 511 (Nolan, 1992) (allowing postdischarge evidence of positive marijuana use test as pertinent to appropriate remedy but not to merits of original discharge); Westinghouse Elec. Corp., 95 LA 881 (Talarico, 1990) (while normally evidence of postdischarge conduct is not relevant, in a drug use situation, it is in fact extremely relevant if the chance exists that the employee may be reinstated); Aeroquip Corp., Sterling Div., 95 LA 31 (Stieber, 1990) (postdischarge resumption of alcoholism program admissible); Northeast Airlines, Inc., 89 LA 943 (Nicolau, 1984) (postdischarge possibility of recovery from alcoholism is relevant to consideration of remedy of reinstatement); Dahlstrom Mfg. Co., Inc., 78 LA 302 (Gootnick, 1982) (postdischarge effort at alcoholism rehabilitation relevant).

Postdischarge drug or alcohol rehabilitation, however, is not always relevant. The fact that an employee subsequently overcame a drinking problem and held a steady, skilled job did not affect the employer's determination that it had cause to terminate the employee on the date of his misconduct.[180]

At what stage the postdischarge evidence is presented may determine whether the evidence is allowed at all.[181] Postdischarge conduct raised for the first time at the arbitration hearing may not be allowed on the basis of prejudice. Notice to the opposing party of the new evidence and ample opportunity for that party to prepare and raise defenses may be important to its admissibility.[182] Even if postdischarge evidence of misconduct is not allowed at the hearing, it may give rise to a separate dischargeable offense that must go through a subsequent grievance process.[183]

## C. Reopening the Record to Accept New Evidence

Occasionally, new evidence, whether after-acquired or postdischarge conduct, will surface after the arbitration hearing has been held but before the award is issued. Absent a contractual provision, whether the arbitrator may reopen the record is within the arbitrator's discretion. Since the decision to reopen a record is discretionary, it is no surprise arbitrators have varied in their approaches.[184] The strictest view demands a "compelling" reason to reopen a case.[185] The most liberal view holds that "technical rules of evidence" do not apply in arbitration proceedings and that to follow them strictly would distort the collective bargaining relationship.[186]

*Westvaco* sets out the following five-part analysis "grounded in common sense" to determine whether to reopen a record to accept newly discovered evidence:

---

[180]Hyster Co., 74 LA 348 (Cox, 1980).

[181]Group W Cable of Chicago, 93 LA 789 (Fischbach, 1989) (references Fairweather's Practice and Procedure in Labor Arbitration, 2d ed., at 298 (BNA Books, 1984), Fairweather distinguishing surprise evidence from new evidence and noting surprise evidence is evidence held back for tactical purposes or harassment).

[182]Browning-Ferris Indus., 77 LA 289 (Shanker, 1981).

[183]Alco Chem. Corp., 92 LA 1159 (Groshong, 1989) (efforts to reopen hearing for newly discovered evidence may be denied on basis subsequent acts of misconduct present separate incidents of misconduct that must go through normal grievance procedure before being made the subject of a hearing).

[184]Westvaco, Va., Folding Box Div., 91 LA 707, 708 (Nolan, 1988) (provides excellent survey of law and various arbitrators' decisions on subject of reopening hearing to take new evidence).

[185]Id. (citations omitted).

[186]Id. (citations omitted).

1. *The request to reopen the hearing must precede the arbitrator's final award.* * * *
2. *The proffered evidence must not have been available with due diligence at the time of the hearing.* * * *
3. *The proffered evidence must be pertinent.*
4. *The proffered evidence must be likely to affect the outcome.*
5. *Admission of the new evidence must not improperly prejudice the other party.*[187]

The first element is important because once an award has been rendered, the arbitrator is without jurisdiction to act. The second element places the burden of due diligence on the offering party. If the party had, or should have had, the evidence at the time of hearing, failure to introduce it may constitute a waiver of the right to have the evidence considered. Requirements three and four are designed to avoid the cost of reopening the proceeding for collateral or duplicative matters. The fifth element is a key requirement. Arbitrators guard against unfairness to the opposing party.[188] Usually if a party has time to respond to the evidence, including the opportunity to cross-examine new witnesses and present its own rebuttal evidence, there will be no improper prejudice.

---

[187]Id. at 709.
[188]Wells Aluminum Corp., 86 LA 983 (Edward Wies, 1986).

Chapter 12

# Remedies for Inappropriate Discipline

## I. General Considerations

Arbitrators have broad authority to fashion remedies for inappropriate discipline. They are constrained only by the contract and the Supreme Court's admonition that the remedy must draw its "essence" from the collective bargaining agreement.[1] Arbitrators provide remedies for inappropriate discipline—whether it is discharge or some other form of discipline—either because there was no "just cause"[2] or because the employer failed to meet the implicit or explicit procedural due process requirements of the collective bargaining agreement.[3] Remedies for due process violations form a continuum. At one extreme, a glaring failure to meet explicit procedural due process requirements can be so prejudicial to the employee that the arbitrator does not have to consider whether there was substantive just cause before overturning the discipline. At the other extreme, a failure to meet a procedural due process requirement that is implicit in the concept of just cause may be harmless error. Remedies for failure to meet both just cause and procedural due process requirements are discussed below.

The actual remedies arbitrators award for inappropriate discipline vary with the specific circumstances. Arbitrators uniformly hold that an employee who is discharged without just cause is entitled to

---

[1]Steelworkers v. Enterprise Wheel & Car Corp., 363 U.S. 593, 46 LRRM 2423, 2425 (1960).
[2]See Chapter 2.
[3]See Chapter 2.

a "make whole" remedy.[4] The make whole remedy attempts to place the employee in the same position she would have been in if the improper discipline had not occurred. In both discharges and other disciplinary actions the arbitrator may provide "partial relief," ranging from reinstatement with less than full back pay to no reinstatement but some monetary damages. The range of available remedies is quite broad. The nature and breadth of the make whole remedy will be discussed first, followed by the considerations arbitrators use in awarding partial relief.

## A. *Make Whole*

Arbitrators almost uniformly award a make whole remedy where there is no just cause for a discharge. They may also award a make whole remedy where the employer fails to provide procedural due process, even where there might be just cause for discharge or discipline.[5] Whether an arbitrator awards a make whole remedy or partial relief generally depends on the egregiousness of the employer's violation of procedural due process. In *General Dynamics Convair Div.,*[6] the arbitrator found that "deviations from the prescribed due process precautions were so pervasive and blatant" that reinstatement with full back pay was a necessary remedy. Terminated for insubordination, the grievant had disobeyed her supervisor's order to permit an inspection of her car for illegal drugs. The contract required a union representative to be summoned prior to searching an employee's vehicle in the company parking lot. Although an employee who refused to submit to an inspection could not be forcibly detained, the employer's security officers detained the grievant for 2 ½ hours before notifying a union steward. Full make whole relief was awarded because "[o]nly [the grievant's] reinstatement with retroactive compensation will compel adherence to the * * * [contractual] due process procedures and, thereby, assure the integrity of the parties' enforcement program."[7]

---

[4]See W. C. Nabors Co. v. NLRB, 323 F.2d 686, 54 LRRM 2259, 2262 (5th Cir., 1963) ("the 'make whole' concept does not turn on whether the pay was wholly obligatory or gratuitous, but on the restoration of the status quo ante"); International Harvester Co., 15 LA 1, 1 (Steward, 1950) (in the absence of contractual provision to the contrary, make whole relief is the general rule at common law and in the developing law of labor relations).

[5]See Kelsey-Hayes Co., 60 LA 9, 15 (Howlett, 1972), quoting Fleming, The Labor Arbitration Process (Univ. of Ill., 1965) (most arbitrators penalize "failure to comply with contractual procedure, thereby encouraging compliance with it").

[6]95 LA 500, 508 (Jones, 1990).

[7]Id. at 508. See also Bake Rite Rolls, 90 LA 1133 (DiLauro, 1988) (company's failure to afford *Weingarten* rights warranted setting aside discharge and award of reinstatement and full back pay); Osborn & Ulland, Inc., 68 LA 1146, 1151 (Beck, 1977) (employer's failure to investigate sufficiently whether employee in fact breached company rule before imposing discipline violates procedural due process and "is a factor, and in some cases, the only factor, in an arbitrator's refusal to sustain a discharge"); Dubuque, Lorenz, Inc., 66 LA 1245, 1251

In *Monterey Coal Co.,*[8] the grievant had signed a "last-chance agreement" in which he consented to be randomly tested for drugs. If he failed the test, he would be terminated without recourse to the grievance and arbitration provisions of the contract. The grievant thereafter failed the drug test, prompting his termination. In reversing the discharge, the arbitrator concluded that "the company was grievously delinquent in its behavior toward the grievant under the procedural terms of the contract"[9] because it failed to provide proof of just cause, refused to hold a meeting within the time specified by the contract, and refused the grievant's request for arbitration.[10] Accordingly, the arbitrator reinstated the grievant with full back pay and seniority, "not on the basis of the substance of the matter" but because of the employer's procedural failings.[11]

## B. Partial Relief[12]

Where the employer's failure to grant procedural due process was less egregious, or where there are mitigating factors, the arbitrator may grant only partial relief.[13] In *Yellow Cab Cooperative Ass'n,*[14] the employer, a taxicab company, lost its insurance coverage. To obtain replacement coverage, it was required by the carrier to submit its employees' driving records for review. On the basis of their driving records, seven grievants were denied coverage by the insurer, thus prompting the employer to terminate them. The arbitrator found that the employer had denied the grievants due process and ordered partial

---

(Sinicropi, 1976) (grievant discharged without hearing); Fabsteel Co., 62 LA 672, 675 (Gowan, 1974) (employer's failure to "carry the required burden of proof with regard to due process" made it "unnecessary for [arbitrator] to pass upon the merits of Company's reasons for terminating the grievant").

[8]96 LA 457, 459 (Feldman, 1990).

[9]Id. at 460.

[10]Id. at 459.

[11]Id. at 460.

[12]For a fuller discussion of reduction in penalty, see section entitled "Reduction in Penalty," this chapter.

[13]Genesee Packaging, 98 LA 777 (Ellmann, 1992) (reinstatement without back pay ordered where employer discharged grievant for failing to follow leave approval procedure when employer had no one available who could authorize leave); Champion Spark Plug Co., 93 LA 1277, 1283 (Dobry, 1989) (grievant reinstated without back pay where employer "utterly failed in the letter of its contractual charge to give notice in writing"); Capitol Hill Hosp., 93 LA 947, 952 (Jones, 1989) (reinstatement without back pay due to "major flaws" in employer's investigative procedures); Chromalloy Am. Corp., 93 LA 828 (Woolf, 1989) (arbitrator weighed employer's flagrant procedural violations against employee's serious misconduct and awarded back pay with no reinstatement); Phillips 66 Co., 93 LA 707 (Goodstein, 1989) (reinstatement with seniority and fringe benefits but no back pay ordered where employer violated its own rules and procedures); Alpha Beta Co., 91 LA 1225 (Wilmoth, 1988) (remedy of back pay but no reinstatement for employer's premature discharge of employee where employer failed to conduct initial investigation); Safeway Stores, Inc., 64 LA 563 (Gould, 1974) (weighing serious procedural violations with severity of infraction warranted back pay without reinstatement).

[14]102 LA 848, 849 (Watkins, 1993).

relief (short-term reinstatement and full back pay), notwithstanding the grievants' lack of insurance coverage.

Specifically, the arbitrator found that the cab company never investigated its drivers' records or put them on notice that a poor driving record would jeopardize their employment, nor did it explore other options for obtaining insurance coverage for the grievants. Accordingly, full back pay and a 40-day reinstatement period, during which the employer was directed to make all reasonable efforts to obtain coverage for the grievants, were warranted. However, if these efforts were unsuccessful, the discharges would go into effect after the expiration of the 40-day period. This decision reflects the arbitrator's careful weighing of the employer's procedural deficiencies, while acknowledging that "the poor records are, after all, the fault of the drivers"[15] and that the increased premiums threatened the survival of the company.

In *KIAM*,[16] the grievant was discharged for sexual harassment of a female co-worker, consisting of letters, repeated verbal overtures, and gifts. The employer argued that the grievant's actions violated its written policy on sexual harassment, as well as public policy. But the arbitrator found that the sexual harassment policy failed to define sexual harassment, describe its elements, or provide examples of sexual harassment. The arbitrator concluded that the company's failure to provide adequate notice of what type of conduct would violate the harassment policy warranted reducing the discharge to a written warning and awarding reinstatement with payment of all lost wages.

In *Anchorage Hilton Hotel*,[17] the arbitrator took into account the employer's procedural errors in his award of reinstatement, without back pay or benefits, of a hotel housekeeper with an otherwise clean record who was discharged for a first-time offense of claiming credit for cleaning a room that she had only partially cleaned. Specifically, the arbitrator noted that the hotel did not have clear guidelines for determining how to count partially cleaned rooms and that the employer had violated the grievant's *Weingarten*[18] rights by refusing to permit a union representative to be present at the investigatory interview.

Arbitrators have also awarded partial remedies, based solely on mitigating factors, where neither the employee's guilt nor the fairness of the employer's procedures is in dispute.[19] In such cases, the typical

---

[15]Id. at 854.

[16]97 LA 617 (Bard, 1991).

[17]102 LA 55 (Landau, 1993).

[18]NLRB v. J. Weingarten, Inc., 95 S.Ct. 959, 88 LRRM 2689 (1975).

[19]See, e.g., General Dynamics, 100 LA 180, 185–87 (Francis, 1992) (grievant discharged for sending threatening letter to wife of supervisor whom she accused of sexual harassment reinstated without back pay where grievant had good work record, supervisor's conduct contributed to grievant's action, employer's failure publicly to discipline supervisor led grievant to believe no action would be taken, and employer imposed disparate treatment on grievant and her supervisor); Hyco, Inc., 66 LA 86, 90 (Nichols, 1976) (Grievant discharged after an epileptic seizure is reinstated without back pay where marital and financial problems may have affected

remedy is reinstatement without back pay.[20] In *Iowa-Illinois Gas & Electric Co.,*[21] for example, the grievant was discharged for excessive absenteeism. The arbitrator found that the employer had treated the grievant "in an altogether fair way," and indeed concluded that "on the basis of the facts before it on April 19, 1990 the Company had just cause to terminate [grievant] * * *."[22] But after his discharge, the grievant sought psychiatric treatment and was found to be suffering from a major depressive disorder. Generally, events occurring after discharge are irrelevant to the question of whether there was just cause. Relying on an exception to the general prohibition of posttermination evidence, the arbitrator found that "the concept of reasonableness embraced within the just cause standard permits [the arbitrator], under the facts as found by him, to consider the post-discharge evidence of rehabilitation."[23] The arbitrator also noted that the grievant's prognosis for recovery was good, that his illness was the sole cause of the absenteeism, that the family problems that proximately caused the illness had been resolved, and that the grievant had a good work record. These circumstances, the arbitrator concluded, warranted partial relief of reinstatement without loss of seniority, but no back pay or other contractual benefits.

In *Amoco Oil Co.,*[24] the arbitrator reinstated, with seniority but no back pay, a grievant who was discharged for obtaining a taxi voucher under false pretenses. The arbitrator concluded that the grievant's action was a "test case" to challenge a change in the company's prior policy of providing taxi vouchers to employees who voluntarily worked overtime. Thus, the grievant was "not guilty of 'theft' in the normal sense of the word because he had to know his unauthorized taxi ride would be discovered at some point."[25] The arbitrator also took account of the grievant's "fine" work record, 22 years of seniority, and expressions of remorse.

In *County of Monroe,*[26] the employer discharged the grievant for absenteeism. The arbitrator found a "special set of facts and extenuating circumstances that should be carefully examined and evaluated

---

grievant's conduct); Thrifty Drug Stores Co., 56 LA 789, 793–94 (Peters, 1971) (grievant who suffered from chronic alcoholism is reinstated without back pay because of his 23 years of service, excellent work record, and high moral character); American Chain & Cable Co., 48 LA 1369, 1372 (Keefe, 1967) (grievant discharged for absenteeism was subsequently diagnosed with fear psychosis and ordered reinstated without back pay upon medical certification of her recovery); St. Regis Paper Co., 12 LA 1023, 1024 (Ralston, Chair, 1949) (grievant who was discharged for leaving work without permission following altercation with co-worker is reinstated without back pay; grievant had good work record and co-worker was partially responsible for altercation).

[20]See, e.g., cases cited in note 19.

[21]95 LA 553 (Volz, 1990).

[22]Id. at 556.

[23]Id. See also Texaco, Inc., 42 LA 408 (Prasow, 1963); Chrysler Corp., 40 LA 935 (Alexander, Chair, 1963).

[24]93 LA 1021 (Allen, 1989).

[25]Id. at 1028.

[26]72 LA 541 (Markowitz, 1979).

in connection with the imposition of a reasonable penalty."[27] The grievant was the sole support of five children. One of her daughters had been suspended from school for violent and threatening behavior, and the grievant had missed time from work to take her daughter for physical and psychological testing. Under these circumstances, the grievant was reinstated without back pay.

## II. Components of a Make Whole Remedy

While reinstatement and back pay are the most common elements of make whole relief, the arbitrator has broad authority to fashion equitable remedies.[28] To make an aggrieved employee whole, arbitrators will generally award some amount of back pay in addition to reinstatement as well as other rights and privileges of employment including seniority, accrued leaves, medical costs/payments, and insurance coverage, as discussed in detail below.

### A. *Traditional Components*

Reinstatement is the central and most common element of the modern remedy for discharge without just cause. The majority rule is that where an arbitrator awards make whole relief, reinstatement will be part of the award. Where a partial remedy is ordered, arbitrators often order reinstatement without back pay and, at times, conditional upon the grievant's demonstration of fitness—physical, mental, or social—for employment.[29]

---

[27]Id. at 543.

[28]See Steelworkers v. Enterprise Wheel & Car Corp., 363 U.S. 593, 46 LRRM 2423, 2425 (1960) (upholding back-pay remedy where contract was silent); Miller Brewing v. Brewery Workers Local 9, 739 F.2d 1159, 1163, 116 LRRM 3130, 3133 (7th Cir., 1984) (Posner, J.), cert. denied, 469 U.S. 1160, 118 LRRM 2192 (1985) (citations omitted) ("Collective bargaining agreements often say little or nothing about the arbitrator's remedial powers; yet it cannot be that he has none; and since he derives all his powers from the agreement, the agreement must implicitly grant him remedial powers when there is no explicit grant."); Minute Maid Co., v. Citrus Workers Local 444, 331 F.2d 280, 56 LRRM 2095 (5th Cir., 1964) (remedy of back pay and reinstatement did not exceed arbitrator's authority where contract was silent as to back pay); Genie Co., 97 LA 542 (Dworkin, 1991) (arbitrator declined to modify agreement by reading contractual language permitting discharge "for cause" to mean that discharge must be for just cause); Yellow Taxi of Minneapolis, 68 LA 26 (O'Connell, 1977) (contract's unambiguous limit on back pay would be respected); Columbus Show Case Co., 64 LA 1148 (Leach, 1975) (contract did not permit back pay beyond date on which grievance was filed). Compare International Harvester Co., 15 LA 1 (Seward, 1950) (specific contractual provisions governing amount and computation of back pay take precedence over arbitrator's general authority to award make whole relief).

[29]See, e.g., Cleveland Elec. Illuminating Co., 100 LA 1039 (Lipson, Chair, 1993) (grievant reinstated subject to medical evaluation; employer must match work to physical ability based on evaluation); General Mills, Inc., 99 LA 143 (Stallworth, 1992) (trial reinstatement during which grievant's fitness for duty is to be evaluated); A.Y. McDonald Mfg. Co., 99 LA 118 (Loebach, 1992) (employer must perform ergonomics evaluation and, if employee cannot be

Back pay is the other essential component of a make whole remedy.[30] The purpose of back pay is "to make the employee whole for the loss sustained by his discharge" and "to put him in exactly the same position financially that he would have been in had the discharge not occurred." In addition to making the grievant whole, back pay may serve a public policy objective of deterrence.[31] The general rule is to award what the grievant would have earned but for the discharge, offset by the grievant's interim earnings.[32] Furthermore, in determining the amount of back pay, most arbitrators take into account the grievant's effort to mitigate damages.[33] As noted above, back pay may be limited by the arbitrator[34] or the parties.[35]

---

reinstated, provide her with test results for workers' compensation claim); Lakeside Jubilee Foods, 95 LA 358 (Berquist, 1990) (reinstatement with no back pay but full benefits conditioned on grievant's treatment for co-dependency problem); Firestone Tire & Rubber Co., 93 LA 381 (Cohen, 1989) (grievant who failed to provide complete and accurate medical history on employment application is reinstated without back pay so long as she is physically able to perform job duties); Amana Refrigeration, Inc., 93 LA 249 (Mikrut, 1989) (employee on workers' compensation reinstated if physically fit to perform work); Rustco Prods. Co., 92 LA 1048 (Watkins, 1989) (grievant's reinstatement conditioned upon his completion of course in race and human relations); Westinghouse Elec. Corp., 91 LA 685 (Talarico, 1988) (reinstatement conditioned on psychiatric counseling). See also discussion in section entitled "Reinstatement Without Back Pay," this chapter.

[30]Golden State Bottling Co. v. NLRB, 414 U.S. 168, 84 LRRM 2839, 2847 (1973), quoting NLRB v. J.H. Rutter-Rex Mfg. Co., 369 U.S. 258, 263, 72 LRRM 2881 (1969) (" 'an order requiring reinstatement and back pay is aimed at "restoring the economic status quo that would have obtained but for company's wrongful refusal to reinstate * * *" ' "); Alliance Mfg. Co., 61 LA 101, 103 (Gibson, 1973). See W.C. Nabors Co. v. NLRB, 323 F.2d 686, 54 LRRM 2259, 2262 (5th Cir., 1963) (back pay "includes the moneys, whether gratuitous or not, which it is reasonably found that the employee would actually have received in the absence of the unlawful discrimination"), cert. denied, 376 U.S. 911, 55 LRRM 2455 (1964).

[31]See General Dynamics Convair Div., 95 LA 500, 500 (Jones, 1990) (back pay, along with reinstatement, necessary to compel employer's adherence to due process). Cf. Hedstrom Co. v. NLRB, 629 F.2d 305, 317, 105 LRRM 2183, 2193 (3d Cir., 1980) ("it is settled that the purpose of a back pay order is to vindicate the public policy embodied in the Act"); NLRB v. Madison Courier, 472 F.2d 1307, 80 LRRM 3377, 3382 (D.C. Cir., 1972) ("The purpose of requiring that the employer make the discriminatee whole in such a case has a two-fold objective. First, the back pay remedy reimburses the innocent employee for the actual losses which he has suffered as a direct result of the employer's improper conduct; second, the order furthers the public interest advanced by the deterrence of such illegal acts.").

[32]See the discussion of computation of back pay in section entitled "Reinstatement With Back-Pay Computation," this chapter.

[33]See the discussion in section entitled "Duty to Mitigate/Interim Earnings," this chapter.

[34]Raynor Mfg. Co., 100 LA 1204 (Fisher, 1993) (back pay for grievant improperly discharged for absenteeism limited to percentage of time he worked prior to discharge based on his attendance record). See, e.g., Atchison, Topeka & Santa Fe Ry., 87 LA 972 (Johnson, 1986) (conditional reinstatement with no back pay); Gulf S. Beverages, Inc., 87 LA 688 (Carraway, 1986) (reinstatement with no back pay if employee agrees to comply with no-beard rule); Longmont Turkey Processors, Inc., 84 LA 638 (Cohen, 1985) (no back pay where employee could not have performed due to disability); Mark Twain Indus., Inc., 74 LA 441 (Stix, 1979) (back-pay award reduced by half).

[35]See Yellow Taxi of Minneapolis, 68 LA 26 (O'Connell, 1977) (contract limited back pay to 10 days); Columbus Show Case Co., 64 LA 1148 (Leach, 1975) (contract prohibited back pay prior to date grievance was presented to foreman).

## B. *Other Possible Components*

In addition to the traditional remedies of reinstatement and back pay, arbitrators have creatively exercised their broad discretion to restore the status quo ante by taking a wide range of remedial actions, including expunging the employee's record;[36] restoring seniority;[37] and awarding lost bonuses, wage increases and overtime pay,[38] vacation, holiday and leave credits,[39] and pension and welfare benefits.[40]

In addition, arbitrators have used their broad discretion to craft other appropriate remedies, including costs of medical care that the employer's health plan would have provided,[41] shift differentials,[42] promotions,[43] and other expenses incurred by the grievant related to the improper discharge.[44]

---

[36]Hy-Vee Food Stores, 102 LA 555 (Berquist, 1994) (employer ordered to expunge employee's records); Ingham Intermediate Sch. Dist., 101 LA 598 (Borland, 1993) (warning expunged); Chivas Prods., Ltd., 101 LA 546 (Kanner, 1993) (discharge expunged); Jacksonville Elec. Auth., 100 LA 1018 (Byars, 1993) (letter of counseling expunged); Utah Power & Light Co., 94 LA 241 (Winograd, 1990) (employee's record cleared).

[37]See Housing Auth. of the County of Monterey, 102 LA 1082 (Staudohar, 1994) (discharge overturned without restoration of seniority); Folsom Return to Custody, Inc., 101 LA 837 (Staudohar, 1993) (reinstatement with seniority but no back pay or benefits); Giant Eagle Mkts. Co., 101 LA 581 (Zobrak, 1993) (employee convicted of selling drugs 8 months prior to hiring, no seniority); Scott Paper Co., 100 LA 1113 (Caraway, 1993) (discharge for off-duty drug use, full make whole remedy including lost seniority); Schulze & Burch Biscuit Co., 100 LA 948 (Goldstein, 1993) (discharge for unemployment fraud, reinstatement with seniority but no back pay or accrued benefits); GTE N., Inc., 98 LA 894 (Dworkin, 1992) (seniority restored).

[38]Michigan State Police, 98 LA 572 (Roumell, 1992) (lost overtime included in remedy); But see W.C. Nabors Co. v. NLRB, 323 F.2d 686, 690, 54 LRRM 2259 (5th Cir., 1963) (enforcing NLRB order including "gratuitous" profit shares in back-pay remedy); Marriott-Host Int'l, 100 LA 1005 (Knowlton, 1992) (wage increase denied); Armour Food Co., 87 LA 250 (1986) (Eisler, 1986) (wage increase limited since, under contract, increase is based not on seniority but on whether employee actually worked or was paid); John Deere Dubuque Tractor Works, 35 LA 495 (Larkin, 1960) (missed overtime included in back pay).

[39]Youngstown Developmental Ctr., 93 LA 1155, 1158 (Sharpe, 1989) (citing cases) ("common for holiday pay to be part of a make whole remedy"); Union Elec. Co., 93 LA 749 (Fowler, 1989) (employee reinstated without back pay is credited with sick leave "bank"); Alliance Mfg. Co., 61 LA 101 (Gibson, 1973) (holiday pay).

[40]Piney Point Transp. Co., 103 LA 1117 (Crable, 1994) (employer ordered to pay front pay and lump-sum fringe benefits to trust funds); Phillips 66 Co., 93 LA 707 (Goodstein, 1989) (fringe benefits awarded); Cowlitz Redi-Mix, 85 LA 745, 753 (Boedecer, 1985) (grievant entitled to back pay without interest and fringe benefits); Engineer Constr. Int'l, 84 LA 11 (Williams, 1984) (grievant granted partial payment of benefits where no just cause for termination).

[41]Riverside Osteopathic Hosp., 98 LA 1044 (McDonald, 1992) (arbitrator ordered payment of retroactive medical benefits, payment of medical bills that would otherwise have been covered, and premiums for third-party insurance coverage).

[42]Brown-Forman Beverage Co., 103 LA 292 (Frockt, 1994) (employee entitled to shift differential bonus); Stone Container Corp., 101 LA 943 (Feldman, 1993) (displaced employees entitled to differential).

[43]Boston Edison Co., 92 LA 374 (Nicolau, 1988) (promotion awarded). See also Underwood Mach. Co., 95 NLRB 1386, 28 LRRM 1447 (1951) (NLRB order finding discriminatee entitled to back pay reflecting promotions that otherwise would have been available but for unlawful discharge).

[44]Marriott-Host Int'l, 100 LA 1005 (Knowlton, 1992) (replacement costs for meals ordered); Northland Greyhound Lines, 23 LA 277 (Levinson, 1954) (transportation expenses to hearing).

## C. Remedies Not Generally Included

As a general rule, arbitrators decline to award damages for emotional distress,[45] except where expressly provided for in the agreement.[46] Nor will arbitrators generally grant consequential damages to compensate grievants for losses that were not proximately caused by the employer's improper actions.[47]

Moreover, arbitrators do not award damages that go beyond making the grievant whole.[48] However, both courts and arbitrators have recognized a limited exception to this rule, based on the public policy of deterring egregious violations of the contract.[49] Punitive damages will also be awarded where provided for by the contract.[50] Although still more the exception than the rule, interest on back pay has been awarded in a number of cases.[51]

---

[45]Union Camp Corp., 104 LA 295 (Nolan, 1994) (arbitrator lacked authority to award damages for emotional distress); Stone Container Corp., 91 LA 1186, 1192 (Ross, 1988) (denying damages for emotional distress).

[46]Klamath County, Or., 90 LA 354, 360 (Levak, 1987) (providing remedy for emotional distress based solely on violation of contract provision that required management to discipline employees in a manner that will not cause undue embarrassment or humiliation).

[47]Marriott-Host Int'l, 100 LA 1005 (Knowlton, 1992) (employee unable to recover losses suffered from inability to finance home lease/purchase). See Hill & Sinicropi, Remedies in Arbitration, 2d ed., 493 (BNA Books, 1991) ("With few exceptions, arbitrators follow the common-law requirement that 'damages' are not recoverable unless they arise naturally from the breach or were contemplated by the parties as a probable result of the breach at the time the contract was made.") But see Southwestern Bell, 61 LA 202 (Wolff, 1973).

[48]See Hill & Sinicropi, Remedies in Arbitration, 2d ed., 436–38 (BNA Books, 1991).

[49]Potashnick Constr. Co., 77 LA 893, 901 (Richardson, 1981) (monetary damages awarded to grievant "because the superintendent in provoking grievant's conduct violated implicit obligations under the collective bargaining agreement"); John Morrell & Co., 69 LA 264, 281 (Conway, 1977) (grievants awarded the value of unpaid leaves of absence that were unreasonably denied). See also Fischer, "Implementation of Arbitration Awards—The Steelworker's View," in Arbitration and the Public Interest, Proceedings of the 24th Annual Meeting of NAA, 126, 133–34 (BNA Books, 1971) (traditional reinstatement plus back-pay remedy simply fails to provide adequate compensation to a grievant who is discharged, since it compensates for neither the time value of lost wages nor the stigma suffered by the grievant); Bethlehem Steel Co., 37 LA 821 (Valtin, 1961) (employer that denied grievant's first choice of vacation schedule must give grievant 2 weeks' vacation pay in addition to the vacation he received).

[50]See Mastrobuono v. Shearson Lehman Hutton, Inc. 115 S.Ct. 1212 (1995) (award containing punitive damages enforced in securities arbitration case); Asbestos Workers Local 34 v. General Pipe Covering, 792 F.2d 96, 122 LRRM 2816, 2819 (8th Cir., 1986) (citation omitted) ("[a]lthough punitive arbitration awards are generally disfavored, * * * courts enforce them where they are authorized by the collective bargaining agreements"); Northshore Invs. v. Directors Guild, 108 LRRM 3010 (C.D. Cal., 1981) (enforcing arbitrator's "punitive" damages award where contract vested arbitrator with the broad power to award "money damages" for contract breach). See also discussion in section entitled "Punitive Damages," this chapter.

[51]Newport Steel Corp., 100 LA 1007 (Gibson, 1993) (grievant's demand for "make-whole" relief "is broad enough to include interest"); National R.R. Passenger Corp., 95 LA 617 (Simons, 1990) (11% interest on back pay); Agriculture Dep't, 93 LA 920 (Seidman, 1989) (back pay with interest ordered); Glover Bottled Gas Corp./Synergy Gas Corp., 91 LA 77 (Simons, 1987) (16% interest added); Markle Mfg. Co., 73 LA 1292 (Williams, 1980) (10% interest). But see Marriott-Host Int'l, 100 LA 1005 (Knowlton, 1992) (no interest); Kings County Truck Lines, 94 LA 875 (Prayzich, 1990) (no interest where contract provides for none and no evidence that employer unduly delayed). See generally Thatcher, "Grievance Arbitration Awards: Where Is the Interest in Interest?" 8 Lab. Law. 255 (1992).

Under the standard of *Alyeska Pipeline Service Co. v. Wilderness Society*,[52] arbitrators have exercised their authority to award attorney fees in cases of bad faith or willful disobedience of a previous award.[53] Likewise, where the contract does not provide a formula for allocation of costs, arbitrators have on occasion awarded all costs against a party that refused to participate until compelled by a court.[54] But where the agreement provides for sharing costs, arbitrators generally do not alter this formula even to punish extreme dilatoriness by one of the parties.[55]

## D. *Reinstatement With Back-Pay Computation*

A full back-pay award is intended to put an aggrieved employee in the same financial position as if the improper suspension or discharge had never occurred.[56] In accomplishing this goal, an amount of money, usually equal to wages lost as a result of improper suspension or discharge, is awarded to the reinstated employee.

*1. Time Period.*   Generally, arbitrators evaluate the reasonableness of the suspension or discharge period and award back pay for the time they deemed excessive or unreasonable.[57] Where the suspended or discharged employee has suffered a physical injury or illness preventing the grievant from being able to work during the

---

[52]421 U.S. 240 (1975) (allowing attorney fees, absent contractual provision, for (1) trustees, (2) willful disobedience of a court order, and (3) bad faith). See Shimman v. Operating Eng'rs Local 18, 744 F.2d 1226, 117 LRRM 2579, 2582 (6th Cir., 1984) (discussing bad faith standard), cert. denied, 469 U.S. 1215, 118 LRRM 2576 (1985).

[53]See Department of Treasury, 79 LA 284 (Roche, 1982) (award of reasonable attorneys' fees based on market value, not actual cost); Leavenworth Times, 71 LA 396, 409 (Bothwell, 1978) ("an arbitrator does have jurisdiction and authority to award damages, including attorneys' fees, under appropriate circumstances, even though the Agreement contains no language authorizing the arbitrator to award damages"). But see Shell Oil Co., 87 LA 473 (Nicholas, 1986) (no attorneys' fees where employer did not act in bad faith).

[54]Munsingwear, Inc., 65 LA 997 (Blum, undated); High & Mighty Farms, 63 LA 992 (Rose, 1974); Jacuzzi Bros., 49 LA 760 (Bothwell, 1967).

[55]But see Indiana Convention Ctr. & Hoosier Dome, 98 LA 713 (Wolff, 1992) (arbitrator ordered company to pay union's share of arbitration costs where employer denied employee *Weingarten* rights); Chromalloy Am. Corp., 93 LA 828, 836 (Woolf, 1989).

[56]E.g., Champion Spark Plug Co., 93 LA 1277, 1285 (Dobry, 1989); United Sec. Indus., 92 LA 951, 954 (Bickner, 1989); Todd Pac. Shipyards, 86 LA 171, 173 (Draznin, 1985); Alliance Mfg. Co., 61 LA 101, 105 (Gibson, 1973); Masonite Corp., 10 LA 854, 855 (McCoy, 1948) (purpose of back pay is to put grievant in exactly the same position financially that he would have been in had the discharge not occurred).

[57]Yellow Cab Coop. Ass'n, 102 LA 848, 854 (Watkins, 1993) (cab drivers discharged for lack of auto insurance were reinstated with back pay for their entire discharge period); Chromalloy Am. Corp., 93 LA 828, 836 (Woolf, 1989) (employer's failure to inform employee of specific charges prior to discharge warranted back pay from date of discharge to first business day following arbitration hearing); Lucky Stores, 91 LA 624, 630 (Ross, 1988) (company's unreasonably lengthy suspension of employee resulted in back-pay award to date of reinstatement less employee's 1-week vacation); P.D.I. Inc., 91 LA 21, 25 (Dworkin, 1988) (company's unreasonable investigatory delay resulted in back-pay award from date of discharge to date of reinstatement less 4 days for suspension pending investigation).

suspension or discharge period, arbitrators may decline to award back pay for the period of disability. In these instances, arbitrators limit the back-pay award to the period during which the employee was physically able to work.[58]

*2. Rate.* The back-pay rate for an improperly suspended or discharged employee is determined by estimating the gross amount of wages the employee would have earned but for the unjust suspension or discharge.[59] There are several methods of calculating gross back pay.

Two of these methods use the grievant's employment history as a guide. First, the "average earnings" formula multiplies the grievant's average earnings per pay period during the preceding year by the number of pay periods in the back-pay period.[60] This formula is appropriate where the nature of the grievant's job, the level of earnings, and the employer's business have all remained relatively constant during the predischarge and back-pay periods.[61]

Second, the "average hours of work" formula calculates the average number of hours worked by the grievant per pay period during a representative period prior to discharge.[62] The "average hours of work" formula is most useful where the grievant has established a regular work pattern and the employer's business is not seasonal

[58]Southwestern Bell Tel. Co., 98 LA 137, 143–44, (Nolan, 1991) (employer ordered to pay employee wages he would have earned from date psychiatrist said he could have returned to work until date of final determination as to his reemployability); KIAM, 97 LA 617, 630 (Bard, 1991) (grievant reinstated with back pay except for period during which he was disabled and unable to work); Dyncorp Fort Rucker Div., 97 LA 572, 578 (Cantor, 1991) (grievant unjustly discharged for alleged failure to report during recovery from automobile accident reinstated with back pay from latest date specified on medical release to return to full workload to date of reinstatement); Excel Corp., 95 LA 1069, 1072 (Shearer, 1990) (improperly discharged disabled employee entitled to back pay from time she identified job she could perform within medical restrictions).

[59]Newport Steel Corp., 100 LA 1007, 1009 (Gibson, 1993) (back pay includes employee's gross earnings but for discharge); Niemand Indus., 94 LA 669, 670 (Nolan, 1990) (back pay reflects amount of money wrongly discharged employee would have made had she not been fired); Darby Printing Co., 49 LA 828, 830 (King, 1967) (back pay is a calculation of earnings grievant would have received if he had worked for company during period in question).

[60]Yellow Cab Coop. Ass'n, 102 LA 848, 854 (Watkins, 1993) (arbitrator determined back-pay rate for taxi drivers whose wages changed on a daily basis by using each driver's average during 6-month period prior to discharge); Menasha Corp., 90 LA 427, 431 (Clark, 1987) (back pay for unjustly discharged employee computed at straight time plus overtime compensation for each month during back-pay period equal to overtime received by grievant in corresponding month of previous year); Darby Printing Co., 49 LA 828, 830–32 (King, 1967) (back pay includes average amount of straight-time pay and overtime pay employee earned per week while he was with employer).

[61]Newport Steel Corp., 100 LA 1007, 1010 (Gibson, 1993) ("average earnings formula" is appropriate where nature of grievant's job, his level of earnings, and employer's business all remained relatively constant during predischarge and back-pay periods); Niemand Indus., 94 LA 669, 670 (Nolan, 1990) (one method of estimating gross pay is to make a projection of average earnings based on grievant's experience before discharge).

[62]Newport Steel Corp., 100 LA 1007, 1010 (Gibson, 1993) ("average hours of work" formula calculates average number of hours worked by grievant per pay period during a representative period prior to discharge). See also Niemand Indus., 94 LA 669, 670 (Nolan, 1990).

or where the employer's wage rates have changed during the back-pay period.[63]

Two additional formulas relied on by arbitrators use other employees' work records during the back-pay period as a guide. First, the "representative employee" formula utilizes as a reference point an employee with comparable earnings who was working prior to discharge and during the back-pay period and whose work, working conditions, and terms of employment are similar to the grievant's.[64] This formula is most useful in cases where there are long back-pay periods involving multiple pay periods and pay changes.[65] Second, the "replacement employee" formula uses the actual earnings of the employee who has replaced the grievant as a reasonable measure of what the grievant would have earned.[66]

Generally, the "representative employee" and "replacement employee" methods are preferred because they automatically make adjustments for additional overtime that may have been available to the grievant during the time of suspension or discharge as well as wage increases that may have come into effect during the time of suspension or discharge.[67] Nevertheless, the "average earnings" and "average hours" formulas will be applied where the grievant's past work record shows chronic absenteeism, refusal of overtime opportunities, or other circumstances indicating that the grievant's weekly income would have been significantly different from that of the replacement or representative employee.[68]

3. *Amount.*   In determining the amount of back pay, arbitrators will include benefits provided for in the collective bargaining agree-

---

[63]Newport Steel Corp., 100 LA 1007, 1010 (Gibson, 1993) ("average hours of work" formula most useful where grievant has established a regular work pattern and employer's business is not seasonal).

[64]Id.; Bethlehem Steel Corp., 81 LA 666 (Seward, 1983) (record of "peer employee" was used to compute average earnings per hour that constructively would have been available to grievant during back-pay period).

[65]Newport Steel Corp., 100 LA 1007, 1010 (Gibson, 1993) ("representative employee" formula most useful in cases where there are long back-pay periods involving different jobs and pay changes).

[66]Vision-Ease, 102 LA 1106 (Mathews, 1994) (lost overtime award based on replacement's actual overtime pay received); Newport Steel Corp., 100 LA 1007, 1010 (Gibson, 1993) ("replacement employee" formula uses actual earnings of employee who has replaced grievant as a reasonable measure of what grievant would have earned); Niemand Indus., 94 LA 669, 670 (Nolan, 1990) (back pay for wrongfully discharged grievant was based upon her replacement's earnings where replacement's seniority and job experience virtually duplicated grievant's); National Metal & Steel Corp., 86 LA 217, 219 (Rothschild, 1985) (improperly demoted employee who lost opportunity for overtime pay was awarded same overtime pay as earned by replacement).

[67]Niemand Indus., 94 LA 669, 670 (Nolan, 1990) (using replacement or peer employee as reference point is preferred because it automatically includes overtime pay and wage raises).

[68]See West Co., 103 LA 452 (Murphy, 1994) (granting overtime where justified by grievant's past record); Seneca Steel Div., 96 LA 838 (Fullmer, 1991) (back pay did not include lost overtime where employee had rejected all overtime offered during year preceding discharge).

ment covering the grievant.[69] For example, back-pay awards may include vacation pay if so provided in the collective bargaining agreement,[70] unless the employee had received unused vacation at the time of discharge.[71] Likewise, paid holidays are generally included in a back-pay award.[72]

On the other hand, arbitrators will often make reductions in back-pay awards where necessary to prevent a grievant from profiting from the suspension or discharge. For example, arbitrators may reduce back-pay awards in order to reflect the grievant's historical employment problems, such as chronic absenteeism.[73] Employers may ask the arbitrator to study the grievant's past record of absences and reduce the award to reflect the percentage of time that the grievant would likely have been absent from work during the back-pay period.[74]

Furthermore, in some cases, arbitrators modify back-pay awards to reflect both parties' level of fault.[75] For example, where a grievant

---

[69]Sparklett Devices, Inc., 90 LA 910, 916 (Fowler, 1988); All Am. Gourmet Co., 88 LA 1241, 1247 (Zobrak, 1987) (grievant reinstated with all wages and benefits including ratification bonus if due). See also Glover Bottled Gas Corp./Synergy Gas Corp., 91 LA 77, 90 (Simons, 1987); Cowlitz Redi-Mix, 85 LA 745, 753–54 (Boedecker, 1985).

[70]CGM Contractors, 93 LA 1159 (Duda, 1989) (reinstated grievant awarded vacation pay as provided in collective bargaining agreement for year in question); Rolling Acres Care Ctr., 91 LA 795 (Dworkin, 1988) (company directed to compensate grievant for 160 hours of vacation pay at rate prescribed for employee's last employment period); Sparklett Devices, Inc., 90 LA 910 (Fowler, 1988) (back-pay award offset to reflect that grievant's termination pay included 2 weeks' paid vacation); Armour Food Co., 87 LA 250 (Eisler, 1986) (parties ordered to credit grievant for days he was entitled to receive pay under collective bargaining agreement including paid vacation); Cowlitz Redi-Mix, 85 LA 745 (Boedecker, 1985) (contractual calculation of vacation pay applied).

[71]Depending upon the contract, arbitrators may permit employers to "offset" back pay with previously paid vacation pay. MRS Transp. Co., 95 LA 514, 518 (Massey, 1990) (if employee had not been improperly discharged, and vacation had been taken during that period of time as required by the contract, employee's earning capacity would have been reduced by equivalent of vacation time and, therefore, offset against back-pay award for amounts already paid as unused vacation was proper).

[72]CGM Contractors, 93 LA 1159 (Duda, 1989) (grievant reinstated with holiday pay). See, e.g., Sparklett Devices, Inc., 90 LA 910 (Fowler, 1988); Armour Food Co., 87 LA 250 (Eisler, 1986); Cowlitz Redi-Mix, 85 LA 745 (Boedecker, 1985); Alliance Mfg. Co., 61 LA 101 (Gibson, 1973).

[73]Raynor Mfg. Co., 100 LA 1204 (Fisher, 1993) (grievant entitled to reinstatement, but abysmal attendance record taken into account in determining amount of back pay). See, e.g., Steadley Co., 89 LA 1049 (Clark, 1987); Plabell Rubber Prods., 89 LA 581 (Ray, 1987); Kansas Power & Light Co., 87 LA 867 (Belcher, 1986); Harbor Furniture Mfg. Co., 85 LA 359 (Richman, 1985); Bethlehem Steel Corp., 71 LA 1003 (Strongin, 1978); Alliance Mfg. Co., 61 LA 101 (Gibson, 1973).

[74]Raynor Mfg. Co., 100 LA 1204 (Fisher, 1993) (back pay reduced by 35% to reflect past absenteeism); Steadley Co., 89 LA 1049 (Clark, 1987) (back pay reduced by 16% to reflect past absenteeism); Plabell Rubber Prods., 89 LA 581 (Ray, 1987) (back pay reduced by 6% to reflect past absenteeism); Kansas Power & Light Co., 87 LA 867 (Belcher, 1986) (back pay reduced by anticipated time that would be lost for all reasons, but not reduced by more than that equal to grievant's absentee record for the 12-month period prior to discharge); Harbor Furniture Mfg. Co., 85 LA 359 (Richman, 1985) (back pay reduced by 15% to reflect prior absenteeism).

[75]Dow Chem. Co., 95 LA 510 (Sartain, 1990) (where grievant deserved severe discipline for his conduct, but employer failed to use progressive discipline, arbitrator awarded one-half back pay); Simplex Prods. Div., 91 LA 356 (Byars, 1988) (grievant reinstated because she had not been warned that her job was in jeopardy, but with only 50% back pay because the reason

and an employer are equally at fault, some arbitrators award one half of full back pay.[76]

In a case where the arbitrator might normally award no back pay but the employer has unreasonably delayed bringing the case to arbitration, thereby unreasonably extending the unemployment period, some amount of back pay may be awarded.[77]

*4. Duty to Mitigate / Interim Earnings.* Employees who are unjustly suspended or discharged are required to mitigate their losses if they wish to receive back pay, regular contractual benefits, accrued leaves, seniority, and other make whole relief. In fact, back pay may be wholly or partially denied to employees who fail to make reasonable efforts to mitigate their damages.[78] Breach of the duty to mitigate damages constitutes an affirmative defense to the payment of back pay. Therefore, many arbitrators rule the employer has the burden of proving that the employee did not make a good faith effort to mitigate.[79]

The duty to mitigate damages does not require a grievant to seek employment in *any* available position. Rather, the duty requires a grievant to seek a position similar in duties, wages, hours, and location to that which was lost.[80] In searching for similar alternative employment, an employee is held to a due diligence standard. Due diligence

---

for discharge was her failure to notify company that she would be unable to return from medical leave on expected date); Panhandle E. Pipeline Co., 88 LA 725 (Yarowsky, 1987) (employee wrongfully discharged for improper receipt of medical benefits reinstated with half back pay due to comparative fault).

[76]Dow Chem. Co., 95 LA 510 (Sartain, 1990); Simplex Prods. Div., 91 LA 356 (Byars, 1988).

[77]Dow Chem. Co., 95 LA 510 (Sartain, 1990) (grievant discharged for sexually harassing co-worker reinstated with back pay equal to one half of wages and benefits actually lost where misconduct was not egregious, employer failed to follow progressive disciplinary procedure, and period off the payroll had been some 2 years). But see Ohio Masonic Home, 94 LA 447 (Volz, 1990) (where grievant and employer shared substantial responsibility for delay in bringing case to arbitration, back pay limited to 3 months' wages).

[78]Kings County Truck Lines, 94 LA 875, 878 (Prayzich, 1990) (when an employee fails to take advantage of reasonable employment opportunities, back pay may be wholly or partially denied), citing Elkouri & Elkouri, How Arbitration Works, 4th ed., 408–09 (BNA Books, 1985); Niemand Indus., 94 LA 669 (Nolan, 1990) (injured employee expected to seek another job; if does so, earnings will be subtracted from damages; if does not, amount that should have been earned will be subtracted from any back-pay award); Cleveland Pneumatic Co., 89 LA 1071, 1075 (Sharpe,1987) (employee not entitled to back pay to extent that he fails to search for alternative work without good reason), citing Phelps Dodge Corp. v. NLRB, 313 U.S. 177, 8 LRRM 439 (1941); Kansas Power & Light Co., 87 LA 867, 872 (Belcher, 1986) (back pay will be reduced if grievant failed to mitigate damages); E.F. Hauserman Co., 64 LA 1065 (Gibson, 1975) (employee not entitled to back pay because he did not use reasonable efforts to mitigate damages).

[79]Youngstown Developmental Ctr., 93 LA 1155, 1159 (Sharpe, 1989) (breach of the duty to mitigate damages is an affirmative defense to payment of back pay); Cleveland Pneumatic Co., 89 LA 1071 (Sharpe, 1987) (breach of duty to mitigate damages is an affirmative defense to the payment of back pay).

[80]Niemand Indus., 94 LA 669, 671 (Nolan, 1990) (employee need accept only similar employment in the same locality with similar conditions and rank); Cleveland Pneumatic Co., 89 LA 1071, 1075 (Sharpe, 1987) (mitigation doctrine does not require that employee seek or accept employment that is dangerous, distasteful, or essentially different from his regular job

does not require the employee to succeed in the pursuit of alternative employment.[81] Rather, due diligence requires the employee to demonstrate a bona fide attempt to mitigate losses, taking into account the employment opportunities available to a person in the employee's particular situation with that person's particular attributes and/or shortcomings.[82]

Although an employee is only obligated to accept *similar* alternative employment, voluntarily leaving *any* interim position (even a dissimilar one) without good cause may constitute a breach of the duty to mitigate damages.[83] Where a grievant voluntarily leaves an interim position without good cause, arbitrators generally reduce the back-pay award by the amount that the employee would have earned had he retained the interim position.[84] In contrast, where an employee voluntarily leaves an interim position in anticipation of impending reinstatement, the duty to mitigate damages is nevertheless fulfilled and the back-pay award remains unaffected.[85]

Generally, where back pay is awarded, it is reduced by any interim earnings in order to prevent grievants from profiting as a result of their discharge.[86] This practice is consistent with the theory behind make whole relief. Make whole relief is not intended to reward or punish either party. Rather, it is intended to allow the parties to resume their employment relationship as if the suspension or discharge had never occurred.

---

or an unreasonable distance from his home), citing NLRB v. Madison Courier, Inc., 472 F.2d 1307, 80 LRRM 3377 (D.C. Cir., 1972); Standard Transformer Co., 51 LA 1110 (Gibson, 1968); McLouth Steel Corp., 23 LA 640 (Parker, 1954).

[81]Niemand Indus., 94 LA 669, 671 (Nolan, 1990) (due diligence requires reasonable effort rather than the highest standard of diligence); Youngstown Developmental Ctr., 93 LA 1155, 1159 (Sharpe, 1989) (duty to mitigate requires a good faith effort, but not success); Cleveland Pneumatic Co., 89 LA 1071, 1075 (Sharpe, 1987) (duty to mitigate requires only a good faith effort and not success).

[82]O'Keeffe's Aluminum Prods., 92 LA 215, 217 (Koven, 1989) (grievant must show that he made a bona fide attempt to mitigate his losses, taking into account the limited employment opportunities available to a person in his particular situation with his particular shortcomings).

[83]Kings County Truck Lines, 94 LA 875, 878 (Prayzich, 1990) (reinstated grievant's back pay reduced by amount equal to wages he would have earned if he had not quit interim employment despite fact that he was not obligated to accept employment in the first place due to its location).

[84]Niemand Indus., 94 LA 669, 671 (Nolan, 1990) (one who quits alternative employment without good reason will not be allowed compensation for forgone hours), citing NLRB v. Mastro Plastics Corp., 354 F.2d 170, 174 n.3, 60 LRRM 2578 (2d Cir., 1965), cert. denied, 384 U.S. 972, 62 LRRM 2242 (1966).

[85]Glover Bottled Gas Corp./Synergy Gas Corp., 91 LA 77 (Simons, 1987) (grievant's departure from interim employment in reasonable reliance upon union agent's report that his discharge grievance had been sustained and his reinstatement had been ordered did not constitute breach of duty to mitigate damages).

[86]Niemand Indus., 94 LA 669 (Nolan, 1990) (employer entitled to deduction from back pay for amount wrongfully discharged grievant actually earned at interim employment). See also Yellow Cab Coop. Ass'n, 102 LA 848, 854 (Watkins, 1993); Youngstown Developmental Ctr., 93 LA 1155 (Sharpe, 1989); Flying Tigers Line, Inc., 91 LA 647 (Concepcion, 1988).

For purposes of back-pay reduction, interim earnings reflect interim vacation and holiday pay,[87] interim retirement benefits,[88] and in many cases interim unemployment compensation.[89] Unless the contract otherwise provides, many arbitrators adopt the National Labor Relations Board (NLRB) approach to unemployment insurance, ruling that it is a nondeductible collateral benefit rather than an alternative source of income.[90] This view has been adopted by the Supreme Court:

> Payments of unemployment compensation were not made to the employees by respondent [employer] but by the state out of state funds derived from taxation. True, these taxes were paid by employers, and thus to some extent respondent helped to create the fund. However, the payments to the employees were not made to discharge any liability or obligation of respondent, but to carry out a policy of social betterment for the benefit of the entire state. * * * We think these facts plainly show the benefits to be collateral.[91]

Accordingly, the preferred view is that state employment compensation payments should not be deducted from back-pay orders where the payments were made out of state funds derived from taxation.[92]

Those arbitrators who do not follow the NLRB approach, however, will reduce back-pay awards by unemployment insurance payments.[93] In fact, an unemployment insurance payment that equals all lost earnings may preclude a back-pay award altogether.[94] In some states, the agency that pays unemployment insurance will require the employee who is reinstated with back pay to return the unemployment insurance benefits.

Generally, when an arbitrator rules that interim earnings are going to be deducted from the back-pay award, the grievant has a

---

[87]Darby Printing Co., 49 LA 831 (King, 1967).

[88]Lakeland Community College, 93 LA 909 (Richard, 1989).

[89]Chrome Deposit Corp., 102 LA 733 (Bethel, 1994); Giddings & Lewis Measurement Sys., 99 LA 17 (Duda, 1992); Quemetco Inc., 96 LA 134 (Darrow, 1990); MRS Transp. Co., 95 LA 514 (Massey, 1990); Dow Chem. Co., 95 LA 510, 514 (Sartain, 1990); Sparklett Devices, Inc., 90 LA 910 (Fowler, 1988).

[90]For cases disallowing employers to deduct unemployment compensation from back pay, see Newport Steel Corp., 100 LA 1007 (Gibson, 1993); Niemand Indus., 94 LA 669 (Nolan, 1990); Armour-Dial, Inc., 76 LA 96 (Aaron, 1980); National Linen Serv., 74 LA 857 (Dunn, 1980); Kaiser Found. Health Plan, 73 LA 1057 (Herring, 1979).

[91]NLRB v. Gullett Gin Co., 340 U.S. 361, 364, 27 LRRM 2230, 2231 (1951) (citations omitted).

[92]Hill & Sinicropi, Remedies in Arbitration, 2d ed. 228–35 (BNA Books, 1991), citing NLRB v. Gullett Gin Co., 340 U.S. 361, 27 LRRM 2230 (1951).

[93]For cases allowing an employer to deduct unemployment compensation from an award of back pay, see Giddings & Lewis Measurement Sys., 99 LA 17 (Duda, 1992); Beverage Distribs., Inc., 96 LA 274 (Dworkin, 1990); O'Keeffe's Aluminum Prods. Inc., 92 LA 215 (Koven, 1989); Glover Bottled Gas Corp./Synergy Gas Corp., 91 LA 77 (Simons, 1987); General Felt Indus., Inc., 74 LA 972 (Carnes, 1979); Alvey, Inc., 74 LA 835 (Roberts, 1980); Dan-Van Rubber, Inc., 68 LA 217 (Rothschild, 1977); Vancouver Plywood Co., 68 LA 205 (Marcus, 1977).

[94]J&L Specialty Prods. Corp., 94 LA 600, 609–10 (Duda, 1990).

duty to disclose information regarding those earnings.[95] Nevertheless, according to one arbitrator, misrepresentation or concealment of interim earnings alone is not enough to preclude all back-pay liability. The arbitrator noted, however, that concealment of interim earnings may cause an arbitrator to reduce a back-pay award. In order to have a back-pay award reduced by concealed interim earnings, the employer must offer proof of concealment.[96]

Ultimately, however, back-pay awards and deductions depend on the arbitrator's discretion. Thus, arbitral silence as to whether certain deductions should be made may be construed as purposeful omission.[97] In light of this rule of construction, it may be argued that no deductions can be made from back-pay awards unless specified by the arbitrator.

*5. Lost Opportunities.* Absent a specific provision in the collective bargaining agreement limiting or otherwise defining how back pay is to be computed,[98] arbitrators may interpret the make whole concept to include compensation for lost overtime and other lost "opportunities." These forms of additional relief may need to be specifically requested in the grievance and at each stage of the grievance-arbitration process.[99]

*a. Overtime.* Lost overtime may be awarded unless it would be too speculative to assume that the employee would have worked some overtime during the back-pay period.[100] One arbitrator stated:

Ordinarily such [overtime] pay would be denied on the ground that the matter is purely conjectural. In this case it is not conjectural. By the Company's own admission Wansley would have been required to work,

---

[95]See also MacMillan Bloedel Containers, 94 LA 992, 995 (Nicholas, 1990) (equity is best served by accepting employee's own statements of income for period of unemployment to extent that they are plausible). See Volz & Goggin, eds., Elkouri & Elkouri, How Arbitration Works, 5th ed., 595 n.371 (BNA Books, 1997) (grievant has duty to reveal facts regarding deduction of outside compensation from computation of back pay).

[96]MacMillan Bloedel Containers, 94 LA 992 (Nicholas, 1990).

[97]Automobile Mechanics Local 701 v. Joe Mitchell Buick, Inc., 930 F.2d 576, 137 LRRM 2121 (7th Cir., 1991).

[98]Yoh Sec., Inc., 85 LA 196 (Goldsmith, 1985) (contract's provision limiting back pay to wages for "straight-time employment" precluded lost overtime award).

[99]Armstrong Air Conditioning, 99 LA 540 (Harlan, 1992) (overtime considered as part of award only if originally included as part of relief requested); Niemand Indus., 94 LA 669 (Nolan, 1990) (despite arbitrator's view that wrongfully discharged employees are "entitled to interest on back pay awards," interest denied because not requested until after original arbitration award on merits).

[100]See also Kaiser Eng'g, 102 LA 1189 (Minni, 1994) (lost overtime denied because "highly speculative"); Arkansas Aluminum Alloys, Inc., 87 LA 273, 277 (Allen, 1986) ("[b]ack pay is to be computed using straight time hours only, unless overtime hours are a regular and normal part of the work schedule"); Milwaukee Sewerage Comm'n, 66 LA 539 (Fleischli, 1976) (overtime awarded because it was undisputed that grievants would have been scheduled to work certain overtime hours); Reed Roller Bit Co., 30 LA 437 (Hebert, 1958) (overtime denied because determination would require conjecture); Masonite Corp., 10 LA 854 (McCoy, 1948) (overtime awarded because not conjectural).

and would have been subject to discipline had he refused. All the other men in his crew worked the extra hours, including the man who took his place. Wansley himself had worked all the hours offered him during the shutdown previous to this one. The facts remove the matter entirely from the field of conjecture.[101]

In determining whether lost overtime is available, arbitrators generally require the party requesting overtime to show that overtime would have been offered and accepted.[102] In addition, whether the overtime is optional or mandatory is one factor in determining whether damages for lost overtime would be speculative.[103] Also relevant are the grievant's attendance record and record of working overtime in the past.[104] Nonetheless, lost overtime pay may still be denied even where a grievant had worked significant overtime in the past, if it would require the arbitrator to speculate that the grievant would have accepted the overtime offered.[105]

b. Other Lost Opportunities.   Arbitrators occasionally include other lost opportunities in awards to prevailing grievants. For instance, missed opportunities for training[106] or promotions[107] may be awarded where they are not speculative.

## E. Reinstatement Without Back Pay

There are a number of circumstances in which arbitrators will direct reinstatement without back pay. In making this decision, arbitrators consider the severity of the employee conduct, whether the employee would be unjustly enriched by a back-pay award, and

---

[101]Masonite Corp., 10 LA 854, 856 (McCoy, 1948).

[102]Standard Brands, 57 LA 448 (Nicholas, 1971) (no basis for overtime award because grievant failed to adduce evidence of availability of overtime opportunities and likelihood of acceptance).

[103]Seneca Steel Div., 96 LA 838 (Fullmer, 1991) (overtime denied where acceptance of overtime was voluntary under contract); Air Treads of Atlanta, Inc., 85 LA 155 (Yancy, 1985) (overtime awarded where contract language required employee to work overtime when "properly notified"); Alliance Mfg. Co., 61 LA 101 (Gibson, 1973) (overtime denied where grievant was not required to work overtime and some of his co-workers had worked no overtime at all); Reed Roller Bit Co., 30 LA 437 (Hebert, 1958) (overtime denied because it was not required and, therefore, would require conjecture).

[104]Armstrong Air Conditioning, 99 LA 540 (Harlan, 1992) (overtime award denied because grievant's high rate of absenteeism and sick days would make determination too speculative).

[105]Shell Oil Co., 87 LA 473 (Nicholas, 1986).

[106]Tanner Cos., 98 LA 530 (Parent, 1991) (reinstating grievants and ordering employer to provide them with training opportunity they had missed because of their improper layoff).

[107]Boston Edison Co., 92 LA 375 (Nicolau, 1988) (reinstating grievant to the position to which she would have been promoted if she had not been wrongfully suspended for failing a drug test under a void drug-testing policy); Georgia Pac. Corp., 88-2 ARB ¶ 8435 (Hewitt, 1988) (reinstating grievant to the job he would have successfully bid had he not been wrongfully discharged); Cleveland, Ohio City Sch. Dist., 82 LA 1302 (Hanes, 1984) (reinstating grievant to the position to which she had been approved for promotion prior to her suspension).

whether the employee followed the proper procedures, as well as other factors.

Where the employee conduct leading to discharge was particularly severe, some arbitrators award reinstatement without back pay. Examples of such severe conduct include involvement in a physical altercation with a co-worker or supervisor,[108] circumvention of collective bargaining channels to voice complaints,[109] consumption of alcohol on the job,[110] and serious violation of work or safety rules.[111]

Arbitrators may decline to award back pay where the award would unjustly enrich the discharged employee. Examples include cases where the employee has already received an equivalent sum via health insurance payments[112] or income from a second or interim job.[113]

Other circumstances in which arbitrators have ordered reinstatement without back pay include cases where employees decline to follow accepted "work now and grieve later" procedure,[114] where employees carelessly submit employment applications containing false information,[115] and where employees purposely violate company rules in order to challenge them in arbitration.[116]

---

[108]Keebler Co., 92 LA 871, 876 (Roumell, 1989) (employee who threatened to physically harm supervisor's family during off-duty altercation reinstated without back pay); Featherlite Mfg. Co., 74 LA 1101, 1103 (Bothwell, 1980) (employee provoked to assault supervisor reinstated without back pay); Affiliated Hosps. of San Francisco, 64 LA 29, 34 (Jacobs, 1975) (employee involved in physical altercation with co-worker in hospital cafeteria reinstated without back pay).

[109]United Cable Television Corp., 92 LA 3, 12 (Koven, 1988) (shop steward who posted defamatory and insubordinate letter on union bulletin board, rather than using the collective bargaining channels to voice his complaints, reinstated without back pay for failure to use appropriate forum for his allegations).

[110]Quaker Oats Co., 96 LA 419, 424 (Marcus, 1991) (employee who violated rule against possession of alcohol on company premises reinstated with "one last chance," but without back pay); Transit Auth. of River City, 95 LA 137, 148 (Dworkin, 1990) (alcoholic bus driver who admittedly consumed two beers 90 minutes prior to reporting to work reinstated to nondriving position without back pay).

[111]Chase Brass & Copper Co., 90 LA 916, 922 (Bressler, 1988) (employee discharged for serious safety violation involving dangerous use of furnace reinstated to different position without back pay); Air Treads, Inc., 86 LA 545, 549 (Allen, 1986) (employee discharged for serious work rule infraction reinstated without back pay).

[112]Schafer Bakeries, 95 LA 759, 767 (Brown, 1990) (employee who improperly made medical insurance claims on behalf of former husband without inquiring about his eligibility for insurance benefits was reinstated, but denied back pay to prevent employee from being unjustly enriched).

[113]Rock Hill Printing & Finishing Co., 64 LA 856, 861 (Whyte, 1975) (employee who was reinstated after being discharged for working a second job during his sick leave was not entitled to back pay from employer in addition to sum earned at second job).

[114]Pepsi Cola Bottling Co., 93 LA 520, 526 (Randell, 1989) (employee who refused to take blood alcohol test in violation of "obey now and grieve later" procedure reinstated without back pay). See, e.g., Fitzsimmons Mfg. Co., 92 LA 609, 616 (Roumell, 1989).

[115]Firestone Tire & Rubber Co., 93 LA 381, 384 (Cohen, 1989) (employee reinstated without back pay where arbitrator found that employee's errors and omissions regarding physical health on employment application were merely careless).

[116]Amoco Oil Co., 93 LA 1021, 1028 (Allen, 1989) (where employee purposely violated company rules in order to challenge them in arbitration, arbitrator awarded reinstatement without back pay).

## F. *Other Components of the Make Whole Remedy*

*1. Accrued Leaves.* Reinstated grievants may also be awarded credit for sick leave, vacation time, and holiday time lost as a result of the improper discharge or discipline. Where employees lose allotted sick days as a result of a lengthy suspension or discharge and are subsequently reinstated, some arbitrators will require that the lost days be added to the next employment period.[117] Similarly, where reinstated grievants' unemployment prevents them from accumulating the requisite number of work hours to earn additional vacation or holiday time for the following year, many arbitrators award credited vacation or holiday time.[118]

*2. Contributions to Retirement.* In addition to regular contractual benefits and accrued leaves, contractually mandated contributions to health and welfare funds, pension funds, and IRAs are normally included in back-pay awards. Generally, these contributions are paid directly to the appropriate fund, rather than to the grievant.[119] In the case of health insurance contributions, however, some arbitrators order reimbursement of actual medical expenses incurred during the period of unemployment rather than ineffective retroactive contributions to the company's health plan.[120] Generally, these reimbursements are provided only where the grievant has made reasonable efforts to mitigate losses. For example, where the employee has attempted to procure private health insurance or to remain enrolled pursuant to COBRA, and has nevertheless incurred medical expenses that would have been avoided had he not been improperly discharged, reimbursement will be ordered.[121]

---

[117]Union Elec. Co., 93 LA 749, 753 (Fowler, 1989) (reinstated employee credited for paid sickness/accident leave); Armour Foods Co., 87 LA 250 (Eisler, 1986) (same).

[118]O'Keeffe's Aluminum Prods., 92 LA 215, 218 (Koven, 1989) (grievant received credit toward vacation for the period of his unemployment); Cowlitz Redi-Mix, 85 LA 745, 752 (Boedecker, 1985) (arbitrator combined hours grievant actually worked and hours grievant would have worked during unemployment period in order to determine the amount of vacation and holiday credit owed).

[119]Automobile Mechanics Local 701 v. Joe Mitchell Buick, Inc., 930 F.2d 576, 578, 137 LRRM 2121 (7th Cir., 1991) (grievants entitled to contributions to health and welfare funds as provided in collective bargaining agreement). See also O'Keeffe's Aluminum Prods., 92 LA 215, 218 (Koven, 1989) (grievant received credit for lost IRA contributions); Glover Bottled Gas Corp./Synergy Gas Corp., 91 LA 77, 93 (Simons, 1987) (grievant awarded reimbursement of lost payments to his pension trust fund account as well as certain amounts under profit-sharing plan).

[120]Riverside Osteopathic Hosp., 98 LA 1044, 1051 (McDonald, 1991) (hospital that improperly denied sickness and accident coverage to disabled nurse during and after union strike ordered to pay sickness and accident benefits, retroactive medical benefits, medical bills, and reimbursement of all payments made to third-party insurance carrier); O'Keeffe's Aluminum Prods., 92 LA 215, 218 (Koven, 1989) (grievant reimbursed for actual medical expenses incurred during unemployment period because health care contributions would not have been paid directly to grievant in any event).

[121]Nursing Home, 88 LA 681, 682–83 (Sedwick, 1987) (employer directed to pay medical bills incurred by grievant for the period that grievant should have been covered by Blue Cross/

*3. Seniority.*   Normally, grievants reinstated receive credit for time off for purposes of calculating length of service or seniority.[122] Seniority credit is usually awarded even where back pay is denied.[123] Occasionally, however, where an employee deserves some punishment for conduct short of discharge, arbitrators will reinstate the employee without seniority for the period of suspension or discharge.[124]

# III. Reduction in Penalty

## A. Authority

The language of many labor agreements expressly or implicitly grants the arbitrator authority to modify the penalty imposed by the employer when it is found to be improper. In other labor agreements, this authority is expressly limited or unclear and the arbitrator's authority to modify the penalty is often a contested issue. Two primary views have been expressed by arbitrators regarding their function in reviewing disciplinary penalties.

One view, adopted by several arbitrators, is that determining the penalty for misconduct is properly a function of management. That is, as stated by one arbitrator, "[t]he Arbitrator should not substitute his judgment for that of management in a case where there is definite cause for discharge."[125]

Another arbitrator articulated the rationale for this principle in the following manner:

> Where an employee has violated a rule or engaged in conduct meriting disciplinary action, it is primarily the function of management to decide upon the proper penalty. If management acts in good faith upon a fair

---

Blue Shield major medical unless grievant did not appropriately mitigate damages). But see Riverside Osteopathic Hosp., 98 LA 1044, 1051 (McDonald, 1991) (disabled nurse did not fail to mitigate damages relating to unpaid medical bills even though she did not continue group medical coverage after receiving notice of her right to do so under COBRA).

[122]Chrome Deposit Corp., 102 LA 733 (Bethel, 1994) (grievant reinstated with full seniority). See, e.g., Yellow Cab Coop. Ass'n, 102 LA 848, 854 (Watkins, 1993); GTE N., 98 LA 894 (Dworkin, 1992); Utah Power & Light Co., 94 LA 233 (Winograd, 1990); Amana Refrigeration, 93 LA 249 (Mikrut, 1989).

[123]Schafer Bakeries, Inc., 95 LA 759 (Brown, 1990) (seniority awarded where back pay denied). See, e.g., Iowa-Illinois Gas & Elec. Co., 95 LA 553 (Volz, 1990); Dow Chem. Co., 95 LA 510 (Sartain, 1990); J&L Specialty Prods. Corp., 94 LA 601 (Duda, 1990); Pepsi Cola Bottling Co., 93 LA 520, 525 (Randall, 1989); Firestone Tire & Rubber Co., 92 LA 381, 384 (Cohen, 1989).

[124]City of Massillon, Ohio, 92 LA 1303, 1305 (Elkin, 1989) (arbitrator ordered grievant reinstated without back pay, benefits, or seniority for discharge period because although discharge was too severe a punishment for grievant's physical altercation with a co-worker, significant penalty was justified). See Volz & Goggin, eds., Elkouri & Elkouri, How Arbitration Works, 5th ed., 940 nn. 260–261 (BNA Books, 1997); Burton Mfg. Co., 82 LA 1228 (Holey, 1984) (insubordinate employee reinstated without back pay, seniority rights, or benefits in order to reduce the severity of his penalty).

[125]White Pine Copper Co., 63-2 ARB ¶ 8548 (Larkin, 1963). See also Franz Food Prods., Inc., 28 LA 543, 548 (Bothwell, 1957).

investigation and fixes a penalty not inconsistent with that imposed in other like cases, an arbitrator should not disturb it. The mere fact that management has imposed a somewhat different penalty or a somewhat more severe penalty than the arbitrator would have, if he had had the decision to make originally, is no justification for changing it. The minds of equally reasonable men differ. A consideration which would weigh heavily with one man will seem of less importance to another. A circumstance which highly aggravates an offense in one man's eyes may be only slight aggravation to another. If an arbitrator could substitute his judgment and discretion for the judgment and discretion honestly exercised by management, then the functions of management would have been abdicated, and unions would take every case to arbitration. The result would be intolerable to employees as to management.[126]

Other arbitrators have termed this the "unreasonable, capricious, or arbitrary action" standard of review. [127]

The majority view is that where the agreement does not impose a clear limitation on the authority to modify a penalty, an arbitrator may reduce the penalty even in the absence of arbitrary, capricious, or discriminatory behavior.[128] Another arbitrator declared that the authority for arbitrators to modify a penalty imposed by management is "irrefutable absent a contractual provision to the contrary."[129] Similarly, another arbitrator stated:

> The discharge penalty requires careful examination. While management's judgment of appropriate penalties is entitled to great weight as part of its function, the Arbitrator, nevertheless, has a mandatory role to examine it and ascertain whether it is arbitrary, discriminatory, contrary to past practice for similar offenses, whether it violates the rules for corrective discipline, or it is draconian in its severity under all the circumstances.[130]

In an early article on arbitration, another arbitrator noted:

> In many disciplinary cases, the reasonableness of the penalty imposed on an employee rather than the existence of proper cause of disciplining

---

[126]Stockholm Pipe Fittings Co., 1 LA 160, 162 (McCoy, 1945). See also Interstate Brands, 97 LA 675, 677 (Ellmann, 1991) (quoting Arbitrator McCoy with approval); Meredith Corp., 78 LA 859, 863 (Talent, 1982) (observing that the McCoy view "has been followed by a substantial and respectable segment of the arbitral community"); North Star Steel Co., 68 LA 114, 123 (Hadlick, 1977) ("[I]t is a function of management to decide upon a proper penalty. It is not the province of the arbitrator to substitute his judgment for the judgment of the Company, if it is established that the management acted in good faith, upon a fair investigation, and fixed a penalty not inconsistent with that imposed in other like cases."); Trans World Airlines, Inc., 41 LA 142, 143–44 (Beatty, 1963) ("an arbitration clause is not an abdication by management of its duties in regard to discipline and discharge and does not grant to the arbitrator authority to redetermine the whole matter by his own standards as if he were making the original decision.").

[127]See JPI Plumbing Prods., 97 LA 386, 388 (Kilroy, 1991); Park Geriatric Village, 81 LA 306, 311 (Lewis, 1983); Porcelain Metals Corp., 73 LA 1133, 1140 (Roberts, 1979).

[128]See Chapter 2 for a review of appropriateness of the penalty as an element of just cause.

[129]General Dynamics, 100 LA 180, 184 (Francis, 1992). See also Kaiser Sand & Gravel, 49 LA 190, 193 (Koven, 1967) (the right to alter a penalty is "inherent in his power to decide the sufficiency of cause").

[130]Interstate Brands, 97 LA 675, 679 (Ellmann, 1991), quoting Harry Casselman.

him is the question the arbitrator must decide. In disciplinary cases generally, therefore, most arbitrators exercise the right to change or modify a penalty if it is found to be improper or too severe, under all circumstances of the situation. This right is deemed to be inherent in the arbitrator's power to discipline and in his authority to finally settle and adjust the dispute before him.[131]

Similar views have been expressed by arbitrators in other cases.[132]

Even under the majority view, when the agreement imposes a clear limitation on the arbitrator's power to modify a penalty, arbitrators respect this limitation. The arbitrator's function under such an agreement is merely to determine whether the employee engaged in conduct giving rise to the discipline. Thus, where a collective bargaining agreement explicitly provided that the "arbitrator may not modify disciplinary penalties," an arbitrator held that his only authority was to decide whether some disciplinary action should have been taken against the grievant.[133]

Before arbitrators will recognize limitations on their ability to modify penalties, however, the agreement must contain clear language that the arbitrator is not to have discretion to reduce a penalty. Language denying the arbitrator "power to add to or subtract from or modify any of the terms of this agreement" will probably not prohibit arbitral discretion.[134] Similarly, language stating that the "Arbitration Committee shall be judicial rather than legislative" did not remove arbitral jurisdiction to modify a penalty.[135]

## B. Factors Considered

Numerous factors may be considered when an arbitrator evaluates a penalty. The most prominent factors are discussed briefly below.[136]

---

[131]Platt, "The Arbitration Process in the Settlement of Labor Disputes," 31 J. Am. Jud. Soc'y 54, 58 (1947).

[132]See Schulze & Burch Biscuit Co., 100 LA 948, 955 (Goldstein, 1993) ("inherent in the power to review is the authority to exercise the right to change or modify a penalty so that it is consonant with all proofs adduced"); Monfort Packing Co., 66 LA 286, 293–94 (Goodman, 1976) ("the concept of just and sufficient cause mandates not only a determination that the employee was guilty of the infraction, but that the reasons for the discharge were fair and just under the circumstances"); Kennecott Copper Corp., 56 LA 924, 926 (Hayes, 1970) (quoting the Platt view with express approval); Kaiser Sand & Gravel, 49 LA 190, 193 (Koven, 1967) (the right to alter a penalty is "inherent in his [the arbitrator's] power to decide the sufficiency of cause"); Mississippi Valley Gas Co., 41 LA 745, 750 (Hebert, 1963) (denying that the arbitrator is merely to determine whether management's action was arbitrary or capricious and declaring that the arbitrator has a responsibility to determine whether the punishment fits the crime).

[133]Allied Paper, Inc., 52 LA 957 (Williams, 1969).

[134]See Lima Elec. Co., Inc., 63 LA 94, 97 (Albrechta, 1974).

[135]International Harvester Co., 53 LA 1197, 1202 (Seinsheimer, 1969).

[136]For a more thorough discussion of these factors, including additional citations, see Volz & Goggin, eds., Elkouri & Elkouri, How Arbitration Works, 5th ed., 910–39 (BNA Books, 1997). Many additional cases are cited at 630–47 in the third edition and at 664–88 in the fourth edition of Elkouri & Elkouri.

*1. Nature of Offense.* An arbitrator's willingness to modify a penalty may vary according to the nature of the offense. Generally, offenses committed by employees are divided into two categories: extremely serious and less serious. As one arbitrator explained:

> Offenses are of two general classes: (1) those extremely serious offenses such as stealing, striking a foreman, persistent refusal to obey a legitimate order, etc., which usually justify summary discharge without the necessity of prior warnings or attempts at corrective discipline; (2) those less serious infractions of plant rules or of proper conduct such as tardiness, absence without permission, careless workmanship, insolence, etc., which call not for discharge for the first offense (and usually not even for the second or third offense) but for some milder penalty aimed at correction.[137]

For extremely serious offenses, arbitrators enforce penalties that meet the seriousness of the offense.[138] In cases of less serious offenses, the concept of corrective or progressive discipline is applied.[139]

*2. Due Process Violations.*[140]   If the employer fails to meet basic requirements of due process when imposing discipline, arbitrators are not likely to sustain the discipline assessed against the employee.[141] The category of due process violation is significant in determining the type of reduction in penalty an arbitrator will require.

a. Procedural.   Many labor agreements prescribe specific procedural prerequisites for discharge or discipline. When the employer contravenes the prescribed requirement, arbitrators generally adopt one of the following three positions: (1) strict compliance with the procedural requirements is required and failure to comply nullifies the entire action; (2) the procedural requirements are of significance only where the employee can show that he or she has been prejudiced by failure to comply; or (3) the procedural requirements are important and any failure to comply will be penalized, but the action taken is not nullified.[142]

In many cases arbitrators have refused to uphold disciplinary action where the employer failed to fulfill a procedural requirement

---

[137]Huntington Chair Corp., 24 LA 490, 491 (McCoy, 1955).

[138]For cases recognizing that summary discharge is proper for serious offenses, see Central Soya Co., 74 LA 1084, 1090 (Cantor, 1980) (threatening a foreman); Alaska Sales & Serv. Co. 73 LA 164, 166 (Axon, 1979) (disloyalty to employer); Liberal Mkt., Inc., 71 LA 148, 151 (Layborne, 1978) (extortion); Factory Servs., Inc., 70 LA 1088, 1091 (Fitch, 1978) (false statements concerning safety maliciously made to regulatory agency); Stansteel Corp., 69 LA 776, 779 (Kaufman, 1977) (possession of marijuana and giving it to fellow employee at work); National Can Corp., 68 LA 351, 352 (Turkus, 1977) ("openly defiant and egregiously insubordinate" conduct).

[139]See Chapter 2 for a full discussion of progressive discipline.

[140]See Chapter 6 for a discussion of the requirements of due process.

[141]For an analysis of specific types of due process violations, see Chapter 2.

[142]Fleming, The Labor Arbitration Process, 139 (1965).

of the agreement, such as providing notice of an investigation,[143] or a requirement for a hearing, or joint discussion prior to the assessment of punishment.[144] In overturning a discharge, one arbitrator explained the importance of strict compliance with the contractual requirements as follows:

> Compliance with this review provision [of the agreement], in my opinion, is a condition precedent to any valid discharge from employment in the absence of "situations of urgency." The review requirement is important because, among other things, it tends to diminish the likelihood of impulsive and arbitrary decisions by supervisors and permits tempers to cool and deliberate judgment to prevail; it encourages careful investigation of the facts by both the Company and the Union; it provides an opportunity whereby the accused may be heard; it permits the presentation, shifting and weighing of all relevant factors; it provides an opportunity to measure the proposed penalty against the alleged offense in the light of the grievant's history, the past treatment by the employer of similar offenses, and other relevant circumstances; it permits consideration of apologies, regrets, and other mitigating circumstances; and enables the parties to consider rehabilitation possibilities.[145]

In a real sense, this contractual requirement of a prior review is a part of contractual "due process," without which a discharge must be held premature and wrongful.[146]

In other cases, arbitrators have found compliance with the spirit of procedural requirements sufficient because the employee was not adversely affected by the employer's failure to comply with the specific procedural requirements.[147] Similarly, the breach of the contractual procedure was held immaterial where the evidence of guilt was very

---

[143]Stroehmann Bakeries, 98 LA 873 (Sands, 1990) (discharge overturned due to inadequate investigation); Champion Spark Plug Co., 93 LA 1277, 1283 (Dobry, 1989) (discharge reduced to suspension where employer technically violated notice-of-charges requirement); Zenith Radio Corp., 47 LA 257, 258 (Griffin, 1966) (duty to notify union prior to discharge).

[144]Capital Hill Hosp., 93 LA 947, 952 (Jones, 1989) (grievant terminated without a fair-minded investigation of the circumstances since she was not given a pretermination opportunity to present her own account of the circumstances); Bethlehem Steel Corp., 54 LA 361, 362–63 (Porter, 1969) (contract gave employee right to present evidence before being discharged); Pittsburgh Steel Co., 47 LA 923, 926 (McDermott, 1966) (failure to give employee or union an opportunity to question the foreman who was the employee's accuser).

[145]Decor Corp., 44 LA 389, 391 (Kates, 1965).

[146]Id.

[147]See Union Oil Co. of Cal., 91 LA 1206, 1208 (Klein, 1988) (to overturn employer's action on procedural grounds, proof must exist that grievant was denied fair consideration of his case due to procedural error; discipline sustained, but employer ordered to pay union's arbitration costs since union was forced to arbitrate because of procedural defect); Central Tel. Co., 76 LA 1137, 1139 (Mead, 1981) (stating that the procedural defect was "technical in nature and has not deprived the grievant of due process"); Cameron Iron Works, 73 LA 878, 881–82 (Marlatt, 1979) (employer "totally ignored" a contract procedural requirement but discharge was sustained since the employee clearly was guilty of a serious offense and had not been prejudiced by the procedural defect); FlintKote Co., 49 LA 810, 816–17 (Block, 1967) (violation was merely technical and did not work to employee's disadvantage).

damaging[148] and where the union waived the contractual requirement by acquiescence.[149]

Even in the absence of procedural requirements, arbitrators have reduced a penalty because the employer failed to make a reasonable investigation or inquiry before assessing punishment.[150] In one such case, the arbitrator observed:

> [I]t is well established in labor arbitration that prior to assessing discipline, management, except in the most obvious and heinous of situations * * * must conduct a fair and impartial investigation of the incident and that a sufficient quantum of evidence or proof must be adduced by the accusing party in order to establish the guilt of the charged party.[151]

Arbitrators have also refused to sustain the penalty when the employer failed to give an employee the chance to be heard.[152] As one arbitrator noted:

> A just cause proviso, standing alone, demands that certain minimal essentials of due process be observed. One at least of those minimum essentials is that the accused have an opportunity, before sentence is carried out, to be heard in his own defense. * * * It is the *process*, not the *result*, which is at issue.[153]

In another case, the arbitrator refused to uphold the penalty where management did not give the employee the opportunity to question his accuser.[154]

b. Rules.[155]   Arbitrators have reduced penalties where the employer failed to consistently apply and enforce or widely disseminate

---

[148]California Elec. Power Co., 11 LA 1 (Prasow, 1948).

[149]Shwayder Bros., 7 LA 552 (Whiting, 1947).

[150]See Carbidie Corp., 100 LA 763, 766 (Felice, 1993) (discharge reduced to suspension where grievant not allowed to explain inconsistencies in time records and employer failed to conduct objective investigation in the matter); Carl Bolander & Sons Co., 100 LA 1, 3 (Reynolds, 1992) (discharge reduced to suspension where no suspension pending investigation or review by higher authorities, rather grievant fired on the spot); Missouri Research Labs., 55 LA 197, 209 (Erbs, 1970) (only one side of the matter was investigated).

[151]Great Midwest Mining Corp., 82 LA 52, 55 (Mikrut, 1984).

[152]McCartney's, Inc., 84 LA 799, 804 (Nelson, 1985).

[153]Id. (emphasis in original). See also United States Steel Corp., 29 LA 272, 277–78 (Babb, 1957) (discharge reversed where employer gave employees no chance to be heard but discharged them summarily upon learning that they had been convicted of larceny by a court).

[154]See also PQ Corp., 101 LA 694, 699 (Pratte, 1993) (penalty reduced where employer failed to give union or employee opportunity to speak with co-worker who was key player in events giving rise to discipline); Interstate Brands, 97 LA 675, 680 (Ellmann, 1991) (penalty reduced where employee not able to confront accuser); Marion Power Shovel Div., 82 LA 1014, 1016 (Kates, 1984); Pittsburgh Steel Co., 47 LA 923, 926 (McDermott, 1966) (penalty reduced where employer failed to give employee or union an opportunity to question the foreman who was the employee's accuser); American Iron & Mach. Works Co., 19 LA 417, 419–20 (Merrill, 1952) (discharge on the basis of a finding by the company physician without giving employee opportunity to present countervailing medical testimony was held improper).

[155]See Chapter 2.

a rule.[156] One arbitrator observed that "[j]ust cause requires that employees be informed of a rule, infraction of which may result in suspension or discharge, unless conduct is so clearly wrong that specific reference is not necessary."[157] Therefore, it has been held that an employer does not have to have specific rules for certain well-recognized proven offenses such as drunkenness, theft, or insubordination.[158]

   i. Warnings.[159]   Arbitrators have refused to sustain penalties where the employer failed to give prior warnings, particularly in discharge cases.[160] Where an employee continues prohibited conduct after having been warned, however, the fact that he was warned clearly stands against him.[161] Arbitrators have emphasized that no prior notice or warning is required where the offense is particularly egregious or legally and morally wrong.[162]

   ii. Lax Enforcement of Rules.[163]   Arbitrators have reduced penalties where the employer over a period of time had condoned violation of the rule.[164] Lax enforcement of rules may lead employees to reasonably believe that the conduct in question is sanctioned by management.[165]

---

[156]Oshita Int'l, 97 LA 592, 596 (Silver, 1991) (employee's discharge reduced to 1-week suspension because employee was not on notice of any general company policy making insubordination a dischargeable offense; no work rules stating insubordination would result in discharge and no other employees had previously been disciplined or discharged for insubordination); Georgia-Pacific Corp., 94 LA 667, 669 (Shearer, 1990) (discharge reduced to suspension for employee who admittedly took fixtures from salvage trailer where employer failed to clearly inform grievant it discontinued practice of giving away salvage items); Armco Inc., 93 LA 561, 562 (Strongin, 1989) (discharge reduced to written reprimand for employee refusing to remove writing from hard hat, in part because company had no rule or policy concerning writing on hard hats supplied by company).

[157]Lockheed Aircraft Corp., 28 LA 829, 831 (Hepburn, 1957). See also Foster Food Prods., 98 LA 854 (D'Spain, 1992) (employer failed to post amended policy).

[158]Philco Corp., 45 LA 437, 441 (Keeler, 1956). See discussions in Chapters 7, 8, and 10.

[159]See Chapter 2.

[160]See Maryland Jockey Club of Baltimore City, 99 LA 1025, 1028 (Farwell, 1992) (reduction of suspension to written warning because employer failed to follow negotiated rules that provided for a warning prior to more severe discipline such as a suspension); Cleaners Hanger Co., 93 LA 526, 529 (Miller, 1989) (discharge reduced to 3-day suspension where grievant received no warning prior to his discharge to improve his work); Glengarry Forest Prods., Ltd., 56 LA 725, 727 (Brown, 1971) (employer not justified in discharging employee who took vacation without securing permission from employer, since employer failed to warn employee after start of unauthorized vacation that his job would be in jeopardy if he did not immediately return to work).

[161]See Potash Co., of Am., 40 LA 582, 585–86 (Abernethy, 1963).

[162]King Soopers, Inc., 101 LA 107, 111 (Snider, 1993) ("[i]t is also well accepted that where the conduct at issue is egregious, such that it would be generally recognized as sexual harassment, no prior notice or warning need be given to the offending employee").

[163]See Chapter 2.

[164]See Champion Spark Plug Co., 93 LA 1277, 1284 (Dobry, 1989) (discharge reduced to suspension of grievant who used abusive language toward supervisor where grievant's behavior was not so different from that which had gone unpunished on numerous previous occasions; management's "lax enforcement was a signal that unacceptable behavior was tolerable").

[165]Great Plains Bag Corp., 83 LA 1281, 1285 (Laybourne, 1984) (discharge for tardiness in reporting to work station held improper where there was no notice that the rule, which had not been enforced for 4 years, was going to be enforced).

Although previously having been lax, an employer can strictly enforce a rule after making it clear that it intends to do so.[166] Furthermore, the arbitration of a case involving discharge for violation of a rule serves clear notice to the employees that in the future this type of misconduct will be deemed a dischargeable offense by the employer.[167]

*3. Delay in Assessing Discipline.*    Arbitrators have reduced penalties because the employer unduly delayed the assessment or enforcement of discipline.[168] One arbitrator stated: "[I]t is a denial of procedural due process and just cause to hold a charge over an employee's head indefinitely and to revive it whenever corroborating or substantiating evidence might eventually surface."[169]

Delays ranging from several weeks up to a year or more have been permitted when the delay was due to employer participation in a police investigation,[170] employee appeals,[171] or when the contract did not provide a time requirement.[172] Similarly, delays have been permitted when they did not result in prejudice to the employee.[173]

*4. Management Also at Fault.*    Where management is also at fault in connection with the employee's wrongful conduct, the arbitrator may reduce the penalty assessed by management.[174] If the conduct

---

[166]Hartman Elec. Mfg. Co., 48 LA 681, 683 (Dyke, 1967); Fairbanks Morse, Inc., 47 LA 224, 226 (Fisher, 1966).

[167]Universal Match Corp., 42 LA 184, 186 (Coffey, 1963).

[168]See Furr's Supermarkets, 95 LA 1021, 1024 (Rezler, 1990); Sunweld Fitting Co., 72 LA 544, 557 (Hawkins, 1979); M.S.L. Indus., Inc., 53 LA 75, 78 (Lehoczky, 1969); Gibson Refrigerator Div., 52 LA 663, 666 (Keefe, 1969); Ed Friedrich, Inc., 37 LA 1003, 1006–07 (Schedler, 1961); Ashland Oil, 28 LA 874, 878 (Bradley, 1957) ("Holding the threat of the penalty over the employee for approximately four months is something of a penalty in itself."); National Carbide Co., 27 LA 128, 130 (Warns, 1956) (discharge set aside where delay in notifying the employee of his discharge made it difficult for him to obtain witnesses in his own behalf).

[169]DeVry Inst. of Tech., 87 LA 1149, 1157 (Berman, 1986).

[170]Id. (employer did not waive its right to impose discipline by failing to act for more than 6 months where the employer was participating in a police investigation and had agreed to take no action against its employees until the police matter was completed).

[171]Southwestern Ill. Coal Corp., 80 LA 806, 807–08 (Hewitt, 1983) (delay was attributed to the grievant's actions in appealing his court conviction).

[172]Rocky Mountain Arsenal, 77 LA 229, 232 (Rockwell, 1981) (stating that there "is no acceptable reason for a delay of approximately nine weeks in imposing a suspension against any employee," but that the "contract in effect at that time had no provision that actions be completed within a certain number of days and therefore there is no violation of the contract").

[173]Gardner-Denver Cooper Indus., 76 LA 26, 30 (Witney, 1980) (3-week "delay in the discharge did not harm the Grievant or prejudice his rights").

[174]See Hess Oil, 98 LA 789 (Hooper, 1992) (A 5-day suspension was reduced to 1-day disciplinary layoff where a 14-year oil refinery employee's alleged negligence in monitoring the control panels caused the refinery unit to shut down. The employee's supervisor ordered him to pay "particular attention" to what the supervisor was doing to correct a problem with another unit. Because of this order the grievant was unable to continue his monitoring of the refinery unit.); Steel Branch Mining, 96 LA 931, 936 (Roberts, 1991) (employer partially responsible because it failed to replace a part it knew was missing; regardless of grievant's unsafe operation of the vehicle, replacement of that part would have avoided any damage or injuries); Southwest Airlines, 93 LA 575, 580 (Morris, 1989) (company partially at fault for not providing painted lines on ramp to show "safe area" to park airplane); Social Sec. Admin., 81 LA 1051, 1053

is particularly egregious, the mere fact that a supervisor is partially at fault may not result in a reduction of penalty.[175]

*5. Discriminatory Treatment.* a. Unequal. It is generally accepted that all employees who engage in the same type of misconduct must be treated essentially the same unless a reasonable basis exists for variation in assessing punishment.[176] Arbitrators have frequently refused to uphold variations in punishment where the differences were not supported by some reasonable basis.[177]

Variations in penalties will be allowed where a reasonable basis exists, such as different degrees of fault or mitigating circumstances affecting some but not all employees. The variations in penalties assessed do not necessarily mean the employer's action has been discriminatory. One arbitrator observed:

> The term "discrimination" connotes a distinction in treatment, especially an unfair distinction. The prohibition against discrimination requires like treatment under like circumstances. In the case of offenses the circumstances include the nature of the offense, the degree of fault and the mitigating and aggravating factors. There is no discrimination, or no departure from the consistent or uniform treatment of employees, merely because of variations in discipline reasonably appropriate to the variations in circumstances. Two employees may refuse a work assignment. For one it is his first offense, there being no prior warning or misconduct standing against his record. The other has been warned and disciplined for the very same offense on numerous occasions. It cannot be seriously contended that discrimination results if identical penalties are not meted out.[178]

---

(Muessig, 1983) (an emotional situation that provoked grievant's outburst was established when an employee was questioned in a public setting that a supervisor "should have known would be confrontational and embarrassing" for the employee).

[175]Gerber Prods Co., 46 LA 956, 959 (Howlett, 1966) (discharge sustained because fact that supervisor was not entirely without fault in an incident was held not to excuse or justify physical assault by employee).

[176]King Soopers, Inc., 101 LA 107, 112 (Snider, 1993) ("It is commonly recognized that work rules must be enforced in a consistent manner; all employees who engage in the same type of misconduct must be treated essentially the same, unless a reasonable or valid basis exists for variations in treatment").

[177]See JPI Plumbing Prods., 97 LA 386, 388–89 (Kilroy, 1991) (discharge reduced to suspension where co-worker who had also been discharged for poor performance on same tank line on same day was reinstated following investigation); Arvin Indus., 96 LA 1185, 1188 (Volz, 1991) (discharge reduced to suspension for employee who violated alcohol policy (first offense) because co-workers whose alcohol-related misconduct was more flagrant received written warnings and 5-day suspensions for first and second offenses); Gold Kist, 94 LA 152, 154 (Byars, 1990) (discharge reduced to written warning where employee received third warning in 6 ½ years for failing to wear gloves while another employee discharged under same rule received three warnings in 3 years before being discharged); T.W. Recreational Servs., 93 LA 302, 310 (Richard, 1989) (company not free to determine discharge was appropriate penalty when it did not discharge other tour guides with less seniority and worse records for similar or more severe breaches of similar duties of care in the past).

[178]Alan Wood Steel Co., 21 LA 843, 849 (Short, 1954). See also Kaiser Steel Corp., 48 LA 1118, 1120 (Block, 1967). In upholding different penalties assessed by management against fight participants, Arbitrator Block noted: "The wisdom of a rule calling for identical penalties to all employees involved in a fight, without regard to culpability, is certainly open to question."

b. *Antiunion.*   In some cases management penalties will be reduced where it appears that antiunion animus contributed to management's action against the employee.[179] Management cannot rid itself of zealous union advocates under the guise of "just cause" discharges.[180] Some arbitrators say that a charge of discrimination because of union activities cannot rest upon mere "surmise, inference or conjecture;"[181] rather evidence is required to sustain such charges.[182]

6. *Employment History.*   In determining the appropriate penalty for an offense, some consideration is usually given to an employee's employment record including both the quality of performance evaluations and lack of discipline as well as length of service.

a. Employment Record.   Arbitrators have reduced penalties in consideration of the employee's good, lengthy past record.[183] Alternatively, an arbitrator's refusal to modify a penalty may be based in part upon the employee's poor past record.[184] There are limitations in considering past offenses. As a rule, arbitrators will not consider past rule infractions where the employee was neither reprimanded[185] nor notified of alleged infractions at the time of their occurrence.[186]

---

[179]See Folsom Return to Custody, Inc., 101 LA 837, 843 (Staudohar, 1993); Steiger Tractor, Inc., 72 LA 175, 179 (O'Connell, 1979) (clear proof existed in the statement of grievant's supervisor that he was mad because grievant went to the union and that he intended to harass grievant "right out of here").

[180]Arden Farms Co., 45 LA 1124, 1130 (Tsukiyama, 1965) (charge of antiunion animus found to be without substance).

[181]New York Racing Ass'n, 43 LA 129, 135 (Scheiber, 1964).

[182]See American Transp. Corp., 81 LA 318, 324 (Nelson, 1983) (stating that to support a charge of antiunion discrimination "there must be evidence and/or powerful inferences reasonably drawn from the evidence"); Thunderbird Inn, 77 LA 849, 852 (Armstrong, 1981) (stating that a charge of antiunion discrimination "requires clear proof"); Steiger Tractor, Inc., 72 LA 175, 179 (O'Connell, 1979) (mere "coincidence" of discipline and assumption of union office, "standing alone," is insufficient to establish antiunion discrimination); Great Atl. & Pac. Tea Co., 45 LA 495, 498 (Livengood, undated) (that grievant was an active union member is not enough to make a case of antiunion discrimination).

[183]See Clow Water Sys., Co., 102 LA 377, 380 (Dworkin, 1994) (employee worked for employer for 15 years without a single disciplinary event); Delmarva Power & Light Co., 100 LA 457, 462 (DiLauro, 1992); General Dynamics, 100 LA 180, 185 (Francis, 1992) (grievant had a record free of any past discipline or of any complaint on the quality of her work during 14-year tenure), Astro-Valcour, 93 LA 91, 97 (Rocha, 1989); Federal-Mogul Corp., 91 LA 1402, 1405 (Nathan, 1988) (grievant had a "clean record" and was not a problem employee; "to discharge her for this first incident would be an overreaction"); Armour Food Co., 86 LA 1197, 1199 (Eisler, 1986) (grievant had good work record with no history of poor job performance).

[184]See Hayes Int'l Corp., 80 LA 1313, 1320 (Traynor, 1983) ("one can conclude from the evidence he has been anything but an exemplary employee"); Electronic Corp. of Am., 3 LA 217, 218–20 (Kaplan, 1946) (neither the incident at the time of discharge nor any other single incident cited by the employer was sufficient to warrant discharge; however, the general pattern of the employee's unsatisfactory conduct, as established by a series of incidents over an extended period, was preponderant evidence justifying discharge).

[185]Western Air Lines, Inc., 37 LA 130, 133 (Wyckoff, 1961).

[186]Carnation Co., 42 LA 568, 570–71 (Miller, 1964) ("Past incidents, for which no formal disciplinary action was taken and no official records maintained, and which cannot at a later date be adequately investigated, cannot be accepted" to support discharge.); Consolidated Vultee Aircraft Corp., 10 LA 907, 908 (Dwyer, 1948).

Nor will arbitrators consider past warnings that have not been put in such form as to make them subject to a grievance.[187]

In some labor agreements the time period during which an employee's work record can be considered is limited.[188] In the absence of express limitation, the employer can generally consider the entire employment history. The more remote the incident, however, the less weight and consideration it receives. While emphasizing the need to consider a grievant's past record, one arbitrator noted:

> We sympathize with the position often taken by unions that there should be some limitation on how far back in the record one should be permitted to go in the matter of digging up old scores. Such historic incidents should be close enough in their relation to the problem involved in the immediate case to warrant consideration.[189]

Another arbitrator held that an employee's attendance record prior to a previous arbitration of his earlier discharge could not be considered in determining the propriety of the second discharge since the first arbitrator "wiped the slate clean."[190]

b. Length of Service.  Long-term service, particularly if the employee has a good record, is a factor clearly in the employee's favor.[191] One arbitrator commented: "Arbitrators often hold that such long term service [13 years] justifies special consideration of alternatives before a discharge is to be considered appropriate."[192] Nonetheless, even long service with the company will not save an employee's job if other factors strongly justify discharge.[193]

---

[187]Duval Corp., 43 LA 102, 106 (Myers, 1964).

[188]See, e.g., Peachtree Doors, 96 LA 828, 834 (Conley, 1991) (arbitrator refused to consider reference to grievant's record for previous years due to presence of "make clean the record" policy in labor agreement); United States Steel Corp., 53 LA 124, 126 (Dybeck, 1969) (employer was penalized for submitting evidence in violation of such provision).

[189]Borg-Warner Corp., 22 LA 589, 596 (Larkin, 1954). In Consolidated Foods Corp., 43 LA 1143, 1149–50 (Klein, 1964), reduced weight was given to discipline assessed before the union came to the plant.

[190]But see Babcock & Wilcox Co., 90 LA 607, 610–11 (Ruben, 1987) (employer permitted to consider an employee's 20-year work record despite a provision in the parties' labor agreement that discipline was "wiped-clean" after 1 year); American Brass Co., 88 LA 161 (Fullmer, 1986).

[191]For cases where this factor was given weight, see Merico, Inc., 98 LA 123, 126 (Silver, 1992) (13-year unblemished employment record); Food Barn Stores, 96 LA 266, 273 (Hilgert, 1990) (11-year "spotless" work record); Lakeside Jubilee Foods, 95 LA 358, 366 (Berquist, 1990) (22-year employee).

[192]Kaiser Permanente, 99 LA 490, 492 (Henner, 1992).

[193]Can-Tex Indus., 90 LA 1230, 1231 (Shearer, 1988) (discharge of 21-year employee with good record upheld where employee sexually harassed co-worker despite warning); Standard Oil Co., 89 LA 1155, 1158 (Feldman, 1987) (upheld discharge of long-term employee who pleaded guilty to drug trafficking); Schlage Lock Co., 88 LA 75 (Wyman, 1986) (just cause existed, under rule prohibiting sexual harassment, for discharge of 32-year employee with unblemished record where employer had practice of discharging both employees and management personnel found to have violated the rule).

## C. Conditional Reinstatement

Arbitrators have used conditional reinstatement to remedy situations where there was just cause for discipline but discharge was an unreasonable penalty under the circumstances. In these cases arbitrators have concluded that even after just cause has been found to discipline an employee, they have discretion to modify a penalty that is too harsh.

This general rule is best illustrated in several cases where problems with alcohol and drug abuse caused the employer to violate company rules. In *Growmark, Inc.,*[194] the employer discharged a truck driver who violated a company attendance policy by missing 5 consecutive days of work without giving notice. The employee had entered a substance abuse treatment program but had not requested medical leave in advance or otherwise informed the employer of his decision to enter the program.

The arbitrator found that just cause required looking at the reason behind the employee's action and the surrounding circumstances.[195] Just cause did not exist in this case because the employee had a good reason to justify his actions. Had he continued to drive without treatment, he would have created a danger to himself and the public. His emotional state, which the arbitrator described as "acute crisis" caused by exhaustion and frustration, also mitigated his failure to follow proper procedures in taking leave. (The arbitrator also noted that leave for substance abuse treatment was generally allowable under company rules[196]). Taking into consideration all these circumstances, the arbitrator awarded reinstatement on the following conditions: (1) the truck driver would have to comply with any company medical directives; and (2) for a 1-year probationary period, the employee was not to be absent from his job without first providing an "express statement of good reason."[197]

Generally, arbitrators do not consider postdischarge conduct.[198] There is, however, a developing trend in drug, alcohol, mental illness, and physical illness cases toward considering the employee's postdischarge conduct to determine whether to award conditional reinstatement instead of affirming a discharge. A reinstatement subject to conditions that prevent future transgressions by the employee (a conditional reinstatement) is sometimes viewed as a more reasonable disciplinary action, where the postdischarge conduct indicates that the employee has been rehabilitated and where the employer has not been significantly injured as a result of the employee's deviation from company rules.

---

[194]100 LA 785, 788 (Ver Ploeg, 1993).

[195]Id. at 789.

[196]Id. at 788.

[197]Id. at 789.

[198]See Chapter 14 for a full discussion of postdischarge conduct.

In *Westinghouse Electric Corp.*[199] an employee was discharged for failing to report to a customer's work site. The employee had relapsed into cocaine addiction and had skipped the work assignment because he knew that he would be required to take a drug test at the work site. The arbitrator found that, among several mitigating circumstances, in the employee's absence from work he had entered and completed a drug treatment program and was now able to return to work.[200] The arbitrator emphasized that evidence of rehabilitation and fitness for work was extremely relevant in deciding to award conditional reinstatement in a substance abuse case.[201]

Although the employer suffered inconvenience because of the failure to report, the arbitrator concluded there was no significant economic harm to the employer. The company did not lose the customer due to the employee's actions. Consequently, there was no just cause for discharge.[202] Instead, the employee was reinstated on the condition that he pass all future drug tests and remain drug free.

Similar criteria for remaining employed have been imposed in conditional reinstatement cases involving mental and physical illness. In *Southwestern Bell Telephone Co.*,[203] an employer was required to reinstate an employee where the company had compelling evidence that the employee had a mental illness (the employee tried to cut off cable television service in order to force the public to consider world peace) prior to discharging the employee, but failed to obtain a medical opinion as to the employee's chances for rehabilitation. The arbitrator reasoned that in cases of physical illness the critical inquiry is whether the employee will be able to return to work in the future, and concluded that evidence of rehabilitation should also be relevant in cases of mental illness.[204] The arbitrator awarded reinstatement conditioned upon the company physician's concluding that the employee was fit for work (in his former position or a comparable one).[205]

Generally, in cases of illness, just cause for discharge is found only where employers have obtained a medical opinion as to the employee's fitness to return to work and to complete the required tasks in a satisfactory way. In *Pepsi-Cola General Bottlers,*[206] an arbitrator awarded conditional reinstatement to a route salesman whose performance had been hindered by a stroke. The company failed to obtain a medical opinion about what accommodations could be made for the employee subsequent to his hospitalization, or his fitness to return

---

[199]95 LA 881 (Talarico, 1990).
[200]Id. at 884.
[201]Id.
[202]Id.
[203]98 LA 137 (Nolan, 1991).
[204]Id. at 142.
[205]Id. at 143.
[206]98 LA 112 (Madden, 1991).

to work at all. The employee was reinstated, conditioned on a medical examination demonstrating that he was able to complete his tasks satisfactorily.[207]

Arbitrators generally favor progressive discipline focusing on rehabilitating an employee rather than the extreme penalty of discharge.[208] The exception to this general rule is where the employee's actions or the circumstances of the case indicate that the potential for rehabilitation is very small. For example, an employee will not be awarded conditional reinstatement if he is simply going through the motions of taking rehabilitative steps. An arbitrator refused conditional reinstatement where the employee had tested positive for marijuana on two separate occasions, one of which occurred during outpatient treatment. When he was subsequently referred to inpatient treatment for his problem, the employee continually denied that he had a drug abuse problem and refused to cooperate with treatment personnel.[209]

In most cases, arbitrators look at years of service and work record as secondary factors in assessing the reasonableness of conditional reinstatement. The central inquiry is whether the employee can return to work in a satisfactory manner. As one arbitrator stated, the central objectives of discipline are rehabilitation of the employee, deterrence of the employee from future misconduct, and deterrence of other employees from similar misconduct.[210]

For acts of insubordination or fighting, if there has only been a single incident that did not cause significant harm to the employer's business, conditional reinstatement may be awarded because there is a reasonable potential for rehabilitation and future satisfactory work.[211]

Generally, when making a conditional reinstatement, arbitrators try to impose conditions on the employee that will motivate the employee to work harder at complying with company rules. For instance, when conditional reinstatement has been ordered in a substance abuse case, it is often conditioned on successful compliance with random drug testing.[212] In *Murcole, Inc.*,[213] an arbitrator reinstated the employee on the condition that the employee be placed on probation for a period of time sufficient for him to understand the seriousness of following the orders of his supervisor.

---

[207]Id. at 116.

[208]Id.

[209]Sterling Chems., 93 LA 953 (Taylor, 1989).

[210]Pepsi-Cola Gen. Bottlers, 98 LA 112, 116 (Madden, 1991).

[211]SK Hand Tool Corp., 98 LA 643 (Hodgson, 1992) (employee discharged after she slapped a payroll administrator; finding discharge to be too severe a penalty where there was only a single incident and no serious physical injury, the arbitrator awarded reinstatement conditioned on the employee not having any altercations within a 30-day probationary period).

[212]Westinghouse Elec. Corp., 95 LA 881 (Talarico, 1990).

[213]99 LA 378, 381 (Darrow, 1992).

The arbitrator will often impose such conditions under a last-chance agreement, which means that the employee has a last chance to comply with management regulations and policies; she might be automatically terminated for failure to meet one of the conditions.[214]

## IV. Review of Last-Chance Agreements[215]

The majority of arbitrators limit their review of disciplinary action under last-chance agreements to the terms of the agreement. These arbitrators favor the proposition that a last-chance agreement can waive or modify an employee's rights under a collective bargaining agreement.[216] The last-chance agreement represents a tradeoff: the employee gets something to which he was not entitled prior to the agreement, continued employment, in return for relinquishing certain employment rights.[217] As long as the lost rights are clearly spelled out in the last-chance agreement, their relinquishment will be upheld by most arbitrators.[218]

The employee may lose the right to have his complaint reviewed for just cause or to have it reviewed at all. The arbitrator's ability to review the disciplinary action is limited by two threshold considerations: (1) whether the last-chance agreement was valid, and (2) whether the terms of the agreement were violated.

One arbitrator outlined five factors to determine whether a last-chance agreement was valid:

(1) Did the employee enter into the last-chance agreement of his own free will?

(2) Was the employee represented by the union when he entered into the agreement?

(3) Did the employee understand the terms of the agreement?

(4) Were the terms (requirements) outlined in the agreement reasonable?

(5) Is the probationary period under the agreement for a reasonable time?[219]

When the arbitrator found these factors were met, the only remaining question was whether the agreement was violated.[220] The

---

[214]Westinghouse Elec. Corp., 95 LA 881, 884 (Talarico, 1990).

[215]Creation of last-chance agreements is covered in Chapter 8.

[216]Butler Mfg. Co., 93 LA 441, 445 (Dworkin, 1989).

[217]Id. at 445.

[218]Id.

[219]Gaylord Container Corp., 97 LA 382, 383 (Goodman, 1991).

[220]Id. The arbitrator found all five factors above were met and concluded on that basis that he had no jurisdiction to review management's decision. The employee was initially discharged due to alcohol abuse and reinstated under a last-chance agreement on the condition

arbitrator's opinion as to whether the violations cited by management were good reasons, bad reasons, or no reason at all for the disciplinary action taken was irrelevant.[221]

In *Merchants Fast Motor Lines*,[222] the arbitrator distilled the test into three parts, holding that last-chance agreements were valid if the terms were (1) clear and unambiguous, (2) understood by both parties, and (3) reasonable. In that case, a truck driver was discharged after a collision. Prior to the collision the driver had been under a last-chance agreement that stated that he would be discharged if he had any future accidents. Even though the employee had not signed the last-chance agreement, the arbitrator held that his admission that he and his union representative understood the terms of the agreement was sufficient to make the agreement valid.[223] The terms imposed were reasonable since the company had a compelling interest in the safety of its drivers.[224] Because the accident itself was undisputed, the arbitrator upheld the discharge.[225]

A minority of arbitrators have held that if just cause is part of the collective bargaining agreement, this provision is in effect as long as the contract is in effect and is not subject to waiver.[226] In *Monterey Coal Co.*,[227] the arbitrator struck a provision from the last-chance agreement (which the employee had signed and understood) that purported to disallow any grievance hearing or arbitration if the company determined that a term of the last-chance agreement had been violated. The arbitrator reinstated the employee because he found this provision contrary to the terms of the collective bargaining agreement, which expressly provided for a grievance hearing and arbitration.[228] Although the provision prohibiting a grievance hearing or arbitration was eliminated, the arbitrator held the remainder of the last-chance agreement enforceable.

Another minority of arbitrators accept the argument that it is possible for the intent or spirit of a last-chance agreement to be followed in spite of a technical violation. This is especially true where the employee has accomplished the desired result of the original disciplinary action and there has been no significant harm to the employer. This reasoning was used where an employee entered a

---

that he not violate any company rules. Although his second discharge was for violating a rule requiring employees to wear safety glasses, the arbitrator did not find the conditions overly broad or unreasonable and upheld the discharge even though the employee was initially discharged for a completely different reason, alcohol abuse.

[221]Butler Mfg. Co., 93 LA 441, 447 (Dworkin, 1989).

[222]99 LA 180, 183 (Marlatt, 1992).

[223]Id.

[224]Id.

[225]Id.

[226]Monterey Coal Co., 96 LA 457 (Feldman, 1990).

[227]Id.

[228]Id.

drug and alcohol abuse program but was dismissed by a program counselor for having a "bad attitude."[229] The employee entered and completed another program and remained drug free. The arbitrator reinstated the employee because he had complied with the intent or spirit of the last-chance agreement. Although he completed an outpatient program instead of a specified inpatient program,[230] the employee was reinstated but remained subject to the terms of the last-chance agreement.[231]

In *Northrop Corp.,*[232] the arbitrator also read the last-chance agreement in conjunction with the collective bargaining agreement. Under the last-chance agreement in this case, any infraction of any company rule would be grounds for immediate discharge. The employee had been accused of violating a company rule against leaving his work station and loitering because he had been talking to other employees on two occasions for excessive amounts of time about personal matters. The time periods involved were approximately 20 minutes.

The arbitrator held that the language "any further infraction" of any company rules had to be read in the context of the collective bargaining terms.[233] The collective bargaining agreement provided that employees would be disciplined for violations of company rules in accord with the nature and frequency of the violations. The arbitrator found that the two incidents were minor in light of the fact that they were isolated incidents that occurred for short periods of time.[234] Minor offenses could not justify the ultimate penalty of discharge, according to the arbitrator, where the employee had corrected the excessive absenteeism problem for which he was originally disciplined.[235] In light of his otherwise outstanding employment record, the arbitrator concluded the employee should be reinstated.[236]

Where an employer discharges an employee for violation of a last-chance agreement, the employer must be able to show that the cited reason for discharge is actually a violation of the last-chance agreement. In *Scott Paper Co.,*[237] a crane operator was reinstated with a last-chance agreement after his discharge for dishonesty and

---

[229]U.S. Steel Corp., Mon Valley Works, 94 LA 1109 (McDaniel, 1990).

[230]Id. at 1115.

[231]It is probably significant that in the cited case the employer implied that the standard of review was a just cause standard by arguing that the company had just cause to fire the employee. The strategy of other employers who have had terminations under a last-chance agreement upheld has been to argue that the employee waived his just cause rights by agreeing to the last-chance provision.

[232]96 LA 149 (Weiss, 1990).

[233]Id.

[234]Id. at 151.

[235]This case differs from *Monterey* in terms of the arbitrator's consideration of the problem that originally initiated disciplinary action.

[236]Northrop Corp., 96 LA 149, 151 (Weiss, 1990).

[237]Scott Paper Co., Southern Operations, 99 LA 624 (Byars, 1992).

absence without permission. Subsequently he was discharged again for "negligent job performance" after he was found sleeping on the job.[238] The arbitrator reinstated the employee, concluding there was no negligence because there was no loss of job performance.[239] The employee had completed his work in the time allotted and his sleeping did not prevent other employees from completing their tasks.[240]

In cases where the arbitrator has reinstated a worker in spite of a violation of a last-chance agreement, the worker usually remains subject to the terms of the last-chance agreement. Where they have ordered reinstatement, most arbitrators have also awarded back pay and no loss of seniority. In some cases, the employee has been subjected to an additional penalty by which that employee can "compensate" the employer for a deviation from the agreement. For example, in *U.S. Steel Corp.*,[241] the employee was required to undergo additional counseling for alcohol and drug abuse. Also, another term was added to his last-chance agreement; any future tardiness, absences, or failures to report would result in immediate termination.[242]

# V. Other Remedies

## A. *Liquidated Damages*

When contracting parties stipulate a specific sum as damages to be awarded for breach of contract, these damages are characterized as liquidated. Liquidated damage provisions are rarely found in collective bargaining agreements. They are usually found in circumstances where a monetary remedy is stipulated for repeated contract violations, especially where no individual can be shown to have suffered a specific loss. Such remedies may be held enforceable only if reasonably proportionate to the loss or injury actually sustained.

For example, in accordance with a formula specified in an agreement, an arbitrator awarded double damages for a repeated work rule violation. Despite the reliance on the specific terms of the parties' agreement, a California court of appeals refused to enforce the award.[243] It held that this provision for liquidated damages violated a state statute forbidding any contract in which damages are set in anticipation of a breach. The court noted there was a statutory exception for contracts where it would be difficult if not impossible to fix

---

[238]Id. at 627.

[239]Id. at 627, 628.

[240]Id. at 627.

[241]U.S. Steel Corp., Mon Valley Works, 94 LA 1109 (McDaniel, 1990).

[242]Id. at 1115, where reinstated employee was denied back pay.

[243]Retail Clerks v. Food Employers Council, 85 Cal. App.3d 286, 99 LRRM 3255 (1978). But see Waggoner v. Northwest Excavating, Inc., 642 F.2d 333, 339, 107 LRRM 2367 (9th Cir., 1981) (court refuses to enforce California statute on attorney fees in LMRA § 301 case).

actual damages. But it found this not to be the case in the contract at hand where no evidence had been presented to show that the parties had even discussed the impracticability of measuring damages.

In other situations, arbitrators have treated union requests for interest on back-pay awards as a form of liquidated damages.[244] Such treatment appears most common in the case of postjudgment interest, which is treated in the nature of a "liquidated" and calculated amount that becomes due by nature of the judgment or award.[245]

## B. Punitive Damages

Arbitrators are ordinarily reluctant or unwilling to award punitive damages, even where discipline or discharge may have been based on personal or antiunion animus.[246] The generally accepted rule in arbitration is that an award of damages should be limited to the amount necessary to make the injured employee whole. The basis for arbitral reluctance to grant punitive damages is that punishment and retribution are foreign to the need for amicable and continuing settlement of disputes by way of the grievance procedure and arbitration process. As a former President of the National Academy of Arbitrators put it, "a grievance is not a traffic ticket. I have no authority to impose a punitive sanction."[247] This position is commonly defended on the basis that a party to a bargaining agreement should not be punished for making a mistake in its administration.

Nevertheless, there are exceptions to this general principle. Most awards of punitive damages appear to have been granted where the contract violation was knowing and repeated [248] or where willful and flagrant.[249] Punitive damages have also been awarded in situations of wrongful discipline and discharge, although, again, they are not common.

Another unusual remedy in discipline cases is a back-pay award without reinstatement.[250]

---

[244]General Elec. Co., 39 LA 897 (Hilpert, 1962).

[245]Osborn & Ulland, Inc., 68 LA 1146 (Beck, 1977); Sears Roebuck & Co., 35 LA 757 (Miller, 1960).

[246]Hill & Sinicropi, Remedies in Arbitration, 2d ed., 436–49 (BNA Books, 1991); Fairweather's Practice & Procedure in Labor Arbitration, 3d ed., Schoonhoven, ed., 343–44 (BNA Books, 1991).

[247]Lucky Stores, Inc., 70-1 ARB ¶ 8271 at 9302 (Feller, 1969).

[248]Mallincrodt Chem. Works, 50 LA 933 (Goldberg, 1968); Bethlehem Steel Co., 31 LA 857 (Valtin, 1961).

[249]Dana Corp., 76 LA 125 (Mittenthal, 1981); Five Star Hardware, 44 LA 944 (Wolff, 1965).

[250]Cases cited in Rehmus, "New Roles for Labor Arbitrators: Pt. II. Justice and the Wrongfully Terminated," in Arbitration 1994: Controversy and Continuity, Proceedings of the 47th Annual Meeting of NAA, 285 (BNA Books, 1994); Safeway Stores, Inc., 64 LA 563 (Gould, 1974); Thorsen Mfg. Co., 55 LA 581 (Koven, 1970).

Both state and federal courts differ on whether an arbitrator's award that is found to be punitive will be enforced. Both the Fifth and Eleventh Circuits courts of appeal allow a punitive award unless prohibited by the collective bargaining agreement.[251] The law in other circuits is unclear,[252] and the Supreme Court has as yet not dealt squarely with the issue.[253]

# VI. Ancillary Relief

## A. *Expungement of Records*

Expungement of records may be a remedy where penalties are determined to be meritless or are significantly reduced.[254] In such cases, the arbitrator orders the employer to remove certain references or documents in the grievant's personnel file or record.[255]

In some cases, the penalty imposed is upheld, but expungement is ordered as to any of the following: references to the penalty, activities leading up to the penalty, or extraneous information. For instance, where the employer prevailed in a proceeding arising from discipline for violation of a call-in rule, the employer was ordered to expunge from the grievant's personnel and disciplinary records all references to a chemical dependency problem and inadequate work performance or attitude. These references were contained in the employer's notes of the grievance procedure and suspension notice. However, the grievant had had no opportunity to respond to these charges because they were extraneous to the grievance.[256]

---

[251]Island Creek Coal Co. v. Mine Workers Dist. 28, 29 F.3d 126, 146 LRRM 2773 (4th Cir., 1994), and cases cited therein.

[252]See Lee v. Chica, 983 F.2d 883 (9th Cir.), cert. denied, 114 S.Ct. 287 (1993).

[253]The Supreme Court in Mastrobuono v. Shearson Lehman Hutton, Inc., 115 S.Ct. 1212, 1217 (1995), enforced an arbitration award containing punitive damages where the "Client Agreement" provided that "any controversy" between the parties arising out of the transaction "shall be settled by arbitration."

[254]Presumably, expungement of a record includes removal along with destruction of that portion of the record removed. See City of N. Miami, 88 LA 1261, 1265 (Davidson, 1987) (removal without destruction of records did not fulfill the "purging requirements" of the parties' contract).

[255]See Foster Food Prods., 98 LA 854, 859 (D'Spain, 1992) (30-day suspension was in violation of labor agreement; therefore, reference to the suspension was ordered removed from the personnel file and instead first written warning letter was ordered placed in file); Merry-weather Foam, 98 LA 611, 616 (Bittel, 1992) (2-day suspension for insubordination reduced to written reprimands and references to alleged insubordination ordered expunged from personnel files); City of Charlotte, 97 LA 1065, 1074 (Borland, 1991) (references to alleged theft/removal of city property were ordered expunged from grievant's personnel file where theft was not proven).

[256]Public Utils. Comm'n of Hibbing, 97 LA 1160, 1167 (Berquist, 1991) (the arbitrator also granted the union and the grievant the right to examine the grievant's personnel record to ensure such references were removed). See also Fort Pitt Bridge Works, 30 LA 633, 635 (Lehoczy, 1958) (suspension was upheld but all reference to the penalty and to the activities leading up to the penalty (walk-out) were ordered expunged from the employees' personnel records because there was no refusal of a direct work order, management did not attempt to stop the employees from walking out, and "social pressures" were present); Ironrite, Inc., 28 LA 394 (Haughton, 1956) (reference to insubordination was ordered expunged from the employee's personnel record because it was not an offense included in the rules).

In an unusual case, expungement was ordered as a mechanism to restore order in the plant where the employer had been lax in the enforcement of its rules. The arbitrator ruled that for purposes of establishing order out of chaos, his award would order (1) that the employer must clear all employee records of all disciplinary entries prior to the date of his award, and (2) that thereafter the employees shall have a responsibility to obey the employer's plant rules and the employer shall have a responsibility to actively enforce them.[257]

## B. *Materials Previously Ordered Expunged*

In some cases, employers will rely on materials that were previously ordered expunged to support the discipline. Arbitrators have modified the penalty meted out by the employer where it was based, in part, on "stale" infractions.[258]

---

[257]Grand Rapids Die Casting Corp., 63 LA 995, 996 (Keefe, 1974).

[258]National Wire Prods. Indus., 96 LA 395, 403 (Dworkin, 1991). But see Iowa Power, Inc., 97 LA 1029, 1031 (Thornell, 1991) (although discipline for prior accident expunged from file pursuant to settlement agreement and therefore inadmissible, accident could be made part of record through witnesses' testimony); Champion Spark Plug Co., 93 LA 1277, 1283 (Dobry, 1989); Bethlehem Steel Corp., 92 LA 857, 860 (Witt, 1988); Southern Cal. Permanente Med. Group, 92 LA 41, 45 (Richman, 1989); Clagon Carbon Corp., 88 LA 347, 349 (Tharp, 1987) (contract specified that records of disciplinary action in employees' personnel files should be removed 2 years after issuance, provided there was no intervening disciplinary action; arbitrator found that discharge was too severe. since he could not consider prior records and present record of disciplinary action was not sufficient); City of Rochester, 82 LA 217, 220 (Lawson, 1984).

Chapter 13

# External Law

## I. Introduction

Although it is generally difficult to identify clear trends in arbitration awards, since the United States Supreme Court's decision in *Alexander v. Gardner-Denver Co.*,[1] arbitrators have appeared to be increasingly willing to rely on external law in resolving discipline and discharge cases involving Title VII and Age Discrimination in Employment Act (ADEA) claims.[2] Historically, arbitrators ignored external law. Even after the enactment of the Civil Rights Act of 1964 and the ADEA, many arbitrators continued to ignore external law.[3] In the early days of the Civil Rights Act, some arbitrators believed that arbitration was not the appropriate forum for alleged acts of discrimination covered by the Act. Thus, comments such as the following were not unusual:

---

[1]415 U.S. 36, 7 FEP Cases 81 (1974).

[2]Volz & Goggin, eds., Elkouri & Elkouri, How Arbitration Works, 5th ed., 47 & n.104 (BNA Books, 1997) (citing arbitral decisions to support the claim that, since *Gardner-Denver* was decided, a "significantly greater number of arbitrators have considered Title VII doctrine" in deciding cases). It is perhaps somewhat unusual that *Gardner-Denver* should have shifted the tide in favor of applying external law in arbitration awards. *Gardner-Denver* reflected a negative attitude toward arbitration, noting that arbitrators have "no general authority to invoke public laws that conflict with the bargain between the parties," and it warned arbitrators that an award based " 'solely upon the arbitrator's view of the requirements of enacted legislation,' rather than on an interpretation of the collective-bargaining agreement" will render the award unenforceable. Gardner-Denver, 415 U.S. at 53, quoting Steelworkers v. Enterprise Wheel & Car Corp., 363 U.S. 593, 597, 46 LRRM 2423 (1960). The Court noted, however, in its famous footnote 21, that "[w]here an arbitral determination gives full consideration to an employee's Title VII rights, a court may properly accord it great weight." Gardner-Denver, 415 U.S. at 60 n.21. Perhaps this strongly worded hint has caused arbitrators to apply Title VII in order to protect their awards from being overturned on appeal.

[3]See, e.g., Allis-Chalmers Corp., 78 LA 17, 19 (Storey, 1982) ("Whether or not there has been a violation of Title VII of the Civil Rights Act of 1964 is a matter for another jurisdiction.").

As to the Civil Rights Act and its enforcement, that is a matter for the EEOC. The Arbitrator's job is to interpret and apply the parties' collective bargaining agreement. As [one arbitrator] noted: "We are not the Equal Employment Opportunity Commission and should not put ourselves in its place in terms of our rights and ability to enforce the law which they administer."[4]

Despite the arbitrator's refusal to consider the Act in his analysis, his decision was consistent with the Act. He upheld the termination of an employee who took an unexcused leave of absence to participate in a fundraiser for a church-affiliated college. In denying the grievance, the arbitrator noted that the employee was not asking for time off to attend religious services. Therefore, just cause supported the termination.

Another arbitrator held that "[t]he determination of [reasonable accommodation and undue hardship] is a matter of law for the proper judicial forum and is not for an Arbitrator whose authority is solely derived from the Agreement."[5] In *Timken Co.*,[6] the arbitrator held that the employer had acted within the terms of the collective bargaining agreement, and directed the employee to go through the proper administrative and judicial forums to contest whether applying the collective bargaining agreement violated the Act.

Perhaps the reluctance of these arbitrators was an implicit acknowledgment of the longstanding judicial mistrust of arbitrators' ability to understand and apply external law.[7] Instead of external law, arbitrators relied on the collective bargaining agreement (CBA), arbitral precedent, the past practices between the parties, the "law of the shop," and their own subjective conceptions of what constitutes discipline or discharge for just cause. The United States Supreme Court authorized this narrow view in its famous pronouncement in *Steelworkers v. Enterprise Wheel & Car Corp.*:[8] "[A]n arbitrator is confined to interpretation and application of the collective bargaining agreement * * *. [H]is award is legitimate only so long as it draws its essence from the collective bargaining agreement."[9]

Although contract interpretation is still the arbitrator's principal task, when a CBA contains an antidiscrimination clause, it may be that the parties have thus bargained (at least in part) for a statutorily appropriate resolution of their dispute. There is an argument that an award that ignores external law does not draw its essence from

---

[4]Kentile Floors, Inc., 66 LA 933, 935 (Larkin, 1976), quoting Ingraham Co., 48 LA 884, 889 (Yagoda, 1966).

[5]Timken Co., 75 LA 801, 805 (Morgan, Jr., 1980).

[6]Id.

[7]See, e.g., Steelworkers v. Warrior & Gulf Navigation Co., 363 U.S. 574, 46 LRRM 2416 (1960) (specialized competence of arbitrators pertains primarily to "the law of the shop, not the law of the land").

[8]363 U.S. 593, 46 LRRM 2423 (1960).

[9]Id. at 597.

the contract and may be subject to vacatur. Other factors that may have increased arbitrators' willingness to refer to external law include the willingness of federal courts to review and vacate arbitral awards that conflict with federal law, the growing pervasiveness of statutory law in all aspects of labor relations, and the inclusion of ever-broader antidiscrimination clauses in CBAs. Thus, arbitrators today generally invoke external law even in the absence of explicit contractual authority. The trend is not uniform. There are still numerous contemporary awards that either simply reject external law or narrowly interpret CBAs to limit the application of external law.

## II. Title VII

### A. General

Where a CBA contains an antidiscrimination clause prohibiting an employer from discriminating on any of the grounds in Title VII, most arbitrators will rely, in varying degrees, on Title VII law (the statute itself, federal case law interpreting it, and, in some instances, EEOC regulations) in formulating their awards. Some arbitrators have based their use of Title VII law on a strict contractual analysis: If the CBA prohibits the employer from discriminating on any of the grounds in Title VII, then the arbitrator, in obeying the duty to draw the essence of the award from the parties' agreement, must apply Title VII to the grievance. As one arbitrator has noted, where a CBA contains a provision prohibiting discrimination, the clause "indicates an intent to incorporate the applicable law on the subject."[10]

Even where a CBA does not contain an explicit antidiscrimination clause that incorporates Title VII, many arbitrators will nevertheless invoke external law. One arbitrator suggested that the concepts of just cause and unlawful discrimination have merged.[11] Arbitrators

---

[10]Rodeway Inn, 102 LA 1003, 1014 (Goldberg, 1994).

[11]See, e.g., Centerville Clinics, Inc., 85 LA 1059, 1062 (Talarico, 1985) (noting that even in a CBA that does not contain an antidiscrimination clause, the issue of discrimination is "necessarily involved in the determination of whether there has been a contract violation" because the concepts of just cause and unlawful discrimination have, for all practical purposes, been merged). Another arbitrator has noted, in applying the ADA to a contract that did not prohibit handicap discrimination, that where a CBA contains merely a "just cause" provision but does not contain an antidiscrimination clause, it makes no logical sense to exclude the entire federal statutory framework in determining what just cause is:

It is well settled that discipline is not just if it is manifestly unfair. But how does one decide what is "fair" and "unfair?" Where does one look for guidelines and principles? One source is arbitral "precedent"—the maxims set forth in nearly a half-century of published decisions on the subject. * * *

Another obvious resource for deciding what does or does not form just cause is basic societal values. * * *

The Arbitrator agrees that technically, he cannot decide whether [the employer] violated the [ADA] when it discharged Grievant. That is a question for the courts. But he is empowered and obligated to decide if Grievant's penalty was just and fair. In making that determination, it is appropriate to look to the [ADA] for guidance.

Thermo King Corp., 102 LA 612, 615 (Dworkin, 1993).

have advanced numerous grounds for relying on external law even in the absence of a CBA containing a reference to Title VII. Indeed, as the *Enterprise Wheel* Court suggested, an arbitrator "may of course look for guidance from many sources."[12] One such source is public policy.

As the Supreme Court first held in *W.R. Grace & Co. v. Rubber Workers Local 759,*[13] and later in *Paperworkers v. Misco, Inc.,*[14] a federal court may not enforce a collective bargaining agreement (and an arbitration award issued thereunder) that is contrary to a "well defined and dominant" public policy which must be ascertained from laws and legal precedent.[15] Although the federal courts are still wrangling over the precise contours of the public policy exception, numerous arbitral awards rely on the explicit (and implicit) public policy considerations embodied in Title VII in formulating their awards. As one arbitrator has noted, "increasingly, arbitration is affected by external law, and if an arbitrator's award is inconsistent with the dictates of 'public policy' as embodied in statutes and administrative regulations, its validity may be challenged through judicial review."[16] This statement is borne out by the fact that numerous appellate courts have set aside arbitral awards that conflict with the public policy considerations in Title VII. In *Newsday v. Long Island Typographical Union No. 915,*[17] an arbitrator found that even though the grievant had verbally and physically harassed female co-workers, the conduct called for progressive discipline rather than termination, and reinstated the grievant. The court of appeals ultimately reversed the award, finding that the arbitrator's decision "disregarded the public policy against sexual harassment in the workplace," condoned employee misconduct, and tended to "perpetuate a hostile, intimidating and offensive work environment."[18] Thus, even in the absence of an antidiscrimination clause in the CBA, public policy may form the basis for applying external law to Title VII grievances.[19]

---

[12]Steelworkers v. Enterprise Wheel & Car Corp., supra note 2, at 597.

[13]461 U.S. 757, 113 LRRM 2641 (1983).

[14]484 U.S. 29, 126 LRRM 3113 (1987).

[15]W.R. Grace at 766.

[16]Fry's Food Stores of Ariz., Inc., 99 LA 1161, 1167 (Hogler, 1992).

[17]915 F.2d 840, 135 LRRM 2659 (2d Cir., 1990), cert. denied, 499 U.S. 922, 136 LRRM 2720 (1991).

[18]Id. at 845. See also Stroehman Bakeries v. Teamsters Local 776, 969 F.2d 1436, 140 LRRM 2625 (3d Cir.) (vacating an award that reinstated a male employee for sexually harassing a customer's employee where the arbitrator found that the employer had not given the grievant a fair opportunity to respond; policy embodied in statutory law may not be ignored by an arbitrator in determining just cause for discharge), cert. denied, 506 U.S. 1022, 141 LRRM 2984 (1992).

[19]See also George Koch Sons, Inc., 102 LA 737, 743 (Brunner, 1994) (where grievant dismissed for unwanted sexual touching of female co-employee, even where CBA had no antidiscrimination language, arbitrator upheld dismissal on basis of "stiff external law").

## B. Awards Applying Title VII Provisions

Although Title VII prohibits discrimination on the grounds of race, color, religion, sex, or national origin, the three most frequently arbitrated claims involve sex (including sexual harassment), race, and religious discrimination. The general principles apply equally to discrimination on the basis of color and national origin. Employers have an affirmative obligation to take reasonable steps to eliminate discrimination or intimidation based on statutorily protected categories.[20]

*1. Sex Discrimination and Sexual Harassment.*    The Equal Employment Opportunity Commission (EEOC) guidelines recognize two kinds of sexual harassment: "quid pro quo" harassment, and harassment occurring as a result of a "hostile environment."[21]

a. Quid Pro Quo.    "Quid pro quo" sexual harassment claims involve allegations that submission to unwelcome sexual advances or requests for sexual favors were made a condition for getting, keeping, or advancing in a job.[22] Perhaps the most frequent allegation advanced under this theory is that the employee refused to submit to a supervisor's sexual advances and was discharged in retaliation for her refusal to engage in a sexual relationship. The EEOC takes the position that an employee may have a valid quid pro quo claim when job benefits are granted to another employee, if the award of benefits was contingent upon participation in a coerced relationship.[23]

---

[20]Snell v. Suffolk County, N.Y., 782 F.2d 1094, 39 FEP Cases 1590 (2d Cir., 1986) (employer tolerated discrimination that destroyed emotional and psychological stability of minority employees); Erebia v. Chrysler Plastic Prods. Corp., 772 F.2d 1250, 37 FEP Cases 1820 (6th Cir., 1985), cert. denied, 475 U.S. 1015, 40 FEP Cases 192 (1986) (employer refused to act on complaints by Hispanic supervisor of racial epithets from employees under his supervision); Walker v. Ford Motor Co., 684 F.2d 1355, 29 FEP Cases 1259 (11th Cir., 1982) (employer tolerated pervasive use of racial slurs and advised black employee that such slurs were "just something a black man would have to deal with in the South"); Bundy v. Jackson, 641 F.2d 934, 24 FEP Cases 1155 (D.C. Cir., 1981) (supervisors knew of sexual harassment and failed to investigate or remedy it); Compston v. Borden, Inc., 424 F.Supp. 157, 17 FEP Cases 310 (S.D. Ohio, 1976) (harassment because of religious beliefs). But see Rabidue v. Texas-American Petrochemicals, 805 F.2d 611, 42 FEP Cases 631 (6th Cir., 1986), cert. denied, 481 U.S. 1041, 43 FEP Cases 1056 (1987) (occasional obscene comments about plaintiff and other women, and the posting of pictures of nude or scantily clad women in work areas did not create hostile environment); Vaughn v. Pool Co. of Tex., Pool Offshore Co. Div., 683 F.2d 922, 29 FEP Cases 1017 (5th Cir., 1982) (no violation where black workers suffered pranks, crude jokes, and verbal abuse, some of which had racial overtones; racial slurs were bantered about without hostility or racial animus, and all employees suffered the same unpleasantness); Washington Scientific Indus., 83 LA 824, 827 (Kapsch, 1984) (desire to forestall future liability based on sexual harassment was insufficient cause to discharge employee who, after unsuccessful attempts to cheer up female co-workers, commented, "I don't think you would even enjoy sex.").

[21]29 C.F.R. pt. 1604.

[22]The EEOC Guidelines define quid pro quo harassment as existing when: (1) submission to such conduct is made either explicitly or implicitly a term or condition of an individual's employment; or (2) submission to or rejection of such conduct by an individual is used as the basis for employment decisions affecting such individual. 29 C.F.R. pt. 1604.11(a).

[23]29 C.F.R. pt. 1604.11(g).

Because the offense involves the perceived ability to affect job benefits, quid pro quo claims do not often arise out of interactions between co-workers. Nor do employers often have occasion to discipline or discharge employees for quid pro quo harassment.[24] There is a risk of such harassment in interactions between "lead" employees and the employees under them. Employees in lead positions can be disciplined for abuse of their authority. In one case a lead employee asked a newspaper carrier if he could be her sugar daddy, put his arm around another carrier, referred to a third as "little girl," and told a lesbian carrier that he could do better. The arbitrator sustained a suspension and reassignment.[25]

b. Hostile Environment.  The law of "hostile environment" claims is based primarily on the Supreme Court's 1986 decision in *Meritor Savings Bank v. Vinson*.[26] In that case, the Court held that a violation could rest on a claim of "hostile environment," regardless of whether the plaintiff suffered tangible job detriment as a result of the harassment.

Hostile environment claims assert that the employer created or condoned an intimidating, hostile, or offensive work environment. The environment may include unwelcome sexual advances, requests for sexual favors, or other verbal or physical conduct of a sexual nature.[27] It may also include acts of physical aggression, intimidation, hostility, or unequal treatment based on sex.[28] Unlike quid pro quo harassment, hostile environment claims do not require a showing of any adverse impact on job benefits. Employers become liable for such harassment if they knew or should have known of the hostile environment. Most sexual harassment charges among co-workers involve claims of hostile environment. For example, an arbitrator upheld the discharge of a long-term male employee who created a hostile environment by referring to a female employee's nipples, tugging at the sweatpants of another female employee, asking sexually explicit questions, and requesting sexual acts of three female employees.[29]

---

[24]Quid pro quo harassment is sometimes raised as a defense to discipline under one of two theories: (1) the actual reason for the discipline is retaliation for resisting supervisory or managerial advances, or (2) the grievant received disparate treatment compared to employees who were involved in coercive workplace liaisons. See the section entitled "Sex Discrimination and Sexual Harassment" in this chapter.

[25]Dayton Newspapers, Inc., 100 LA 48 (Strasshofer, 1992).

[26]106 S.Ct. 2399, 40 FEP Cases 1822 (1986) (supervisor allegedly made repeated demands for sexual favors, fondled plaintiff in front of other employees, exposed himself to her, and forcibly raped her on several occasions).

[27]The EEOC Guidelines define "hostile environment" sexual harassment as occurring when "conduct has the purpose or effect of unreasonably interfering with an individual's work performance or creating an intimidating, hostile, or offensive work environment." 29 C.F.R. pt. 1604.11(a)(3).

[28]Hall v. Gus Constr. Co., 842 F.2d 1010, 1013–14, 46 FEP Cases 573 (8th Cir., 1988); Hicks v. Gates Rubber Co., 833 F.2d 1406, 1415, 45 FEP Cases 608 (10th Cir., 1987), appeal after remand, 928 F.2d 966, 59 FEP Cases 1787 (10th Cir., 1991).

[29]Steuben Rural Elec. Corp., 98 LA 337 (La Manna, 1991).

But repeating off-color sexual jokes to a female employee who was not offended by them did not contribute to a hostile environment.[30]

c. "Reasonable Victim" Standard.   In the lower courts, early post-*Meritor* cases applied a mixture of objective and subjective standards in evaluating claims of hostile environment. To prevail, a plaintiff had to establish (1) that a reasonable person would have been offended, and (2) that the plaintiff was actually offended and suffered injury.[31] The EEOC vigorously challenged that standard in 1990, arguing that a strictly objective standard should be used without any evaluation of actual injury. The Ninth Circuit rejected both the traditional test and the EEOC's "reasonable person" test in *Ellison v. Brady*.[32] Instead, it held that sexually harassing conduct must be evaluated from the perspective of a "reasonable woman." It noted that the "reasonable person" standard ignored differing perspectives and experiences of men and women. The "reasonable woman" standard has since come to be referred to as the "reasonable victim" standard, in recognition of the possibility that men, as well as women, may suffer sexual harassment.

The Supreme Court reaffirmed and clarified "reasonable person" terminology in *Harris v. Forklift Systems, Inc.*[33] The Court rejected the need for proof of tangible psychological or economic injury if the conduct was not "severe or pervasive enough to create an objectively hostile or abusive work environment—an environment that a reasonable person would find hostile or abusive * * *."[34] Under the test enunciated by the Court, sexual harassment would be established if "the environment would reasonably be perceived, and is perceived, as hostile or abusive."[35]

d. Arbitration Awards in Sex Discrimination.   The most frequently arbitrated discrimination claims under Title VII involve sex discrimination. Although there are variations, three basic patterns recur throughout published awards: (1) grievances alleging that the employee was improperly disciplined or discharged on the basis of sex, (2) grievances alleging that the employer's acceptance of a sexually hostile environment without disciplining the offending employee constitutes sexual harassment, and (3) grievances alleging improper discipline or discharge of an employee accused of sexually harassing a co-employee.

---

[30]Ralph's Grocery Co., 100 LA 63 (Kaufman, 1992) (reinstatement without back pay ordered for discharged assistant manager).

[31]Rabidue v. Texas-American Petrochemicals, 805 F.2d 611, 42 FEP Cases 631 (6th Cir., 1986), cert. denied, 481 U.S. 1041, 43 FEP Cases 1056 (1987) (occasional obscene comments about plaintiff and other women, and the posting of pictures of nude or scantily clad women in work areas, did not create hostile environment).

[32]924 F.2d 872, 54 FEP Cases 1346 (9th Cir., 1991).

[33]114 S.Ct. 367, 63 FEP Cases 225 (1993).

[34]Id., 63 FEP Cases at 227.

[35]Id. at 228.

Arbitrators have generally applied the standards set out by the courts when deciding whether there was just cause to discipline an employee for sexual harassment. A wide range of conduct—verbal, physical, written, and visual—has been asserted to have contributed to a hostile environment.[36] Harassing verbal conduct includes sexual teasing, jokes, remarks, or questions; phone calls of a sexual nature; and pressure for sexual favors or dates. In one case an arbitrator found just cause to discharge a male long-term employee who asked sexually explicit questions and requested sexual acts of three female co-workers. No progressive discipline was required because the sexual harassment policy permitted discharge based on the severity of the offense. The arbitrator found this conduct posed a possible imminent danger to co-workers, and the employee continued in the behavior even though co-workers rejected it.[37] Another arbitrator upheld the discharge of a male employee who referred to a female co-worker in lewd, sexually demeaning terms. The remark was made in anger to someone he knew or reasonably should have known would report it to the female, and he had been warned against using offensive language 4 months earlier and was on a last-chance agreement.[38] Even without explicit, lewd, or demeaning language, an arbitrator upheld the discharge of a male employee who made persistent unwanted advances to female employees, forcing them to waste time in attempts to avoid him.[39]

In *Superior Coffee & Foods*,[40] an employer discharged a male employee for grabbing several female employees. The union grieved the dismissal solely on the basis of prior arbitral awards that ordered reinstatement of employees guilty of even more egregious sexually oriented conduct. The arbitrator rejected these precedents and upheld the discharge on the basis that courts should overturn any "labor arbitration awards thought to be inconsistent with today's sexual-harassment mores, as reflected in the well-known federal and state legislation prohibiting sex discrimination and sexual harassment."[41] The arbitrator cited several Title VII cases and quoted extensively from the EEOC's guidelines on sexual harassment to demonstrate the public policy involved.

Similarly, in *EZ Communications, Inc.*,[42] a radio announcer was discharged after she walked off the job in response to unwelcome

---

[36]Schlage Lock Co., 88 LA 75, 78–79 (Wyman, 1986).

[37]Steuben Rural Elec. Corp., 98 LA 337 (La Manna, 1991).

[38]Flexsteel Indus., Inc., 94 LA 497 (Briggs, 1990).

[39]United Elec. Supply Co., 82 LA 921 (Madden, 1984).

[40]103 LA 609 (Alleyne, 1994).

[41]Id. at 613, citing Newsday, Inc. v. Long Island Typographical Union 915, 915 F.2d 840, 135 LRRM 2659 (2d Cir., 1990), cert. denied, 499 U.S. 922, 136 LRRM 2720 (1991); Stroehman Bakeries v. Teamsters Local 776, 969 F.2d 1436, 140 LRRM 2625 (3d Cir.), cert. denied, 506 U.S. 1022, 141 LRRM 2984 (1992).

[42]91 LA 1097 (Talarico, 1988).

sexual banter directed at her by her co-employees. The CBA permitted the immediate discharge of an employee for "flagrant neglect of duty" and the forfeiture of all severance benefits. The CBA also acknowledged the parties' support for the EEOC guidelines, including those relating to sex discrimination. The employee was denied severance because her walking off the job allegedly constituted a flagrant neglect of duty. She grieved, alleging that the laws prohibiting sexual harassment authorized her walkout, notwithstanding her alleged neglect of duty. The arbitrator ruled in her favor, noting that the issue was governed by federal "sexual harassment laws," saying: "An employee no longer has to put up with a hostile work environment that is created on the basis of sex, be it in the form of jokes, comments, suggestions, touching, etc."[43]

Harassing physical conduct includes kissing,[44] touching,[45] grabbing,[46] indecent exposure,[47] and indecent gestures.[48] Employees also may run afoul of sexual harassment policies when they write letters or notes suggesting sexual liaisons or inquire or comment on the victim's sexual habits.[49] Finally, visual conduct includes displaying pornographic materials at work and directing sexually suggestive looks or gestures at the victim.[50] In applying Title VII in sex discrimination cases, arbitrators are beginning to develop a body of precedent

---

[43]Id. at 1100.

[44]Honeywell, Inc., 95 LA 1097 (Gallagher, 1990) (discharge reduced to suspension, where white male security guard allegedly continued to harass two female guards after being warned twice against making inappropriate ethnic and sexual remarks); Care Inns, Inc. dba Care Inn Nursing Home, 81 LA 687 (Taylor, 1983) (just cause existed to discharge black janitor who forcibly grabbed arm of white nurse's aide, leaned over, and kissed her on the cheek while she was preparing a patient for bath).

[45]Rockwell Int'l Corp., 85 LA 246 (Feldman, 1985) (discharge for sexual harassment warranted where employee touched three female employees without authorization and used body language that made them uncomfortable).

[46]Zia Co., 82 LA 640 (Daughton, 1984) (just cause existed to discharge 24-year custodial crew member for grabbing, hugging, and kissing co-worker on three occasions in trailer in work area).

[47]Porter Equip. Co., 86 LA 1253 (Liberman, 1986) (just cause existed to discharge employee who pulled hand of female co-worker toward his exposed penis). Compare Hyatt Hotels Palo Alto, 85 LA 11 (Oestreich, 1985) (discharge reduced to 15-day suspension where hotel assistant banquet manager exposed himself to female employee during work hours and investigation disclosed prior incidents of sexual harassment).

[48]Meijer, Inc., 83 LA 570, 573 (Ellmann, 1984) (discharge too severe a penalty for employee who embraced fellow employee and gave a "little bit of a hump motion").

[49]General Dynamics, 100 LA 180 (Francis, 1992) (just cause existed to discipline employee who sent letter to supervisor's wife describing supervisor's alleged sexual comments to employee); Dayton Newspapers, 100 LA 48 (Strasshofer, 1992) (suspension upheld where employee asked lesbian co-worker about what sexual positions she used and asked other co-worker whether she had ever had an affair and what type of sex acts did she enjoy).

[50]Fruehauf Trailer Corp., 93-2 ARB ¶ 3584 (Traynor, 1993) (upheld suspension of employee who drew sexually offensive cartoon suggestive of coworkers involved in a sexually explicit act); Machinists, 92-1 ARB ¶ 8243 (DiLauro, 1991) (staring at co-worker may constitute sexual harassment).

about the discipline appropriate to different forms of sexual harassment.[51]

Certain other forms of behavior cannot be clearly defined as sexual harassment. Where the employer's sexual harassment policy does not give examples of sexual harassment, arbitrators have held that employees were not on notice that the less severe forms of conduct constituted sexual harassment. Arbitrators apply the principle that conduct that cannot be automatically recognized as sexual harassment is a basis for discipline only if the employee persists in that behavior after being made aware the conduct is considered objectionable. Thus, the comment that a frozen dinner that a co-worker placed in a microwave was still hard was not a blatant reference to an erect male sex organ and was not punishable as sexual harassment in the absence of a prior warning.[52] However, grievant's numerous comments on the attire or appearance of a co-worker is a factor that can be considered in determining the appropriate discipline.[53]

Still other conduct is widely recognized not to be sexual harassment, even though gender and sexual relations are involved. Where the conduct is perceived by both the accused and the alleged victim as a joke, otherwise-objectionable conduct is not sexual harassment.[54] Some conduct, however, may run afoul of other rules, such as those prohibiting horseplay. Finally, some conduct is dismissed as too isolated or minor to create a hostile environment.

---

[51]See, e.g., City of Havre, Mont., 100 LA 866 (Levak, 1992) (noting that, based on federal law, dismissal is the appropriate penalty for unwanted sexual touching, and suspension is the appropriate penalty for harassment involving sexually offensive language and gestures).

[52]King Soopers, Inc., 86 LA 254 (Sass, 1985). See KIAM, 97 LA 617 (Bard, 1991) (No just cause for discharge of male employee for violating sexual harassment policy, even though he created a hostile environment for female co-worker and had constructive notice of the policy, which had been in effect and posted for 2 years. The policy did not define, describe, or provide examples of sexual harassment; enforcement was lax, the grievant was not warned of possible discipline or discharge, and progressive discipline was warranted. Supervisory statement that as a gentleman, you have got to stop and leave her alone is not a warning for purposes of progressive discipline because it made no reference to the sexual harassment policy or possible discipline if the conduct continued); Dow Chem. Co., 95 LA 510 (Sartain, 1990) (discharge too severe for black male employee, despite proof he sexually harassed three female co-workers; grievant had been warned his conduct was unacceptable, but it was limited to kidding with sexual innuendo; second warning letter did not constitute a clear and forceful final warning).

[53]See, e.g., United Elec. Supply Co., 82 LA 921 (Madden, 1984), and Renton Sch. Dist., 102 LA 854 (Wilkinson, 1994) (in both cases the grievants' numerous comments regarding female co-workers' dress and attire were a factor used to uphold the discharge).

[54]RMS Techs., Inc., 94 LA 297 (Nicholas, 1990) (not "outrageous conduct" warranting discharge to bring in copy of National Lampoon, read it on lunch break, and leave it in area to which others had ready access; disruption of work occurred only when magazine was retrieved from trash and reviewed by several female employees; employer had no objective standard for prohibitive racial, ethnic, or sexist printed matter; employer took no action against others who brought in similar materials); Louisville Gas & Elec. Co., 81 LA 730 (Stonehouse, 1983) (not sexual harassment to point piece of metal rod at female co-worker and ask how she would like to have it stuck up in her a— so her temperature could be taken, following similar remark made to male employee; female took it to be a joke; grievant did not intend to intimidate or harass).

Not all decisions based on an employee's sex are barred by Title VII. The Act provides that "it shall not be an unlawful employment practice for an employer to hire and employ employees * * * on the basis of * * * religion, sex or national origin in those certain instances where religion, sex or national origin is a bona fide occupational qualification reasonably necessary to the normal operation of that particular business or enterprise * * *."[55] This is known as the bona fide occupational qualification (BFOQ) exception. Arbitrators have applied Title VII's BFOQ exception to permit an employer to discriminate on the basis of sex where such discrimination is reasonably necessary for the operation of the employer's business.[56] Although not all arbitral decisions apply the BFOQ exception, some arbitrators carefully analyze the BFOQ. For example, in *Western School District Board of Education*,[57] a school district refused to transfer a male teacher to the position of a female high school guidance counselor. The district historically employed same-sex counselors for its male and female students and limited the position to female applicants, based on a BFOQ theory. In determining that the school district improperly relied on sex as a basis for filling the position, the arbitrator relied on Title VII and the EEOC's regulations painstakingly analyzing the BFOQ exception. Applying the BFOQ very narrowly, the arbitrator ruled that the grievant made out a prima facie case of discrimination and that the school district failed to meet its burden of proof on the BFOQ affirmative defense.

*2. Race Discrimination.*    Many charges of racial and ethnic harassment involve slurs and similar abusive language. For instance, calling a black co-worker "boy" resulted in a 30-day suspension for a white employee.[58] Posting a sign that alleged the black human resources director was an "Uncle Tom" led to a 60-day suspension for a white employee.[59] Similarly, a black female worker who told a white female worker, "I'll get your white ass," was suspended, while another black female received a warning for calling a co-worker "white bitch."[60] Occasionally, employees receive discipline for singling out minority

---

[55]42 U.S.C. § 2000e-2(e) (1994).

[56]See, e.g., Southern Cal. Gas Co., 91 LA 100 (Collins, 1988) (employer did not violate nondiscrimination clause where it denied a female employee a promotion because she did not meet the job's minimum qualifications, the qualifications were reasonable, and there was no evidence that the requirements had an adverse impact on female employees).

[57]94 LA 681 (Kanner, 1990).

[58]Thermos Co., 100 LA 27 (Cerone, 1992).

[59]TRW, Inc., 99 LA 1216 (Fullmer, 1992).

[60]Emery Air Freight Corp., 94 LA 1023 (Feldman, 1990). See Hannaford Bros. Co., 93 LA 721 (Chandler, 1989) (just cause existed to discharge employee who repeatedly harassed co-workers by name calling, military and ethnic slurs, and obscene gestures and comments regarding sexual preference, whether or not conduct constituted sexual harassment; remarks intimidated victims so as to adversely affect production, employee lied in denying charges during investigation, rules prohibited harassment, and employer had policy of terminating flagrant violators).

co-workers for particularly unpleasant or hazardous work. For instance, an arbitrator upheld the suspension of a lead worker who singled out a black college student to paint a gas pump and work on an admittedly dangerous separator while it was being tested.[61] A pattern of harassment may be asserted by its target as a defense to otherwise-prohibited workplace altercations. A Hispanic employee who was discharged for fighting was reinstated because the other employee provoked him with repeated racial slurs.[62]

Although there are fewer recent arbitrations involving race discrimination than sex discrimination, the reported awards generally apply Title VII doctrine, even in the absence of an explicit antidiscrimination clause in the CBA.[63] Some arbitrators apply Title VII rigorously. In *City of Berkeley*,[64] the CBA contained a provision prohibiting discriminating on the basis of race. When the city established a new position, four employees applied for it, including the grievant, an African-American male. When the position was given to a white male (who, it was later discovered, did not meet the job's experience requirements), the union grieved, arguing both "disparate treatment" and "disparate impact" discrimination.[65] With respect to the disparate treatment claim, the arbitrator applied the *McDonnell Douglas* burden of proof test to the facts[66] and found that although the grievant had established a prima facie case, the city had met its burden of showing that its reasons for promoting the white employee were legitimate (he had a superior work record), and the grievant was unable to prove that the employer's stated reason was pretextual. With respect to the disparate impact claim, the grievant pointed to statistics showing that African-Americans were statistically underrepresented in the city's work force as a whole. However, the employer adduced statistics that showed that it had met or exceeded its affirmative action goals based on the relevant labor markets. Accordingly, the arbitrator denied the grievance.

---

[61]Atlantic Richfield Co., 81 LA 861 (Nicholas, 1983).

[62]McDonnell Douglas Space Sys. Co., 92 LA 1107 (Herring, 1989). See P.D.I., Inc., 91 LA 21 (Dworkin, 1988) (no just cause for discharge where white female employee withstood 2 days of outrageous verbal abuse from black co-worker, then used a vulgar term in begging co-worker to stop; grievant used acceptable shop talk and did not break any rule; employer discharged both employees, largely out of a desire to maintain workplace harmony and avoid the appearance of racial discrimination).

[63]See, e.g., Arkansas Power & Light Co., 89 LA 1028 (Woolf, 1988) (arbitrator may consider racial bias even where contract does not prohibit racial discrimination).

[64]94 LA 1198 (Bogue, 1990).

[65]Disparate treatment discrimination involves an employment practice that, on its face, is discriminatory (e.g., the preference of one racial group over another). Disparate impact discrimination involves a facially neutral employment practice that, in practice, results in a pattern of racial discrimination (e.g., job qualification tests that tend to exclude minorities at a much higher rate than nonminorities). Although both types of discrimination are prohibited under Title VII, the procedures that have evolved to prove the two claims are significantly different under federal law.

[66]McDonnell Douglas Corp. v. Green, 411 U.S. 792, 5 FEP Cases 965 (1973). See Chapter 14.

Other arbitrators have been less rigorous in their application of Title VII. In *Pacific Airmotive Corp.*,[67] the grievant, an African-American male, was demoted from a supervisory position shortly after he had been promoted. Although the arbitrator noted that discrimination was strongly suggested by the grievant's testimony, he placed a minimal burden on the employer to rebut the inference of discrimination. Because a superior who made an apparently racist remark "explained" it, and that same supervisor was initially responsible for promoting the grievant, the arbitrator dismissed the grievance. There was no discussion of Title VII law in the award.

Generally, where a disparate impact claim is involved, arbitrators do not evaluate proofs as rigorously as federal judges. In *Sifco Industries, Steel Improvement & Forge Div.*,[68] an employer laid off two minority employees who failed written portions of competency tests. They both passed the practical portion of the test, and one of the employees obtained a perfect score. Nevertheless, the arbitrator ruled, without any analysis of the test's possible bias against minorities, that because four other employees passed the test, including one minority, the test was not discriminatory.[69]

*3. Religious Discrimination.* a. Scope of Protection. Section 701(j) of the Act defines the term "religion" in part as "[a]ll aspects of religious observance and practice, as well as belief * * *."[70] The Act does not require that an individual be of a particular faith to be protected. Thus, intensely personal convictions including moral or ethical beliefs that are sincerely held with the strength of traditional religious views come within the meaning of a religious belief even if other individuals find the beliefs incomprehensible or incorrect.[71] The Act does not exclude employees who adopt or convert to beliefs during the course of employment.[72] Further, it is irrelevant that one member of a religion is willing to perform some act that is contrary to another's

---

[67]95 LA 777 (Kaufman, 1990).

[68]97 LA 244 (Fullmer, 1991).

[69]Title VII's procedures for resolving a disparate impact case are more involved and generally place a heavier burden on the employer to justify a practice that has discriminatory effects. First, the complaining party must make a prima facie case by showing that the employer "uses a particular employment practice that causes a disparate impact on the basis of race, color, religion, sex or national origin." 42 U.S.C. § 2000e-2(k)(1)(A)(i). Once the complainant has made the prima facie case, the burden shifts to the employer to persuade the court that the challenged practice is "job related for the position in question and consistent with business necessity." *Id.* If the employer is successful, then the burden shifts to the complainant to show that the challenged practice is not job-related. However, even if the complainant fails at this stage, he can nevertheless still prevail by demonstrating the efficacy of a different procedure lacking a discriminatory impact. Griggs v. Duke Power Co., 401 U.S. 424, 3 FEP Cases 175 (1971).

[70]42 U.S.C. § 2000e(j).

[71]EEOC Dec. No. 76-104 (Apr. 2, 1976), CCH EEOC Decisions (1983) ¶ 6500; 29 C.F.R. § 1605.1.

[72]Draper v. United States Pipe & Foundry Co., 527 F.2d 515, 518, 11 FEP Cases 1106 (6th Cir., 1975).

interpretation of the commands of their common faith. The important factor is the belief of the claimant employee.[73]

Another important factor in determining whether an activity is protected is whether the activity is mandated by, or is a cardinal principle of, the religion. Thus, working on a church play does not constitute a religious activity.[74] And attendance at a religious convention or meeting that is motivated solely by personal considerations is not protected.[75] Conversely, monthly religious meetings that an employee is required to attend as part of his pastoral duties are protected.[76] Other protected activities include religious holy days such as the Jewish High Holy days of Yom Kippur and Rosh Hashanah, and the Day of Atonement and Feast of Tabernacles observed by the Worldwide Church of God.[77] The Saturday and Sunday Sabbaths observed by many religions are also subject to certain protections.[78] However, religious activity does not protect an employee from being required to work Sundays where that employee's religion does not observe any day as a Sabbath, nor do its tenets prohibit members from working on Sundays.[79]

To prevail on a religious discrimination claim, the employee must prove: (1) that the employee has a bona fide belief that compliance with an employment requirement is contrary to his or her religious faith, (2) that the employee has informed the employer about the conflict, and (3) that the employee was discharged because of his or her refusal to comply with the employment requirement.[80]

b. Reasonable Accommodation. The employer must demonstrate that it made a reasonable accommodation or that it cannot do so without suffering undue hardship.[81] According to the Supreme Court, "any reasonable accommodation by the employer is sufficient," and if an employer has made any reasonable accommodation, it need

---

[73]Thomas v. Review Bd. of the Ind. Employment Sec. Div., 101 S.Ct. 1425, 25 FEP Cases 629 (1981).

[74]Wessling v. Kroger Co., 554 F.Supp. 548, 552, 30 FEP Cases 1222 (E.D. Mich., 1982).

[75]Haig v. Everett, 8 Ark. App. 255, 650 S.W.2d 593 (1983); Clorox Co., 92 ARB ¶ 8455 (Byars, 1992).

[76]Weitkenaut v. Goodyear Tire & Rubber Co., 381 F.Supp. 1284, 10 FEP Cases 513 (D. Vt., 1974).

[77]EEOC Dec. No. 76-116 (July 7, 1976), CCH EEOC Decisions (1983) ¶ 6681; EEOC v. Universal Mfg. Corp., 914 F.2d 71, 53 FEP Cases 1811 (5th Cir., 1990); Willey v. Maben Mfg., Inc., 479 F.Supp. 634 (N.D. Miss., 1979).

[78]EEOC v. Hacienda Hotel, 881 F.2d 1504, 1513–14, 50 FEP Cases 877 (9th Cir., 1989); Lake v. B.F. Goodrich Co., 837 F.2d 449, 46 FEP Cases 569 (11th Cir.), cert. denied, 109 S.Ct. 76, 47 FEP Cases 1592 (1988); Smith v. Pyro Mining Co., 827 F.2d 1081, 1086, 44 FEP Cases 1152 (6th Cir., 1987), cert. denied, 108 S.Ct. 1293, 46 FEP Cases 600 (1988).

[79]EEOC v. Chrysler Corp., 652 F.Supp. 1523, 1529, 45 FEP Cases 513 (N.D. Ohio, 1987).

[80]Smith v. Pyro Mining Co., 827 F.2d 1081, 1086, 44 FEP Cases 1152 (6th Cir., 1987), cert. denied, 108 S.Ct. 1293, 46 FEP Cases 600 (1988); Johnson v. Angelica Uniform Group, Inc., 762 F.2d 671, 673, 37 FEP Cases 1409 (8th Cir., 1985); Brener v. Diagnostic Ctr. Hosp., 671 F.2d 141, 144, 28 FEP Cases 907 (5th Cir., 1982); Burns v. Southern Pac. Transp. Co., 589 F.2d 403, 405, 17 FEP Cases 1648 (9th Cir., 1978), cert. denied, 99 S.Ct. 843, 18 FEP Cases 1430 (1979).

[81]EEOC v. Chrysler Corp., 652 F.Supp. 1523, 1527, 45 FEP Cases 513 (N.D. Ohio, 1987).

not show that "each of the employee's alternative accommodations would result in undue hardship."[82] Thus, Title VII does not require employers to accommodate religious practices of an employee in the way that the employee would like to be accommodated.[83] Nor is the employer required to spare the employee any cost or give an employee a choice among several accommodations.[84]

Reasonable accommodations include the following: providing the employee the option to take the necessary time off in the form of unpaid leave;[85] permitting voluntary shift substitutes and "swaps";[86] creating flexible scheduling, i.e., "flexible arrival and departure times, floating or optional holidays, flexible work breaks, use of lunch time in exchange for early departure, staggered work hours, and permitting an employee to make up lost time due to the observance of religious practices";[87] and contacting the union to determine if the employee may be assigned to another position or if the union will allow an exception to the seniority provisions of the collective bargaining agreement.[88] However, an employer that operates 24 hours a day and has thousands of employees may be required to be more accommodating on the theory that it has the available resources.[89]

While it is not the employee's responsibility to arrange the accommodation,[90] the employee is expected to cooperate with the employer

[82] Ansonia Bd. of Educ. v. Philbrook, 107 S.Ct. 367, 42 FEP Cases 359, 363 (1986).

[83]Pinsker v. Adams & Arapahoe Counties Joint Dist. 28J, 735 F.2d 388, 390, 34 FEP Cases 1570 (10th Cir., 1984).

[84]Id. at 390–91; Mathewson v. Florida Game & Fresh Water Fish Comm'n, 693 F.Supp. 1044, 1050, 46 FEP Cases 917 (M.D. Fla., 1988), aff'd mem., 871 F.2d 123, 49 FEP Cases 1512 (11th Cir., 1989).

[85]Ansonia Bd. of Educ. v. Philbrook, 107 S.Ct. 367, 42 FEP Cases 359 (1986). "But unpaid leave is not a reasonable accommodation when paid leave is provided for all purposes *except* religious ones." Id., 42 FEP Cases at 364 (emphasis in original).

[86]Huston v. Auto Workers Local 93, 559 F.2d 477, 478, 480–81, 15 FEP Cases 326 (8th Cir., 1977); 29 C.F.R. §1605.2(d)(i). It is not the employee's responsibility to arrange for a replacement. Lake v. B.F. Goodrich Co., 837 F.2d 449, 451, 46 FEP Cases 569 (11th Cir.), cert. denied, 109 S.Ct. 76, 47 FEP Cases 1592 (1988).

[87]29 C.F.R. §1605.2(d)(ii). State and federal wage and hour laws must be considered before any of these flexible scheduling options are implemented.

[88]29 C.F.R. §1605.2(d)(iii); Trans World Airlines, Inc. v. Hardison, 97 S.Ct. 2264, 14 FEP Cases 1697 (1977). The airline discharged an employee after he refused to work on Saturdays because of his religion. The carrier approached the union regarding the possible accommodation of the employee under the collective bargaining agreement, but the union was unwilling to violate the seniority provisions. A proposal that the employee work only 4 days a week was rejected by the company on the grounds that it needed to staff the weekend position, and the carrier refused to employ someone not regularly assigned to work Saturdays because it would have been required to pay premium wages to do so. Id., 14 FEP Cases at 1699. The Court upheld the discharge.

[89]EEOC Dec. No. 76-116 (July 7, 1976), CCH EEOC Decisions (1983) ¶ 6681 (employer with thousands of employees that operated 24 hours a day every day of the year violated Title VII by offering a Jewish employee leave without pay on two Jewish holidays rather than assigning her to work on Christmas and Good Friday and allowing paid holidays for the two Jewish holidays).

[90]Lake v. B.F. Goodrich Co. 837 F.2d 449, 451, 46 FEP Cases 569 (11th Cir.), cert. denied, 109 S.Ct. 76, 47 FEP Cases 1592 (1988).

in reaching an accommodation.[91] However, an employee is not required to ask another to work on a Sabbath when the employee's belief makes such a request sinful.[92]

Requiring an employer to bear "more than de minimis cost to accommodate an employee's religious preferences," such as payment of overtime pay to another employee, constitutes an undue hardship under the statute.[93] Undue hardship is also evidenced by an actual imposition on co-workers or a disruption of the work routine.[94] The mere fact that some employees may grumble is inadequate.[95] Further, employers are not required by Title VII to carve out special exceptions to a seniority system in order to help employees meet religious objectives; such favoritism at the expense of other employees who are entitled to the benefits of any seniority system is clearly not required by Title VII and may in fact result in reverse discrimination.[96]

The duty to accommodate does not "require an employer to discriminate against some employees in order to enable others to observe their Sabbath."[97] Thus, "Sabbath observers are not 'favored' over co-workers, any more than injured workers are 'favored' when given disability leave. The law simply alleviates for them a conflict of loyalties not faced by their secular co-workers."[98] As with any form of discrimination and the employer's attempt to create accommodations,

---

[91]An employee cannot shirk his duties to try to accommodate himself or to cooperate with his employer in reaching an accommodation by a mere recalcitrant citation of religious precepts. Nor can he thereby shift all responsibility for accommodation to his employer. Where an employee refuses to attempt to accommodate his own beliefs or to cooperate with his employer's attempt to reach a reasonable accommodation, he may render an accommodation impossible. In such a case, the employee himself is responsible for any failure of accommodation and his employer should not be held liable for such failure. Chrysler Corp. v. Mann, 561 F.2d 1282, 1285, 15 FEP Cases 788 (8th Cir., 1977), cert. denied, 98 S.Ct. 778, 16 FEP Cases 501 (1978). See also Hudson v. Western Airlines, Inc., 851 F.2d 261, 266–67, 47 FEP Cases 295 (9th Cir., 1988); Smith v. Pyro Mining Co., 827 F.2d 1081, 1085, 44 FEP Cases 1152 (6th Cir., 1987), cert. denied, 108 S.Ct. 1293, 46 FEP Cases 600 (1988); Wren v. T.I.M.E.-D.C., Inc., 453 F.Supp. 582, 584, 19 FEP Cases 582 (E.D. Mo., 1978), aff'd, 595 F.2d 441 (8th Cir., 1979).

[92]Smith v. Pyro Mining Co., 827 F.2d 1081, 1088, 44 FEP Case 1152 (6th Cir., 1987), cert. denied, 108 S.Ct. 1293, 46 FEP Cases 600 (1988); EEOC v. J.P. Stevens & Co., 740 F.Supp. 1135, 1138, 53 FEP Cases 768 (M.D.N.C., 1990).

[93]Trans World Airlines, Inc. v. Hardison, 97 S.Ct. 2264, 14 FEP Cases 1697 (1977). While an employer is required to incur regular overtime charges, the EEOC will presume that the infrequent payment of premium wages for a substitute or the payment of premium wages while a more permanent accommodation is being sought are costs that an employer can be required to bear as a means of providing a reasonable accommodation. Further, the Commission will presume that generally the payment of administrative costs necessary for providing the accommodation will not constitute more than a de minimis cost. Administrative costs, for example, include those costs involved in rearranging schedules and recording substitutions for payroll purposes. 29 C.F.R. §1605.2(e)(1).

[94]Brener v. Diagnostic Ctr. Hosp., 671 F.2d 141, 146, 28 FEP Cases 907 (5th Cir., 1982).

[95]Burns v. Southern Pac. Transp. Co., 589 F.2d 403, 407, 17 FEP Cases 1648 (9th Cir., 1978), cert. denied, 99 S.Ct. 843, 18 FEP Cases 1430 (1979).

[96]Gibson v. Missouri Pac. R.R., 620 F.Supp. 85, 87–88, 39 FEP Cases 369 (E.D. Ark., 1985).

[97]Trans World Airlines, Inc. v. Hardison, 97 S.Ct. 2264, 14 FEP Cases 1697 (1977).

[98]McConnell, "Religious Participation in Public Programs: Religious Freedom as a Crossroads," 59 U. Chi. L. Rev. 115, 125 (1992), discussing Estate of Thornton v. Caldor, Inc., 105 S.Ct. 2914, 38 FEP Cases 1 (1985).

one must be careful to avoid the pitfall of reverse discrimination. Thus, it is appropriate to allow an employee to take an unpaid personal day for a religious holiday rather than provide an employee of a minority faith an additional paid holiday that is not provided to employees of other faiths.[99]

Cases of religious discrimination typically involve the discipline or discharge of an employee who is absent from work to observe a religious holiday. Arbitrators generally apply Title VII's standards to these cases. Even in those cases where the Act is not referenced, the arbitrator's decision is frequently consistent with the primary tenets and policies of the Act.[100] For example, in *H. K. Porter Co.,*[101] the arbitrator held that public policy imposed an obligation on the employer to reasonably accommodate an employee's need for 1 day off to attend a special church service.

Similarly, in *Reynolds & Reynolds Co.,*[102] the arbitrator upheld the discharge of an employee who insisted on leaving work early twice a week to attend a meeting for Jehovah's Witnesses. The factors considered by the arbitrator were that the employee did not cooperate with the employer, the need of the employee to leave early twice a week was overly burdensome on the employer during the busy season, and accommodating the grievant would result in discrimination against other employees.

As more and more courts have analyzed the Act, more information and interpretive decisions have become available to arbitrators. Consequently, arbitrators are becoming more comfortable with the Act and there are very few recent decisions involving discipline for absences for religious reasons where the Act is not discussed and analyzed by the arbitrators.[103] Thus, one arbitrator held that "he is bound by the Guidelines of the EEOC, the agency charged by Congress with responsibility for ensuring compliance with the Act * * *."[104] Further, under this more recent line of decisions, "an Employer [is] not required to enforce a provision [of the collective bargaining agreement] that was discriminatory in violation of Title VII."[105] An arbitrator, however,

---

[99]Pinsker v. Adams & Arapahoe Counties Joint Dist. 28J, 735 F.2d 388, 390–91, 34 FEP Cases 1570 (10th Cir., 1984). It is interesting to note that members of mainstream religions may have little or no need for accommodation. McConnell, "Accommodation of Religion: An Update and a Response to the Critics," 60 Geo. Wash. L. Rev. 685, 733 (March, 1992). Thus, for example, Christmas is designated as a national holiday.

[100]H.K. Porter Co., 83-2 ARB ¶ 8439 (Shanker, 1983); Reynolds & Reynolds Co., 63 LA 157 (High, 1974). But see Walker Mfg. Co., 60 LA 525 (Simon, 1973) (employer held to have acted properly under the CBA by terminating an employee who refused to work Sundays despite the employee's religious beliefs; arbitrator admitted that the decision was unfortunate from a policy perspective and suggested reemployment since grievant was a valuable employee).

[101]83-2 ARB ¶ 8439 (Shanker, 1983).

[102]63 LA 157 (High, 1974).

[103]See Moonlight Mushrooms, Inc., 93-2 ARB ¶ 3554 (Dean, Jr., 1993); United States Playing Card Co., 87 LA 937 (Duda, 1986); New York Dep't of Envtl. Conservation, 87 LA 848 (Babiskin, 1986); Alabama By-Products Corp., 79 LA 1320 (Clarke, 1982).

[104]Alabama By-Products Corp., 79 LA 1320, 1325–26 (Clarke, 1982).

[105]United States Playing Card Co., 87 LA 937, 943 (Duda, 1986).

is without jurisdiction to consider a discrimination claim that was already decided by the EEOC or a comparable state agency, though an arbitrator may decide the question of a contract breach.[106]

While arbitrators generally analyze the Act, they are not always entirely accurate. In *Moonlight Mushrooms, Inc.,*[107] the grievant, a Seventh Day Adventist, was discharged for excessive unexcused absences on Saturdays. The grievant argued that his religion prohibited him from working on Saturdays and that the discharge violated Title VII. The arbitrator relied on Title VII case law, which requires that an employer reasonably accommodate an employee's religious observance, unless such accommodation would result in an undue hardship on the employer's business. Finding that the employer's business required employees to work whenever mushrooms were ready for harvesting, and that any one employee's absence could jeopardize the crop, the arbitrator ruled that the employer reasonably accommodated grievant by allowing him to attempt to trade his Saturday hours for the weekday hours of other employees. This accommodation does not appear to be as substantial as the types of accommodations approved in federal religious discrimination cases.[108]

Other arbitral awards have applied Title VII's standards in religion cases more rigorously. In *Centerville Clinics, Inc.,*[109] a dental clinic discharged a dental assistant who refused to work on Saturdays for religious reasons. Although the CBA did not contain an antidiscrimination clause, the arbitrator applied Title VII's religious discrimination provisions because they are "necessarily involved in the determination of whether there has been a contract violation."[110] In applying Title VII's religious discrimination provisions and Supreme Court precedent,[111] the arbitrator balanced the employer's reasonable accommodation against the undue hardship of never having her available on Saturdays. The arbitrator found that the latter option would result in an undue burden on the employer and denied the grievance.

Relying on the cases interpreting the Act and the EEOC Guidelines, another arbitrator addressed the issue of reasonable accommodation in *Alabama By-Products Corp.*[112] In this case, the employee

---

[106]JPI Transp. Prods., Inc., 93 LA 716 (Kindig, 1989) (In light of the dismissal of the discrimination charge by both the EEOC and the Ohio Civil Rights Commission, Arbitrator Kindig focused on whether the employee was terminated in accordance with the terms of the employer's attendance policy.).

[107]101 LA 421 (Dean, 1993).

[108]See, e.g., Beadle v. Hillsborough County Sheriff's Dep't, 29 F.3d 589, 65 FEP Cases 1069 (11th Cir., 1994) (where employee could not work after sundown on Friday evening for religious reasons, employer's offering of neutral shift rotation in addition to actively assisting the employee to arrange shift swap was reasonable accommodation), cert. denied, 115 S.Ct. 2001, 67 FEP Cases 1344 (1995).

[109]85 LA 1059 (Talarico, 1985).

[110]Id. at 1062.

[111]Trans World Airlines v. Hardison, 97 S.Ct. 2264, 14 FEP Cases 1697 (1977).

[112]79 LA 1320 (Clarke, 1982).

was an ordained minister of the Church of God and his duties included preaching at funerals whenever a church member requested him to do so. The employee was disciplined for absences when he was preaching at funerals. The employer contended that it reasonably accommodated the employee's religious beliefs by allowing him to use a personal day or a vacation day, rather than permitting an excused absence. Relying on the EEOC Guidelines, the arbitrator held that the preaching was protected by the Act and that the personal/vacation day option was not a reasonable accommodation. Accordingly, since there was no evidence of hardship to the employer, the arbitrator directed that the unexcused absences be removed from the employee's record.

In *JPI Transportation Products,*[113] an employee discharged for violation of an absenteeism policy alleged that his absences were due to his observance of the Sabbath as required by the tenets of his church, the Worldwide Church of God. The state civil rights commission had dismissed the grievant's discrimination charge, finding that the employer had reasonably accommodated the employee's religious need. While some of grievant's absences were for Sabbath observance, the arbitrator found that the employer administered the attendance policy consistently, issued appropriate warnings, and reasonably accommodated the employee's religious needs. The arbitrator noted that irrespective of the reason for which the grievant refused to work Saturdays, he had placed himself "well into the disciplinary procedure" prior to joining the church. The arbitrator also noted that the grievant could not have been excused from rotating Saturday work without violating the contract.

In *Bronx-Lebanon Hospital Center,*[114] an employee was denied leave and ordered to report to work on Good Friday, but she attended Roman Catholic services instead. The arbitrator concluded that it was unnecessary to reach the issue of religious discrimination because the grievant's faith did not preclude working on Good Friday. The grievant's choice to attend services was one of religious preference and not religious obligation.

The question of employee cooperation with the employer's attempt to provide a reasonable accommodation under the Act was analyzed in *New York Department of Environmental Conservation.*[115] After a review of multiple cases interpreting the Act, the arbitrator ruled that "Title VII is premised on 'bilateral cooperation.' The employee has a correlative duty to make a good faith effort to satisfy his needs through the means offered by the employer. A reasonable accommodation need not be on the employee's terms only."[116]

---

[113]93 LA 716 (Kindig, 1989).

[114]90 LA 1216 (Babiskin, 1988).

[115]87 LA 848 (Babiskin, 1986).

[116]Id. at 851. See also Georgia Power Co., 94 LA 1303 (Baroni, 1990).

c. Harassment.   Religious harassment takes the form of abusive gestures and comments about the employee, or conduct directed toward religious dress, icons, or other outward manifestations.[117] Employees have also been disciplined for antagonizing co-workers by preaching on the job.[118] But an employee's use of foul language was not harassment of a born-again Christian where the employee subjected everyone in the plant to such language and did not intend to harass the other employee.[119]

d. Questions Concerning Religious Beliefs.   Employers are generally permitted to inquire about an employee's religious beliefs only to the extent necessary to determine whether the employee's belief requires absence from work on a given day.[120] At least one arbitrator has held that

> [i]t is * * * within the scope of proper supervisory inquiry to ask an employee what the religious significance of a particular day is to the employee. Moreover, where an employee makes it clear that he or she is a member of an organized religion, and professes no personal beliefs apart from the tenets of that religion, it is not improper for supervisors to consider the tenets of that religion to assist them in determining whether the employee's [sic] sincerely holds a personal belief which requires him or her to refrain from work on a particular day.[121]

4. Sexual Preference Harassment.   Some state and local laws prohibit workplace discrimination based on sexual preference. Employees who violate this prohibition may be subject to discipline. For example, a male employee who asked a male co-worker if he had semen dripping from his asshole was discharged, despite the employee claiming it was a joke. The contract incorporated a city ordinance prohibiting discrimination based on sexual or affectional preference.[122]

5. Disability-Based Harassment.   The Americans with Disabilities Act (ADA)[123] prohibits employers from discriminating against a "qualified individual with a disability" because of that disability, in

---

[117]See generally 29 C.F.R. § 1609.1(b).

[118]United Parcel Serv., 76 LA 244 (Darrow, 1981).

[119]Bethlehem Structural Prods. Corp., 105 LA 205 (Witt, 1995).

[120]Social Sec. Admin., 79 LA 449 (Mittelman, 1982) (federal agency that suspected employees of taking advantage of liberal policy with respect to requests for religious time off properly directed supervisors to determine sincerity of requests by asking those employees whether request was based on personal religious beliefs and whether personal religious belief required absence from work for period requested).

[121]Id. at 456.

[122]Fry's Food Stores of Arizona, Inc., 99 LA 1161 (Hogler, 1992). See Philip Morris, 94 LA 826 (Baroni, 1990) (just cause existed for written warning to male employees where female employee reported they made animal sounds and comments about faggot truck; conduct was part of year-long pattern of offensive remarks and behavior directed at co-worker and her husband, derogated husband's sexual preference, and forced co-worker to take medical leave of absence for mental distress).

[123]29 U.S.C. §12101 et seq.

"job application procedures, the hiring, advancement, or discharge of employees, employee compensation, job training, and other terms, conditions, and privileges of employment." EEOC regulations interpreting the ADA make it unlawful to "coerce, intimidate, threaten, harass or interfere with any individual in the exercise or enjoyment of, or because that individual aided or encouraged any other individual in the exercise of, any right granted or protected by this part."[124] The courts are still working out the degree of severity required to make harassment based on disability actionable.[125] To date, reported arbitral cases do not address the issue of discipline for harassment of disabled co-workers.

*6. Awards Disregarding Title VII.*   Some arbitrators still ignore external law in resolving Title VII type grievances. This position is embodied in the following statement contained in a 1982 award: "Whether or not there has been a violation of Title VII of the Civil Rights Act of 1964 is a matter for another jurisdiction."[126] Some arbitrators have relied on a strict interpretation of a CBA's antidiscrimination clause in order to avoid reference to external law. Where a CBA identified specific types of prohibited discriminatory activities, conduct that was not covered by the clause was held to be an insufficient basis for discharge.[127]

Other awards have rejected Title VII even where there is a contractual basis for applying it. In an unrepresentative decision, *Godchaux-Henderson Sugar Co.*,[128] the grievant was discharged for essentially threatening to rape a female co-employee. The company's work rules prohibited immoral or indecent behavior. Even though the grievant admitted that he had made repeated sexual advances to the female employee, the arbitrator refused to sustain the discharge. He found that "when the company brings a young female employee into the plant and allows her unsupervised freedom to invite male employees to her work place for conversation and play, trouble is inevitable."[129] In passing, the arbitrator noted that the company is not the guardian of the morals of its employees.[130]

---

[124]29 C.F.R. §1630.12(b).

[125]See, e.g., Schaff v. Shalala, 3 AD Cases 770 (D. Md. 1994) (allegations that employees mocked visually impaired employee by waving badges in front of his face, swapping seats at lunch, and making him look incompetent during meeting are so relatively minor as to fail to establish existence of hostile work environment).

[126]Allis-Chalmers Corp., 78 LA 17, 19 (Storey, 1982).

[127]See, e.g., County of Orange, 76 LA 1040, 1043 (Tamoush, 1981) (refusing to find sexual preference discrimination under labor contract that did not prohibit such conduct; arbitrator noted that he should "not engage in 'legislative innovation' when the parties have so clearly provided a specific listing of prohibited discrimination in protected groups not merely for illustration, but to provide specific limits").

[128]75 LA 377 (Barnhart, 1980).

[129]Id. at 380.

[130]Cf. Newsday, Inc. v. Long Island Typographical Union, 915, 915 F.2d 840, 135 LRRM 2659 (2d Cir., 1990), cert. denied, 499 U.S. 922, 136 LRRM 2720 (1991) (employer has "legal

Similarly, in *KIAM*,[131] an employee was discharged after he repeatedly made unwelcome sexual advances to a female co-worker. The arbitrator first noted that an employer is obligated to promulgate sexual discrimination policies because external law makes sexual discrimination illegal. After acknowledging that the grievant's conduct resulted in a hostile work environment, the arbitrator refused to uphold the discharge. In essence, the arbitrator focused on the reasonableness of the work rules in question, rather than on the applicability of Title VII. "[V]iolation of [Title VII] is not *per se* the standard by which the Arbitrator is obligated to judge the grievant's behavior, [it is] only one standard by which the Arbitrator may judge the reasonableness of the work rule."[132] In short, the arbitrator held that the existence of sexual harassment does not automatically confer the right of discharge.[133] Thus, the arbitrator found no just cause for dismissal because the company's sexual discrimination policy did not adequately inform the employees of what was expected of them, the consequences of wrongdoing, and the mechanism for enforcement of the policy. There was "no doubt in the Arbitrator's mind" that the grievant's conduct resulted in a hostile work environment.[134] Furthermore, in rejecting the company's public policy argument, he found that public policy does not mandate the termination of a harassing employee. "[I]f the harasser is governed by a collective bargaining agreement where just cause is provided it is ultimately for an arbitrator to determine the appropriate penalty to be imposed consistent with the stated purposes of the written policy and considerations of justice."[135]

## III. Age Discrimination in Employment Act

The same general approach to Title VII claims is found in arbitral awards involving age discrimination claims under the Age Discrimination in Employment Act (ADEA). The typical age discrimination grievance involves an employee in the protected age class (over 40 years of age) who is discharged, disciplined, or passed over for a promotion in favor of a nonprotected employee with greater seniority,

---

duty to eliminate sexual harassment in the workplace"). EEOC sexual harassment guidelines make it clear that an employer does have an affirmative duty to act as a moral guardian: "An employer should take all steps necessary to prevent sexual harassment from occurring, such as affirmatively raising the subject, expressing strong disapproval, developing appropriate sanctions, informing employees of their right to raise and how to raise the issue of harassment under Title VII, and developing methods to sensitize all concerned." 29 C.F.R. §1604.11(f)(1995).

[131]97 LA 617 (Bard, 1991).

[132]Id. at 625.

[133]Id. at 630.

[134]Id.

[135]Id. at 626.

ostensibly superior job skills, or a better disciplinary record. In *Alpha Beta Co.,*[136] the grievant, a 50-year-old male, was passed over for a promotion in favor of a much younger employee with greater seniority. The CBA contained a broad antidiscrimination clause prohibiting all forms of discrimination under federal law, including age discrimination, and a standard clause providing that senior qualified employees should receive job openings. There was uncontradicted testimony that one of the grievant's supervisors stated that the grievant did not get the job because a "younger, more agile person" was needed. The arbitrator found that even though age discrimination probably played a role in the decision, there were also legitimate, performance-based reasons for the action—in other words, it was a mixed motive case.[137] Relying on the then-governing *Price Waterhouse*[138] burden of proof test, the arbitrator found that the burden was on the employer to prove, by a preponderance of the evidence, that it would have made the same decision based on the legitimate reason alone.[139] The arbitrator denied the grievance because in the absence of the discriminatory motive, the CBA's seniority clause would have required the employer to give the job to the senior employee.

As with Title VII, the ADEA has a bona fide occupational qualification (BFOQ) exception that permits employment decisions based on age where "age is a bona fide occupational qualification reasonably necessary to the normal operation of the particular business * * * ."[140] In *Arab Electric Cooperative,*[141] the employer instituted a lineman apprenticeship program that only permitted participants under age 26. Two grievants senior to those admitted were older than 26 and were denied admission.[142] Although the CBA contained a provision prohibiting age discrimination, the employer's stated basis for limiting the program to individuals less than 26 years of age was the acknowledged danger of the job. The arbitrator denied the grievance on the basis of a BFOQ and the federal regulation that excepts bona fide apprenticeship programs from the Act's coverage.[143]

---

[136]92 LA 1301 (Wilmoth, 1989).

[137]A mixed-motive case involves an employment decision based in part on legitimate reasons and in part on illegal considerations.

[138]Price Waterhouse v. Hopkins, 490 U.S. 228, 49 FEP Cases 954 (1989).

[139]Prior to the 1991 amendments to Title VII, in a mixed-motive case the employer could avoid liability by demonstrating, by a preponderance of the evidence, that it would have made the same employment decision in the absence of the discriminatory motivation. Subsequent to the 1991 amendments to Title VII, if it is shown that discrimination played any role in the employer's practice, then such a practice is automatically unlawful. 42 U.S.C. §2000e-2(m). However, if the employer can also show legitimate reasons for the action, then the remedies available to the employee are limited. 42 U.S.C. §2000e-5(g)(2)(B).

[140]29 U.S.C. §623(f).

[141]97 LA 1074 (King, 1991).

[142]Although the age of the grievants is not stated in the decision, the arbitrator appeared to rely on the ADEA in formulating his analysis, so this decision is relevant on this issue.

[143]29 C.F.R. §1625.13.

# IV. Americans with Disabilities Act

In 1990 Congress enacted the Americans with Disabilities Act (ADA).[144] It prohibits employment discrimination against qualified individuals with physical or mental disabilities. As with other statutes, the ADA presents the possibility of its requirements conflicting with a CBA.

## A. *Awards Applying ADA*

In *Cleveland Electric Illuminating Co.,*[145] the arbitrator applied the ADA's reasonable accommodation requirement to a CBA clause that provided that an employee who is incapacitated for regular work must be placed in "any work he can do." The arbitrator held that the company did not go far enough in attempting to find the grievant work that did not include pole climbing after his accident.

In *Thrifty Cos.,*[146] the arbitrator sustained the grievance where the company, which had no absenteeism policy, discharged the grievant for excessive absences. The grievant suffered from diabetes and was unable to perform her responsibilities. The arbitrator stated that because the ADA requires a company to take an employee's disability into account, the company was unreasonable in not considering the grievant's physical condition. Therefore, the arbitrator determined that the company lacked just cause to terminate the grievant.[147]

After a 6-month medical leave of absence the grievant was placed in a part-time, light-work position for approximately 1 year before she was returned to a full-time position. The union argued that the company violated the CBA and the ADA by failing to place her in a full-time position upon her return to work. The arbitrator denied the grievance in part, finding that the company satisfied the CBA and the ADA by placing grievant in a part-time position, and granted it in part, holding that the company should have returned her to full-time status sooner.[148]

In *Kaiser Aluminum & Chemical Corp.,*[149] the grievant was a kleptomaniac who stole from the company for 15 to 18 years. The arbitrator noted that "[i]t is highly significant that employers need not make 'reasonable accommodation' for employees suffering from kleptomania under the Americans with Disability Act. In short, even

---

[144]42 U.S.C. §12101 et seq. (1990).

[145]100 LA 1039 (Lipson, 1993).

[146]103 LA 317 (Staudohar, 1994).

[147]See also Laidlaw Transit, Inc., 104 LA 302 (Concepcion, 1995) (grievant was not discharged for insubordination because he was never warned that he would be terminated if he failed to take medication to control his disability).

[148]Consentino's Brywood Price Chopper, 104 LA 187 (Thornell, 1995).

[149]99 LA 609 (Goldberg, 1992).

if kleptomania is shown, it is not a recognized defense to a termination based on theft at the workplace."[150]

In *City of Dearborn Heights*,[151] the police department reassigned a night shift officer suffering from life-threatening diabetes to the day shift as a reasonable accommodation under the ADA. The union filed a grievance because two other officers were reassigned to other shifts in violation of their seniority. The arbitrator denied the grievance because the ADA takes precedence over seniority.[152]

In *Thermo King Corp.*,[153] the company previously entered into a last-chance arrangement with the grievant, who was suffering from chronic depression. Applying the ADA, the arbitrator denied the grievance because the ADA does not impose an obligation on a company to tolerate repeated absences whenever the grievant's alcohol/drug dependency makes it difficult to keep on schedule.[154]

In *Meijer, Inc.*,[155] a 24-year-old grievant who suffered from bipolar affective disorder was discharged for making offensive remarks to a customer. The arbitrator determined that the grievant's illness contributed to the incident and held that since he failed to seek treatment and take required medication that would have prevented the episode, the company did not have to accommodate the grievant.

## B. Awards Not Applying ADA

Upon returning from a medical leave, the grievant was assigned to a different shift because she had been subjected to sexual harassment on her previous shift. The displaced employee's grievance was upheld in *Stone Container Corp.*[156] In the absence of a nondiscrimination clause in the contract, the arbitrator refused to apply the ADA, stating that "if the contract of collective bargaining allows the arbitrator to determine the answers of the grievance under the law of the land, then the contract needs to say so."[157] Under the facts of this case, it did not.[158]

---

[150]Id. at 614.

[151]101 LA 809 (Kanner, 1993).

[152]See also San Francisco Unified Sch. Dist., 104 LA 215 (Bogue, 1995) (arbitrator looked to ADA standard of reasonable accommodation to determine whether school district acted properly to find job for teacher with multiple sclerosis).

[153]102 LA 612 (Dworkin, 1993).

[154]See also American Sterilizer Co., 104 LA 921 (Dissen, 1995) (arbitrator looked to ADA and denied grievance where employer refused to create special half-day position for disabled employee; ADA does not have purpose of creating new job categories or restructuring existing ones in such a way as to wreak havoc on the current employment system and the CBA).

[155]103 LA 834 (Daniel, 1994).

[156]101 LA 943 (Feldman, 1993).

[157]Id. at 947.

[158]See also Multi-Clean, Inc., 102 LA 463 (Miller, 1993) (arbitrator lacked authority to determine whether employer's refusal to return a disabled employee to work violated the ADA

Another arbitrator refused to apply the ADA in *Altoona Hospital*.[159] After a year-long leave of absence, two doctors certified that the grievant was capable of performing the duties of her position, but her personal physician placed restrictions on her return to work. The company took the position that there was no vacancy for an employee with her limited capacity. The arbitrator refused to apply the ADA, despite a broad nondiscrimination clause in the CBA, stating that the CBA was the sole source of authority in the matter.

## V. Family and Medical Leave Act

In 1993, Congress enacted the Family and Medical Leave Act (FMLA).[160] It was designed to provide job protection for employees who needed time off because of the birth or adoption of a child, to care for a member of their immediate family who has a serious health condition, or because of the employee's serious health condition. This law could pose a conflict with the leave of absence provision in a CBA, which may result in a significant number of arbitrations.

The Fourth Circuit has held that a lawsuit under the FMLA must be stayed pending the outcome of arbitration.[161] While on an FMLA leave, the employee signed an acknowledgment form for a new employee handbook that included an agreement to submit all employment disputes to arbitration. The employee was discharged and sued. The hospital's motion to stay the action pending arbitration was denied. On appeal, the Fourth Circuit cited the Supreme Court's endorsement of the liberal policy favoring arbitration for claims created by contract or by statute. It held that in agreeing to arbitrate a statutory claim, the employee did not give up the rights afforded by statute but only agreed to submit to an arbitral rather than judicial forum.

In *Grand Haven Stamped Products Co.,*[162] the grievant was required to use accrued vacation time for an FMLA leave. Since both the union and the employer relied on interpretations of the FMLA, the arbitrator found it necessary to review the FMLA before analyzing the contractual dispute. Although the FMLA allowed employers to require the use of accrued vacation leave, that right must be interpreted within the context of the CBA. The arbitrator ruled that the CBA vacation clause grants employees the right to take their vacation

---

where CBA limited arbitral jurisdiction to its terms); Exxon Co., U.S.A., 101 LA 997 (Sergent, 1993) (arbitrator refused to apply the ADA because CBA limited grievances to matters arising only out of the interpretation or application of CBA).

[159]102 LA 650 (Jones, 1993).

[160]26 U.S.C. §2601.

[161]O'Neil v. Hilton Head Hosp., 115 F.3d 272 (4th Cir., 1977).

[162]107 LA 131 (Daniel, 1996).

whenever they wish, subject to restrictions that were not applicable here. Therefore, the grievance was sustained.

In *Oxboro Clinic,*[163] the grievant was denied a job because of excessive absenteeism (due partly to migraine headaches), despite meeting the requirements for the position. The arbitrator sustained the grievance, stating that her absences for other reasons would have been borderline and the migraines could not be counted because they were covered by the FMLA.

In *Lau,*[164] the grievant was discharged for violating the absenteeism policy that was based on a 12-point system, excluding personal leaves required under the FMLA. The grievant claimed that her last points were incorrectly assessed because the absences were covered by the FMLA. The arbitrator denied the grievance because the grievant did not comply with the FMLA policy that required that the application for leave be submitted with documentation.[165]

## VI. Title VII and ADEA Procedures and Remedies

Even where arbitrators expressly rely on Title VII and the ADEA in resolving discipline and discharge cases, the statutes are not always followed in their entirety. Many arbitral decisions[166] follow the burden of proof approach announced by the Supreme Court in *McDonnell Douglas Corp. v. Green.*[167] In disparate treatment cases, where there is no direct evidence of discriminatory intent, this burden generally requires the complainant to carry the initial burden of establishing a prima facie case of discrimination: (1) that the employee is a member of a protected class, (2) that the employee was subjected to an adverse employment action, and (3) that a member of the nonprotected class was the beneficiary of a favorable employment action. If the prima facie case is proved, the burden shifts to the employer to articulate some legitimate, nondiscriminatory reason for the action. If the employer meets this burden, then the employee must prove that the reasons offered by the employer were a pretext for discrimination. Throughout, the complainant has the ultimate burden of persuading the trier of fact that the employer intentionally discriminated. However, where there is direct evidence of discrimination, or where the claim involves disparate impact, the *McDonnell Douglas* test does not apply.

---

[163]108 LA 11 (Jacobowski, 1997).

[164]108 LA 136 (Krislov, 1996).

[165]For other awards that discuss the FMLA, see Oxboro Clinic, Bloomington, Minn., 108 LA 11 (Jacobowski, 1997), and Springfield Ass'n of Retarded Citizens, 103 LA 1136 (Hoh, 1996).

[166]See, e.g., Chicago Transit Auth., 95 LA 753 (Goldstein, 1990) (adopting *McDonnell Douglas* burden of proof approach to arbitration of Title VII claims).

[167]411 U.S. 792, 5 FEP Cases 965 (1973).

Not all arbitrators follow the *McDonnell Douglas* approach. In arbitration the burden of proof is on the employer to prove legitimate reasons for a discharge.[168] As one arbitrator noted, where a discharge involved sexual harassment, the employer still has the burden of proof and the "overwhelming focus of the evidence on [the grievant] does not shift that burden of proof."[169] In *Paris Printing Co.,*[170] the company reduced its force and laid off a senior employee who could not operate certain machinery, while retaining a junior employee who could. Although the CBA did not explicitly refer to the ADEA, the arbitrator first noted that external law is a relevant factor in interpreting a CBA. In sustaining the layoff and citing several appellate court ADEA cases, the arbitrator said the grievant had the burden of establishing he was qualified for the position. The arbitrator further noted that if the grievant had shown the company's actions were merely pretextual he would have prevailed. Because the employee offered no such evidence, the arbitrator found the company had a legitimate, nondiscriminatory motive for retaining the junior employee.

Even where arbitrators expressly rely on external law, the wide range of remedies available to aggrieved employees under Title VII and the ADEA are generally not available in arbitration. Arbitrators generally do not award attorneys' fees, punitive damages, or interest, even though such remedies are available under Title VII and the ADEA.[171] In *Union Camp Corp.,*[172] the CBA prohibited sex discrimination and stated that it was subject to "any changes made necessary by reason of enactment of Federal or State legislation."[173] The arbitrator refused to award compensatory damages to sexual harassment grievants, even though the 1991 amendments to Title VII expressly authorize damages.[174] In refusing to award compensatory damages for emotional distress, the arbitrator noted that the CBA did not expressly provide for an award of compensatory damages by an arbitrator; "nothing in it reveals an intention to vest arbitrators with all the powers of a federal judge."[175] The arbitrator stated that if the parties had intended compensatory damages to be a possible remedy, they could have adopted the full statutory scheme.

---

[168]See, e.g., Fry's Food Stores of Ariz., Inc., 99 LA 1161 (Hogler, 1992) (management generally has the burden of proving just cause in terminating employees).

[169]Rodeway Inn, 102 LA 1003, 1013 (Goldberg, 1994).

[170]94 LA 951 (Berger, 1990).

[171]See, e.g., Volz & Goggin, eds., Elkouri & Elkouri, How Arbitration Works, 5th ed., 589–91 (BNA Books, 1997) (generally, attorney's fees, interest, and punitive damages are not available in arbitration unless there is explicit contractual language authorizing such items).

[172]104 LA 295 (Nolan, 1995).

[173]Id. at 301.

[174]42 U.S.C. §1981A.

[175]104 LA at 301.

# VII. Forum Shopping: Court or Arbitration

In addition to the EEOC and federal court remedy provided by law, if the employee is covered by a collective bargaining agreement or a written employment agreement, there may be an additional contractual remedy. The Supreme Court first addressed this issue in *Alexander v. Gardner-Denver Co.*[176] In that case, the Court held that an employee covered by a collective bargaining agreement may file a Title VII action against the employer, whether or not the employee had previously invoked the contractual grievance-arbitration procedure. Cases subsequent to *Gardner-Denver* applied its holding to other statutory causes of action.[177] In *Gilmer v. Interstate/Johnson Lane Corp.,*[178] a noncollective bargaining case, the Supreme Court held that a claim brought under the ADEA was subject to compulsory arbitration pursuant to a written employment agreement and could not be relitigated in a federal court.

In *Gardner-Denver,* the Supreme Court held that an employee's right to pursue a Title VII action is not foreclosed by first submitting the claim to arbitration under a nondiscrimination clause of a collective bargaining agreement. The Court noted that grievance arbitration seeks to vindicate the contractual rights of a collective group (the union), while Title VII protects an individual's statutory rights. Therefore, if the arbitration precluded a statutory claim, it would sacrifice individual statutory rights in favor of collective contractual rights, thus defeating the "paramount congressional purpose behind Title VII."[179]

The Court viewed arbitration as an essentially flawed method for resolving statutory claims. It noted that an arbitrator's authority is limited to contractual obligations,[180] that the arbitrator's expertise is "the law of the shop, not the law of the land,"[181] that "the usual rules of evidence do not apply; and [that] rights and procedures common to civil trials, such as discovery, compulsory process, cross-examination, and testimony under oath, are often severely limited or unavailable."[182] The Court concluded that the only way to safeguard employees' statutory rights is to ensure that a judicial forum is always available.

---

[176]415 U.S. 36, 7 FEP Cases 81 (1974).

[177]McDonald v. City of West Branch, 466 U.S. 284, 115 LRRM 3646 (1984) (availability of both 42 U.S.C. §1983 and arbitration remedies); Barrentine v. Arkansas-Best Freight Sys., Inc. 450 U.S. 728, 24 WH Cases 1284 (1981) (availability of both Fair Labor Standards Act and arbitration remedies).

[178]500 U.S. 20, 55 FEP Cases 1116 (1991).

[179]Alexander v. Gardner-Denver Co., 415 U.S. 36, 51, 7 FEP Cases 81 (1974).

[180]Id. at 53–54, 56–57.

[181]Id. at 57.

[182]Id. at 57–58.

*Gilmer* reflects the Supreme Court's radically changed attitude toward arbitration as a means of resolving statutory claims. In *Gilmer,* the plaintiff was a registered representative employed by a securities firm. His registration application with the New York Stock Exchange contained an arbitration clause providing for mandatory arbitration of all disputes arising out of his employment or termination. When he was terminated at age 62, he filed an ADEA charge with the EEOC and a subsequent suit in district court. The employer moved to compel arbitration on the basis of the arbitration clause contained in the plaintiff's registration application.[183]

The Supreme Court upheld compelling arbitration and rejected virtually all the theoretical underpinnings that supported its decision in *Gardner-Denver* when it noted that this "'mistrust of the arbitral process' was a historic relic "undermined by our recent arbitration decisions."[184] The Court found the broad policy in favor of arbitration contained in the Federal Arbitration Act (FAA) overcame Congress's intent to have statutory claims resolved in a judicial forum.[185]

The Court rejected the employee's reliance on *Gardner-Denver* by distinguishing it on three bases:

> First, [the *Gardner-Denver* line of cases] did not involve the issue of the enforceability of an agreement to arbitrate statutory claims. Rather, they involved the quite different issue whether arbitration of contract-based claims precluded subsequent judicial resolution of statutory

---

[183]9 U.S.C. §1 et seq.

[184]Gilmer v. Interstate/Johnson Lane Corp., 500 U.S. 20, 34 n.5, 55 FEP Cases 1116 (1991), quoting Shearson/American Express v. McMahon, 482 U.S. 220, 231–32 (1987).

[185]*Gilmer's* holding was based, in part, on the fact that, because the plaintiff's arbitration agreement was not contained in his contract with his employer but was in his registration application with the New York Stock Exchange, his agreement to arbitrate was not in a "contract of employment" and thus was subject to the FAA. The FAA excludes from its coverage "contracts of employment of seamen, railroad employees, or any other class of workers engaged in foreign or interstate commerce." 9 U.S.C. §1. Thus, because Gilmer's agreement to arbitrate was not contained in his contract of employment, the FAA was deemed applicable. The court cited its liberal policy favoring arbitration as support for its holding that arbitration was the employee's exclusive remedy. The Court left open, though, the issue of the scope of the FAA's exclusion of all "contracts of employment." Thus, depending on the scope of the FAA's exclusion, the *Gilmer* holding may be a narrow one and may only be applicable to contracts outside the employment context. The circuit courts are split on the issue of the scope of the FAA's exclusion of employment contracts. Several circuit courts have construed this exclusion narrowly. See, e.g., Miller Brewing Co. v. Brewery Workers Local 9, 739 F.2d 1159, 1162, 116 LRRM 3130 (7th Cir., 1984), cert. denied, 469 U.S. 1160, 118 LRRM 2192 (1985) (exclusion limited to "workers employed in the transportation industries"); Erving v. Virginia Squires Basketball Club, 468 F.2d 1064, 1069 (2d Cir., 1972) (exclusion limited to "those actually in the transportation industry"); Dickstein v. DuPont, 443 F.2d 783, 785 (1st Cir., 1971) (limiting exclusion to "employees * * * involved in, or closely related to, the actual movement of goods in interstate commerce"); Golenia v. Bob Baker Toyota, 915 F.Supp. 201 (S.D. Cal., 1996) (exclusionary clause in §1 of FAA should be narrowly construed to cover only workers directly involved in the interstate transportation of goods). Other courts have given a more expansive interpretation to the exclusion. See, e.g., Pritzker v. Merrill Lynch, Pierce, Fenner & Smith, 7 F.3d 1110, 1119–20 (3d Cir., 1993) (in dicta, "'contracts of employment' are explicitly exempted from the FAA"); Willis v. Dean Witter Reynolds, Inc., 948 F.2d 305, 310–12, 57 FEP Cases 386 (6th Cir., 1991) (all employment contracts excluded from FAA coverage).

claims. Since the employees there had not agreed to arbitrate their statutory claims, and the labor arbitrators were not authorized to resolve such claims, the arbitration in those cases understandably was held not to preclude subsequent statutory actions. Second, because the arbitration in those cases occurred in the context of a collective-bargaining agreement, the claimants there were represented by their unions in the arbitration proceedings. An important concern therefore was the tension between collective representation and individual statutory rights, a concern not applicable to the present case. Finally, those cases were not decided under the FAA, which * * * reflects a "liberal federal policy favoring arbitration agreements."[186]

Accordingly, the Court concluded that it should enforce arbitration agreements that prohibit employees from pursuing their discrimination claims in federal court.

The narrow holding of *Gardner-Denver* appears to survive *Gilmer:* most courts have held that union employees are not barred from pursuing their statutory claims in court as a result of a prior submission of a claim to arbitration. For example, in *Griffith v. Keystone Steel & Wire Co.,*[187] a union employee brought a Title VII claim without submitting a grievance. The employer moved to dismiss, citing *Gilmer.* The court rejected *Gilmer's* relevancy, noting that unlike the plaintiff in *Gilmer,* the plaintiff did not sign an individual agreement to arbitrate.[188] Relying on *Gardner-Denver,* the court denied the employer's motion to dismiss.[189]

In one case, a court barred the judicial resolution of statutory claims where the employee was subject to an arbitration agreement contained in a CBA. In *Austin v. Owens-Brockway Glass Container, Inc.,*[190] an employee filed an ADA and Title VII action without submitting her claim to arbitration as required by the CBA. The employer moved for summary judgment on the ground that the employee's failure to use the grievance arbitration procedure set forth in the CBA barred her from filing a claim in federal court. The employer also cited *Gilmer* to support its position, along with the 1991 amendments to the Civil Rights Act, which state Congress's preference for

---

[186]500 U.S. at 35 (citations omitted), quoting Mitsubishi Motors Corp. v. Soler Chrysler-Plymouth, 473 U.S. 614, 625 (1985).

[187]858 F.Supp. 802, 66 FEP Cases 227 (C.D. Ill., 1984).

[188]Id. at 804.

[189]See also Tran v. Tran, 54 F.3d 115, 149 LRRM 2350 (2d Cir., 1995) (FLSA claim is not required to be submitted to labor contract arbitration provision); Martin Marietta Corp., Aero & Naval Sys. v. Maryland Comm'n on Human Relations, 38 F.3d 1392, 1402, 147 LRRM 2645 (4th Cir., 1994) (*Gilmer* does not prohibit employee subject to CBA from pursuing state law discrimination claims); Bates v. Long Island R.R., 997 F.2d 1028, 1034–35, 143 LRRM 2767 (2d Cir.), cert. denied, 114 S.Ct. 550, 144 LRRM 2872 (1993) (*Gilmer* does not prohibit railroad workers subject to CBA from filing action under the Rehabilitation Act); Bolden v. Southeastern Pa. Transp. Auth., 953 F.2d 807, 825–26, 139 LRRM 2118 (3d Cir., 1991), cert. denied, 112 S.Ct. 2281, 143 LRRM 2304 (1992) (arbitration agreement in CBA did not bar employee from pursuing §1983 claim).

[190]844 F.Supp. 1103, 145 LRRM 2445 (W.D. Va., 1994).

arbitral resolution of discrimination claims. Without referring to *Gardner-Denver,* the court held that because the CBA provided for mandatory arbitration of all disputes, the plaintiff's failure to grieve constituted a waiver of her right to file suit. It then granted summary judgment to the employer. On appeal, the Fourth Circuit affirmed.[191] Although the Fourth Circuit referred to *Gardner-Denver,* it simply rejected it, finding that the employee was a party to the CBA, by virtue of her union membership. Thus, she voluntarily agreed to submit her claim to arbitration. This is the only decision that has held that an arbitration clause in a collective bargaining agreement waives an employee's rights to litigate statutory claims.

It is unclear from *Owens-Brockway* whether an arbitration clause absolutely waives a judicial forum or whether an employee must exhaust his remedies under the grievance-arbitration procedure before filing a lawsuit. By its reliance on *Gilmer,* though, the opinion suggests that an arbitration clause constitutes a complete waiver. Indeed, a recent district court case relying on *Owens-Brockway* held that a union employee is limited to arbitration and may not file a federal action unless the employee can show that the union's arbitration of the ADA claim breached its duty of fair representation and seriously undermined the integrity of the arbitration process.[192]

In an opinion from the Third Circuit, *Martin v. Dana Corp.,*[193] an employee was subject to a grievance-arbitration procedure that required him to process all equal employment claims through that procedure. The CBA contained a unique provision that allowed the union or the employee to invoke the procedure. Since the employee had the right to invoke the grievance-arbitration procedure, the court found *Gardner-Denver's* concern for the individual's rights were not implicated and the employee was barred from filing suit.

These cases appear to be anomalous. Most courts have held that *Gardner-Denver* is still the law regarding employees covered by a CBA and that an employee can sue notwithstanding the existence of an arbitration clause covering employment discrimination disputes in the agreement.[194]

Although some courts have held that the arbitration clause in an employee handbook need not expressly refer to statutory discrimination claims in order to be deemed to cover such (disability)

---

[191]Austin v. Owens-Brockway Glass Container, Inc., 78 Fd.3d 875, 151 LRRM 2673 (4th Cir.), cert. denied, 117 S.Ct. 432, 153 LRRM 2960 (1996).

[192]Moore v. Duke Power, 155 LRRM 2412 (W.D.N.C., 1997).

[193]1997 WL 313054 (3d Cir., 1997).

[194]See e.g., Harrison v. Eddy Potash, Inc., 112 F.3d 1437, 156 LRRM 2033 (10th Cir., 1997); Pryner v. Tractor Supply Co., 109 F.3d 354, 154 LRRM 2806 (7th Cir., 1997); Varner v. National Super Mkts., 94 F.3d 1209, 71 FEP Cases 1367 (8th Cir., 1996); Tran v. Tran, 54 F.3d 115, 149 LRRM 2350 (2d Cir., 1995), cert. denied, 116 S.Ct. 1417, 151 LRRM 3056 (1996).

claims,[195] many courts have required explicit reference to statutory claims.[196]

In another case, *EEOC v. River Oaks Imaging & Diagnostic*,[197] the EEOC obtained an injunction prohibiting an employer from requiring its employees to sign employment agreements. The Michigan Supreme Court held in *Heurtebise v. Reliable Business Computers, Inc.*,[198] that where a handbook contained a standard "at-will" contract disclaimer clause along with a mandatory arbitration clause, the arbitration clause was unenforceable because the disclaimer clause demonstrated that the employer did not intend to be bound by any portion of the handbook, including the arbitration clause.

Some courts have held that continuing employment is sufficient consideration to support an arbitration agreement signed after starting work. In *Patterson v. Tenet Healthcare*,[199] the court held that an arbitration clause printed on a separate page on a tear-out sheet contained in an employee handbook was enforceable. Although the court noted that arbitration clauses contained in employee handbooks qualified by disclaimers are generally unenforceable because such disclaimers vitiate the arbitration clause, this arbitration clause was in a separate document that the employee, by signing, agreed to. The court enforced the arbitration agreement. In *Great Western Mortgage Corp. v. Peacock*,[200] the court found that the plaintiff, a college graduate, admitted signing an arbitration agreement after beginning work, and then voluntarily filed for arbitration. The court enforced the arbitration agreement. The court found no evidence that the employee was coerced into signing the agreement.

Similarly, in *Johnson v. Hubbard Broadcasting, Inc.*,[201] an employee signed an arbitration agreement that contained a provision limiting her relief to out-of-pocket damages. The court refused to decide the issue of whether the damages limitation rendered the agreement unenforceable. Instead it remanded the issue to the arbitrator, noting that "should the arbitrator find that the terms of the arbitration agreement deny [plaintiff] the opportunity to recover the full array of statutory remedies established under state and federal law, the agreement would contravene federally and state established

---

[195]Golenia v. Bob Baker Toyota, 915 F.Supp. 201 (S.D. Cal., 1996).

[196]See, e.g., Caldwell v. KFC Corp., 958 F.Supp. 962, 74 FEP Cases 1045 (D.N.J., 1997) (where arbitration clause simply covered disputes arising out of termination, sexual harassment claim not arbitrable); Rudolph v. Alamo Rent A Car, Inc., 952 F.Supp., 311, 73 FEP Cases 25 (E.D. Va., 1997) (where parties did not agree to arbitrate statutory claims in arbitration agreement, employee allowed to pursue sexual harassment claim in federal court); Hoffman v. Aaron Kamhi, Inc., 927 F.Supp. 640 (S.D.N.Y., 1996) (where arbitration clause did not refer to civil rights or discrimination claims, employee not required to arbitrate FMLA or ADA claims).

[197]67 FEP Cases 1243 (S.D. Tex., 1995).

[198]452 Mich. 405, 550 N.W.2d 243 (1996).

[199]113 F.3d 832, 73 FEP Cases 1822 (8th Cir., 1997).

[200]110 F.3d 222, 73 FEP Cases 856 (3d Cir., 1997).

[201]940 F.Supp. 1447, 73 FEP Cases 8 (D. Minn., 1996).

remedial measures, possibly rendering the agreement unenforceable as unconscionable."[202]

## VIII.  Drug Testing

### A.  *General*

The Omnibus Transportation Employee Testing Act of 1988 and 1991[203] imposes a requirement on all Department of Transportation agencies to establish mandatory testing guidelines for employers under their respective jurisdictions.[204] In addition, Congress has mandated drug and/or alcohol testing programs for licensees and contractors of certain government agencies whose operations raise public safety concerns, including the National Aeronautics & Space Administration,[205] the Department of Defense,[206] the Nuclear Regulatory Commission,[207] and the Department of Energy.[208] Finally, all federal agencies are required to establish drug-testing programs for their employees pursuant to Executive Order No. 12,564, issued in 1986 under authority granted by Congress in 5 U.S.C. § 7301.[209]

Testing programs established under these and earlier statutes and regulations were subjected to Fourth Amendment challenges. Some challenges were successful in narrowing the range of employees who could be subjected to federally mandated drug testing,[210] and in

---

[202]Id. at 1462.

[203]45 U.S.C. §431(r) (railroad), 49 U.S.C. App. §1434 (aviation), 49 U.S.C. App. §1618(a) (mass transportation), 49 U.S.C. §2717 (commercial motor vehicles).

[204]General guidelines for testing procedures in all DOT agencies are set forth in 49 C.F.R. Part 40. Each agency has also promulgated its own guidelines concerning the implementation of testing programs among employers covered by that agency. See 46 C.F.R. Part 16 (Coast Guard); 49 C.F.R. §391.81 et seq. (Federal Highway Administration); 49 C.F.R. Part 653 (Federal Transit Administration); 14 C.F.R. Part 121, Appx. 1 (Federal Aviation Administration); 49 C.F.R. Part 219 (Federal Railroad Administration); and 49 C.F.R. Part 199 (Research and Special Programs Administration, covering pipeline operators).

[205]42 U.S.C. Ch. 26, National Space Program.

[206]48 C.F.R. §223.570, §252.223-7004 (1992).

[207]10 C.F.R. pt. 26 (1989).

[208]10 C.F.R. pt. 707 & 48 C.F.R. §923.5 (1992).

[209]5 U.S.C. §7301 provides that "[t]he President may prescribe regulations for the conduct of employees in the executive branch."
    In 1988, Congress also passed the Drug-Free Workplace Act for grantees and contractors of all federal agencies, 41 U.S.C. §701 et seq. This Act only requires covered employers to certify that they will provide a drug-free workplace and does not require the establishment of testing programs.

[210]See, e.g., Harmon v. Thornburgh, 878 F.2d 484, 492–93 (D.C. Cir., 1989), cert. denied, 110 S.Ct. 865 (1990); Government Employees (AFGE) v. Sullivan, 787 F.Supp. 255, 257 (D.D.C., 1992); Government Employees (AFGE) v. Derwinski, 777 F.Supp. 1493, 1500–01 (N.D. Cal., 1991).

narrowing the scope of acceptable testing procedures.[211] In *Skinner v. Railway Labor Executives Ass'n*[212] and *Treasury Employees v. Von Raab,*[213] however, the Supreme Court made it clear that testing programs falling within certain guidelines are constitutionally permissible. Thus, testing programs appear to be generally permissible where tested employees are engaged in work that poses a particular security or public safety concern; where the intrusion on an employee's privacy is not excessive (e.g., blood testing for alcohol is not used where breath testing is available and is equally effective); and where the procedure for analyzing and utilizing test results includes adequate technological and procedural safeguards.

## B. Arbitration and Public Policy

Cases involving discipline based on federally mandated drug or alcohol testing present both statutory and contractual issues. The federal statutes and regulations governing private industry address whether violations have occurred, but leave the parties to determine the consequences of those violations.[214] Many cases pose statutory issues that must be resolved before the arbitrator can even reach the contractual elements of the dispute. Where an arbitrator's award contradicts a statutory requirement or an authoritative interpretation of such a requirement, that award may be subject to vacatur.[215]

Cases involving the "public policy exception" set forth in the Supreme Court's decisions in *W.R. Grace & Co. v. Rubber Workers*

---

[211]See, e.g., Government Employees (AFGE) v. Derwinski, 777 F. Supp. 1493, 1502 (N.D. Cal., 1991); Government Employees (AFGE) v. Sullivan, 744 F.Supp. 294, 301 (D.D.C., 1990).

[212]489 U.S. 602, 130 LRRM 2857 (1989).

[213]489 U.S. 656, 4 IER Cases 246 (1989).

[214]The NLRB General Counsel has opined that drug and alcohol testing programs are a mandatory subject of bargaining. See Op. Gen. Couns., Sept. 8, 1987. See also Kysor/Cadillac Div., 307 NLRB 598, 140 LRRM 1127 (1992); Coastal Chem. Co., 304 NLRB 556, 138 LRRM 1328 (1991); Storer Communications, 297 NLRB 296, 133 LRRM 1052 (1989). In certain cases, however, an employer's unilateral imposition of a testing program has been upheld based on a contract's management rights clause. See, e.g., Chicago Tribune Co. v. NLRB, 974 F.2d 933, 141 LRRM 2209 (7th Cir., 1992); Southern Cal. Edison Co., 310 NLRB 1229, 143 LRRM 1073 (1993) (on the longstanding and unchallenged existence of that program); Bath Iron Works Corp., 302 NLRB 898, 137 LRRM 1124 (1991).

Under the Railway Labor Act, which applies a different approach to the duty to bargain, the courts found disputes over an employer's unilateral implementation of a drug or alcohol testing program "minor" disputes, subject to compulsory arbitration. Allied Pilots Ass'n v. American Airlines, Inc., 898 F.2d 462, 134 LRRM 2148 (5th Cir., 1990); Teamsters v. Southwest Airlines, 875 F.2d 1129, 131 LRRM 2761 (5th Cir., 1989) (en banc).

[215]See, e.g., Interstate Brands Corp. v. Local 441, Retail, Wholesale & Dep't Store Union Local 441, 39 F.3d 1159, 148 LRRM 2086 (11th Cir., 1994) (vacating arbitrator's award based on erroneous interpretation of DOT regulations concerning chain-of-custody requirements in handling of urine specimen). But see Frank v. Department of Transp., 35 F.3d 1554 (Fed. Cir., 1994) (court defers to arbitrator's interpretation of FAA regulations in finding that possible tampering did not require dismissal of positive drug test).

*Local 759*[216] and *Paperworkers v. Misco, Inc.,*[217] provide still greater difficulties. The Court established a standard for federal courts vacating an arbitrator's award for violating a "well-defined and dominant public policy."[218] The public policy must "be ascertained by reference to the laws and legal precedents and not from general considerations of supposed public interests."[219] The Court in *Misco* reserved the question of whether this "public policy exception" was limited to where an arbitrator's award violates "positive law."[220] Some later courts of appeals cases adopted a broader view of the exception that includes "well-defined and dominant" public policies even when they are not dictated by positive law.[221]

Courts have applied this broader version of the public policy exception in vacating awards involving drug or alcohol testing that the court concludes violate the spirit of a federal statute. Thus, in *Exxon Shipping Co. v. Exxon Seaman's Union (Exxon I),*[222] an arbitration panel ordered reinstatement of a helmsman who tested positive for drugs under the company's definition of a positive test, but not under the Coast Guard's less-stringent standard. The court rejected the arbitration panel's order of reinstatement and explained that "the award reinstating [the grievant] violates the public policy protecting the public and the environment against operation of vessels by drug users."[223]

The Third Circuit again reached this conclusion in a case bearing "a striking factual resemblance to" *Exxon I.* In *Exxon Shipping Co. v. Exxon's Seamen's Union (Exxon II),*[224] the court vacated an arbitrator's award reinstating a seaman who tested positive for alcohol (while on duty) at a level far above that permitted by the collective bargaining agreement or by applicable Coast Guard regulations. The court acknowledged, "we are aware of no statute or regulation that directly prohibits the owner or operator of an oil tanker from continuing to employ a crew member who is found to be intoxicated on duty."[225] The court noted the consequences that might befall an employer that continues to place employees in safety-sensitive positions after those employees have been shown to be drug or alcohol abusers. Because of the legal risks to the employer, and the legal authorities proscribing

[216]461 U.S. 757, 113 LRRM 2641 (1983).

[217]484 U.S. 29, 126 LRRM 3113 (1987).

[218]Id. at 43, citing W.R. Grace v. Rubber Workers Local 759, 461 U.S. 757, 766, 113 LRRM 2641 (1983).

[219]Id.

[220]Paperworkers v. Misco., Inc., 484 U.S. 29, 45 n.12, 126 LRRM 3113 (1987).

[221]See discussion in Exxon Shipping Co. v. Exxon Seamen's Union (Exxon I), 993 F.2d 357, 363, 143 LRRM 2312 (3d Cir., 1993).

[222]Id.

[223]Id. at 364.

[224]11 F.3d 1189, 144 LRRM 2955 (3d Cir., 1993).

[225]Id. at 1195.

alcohol use, the court favored a public policy "that owners and operators of oil tankers should be permitted to discharge crew members who are found to be intoxicated while on duty."[226]

Arbitration decisions in this area often involve statutory interpretation,[227] with arbitrators using statutes and regulations like courts applying public policy. For example, some arbitrators, when assessing the validity of an employer's decision to discharge an employee for drug or alcohol use, note the existence of regulations that, even where not directly applicable, still show a strong policy concern for safety and support the employer's decision.[228] Similarly, some arbitrators note that while regulations may not require the particular discipline taken, the regulation may nonetheless impose a burden on the employer. This helps persuade the arbitrator that the employer is justified in imposing disciplinary measures.[229]

While some arbitrators cite testing statutes or regulations as persuasive in deciding discipline issues, many arbitrators only look to them as a basis for discipline to the extent the employer's policy or the collective bargaining agreement directly requires discipline. For instance, where the statute or regulation requires only a limited action, the arbitrator may choose to uphold only that action,[230] despite the employer's assertion that the statute requires more. Where no personnel action is required by the applicable statute or regulation, some arbitrators will treat a positive test result the same way they treat any other violation of the contract and look only at specific

---

[226]Id. at 1196. Other courts have taken the same approach and reached similar results in cases not involving testing statutes or regulations but involving drug or alcohol use at levels prohibited by statute or regulation where discipline was not specifically mandated by the statute or regulation. See, e.g., Delta Air Lines v. Air Line Pilots, 861 F.2d 665, 130 LRRM 2014 (11th Cir., 1988), cert. denied, 493 U.S. 871, 132 LRRM 2623 (1989); Meat Cutters Local 540 v. Great W. Food Co., 712 F.2d 122, 114 LRRM 2001 (5th Cir., 1983). See also Gulf Coast Indus. Workers v. Exxon Co., USA, 991 F.2d 244, 143 LRRM 2375 (5th Cir.) (employer's requirement to comply with Drug-Free Workplace Act for Federal Contractors, 41 U.S.C. §§701–707 (1988) and Department of Defense regulations, 48 C.F.R. §223.5 (1992), together with other legal authorities, supports public policy against continued employment of recidivist drug user even though no specific statutory violation occurred), cert. denied, 114 S.Ct. 441, 144 LRRM 2680 (1993).

[227]See, e.g., Mason & Hangar-Silas Mason Co., 103 LA 371 (Cipolla, 1994) (employer failed to comply with DOE regulation concerning informing employee of right to retest; arbitrator denied reinstatement because of positive drug test, but required back pay to remedy employer's violation of regulations); Moore-Handley, Inc., 102 LA 813 (Grooms, 1994) (overturning discharge for "refusal" to test based on employer's failure to follow DOT procedures properly).

[228]See, e.g., Columbia Gas of Ohio, 102 LA 85 (Cohen, 1993) (discharge for positive drug test validated in part by fact that employer is in safety-sensitive industry under DOT regulation); Southern Union Gas Co., 100 LA 964 (Baroni, 1993) (citing DOT regulations as support for importance of strictly enforcing safety rules in industry; upholds discharge for failing return-to-work test after rehabilitation).

[229]See, e.g., Columbia Gas of Pa., 102 LA 513, 516 (Duff, 1994) (upholding discharge based in part on fact that "[t]he Grievant's illegal off-the-job use of the drug cocaine adversely affected the Company because it had to remove him twice from his job according to DOT regulations").

[230]See, e.g., Lockheed Missiles & Space Co., 101 LA 804 (Gentile, 1993) (upholding suspension for period where DOT regulations prevented employee's recertification and return to work, but overturning discharge or any additional discipline because no finding that grievant was "under the influence" as required by company policy).

contract terms in deciding on appropriate discipline.[231] Indeed, some arbitrators will not even apply potentially relevant DOT regulations and standards unless the contract specifically requires them to do so.[232]

# IX.  Federal Antiretaliation Statutes

The following federal statutes protect employee conduct aimed at advancing the interests of the statute or federal public policy:

1.  Discrimination Statutes.
    a.  Title VII of the Civil Rights Act of 1964, as amended[233] (Title VII);
    b.  Section 1981 of the Civil Rights Act of 1866[234] (Section 1981);
    c.  The Age Discrimination in Employment Act of 1967[235] (ADEA); and
    d.  The Americans with Disabilities Act of 1990[236] (ADA).
2.  The Occupational Safety and Health Act[237] (OSHA).
3.  The Fair Labor Standards Act[238] (FLSA).
4.  Executive Order 11,246 and Statutes Applying to Government Contractors.
5.  The Federal Whistleblower's Protection Act.[239]

The overwhelming majority of claims raised under these statutes are disposed of in court proceedings as opposed to arbitration.

The statutes contain provisions protecting employees from retaliation where the employees file a charge, testify, assist, or participate

---

[231]See, e.g., Amerigas, 102 LA 1185 (Marino, 1994) (one positive test under FHWA regulation not sufficient to justify discharge; in the absence of a negotiated CBA clause specifically authorizing discharge, arbitrator refused to apply unilaterally imposed drug-testing rules not specifically required by regulations because they are a mandatory subject of bargaining under NLRB rules); Georgia-Pacific Corp., 100 LA 713 (Hockenberry, 1993) (discharge due to violation of DOT regulations reduced to one-time leave based on arbitrator's reading of the collective bargaining agreement).

[232]See, e.g., United Parcel Serv., 101 LA 589 (Briggs, 1993) (driver tested with blood alcohol content of 0.053 not "under the influence" based on DOT's 0.04 standard, and therefore could not be discharged under contract provision, where contract does not specify that DOT standard rather than state motor vehicle standard applies).

[233]42 U.S.C. §2000e et seq. (1994).

[234]42 U.S.C. §1981 et seq. (1994).

[235]29 U.S.C. §621 et seq. (1994).

[236]42 U.S.C. §12203 (1994).

[237]29 U.S.C. §660 et seq. (1994).

[238]29 U.S.C. §215 et seq. (1994).

[239]5 U.S.C. §2302 (1994).

in any investigation, proceeding, or hearing under the statute.[240] For example, Title VII provides that it is unlawful for

> [a]n employer to discriminate against any of his employees or applicants for employment * * * because he has opposed any practice made an unlawful employment practice [by Title VII], or because he has made a charge, testified, assisted, or participated in any manner in an investigation, proceeding, or hearing under [Title VII].[241]

The prohibitions of retaliation in the ADEA and the ADA track the language of Title VII.[242] These antidiscrimination statutes protect two separate categories of employee activity from retaliation by employers: "participation conduct" and "opposition conduct."

Participation conduct includes filing charge with a state or federal fair employment practices agency or participating in an agency investigation of allegedly discriminatory conduct. Court decisions have consistently held that an employee is protected even if the Title VII charge contains false statements[243] or is ultimately proven to be without merit.[244] Opposition conduct consists of activity taken by an employee to protest or oppose illegal discrimination without having filed a formal charge.

Labor arbitrators have applied the participation conduct doctrine to retaliation grievances. In *Social Security Administration Data Operations Center,*[245] the arbitrator upheld a union steward's right to file a grievance alleging that he was passed over for a promotion because he filed an EEOC complaint. On the merits, however, the

---

[240]Unlike the other statutes, §1981 does not contain specific provisions prohibiting retaliation; however, the Civil Rights Restoration Act of 1991 amended the definition of "make and enforce contracts" to include "the making, performance, modifications and termination of contracts, and the enjoyment of all benefits, privileges, terms and conditions of the contractual relationship." 42 U.S.C. §1981(b) (1994). It appears that discrimination in the form of retaliation against an employee who has brought a claim of discrimination would be prohibited by §1981. What is unclear is whether courts will permit a cause of action to be brought under §1981 by one who has opposed racial discrimination directed at others. The Civil Rights Act of 1991 vitiated the Supreme Court's narrow interpretation of the Act as set forth in Patterson v. McLean Credit Union, 491 U.S. 164, 49 FEP Cases 1814 (1989), which limited §1981 actions to causes arising from the initial making of a contract or where the right to enforce contractual obligations was impaired on a discriminatory basis. In view of the 1991 amendments, it seems likely that many courts will follow the line of cases prior to *Patterson* that permitted a cause of action to be brought under §1981 by an employee who has opposed racial discrimination directed at others. See, e.g., Pinkard v. Pullman-Standard Div., 678 F.2d 1211, 29 FEP Cases 216 (5th Cir., 1982), cert denied, 459 U.S. 1105, 30 FEP Cases 1048 (1983); Setser v. Novack Inv. Co., 638 F.2d 1137, 24 FEP Cases 1793 (8th Cir., 1981); Winston v. Lear-Siegler, Inc. 558 F.2d 1266, 15 FEP Cases 306 (6th Cir., 1977).

[241]42 U.S.C. §2000e-3(a) (1994).

[242]29 U.S.C. §623(d) (1994) (ADEA) and 42 U.S.C. §12203(a) (1994) (ADA). Section 12203(b) of the ADA also prohibits interference, coercion, or intimidation of any individual seeking to exercise his or her rights under the ADA.

[243]Pettway v. American Cast Iron Pipe Co., 411 F.2d 998, 1 FEP Cases 752 (5th Cir., 1969).

[244]Moyo v. Gomez, 32 F.3d 1382, 65 FEP Cases 821 (9th Cir., 1994), cert. denied, 115 S.Ct. 732, 68 FEP Cases 1536 (1995).

[245]91 LA 435 (Shieber, 1988).

arbitrator denied the grievance, finding that the grievant failed to meet the burden of proof under *Texas Department of Community Affairs v. Burdine.*[246] A successful retaliation grievance was alleged in *Rodeway Inn.*[247] The CBA contained a broad antidiscrimination clause. After a thorough discussion of retaliation law, the arbitrator sustained the grievance, which alleged that the employee was fired because she complained about sexual harassment directed against her by the owner of her company. The arbitrator held that the grievant had an unfettered and protected right to voice reasonably based sexual harassment complaints to co-workers, to her union, and ultimately to the EEOC. A minority of arbitrators currently apply federal retaliation law to discrimination-based grievances. As more and more CBAs include broad antidiscrimination clauses, successful retaliation grievances are likely to become more prevalent.

## X. State Statutes

Forty-seven states have comprehensive fair employment practices or civil rights statutes protecting employees from discrimination because of age, race, religion, color, national origin, and disability. Only Alabama, Georgia, and Mississippi do not. Many states have protections broader than the protected classifications under Title VII, including, for example, marital status[248] and sexual orientation[249] as protected categories. Most state antidiscrimination statutes prohibit retaliation against employees who oppose practices forbidden by state antidiscrimination laws or employees who participate in proceedings under the state statutes.[250]

A majority of states have explicit statutory prohibitions against discrimination or retaliation against employees for pursuit or receipt of workers' compensation benefits as well as participation in proceedings under state workers' compensation laws.[251] Some states require

---

[246]450 U.S. 248, 25 FEP Cases 113 (1981). The arbitrator noted that the burden-of-proof rules announced in *Burdine* are "applicable under a collective bargaining agreement in which a claim of discrimination based on retaliation for [the] * * * filing of EEO complaints is made." 91 LA at 436.

[247]102 LA 1003 (Goldberg, 1994).

[248]See, e.g., Cal. Gov't Code §12900 et seq. (West 1980 & Supp. 1990); N.Y. Exec. Law §§290 et seq. (McKinney 1982).

[249]Nineteen states have some form of protection against sexual-orientation discrimination. Most states that ban discrimination on the basis of sexual orientation do so only in state employment or public works contracts. However, several states bar sexual-orientation discrimination in all forms of employment. See, e.g., Mass. Gen. L., ch. 151B, §4 (1992); Cal. Lab. Code §1102.1 (Deering 1991); Haw. Rev. Stat. §378-1 (1985).

[250]See, e.g., Ohio Rev. Code Ann. §4112.02 (barring discrimination against individuals who have opposed unlawful discriminatory practice).

[251]See, e.g., N.J. Rev. Stat. Ann. §24:15-39.1 (West 1988) (prohibiting discharge or other discrimination against employee for claiming workers' compensation benefits or for testifying at a workers' compensation hearing).

employees covered by collective bargaining agreements to exhaust their contractual remedies before pursuing an independent action under state law.[252]

With few exceptions, states have enacted statutes prohibiting employers from disciplining employees who are absent from the workplace for the purposes of voting,[253] serving as an election official,[254] or serving as a juror.[255] Many states have statutes prohibiting adverse employment action against employees called away from their jobs to serve in the National Guard or military reserves.[256] In recent years, by statute, several states have protected "whistleblower" employees who complain of state occupational safety and health law violations.[257]

Arbitrators are increasingly recognizing the applicability of state statutes to grievances, especially where the CBA in question incorporates external law. For example, arbitrators have frequently applied the antiretaliation provisions of state workers' compensation laws to grievances involving the discharge of employees who were collecting workers' compensation. Although many arbitrators have considered state workers' compensation laws, most arbitrators have rejected grievants' reliance on these statutes. For example, in *ITT Automotive*,[258] the worker's grievance protesting a transfer that was based on a workers' compensation claim was rejected because the transfer was rationally related to the company's stated basis for the transfer. In *Dunlop Tire Corp.*,[259] the grievant claimed that the discipline was in retaliation for filing a workers' compensation claim as opposed to violating company rules. The grievance was denied because the statute only prohibits the termination, not the discipline, of an employee who files a workers' compensation claim. Arbitrators also consider state sex discrimination laws and other state discrimination laws. In *Security Pacific Bank*,[260] the grievance alleging retaliatory discharge under Arizona civil rights law was denied because the grievant failed to demonstrate a causal connection between filing of the claim and the adverse employment action. The employer presented nondiscriminatory reasons for discharge. As discussed earlier in the section on the arbitration of Title VII claims, however, arbitrators are generally

---

[252]See, e.g., Alaska Stat. §09.43.010 (1994) (mandatory arbitration covering all disputes under a labor contract); but see 820 ILCS §35/2 (1993) (all matters shall be arbitrated except those involving questions that may be the subject of a civil action).

[253]See, e.g., Ga. Code Ann. §21-2-404 (1987).

[254]See, e.g., Neb. Rev. Stat. §§32-1050, 32-1050.1 (1988).

[255]See, e.g., 705 ILCS 305/4.1 (1992).

[256]See, e.g., Wis. Stat. Ann. §111.321 (West 1988) (prohibiting discrimination based on membership in National Guard, state defense force, or reserve forces).

[257]See, e.g., Md. Code Ann. (Lab. & Empl.) §5-604 (1991) (prohibiting discrimination against employee who files a complaint, testifies in a proceeding, or exercises any rights under the state's occupational and health laws).

[258]105 LA 11 (Shanker, 1995).

[259]94 LA 365 (Kindig, 1990).

[260]100 LA 145 (Forbes, 1992).

hesitant to apply external law (either state or federal) in labor arbitration in the absence of an explicit CBA provision incorporating external law. In *Owens-Illinois*,[261] the arbitrator stated that workers' compensation is a creature of state statute, not of the contract. Since state law provides for the enforcement of the employee's rights, that is the sole and exclusive procedure for enforcing those rights.

## XI. Lie Detectors and Monitoring

The question of the weight an arbitrator should accord the various tools that may be used in assessing such factors as an employee's psychological state, truthfulness, or honesty implicates a wide variety of competing interests. The employer wants to assess whether an employee is fit to work or return to work, poses a danger to herself or others, or is involved in theft or other activities antithetical to the goals of the organization. The employee wants to be assured that the employer does not intrude on her private life any more than necessary. Where mechanical or pen-and-paper tests are involved, the arbitrator must also deal with questions of reliability, probity, and equity.

### A. Lie Detectors

*1. The Employee Polygraph Protection Act of 1988.*   The Federal Employee Polygraph Protection Act of 1988[262] prohibits most private sector employers from using polygraph examinations either for preemployment screening or to test current employees except in certain specially defined situations under carefully drawn restrictions.[263] Under the Act's provisions, covered employers may not directly or indirectly require, request, suggest, or cause any employee or prospective employee to submit to or take a lie detector test. These employers may not use or even inquire about the results of lie detector tests obtained by others. Nor may they discharge, discipline, threaten, or discriminate against any employee or prospective employee who refuses to take or fails a test or who exercises any rights under the Act.

*2. State Laws.*   Many states strictly limit private employers' rights to request or use lie detectors; others do not address the subject at all. Thus, under state law alone, some employers are free to utilize

---

[261]83 LA 1265, 1269 (Cantor, 1984).

[262]29 U.S.C. §2001 et seq. (1993).

[263](1) The investigation involves economic loss to the employers; (2) the employee given the test has access to the property that is the subject of the investigation; (3) the employer has a reasonable suspicion that the employee was involved in the incident under investigation; and (4) the employer provides a statement identifying the specific incident under investigation to the employee 48 hours in advance of the administration of the test.

lie detector tests as they see fit,[264] while others are prohibited from requiring or using lie detector examinations or from even suggesting, recommending, influencing, asking, or threatening to administer such a test.[265] Several states further seek to protect employees by prohibiting reference to or the use of lie detector tests in court proceedings. Where a state law prohibits referring to or introducing lie detector test results in court proceedings, an arbitrator may be reluctant to admit or to give any weight to lie detector evidence.[266]

The Employee Polygraph Protection Act does not preempt any state law, local ordinance, or collective bargaining agreement that places more severe restrictions on a private sector employer's use of lie detector tests than does the Act.[267] Thus, the employee has the benefit of those provisions of applicable state or federal law or of a relevant collective bargaining agreement that most restrict the use of a lie detector test.

*3. Arbitration Awards.* a. In General. The majority of arbitrators do not regard lie detector test results as probative. Many reject lie detector evidence because they consider it to be inherently unreliable.[268] Others accord lie detector results little weight, noting that "such evidence has not attained scientific acceptance as a reliable and accurate means of ascertaining truth or deception," but will admit it into evidence for limited purposes.[269] In general, however, even arbitrators in the latter group decline to accord this evidence any weight when the employer has relied solely on test results to support disciplinary action against an employee.[270] The minority of arbitrators who admit lie detector results into evidence often require evidence of the lie detector test examiner's experience and the accuracy of the test reports themselves.[271] In addition, given the hearsay nature of

---

[264]Of course, subject in the vast number of cases to the provisions of the federal act.

[265]See Finkin, Privacy in Employment Law, 220-51 (BNA Books, 1995), for the full text of state laws concerning lie detector and/or polygraph tests.

[266]See Deer Lakes Sch. Dist., 94 LA 334 (Hewitt, 1989) (since the courts of the Commonwealth of Pennsylvania do not permit the introduction into evidence of lie detector results or even permit any reference to a lie detector examination to be made before a finder of fact, the arbitrator discounted the polygraph results submitted to him in this case).

[267]29 U.S.C. §2009 (1993).

[268]Abbott-Northwestern Hosp., 94 LA 621 (Berquist, 1990); Texas City Ref., Inc., 89 LA 1159 (Milentz, 1987); World Airways, Inc., 78 LA 454 (Jones, 1982).

[269]Reynolds Metals Co., 85 LA 1046, 1052 (Taylor, 1985).

[270]Bunker Ramo Corp., 76 LA 857 (Hon, 1981); Purolator Armored, Inc., 75 LA 331 (Dolnick, 1980), citing Mount Sinai Hosp. Med. Ctr., 73 LA 297 (Dolnick, 1979) (where the sole factor to justify the company's position is the recommendation of a polygraph examiner, it must be weighed with caution); Bowman Transp., Inc., 64 LA 453, 457 (Hon, 1975).

[271]A.R.A. Mfg. Co., 87 LA 182 (Woolf, 1986) (polygraph examination of employee who allegedly observed grievant take a compressor was given no weight in determining the propriety of grievant's discharge, where the lie detector examiner failed to submit evidence of required testing experience, the examiner's report did not contain sufficient information to determine his qualifications as an expert witness, the arbitrator was not told the sequence and clarity of the examiner's questions or given any raw data that was evaluated, and the examiner had not sworn to the accuracy of his reports).

the test results arbitrators may require that the grievant's representative be given the opportunity to cross-examine the individual who administered the lie detector examination.[272]

b. As Corroborative Evidence.    Even arbitrators who prefer to rely on other types of evidence may admit the results of a lie detector test for corroboration. One arbitrator permitted the introduction of the results of a lie detector test for the sole purpose of verifying the credibility of testimony.[273]

c. Grievant's Request to Submit to Lie Detector Test.    In some circumstances an employee may volunteer for a polygraph or other lie detector test. For example, an employee who has been disciplined for wrongdoing may request, or even demand, that the employer administer a lie detector test to establish his or her innocence. In *Abbott-Northwestern Hospital*,[274] the arbitrator reasoned that an employer should not be required to accede to a grievant's request for a lie detector test during an investigation of the grievant's alleged theft of a company answering machine because "it is not reliable and usurps the function of the arbitrator in the findings of fact and conclusions of law and his opinion."[275] It should also be noted that an employer's failure to grant such a request may not be relied upon by the grievant as evidence of his or her innocence.[276]

d. Grievant's Refusal to Submit to Lie Detector Test.    Arbitrators have consistently refused to uphold an employer's disciplinary action against an employee who refuses to submit to a lie detector test.[277] Moreover, an employee can refuse to take a lie detector test, or terminate a lie detector test, and the employee's action is ordinarily inadmissible to create a presumption of guilt.[278]

---

[272]Houston Lighting & Power Co., 87 LA 478 (Howell, 1986) (practitioners who desire to make use of the results of lie detector tests are advised to ensure, among other conditions, that the test examiner is available for cross-examination). See also Consumer Plastics Corp., 88 LA 208 (Garnholz, 1987) (no weight was given to a lie detector test voluntarily taken by the company's undercover agent and offered into evidence because a union representative was not present to cross-examine the agent when the test was administered).

[273]City of Miami, 92 LA 175, 180 (Abrams, 1989) (lie detector evidence should be considered as just another piece of information an arbitrator might find useful in determining credibility of witnesses). See also Texas City Ref., 89 LA 1159 (Milentz, 1987) (employer was not required to grant request for a lie detector test of employee whom it discharged after second positive drug screen results but who consistently denied using drugs; lie detector tests have been found to be unreliable and their use to refute or confirm findings of sophisticated and scientific drug-testing procedure would be meaningless).

[274]94 LA 621 (Berquist, 1990).

[275]Id. at 628.

[276]Kellogg Co., 93 LA 884, 892 (Clarke, 1989) (noting that employee's offer to take polygraph test not worthy of any evidentiary weight).

[277]Mississippi Power Co., 90 LA 220, 222 (Jewett, 1987), quoting Arbitrator Edgar Jones, Jr., in Elkouri & Elkouri, How Arbitration Works, 315–16 (BNA Books, 1987): "Under the overwhelming weight of arbitral authority employees are not to be penalized for refusal to take lie detector tests; and where an employee does submit to lie detector testing, the test results should be given little or no weight in arbitration."

[278]Id. (grievant's decision to terminate a lie detector test after being informed that the results of the first part of the test were considered deceptive did not establish his guilt, where

## B. Monitoring

*1. Personnel Files and Evaluations.* Employer requirements that certain personal information be maintained in personnel files generally will be upheld, so long as the requirements are reasonable and do not violate the collective bargaining agreement. For example, in *Texas Utilities Electric Co.,*[279] the arbitrator found reasonable a requirement that employees inform supervisors of the use of prescription drugs, including type and dosage, provided the information was treated as confidential. The arbitrator found the rule reasonable because it applied only to medications that affect performance and the information was necessary to ensure safety in the hazardous environment of a gas plant.[280]

An arbitrator upheld a company requirement for a comprehensive annual physical examination program (which included a physical exam and family medical history), where the management rights clause reserved the company's right to set reasonable guidelines for employee physical fitness. Specifically, the arbitrator found the employer could monitor the health of its guard-fire fighters.[281]

*2. Surveillance.* The Omnibus Crime Control and Safe Street Act of 1968, as amended by the Electronic Communications Privacy Act of 1986 (ECPA), restricts wiretapping.[282] In addition, several states have express restrictions on the use of a variety of electronic surveillance devices,[283] or common-law privacy protections. Surveillance for the purpose of monitoring employees' union activity violates the National Labor Relations Act.[284]

---

grievant took the test without having a union representative present and was free to terminate the lie detector test at any time without prejudice to himself).

[279]90 LA 625 (Allen, 1988).

[280]Id.

[281]FMC, Northern Ordinance Div., 90 LA 834 (Bognanno, 1988).

[282]18 U.S.C. §§2510-20, 2701-11. Title III of the federal wiretapping statute prohibits the interception, disclosure, or intentional use of oral, wire, and electronic communications by both private and public parties without prior judicial consent. As amended by the ECPA, Title III provides that the individual whose communication was intercepted in violation of the Act can recover a minimum of $100 per day for each violation or $10,000, whichever is greater. Punitive damages, reasonable attorneys' fees and other costs of litigation as well as criminal penalties can also be recovered.

[283]For example, Connecticut's statute prohibits the use of electronic surveillance devices in certain situations. Conn. Gen. Stat. §31-48b prevents employers from conducting surveillance in areas set aside for the health or personal comfort of the employees, such as restrooms, or in areas used for the purpose of safeguarding employee possessions, such as locker rooms, or in lounges. See also Nev. Rev. Stat. §53-13.160(1) (unlawful to hire detectives or "spotters" for purpose of investigating employees and reporting to employer information about employees that involves a question of integrity, honesty, or breach of employer rules unless the employer gives notice and hearing to the employee, at which hearing employee has opportunity to confront person making report).

[284]29 U.S.C. §158(a)(1). States may also prohibit such conduct. See, e.g., Hawaii Employment Relations Act, Haw. Rev. Stat. §377-6(10) (unfair labor practice to spy on employees exercising rights protected by the Act); New York State Employment Relations Act, N.Y. Lab. Law Art. 20, §704 (Consol. 1991) (unfair labor practice to spy on or keep under surveillance any activities of employees or their representatives in the exercise of rights protected by the

Central Michigan University investigated a professor who allegedly assigned passing grades to Middle Eastern students who had not fulfilled course requirements.[285] The investigation revealed that student plagiarism existed with the professor's knowledge and consent. The professor permitted Middle Eastern students to ignore syllabus requirements and still receive a C for the course. The Faculty Association contended that the professor had been subject to "surreptitious surveillance" by the university. The arbitrator concluded that the surreptitious observations were reasonable as the professor was notified of the investigation 4 months before its completion, observations were made by openly walking past the door of the classroom and noting who was in attendance, and the university made three requests for additional information from the professor during the investigation.[286]

*3. Searches.*   The Fourth Amendment of the United States Constitution contains protections against unreasonable searches and seizures. Those protections apply when the governmental entity acts as an employer. In general, the Fourth Amendment protections do not apply to nongovernmental actors and do not apply, except by analogy, to private sector employers.[287] Some state constitutions, however, contain rights of privacy that may apply in the employment context in the private sector.

If the management rights clause reserves the right to maintain a safe working environment or ensure the efficient operation of the business, searches of employees or their property are frequently held to be a reserved right. As a result, searches to discover or deter employee theft or other illegal conduct (e.g., possession of weapons or drugs), have been upheld by arbitrators. To uphold these searches arbitrators usually require: (1) a broad management rights provision, (2) notice to employees that they may be subject to search, and (3) fairness in the searches themselves. Where employers have had serious problems with thefts, or where there is other reasonable cause, a rule or practice requiring employees to submit to searches may be upheld if the employer has reasonable cause and the searches are conducted fairly.

In *Pacific Southwest Air Lines,*[288] there was a broad management rights clause and a company policy allowing searches of employees' personal possessions. The company policy, however, specifically precluded the company from conducting "random" searches without specific reasonable grounds. Nevertheless, the company engaged in

Act); R.I. Gen. Laws §28-7-13 (same). Discussion of the National Labor Relations Act and unfair labor practices is beyond the scope of this chapter.

[285]Central Mich. Univ., 101 LA 66 (House, 1993).

[286]Id.

[287]Union Oil Co. of Cal., 99 LA 1137 (McKay, 1992) (application of exclusionary rule to private employer is appropriate only where employer's conduct is unfair or violates fundamental concepts of due process or fair play).

[288]87 LA 701 (Rothschild, 1986).

searches of an entire shift of employees after they clocked out for the day but before they left company property. The union objected, saying this way was an impermissible "random" search that the company's policy prohibited. The company argued that a search of all employees on a shift is a uniform, not a random, search. The arbitrator found the searches consistent with the written policy and not "random" in the ordinary and accepted meaning of that word. He was, however, critical of the purpose expressed for the search (to let the employees know the company was aware of the pilferage and was determined to have it stopped) and the lack of notice provided either to the union or the employees.[289] Several other arbitrators have upheld the propriety of an employer's search of an employee's person or belongings where there is an established company policy permitting the search and where the search is not unreasonable, arbitrary, or capricious.[290]

The propriety of a search may turn on the employees' expectation of privacy. A company had no express rule permitting it to search employee toolboxes, but there was a past practice of opening employees' toolboxes either to remove tools needed for other employees or to protect against theft. When the company discovered increased theft, however, it required employees to purchase their own locks for their toolboxes. The arbitrator said that this requirement gave the employees a higher expectation of privacy in their toolboxes. The arbitrator held that the employer could search them only if it had a reasonable basis for believing there was a violation of a published rule of conduct.[291]

*4. Electronic Interception and Nonelectronic Eavesdropping.*[292] Federal wiretapping law contains a "prior consent" exception[293] that permits an employer "to intercept a wire, oral or electronic communication where such person is a party to the communication or where

---

[289]Id.

[290]Folsom Return to Custody, Inc., 101 LA 837 (Staudohar, 1993) (company did not violate collective bargaining agreement by searching employee's car for weapon because established company policy permitted search for purpose of maintaining health and safety of employees and employee was aware of possible discipline for having a weapon in his car); Vista Chem. Co., 92 LA 329 (Duff, 1989) (substance abuse policy that permits searches of employees' clothing based on reasonable suspicion is proper, where such searches are permitted only to the extent necessary to ensure safe and productive conduct of employer's business; possibility that employees will improperly be subjected to humiliation and indignity is not sufficient to deprive employer of such a fundamental weapon to deter theft); Kraft, Inc., 82 LA 360 (Denson, 1984) (determining propriety of search requires a balance between the legitimate interests of the employer and the personal dignity of the employee); American Welding & Mfg. Co., 89 LA 247 (Dworkin, 1987) (employer's search of employee's lunchbox, which was inside employee's toolbox, did not violate due process or the collective bargaining agreement as reasonable searches to prevent theft were permitted); but see, e.g., Utah Power & Light Co., 94 LA 233 (Winograd, 1990) (absenteeism alone does not provide necessary probable cause for requiring drug test of employee, and application of "obey now, grieve later" rule would render employee's expectation of privacy meaningless, since employee who submits to test cannot "undo" that invasion of privacy by successfully prosecuting grievance).

[291]Kawneer Co., 86 LA 297, 300-01 (Alexander, 1985).

[292]18 U.S.C. §§2510-20, 2701-11.

[293]18 U.S.C. §2511(2)(d).

one of the parties to the communication has given prior consent to such interception * * *." The exception, however, does not allow an employer to rely on its own consent in monitoring employees' telephone conversations with third parties.

Some states may have similar prohibitions and may even prohibit conduct that is permissible under federal law.

Although few arbitrators have directly addressed the issue of telephone monitoring, one arbitrator considered whether an employee was aware that her conversation was being recorded and could be revealed. In a taped call initiated by her former supervisor, a 911 communicator laughed enthusiastically at the caller's racially insensitive song parody about a housing complex fire in which five black children died.[294] The employer suspended the 911 communicator for "failure to exercise good judgment." The discipline was overturned. The work rule concerning the exercise of "good judgment" was deemed too vague and a previous counseling for the same matter was deemed to be a disciplinary reprimand. Thus, the arbitrator concluded the later suspension was impermissible double jeopardy.

Arbitrators have addressed the use of cameras in the workplace to monitor employees and have generally ruled that employers are within contractual limits when using video surveillance for certain purposes. For example, in *Emporium-Capwell,*[295] the arbitrator sanctioned the use of a camera that monitored a cash register when shortages were occurring. The camera continuously recorded, but was not regularly monitored. When shortages occurred, the day's videotape was reviewed and showed the employee removing money from the cash drawer and not replacing it. The video, in effect, gave a picture to back up the cash register receipts.

   5. *Computerized Monitoring.*   Technological advances make it possible for employers to measure workplace efficiency by monitoring, among other things, employees' actual use of computer terminals. This capability raises concerns about an employee's right to privacy when using computer equipment at work. An employer installed a device that monitors gas, mileage, and other information about a driver's performance into its delivery trucks, without negotiating with the union.[296] Using the device required drivers to enter each location into a computerized console. Despite the employer's right to monitor employees' performance, the arbitrator held that implementing this computerized device amounted to a change in the "method of delivery" and the collective bargaining agreement required that the employer and union negotiate over changes in methods of delivery.[297] The arbitrator did not declare this type of monitoring unreasonable but,

---

[294]Dane County, Wis., 97 LA 221 (Flaten, 1991).

[295]91 LA 845 (Concepcion, 1988).

[296]Schwebel Baking Co., 100 LA 1197 (Cohen, 1992).

[297]Id.

rather, struck down the implementation of the device based on other collective bargaining provisions.[298]

*6. e-mail.* The protections afforded by the Fourth Amendment of the Constitution of the United States against unreasonable searches and seizures by governmental employers arguably applies to a governmental employer's monitoring of e-mail and other forms of electronic communication. There must, however, be a reasonable expectation by the employee that her e-mail communications will be private. The Electronic Communications Privacy Act of 1986 (ECPA)[299] protects oral, wire, and electronic communications from interception by, and disclosure to, third parties under statutorily defined circumstances (subject to several statutory exceptions). Under this law, the reasonableness of the employee's expectation of privacy attached to the communication will affect the employer's right to monitor the communication and the extent to which the employer may be liable for such monitoring. There are few arbitration decisions in this area.

One reported case concerned a supervisor's expectation of privacy in his personal computer "basket" of mail.[300] The arbitrator had to decide "whether entering a computer basket on a computer program carries with it the same expectations of privacy as rifling through a supervisor's desk."[301] The arbitrator acknowledged that the scenarios presented some similarities, but noted some significant differences. The rule was that employees have access to anything on the computer so long as it is not electronically blocked. The arbitrator noted the supervisor's expectation that his personal computer basket would be electronically isolated so that employees would not have access to it.[302] As a result, the arbitrator found a 2-week suspension of an employee who entered his supervisor's computer basket and copied a private document too severe under the collective bargaining agreement.[303]

---

[298]Where a similar device was installed on police vehicles by a Connecticut municipality, the State Board of Labor Relations ruled that the installation of such a monitoring device was a permissible prophylactic procedure (one designed to monitor contractual obligations for enforcement purposes) and did not rise to the level of a mandatory subject of bargaining. Town of Stratford Police Dep't, Dec. No. 1833 (1979).

[299]18 U.S.C. §§2510 et seq.

[300]Press Democrat Publ'g Co., 93 LA 969 (McKay, 1989).

[301]Id. at 975.

[302]Id.

[303]Id. at 977.

Chapter 14

# Finality of Awards and Court Actions

## I. Introduction

When the parties invoke their arbitration agreement, they expect the arbitrator to issue an award resolving the dispute. In discipline and discharge cases, this will typically mean a ruling that either affirms or rejects the employer's action.

When the arbitrator issues an award, however, that does not necessarily end the proceeding. Each side must decide how to respond to the arbitrator's ruling, and the nature of that response determines what further actions the employer and union may take. In an overwhelming number of cases, the response of the parties is to comply with the arbitrator's award.[1] This is understandable since labor arbitration is a continuing process that requires mutual respect and cooperation to succeed. This can best be achieved by following the award's directives: where the grievance has been denied, the union will drop the issue; where a discharged employee has been reinstated with back pay, the employer will return the grievant to his or her former position and provide compensation commensurate with the award.

Nevertheless, in a small number of cases one or both parties may seek review of the arbitrator's award. The arbitrator may, for example, be requested by one or both sides to reconsider or clarify the award. Or the prevailing party may institute legal proceedings to confirm the arbitrator's award and to enforce its terms if the losing party has

---

[1]Recent research suggests that only approximately 1% of all labor arbitration awards lead to legal action to overturn them. Feuille, LeRoy, & Chandler, "Judicial Review of Arbitration Awards: Some Evidence," 41 Lab. L.J. 477, 481 (1990).

failed to comply. Alternatively, the losing party may institute legal proceedings to vacate the award to free itself of any obligations contained in the arbitrator's ruling.

When such actions are brought, courts will normally defer to the arbitrator's decision. Prevailing legal principles direct the courts not to second-guess arbitrator rulings for factual or legal error. This is due in part to the belief that since the parties have agreed to abide by the arbitrator's decision, judicial scrutiny should not undercut that agreement. Nevertheless, courts have developed some limited exceptions to the general rule that they will not interfere with arbitration awards. These exceptions include doctrines that permit courts to review whether the arbitrator adhered to the limits on his or her contractual authority, whether the terms of the award violate public policy, and whether the arbitrator adhered to established procedural standards. Where the requirements of any of these doctrines are not met, the arbitrator's award may be subjected to judicial review.

While this chapter will present an overview of the legal principles governing the review of arbitration awards in discipline and discharge cases, it should be understood that voluntary compliance by the parties is the norm. And even where review is sought, most proceedings end with the arbitrator's award being enforced as written.

## II. Resubmission and Clarification of Arbitration Awards

If one or both parties are dissatisfied with the award, they may seek to have the arbitrator reconsider the ruling. This may be the result of a desire to have the arbitrator change the award or because the award is unclear and the parties do not know how to comply. Where both parties consent to have the arbitrator reconsider or clarify the award, no legal problems arise. The legal doctrine of *functus officio* applies, however, if one of the parties objects.

The doctrine of *functus officio* provides that unless both parties consent, the arbitrator's jurisdiction ceases when a "final" award is issued.[2] The principle is designed primarily to assure the award's

---

[2]The rule, its policies, and progeny are discussed in "Modification and Correction of an Award by the Arbitrator," Fairweather's Practice and Procedure in Labor Arbitration, 3d ed., 383, Schoonhoven, ed. (BNA Books, 1991); Eischen, Interim Awards and Retention of Jurisdiction," and "Modification and Correction of the Award" in Labor & Employment Arbitration, Bornstein & Gosline, eds., §1.04[4] & [5] (Matthew Bender, 1990); Werner & Holtzman, "Clarification of Arbitration Awards, 3 Lab. Law. 183 (1987); Gosline, "Re-Exhaustion of Arbitration Procedures as Appropriate Course for Resolving Back Pay Issues Arising as a Result of Resolution of Grievance," 59 A.L.R. Fed 501 (1982); Dilts, "Award Clarification: An Ethical Dilemma," 33 Lab. L.J. 366 (1982); Schrieber, "The Doctrine of *Functus Officio* With Particular Relation to Labor Arbitration," 23 Lab. L.J. 638 (1972); Busch, "Does the Arbitrator's Function Survive His Award?" 16 Arb. J. 31 (1961); Jones, "Arbitration and the Doctrine of Possible Error," 11 Lab. L.J. 1023 (1960).

finality; to preclude the parties from indirect attempts to appeal, relitigate, or submit new issues; and to avoid the appearance of nest feathering by the arbitrator.[3]

*Functus officio* is an ethical standard for arbitrators who are members of the National Academy of Arbitrators (NAA) or who serve under appointment by the Federal Mediation and Conciliation Service (FMCS) or the American Arbitration Association (AAA). This standard is found at Section 6 (D)(1) of the Code of Professional Responsibility for Arbitrators of Labor-Management Disputes, which provides: "No clarification or interpretation of an award is permissible without the consent of both parties." Indeed, on March 3, 1980, the FMCS wrote the arbitrators on its roster:

> The submission of a Decision removes an arbitrator from further authority for a particular matter. Absent a *joint* request, any response by an arbitrator to both parties [should] be limited to stating the function of the office ceases with the Decision submission. Even an abbreviated explanation is too much.[4]

Nevertheless, there are circumstances where *functus officio* does not apply or where it is disregarded to achieve the proper practical result. For example, evident errors in form that do not affect the merits of the original controversy often are corrected at the request of one party or sua sponte by the arbitrator. The NAA's Advisory Opinion No. 20[5] states that correcting the identity of employees, backpay calculations, and "other corrections of similar evident clerical mistakes or computational errors" does not violate Section 6(D)(1)'s prohibition against "clarification or interpretation of an award." The opinion concludes that such corrections are consistent with common and statutory law and are necessary to avoid unfair burdens on the parties and misuse of the arbitration process.

Parties rarely present evidence concerning the appropriate remedy when litigating the merits of a disciplinary dispute. Consequently, arbitrators commonly define a remedy in general terms and specifically retain jurisdiction over any dispute that may arise concerning its administration or implementation. Many arbitrators solicit a stipulation during the hearing to grant them continued jurisdiction over

---

[3]One critic describes the doctrine as "talismanic ritualism" resulting from a "medieval pathology" and used so arbitrators do not have to face their mistakes. Ellmann, *"Functus Officio* Under the Code of Professional Responsibility: The Ethics of Staying Wrong," in Proceedings of the 45th Annual Meeting of NAA, 190 (BNA Books, 1993). Less derogatory but detailed discussions are Rehmus, "The Code and Postaward Arbitral Discretion," in Proceedings of the 42nd Annual Meeting of NAA, 127 (BNA Books, 1990); Crane, "The Use and Abuse of Arbitral Power," in Proceedings of the 25th Annual Meeting of NAA, 66 (BNA Books, 1973); Seitz, "Problems of the Finality of Awards, or *Functus Officio* and All That," Proceedings of the 17th Annual Meeting of NAA, 165 (BNA Books, 1964).

[4]Quoted in Volz & Goggin, eds., Elkouri & Elkouri, How Arbitration Works, 5th ed., 388 n.309 (BNA Books, 1997).

[5]93 LA 1319 (1989).

the remedy if the grievance is sustained. A substantial number of arbitrators simply announce that they are retaining jurisdiction when they issue an award that contains an affirmative remedy.[6]

Various theories support an arbitrator who retains jurisdiction over an affirmative remedy. For example, national labor policy may require it. In *Steelworkers v. Enterprise Wheel & Car Corp.,*[7] the Supreme Court sustained the Fourth Circuit's ruling[8] that labor arbitration obligates the parties to complete an arbitration so monetary amounts due grievants will be definitely ascertained.

A more frequent rationale is that retained jurisdiction is "unfinished business." By defining a remedy broadly and remanding it to the parties, an arbitrator does not speak "finally" on the remedial issue. Rather, the parties are given the first opportunity to reach an agreement, but if they are unable to do so, either party may reinvoke the arbitrator's original authority to decide the remedial issue. Given the consensus on back pay and other monetary "make whole" remedies, parties generally are able to resolve remedial issues without returning to the arbitrator. Yet, even where there is little reason to expect agreement, it is beneficial to provide the parties with an opportunity to define and resolve any remaining differences after their consideration of the award's merits.[9]

Courts do not allow a party to return to arbitration to relitigate issues that have been decided clearly.[10] However, they frequently direct the parties to resubmit an ambiguous or incomplete award to the arbitrator for clarification or interpretation.[11] Courts sidestep technical application of the *functus officio* doctrine in favor of finally resolving the dispute without prejudicing either of the parties for the arbitrator's initial failure to render a definitive award. The Ninth Circuit explained that where the parties have elected to submit their

---

[6]The scope of retained jurisdiction should be defined narrowly and for a specific time. Rehmus, "The Code and Postaward Arbitral Discretion," in Proceedings of the 42nd Annual Meeting of NAA, 127, 136–37, 139 (BNA Books, 1990); Hill & Sinicropi, "Option to Remand Back Pay Issue," Remedies in Arbitration, 2nd ed., 57–60 (BNA Books, 1991).

[7]363 U.S. 593, 46 LRRM 2423 (1960).

[8]269 F.2d 327, 44 LRRM 2349 (4th Cir., 1959).

[9]Cf. Young's Commercial Transfer, 101 LA 993 (McCurdy, 1993).

[10]See e.g., McClatchy Newspapers v. Central Valley Typographical Union, 46, 686, F.2d 731, 111 LRRM 2254 (9th Cir.), cert. denied, 459 U.S. 1071, 111 LRRM 3064 (1982); Washington-Baltimore Newspaper Guild Local 35 v. Washington Post Co., 442 F.2d 1234, 76 LRRM 2274 (D.C. Cir., 1971); Hotel & Restaurant Employees Local 878 v. Cullop, 146 LRRM 3086 (D. Alaska, 1994).

[11]In analyzing ambiguity, the judicial focus should be on the arbitrator's award and not the rationale for reaching the award; otherwise there is danger that a party will use the process as a guise to relitigate an adverse decision. In assessing incomplete awards, courts should determine the issues originally submitted, and, if not answered, order that they be resubmitted to the arbitrator as unfinished business. See Teamsters Local 312 v. Matlack, Inc., 118 F.3d 985, 155 LRRM 2738 (3d Cir., 1997) (clarification exception to *functus officio* doctrine); Teamsters Local 631 v. Silver State Disposal Serv., Inc., 109 F.3d 1409, 154 LRRM 2865 (9th Cir., 1997) (completion exception to *functus officio* doctrine).

disputes to arbitration, they should be completely resolved by arbitration, rather than only partially resolved. In some cases carrying out this philosophy will require remanding the matter to the arbitrators.[12] As Judge Posner noted in *Ethyl Corp. v. Steelworkers*,[13] *functus officio* does not receive a "fastidious" analysis if a court determines an award needs clarification.[14]

A helpful analysis of the *functus officio* doctrine is contained in an opinion by Judge Posner in *Excelsior Foundry Co.*[15] The dispute arose over the interpretation of an arbitrator's reinstatement award allowing an employee 60 days to complete an approved rehabilitation program. The employee's enrollment in the program was delayed because of the need for clarification concerning who would pay program costs. When he finally enrolled, it was already too late to complete the program within the required 60 days. A union representative had unilaterally called the arbitrator who then wrote to both parties that it was his intent that the 60-day period run from his clarification of the award settling the dispute over who would pay for the costs of the rehabilitation program, not from the date of the original award. The company, however, refused to reinstate the employee following his completion of the program, and subsequently the district court granted summary judgment to the company in the union's suit to compel enforcement. The court concluded that the *functus officio* doctrine barred the arbitrator from extending the period for completion of the rehabilitation program.

Since the parties had not agreed to return to the arbitrator, Judge Posner concluded that the legitimacy of the arbitrator's decision rested upon the application of the *functus officio* doctrine. In the course of his ruling, Judge Posner questioned whether the doctrine continues to exist in labor arbitration, based as it is on the analogy of arbitrators as judges who, if they resign their office, cannot rule on requests to reconsider or amend their decisions. Judge Posner saw the analogy as flawed because review will be available to a litigant before another judge even if the original judge is not available to reconsider his or her decision. The *functus officio* doctrine in labor arbitration, however, deprives the parties of any opportunity to seek

---

[12]Hanford Atomic Metal Trades Council v. General Elec. Co., 353 F.2d 302, 307, 61 LRRM 2004 (9th Cir., 1965).

[13]768 F.2d 180, 119 LRRM 3566 (7th Cir., 1985).

[14]See also Red Star Express Lines v. Teamsters Local 170, 809 F.2d 103, 124 LRRM 2361 (1st Cir., 1987) (indirectly approves arbitrator reopening a hearing based on unilateral management request to consider the back-pay formula); Steelworkers v. Ideal Cement Co. Div., 762 F.2d 837, 119 LRRM 2774 (10th Cir., 1985) (court declined to decide whether *functus officio* is part of substantive federal labor law); Courier-Citizen v. Graphic Communications Local 11, 702 F.2d 273, 112 LRRM 3122 (1st Cir., 1983) (strict common law doctrine of *functus officio* does not apply to substantive law of labor relations); Grand Rapids Die Casting Corp. v. Auto Workers Local 159, 684 F.2d 413, 111 LRRM 2137 (6th Cir., 1982).

[15]Glass & Pottery Workers Local 182B v. Excelsior Foundry Co., 56 F.3d 844, 149 LRRM 2538 (7th Cir., 1995).

reconsideration, clarification, amendment, or any other modification of the award. Such a rule might serve a useful purpose in deterring ex parte communications with arbitrators after the award has been issued, but this would be inconsistent with the general recognition that courts and adjudicative agencies have "the inherent power to reconsider * * * decisions within a reasonable time."[16]

Judge Posner observed that in recognition of these concerns loopholes exist in the *functus officio* doctrine. For example, the facts of the *Excelsior Foundry Co.* case could be characterized as an effort to interpret as opposed to alter the award, and therefore returning to the arbitrator would not be barred by the *functus officio* doctrine. As long as such an effort is made within a reasonable time, which Judge Posner concluded existed in the facts before him, clarification by the arbitrator is permissible. But in a larger sense, Judge Posner believed that

> [s]ince the case for the exceptions seems stronger than the case for the rule, perhaps the time has come to discard the rule. It is judge-made; it can be judge-unmade.[17]

Since such a ruling was not necessary for the disposition of the case and had not been asked for by the parties, Judge Posner was content to issue his decision based upon existing principles. However, his discussion of the sources and role of the *functus officio* doctrine raises serious questions as to its continuing viability.

## III. Standards for the Review of Arbitration Awards

### A. *Evolution of Supreme Court Doctrine*

Prior to 1947, the only source of federal judicial authority to review arbitration awards was the Federal Arbitration Act (FAA).[18] The FAA establishes specific standards for courts to employ when considering a challenge to the decision of an arbitrator, providing in pertinent part that an award may be vacated:

(1) Where the award was procured by corruption, fraud, or undue means.

(2) Where there was evident partiality or corruption in the arbitrators, or either of them.

(3) Where the arbitrators were guilty of misconduct in refusing to postpone the hearing, upon sufficient cause shown, or in refusing to hear evidence pertinent and material to the controversy;

---

[16]Id., 149 LRRM at 2541.

[17]Id.

[18]9 U.S.C. §1(a) (1970).

or of any other misbehavior by which the rights of any party have been prejudiced.

(4) Where the arbitrators exceeded their powers, or so imperfectly executed them that a mutual, final, and definite award upon the subject matters submitted was not made.[19]

The legislation specifically excludes coverage for contracts of employment involving "workers engaged in foreign or interstate commerce,"[20] and collective bargaining agreements generally have been viewed as outside of the scope of the Act's provisions.[21]

The issue of labor contract enforcement was addressed by Congress in the 1947 Labor Management Relations Act which included Section 301, which grants federal courts jurisdiction to entertain suits alleging collective bargaining agreement violations.[22] Ultimately, the Supreme Court interpreted this provision to mean that federal courts were required to develop a body of federal common law to govern the interpretation of labor contracts and that one of its components was to be federal court authority to enforce agreements to arbitrate labor contract disputes.[23]

While this principle compels the parties to arbitrate their collective bargaining agreement disputes,[24] it does not directly address

---

[19]9 U.S.C. §10.

[20]9 U.S.C. §1. While some courts have read the exclusion broadly to cover all employment contracts involving interstate or foreign commerce (see, e.g., Stokes v. Merrill Lynch, 523 F.2d 433 (6th Cir., 1975); Dickstein v. DuPont, 443 F.2d 783 (1st Cir., 1971)), other courts have concluded that the exclusion only applies to transportation workers and others who have a direct part in movement of goods in interstate commerce. See, e.g., Postal Workers v. United States Postal Serv., 823 F.2d 466, 126 LRRM 2263 (11th Cir., 1987); Signal-Stat Corp. v. Electrical Workers (UE) Local 475, 235 F.2d 298, 38 LRRM 2378 (2d Cir., 1956), cert. denied, 354 U.S. 911, 40 LRRM 2200 (1957). The U.S. Supreme Court enforced an arbitration clause involving an employment dispute in Gilmer v. Interstate/Johnson Lane Corp., 500 U.S. 20, 55 FEP Cases 1116 (1991), but the arbitration agreement was contained in a registration statement Gilmer signed with the New York Stock Exchange, rather than an employment contract. Therefore, the impact of the employment contract exclusion as applied to individual employment contracts executed between the employer and employee was left unresolved.

[21]See Food & Commercial Workers, Local 7R v. Safeway Stores, Inc., 889 F.2d 940, 132 LRRM 3090 (10th Cir., 1989). Many cases refer to the Act for guidance, E.g., Posadas de P.R. Assocs. v. Asociacion de Empleados de Casino de P.R., 873 F.2d 479, 131 LRRM 2223 (1st Cir., 1989).

[22]Section 301 provides that "[s]uits for violation of contracts between an employer and a labor organization * * * may be brought in any district court of the United States having jurisdiction of the parties, without respect to the amount in controversy or without regard to the citizenship of the parties." 29 U.S.C. §185(a).

[23]Teamsters Local 174 v. Lucas Flour Co., 82 S.Ct. 571, 49 LRRM 2717 (1962); Charles Dowd Box Co. v. Courtney, 82 S.Ct. 519, 49 LRRM 2619 (1962); Textile Workers v. Lincoln Mills, 353 U.S. 448, 40 LRRM 2113 (1957).

[24]In two 1960 decisions involving arbitration clauses in Steelworkers union contracts, the Supreme Court created a presumption in favor of the arbitrability of grievances, observing that "[a]n order to arbitrate the particular grievance should not be denied unless it may be said with positive assurance that the arbitration clause is not susceptible of an interpretation that covers the asserted dispute. Doubts should be resolved in favor of coverage." Steelworkers v. Warrior & Gulf Navigation Co., 363 U.S. 574, 582, 46 LRRM 2416 (1960). See also Steelworkers v. American Mfg. Co., 363 U.S. 564, 569, 46 LRRM 2414 (1960).

the enforceability of the labor arbitrator's award. That question was presented in *Steelworkers v. Enterprise Wheel & Car Corp.*[25] There the parties had signed a collective bargaining agreement that included a broad arbitration clause governing "any differences 'as to the meaning and application'" of the contract and providing "that the arbitrator's decision 'shall be final and binding on the parties.'"[26] The company, however, had previously refused to arbitrate the grievance until it was compelled to do so by court order. Thereafter, it refused to comply with the arbitrator's award. The federal district court ordered enforcement of the arbitrator's ruling, but the court of appeals reversed the district court and held the award unenforceable.

The response of the Supreme Court was to reject the interventionist approach of the court of appeals. It succinctly observed:

> The refusal of courts to review the merits of an arbitration award is the proper approach to arbitration under collective bargaining agreements. The federal policy of settling labor disputes by arbitration would be undermined if courts had the final say on the merits of the awards.[27]

The Court explained that "arbitrators under these collective agreements are indispensable agencies in a continuous collective bargaining process."[28] They are chosen for their expertise, and it is appropriate for them to apply their "knowledge of the custom and practices of a particular factory or of a particular industry"[29] in reaching their decisions.

Under *Enterprise Wheel*, therefore, arbitrators have wide-ranging authority in the interpretation of collective bargaining agreements and can bring their "informed judgment to bear in order to reach a fair solution of a problem."[30] Moreover, the merits of their conclusions are not subject to judicial review. The only limitation is that the arbitrator must interpret the contract in reaching his or her decision. As the Court observed:

> [A]n arbitrator is confined to interpretation and application of the collective bargaining agreement; he does not sit to dispense his own brand of industrial justice. He may of course look for guidance from many sources, yet his award is legitimate only so long as it draws its essence from the collective bargaining agreement. When the arbitrator's words manifest an infidelity to this obligation, courts have no choice but to refuse enforcement of the award.[31]

---

[25]363 U.S. 593, 46 LRRM 2423 (1960).
[26]Id. at 594.
[27]Id. at 596.
[28]Id.
[29]Id.
[30]Id. at 597.
[31]Id.

Judicial review standards for labor arbitration awards were again addressed by the Supreme Court in *Paperworkers v. Misco, Inc.*[32] Here the employer, which operated a paper-converting plant, discharged an employee whose job involved the operation of hazardous machinery. The employee had informed the company that he had been arrested for the possession of marijuana in his home, and later investigation by the company disclosed that he had also been found in the back seat of a friend's vehicle in the company parking lot, "with marijuana smoke in the air and a lighted marijuana cigarette in the frontseat ashtray."[33] The company's position was that these events violated the company's rule against having narcotics on company property. Not until shortly before the hearing did the company become aware that the employee had also been arrested for marijuana possession based upon marijuana gleanings found by police in his own car, which had also been located in the company's parking lot.

After the employee was discharged, he filed a grievance that the company rejected. Thereafter, the arbitrator concluded that the company lacked the just cause required for termination under the applicable collective bargaining agreement. He awarded the employee reinstatement with back pay and full seniority. The arbitrator refused to consider the evidence of marijuana gleanings found in the employee's car because this was unknown to the company at the time of the discharge. The remaining evidence, in the arbitrator's judgment, failed to establish that the employee was in possession of narcotics on company property in violation of company rules. Both the district court and court of appeals, however, refused to enforce the award. In particular, the court of appeals concluded that the arbitrator's narrow focus on "procedural rights" led to an erroneous conclusion. In the court's judgment, the employee had brought drugs onto company premises, as evidenced by his apprehension in a car filled with marijuana smoke and by the discovery of marijuana in his own vehicle.

In reversing the court of appeals, the Supreme Court reaffirmed that "courts are not authorized to reconsider the merits of an award even though the parties may allege that the award rests on errors of fact or on misinterpretation of the contract."[34] Rather, since the parties have contracted to have disputes settled by an arbitrator chosen by them rather than by a judge, it is the arbitrator's view of the facts and of the meaning of the contract that they have agreed to accept. Courts thus do not sit to hear claims of factual or legal error by an arbitrator as an appellate court does in reviewing decisions of lower courts. To resolve disputes about the application of a collective bargaining agreement, an arbitrator must find facts and a court may not reject those findings simply because it disagrees with them. The

---

[32]484 U.S. 29, 126 LRRM 3113 (1987).

[33]Id. at 29.

[34]Id. at 36.

same is true of the arbitrator's interpretation of the contract. The arbitrator may not ignore the plain language of the contract, but the parties have authorized the arbitrator to give meaning to the language of the agreement, and a court should not reject an award on the ground that the arbitrator misread the contract.[35] Using this standard, the Court concluded that the court of appeals had improperly reevaluated the arbitrator's factual conclusions and overall interpretation of the contract.

In addition to reaffirming that courts are not to review the merits of labor arbitration awards, *Misco* considered whether courts can refuse to enforce the arbitrator's ruling on the basis of public policy considerations. The court of appeals in *Misco* relied on the public policy "against the operation of dangerous machinery by persons under the influence of drugs or alcohol"[36] and held that no award reinstating an employee violating this policy can be enforced. While conceding that public policy can justify the rejection of an arbitration award,[37] the Court found it inapplicable to the facts in *Misco*. It cautioned that the public policy must be "'explicit'" as well as "'well defined and dominant,'"[38] and that it "is to be ascertained by 'reference to the laws and legal precedents and not from general considerations of supposed public interests.'"[39] The court of appeals' unsupported public policy determination failed to meet this standard, and the available evidence was not sufficient to establish a violation of the asserted public policy.

## B. Deference to the Arbitration Award

Although the *Enterprise Wheel* and *Misco* Supreme Court decisions were more than 25 years apart, the two cases are similar in their treatment of judicial review standards for labor arbitration awards. In each case, the Court directed trial and appellate tribunals to limit their scrutiny of the labor arbitration process and to specifically avoid second-guessing the arbitrator's substantive judgment. The parties chose an arbitrator to interpret their contract: only if he or she fails to perform that function, or does so in a fashion that contravenes a well-defined and dominant public policy, can a court properly reject the award.

---

[35]Id. at 37–38, referring to Steelworkers v. Enterprise Wheel & Car Corp., 363 U.S. 593, 599, 46 LRRM 2423 (1960).

[36]Misco, Inc. v. Paperworkers, 768 F.2d 739, 743, 120 LRRM 2119 (5th Cir., 1985), rev'd, 484 U.S. 29, 126 LRRM 3113 (1987).

[37]Paperworkers v. Misco, Inc., 484 U.S. 29, 42, 126 LRRM 3113 (1987), citing W. R. Grace & Co. v. Rubber Workers Local 759, 461 U.S. 757, 766, 113 LRRM 2641 (1983).

[38]Paperworkers v. Misco, Inc.; 484 U.S. 29, 42, 126 LRRM 3113 (1987), quoting W.R. Grace & Co. v. Rubber Workers Local 759, 461 U.S. 757, 766, 113 LRRM 2641 (1983).

[39]Id., quoting W.R. Grace & Co. v. Rubber Workers Local 759, 461 U.S. 757, 766, 113 LRRM 2641 (1983), quoting Muschany v. United States, 324 U.S. 49, 66 (1945).

In many cases lower federal courts have found little difficulty in disposing of challenges to labor arbitration awards by simply repeating the admonition of the Supreme Court to avoid review of the merits of the award.[40] The courts identify the award as drawing its essence from the labor contract and proceed to grant enforcement.[41] Not only does this approach make disposition of the challenge straightforward, it also sends a clear message to employers and union representatives that the judiciary is not available to thwart the speed and efficiency of the labor arbitration process.

In other situations, however, courts have been willing to reject arbitration awards in circumstances that appear inconsistent with Supreme Court standards.[42] In *Torrington Co. v. Metal Products Workers Local 1645*,[43] the court illustrates this approach. The company unilaterally discontinued a 20-year unwritten practice of providing time off with pay to allow employees to vote. In response, the union protested but did not file a contract grievance. The issue was addressed in the next round of contract negotiations, which resulted in agreement by the parties to continue the old contract with specific amendments. Despite early union proposals to include voting pay in the agreement, no language covering the issue of paid voting time was incorporated. Thereafter, when the company refused to provide voting pay, the union filed a grievance and the matter was ultimately referred to arbitration.

The arbitrator concluded that the company's refusal of voting pay violated the contract. In his view, the uninterrupted 20-year practice was part of the company's contractual obligation that could not be discontinued without union consent. No such consent could be found in the contract negotiation process. The Second Circuit refused to enforce the award. It ruled that the arbitrator's decision exceeded his authority under the contract. In the court's view, the issue was whether the arbitrator had jurisdiction to rule that past practices had become part of the company's contractual obligation to its employees.[44] Courts are entitled to review an arbitrator's decision on the scope of

[40]See, e.g., Glass & Pottery Workers v. Owens-Illinois, Inc., 758 F.Supp. 962, 136 LRRM 2397 (D.N.J., 1991); Paperworkers v. Gaylord Container Corp., 755 F.Supp. 158, 136 LRRM 2570 (E.D. La., 1991).

[41]See Trevathan v. Newport News Shipbuilding & Drydock Co., 752 F.Supp. 698, 700, 139 LRRM 2990 (E.D. Va., 1990) (holding plaintiff not entitled to relief because "[h]e seeks to have the Court substitute its judgment for that of the arbitrator").

[42]One commentator has observed that notwithstanding ritual invocation of the various verbal formulations of the finality principle, reviewing courts frequently do explore the merits of arbitral interpretation, either as an independent ground to sustain a determination to enforce an award or as an indication of default justifying denial of enforcement. Kaden, "Judges and Arbitrators: Observations on the Scope of Judicial Review," 80 Colum. L. Rev. 267, 270–71 (1980).

[43]362 F.2d 677, 62 LRRM 2495 (2d Cir., 1966).

[44]"[W]e hold that the question of an arbitrator's authority is subject to judicial review, and that the arbitrator's decision that he has authority should not be accepted where the reviewing court can clearly perceive that he has derived that authority from sources outside the collective bargaining agreement at issue." Id. at 680.

his or her jurisdiction. According to the court, that is what it did here, as opposed to ruling on the merits of the award. The distinction, however, is at best a subtle one.

The same reasoning can be seen in more recent cases, such as *Leed Architectural Products, Inc. v. Steelworkers Local 6674*.[45] Here, an arbitrator found that the company violated the collective bargaining agreement when it paid one employee in excess of the wage rate the parties had agreed upon—a determination that, according to the court, drew its essence from the contract and was entitled to judicial deference. The court, however, concluded that the arbitrator exceeded his authority by ordering the company to pay other employees the same higher rate, rather than rescind the single employee's pay raise. The agreement provided for a defined wage rate, and by allowing the increase given to one employee to raise the wage levels of equivalent employees, the arbitrator violated his obligation to confine himself to the interpretation of the agreement without adding, subtracting, or modifying it in any way. Despite the usually wide latitude given to arbitrators in framing remedies, the court concluded that this arbitrator lacked authority to remedy the company's contract violation in this manner.

In *Delta Queen Steamboat Co.*,[46] the company discharged the captain of a riverboat excursion vessel for neglect that caused a near collision. Despite a finding that the captain's conduct involved gross carelessness, the arbitrator ordered reinstatement because of his 40-year unblemished record and the disparity between the discipline imposed upon him and other employees involved in mishaps. The company challenged the arbitrator's decision in federal district court, maintaining that he exceeded his jurisdiction, since the contract provided that discipline for proper cause was the sole responsibility of the company. The district court agreed and vacated the award. Its decision was upheld by a panel of the Fifth Circuit. The court read the contract to divest the arbitrator of jurisdiction to reverse the company's disciplinary decision once he found proper cause, which was implicit in his conclusion that the captain's conduct reflected gross carelessness.

Dissenting from the denial of a rehearing en banc, however, Judge Williams maintained there was no basis in the contract to justify withdrawing the degree of discipline from the reach of the arbitration clause.[47] He pointed to other provisions of the collective bargaining agreement that subjected discharge cases to the grievance machinery of the contract, and concluded that the term "case" could include

[45]916 F.2d 63, 135 LRRM 2766 (2d Cir., 1990).

[46]Delta Queen Steamboat Co. v. Marine Eng'rs Dist. 2, 889 F.2d 599, 133 LRRM 2077 (5th Cir., 1989), reh'g denied en banc, 897 F.2d 746, 134 LRRM 2080 (5th Cir., 1990).

[47]Delta Queen Steamboat Co. v. Marine Eng'rs Dist. 2, 897 F.2d 746, 134 LRRM 2080 (5th Cir., 1990) (Williams, J., dissenting from denial of rehearing en banc).

punishment as well as liability. This represents an arbitral construction of the contract that is entitled to judicial deference. Finally, Judge Williams criticized the tendency to assert that an "incorrect interpretation of the contract means that the arbitrator exceeded his or her jurisdiction,"[48] an approach, he concluded, that would send the wrong signal to the losing parties in labor arbitration proceedings.[49]

## C. *Exceptions to the Deference Standard*

In some instances, lower courts appear to have ignored the Supreme Court admonition that the merits of an arbitrator's award should not be subject to review. These can be characterized as cases in which the courts have concluded that an arbitrator ignored the plain language of the contract or acted in manifest disregard of the law.[50] The courts apparently felt the arbitrator was so obviously wrong in his or her ruling, or so totally indifferent to controlling legal principles, that the award could not be allowed to stand.

In *Tennessee Valley Authority v. Salary Policy Employee Panel,*[51] for example, the arbitrator concluded that an employee had been properly terminated for travel voucher fraud, but that the duration of her suspension without pay pending investigation was excessive. Her discharge was upheld, but the arbitrator awarded her 4 weeks of back pay. The TVA sought to vacate the award, and the district court observed that its authority to reject the arbitrator's judgment extended to situations in which:

(1) an award conflicts with express terms of the collective bargaining agreement,

(2) an award imposes additional requirements that are not expressly provided in the agreement,

(3) an award is without rational support or cannot be rationally derived from the terms of the agreement, and

(4) an award is based on general considerations of fairness and equity instead of the precise terms of the agreement * * *.[52]

In the court's view, an arbitration award that implicitly alters plain or unambiguous contractual language does not draw its essence from the collective bargaining agreement. Thus, it may not be judicially

---

[48]Id. at 750, 134 LRRM at 2083.

[49]See also Exxon Corp. v. Esso Workers' Union, 118 F.3d 841, 155 LRRM 2782 (1st Cir., 1997).

[50]Contico Int'l Inc. v. Leather Goods Workers Local 160, 738 F.Supp. 1262, 135 LRRM 2091 (E.D. Mo., 1990); Mangan v. Owens Truckmen, Inc., 715 F.Supp. 436 (E.D. N.Y., 1989).

[51]136 LRRM 2533 (E.D. Tenn., 1989), aff'd, 917 F.2d 564, 136 LRRM 2543 (6th Cir., 1990).

[52]Id. at 2535, citing Dobbs, Inc. v. Teamsters Local 614, 813 F.2d 85, 124 LRRM 2827 (6th Cir., 1987); Cement Divs., National Gypsum Co. v. Steelworkers Local 135, 793 F.2d 759, 766, 123 LRRM 2015 (6th Cir., 1986).

enforced.[53] Using this approach, the court vacated the back-pay award because it concluded that the arbitrator wrongly interpreted the contractual promptness requirement to apply to suspensions pending investigation.[54]

The opinion of the Eighth Circuit Court of Appeals in *George A. Hormel & Co. v. Food & Commercial Workers Local 9*[55] illustrates a somewhat more circumscribed approach to judicial review, but one that nevertheless asserts authority to evaluate the merits of the arbitrator's award. The dispute arose out of the company's decision to end hog-slaughtering operations at its plant in Austin, Minnesota. It then remodeled the facility, leased part of it to another company, and proceeded to purchase slaughtered meat from the lessee for its own processing and packaging. An arbitrator agreed with the union's claim that the contract required any slaughtering taking place within the company's facility to be performed by union members, even in the context of the leasing arrangement. The company, by contrast, maintained that the contract language pertaining to leasing and subcontracting was so clear and unambiguous that it was not susceptible to the construction given.[56]

When the company's challenge to the arbitration award came before the Eighth Circuit Court of Appeals for review, the court cited law from the Tenth Circuit calling for deference to an award "'unless it can be said with positive assurance that the contract is not susceptible to the arbitrator's interpretation.'"[57] The court then concluded that such a standard, on its own, would not warrant interfering with the arbitrator's judgment. Nevertheless, the court observed that

> where the award's result is one so contrary to common experience and logic that it is more likely than not that such result was not the intent of the parties, and where *additional* facts exist that strongly indicate that the arbitrator did not premise his award on the contract, notwithstanding his words to the contrary,[58]

vacation of the award would be appropriate. The Eighth Circuit found this to be the proper solution in *Hormel*, relying upon the "additional facts" that the arbitrator failed to discuss contract language the court

---

[53]Id., citing Electrical Workers (IBEW) Local 1842 v. Cincinnati Elecs. Corp., 808 F.2d 1201, 124 LRRM 2473 (6th Cir., 1987).

[54]136 LRRM at 2536. The court also concluded that a just cause standard of review did not apply to suspensions pending investigation, as opposed to disciplinary suspensions, and that the arbitrator's finding that the grievant was prejudiced by delay lacked evidentiary support. Id.

[55]879 F.2d 347, 131 LRRM 3018 (8th Cir., 1989).

[56]Id. at 350.

[57]Id., quoting Sterling Colo. Beef Co. v. Food & Commercial Workers Local 7, 767 F.2d 718, 720, 119 LRRM 3303 (10th Cir., 1985); accord NCR Corp. v. Machinists Lodge 70, 128 LRRM 3024, 3027–28 (D. Kan., 1988).

[58]879 F.2d at 350 (emphasis in original).

felt was relevant and gave no explanation of how the contract was construed without such a discussion.

The difficulty that is apparent every time a court rejects an arbitration award as inconsistent with "the clear" terms of the contract is that "clarity" is subjective. In *Berklee College of Music v. Teachers Local 4412,*[59] for example, the contract required grievances to be filed within 10 days and provided that time limits were only waivable with written mutual consent. The union filed a grievance several days beyond the limit, and there had been no waiver of the deadline. Nevertheless, because the contact did not specify the legal consequences of a late filing, the arbitrator concluded that he had the authority to ignore de minimis violations.

In enforcing the award, the First Circuit observed that other provisions of the contract demonstrated that the parties knew how to specify the consequences of nonaction but had failed to do so when dealing with the initial filing of a grievance. Moreover, the courts have found ways around seemingly absolute time limits, and this background could be applied to labor contract grievances as well. Even the mutual consent requirement could be explained as related to claims of waiver by the parties but irrelevant to the application of tolling principles by the arbitrator. Whether right or wrong, the court's arguments are certainly interpretations of the contract, which the Supreme Court left to the nonreviewable discretion of the arbitrator.

In a forceful dissent, Judge Acosta maintained that the award fell within the range of decisions subject to judicial intervention.[60] He found that the contractual requirements were unambiguous and that the arbitrator improperly "decided that the words of the Agreement meant what he chose them to mean."[61] Judge Acosta cautioned that "reason must still rule the use and intent of our juridical language lest we fall prey to Lewis Carroll's famous exposition that the question is not what a word means but which is to be master: the word or its user."[62] As the judge noted, arbitrators should not behave like Humpty Dumpty, who said to Alice: "When *I* use a word * * * it means just what I choose it to mean—neither more nor less."[63]

## D. Public Policy Review

There are fewer public policy challenges to labor arbitration awards (as opposed to "essence of the contract" challenges,[64] but there

---

[59]858 F.2d 31, 129 LRRM 2465 (1st Cir., 1988), cert. denied, 493 U.S. 810, 132 LRRM 2623 (1989).

[60]Id. at 34 (Acosta, J., dissenting).

[61]Id. at 35.

[62]Id.

[63]Id. at 35 n.3, quoting Carroll, Through the Looking Glass, 186–87 (Signet Classics, 1960).

[64]See Berger, "Judicial Review of Labor Arbitration Awards Practices, Policies and Sanctions," 10 Hofstra Lab. L.J. 245, nn.130 & 152 (1992).

are cases in which this is an exclusive or contributing theory in analyzing the enforceability of the award.[65] Since *Misco*,[66] however, those courts that have relied on public policy to reject labor arbitration awards have been careful to delineate the source of the public policy on which they rely. They refer to statutes and regulations to support the existence of the public policy.[67] But the courts remain split as to how the public policy must relate to the arbitration award.[68] For some, the award itself must violate public policy,[69] a standard unlikely to be met since statutes and regulations do not typically address the specific issues labor arbitrators confront. Other courts, however, are satisfied if the public policy simply relates to the arbitrator's award, even if there is no direct conflict.[70]

The panel and en banc rulings of the Ninth Circuit Court of Appeals in *Stead Motors*[71] illustrate the two positions. The Ninth Circuit panel refused to enforce an arbitrator's award reinstating an auto mechanic who had failed to properly tighten the lug nuts on the

[65]After the Supreme Court confirmed the validity of the public policy rationale for vacating arbitration awards in W. R. Grace & Co. v. Rubber Workers Local 759, 461 U.S. 757, 113 LRRM 2641 (1983), a number of appellate courts took advantage of the opportunity to reverse labor arbitrator decisions. E.g., United States Postal Serv. v. Letter Carriers, 810 F.2d 1239, 124 LRRM 2644 (D.C. Cir., 1987), cert. dismissed, 485 U.S. 680, 128 LRRM 2144 (1988); United States Postal Serv. v. Postal Workers, 736 F.2d 822, 116 LRRM 2870 (1st Cir., 1984); Meat Cutters Local 540 v. Great W. Food Co., 712 F.2d 122, 114 LRRM 2001 (5th Cir., 1983). Ultimately, the Court tightened the standards in *Misco* by requiring that the public policy be clearly articulated in law before it could be used to vacate an award. There remains strong support for the position that public policy reversal is only justified where the arbitrator's award would violate a statute, regulation, or other form of positive law. Edwards, "Judicial Review of Labor Arbitration Awards: The Clash Between the Public Policy Exception and the Duty to Bargain," 64 Chi.-Kent L. Rev. 3 (1988).

[66]See discussion of Paperworkers v. Misco, Inc., 484 U.S. 29, 126 LRRM 3113 (1987), at supra notes 32–39.

[67]E.g., Newsday, Inc. v. Long Island Typographical Union Local 915, 915 F.2d 840, 135 LRRM 2659 (2d Cir., 1990), cert. denied, 499 U.S. 922, 136 LRRM 2720 (1991); Delta Air Lines, Inc. v. Air Line Pilots, 861 F.2d 665, 130 LRRM 2014 (11th Cir., 1988), cert. denied, 110 S.Ct. 201, 132 LRRM 2623 (1989); Iowa Elec. Light & Power Co. v. Electrical Workers (IBEW) Local 204, 834 F.2d 1424, 127 LRRM 2049 (8th Cir., 1987).

[68]See, e.g., Interstate Brands Corp. v. Teamsters Local 135, 909 F.2d 885, 135 LRRM 2006 (6th Cir., 1990), cert. denied, 499 U.S. 905, 136 LRRM 2648 (1991); Stead Motors of Walnut Creek v. Machinists Lodge 1173, 886 F.2d 1200, 132 LRRM 2689 (9th Cir., 1989). But see Newsday, Inc. v. Long Island Typographical Union Local 915, 915 F.2d 840, 135 LRRM 2659 (2d Cir., 1990), cert. denied, 499 U.S. 922, 136 LRRM 2720 (1991); Delta Air Lines, Inc. v. Air Line Pilots, 861 F.2d 665, 130 LRRM 2014 (11th Cir., 1988), cert. denied, 110 S.Ct. 201, 132 LRRM 2623 (1989).

[69]E.g., Interstate Brands Corp. v. Teamsters Local 135, 909 F.2d 885, 135 LRRM 2006 (6th Cir., 1990), cert. denied, 499 U.S. 905, 136 LRRM 2648 (1991); Stead Motors of Walnut Creek v. Machinists Lodge 1173, 886 F.2d 1200, 132 LRRM 2689 (9th Cir., 1989); United States Postal Serv. v. Letter Carriers, 839 F.2d 146, 127 LRRM 2593 (3d Cir., 1988).

[70]E.g., Newsday, Inc. v. Long Island Typographical Union Local 915, 915 F.2d 840, 135 LRRM 2659 (2d Cir., 1990), cert. denied, 499 U.S. 922, 136 LRRM 2720 (1991); Iowa Elec. Light & Power Co. v. Electrical Workers (IBEW) Local 204, 834 F.2d 1424, 127 LRRM 2049 (8th Cir., 1987).

[71]Stead Motors of Walnut Creek v. Machinists Lodge 1173, 886 F.2d 1200, 132 LRRM 2689 (9th Cir., 1989) (the panel decision is reported at Stead Motors of Walnut Creek v. Machinists Lodge 1173, 843 F.2d 357, 127 LRRM 3213 (9th Cir., 1988)).

wheel of a car. The mechanic had previously been involved in a similar incident. He also ignored clear instructions from his supervisor on how to tighten lug nuts. The panel found the award to violate California public policies in favor of the operation of safe vehicles on the roads as well as safety requirements implicit in state licensing of auto repair businesses. The Ninth Circuit sitting en banc reversed the panel, however, because it could find no specific public policy violated by the arbitrator's reinstatement award. The Ninth Circuit found that even if California had a public policy requiring all vehicles operated on public roads to be in a safe condition, reinstating a mechanic who was discharged for releasing a vehicle in an unsafe condition did not contravene any explicit part of that policy.

Public policy has been at issue in a number of cases involving reinstatement of employees who engaged in unsafe acts. The Eighth Circuit Court of Appeals, for example, dealt with a nuclear power plant employee who had been fired for safety violations but was later reinstated by an arbitrator because of lax company training procedures.[72] The court found that the extensive safety regulations governing the nuclear power industry presented a well-defined and dominant public policy that the reinstatement award offended. In contrast, the District of Columbia Court of Appeals refused to overturn an arbitration award that reinstated a pilot found to have flown under the influence of alcohol, where the award was conditioned on the pilot's recertification by the Federal Aviation Administration.[73]

Some recent decisions indicate that use of the public policy theory may be expanding. One court vacated an award reinstating an employee found to have engaged in sexual harassment because of its view of the strong public policy against sexual harassment.[74] Another court vacated an award in a sexual harassment case because the arbitrator did not address the sexual harassment issue.[75] The arbitrator ruled that the company violated its contractual obligation to investigate the facts before terminating an employee. Because he found that the company violated the employee's contractual due process rights, the arbitrator did not consider the question of whether any sexual harassment took place. The Third Circuit vacated the award on the grounds that the public policy against sexual harassment required the arbitrator to decide whether sexual harassment occurred, despite a dispositive procedural issue. These cases go beyond

---

[72]Iowa Elec. Light & Power Co. v. Electrical Workers (IBEW) Local 204, 834 F.2d 1424, 127 LRRM 2049 (8th Cir., 1987).

[73]Northwest Airlines v. Air Line Pilots, 808 F.2d 76, 124 LRRM 2300 (D.C. Cir., 1987). A contrary decision involving a pilot reinstated following his discharge for flying under the influence of alcohol was reached in Delta Air Lines, Inc. v. Air Line Pilots, 861 F.2d 665, 130 LRRM 2014 (11th Cir., 1988), cert. denied, 110 S.Ct. 201, 132 LRRM 2623 (1989).

[74] Newsday, Inc. v. Long Island Typographical Union Local 915, 915 F.2d 840, 135 LRRM 2659 (2d Cir., 1990), cert. denied, 499 U.S. 922, 136 LRRM 2720 (1991).

[75]Stroehmann Bakeries, Inc. v. Teamsters Local 776, 762 F.Supp. 1187, 136 LRRM 2874 (M.D. Pa., 1991), aff'd, 969 F.2d 1436, 140 LRRM 2625 (3d Cir., 1992).

safety risks, relying upon the public policy against sexual harassment contained in antidiscrimination laws. Although there is no explicit legal barrier to reinstating employees who have been accused of, or have engaged in, sexual harassment, courts concluded that interference with the arbitration process is nevertheless permissible because of "public policy."

### E. Procedural Grounds for Denying Enforcement: Arbitrator and Party Misconduct and Defects in Proceedings

Courts will not enforce awards procured through fraud or corruption, or awards rendered as a result of the "evident partiality" of the arbitrator. The party asserting one of these defenses, however, must establish facts that demonstrate that fraud, corruption, or partiality influenced the outcome of the arbitration. The mere appearance of fraud is not sufficient to vacate an award. The protesting party must present verifiable facts to support the allegation of fraud, by identifying witnesses, presenting affidavits, or producing other documentation that supports the claim.[76]

Even if fraud is established, a nexus must be demonstrated between the fraud and the decision before it can serve as the basis for a reversal.[77] In a case arising out of Section 3, Subsection 1(q) of the Railway Labor Act, a discharged employee sought judicial review of the National Railway Adjustment Board's (NRAB) summary rejection of his claim for wrongful termination in violation of the collective bargaining agreement. The employee argued that the NRAB's findings and order were a product of fraud or corruption.[78] The complaint alleged that a management member of the employer who served on the NRAB panel had deliberately misrepresented facts to the board by knowingly providing them with false information, which was used as the basis for the board's decision to abolish the employee's job. On appeal, the Fifth Circuit found that these allegations fell within the ambit of Section 3 of the Railway Labor Act, which provides for judicial review of an NRAB order that is the product of fraud or corruption by a member of the division responsible for the order. Accordingly,

---

[76]In upholding a foreign arbitration award against challenges of fraud, a district court stated that even where the opposing party purposefully withheld evidence from the arbitration panel—which likely affected the outcome of the arbitration—the protesting party was not entitled to invoke fraud as a defense where it was aware of the pendency of arbitration proceedings and opted not to attend and present evidence of the contested agreement itself. Failure of the foreign corporation to prove the case for an absent party does not constitute fraud. Biotronik Messund Therapiegeraete GmbH & Co. v. Medford Med. Instrument Co., 415 F.Supp. 133 (D.N.J., 1976).

[77]A.G. Edwards & Sons, Inc. v. McCullough, 764 F.Supp. 1365 (D. Ariz., 1991); Forsythe Int'l v. Gibbs Oil Co., 915 F.2d 1017 (5th Cir., 1990).

[78]Hayes v. Western Weighting & Inspection Bureau, 838 F.2d 1434, 127 LRRM 3000 (5th Cir., 1988).

the lower court's dismissal was vacated, and the case was remanded for further proceedings on the threshold issue of fraud or corruption. A claim of impropriety on the part of an arbitrator demonstrating "evident partiality" carries a heavy burden of proof. In order to have an award vacated due to arbitrator partiality, the complaining party must establish that the arbitrator had a personal interest in the proceedings that biased her judgment[79] or that she engaged in ex parte contacts that tainted the decision.[80] Such conflicts of interest may arise out of business associations or personal affiliations that lead a party to reasonably believe the arbitrator incapable of rendering an impartial decision. Again, as in cases alleging fraud, the mere appearance of impropriety, in the absence of specific facts indicating improper motive, is insufficient grounds for vacating an award.[81]

The standard for determining whether the arbitrator was biased turns on whether a reasonable person would conclude that the arbitrator was partial to the opposing party.[82] This determination should be made after considering the "totality of circumstances" surrounding the alleged bias, including peculiar commercial practices in a geographic area, the arbitrator's financial interest in the arbitration, the nature of the relationship between the arbitrator and the purported favored party, and whether any such relationship existed during the arbitration process.[83] Arbitrators have an obligation to disclose affiliations or dealings with a party to the arbitration that might create the appearance of potential bias.[84] Failure to make the requisite disclosure may be viewed as an indication of "evident partiality" by the courts.

Circumstances in which "evident partiality" has been found are varied and depend upon the specific facts and surrounding environment of the case. They include arbitration proceedings where an undisclosed father-son relationship existed between the arbitrator and an officer of the union with which the complaining party was affiliated,[85] where the arbitrator had ex parte meetings with a party to discuss defenses and potential documentary evidence prior to the

---

[79]Austin South I. Ltd. v. Barton-Malow Co., 799 F.Supp. 1135 (M.D. Fla., 1992).

[80]M&A Elec. Power Coop. v. Electrical Workers (IBEW) Local 702, 977 F.2d 1235, 141 LRRM 2512 (8th Cir., 1992); Metropolitan Property & Cas. Ins. Co. v. J.C. Penney Cas. Ins. Co., 780 F.Supp. 885 (D. Conn., 1991).

[81]Sheet Metal Workers Local 420 v. Kinney Air Conditioning Co., 756 F.2d 742, 118 LRRM 3398 (9th Cir., 1985).

[82] C.T. Shipping, Ltd. v. DMI (U.S.A.) Ltd., 774 F.Supp. 146 (S.D.N.Y. 1991); Apperson v. Fleet Carrier Corp., 879 F.2d 1344, 131 LRRM 3079 (6th Cir., 1989), cert. denied, 110 S.Ct. 2206 (1990).

[83]United States v. Teamsters, 814 F.Supp. 1165, 143 LRRM 2890 (S.D.N.Y., 1993); Pompano-Windy City Partners, Ltd. v. Bear Stearns & Co., 794 F.Supp. 1265 (S.D.N.Y., 1992).

[84]Graphic Arts v. Haddon Craftsmen, Inc., 489 F.Supp. 1088 (D.C. Pa., 1979); Sanko S.S. Co. v. Cook Indus., Inc., 495 F.2d 1260 (2d Cir., 1973).

[85]Morelite Constr. Corp. v. New York City Dist. Council Carpenters Benefit Fund, 748 F.2d 79, 117 LRRM 3009 (2d Cir., 1984).

selection of an arbitration panel,[86] and where the chairman of the arbitration panel was personally involved in separate, ongoing proceedings that involved a party to the dispute.[87]

Despite these examples, relationships or situations that may cause suspicion about the arbitrator's partiality do not result in vacation of an award if the fundamental fairness of the proceeding is not impaired.[88] Ongoing or prior associations lacking a reasonable relationship to the case at issue, or circumstances that may arise during the pendency of the proceedings that do not impact the outcome of the arbitration, do not require disqualification of the arbitrator if he had no financial interest in the outcome.[89] When an arbitrator satisfies the obligation to disclose any circumstances likely to create a presumption of bias, the award cannot be set aside on grounds of impropriety.[90] Likewise, where a party to the dispute is aware of a potentially prejudicial relationship between the arbitrator and the opposing party and does not raise an objection during the course of the proceedings, the party waives the right to assert the defense later. [91]

Arbitrator misconduct encompasses due process violations, or other procedural deprivations, rather than the type of fraud, corruption, or partiality discussed above. At its core, the prohibition against arbitrator misconduct is designed to ensure that a fundamentally fair hearing is made available to all parties.[92] For example, either party may, from time to time, request a postponement or an adjournment of a hearing, and the arbitrator is responsible for deciding whether to grant such a request. The arbitrator's decision on the matter, if manifestly unfair or prejudicial to one party, may amount to misconduct. Arbitrators, however, are afforded reasonable discretion in such matters. Thus, for example, where an arbitrator refuses to grant a discharged employee an adjournment after previous adjournments have been granted, there is no misconduct.[93]

---

[86]Metropolitan Property & Cas. Ins. Co. v. J.C. Penney Cas. Ins. Co., 780 F.Supp. 885 (D. Conn., 1991).

[87]Sun Ref. & Mktg. Co. v. Statheros Shipping Corp. of Monrovia, Liberia, 761 F.Supp. 293 (S.D.N.Y.), aff'd, 948 F.2d 1277 (2d Cir., 1991).

[88]Amerada Hess Corp. v. Federal Labor Union Local 22026, 385 F.Supp. 279, 87 LRRM 2698 (D.N.J., 1974).

[89]Peoples Sec. Life Ins. Co. v. Monumental Life Ins. Co., 991 F.2d 141 (4th Cir., 1993); Trustees of Pressmen Local 72 Indus. Pension Fund v. Judd & Detweiler, Inc., 736 F.Supp. 1351 (D.Md., 1988); Merit Ins. Co. v. Leatherby Ins. Co., 714 F.2d 673 (7th Cir.), cert. denied, 104 S.Ct. 529 (1983), mandate amended, 728 F.2d 943 (2d Cir., 1984); International Produce, Inc. v. A/S Rosshavet, 638 F.2d 548 (2d Cir.), cert. denied, 101 S.Ct. 3006 (1981).

[90]Reed & Marin, Inc. v. Westinghouse Elec. Corp., 439 F.2d 1268, 1275 (2d Cir., 1971).

[91]UCO Terminals, Inc. v. Apex Oil Co., 583 F.Supp. 1213 (S.D.N.Y.), aff'd, 751 F.2d 371 (2d Cir., 1984); Cook Indus., Inc. v. C. Itoh & Co. (Am.) Inc., 449 F.2d 106 (2d Cir., 1971), cert. denied, 92 S.Ct. 957 (1972).

[92]A fundamentally fair arbitration hearing need not follow the rules established for judicial proceedings. Roche v. Service Employees Local 32B-32J, 755 F.Supp. 622, 624, 140 LRRM 3056 (S.D.N.Y., 1991), quoting Bell Aerospace Co. Div. v. Auto Workers Local 516, 500 F.2d 921, 923, 86 LRRM 3240 (2d Cir., 1974).

[93]Id.

An arbitrator's decision on procedural matters may at times be found to have been faulty, but that does not automatically mean the misconduct warrants reversal. The misconduct must be scrutinized to determine whether it tainted the outcome of the arbitration. The burden is on the moving party to prove that the award, as issued, was tainted as a result of the alleged misconduct. For example, in upholding an award over a claim of procedural misconduct by the arbitrator, the Eighth Circuit Court of Appeals stated:

> We agree with the district court that the arbitrator acted improperly in consulting with the International Officer of the Operating Engineers Union. Arbitrators must meticulously refrain from such outside-the-record consultations if the arbitration process is to continue to be respected and used by labor and management. Nevertheless, we are convinced, as was the district court, that the post-hearing consultation did not taint the arbitrator's decision.[94]

Some arbitration agreements provide for time limits within which the arbitrator must issue an award. Some also provide that the parties may extend the time limits by mutual agreement. Inclusion of these types of provisions raises a question as to whether an arbitrator's unconsented delay in issuing his award prejudices one of the parties sufficiently to warrant vacation of the award on the grounds of arbitrator misconduct. The dilemma faced by the parties to an arbitration in such a case is whether to object to the delay as it occurs, not knowing which party the ultimate award will favor, or to wait until the award is issued and then object only if the award is unfavorable. Courts have not been receptive to the complaints of those who choose to wait to object until they receive an adverse award. In an employee discharge case where the arbitrator waited 44 days to issue the award in favor of the employee, in lieu of the 3 days stipulated in the contract, the Fifth Circuit held:

> To hold that the company could wait 44 days without protesting the failure of the arbitrator to render his decision and then, when the adverse award was handed down to allow the company to attack it on these grounds would run counter to the express federal labor policy in favor of encouraging arbitration. Moreover, we would be extremely loath to penalize the beneficiary of the award because of the lapse of time over which he had no possible control.[95]

---

[94]M&A Elec. Power Coop. v. Electrical Workers (IBEW) Local 702, 977 F.2d 1235, 1237, 141 LRRM 2512 (8th Cir., 1992) (footnote omitted).

[95]Machinists Lodge 725 v. Mooney Aircraft, Inc., 410 F.2d 681, 683, 71 LRRM 2121 (5th Cir., 1969). See also Nagle v. John Hancock Mut. Life Ins. Co., 767 F.Supp. 67 (S.D.N.Y., 1991) (arbitration agreement provided that if the award was not timely rendered, either party could demand in writing that the award be issued within 10 days and could terminate the arbitration if the demand was not met; however, as the petitioner never complied with these provisions, the court denied the motion to vacate).

A motion to vacate due to arbitrator delay may be filed, only after submission of a timely written protest to the arbitrator, prior to the issuance of an award.


# IV. Statute of Limitations for Confirming and Vacating Arbitration Awards

Section 301 of the Labor Management Relations Act (LMRA) provides for federal jurisdiction over suits for violation of contracts between an employer and a labor organization,[96] but it does not establish a statute of limitations for such actions. The general rule where Congress fails to provide a statute of limitations is for the court to borrow the most suitable limitations period from state law.[97] State limitations may on occasion be "unsatisfactory vehicles for the enforcement of federal law."[98] This means identifying whether a statute of limitations should be borrowed from state or federal law to govern these actions, and which law within the state or federal framework should be relied on to supply that limitations period.


## A. *Limitations Period for Unfair Representation Actions Under LMRA Section 301*

In *Del Costello v. Teamsters,*[99] the Supreme Court ruled on the applicable statute of limitations under Section 301 of the LMRA for an unfair representation lawsuit brought by employees against their employers for breach of contract and against their unions for unfair representation. The Court found that in light of the unique "hybrid" nature of the suit, which included claims against the employer and union for substantially different wrongs, state law did not provide an analogous action from which a limitations period could be satisfactorily borrowed.

Consequently, the Court found it necessary to look to federal law to supply a limitations period. It chose the 6-month limitations period from Section 10(b) of the National Labor Relations Act (NLRA) as the most suitable because it was designed to accommodate a balance of interests very similar to those involved in the hybrid case under

---

[96]29 U.S.C. § 185(a).

[97]North Star Steel Co. v. Thomas, 63 USLW 4465 (1995); Reed v. Transportation Union, 488 U.S. 319, 323, 130 LRRM 2137 (1989); Auto Workers v. Hoosier Cardinal Corp., 86 S.Ct. 1107, 1112, 61 LRRM 2545 (1966).

[98]DelCostello v. Teamsters, 462 U.S. 151, 161, 113 LRRM 2737 (1983).

[99]Id.

consideration.[100] The *DelCostello* Court did not indicate what statute of limitations would apply to other types of actions under Section 301 that do not have the unique characteristics associated with hybrid cases involving claims of a breach of contract by the employer coupled with unfair representation by the union.

In an earlier decision, *Auto Workers v. Hoosier Cardinal Corp.*,[101] the Supreme Court considered the application of a statute of limitations to a straightforward Section 301 action claiming an employer's breach of a collective bargaining agreement. There was no clause in the agreement requiring the parties to submit their disputes to arbitration and the suit was brought by the union itself. In *Hoosier*, the Court held that Indiana's 6-year limitations period for actions on unwritten contracts governed the claim even though the effect was that there would be no uniform statute of limitations that would govern similar Section 301 actions in other judicial districts. The holding in *Hoosier* was reaffirmed by the Court in *DelCostello* and stands as proof that the Court does not intend federal law to govern the statute of limitations for all Section 301 actions.[102]

## B. Court of Appeals Decisions in Actions to Confirm and Vacate Arbitration Awards

While the circuit courts have followed *DelCostello* by strictly applying the 6-month statute of limitations from Section 10(b) of the NLRA to hybrid cases under Section 301,[103] every circuit has held that the *DelCostello* Court's use of the NLRA limitations period does not extend to cases to enforce or vacate arbitration awards arising under the same section. All of the circuits have distinguished the hybrid cases addressed by the *DelCostello* decision from straightforward actions to enforce or vacate arbitration awards.

All but two circuits have consistently borrowed a limitations period from an analogous state law in actions to enforce or vacate an award under Section 301, where an analogous state law statute of

---

[100]Id. at 171, quoting United Parcel Serv. v. Mitchell, 451 U.S. 56, 67–69, 70–71, 107 LRRM 2001 (1981), (Stewart, J., concurring in judgment). *Mitchell* held that state limitations law regarding vacation of arbitration awards should be applied to hybrid cases. The *DelCostello* Court distinguished *Mitchell* by noting that the union in that case had not appealed the arbitration panel's finding of a violation of the duty of fair representation; thus the only issue that reached the Court concerned the employee's § 301 breach-of-contract claim against his employer. 462 U.S. at 154 n.1.

[101]383 U.S. 696, 61 LRRM 2545 (1966).

[102]462 U.S. at 161–63.

[103]See, e.g., Barnett v. United Air Lines, Inc., 738 F.2d 358, 116 LRRM 2890 (10th Cir.), cert. denied, 469 U.S. 1087, 117 LRRM 3232 (1984); Perez v. Dana Corp., Parish Frame Div., 718 F.2d 581, 114 LRRM 2814 (3d Cir., 1983).

limitations has been available.[104] The reasoning given in these cases has been that the concerns that led to the Court's holding in *Del-Costello* are not relevant to actions to enforce or vacate an arbitration award. First, state law will almost always provide an analogous cause of action from which to borrow a limitations period in a Section 301 action to enforce or vacate an arbitration award.[105] Second, the relatively short limitations period for actions to vacate arbitration awards (usually between 30 and 90 days) is not at odds with the purpose of the federal statute to achieve finality of private settlements. Finally, as the parties to an action to enforce or vacate an arbitration award are generally the union and the employer, both of whom are knowledgeable and experienced in collective bargaining matters, as well as usually represented by legal counsel, the need for a longer limitations period to accommodate the inexperienced and unrepresented employee more often found in unfair representation cases such as *Del-Costello* is not present.[106]

The Sixth and Eleventh Circuits are the only circuits to express disagreement with the majority view that Section 301 actions to enforce or vacate arbitration awards should be governed by limitations periods borrowed from analogous state laws.[107] In *Occidental Chemical Corp. v. Chemical Workers,*[108] the Sixth Circuit was asked to determine which statute of limitations should govern an employee's action

---

[104]See, e.g., Burns Int'l Sec. Servs., Inc. v. Plant Guard Workers, 47 F.3d 14, 148 LRRM 2317 (2d Cir., 1994); Longshoremen (ILA) Local 953 v. Cataneo, Inc., 990 F.2d 794, 143 LRRM 2025 (4th Cir., 1993); Service Employees Local 36 v. City Cleaning Co., 982 F.2d 89, 142 LRRM 2158 (3d Cir., 1992); Harry Hoffman Printing, Inc. v. Graphic Communications Local 261, 912 F.2d 608, 135 LRRM 2774 (2d Cir., 1990); Electrical Workers (IBEW) Local 2 v. Anderson Underground Constr., Inc., 907 F.2d 74, 134 LRRM 2726 (8th Cir., 1990); Posadas de P.R. Assocs. v. Asociacion de Empleados de Casino de P.R., 873 F.2d 479, 131 LRRM 2223 (1st Cir., 1989); Operating Eng'rs Local 150 v. Centor Contractors, Inc., 831 F.2d 1309, 126 LRRM 2548 (7th Cir., 1987); Electrical Workers (IBEW) Local 969 v. Babcock & Wilcox, 826 F.2d 962, 126 LRRM 2482 (10th Cir., 1987); Plumbers' Pension Fund Local 130 v. Domas Mechanical Contractors, Inc., 778 F.2d 1266 (7th Cir., 1985); Carpenters Local 1020 v. FMC Corp., 724 F.2d 815, 115 LRRM 2582 (9th Cir., 1984); Electrical Workers (IUE) v. Ingram Mfg. Co., 715 F.2d 886, 114 LRRM 3083 (5th Cir., 1983), cert. denied, 466 U.S. 928, 115 LRRM 3416 (1984).

[105]But see Sheet Metal Workers Local 33 v. Power City Plumbing & Heating, 934 F.2d 557, 137 LRRM 2549 (4th Cir., 1991) (court borrowed 3-month limitations period from the Federal Arbitration Act to govern employer's motion to vacate the arbitrator's award because West Virginia did not have a limitations period covering actions to vacate arbitration awards); Occidental Chem. Corp. v. Chemical Workers, 853 F.2d 1310, 128 LRRM 3161 (6th Cir., 1988) (court borrowed 3-month limitations period from Federal Arbitration Act to govern employer's action to vacate arbitration award because Michigan's arbitration act specifically excluded labor contracts from its coverage).

[106]See Posadas de P.R. Assocs. v. Asociacion de Empleados de Casino de P.R., 873 F.2d 479, 131 LRRM 2223 (1st Cir., 1989) (applying Puerto Rico's judicially created 30-day time bar for vacating arbitration awards to actions under § 301 to vacate arbitration awards).

[107]But see Champion Int'l Corp. v. Paperworkers Local 371, 779 F.2d 328, 121 LRRM 2449 (6th Cir., 1985) (applying Tennessee's 90-day statute of limitations to employer's action to vacate arbitration award).

[108]853 F.2d 1310, 128 LRRM 3161 (6th Cir., 1988). The *Occidental Chem.* ruling was followed in Bacashihua v. United States Postal Serv., 859 F.2d 402, 129 LRRM 2620 (6th Cir., 1988).

to vacate an arbitrator's award and the union's attempts to enforce the award. The court looked to Michigan's statute for challenging arbitration decisions, but rejected application of its time bar because the statute explicitly excluded coverage of labor contracts.[109] It concluded that the 3-month statute of limitations in Section 12 of the FAA should govern the employer's action to vacate the arbitration award because it also advanced the policy of bringing about a quick resolution of labor disputes as intended under Section 301, as well as providing uniformity among nonhybrid Section 301 actions.

In *Postal Workers v. U.S. Postal Service,*[110] the Eleventh Circuit opted to depart from the course taken by most other circuits and to also apply the 3-month statute of limitations provided in the FAA to nonhybrid Section 301 actions to vacate or enforce arbitration awards. Since *Postal Workers* was decided in 1987, the Eleventh Circuit has applied a state statute of limitations to an action by a union to enforce an arbitration award under Section 301[111] and to a union's suit to compel arbitration of a dispute under Section 301.[112] But the Eleventh Circuit apparently continues to view actions to modify or vacate arbitration awards under Section 301 as controlled by the 3-month statute of limitations in Section 12 of the FAA.[113]

## V. The Role of Arbitration Precedents

Parties to a collective bargaining agreement may find themselves confronting a grievance that was the subject of a previous arbitration award between the same union and employer, and under the same labor contract. The party that prevailed in the earlier proceeding usually wants the prior ruling to control the disposition of the later case. Courts have taken various positions on the question of whether the prior award should be given res judicata status or treated with deference in the subsequent proceeding.

In *Westinghouse Elevators of Puerto Rico v. S.I.U. de Puerto Rico,*[114] the issue before the First Circuit was whether a subsequent arbitrator was bound by the decision in earlier arbitration over the same contractual provision between the same parties. The employer argued that the prior arbitration decision had become part of the contract between the parties because since the earlier decision was

---

[109]853 F.2d at 1315.

[110]823 F.2d 466, 475, 126 LRRM 2263 (11th Cir., 1987).

[111]Bakery, Confectionery & Tobacco Workers Local 362-T v. Brown & Williamson Tobacco Corp., 971 F.2d 652, 141 LRRM 2248 (11th Cir., 1992).

[112]Paperworkers Local 395 v. ITT Rayonier, Inc., 931 F.2d 832, 137 LRRM 2614 (11th Cir., 1991).

[113]Supra note 111.

[114]583 F.2d 1184, 99 LRRM 2651 (1st Cir., 1978).

rendered, the identical language had been adopted in all successive contracts. The employer insisted that the second arbitrator had "no authority to change the terms of the contract by rendering an entirely different interpretation" of the identical contract language.[115]

The First Circuit rejected the employer's theory of incorporation into the contract, observing:

> Unless the Parties agree otherwise in their contract, an arbitrator's award rendered in a prior arbitration proceeding—even between the same parties—does not stop either party from raising the same issue in a subsequent arbitration; nor does it bar the arbitrator from determining the same or similar issue anew. The arbitrator may consider prior awards between the same parties or between other parties if offered in the proceeding before him, but he is not bound to follow them.[116]

The First Court concluded that the second arbitrator did not exceed his authority in reaching a different interpretation of the disputed contract language and held that an arbitration award is not subject to judicial review simply because it reaches a result directly contrary to a previous arbitration award covering the same collective bargaining provisions.

The U.S. Supreme Court considered the same question in *W.R. Grace & Co. v. Rubber Workers Local 759*,[117] holding that where the arbitrator's award "draws its essence from the collective bargaining agreement," and is a reasonable interpretation of its meaning, it is not invalid simply because it reaches a different conclusion than a prior arbitration award, even where the prior award involved the same parties and the same contractual issues.[118] Other jurisdictions have followed this rule in numerous subsequent decisions.[119]

Additional support for the proposition that arbitrators are not bound by principles of stare decisis is found in the Code of Professional Responsibility for Arbitrators. Under the heading "Reliance by an Arbitrator on Other Arbitration Awards or on Independent Research," the Code states:

> 1. An arbitrator must assume full personal responsibility for the decision in each case decided.
>
>    a. The extent, if any, to which an arbitrator properly may rely on precedent, on guidance of other awards, or on independent research is dependent primarily on the policies of the parties

---

[115]Id. at 1186.

[116]Id. at 1187, quoting Federal Bearings Co., Inc., 22 LA 721, 725–27 (Justin, 1954).

[117]461 U.S. 757, 113 LRRM 2641 (1983).

[118]Id. at 764–66.

[119]See, e.g., Laborers Local 504 v. Roadmaster Corp., 916 F.2d 1161, 135 LRRM 2831 (7th Cir., 1990); Trailways Lines, Inc. v. Trailways, Inc. Joint Council, 817 F.2d 1333, 125 LRRM 2364 (8th Cir. 1987); McGraw Edison v. Electrical Workers (IUE) Local 1104, 767 F.2d

on these matters, as expressed in the contract, or other agreement, or at the hearing.

b. When the mutual desires of the parties are not known or when the parties express differing opinions or policies, the arbitrator may exercise discretion as to these matters, consistent with acceptance of full responsibility for the award.[120]

Nothing in this passage implies that an arbitrator is bound by poor decisions. At most, it authorizes arbitrators to exercise independent discretion concerning the use of precedents where the parties have not mutually agreed to the contrary. Numerous other labor authorities have also reached the conclusion that arbitrators are not bound by principles of stare decisis.[121]

While there are abundant authorities stating that arbitration decisions do not carry the binding force of judicial precedent, there are also a number of authorities espousing the view that prior arbitration decisions *should* be given deference where the parties are the same; no substantial change has occurred in the facts, circumstances, or the contract language; and the parties have renegotiated their contract and made no relevant changes since the prior award was rendered.[122] Indeed, a survey of labor arbitrators revealed that 77 percent of the 238 polled believed that precedents should be given some weight, even those decided under other contracts.[123] Some of the reasons given for deferring to prior arbitration awards include: (1) a preference for consistency so that parties can predict how similar disputes will be resolved in the future, (2) reliance on the authority of prior awards, (3) ensuring accountability of arbitrators, (4) deference to the reasoning and principles enunciated by respected arbitrators previously faced with the same or similar issue, and (5) the fact

---

485, 119 LRRM 3403 (8th Cir., 1985); Electrical Workers (IBEW) Local 199 v. United Tel. Co. of Fla., 738 F.2d 1564, 117 LRRM 2094 (11th Cir., 1984); Wyman-Gordon Co. v. Steelworkers, 613 F.Supp. 626 (N.D. Ill., 1985). *Trailways Lines,* however, suggested that the second arbitrator should consider the first award and explain its inapplicability.

[120]Code of Professional Responsibility for Arbitrators of Labor Management Disputes, ch. 2, §G (May 30, 1996).

[121]See, e.g., McQuay-Perfex, Inc., 93 LA 865 (Bard, 1989); Wright Air Force Base, 24 FLRA 875 (1986); Madison Mut. Ins. Co., 81 LA 519 (Mangeot, 1983). But cf. Southeastern Pa. Transp. Auth., 100 LA 767 (Goulet, 1992) (holding second arbitrator bound by award of the first where dispute involved same parties, same contract, same issue, and same cause of action); City of N. Miami, 88 LA 815 (Bressler, 1987) (recognizing no distinction between application of principles of res judicata or stare decisis in arbitration versus judicial proceedings); Hotel & Restaurant Employees Local 226, 281 NLRB 284, 124 LRRM 1142 (1986) (union was ordered to supply unreported arbitration decisions involving employer/members to complainant Nevada Resort Association (NRA) because of the recognized practice of NRA/union panel arbitrators to consider themselves bound by stare decisis); North Star Steel Co., 87 LA 40 (Miller, 1986) (making no distinction between application of principles of stare decisis or res judicata in judicial versus arbitral decisions). See generally Heinsz, "Grieve it Again: Of Stare Decisis, Res Judicata and Collateral Estoppel in Labor Arbitration," 38 B.C. L. Rev. 275 (1997).

[122]For additional discussion of this topic, see Chapter 11.

[123]Volz & Goggin, eds., Elkouri & Elkouri, How Arbitration Works, 5th ed., 605 (BNA Books, 1997).

that many disputes may be disposed of before arbitration if parties agree on the authoritative weight to be accorded to precedential decisions.

On the other hand, there are certain drawbacks associated with blind, unthinking deference to prior arbitration awards. Some of the pitfalls of excessive or unwarranted deference include the repetition of reasoning or contract construction that was faulty the first time it was applied, and the inflexible application of a decision that, though appropriate under the facts of the prior dispute, is not sound in light of the circumstances involved in the later dispute.

It is common practice for the parties to an arbitration to cite and provide copies of prior arbitration awards to the arbitrator for guidance. It is generally thought that the arbitrator should consider these decisions and accord them appropriate weight based on factors such as whether they were decided under the same contract provisions and between the same parties and whether the contract has been renegotiated since the prior award with no relevant change in language.[124] On the other hand, deference would not be warranted where (1) the earlier arbitrator exceeded his or her authority; (2) the reasoning in the earlier decision was obviously faulty or biased; (3) the earlier arbitrator did not have, or refused to hear, relevant evidence available in the later arbitration; (4) the earlier decision is itself in conflict with other award(s); or (5) the issue is affected by contract language or some other factor that has changed in the interim.[125] Numerous arbitrators have followed these general standards.[126]

The consensus of the arbitrator community is that while prior arbitration decisions are not technically binding, decisions of prior arbitrators interpreting the same contract language between the same parties should be given considerable weight and should be followed absent a substantial change in facts, circumstances, or contract language warranting different treatment of the later dispute. This is the favored approach, with variance justified only in narrow circumstances. As one arbitrator observed:

> The arbitration process would hardly survive the erosion of confidence in its effectiveness were second thought arbitrators freely to set aside first impression arbitral awards so that awards would lose their acceptability as being final and binding. It is not surprising, therefore, that it is unusual, indeed rare, for a later arbitrator to find the earlier

---

[124]Monarch Tile, 101 LA 585 (Hooper, 1993).

[125]Id.

[126]See, e.g., Connecticut Light & Power v. Electrical Workers (IBEW) Local 420, 718 F.2d 14, 114 LRRM 2770 (2d Cir., 1983) (prior award not followed because "analytically unsound"); McQuay-Perfex, Inc., 93 LA 865 (Bard, 1989) (arbitrator not bound by prior award because of prior arbitrator's clear error in interpreting an earlier decision); North Star Steel Co., 87 LA 40 (Miller, 1986) (prior award not followed because different issues were presented); Madison Mut. Ins. Co., 81 LA 519 (Mangeot, 1983) (prior arbitration award not followed because facts were substantially different).

award not final and binding. Even so, however, there do arise circumstances in which the occasion seems compelling to the later arbitrator to disregard or modify the earlier award. After all, it is the integrity and intelligence of each arbitrator that are commissioned by the disputants who jointly select each to make his or her own appraisal and decision.[127]

# VI.  Deferral to Arbitration

In some circumstances, actions taken by an employer may constitute both breaches of a labor contract subject to arbitration and an unfair labor practice violating the National Labor Relations Act. In response to this problem, the National Labor Relations Board (NLRB) has developed a policy of accommodating the duplicate jurisdiction by requiring in many instances that the parties utilize available arbitration procedures instead of invoking the statute's unfair labor practice machinery. Moreover, once an arbitrator has issued a ruling, the Board will defer to the arbitrator's decision if certain criteria are met. This process can be significant in cases where an employee maintains that his or her discipline or discharge violates one of the provisions of Section 8(a) of the National Labor Relations Act.[128]

In response to the argument that the Board's jurisdiction over unfair labor practices bars consideration of a parallel labor contract claim in another forum, the Supreme Court specifically held that the Board's jurisdiction is not exclusive when issues relating to the interpretation of a labor agreement arise.[129] Subsequently, in a case involving a labor contract dispute that also could be characterized as a representational or jurisdictional question under the National Labor Relations Act, the Supreme Court held that the arbitrator could nevertheless proceed to consider whether there had been a collective bargaining agreement violation.[130] In short, the Board's authority over unfair labor practices does not preempt an arbitrator's consideration of labor contract claims that raise parallel issues.

Despite the fact that the existence of an arbitrable contract grievance does not oust the NLRB of jurisdiction to rule on a parallel

---

[127]McQuay-Perfex Inc., 93 LA 865, 870–71 (Bard, 1989), quoting Todd Shipyards Corp., 16 LA 27, 28 (Jones, 1977).

[128]This may arise where it is claimed that discipline was imposed because of an employee's union activity in violation of §8 (a) (3) of the NLRA, or where discipline will interfere, restrain, or coerce the exercise of rights protected by §7, a result that is barred by §8 (a) (1) of the Act.

[129]Smith v. Evening News Ass'n, 371 U.S. 195, 51 LRRM 2646 (1962). The contract in question, however, had no arbitration clause.

[130]Carey v. Westinghouse Elec. Corp., 375 U.S. 261, 55 LRRM 2042 (1964). Arbitration was ordered even though only one of two unions involved in the dispute was to be a formal party to the proceeding. The Court noted that the arbitrator's ruling could end the dispute as a practical matter, but nevertheless recognized that any conflict between the arbitrator and the Board would require that the Board's ruling take precedence.

unfair labor practice charge, the Board has developed a policy of selective deference to the arbitration process. This includes deference to arbitration awards already issued, deference to an arbitration process already invoked, and perhaps most controversially, deference to the availability of an arbitration alternative the grieving party has chosen to avoid. In each instance, however, the Board has developed standards and criteria to govern the exercise of its discretion, so that in not all cases will the Board decline to exercise its jurisdiction. Moreover, in certain areas the Board has chosen not to defer to the arbitration process at all because of special considerations.

Although the Board initially refused to accept arbitrator decisions on matters subject to Board jurisdiction even where the arbitrator had ordered a discriminatorily discharged employee to be reinstated,[131] it reversed itself in *Spielberg Manufacturing Co.*[132]

Specifically, the Board concluded that before deference can be given to an arbitration award already rendered, the proceedings must have been fair and regular, all parties must have agreed to be bound, and the decision of the arbitrator must not have been repugnant to the purposes and policies of the Act. Subsequently, the Board added an additional standard requiring that the issue involved in the unfair labor practice case must have been presented to the arbitrator and considered in the arbitration decision and award.[133] However, under current law, it is sufficient for deference that the issues be factually parallel and that the relevant facts were presented to the arbitrator.[134]

## A. *Parallel Issues*

Initially, in cases where the unfair labor practice issue had been neither presented to nor considered by the arbitrator,[135] or where the arbitrator specifically declined to rule on the unfair labor practice issue,[136] the Board refused to defer to the arbitration award. The impact of this approach, however, was to give the parties the power to ensure Board consideration of their case by withholding the presentation of the unfair labor practice issue from the arbitrator. Therefore, the Board changed its position and held that absent unusual circumstances, such as both parties agreeing to exclude statutory issues or the arbitrator declining to consider them, deferral would be required where the labor contract and unfair labor practice issues were parallel.[137]

---

[131]See Rieke Metal Prods. Corp., 40 NLRB 867, 10 LRRM 82 (1942).

[132]112 NLRB 1080, 36 LRRM 1152 (1955).

[133]Raytheon Co., 140 NLRB 883, 52 LRRM 1129 (1963), set aside on other grounds, 326 F.2d 471, 55 LRRM 2101 (1st Cir., 1964).

[134]Olin Corp., 268 NLRB 573, 115 LRRM 1056 (1984).

[135]Ford Motor Co., 131 NLRB 1462, 48 LRRM 1280 (1961).

[136]Monsanto Chem. Co., 130 NLRB 1097, 47 LRRM 1451 (1961).

[137]Electronic Reproduction Serv. Corp., 213 NLRB 758, 87 LRRM 1211 (1974).

This broadened policy of deference to arbitration awards was reversed by the Board in 1980.[138] But in 1984, the Board returned to its policy of expanded deference in *Olin Corp.*[139] There the Board held that the requirement that the unfair labor practice issue be presented to and considered by the arbitrator would be deemed satisfied if the unfair labor practice and contractual issues were factually parallel and general facts relevant to resolving the unfair labor practice issue were presented to the arbitrator. The impact of the *Olin* decision is to eliminate the need for explicit consideration of statutory questions by the arbitrator as a precondition for deferral. Rather, it is sufficient that the arbitrator consider factual issues that would also be presented to the Board in an unfair labor practice proceeding. The party objecting to deferral has the burden of establishing that this did not occur.[140]

## B. *Fair and Regular Proceedings*

As a condition for deferral, the Board also requires that the arbitration be fair and regular. This ensures that minimum due process standards have been followed. This requirement is violated in cases where insufficient time has been given for preparation[141] or where rights of confrontation and cross-examination were denied.[142] Hostility and bias are also grounds for the Board to refuse deferral.[143]

## C. *The Parties' Agreement to Be Bound*

The *Spielberg* deferral standards require that the parties agreed to be bound by the arbitrator's ruling as a precondition for deferral. Where there has been such an agreement, the award possesses a sufficient degree of finality so that Board consideration of the merits of the unfair labor practice issue is not required. In the normal collective bargaining context, this requirement is not an obstacle, because the arbitration clause of the labor contract establishes the necessary mutual agreement for finality. If there is not a general arbitration clause

---

[138]Suburban Motor Freight, 247 NLRB 146, 103 LRRM 1113 (1980).

[139]268 NLRB 573, 115 LRRM 1056 (1984). *Olin* was followed in Anderson Sand & Gravel Co., 277 NLRB 1204, 121 LRRM 1069 (1985), and Reichhold Chems., 275 NLRB 1414, 120 LRRM 1037 (1985).

[140]268 NLRB at 574.

[141]Gateway Transp. Co., 137 NLRB 1763, 50 LRRM 1495 (1962).

[142]See Versi Craft Corp., 227 NLRB 877, 94 LRRM 1207 (1977); Honolulu Star-Bulletin, 123 NLRB 395, 43 LRRM 1449 (1959), enforcement denied on other grounds, 274 F.2d 567, 45 LRRM 2184 (D.C. Cir., 1959).

[143]See Russ Togs, Inc., 253 NLRB 767, 106 LRRM 1067 (1980); Brown Co., 243 NLRB 769, 101 LRRM 1608 (1979), aff'd in pertinent part, 663 F.2d 1978, 109 LRRM 2663 (9th Cir., 1981); Mason & Dixon Lines, 237 NLRB 6, 98 LRRM 1540 (1978).

in the parties' labor contract, the deferral standards require that the parties agree to accept the arbitrator's decision in the specific dispute. The agreement to be bound by the arbitrator's ruling applies to the employer and the labor union; there is no need for concurrence by individual grievants.[144]

## D. *Repugnancy to the Policies of the Act*

The Board reviews an arbitration award to determine whether it is repugnant to the policies of the Act. The Board has held that the "test of repugnancy under *Spielberg* is not whether the Board would have reached the same result as an arbitrator, but whether the arbitrator's award is palpably wrong as a matter of law."[145] The standard was reaffirmed in *Olin*, where the Board explained that the test focuses on whether the arbitrator's award was "susceptible to an interpretation consistent with the Act."[146]

Using this standard, the Board has refused to defer to arbitrator rulings that involve the waiver of rights under Section 7 of the Act,[147] and where the arbitrator's award upheld restrictions on the right of employees to seek access to NLRB procedures.[148] Cases since *Olin*, such as *United States Postal Service*,[149] indicate that deference will occur even if an arbitration award is not fully consistent with Board precedent.

## E. *Excluded Cases*

Although the Supreme Court has indicated it would support deferral in representation cases,[150] the Board has declined to defer to arbitration awards in representation cases.[151] A similar approach has been taken with arbitration awards involving violations of Section 8

---

[144]Great Scott Supermarkets, 206 NLRB 447, 84 LRRM 1563 (1973).

[145]Inland Steel Co., 263 NLRB 1091, 111 LRRM 1193 (1982) (footnote omitted).

[146]Olin Corp., 268 NLRB 573, 574, 115 LRRM 1056 (1984).

[147]Ford Motor Co., Rouge Complex, 233 NLRB 698, 96 LRRM 1513 (1977); but see Pincus Bros., Inc.—Maxwell, 237 NLRB 1063, 99 LRRM 1099 (1978), enforcement denied, 620 F.2d 367, 104 LRRM 2001 (3d Cir., 1980).

[148]E.g., Texaco, Inc., 233 NLRB 375, 96 LRRM 1534 (1977); Virginia-Carolina Freight Lines, 155 NLRB 447, 60 LRRM 1331 (1965).

[149]275 NLRB 430, 119 LRRM 1153 (1985). Awards not susceptible to an interpretation consistent with the Act will be denied enforcement. See Manitowoc Eng'g Co., 291 NLRB 915, 130 LRRM 1072 (1988).

[150]Carey v. Westinghouse Elec. Corp., 375 U.S. 261, 55 LRRM 2042 (1964).

[151]Commonwealth Gas Co., 218 NLRB 857, 89 LRRM 1613 (1975); Hershey Foods Corp., 208 NLRB 452, 85 LRRM 1312 (1974), enforced, 506 F.2d 1052, 90 LRRM 2890 (3d Cir., 1974).

(a) (2), which prohibits the unlawful domination of or assistance to a union.[152]

More significantly, in discharge and discipline arbitrations the Board has held that it will not defer to an award that involves an allegation of conduct violating Section 8 (a) (4) of the Act. That section bars discrimination against employees who have filed charges or given testimony pursuant to the Act. Thus, in order to protect the integrity of the Board's procedures, it has adopted a policy of not deferring in such cases.[153]

## F. Prearbitration Deferral

Although the Board had developed a policy of deferring to arbitration awards already rendered, the Board announced in *Collyer Insulated Wire*[154] that it would adopt a policy of deferring to an arbitration process not yet completed or invoked. *Collyer* itself involved application of the policy to a refusal-to-bargain charge under Section 8 (a) (5) of the Act. But in order to provide protection to the affected employees, jurisdiction was retained, to be exercised if the dispute was not settled or submitted to arbitration promptly, or if the *Spielberg* standards were not satisfied in any award ultimately issued.

Subsequently, discipline and discharge cases arising under Section 8 (a) (1) and (3) of the Act were included in the prearbitration deferral policy.[155] The Board relied upon "the reasonableness of the assumption that the arbitration procedure will resolve this dispute in a manner consistent with the standards of *Spielberg*."[156] The deferral policy assumes the arbitrator has sufficient remedial power to fashion a remedy that will also cover the parallel unfair labor practice charge.[157] However, the Board has held that a refusal to arbitrate or waive procedural defenses will preclude deferral.[158] Early on, the *Collyer* doctrine received approval from the appellate courts.[159] This support was recently reaffirmed by the District of Columbia Court of Appeals, which stated that the NLRA and the LMRA do not preclude the Board from requiring a claimant to exhaust contractual grievance

---

[152]Servair, Inc., 236 NLRB 1278, 99 LRRM 1259 (1978), enforced in part, 607 F.2d 258, 102 LRRM 2705 (9th Cir., 1979).

[153]Filmation Assocs., 227 NLRB 1721, 94 LRRM 1470 (1977).

[154]192 NLRB 837, 77 LRRM 1931 (1971).

[155]National Radio Co., 198 NLRB 527, 80 LRRM 1718 (1972).

[156]Id. at 531.

[157]Hoffman Air & Filtration Sys. Div., Clarkson Indus., 312 NLRB 349, 144 LRRM 1215 (1993).

[158]Tel Plus Long Island, 313 NLRB No. 47, 145 LRRM 1158 (1993).

[159]E.g., Enterprise Publ'g Co. v. NLRB, 493 F.2d 1024, 85 LRRM 2746 (1st Cir., 1974); Associated Press v. NLRB, 492 F.2d 662, 85 LRRM 2440 (D.C. Cir., 1974).

remedies before the Board hears a Section 8 (a) (3) discrimination claim. In its opinion the court observed:

> We also find that the Board's deferment policy is reasonable and is informed by a permissible construction of the Board's various statutory obligations, and that the Board's order in this case was wholly consistent with that policy.[160]

---

[160]Hammontree v. NLRB, 925 F.2d 1486, 1500, 136 LRRM 2478 (D.C. Cir., 1991).

# Table of Court Cases

*This table is alphabetized letter-by-letter (e.g., Northshore precedes North Star). References are to chapter and footnote number (e.g., **14:** 88 refers to footnote 88 in chapter 14).*

# G

Gardner v. Broderick, 392 U.S. 273 (1968) *5:* 203–04

Garrity v. New Jersey, 385 U.S. 493 (1967) *5:* 201–02

George A. Hormel & Co. v. Food & Commercial Workers Local 9, 879 F.2d 347, 131 LRRM 3018 (8th Cir. 1989) *14:* 55–58

Gibson v. Missouri Pac. R.R., 620 F. Supp. 85, 39 FEP Cases 369 (E.D. Ark. 1985) *13:* 96

Gilmer v. Interstate/Johnson Lane Corp., 500 U.S. 20, 55 FEP Cases 1116 (1991) *13:* 178, 184–86; *14:* 20

Glass & Pottery Workers
—v. Owens-Illinois, Inc., 758 F. Supp. 962, 136 LRRM 2397 (D.N.J. 1991) *14:* 40
—Local 182B v. Excelsior Foundry Co., 56 F.3d 844, 149 LRRM 2538 (7th Cir. 1995) *14:* 15–17

Golden State Bottling Co. v. NLRB, 414 U.S. 168, 84 LRRM 2839 (1973) *12:* 30

Goldman v. Weinberger, 106 S. Ct. 1310, 40 FEP Cases 543 (1986) *8:* 283

Golenia v. Bob Baker Toyota, 915 F. Supp. 201 (S.D. Cal. 1996) *13:* 185, 195

Government Employees (AFGE)
—v. Derwinski, 777 F. Supp. 1493 (N.D. Cal. 1991) *13:* 210–11
—v. Sullivan
— —744 F. Supp. 294 (D.D.C. 1990) *13:* 211
— —787 F. Supp. 255 (D.D.C. 1992) *13:* 210

Grand Rapids Die Casting Corp. v. Auto Workers Local 159, 684 F.2d 413, 111 LRRM 2137 (6th Cir. 1982) *14:* 14

Graphic Arts v. Haddon Craftsmen, Inc., 489 F. Supp. 1088 (D.C. Pa. 1979) *14:* 84

Great W. Mortgage Corp. v. Peacock, 110 F.3d 222, 73 FEP Cases 856 (3d Cir. 1997) *13:* 200

Griffith v. Keystone Steel & Wire Co., 858 F. Supp. 802, 66 FEP Cases 227 (C.D. Ill. 1984) *13:* 187–88

Griggs v. Duke Power Co., 401 U.S. 424, 3 FEP Cases 175 (1971) *13:* 69

Gulf Coast Indus. Workers v. Exxon Co., USA, 991 F.2d 244, 143 LRRM 2375 (5th Cir.), *cert. denied,* 114 S. Ct. 441, 144 LRRM 2680 (1993) *13:* 226

Gullett Gin Co.; NLRB v., 340 U.S. 361, 27 LRRM 2230 (1951) *12:* 91–92

# H

Hacienda Hotel; EEOC v., 881 F.2d 1504, 50 FEP Cases 877 (9th Cir. 1989) *13:* 78

Haig v. Everett, 8 Ark. App. 255, 650 S.W.2d 593 (1983) *13:* 75

Hall v. Gus Constr. Co., 842 F.2d 1010, 46 FEP Cases 573 (8th Cir. 1988) *13:* 28

Hammontree v. NLRB, 925 F.2d 1486, 136 LRRM 2478 (D.C. Cir. 1991) *14:* 160

Hanford Atomic Metal Trades Council v. General Elec. Co., 353 F.2d 302, 61 LRRM 2004 (9th Cir. 1965) *14:* 12

Harmon v. Thornburgh, 878 F.2d 484 (D.C. Cir. 1989), *cert. denied,* 110 S. Ct. 865 (1990) *13:* 210

Harris v. Forklift Systems, Inc., 114 S. Ct. 367, 63 FEP Cases 225 (1993) *13:* 33–35

Harrison v. Eddy Potash, Inc., 112 F.3d 1437, 156 LRRM 2033 (10th Cir. 1997) *13:* 194

Harry Hoffman Printing, Inc. v. Graphic Communications Local 261, 912 F.2d 608, 135 LRRM 2774 (2d Cir. 1990) *14:* 104

Hayes v. Western Weighting & Inspection Bureau, 838 F.2d 1434, 127 LRRM 3000 (5th Cir. 1988) *14:* 78

Hedstrom Co. v. NLRB, 629 F.2d 305, 105 LRRM 2183 (3d Cir. 1980) *12:* 31

Hershey Foods Corp., 208 NLRB 452, 85 LRRM 1312 (1974), *enforced,* 506 F.2d 1052, 90 LRRM 2890 (3d Cir. 1974) *14:* 151

Heurtebise v. Reliable Bus. Computers, Inc., 452 Mich. 405, 550 N.W.2d 243 (1996) *13:* 198

Hicks v. Gates Rubber Co., 833 F.2d 1406, 45 FEP Cases 608 (10th Cir. 1987), *appeal after remand,* 928 F.2d 966, 59 FEP Cases 1787 (10th Cir. 1991) *13:* 28

Hoffman v. Aaron Kamhi Inc., 927 F. Supp. 640 (S.D.N.Y. 1996) *13:* 196

Honolulu Star-Bulletin, 123 NLRB 395, 43 LRRM 1449 (1959), *enforcement denied,* 274 F.2d 567, 45 LRRM 2184 (D.C. Cir. 1959) *14:* 142

Hoska v. Department of Army, 677 F.2d 131 (D.C. Cir. 1982) *9:* 75

Hotel & Restaurant Employees Local 878 v. Cullop, 146 LRRM 3086 (D. Alaska 1994) *14:* 10

Hudson v. Western Airlines, Inc., 851 F.2d 261, 47 FEP Cases 295 (9th Cir. 1988) *13:* 91

Ohio Edison Co. v. Ohio Joint Council, 947 F.2d 786, 138 LRRM 2823 (6th Cir. 1991)  *6:* 240

O'Neil v. Hilton Head Hosp., 115 F.3d 272 (4th Cir. 1977)  *13:* 161

Operating Eng'rs Local 150 v. Centor Contractors, Inc., 831 F.2d 1309, 126 LRRM 2548 (7th Cir. 1987)  *14:* 104

# P

Paperworkers
—v. Gaylord Container Corp., 755 F. Supp. 158, 136 LRRM 2570 (E.D. La. 1991)  *14:* 40
—Local 395 v. ITT Rayonier, Inc., 931 F.2d 832, 137 LRRM 2614 (11th Cir. 1991)  *14:* 112

Patterson
—v. McLean Credit Union, 491 U.S. 164, 49 FEP Cases 1814 (1989)  *13:* 240
—v. Tenet Healthcare, 113 F.3d 832, 73 FEP Cases 1822 (8th Cir. 1997)  *13:* 199

Pechacek v. Minnesota State Lottery, 497 N.W.2d 243 (Minn. 1993)  *9:* 63–64

Pence v. Rosenquist, 573 F.2d 395 (7th Cir. 1978)  *8:* 279

Peoples Sec. Life Ins. Co. v. Monumental Life Ins. Co., 991 F.2d 141 (4th Cir. 1993)  *14:* 89

Perez v. Dana Corp., Parish Frame Div., 718 F.2d 581, 114 LRRM 2814 (3d Cir. 1983)  *14:* 103

Pettway v. American Cast Iron Pipe Co., 411 F.2d 998, 1 FEP Cases 752 (5th Cir. 1969)  *13:* 243

Phelps Dodge Corp. v. NLRB, 313 U.S. 177, 8 LRRM 439 (1941)  *12:* 78

Phillips v. State Bd. of Regents of State Univ. & Community College Sys., 863 S.W.3d 45 (Tenn. 1993)  *4:* 17

Pincus Bros., Inc.—Maxwell, 237 NLRB 1063, 99 LRRM 1099 (1978), *enforcement denied,* 620 F.2d 367, 104 LRRM 2001 (3d Cir. 1980)  *14:* 147

Pinkard v. Pullman-Standard Div., 678 F.2d 1211, 29 FEP Cases 216 (5th Cir. 1982), *cert. denied,* 459 U.S. 1105, 30 FEP Cases 1048 (1983)  *13:* 240

Pinsker v. Adams & Arapahoe Counties Joint Dist. 28J, 735 F.2d 388, 34 FEP Cases 1570 (10th Cir. 1984)  *13:* 83–84, 99

Plumbers' Pension Fund Local 130 v. Domas Mechanical Contractors, Inc., 778 F.2d 1266 (7th Cir. 1985)  *14:* 104

Pompano-Windy City Partners, Ltd. v. Bear Stearns & Co., 794 F. Supp. 1265 (S.D.N.Y. 1992)  *14:* 83

Posadas de P.R. Assocs. v. Asociacion de Empleados de Casino de P.R., 873 F.2d 479, 131 LRRM 2223 (1st Cir. 1989)  *14:* 21, 104, 106

Post v. Harper, 980 F.2d 491 (8th Cir. 1992)  *2:* 37

Postal Workers v. United States Postal Serv., 823 F.2d 466, 126 LRRM 2263 (11th Cir. 1987)  *14:* 20, 110

Price Waterhouse v. Hopkins, 490 U.S. 228, 49 FEP Cases 954 (1989)  *13:* 138

Pritzker v. Merrill Lynch, Pierce, Fenner & Smith, 7 F.3d 1110 (3d Cir. 1993)  *13:* 185

Pryner v. Tractor Supply Co., 109 F.3d 354, 154 LRRM 2806 (7th Cir. 1997)  *13:* 194

Puzick v. City of Colorado Springs, 680 P.2d 1283 (Colo. Ct. App. 1983)  *9:* 59

# R

Rabidue v. Texas-American Petrochemicals, 805 F.2d 611, 42 FEP Cases 631 (6th Cir. 1986), *cert. denied,* 481 U.S. 1041, 43 FEP Cases 1056 (1987)  *13:* 20, 31

Rathert v. Village of Peotone, 903 F.2d 510 (7th Cir.), *cert. denied,* 498 U.S. 921 (1990)  *8:* 281

Raytheon Co., 140 NLRB 883, 52 LRRM 1129 (1963), *set aside,* 326 F.2d 471, 55 LRRM 2101 (1st Cir. 1964)  *14:* 133

Red Star Express Lines v. Teamsters Local 170, 809 F.2d 103, 124 LRRM 2361 (1st Cir. 1987)  *14:* 14

Reed v. Transportation Union, 488 U.S. 319, 130 LRRM 2137 (1989)  *14:* 97

Reed & Martin, Inc. v. Westinghouse Elec. Corp., 439 F.2d 1268 (2d Cir. 1971)  *14:* 90

Retail Clerks v. Food Employers Council, 85 Cal. App. 3d 286, 99 LRRM 3255 (1978)  *12:* 243

River Oaks Imaging & Diagnostic; EEOC v., 67 FEP Cases 1243 (S.D. Tex. 1995)  *13:* 197

Robinson v. Jacksonville Shipyards, Inc., 760 F. Supp. 1486 (M.D. Fla. 1991)  *2:* 360

Roche v. Service Employees Local 32B-32J, 755 F. Supp. 622, 140 LRRM 3056 (S.D.N.Y. 1991)  *14:* 92–93

# T

Teamsters
—v. Southwest Airlines, 875 F.2d 1129, 131 LRRM 2761 (5th Cir. 1989)  *13:* 214
—United States v., 814 F. Supp. 1165, 143 LRRM 2890 (S.D.N.Y. 1993)  *14:* 83
—Local 174 v. Lucas Flour Co., 82 S. Ct. 571, 49 LRRM 2717 (1962)  *14:* 23
—Local 312 v. Matlack, Inc., 118 F.3d 985, 155 LRRM 2738 (3d Cir. 1997)  *14:* 11
—Local 631 v. Silver State Disposal Serv., Inc., 109 F.3d 1409, 154 LRRM 2865 (9th Cir. 1997)  *14:* 11
Tennessee Valley Auth. v. Salary Policy Employee Panel, 136 LRRM 2533 (E.D. Tenn. 1989), *aff'd,* 917 F.2d 564, 136 LRRM 2543 (6th Cir. 1990)  *14:* 51–54
Texas Dep't of Community Affairs, 450 U.S. 248, 25 FEP Cases 113 (1981)  *13:* 246
Textile Workers v. Lincoln Mills, 353 U.S. 448, 40 LRRM 2113 (1957)  *14:* 23
Thomas v. Review Bd. of the Ind. Employment Sec. Div., 101 S. Ct. 1425, 25 FEP Cases 629 (1981)  *13:* 73
Tootsie Roll Indus., Inc. v. Bakery, Confectionery & Tobacco Workers Local 1, 832 F.2d 81, 126 LRRM 270 (7th Cir. 1987)  *2:* 250
Torrington Co. v. Metal Prods. Workers Local 1645, 362 F.2d 677, 62 LRRM 2495 (2d Cir. 1966)  *14:* 43–44
Trailways Lines, Inc. v. Trailways, Inc. Joint Council, 817 F.2d 1333, 125 LRRM 2364 (8th Cir. 1987)  *14:* 119
Tran v. Tran, 54 F.3d 115, 149 LRRM 2350 (2d Cir. 1995), *cert. denied,* 116 S. Ct. 1417, 151 LRRM 3056 (1996)  *13:* 189, 194
Trans World Airlines v. Hardison, 97 S. Ct. 2264, 14 FEP Cases 1697 (1977)  *13:* 88, 93, 97, 111
Treasury Employees v. Von Raab, 489 U.S. 656, 4 IER Cases 246 (1989)  *13:* 213
Trevathan v. Newport News Shipbuilding & Drydock Co., 752 F. Supp. 698, 139 LRRM 2990 (E.D. Va. 1990), *aff'd,* 944 F.2d 902, 139 LRRM 3000, text at Westlaw 91-2005 (4th Cir. 1991)  *7:* 89, 127; *14:* 41
Trustees of Pressmen Local 72 Indus. Pension Fund v. Judd & Detweiler,

Inc., 736 F. Supp. 1351 (D. Md. 1988)  *14:* 89

# U

UCO Terminals, Inc. v. Apex Oil Co., 583 F. Supp. 1213 (S.D.N.Y.), *aff'd,* 751 F.2d 371 (2d Cir. 1984)  *14:* 91
United Parcel Serv. v. Mitchell, 451 U.S. 56, 107 LRRM 2001 (1981)  *14:* 100
United States v. *See name of opposing party*
United States Postal Serv.
—v. Letter Carriers
——810 F.2d 1239, 124 LRRM 2644 (D.C. Cir. 1987), *cert. dismissed,* 485 U.S. 680, 128 LRRM 2144 (1988)  *14:* 65
——839 F.2d 146, 127 LRRM 2593 (3d Cir. 1988)  *14:* 69
—v. Postal Workers, 736 F.2d 822, 116 LRRM 2870 (1st Cir. 1984)  *14:* 65
Universal Mfg. Corp.; EEOC v., 914 F.2d 71, 53 FEP Cases 1811 (5th Cir. 1990)  *13:* 77

# V

Varner v. National Super Mkts., 94 F.3d 1209, 71 FEP Cases 1367 (8th Cir. 1996)  *13:* 194
Vaughn v. Pool Co. of Tex., Pool Offshore Co. Div., 683 F.2d 922, 29 FEP Cases 1017 (5th Cir. 1982)  *13:* 20

# W

Waggoner v. Northwest Excavating, Inc., 642 F.2d 333, 107 LRRM 2367 (9th Cir. 1981)  *12:* 243
Walker v. Ford Motor Co., 684 F.2d 1355, 29 FEP Cases 1259 (11th Cir. 1982)  *13:* 20
Washington-Baltimore Newspaper Guild Local 35 v. Washington Post Co., 442 F.2d 1234, 76 LRRM 2274 (D.C. Cir. 1971)  *14:* 10
W.C. Nabors Co. v. NLRB, 323 F.2d 686, 54 LRRM 2259 (5th Cir. 1963), *cert. denied,* 376 U.S. 911, 55 LRRM 2455 (1964)  *12:* 4, 30, 38
Weitkenaut v. Goodyear Tire & Rubber Co., 381 F. Supp. 1284, 10 FEP Cases 513 (D. Vt. 1974)  *13:* 76

## Z

# Index

This index is alphabetized word-by-word (e.g., Labor Management Relations Act precedes Laboratory procedures). References are to page numbers.

505

**Abusive language,** 278–79. *See also*
  Inappropriate language
**Accidents**
  discipline for, 259–60
  drug test, triggering, 209, 260
  employee misconduct causing,
    259–60
  reports, 260
**Acquired immune deficiency
  syndrome, refusal to work
  due to fear of AIDS
  contagion,** 174–75
**ADA.** *See* Americans with Disabilities
  Act
**ADEA.** *See* Age Discrimination in
  Employment Act
**Administrative tribunals,
  arbitration issue already
  decided in,** 360–61
**Advocate's role in arbitration,** 1–27
  analyzing case, 3
    case matrix, use, 3–14
  arbitrator, choosing, 2, 14–23
    availability, 22–23
    colleagues, consulting, 19–22
    reading awards of, 16–19
  case matrix, use, 7–9
    hypothetical case, 9–14
  comprehension aids, providing to
    arbitrator, 26–27
  evaluating case, 3
    case matrix, use, 7–14
  investigating case, 2–3
  opening statements, 25–26
  preparation for, 23–24
  presenting case, 24–27
  researching case, 2–3
  witness sequestration, 26
**Age Discrimination in Employment
  Act (ADEA),** 411–13, 432–33,
    437–38, 448–50
**Agreements**
  arbitration, for, 439–44
  collective bargaining agreements. *See*
    Collective bargaining
    agreements
  last-chance agreements. *See* Last-
    chance agreements
**AIDS, refusal to work due to fear
  of contagion,** 174–75
**Alcohol use by employees.** *See*
  Substance abuse
**American Arbitration Association**
  *functus officio* doctrine, 463
  Voluntary Labor Arbitration Rules,
    333–34
**Americans with Disabilities Act
  (ADA),** 93, 133, 344–45,
    448–50

  awards, 434–36
  harassment of individual with
    disability, 430–31
**Annulment theory, job application
  falsification,** 246–47
**Antiretaliation statutes,** 448–50
**Appearance standards.** *See* Dress
  and grooming codes
**Applicants, falsification by.** *See* Job
  applicants, falsification by
**Arbitration**
  agreements to arbitrate, 439–44
  arbitrators. *See* Arbitrators
  awards. *See* Awards
  deferral to arbitration, 489–94
  opening statements, 25–26
  procedure, 335–39
  rolling hypothesis, 24–26
**Arbitrators**
  availability, 22–23
  awards by. *See* Awards
  behavior at hearing, 19–22
  bias tainting award, 479–80
  choosing, 2, 14–23
    availability, 22–23
    colleagues, consulting, 19–22
    reading awards of, 16–19
  complex theories, willingness to
    understand, 21
  comprehension aids, advocate
    providing to, 26–27
  educability, 21
  evidence, control of, 20–21
  faulty decision, 481
  inappropriate intrusion into case, 21
  jurisdiction, *functus officio* doctrine,
    462–64
  mediation, urging, 21
  misconduct, 480–81
  partiality tainting award, 479–80
  posthearing conduct, 21–22
  prior decisions, subsequent arbitrator
    not bound by, 485–88
  rolling hypothesis, 24–26
  substance abuse last-chance
    agreements, role, 218
**Artistic judgment, discharge based
  on,** 345
**Attendance**
  absences. *See* Absences
  policies. *See* Attendance policies
  tardiness. *See* Tardiness
**Attendance policies,** 93–132
  bereavement, 106–07
  collective bargaining, 94
  due process issues, 95–96
  employer-created, 93–97
  just cause, policy conflicting with, 96
  "no fault," 94